DECARBONISATION AND THE EN

This timely collection of essays examines the legal and regulatory dynamics of energy transitions in the context of emerging trends towards decarbonisation and the global increase in low-carbon energy solutions. The book explores this topic by considering the applicable energy law and policy frameworks in both:

(i) highly industrialised and major economies such as the US, EU, China and Australia; and
(ii) resource-rich developing countries such as Nigeria and regions like Southern Africa.

Comprising 16 chapters, the book delves into the trade-offs and regulatory complexities of carbon constraints in conventional energy supply systems, while maintaining a reliable and secure energy system that is equally sustainable (ie decarbonised). It highlights the importance of ensuring affordable access to energy services in developing economies as the energy transitions unfold and explores the potentials of emerging technologies such as power-to-gas and Carbon Capture and Storage. Additionally, the book also considers the international investment law implications of energy decarbonisation.

Focusing on the nexus between law, regulation and institutions, it adopts a novel contextual approach to examine how and to what extent institutions can effectively facilitate more reliable, sustainable and secure energy supply systems in the twenty-first century. In a unique, holistic way, the book portrays the conventional hydrocarbon-based energy supply industry in a largely international and interconnected context. It highlights the costs, benefits and losses that may arise as the transition towards decarbonisation unfolds depending on the pathways and solutions adopted. With chapters written by leading experts in energy law and policy, the reader-friendly style and engaging discussions will benefit an international audience of policymakers, academics, students and advisers looking for a more incisive understanding of the issues involved in energy transitions and the decarbonisation of energy systems.

Global Energy Law and Policy: Volume 1

Global Energy Law and Policy

Series Editors
Peter D Cameron
Pieter Bekker
Volker Roeben

Energy policy and energy law are undergoing rapid global transformation, characterised by the push in favour of decarbonisation. The 2015 Sustainable Development Goals and the 2015 Paris Agreement on international climate action have forged a consensus for a pathway to a universal just transition towards a low-carbon economy for all states and all societies.

This series publishes conceptual work that help academics, legal practitioners and decision-makers to make sense of these transformational changes. The perspective of the series is global. It welcomes contributions on international law, regional law (for example, from the EU, US and ASEAN regions), and the domestic law of all states with emphasis on comparative works that identify horizontal trends, and including transnational law. The series' scope is comprehensive, embracing both public and commercial law on energy in all forms and sources and throughout the energy life-cycle from extraction, production, operation, consumption and waste management/decommissioning. The series is a forum for innovative interdisciplinary work that uses the insights of cognate disciplines to achieve a better understanding of energy law and policy in the 21st century.

Recent titles in this series:

The Global Energy Transition: Law, Policy and Economics for Energy in the 21st Century
edited by Peter D Cameron, Xiaoyi Mu and Volker Roeben

The Law and Governance of Mining and Minerals: A Global Perspective
by Ana Elizabeth Bastida

National Climate Change Acts: The Emergence, Form and Nature of National Framework Climate Legislation
edited by Thomas L Muinzer

Decarbonisation and the Energy Industry

Law, Policy and Regulation in Low-Carbon Energy Markets

Edited by
Tade Oyewunmi
Penelope Crossley
Frédéric Gilles Sourgens
and
Kim Talus

·HART·
OXFORD · LONDON · NEW YORK · NEW DELHI · SYDNEY

HART PUBLISHING
Bloomsbury Publishing Plc
Kemp House, Chawley Park, Cumnor Hill, Oxford, OX2 9PH, UK
1385 Broadway, New York, NY 10018, USA
29 Earlsfort Terrace, Dublin 2, Ireland

HART PUBLISHING, the Hart/Stag logo, BLOOMSBURY and the Diana logo are
trademarks of Bloomsbury Publishing Plc

First published in Great Britain 2020

First published in hardback, 2020
Paperback edition, 2022

Copyright © The Editors and Contributors severally 2020

The Editors and Contributors have asserted their right under the Copyright, Designs and
Patents Act 1988 to be identified as Authors of this work.

All rights reserved. No part of this publication may be reproduced or transmitted in any form or by
any means, electronic or mechanical, including photocopying, recording, or any information
storage or retrieval system, without prior permission in writing from the publishers.

While every care has been taken to ensure the accuracy of this work, no responsibility for loss or
damage occasioned to any person acting or refraining from action as a result of any statement in it
can be accepted by the authors, editors or publishers.

All UK Government legislation and other public sector information used in the work is Crown
Copyright ©. All House of Lords and House of Commons information used in the work is
Parliamentary Copyright ©. This information is reused under the terms of the Open Government
Licence v3.0 (http://www.nationalarchives.gov.uk/doc/open-government-licence/version/3) except
where otherwise stated.

All Eur-lex material used in the work is © European
Union, http://eur-lex.europa.eu/, 1998–2022.

A catalogue record for this book is available from the British Library.

Library of Congress Cataloging-in-Publication Data

Names: Oyewunmi, Tade, editor. | Crossley, Penelope, editor. |
Sourgens, Frédéric Gilles, editor. | Talus, Kim, editor.
Title: Decarbonisation and the energy industry : law, policy, and regulation in low-carbon energy
markets / edited by Tade Oyewunmi, Penelope Crossley, Frédéric Gilles Sourgens and Kim Talus.
Other titles: Decarbonization and the energy industry
Description: Oxford, UK ; New York, NY : Hart Publishing, an imprint of Bloomsbury Publishing, 2020. |
Series: Global energy law and policy ; volume 1 | Includes bibliographical references and index.
Identifiers: LCCN 2020028706 (print) | LCCN 2020028707 (ebook) |
ISBN 9781509932900 (hardback) | ISBN 9781509932917 (ePDF) |
ISBN 9781509932924 (Epub)
Subjects: LCSH: Energy industries—Law and legislation. | Energy development—Law
and legislation. | Power resources—Law and legislation. | Carbon sequestration—Law
and legislation. | Carbon dioxide mitigation—Law and legislation.
Classification: LCC K3981 .D43 2020 (print) | LCC K3981 (ebook) | DDC 346.04/679—dc23
LC record available at https://lccn.loc.gov/2020028706
LC ebook record available at https://lccn.loc.gov/2020028707

ISBN: HB: 978-1-50993-290-0
PB: 978-1-50994-548-1
ePDF: 978-1-50993-291-7
ePub: 978-1-50993-292-4

Typeset by Compuscript Ltd, Shannon

To find out more about our authors and books visit www.hartpublishing.co.uk. Here you will find
extracts, author information, details of forthcoming events and the option to sign up for our newsletters.

TABLE OF CONTENTS

List of Contributors vii

Introduction: Energy in a Carbon-Constrained World.. 1
    Tade Oyewunmi, Penelope Crossley, Kim Talus and Frédéric Sourgens

PART I
ENHANCING SECURE AND RELIABLE ACCESS TO SUSTAINABLE ENERGY SYSTEMS IN THE TWENTY-FIRST CENTURY

1. *Tradeoffs and Tensions in the American Energy Transition* 15
    David B Spence

2. *The US Gas Supply Boom under Carbon Constraints: Examining the Role of Regulatory Institutions* 37
    Tade Oyewunmi

3. *Decarbonising Gas and Electricity Systems: An Outlook on Power-to-Gas and other Technology-Based Solutions* 69
    Tade Oyewunmi

4. *Economic Waste and Environmental Problems: Natural Gas Flaring in Texas*.. 107
    Kim Talus and Cheri R Hasz

5. *Global Governance Networks for Climate Change and Energy Investments*.. 123
    Frédéric Gilles Sourgens

6. *Investment Law and Decarbonisation* 157
    Diane Desierto and Frédéric Gilles Sourgens

7. *Private Mineral Rights and Africa's Shale Gas* 177
    Emeka Duruigbo

8. *International Oil and Gas Operators and Decarbonisation* 201
    Peter Kayode Oniemola

9. *The Carbon Taxation Conundrum* 221
    Frédéric Gilles Sourgens and Lori A McMillan

PART II
ENERGY TRANSITIONS: LAW AND REGULATION IN SELECTED COUNTRIES AND REGIONS

10. *A Primer on United States Energy and Decarbonisation Policy*......................245
    Troy A Rule

11. *The Integration of Renewable Energy Sources in the EU Electricity Grid: Adapting Current Market Rules to 'New Market Realities'*...............................263
    Sirja-Leena Penttinen and Leonie Reins

12. *Regulating Energy Supply in China*..283
    Philip Andrews-Speed

13. *Energy Law and Regulation in Nigeria – Prospects for Reliable Electricity Supply*..307
    Tade Oyewunmi and Ivie Ehanmo

14. *Australian Electricity Law and Policy in a Time of Energy Market Transition, National Emergency and Climate Crisis*...337
    Penelope Crossley

15. *Canada's Emerging LNG Export Industry and the Project Approval Challenge*..353
    Rudiger Tscherning

16. *Challenges and Opportunities for Energy Transitions and Decarbonisation in Southern African Countries*...377
    Victoria R Nalule and Smith I Azubuike

Conclusion: An Exposition of a Contextual Approach to Energy and Decarbonisation..401
Penelope Crossley, Tade Oyewunmi, Kim Talus and Frédéric Sourgens

Index..409

LIST OF CONTRIBUTORS

Dr Philip Andrews-Speed, Senior Principal Fellow at the Energy Studies Institute, National University of Singapore. He has 38 years in the field of energy and resources law, starting his career as a mineral and oil exploration geologist before moving into the field of international energy and resource governance, with a focus on China.

Dr Smith I Azubuike, Barrister and Solicitor of the Supreme Court of Nigeria. He is currently Champions Coordinator at the Extractives Hub, CEPMLP, University of Dundee and teaches English Law of Contract at the Dundee Law School.

Dr Penelope Crossley, Associate Professor of Law, Sydney University Law School, Australia. She is a leading expert in Australian and comparative international law for renewable energy and electricity market governance. She is the Senior Industry Advisor to the Australian Energy Storage Alliance, as well as the Chair of the Product Listing Review Panel for the Clean Energy Council.

Dr Diane A Desierto, Associate Professor of Human Rights Law and Global Affairs at the Keough School of Global Affairs at the University of Notre Dame. She teaches International Law and Human Rights; Human Rights, Sustainability and the Global Commons; Trade, Investment and Human Rights; and Economic, Social and Cultural Rights.

Emeka Duruigbo, Professor of Law at the Thurgood Marshall School of Law, Texas Southern University, Houston, Texas, USA. He is a leading scholar and advocate in Energy Law, Business Law and International Economic Law. He is an Education Advisory Board member of the Institute for Energy Law and the Association of International Petroleum Negotiators (AIPN).

Ivie Ehanmo, Partner in the law firm of George Etomi & Partners, Lagos, Nigeria. She is an energy law and policy expert and provides legal, regulatory, governance and transaction advisory support to global institutions and agencies such as the World Bank and the US Agency for International Development.

Cheri R Hasz, JD Candidate at Tulane Law School, New Orleans, Louisiana, USA. She has about 5 years experience in the US oil and gas industry prior to commencing her JD program at Tulane.

Lori A McMillan, Professor of Law at Washburn University School of Law, Kansas, USA. Professor McMillan teaches taxation law and policy, and her experience includes working as a tax and business law Attorney and a Visiting Professor in Canada.

List of Contributors

Dr Victoria R Nalule, Energy and Mining professional and consultant. She is the Founder and Executive Director of the African Energy and Minerals Management Initiative, and also a Research Fellow with the Extractives Hub project, at the Centre for Energy, Petroleum & Mineral Law & Policy, University of Dundee, UK.

Dr Peter Oniemola, Lecturer in the Faculty of Law, University of Ibadan, Nigeria, and the Energy Law Programme Coordinator at the Centre for Petroleum, Energy Economics and Law, University of Ibadan, Nigeria.

Dr Tade Oyewunmi, Assistant Professor of Energy Law and Policy and Senior Research Fellow at the Institute for Energy and the Environment, Vermont Law School, Vermont, USA. He is an academic advisory board member of the Center for American and International Law's Institute for Energy Law. He is also a member of the AIPN.

Dr Sirja-Leena Penttinen, Assistant Director, Adjunct Professor at the Center for Energy Law, Tulane University Law School, New Orleans, LA, USA. She is also a Senior Lecturer in European Energy Law at the University of Eastern Finland (UEF) Law School, Joensuu, Finland.

Dr Leonie Reins, Assistant Professor at the Tilburg Institute for Law, Technology, and Society (TILT), Tilburg Law School, the Netherlands. Leonie's research focuses on the intersections of energy and environmental law.

Troy A Rule, Professor of Law and the Joseph Feller Memorial Chair in Law and Sustainability at Arizona State University's Sandra Day O'Connor College of Law, Phoenix, Arizona, USA.

Frédéric Gilles Sourgens, Senator Robert J Dole Distinguished Professor of Law and Director of Washburn University Law School's Oil and Gas Law Center. He serves as Editor-in-Chief of *Investment Claims* (Oxford University Press). He is co-chair for the American Society of International Law's Private International Law Interest Group and a member of the Academic Council of CAIL's Institute for Transnational Arbitration.

David Spence, Baker Botts Chair in Law at the University of Texas School of Law, and Professor of Business Government & Society at the McCombs School of Business, Austin, Texas, USA. He is a leading scholar in the areas of law and politics of energy regulation, and the environmental regulation of the oil and gas industry and electric utilities.

Dr Kim Talus, James McCulloch Chair in Energy Law at Tulane University, Director of Tulane Center for Energy Law, Professor of European Energy Law at UEF Law School and Professor of Energy Law at University of Helsinki, Finland. He is also the Editor-in-Chief of the *Oil, Gas and Energy Law (OGEL)* journal.

Dr Rudiger Tscherning, Assistant Professor, Faculty of Law, University of Calgary, Canada. Dr Tscherning researches and teaches in the areas of energy and natural resources law, infrastructure and construction law, private international law (the conflict of laws) and the transportation of energy and commodities.

Introduction: Energy in a Carbon-Constrained World

TADE OYEWUNMI, PENELOPE CROSSLEY, KIM TALUS AND FRÉDÉRIC SOURGENS

Energy does not have a physical attribute comparable to items that could, for example, be gathered into a bag or boxed up such as potatoes or a bundle of gold coins. Rather, the simplest definition of 'energy' is *'the capacity to do work'* which takes various forms such as kinetic energy associated with motion, chemical energy stored in materials that is released following a chemical reaction such as in batteries,[1] thermal energy associated with heat and temperature, electrical energy resulting from the flow of electric charge commonly referred to as electricity, and radiant energy associated with light and radiation, eg solar. Over the course of the past century, electrical energy has emerged as a vital form of energy created from primary sources such as gas, water (hydro), wind and coal by generating electricity as a secondary energy source.[2] Thus, energy and in particular electricity has constituted the mainstay to modern standards of living and economic development globally. It is required to turn on lights, cook, heat spaces in cold regions or for cooling purposes in temperate regions, as well as being needed to move machinery in a manufacturing process. As a system for meeting demand, energy supply comprises the extraction and processing of primary sources such as hydro, wind and natural gas, followed by the conversion or processing, then transmission and distribution as a final and useable form such as electricity or transportation fuel.

The industries and operations that evolved through this system(s) of energy supply generally did not evolve or develop as an integrated whole. For example, the oil and gas industry historically advanced with its own unique attributes and largely international outlook over the years, while electricity supply evolved mostly with a local, national and in some cases regional outlook, with its own peculiar features and stakeholders.[3] However, the growing utilisation and commercialisation of

---

[1] Kevin B Jones, Benjamin B Jervey and Matthew Roche, *The Electric Battery: Charging Forward to a Low-Carbon Future* (Praeger, 2017) 1–212.
[2] Tade Oyewunmi, *Regulating Gas Supply to Power Markets: Transnational Approaches to Competitiveness and Security of Supply* (Wolters Kluwer, 2018) 360.
[3] Ibid 14–30.

resources such as natural gas since the 1990s and technological advancements in the electricity sector such as Combined-Cycle Gas Turbines allowing for more efficiency and less pollution enhanced several types of transitions. There has been a more or less global shift with growing interconnectedness between energy sectors such a gas and electricity markets, including gas and electricity market reforms to enhance the competitiveness and security of energy supply.[4]

More recently, factors such as climate change mitigation and the need to curb energy-related greenhouse gas (GHG) emissions,[5] the falling costs of renewables (eg wind and solar), progress in energy efficiency and demand-side management programmes and electrification of things such as transportation and residential energy uses instigated an evolving set of transitional energy systems and markets, especially in the context of organisational and regulatory paradigms for such energy supply systems.[6] The shift ranges from systems and markets dominated by centralisation and vertical integration, towards the promotion of open access to networks to promote competition and viability and now to the growth in renewables to enhance a clean and sustainable energy system. One general feature of the latest evolving trend(s) is the increase of off-grid or distributed and decentralised systems powered by renewables such as rooftop solar and advanced storage battery and scenarios where erstwhile consumers could become more active in demand-side management, etc.

I. A Contextual Narrative for Energy Transitions and Decarbonisation

Accordingly, this handbook examines the legal and regulatory dynamics of energy transitions in the context of emerging trends towards decarbonisation and

---

[4] Kim Talus, *EU Energy Law and Policy: A Critical Account* 352 (Oxford University Press, 2013); Kim Talus, 'Long-Term Natural Gas Contracts and Antitrust Law in the European Union and the United States' (2011) 4(3) *Journal of World Energy Law and Business* 260–315; David B Spence, 'Naive Energy Markets' (2016–2017) 92 *Notre Dame Law Review* 973–1030; Yinka Omorogbe, 'Alternative Regulation and Governance Reform in Resource-Rich Developing Countries of Africa' in Barry Barton et al (eds), *Regulating Energy and Natural Resources* (Oxford University Press, 2006) 39–65; Paul Joskow, 'Restructuring, Competition and Regulatory Reform in the U.S. Electricity Sector' (1997) 11(3) *Journal of Economic Perspectives* 119–38.

[5] See the US Environmental Protection Agency (EPA), 'Inventory of Greenhouse Gas Emissions and Sinks 1990–2017' (430-R-19-001, 11 April 2019) 10–86, 1–3. The Intergovernmental Panel on Climate Change (IPCC) concluded in its most recent scientific assessment report that it is extremely likely that human influences have been the dominant cause of global warming since the mid-20th century, thereby increasing the threat of climate change impact. The report further states that 'If greenhouse gas concentrations continue to increase, climate models predict that the average temperature at the Earth's surface is likely to increase from 0.5 to 8.6 degrees Fahrenheit above 1986 through 2005 levels by the end of this century, **depending on future emissions and the responsiveness of the climate system**' (emphasis added).

[6] Dieter Helm, *Burn Out: The Endgame for Fossil Fuels* (Cambridge University Press, 2017); Jonathan Stern, *The Future of Gas in Decarbonising European Energy Markets – the Need for a New Approach* (Oxford Institute for Energy Studies, NG 116, January 2017) 1–37.

growth in low-carbon energy sources globally. It explores the tradeoffs and regulatory complexities of carbon-constraints and systemic changes to conventional hydrocarbon-based energy supply frameworks in:

i. highly industrialised and developed economies such as the US, EU and Australia; and
ii. resource-rich developing countries such as Nigeria, regions such as Southern Africa and major global economic powerhouses such as China.

Generally, the legal, regulatory and policy framework governing energy supply systems involve:

a) ensuring suppliers and operators earn just and reasonable returns on investments and affordable prices for consumers;
b) reliability and security of supply; and
c) protection from environmental harm and sustainability.

The push towards a more sustainable system of supply that is now reflected in the climate change mitigation and GHG emission reduction debate is typically framed as purely a 'climate change' and 'environmental law' problem. However, this handbook shows it is much more than these, rather it is equally an energy institutions, law and policy problem. While the abovementioned three dimensions of energy law and policy would often seem counteracting, they are not mutually exclusive in reality.

Arguably, what stands in the way of successful climate change mitigation efforts is that both economic activity and economic development depend upon energy.[7] In view of the fact that the bulk of extant energy infrastructure and the cheapest form of energy is GHG intensive, any attempt to reduce energy-related emissions therefore has an immediate and tangible impact on economic activity.[8] Recently, the yellow vest protests in France fighting against the imposition of carbon taxes by the French Government demonstrated an additional unintended consequence of a pure environmental law solution: the imposition of the classical environmental law principle that the polluter should pay for the clean-up of their pollution through some form of carbon tax. This disproportionately affects poorer members of society and potentially deprives less developed states of the ability to fully industrialise.[9]

The search for a workable balance between the mainstream dimensions of energy policy and its interlinkages with climate and environmental law is particularly difficult in today's energy markets. The energy world is currently going through a number of fundamental transitions, the most significant one being the transition towards a more sustainable energy system in which the main or an increasing amount of energy is sourced from low and zero-carbon sources such as

---

[7] Frédéric Gilles Sourgens, 'Geo-Markets' (2020) *Virginia Environmental Law Journal* (forthcoming).
[8] *Ibid.*
[9] *Ibid.*

solar and wind, equally leading to a more decentralised and distributed system; in sharp contrast with the main paradigms that we have seen over the past century.[10] Almost all countries have hitherto relied mainly on conventional energy systems fuelled by hydrocarbon sources such as coal, oil and gas, while the developing and emerging economies are increasingly becoming centres of economic growth, urbanisation and rising energy demand. The industry and markets that developed in the context of production, supply and utilisation of hydrocarbons for energy (electricity and heat) purposes have been critical drivers of modernisation, industrial and economic growth. The modern economy was built on hydrocarbons.

Regardless, it is important to note that the externalities attributable to the hydrocarbon-based supply chain are a significant source of GHG emissions such as carbon dioxide and methane. In the US for example, the largest source of GHG emissions from human activities is attributed to the combustion of hydrocarbons such as oil and coal for electricity, heat and transportation. In this regard, transportation, electricity production, industry, commercial and residential and agriculture respectively accounted for 28.9 per cent, 27.5 per cent, 22.2 per cent, 11.6 per cent and 9.0 per cent of overall anthropogenic 2017 GHG emissions, while land use and forestry led to the offset of about 11.1 per cent of 2017 GHG emissions. Land areas can act as a sink (absorbing CO_2 from the atmosphere) or a source of GHG emissions.[11] It is noted that the trend started to decline from 2014, arguably as a result of the energy transitions towards less carbon intensive sources, including energy efficiency and conservation and as the electrification of things in various key demand sectors gained traction.[12] A declining trend is also reported for the electric power sector emissions from 2014 onwards compared to the rise in emissions attributable to other sectors such as transportation, while emissions from agriculture, industry, commercial and residential uses remained relatively flat or the same.

The decrease in CO_2 emissions from fossil fuel combustion is attributable to factors such as a continued shift from coal to natural gas in the electricity and heat sector, increased use of zero-carbon renewables in the electric power sector, and fluctuations in demand and energy usage and efficiency, etc.[13] As the use of zero-carbon renewables increase, the carbon-intensity of energy supply systems

---

[10] 'Energy system' here includes generation, transmission and distribution as well as end-use. Moving to a more sustainable energy system requires changes in all these areas including introduction of renewable energy, energy efficiency measures, adaptation of network regulation and so on.

[11] The US Environmental Protection Agency (EPA), *Sources of Greenhouse Gas Emissions*, available at www.epa.gov/ghgemissions/sources-greenhouse-gas-emissions; See also US EPA, *Inventory of Greenhouse Gas Emissions and Sinks 1990–2017* (n 5), ES-18 (2019); and the International Energy Agency (IEA), *Energy Policies of IEA Countries: The United States 2019 Review* (IEA Publications, 2019) 279, 43–44.

[12] US EPA, *Inventory of Greenhouse Gas Emissions and Sinks 1990–2017* (n 5), 10–86, ES-18.

[13] The International Energy Agency (IEA), 'Global Energy & CO_2 Status Report 2019: The Latest Trends in Energy and Emissions in 2018' (2019) at www.iea.org/reports/global-energy-and-co2-status-report-2019/emissions#abstract (last accessed 1 April 2020)).

also decrease. Unfortunately for the environmental enthusiast, coal-fired electricity generation which accounts for 30 per cent of global CO_2 emissions and most generating plants found in the major economic growth centres, such as in Asia, have a long lifespan. Most coal-power generation assets are just about 12 years old even though the average economic life-span of these assets is about 40 years.[14] On a positive note, economics and policy shifts have inspired a major global growth in switching from coal to gas-fired power generation, thereby reducing the carbon intensity of global energy use by more than half of what it would have been as at 2018.[15]

While renewable energy technologies have matured and the prices have fallen, it is unlikely that renewable energy alone can meet the extant and growing energy demand in the world without imposing the sort of costs and energy justice or equity issues that could have been avoided if the low carbon traditional energy systems are restructured and thus evolve in a sustainable and efficient manner through innovative technological solutions such as hydrogen-compatible networks, power-to-gas, carbon capture, and utilisation or storage. Conversely, existing super majors evolve into 'energy companies' rather than just profit-centred fossil fuel vendors. Given the complexities of climate change mitigation and the growing calls to hold the energy, oil and gas industry accountable as a significant contributor, it is imperative to ask whether operators in the energy, oil and gas sector should be viewed as 'the problem', only 'part of the problem', or if they should be considered as an essential 'part of the solution'?[16]

Looking ahead, natural gas which is the most environmentally-friendly and efficient hydrocarbon when utilised for electricity and other energy purposes and renewables is poised to play a significant role in the evolving low-carbon energy mixes of various countries and as the global transition in the structure of energy markets unfold. The two plausible alternative pathways in the unfolding transitions towards a zero- or low-carbon energy supply future are:

a) The 'decarbonised natural gas' pathway: in this regard, natural gas exploration, production and affiliated networks which currently play a crucial role in global energy supply, adapts to the requirements of a decarbonised system. This calls for supporting a market-led, cost-reflective approach to the regulation and policies promoting decarbonisation, which should also enable technological and innovative ways towards eliminating and curbing unwanted GHG and methane emissions that arise along the value chain through leaks, flaring or venting. It is instructive to note the unfolding industry-led developments in carbon capture utilisation and storage (CCUS), carbon recycling, methane reformation, renewable natural gas, power-to-gas and hydrogen, etc; and

---

[14] *Ibid.*
[15] *Ibid.*
[16] The International Energy Agency (IEA), 'The Oil and Gas Industry in Energy Transitions: World Energy Outlook Special Report' (IEA Publications, 2020) 164.

b) The 'All-Electric' pathway in which electricity from 'carbon-free' renewables or energy systems such as nuclear or bioenergy comprises the only means of reaching the objectives of climate change mitigation. This appears to be the most radical and costly path towards ensuring sustainability in energy supply and long-term climate change mitigation goals. Additionally, most discussions suggesting such a pathway, including banning exploration and production of hydrocarbons, do not comprehensively address the costs and risks of intermittency in the utilisation of renewables and organisation of an increasingly distributed or decentralised system; the ability or affordability to store energy in batteries for the medium to long-term; the embodied 'emissions' and 'environmental impacts' of large-scale deployment of popular clean-energy systems such as solar photovotalic (PV) systems and wind farms as opposed to other clean sources like nuclear and hydro; the lingering energy access, affordability, justice and equity issues still hampering the developing economies mostly in Sub-Saharan Africa.

A more balanced and pragmatic energy systems transition process would require a coherent and comprehensive set of policies and regulatory instruments that enhance timely investment in cleaner, smarter and more efficient energy technologies in both the natural gas and renewable energy industry context. Industry operators in the petroleum industry will also need to adapt portfolios and practices to meet the needs of the times going forward. To survive the transitions, some will have to remodel into 'energy systems and services' companies rather than just crude oil and fossil fuel vendors. Curtailing operational practices such as flaring and venting of natural gas (which comprises mostly of methane) and CO_2; electrifying upstream and midstream operations; installing renewable-based systems in upstream and midstream operations; investing in CCUS units at significant points of CO_2 emissions; injecting CO_2 in enhanced oil recovery operations; and using low-carbon hydrogen in place of hydrogen produced using natural gas could presumably be the lowest cost options to cutting energy-related emissions.

Policymakers, industry operators, lawyers, academics, stakeholders and students engaged in energy-related matters are increasingly puzzled by questions such as:

i. Who and what determines which primary energy resources are developed in a low-carbon and transitional context?
ii. What projects are approved and what are the institutional and policy factors that support timely investments in the necessary cleaner and more efficient energy sources?
iii. How should law and policy deal with any issues bordering on stranded assets and investments attributable to the energy transitions and decarbonisation?
iv. Will consumers be better protected in the emerging scenarios and as prosumers?
v. How will existing transmission and distribution network operators adapt to the new role of 'active' consumers, smart meters and other transitional issues?

vi. Can major international oil and gas companies typically involved in hydrocarbon exploration and production efficiently adapt to the new environment and what is the role of international energy and investment law going forward?
vii. How should law and policy in hydrocarbon-rich emerging or developing countries adapt to an 'all-electric' or 'decarbonised natural gas' pathway?
viii. What suite of investment incentives will be required for developing technologies such as CCUS, carbon recycling and hydrogen compatible gas networks or power-to-gas?
ix. What are the necessary considerations for policymakers and institutions in imposing environmental or climate change-related measures?

Several questions relating to the direct and indirect environmental implications of permitting and approval of liquefied natural gas export projects from the US have also been raised recently.

II. A Look at Institutions and Regulation for Energy and Decarbonisation

This book takes a unique approach to the energy supply systems of the future. Unlike most other texts and works in the field, this book portrays the conventional (hydrocarbon-based) energy supply industry holistically (as it is) and highlights the need for a contextual approach to law and regulation in the pursuit of reliability and security of energy supply which are essential issues that typically arise due to increased utilisation of intermittent renewable energy sources (especially, wind and solar) and smart electricity systems globally. Often, questions relating to climate change mitigation and energy transitions are considered from either a purely climate change environmentalist perspective or the purview of mainstream conventional energy industry proponent(s). This research handbook proposes a holistic and balanced idea of the evolving twenty-first century energy supply industry as an interconnected and international value chain in which costs, benefits and losses accrue as the transition to a zero and low-carbon system unfolds.

The book highlights the role of law and organisational institutions in the context of securing timely and reliable energy supply, its sustainability and competitiveness. The originality of this handbook is its discussion of the different role(s) that main conventional energy sources such as gas plays as a transitional (and possibly even post-transitional) fuel and how different countries are grappling with the transition and integrating large volumes of renewables onto their grids. While chapter 14 briefly discusses the scrapping of a national carbon tax in Australia and chapter 12 highlights the introduction of a 'carbon emissions trading scheme' in China, the handbook does not delve into the complexities of climate-centred debates such as international climate finance. Chapter nine on the carbon taxation conundrum considers 'taxation as a regulatory tool' and means of achieving energy decarbonisation policy objectives. Considering the theme and approach of the book, the authors focused primarily on the institutional and regulatory dynamics of an evolving energy supply system in specific contexts.

While there are some academic and industry-led commentaries on various aspects of the issues raised above, there is yet to be a holistic 'law-in-context' approach. By and large, there is yet to be any significant research studies focused on the nexus between law, regulation and institutions which examines: (i) the role of such institutions in managing the transition in a fair and efficient manner; and (ii) the costs and benefits of pursuing the agenda of decarbonisation on the conventional hydrocarbon-based energy industry. Written within 16 chapters, this book seeks to examine this particular set of issues and the discussion is framed around two parts:

I. Enhancing Secure and Reliable Access to Sustainable Energy Systems in the Twenty-First Century.
II. Energy Transitions: Law and Regulation in Selected Countries and Regions.

Chapters one to nine comprise the first part, while chapters ten to 16 make up the second part.

The chapters for North America examine US energy and climate policies and their interaction, including an overview of the scope and main components of the US energy industry and the regulatory structures that govern it and then discusses the primary policy strategies that the US Federal Government and state and local governments have been employing over the past decade, bordering on the transition towards a more sustainable and low-carbon energy supply industry.

Chapter one by David Spence highlights the unique structure of the American electricity sector. This chapter also explores the political-economic dynamics that suppress the kind of dialogue that might help policymakers grapple with the trade-offs associated with a rapid green transition from a system that relies mainly on hydrocarbons towards one that predominantly comprises low- or zero-carbon energy sources.

In chapters two and three respectively, Tade Oyewunmi examines the legal and regulatory issues encountered in the context of: (i) the US gas supply boom under carbon-constraints; and (ii) power-to-gas, carbon capture, storage and utilisation (CCUS), negative emissions technology and other innovative solutions for decarbonisation. Chapter three in particular underscores the need to develop and adopt rules and necessary policy initiatives that will enhance technologies such as power-to-gas and CCUS as a pragmatic way of integrating alternative sources of energy and decarbonisation.

One of the issues in the US also includes gas flaring and its regulation. While international efforts are directed towards the reduction of flaring where possible, the recent practice of the Texas Railroad Commission (Railroad Commission) offers an alternative scenario. The volumes of gas flared in Texas have grown exponentially over the last few years and the Railroad Commission's relaxed attitude towards flaring of natural gas has gathered national and international attention. In chapter four, Kim Talus and Cheri R Hasz provide an account of the regulatory framework for gas flaring in Texas. They also examine pre- and post-1990 regulatory practices by the Railroad Commission and seek to explain some of the reasons behind the relaxed approach of the Railroad Commission towards flaring of associated gas.

Chapter 15 by Rudiger Tscherning examines the emergence of Canada's liquefied natural gas (LNG) industry, the myriad of regulatory challenges arising from Canada's federal to provincial decision-making process (including aggressive reforms proposed for the approval of energy projects at federal level), federal GHG and British Columbia's environmental agenda and the drastic GHG emission reduction targets recently announced, as well as the question of navigation from BC export terminals. The central argument is that Canada may be entering the LNG market too late, in unpredictable times, thereby leading to project delays and significant challenges to potential buyers.

Chapter 11, by Sirja-Leena Penttinen and Leonie Reins, focuses on legal issues and experience in the European Union regarding the integration of renewable energy into the electricity grid to facilitate the energy transition towards a low-carbon society. More concretely, it discusses new technologies aimed at ensuring grid flexibility and also includes some examples from the EU Member States. In addition, it examines the regulatory framework adopted (and which is currently under revision) to facilitate the progress towards a 'green' electricity grid.

In the Asia Pacific region, Penelope Crossley's chapter 14 on Australia has been written with largest bushfires in the country's history as a backdrop. The chapter discusses the conflicting objectives of Australia's approach to energy, the implications of the failure to integrate energy and climate law and how the worst drought and bushfires in Australia's history may change future regulation of the energy sector and Australia's approach to climate change.

No book on energy transition and decarbonisation in the twenty-first century could be complete without considering China. China's energy sector continues to be dominated by the State – through the ownership of the major producers and consumers of energy, the provision of finance, the approval of projects, and the control of some energy prices. Although the Government has been steadily increasing the role of economic policy instruments in this sector, administrative tools remain the preferred approach. Thus, China's relative success in curbing the use of coal and promoting natural gas and renewable energy has depended greatly on a combination of plans, regulations, decrees, preferential loans and subsidies. However, the efficacy of this approach has been frequently undermined by local governments and state-owned companies, not least because of the continued low cost of coal and the economic importance of the coal industry in many places. The Government is currently introducing several market mechanisms, including a power market and a carbon emissions trading scheme. These are unlikely to have a significant impact on the fuel mix, at least in the short-term, due to the predominance of state-owned enterprises in the power industry and the interference in these markets by local governments.

For Africa, the book centres around chapters on Nigeria and the Southern Africa region (chapters 13 and 16 respectively). The chapter on Nigeria, written by Ivie Ehanmo and Tade Oyewunmi, examines the regulatory framework governing the Nigerian Electricity Supply Industry (NESI) with particular emphasis on the development of on-grid and off-grid electricity systems. The chapter discusses the bottlenecks to power transmission of the recently privatised grid-based systems, and highlights the complexities of promoting access to reliable and affordable energy services. This context involves a developing economy, which is also the biggest economy in Africa, that is equally rich in hydrocarbons and thus rely considerably on natural gas for electricity generation. Nigeria has been the biggest oil and gas producer and resource-rich country on the continent for decades. Despite the structural reforms, liberalisation and partial privatisation of the Nigerian electricity supply industry under the 2001 National Electric Power Policy and the Electric Power Sector Reform Act 2005, there are several teething issues such as liquidity and curtailing transmission and distribution losses for grid-based energy systems. The chapter evaluates the framework for off-grid systems, which are designed to be powered mainly by renewables, including the various challenges and ends by proffering some plausible solutions.

The chapter examining the challenges and opportunities for energy transitions and decarbonisation in Southern African countries, by Victoria Nalule and Smith Azubuike, focuses on countries within the Southern African Development Community (SADC). The main objective of SADC is to achieve development, economic growth and alleviate poverty through regional integration. Such goals undeniably include access to modern energy in a secure, reliable and affordable way. For several decades, the dominant source of energy for grid-based electricity in the region is coal, followed by hydro. There is also the Southern African Power Pool (SAPP) whose electricity supply is dominated by generation from South Africa, a country that is highly dependent on coal, and a growing influence of oil, gas and renewables. As of 2019, coal made up 65.7 per cent of the primary energy in South Africa followed by crude oil at 21.6 per cent. There have been recent attempts to restructure and promote private sector participation, improve energy access to more affordable and universal energy access, especially to the rural areas, and a shift towards off-grid applications powered mostly by renewables. As with Nigeria, the most pressing issues in the region would be to ensure a just and fair transition that recognises and addresses the need for development powered by affordable access to energy and reliable energy services, while preventing environmental externalities as reasonably possible.

Chapter seven on private mineral rights and shale resources in Africa by Emeka Duruigbo examines the role played by private mineral ownership in the Shale Revolution. It argues that the absence of private ownership is an obstacle that needs to be overcome for shale gas development to thrive abroad. Nevertheless, the problem is not insurmountable. Policymakers simply need to consider private ownership of minerals or introduce effective substitutes to overcome the impediment, facilitate the development of these resources and reap the expected gains for the economy and environment. The chapter proposes one such substitute, namely Civic Shares.

Chapter eight on international oil and gas operators and decarbonisation by Peter Oniemola focuses on the impact of climate change initiatives internationally and their impact on traditional oil and gas companies. It looks further at what the international legal regime on climate change can offer to a change in the development of a regime for support of clean energy technologies through the sustainable development and market-based options that can be used under the Paris Agreement. Thereafter it discusses the trends in decarbonisation and how international oil and gas operators are affected. It examines measures for preparedness of states and the international oil and gas operators in the push towards decarbonisation and concludes on the need to follow decarbonisation paths.

Chapter five on global governance networks for climate change and energy investments by Frédéric Gilles Sourgens submits that the very task of decarbonisation governance cannot be monolithic. It cannot look at a single actor to bring about the desired result. It is instead made up of interweaving, intercommunicating and frequently competing governance networks. This chapter outlines what governance networks are involved in the decarbonisation process. The chapter further explains how these networks interact with each other so as to (hopefully) balance the maddeningly simple carbon equation of less out than in.

Chapter six by Diane Desierto and Frederic G Sourgens on energy decarbonisation and international investment law points out that an investment law and energy regime should strive to act as a catalyst for human development rather than simply as an aggregator of economic growth. The chapter appraises the role of investment law in global policy processes aimed at decarbonisation. It expounds on the concept of positive invocation of investment law for green energy development and the role of investment law in the reliance of investment protection to bind states to their promises to incentivise 'green' energy generation capacity such as solar power. Arguably, a design problem exists in the quest for energy decarbonisation to the extent that conventional energy systems (such as coal) responsible for most of the energy-related GHG emissions have a long life duration. The chapter further considers how investment law could better support human development in the context of decarbonisation. It highlights that decarbonisation cannot be achieved by the community of states alone, rather, as with the discussions in the global governance networks, it requires the input of all stakeholders.

In chapter nine on carbon taxation, Frederic G Sourgens and Lori A McMillan argue that it is not enough, that a goal is identified for policy and law to achieve – even if it is a laudable goal with a large consensus behind it such as taxing carbon emissions. Care must be taken that the legislation – in this case a tax provision for energy related decarbonisation – is sufficiently well-crafted to ensure that the underlying policy objective is in fact reached in a just, fair and reasonable way, ie it does so in the least harmful manner. In short, tax policy requires us to test that the tax and the carbon price set thereby really does what it promises – in this case to bring about a reduction in carbon emissions and attendant pollution, or at the very least force polluters to internalise the negative externalities they are creating. However, consideration must also be given to who actually bears the incidence of the tax, and whether there are consequences aside from the policy goal itself. In short, all sides must be identified and weighed when crafting a response to a problem through taxation as a regulatory tool. It is important to note that in setting a carbon price through taxation, a price that is significantly less than the 'true costs' would most likely not achieve the necessary goals of decarbonisation it sets out to meet. Rather it would create externalities of its own without absorbing the externalities of carbon emissions.

PART I

Enhancing Secure and Reliable Access to Sustainable Energy Systems in the Twenty-First Century

1

Tradeoffs and Tensions in the American Energy Transition

DAVID B SPENCE*

I. Introduction

Median public opinion in the United States on the question of the importance and urgency of action to address climate change has lagged behind most of the world's industrialised democracies. About six in ten US adults say they would 'favour' or 'strongly favour' policies that dramatically reduce the country's use of fossil fuels as a way to reduce greenhouse gas emissions and address climate change,[1] and a similar percentage see climate change as a 'major threat'.[2] By contrast there is near unanimity in support of those positions in most of western Europe.[3] Nevertheless, concern over climate is on the rise everywhere, and American climate policy is characterised by the lack of a durable national carbon policy, on the one hand, and a robust policy dialogue about policy change (mostly at the sub-national level), on the other. Within the last few years new plans to rapidly decarbonise the energy sector are peppering policy discourse and state and local law. These developments may reflect a growing sense that this is a particularly propitious moment to reduce carbon emissions from the electricity sector, because low-carbon electric generation resources have declined precipitously in price, stimulating customer demand for cheap, clean wind and solar power. At the same time, rapid decarbonisation presents difficult value choices for policymakers about how to manage persistent

---

*This chapter adapts and develops arguments and analyses first presented by the author in a 2017 conference at the University of Pennsylvania Wharton School and in a 2019 article published in the *Notre Dame Law Review*. The author wishes to thank Reem Ali for her research assistance in the preparation of this chapter.

[1] J McCarthy, 'Most Americans Support Reducing Fossil Fuel Use' (*Gallup*, 22 March 2019) available at https://news.gallup.com/poll/248006/americans-support-reducing-fossil-fuel.aspx.

[2] F Moira and H Christine, 'A Look at How People around the World View Climate Change' (*Pew Research* Center, 18 April 2019) available at www.pewresearch.org/fact-tank/2019/04/18/a-look-at-how-people-around-the-world-view-climate-change/.

[3] European Social Survey, 'European Attitudes to Climate Change and Energy: Topline Results from Round 8 of the European Social Survey' (September 2018) available at www.europeansocialsurvey.org/docs/findings/ESS8_toplines_issue_9_climatechange.pdf.

tradeoffs in the energy sector between the objective of reducing carbon emissions, on the one hand, and providing a reliable, affordable energy supply, on the other.

Every policy choice made in the cause of decarbonisation implicates – that is, represents an implicit decision about – these tradeoffs. Each decision will make energy more or less expensive and/or reliable for some people. These choices ought to be an explicit part of the process of choosing energy-related decarbonisation policies but remain obscured in the current American policy dialogue. That fact can be ascribed to two forces shaping the American policymaking environment. The first is the ideological hyper-polarisation of American political parties and partisans. While six in ten Americans view climate change as an important threat, only three in ten Republicans (versus eight in ten Democrats) typically hold the same view. The second force is the rise of digital information dissemination and social media networks as the dominant platforms on which public policy discussion takes place. Together these forces lead us to ignore or assume away tradeoffs, which is likely to slow progress toward reducing carbon emissions from the electricity sector (and other sectors) in the end. After a brief description of the unique structure of the American electricity sector, this chapter explores the political-economic dynamics that suppress the kind of dialogue that might help policymakers grapple with the tradeoffs associated with a rapid green transition from a system that relies mainly on hydrocarbons towards one that predominantly comprises low- or zero-carbon energy sources.

II. The American Electricity Sector

The provision of electricity service in the United States has always been dominated by private ownership – specifically investor-owned utilities (IOUs).[4] An early 'public power' movement led some cities and towns to provide electricity service within their boundaries, but these municipal utilities have been the exception to the rule.[5] As with the railroads, most late-nineteenth and early twentieth century states and municipalities sought to attract private investment in the provision of electricity services by offering investors a government-chartered monopoly and a fair return (via regulated rates) on their prudently made investments. In return, IOUs understood that their returns would be no greater than those required to provide reliable service, that they would be required to serve all customers within their territories, and that they would be prohibited from discriminating by price within customer classes. By the early part of the twentieth century, IOUs provided electric service in most of the places where it made economic sense to do so: that is,

---

[4] J Wasik, *Merchant of Power Sam Insull, Thomas Edison, and the Creation of the Modern Metropolis* (Palgrave Macmillan, 2015).
[5] A Richardson and J Kelly, 'The Relevance and Importance of Public Power in the United States' (2005) 19 *Natural Resources & Environment* 54.

where there was sufficient population density and wealth to make the provision of service profitable according to these ratemaking rules. State public utility commissions regulated the terms and conditions (including price) by which IOUs provided monopoly service to customers within their territories. The Rural Electrification Act, part of the New Deal,[6] eventually provided a mechanism to bring electricity to poorer, more sparsely populated parts of the country not served by IOUs or municipal utilities, by facilitating the creation of rural electricity co-ops.[7]

By the second half of the twentieth century, virtually everyone in the United States received electricity service from a monopoly provider whose large, generating stations delivered power over the 'network-bound' largely centralised electric grid. About three-quarters of American customers were served by IOUs, with the remainder being served by municipal utilities and rural co-ops. IOUs were typically vertically-integrated in that they generated most of the power that they sold to their customers' municipal utilities and co-ops sometimes generated their own power, but often purchased power at wholesale from IOUs, and IOUs sometimes purchased power at wholesale from each other. These individual utility-owned systems were stitched together over time into a vast American electric grid that comprises three large grids: one covering the eastern part of the country, a second covering the western part, and a third that exists entirely within the state of Texas so that Texas may avoid certain aspects of federal regulation by refraining from interstate commerce in electricity.[8]

Because American customers were served by monopolies, regulators set the price of electricity. Regulatory jurisdiction in this system is bifurcated. The US Federal Power Act (FPA) gives the Federal Energy Regulatory Commission (FERC) ratemaking jurisdiction over wholesale sales and the transmission of electricity in interstate commerce; it reserves to the states the authority to site generators and set rates for retail sales and distribution. Both the FPA and its state analogues require that rates be 'just and reasonable', language that courts have interpreted to mandate a kind of qualified cost-minimisation rule. That is, utilities are entitled to earn a return on investment sufficient to provide reliable service to customers, but no more than that.[9] Critics of rate regulation note that this rule provides IOUs with an incentive to overinvest in assets or capital which may not be necessary for maintaining the basic reliability obligation; information asymmetries between IOUs and regulators may facilitate that overinvestment – a phenomena known within economics as the Averch-Johnson effect.[10] Worry about the Averch-Johnson

---

[6] The 'New Deal' is the name historians have given to the legislative programme proposed by President Franklin D Roosevelt to lift the United States from depression in the 1930s.
[7] JB Eisen et al, *Energy, Economics and the Environment: Cases and Materials* (Foundation Press, 2015) 29–73.
[8] DB Spence and D Bush, 'Why Does ERCOT Have Only One Regulator?' in LL Kiesling and And Kleit (eds), *Electricity Restructuring: The Texas Story* (Aei Press, 2009).
[9] *FCP v Hope Natural Gas Co*, 320 US 591 (1944).
[10] H Averch and L Johnson, 'Behavior of the Firm Subject to External Regulatory Constraint' (1962) 52 *The American Economic Review* 1052.

effect comprised part of the argument for the late twentieth century move toward competition and market pricing in the electricity sector.[11]

Regardless, electric utilities have assiduously followed the cost-minimisation rule in the way they dispatch (use) power plants to satisfy demand that fluctuates over the course of the day, or the year. Because electricity cannot be stored at commercial quantities, the electric grid must be kept in balance at all times in order to ensure reliable service.[12] Therefore, as consumer demand for electricity varies, grid operators must match those variations by varying the amount of electricity that generators dispatch to the grid in real time. And because individual utility systems are interconnected, this balancing takes place continuously across each of the three major American grids (Eastern Interconnect, Western Interconnect and Texas). Grid operators dispatch the available generators with the lowest marginal costs first, subject to the need to maintain reliability, a practice known in the industry as the 'security constrained economic dispatch' (SCED) rule.[13]

The SCED rule minimises costs because once the upfront capital costs of a generating unit are sunk, it is economically rational for the seller to minimise its marginal costs. For most generating units, the primary component of marginal costs is fuel (eg in a gas-fired or coal-fired unit, the costs attributed to the delivery through pipelines and the wholesale price of 'gas volumes' or coal respectively used as fuel). Therefore, dispatch order has been heavily influenced by historical fluctuations in the relative price of electric generation fuels. However, under traditional rate regulation, ratepayers pay not only for fuel costs but for capital costs and all of the other costs of providing electric service. Theoretically, IOUs and regulators minimised long run total costs to ratepayers by approving the construction of a diverse portfolio of generating plants that would be flexible enough to maintain reliable service and hedge against drastic changes in relative fuel prices. In any case, courts deem these cost minimisation rules to be required by the 'just and reasonable' rate requirement in public utility statutes.[14]

Beginning in the 1990s, regulators and state legislatures sought to introduce competition and market pricing into the electricity sector. The FERC took action in the mid-1990s to: (i) 'unbundle' (force the separation of) electricity transmission from wholesale power sales, forcing IOUs to open up access to the transmission grid to third parties, thereby introducing competition into wholesale power markets; and (ii) authorise wholesale sales of power at market (rather than administratively-set) prices. Around the same time, a minority of states – including California, Texas, New York and much of New England – took parallel

---

[11] SG Breyer and PW MacAvoy, *Energy Regulation by the Federal Power Commission* (Brookings Institution, 1974).

[12] That is, in order to keep the lights on, the American alternating current grid must be kept at a frequency of 60 Hz; if it deviates too far from this target, it fails. This is a feature of all alternating current grids, though some balance at frequencies other than 60Hz (North American Electric Reliability Corporation, 2011).

[13] Eisen et al (n 7) 695.

[14] Eisen et al (n 7) 695.

regulatory action to unbundle their retail markets, introducing competition and market pricing into retail sales. These moves jump-started previously moribund bulk power markets, as retailers started seeking power supplies from new and geographically-distant sources. This in turn stimulated the FERC to nudge IOUs to create regional governance institutions for wholesale power markets. Those governance institutions, known variously as Regional Transmission Organisations (RTOs) or Independent System Operators (ISOs), are non-profit associations of IOUs which manage the operation of regional transmission grids and oversee the operation of competitive wholesale power markets.[15] In RTO markets wholesale prices are set by supply and demand and vary across both time and locations on the regional system. This depends upon the cost of the marginal generator supplying power to that location and any congestion constraints impeding the flow of power to that location. In this way, the SCED rule is reflected in the connection between wholesale spot prices and the marginal cost of supplying power to specific places at specific times.

The spectacular failure of California's newly-competitive power market in late 2000 and early 2001 slowed the move toward restructuring in the other states, such that electricity markets in the United States now fall into one of three categories:

a) *traditional markets*, where rate regulation and vertically integrated monopolies continue to prevail;
b) *fully competitive markets*, where both wholesale and retail power markets are characterised by competition and market pricing; and
c) *hybrid markets*, where competition and market pricing reigns in wholesale power markets, but retail prices continue to be regulated.

Thus, twenty-first century American electricity markets are a polyglot. In many of the south-eastern states (traditional markets), customers continue to pay a single, regulated, volumetric rate for bundled service provided (and mostly generated) by their monopoly IOU. In that way, those markets incentivise investment in generation as they always have.

In fully competitive regions such as in New England, or states like Texas and New York, retail customers can shop for power from among a wide variety of retail sellers competing for their business. They pay a market price for power and a separate (regulated) fee to the monopoly provider of transmission and distribution services. Generators must recoup their costs from power sales (in New England and New York, but not in Texas) and they have the potential to earn capacity payments designed to incentivise sufficient generation reserves. Retailers secure the power they need to serve their customers on competitive wholesale markets overseen by RTOs/ISOs, like the New England ISO (ISONE), the Electric Reliability Council of Texas (ERCOT) or the New York ISO, respectively. Lastly, in hybrid states like

---

[15] DB Spence, 'Can Law Manage Competitive Energy Markets?' (2008) 93 *Cornell Law Review* 767; W Boyd, 'Public Utility and the Low-Carbon Future' (2014) 61 *UCLA Law Review* 1616.

Minnesota and Wisconsin, monopoly utilities continue to provide retail service at regulated rates, but purchase most of the power they sell to their customers on competitive wholesale markets overseen by the Midcontinent ISO.

III. The Green Transition in the United States

A. Regulatory Developments and Policy Momentum

As already noted, a clear majority of the American citizenry now accepts the reality and seriousness of climate change, but that national majority opinion is not reflected in national policy. After Congress failed to address carbon emissions in 2010,[16] the Obama Administration's so-called 'Clean Power Plan' (CPP) took the first steps toward regulating carbon emissions from the electricity sector by establishing guidelines for states' plans to limit carbon dioxide emissions from existing power plants.[17] The Trump Environmental Protection Agency (EPA), however, repealed the CPP in June 2019 and replaced it with its Affordable Clean Energy (ACE) rule,[18] which relaxes the CPP's limits on fossil-fuelled power plants.[19] The ACE rule reflects the preferences of a majority of Republican voters and politicians, who continue to oppose policies to reduce carbon emissions. Because of the lack of a coherent federal carbon emissions policy, what climate policy momentum exists in the United States can be found in state and local governments, or in academic and activist policy networks.

In recent years several states have established ambitious decarbonisation goals. In California, Governor Jerry Brown signed a bill mandating 50 per cent of California's electricity to be powered by renewable resources by 2025 and 60 per cent by 2030, while calling for a 'bold path' toward 100 per cent zero-carbon electricity by 2045.[20] Hawaii has established a goal of 100 per cent renewable electricity sources by 2045.[21] New York State's Climate Leadership and Community Protection Act calls for all the state's electricity to come from carbon-free sources

---

[16] Legislation to establish a cap and trade system for carbon emissions passed in the US House of Representatives in 2009, but failed in the Senate in 2010. H.R.2454–American Clean Energy and Security Act of 2009, available at www.congress.gov/bill/111th-congress/house-bill/2454.

[17] Environmental Protection Agency (EPA), 'Carbon Pollution Emission Guidelines for Existing Stationary Sources: Electric Utility Generating Units' (*EPA*, 23 Oct 2015), available at www.federalregister.gov/documents/2015/10/23/2015-22842/carbon-pollution-emission-guidelines-for-existing-stationary-sources-electric-utility-generating.

[18] EPA, 'Electric Utility Generating Units: Repealing the Clean Power Plan' (*EPA*, 19 June 2019), available at www.epa.gov/stationary-sources-air-pollution/electric-utility-generating-units-repealing-clean-power-plan#additional-resources.

[19] EPA, 'Affordable Clean Energy Rule' (*EPA*, 19 July 2019), available at www.epa.gov/stationary-sources-air-pollution/affordable-clean-energy-rule.

[20] California Public Utilities Code (hereinafter 'Cal. Pub. Util. Code') § 399.11 (2019); Cal. Pub. Util. Code § 399.15 (2019); Cal. Pub. Util. Code § 399.30 (2019).

[21] Hawaii Revised Statutes (hereinafter 'Haw. Rev. Stat.') § 269–92.

by 2030, and for 70 per cent of which must be from renewable sources.[22] The State of Washington's 2019 Clean Energy Transformation Act requires all electric utilities in Washington to transition to carbon-neutral electricity by 2030.[23] New Mexico has mandated that the state's publicly regulated utilities receive all of their electricity from carbon-free sources by 2045.[24] And other states are establishing ambitious goals that nevertheless stop short of complete elimination of carbon emissions: for example, Minnesota law establishes a goal of reducing greenhouse gas emissions by 80 per cent by 2050.[25] Each of these state programmes is unique, establishing slightly different goals and timetables, and covering different combinations of business sectors, reflecting the absence of national policy in the federal American system.

In some places, the momentum for a green transition comes not from top-down policies but by bottom-up market demand. Conservative Republican Texas has more than three times as much wind-generating capacity as any other state, thanks to ample wind resources, low regulatory barriers to entry for generators, and the state's decision to build transmission lines to remote parts of west and north Texas where wind resources are strongest. The green transition is also happening at the local level. Aspen, Colorado, Georgetown, Texas and more than 100 other American cities have pledged to meet their electricity needs using '100 percent renewable' energy.[26] And several major IOUs have pledged to rapidly reduce their reliance on fossil fuels: Xcel Energy, serving parts of Minnesota and Colorado, has pledged to rely only on generation that emits no carbon dioxide at all (100 per cent emission reduction) by 2050.[27]

Another source of pressure for a more vigorous national climate policy comes from activist groups and other non-governmental organisations (NGOs) whose influence has been felt in the race for the Democratic Party nomination for the presidency in 2020. An NGO called the Sunrise Movement pushed the issue to the forefront with their 2018 proposal for a 'Green New Deal',[28] and in 2019 presidential candidates began embracing its terms in an attempt to attract the support of Democratic Party voters. Almost all of the presidential candidate plans call for the elimination of carbon emissions from the electricity sector by 2050,[29] and

---

[22] New York Environmental Conservation Law § 75–0103 (McKinney).
[23] Washington Revised Code Ann. § 19.285.040.
[24] Energy Transition Act, 2019 Bill Text NM S.B. 489 (official classification pending).
[25] Minnesota Statutes § 216H.02.
[26] '100% Commitments in Cities, Counties, & States' (*Sierra Club*, 5 April 2019) available at www.sierraclub.org/ready-for-100/commitments.
[27] 'Building a Carbon Free Future' (*Xcel Energy*, 2019) available at www.xcelenergy.com/staticfiles/xe/PDF/Xcel Energy Carbon Report -Feb 2019.pdf.
[28] See D Roberts, 'The Green New Deal, Explained' (*Vox*, 30 March 2019), available at www.vox.com/energy-and-environment/2018/12/21/18144138/green-new-deal-alexandria-ocasio-cortez.
[29] L Bloomer and C McCoy, 'In Which We Compare Democratic Presidential Candidates' Climate Plans – Environmental & Energy Law Program' (*Harvard Law School*, 5 September 2019), available at https://eelp.law.harvard.edu/2019/09/in-which-we-compare-democratic-presidential-candidates-climate-plans/.

some would aim to do so using only renewable energy (no nuclear or fossil-fuelled power).[30]

These bolder climate policy ambitions have been fed in part by aggressive rapid-decarbonisation plans and ideologies emerging from academia, some of which call for the construction of massive amounts of renewable energy infrastructure – a huge continental system of renewable generators connected by a new transmission network.[31] Furthermore, now that renewables are price competitive with traditional energy sources in many places, corporate customers are demanding more clean energy.[32] For example, the desire for cheap renewable power is driving proposals to build new transmission capacity linking: (i) the windy central plains to load centres to the East – cities like Minneapolis, Chicago, St Louis and Houston – where consumers want utility-scale wind power;[33] and (ii) transmission linking Texas wind power to consumers in the south-eastern gulf coast states.[34] Indeed, it may be that willing developer-sellers and corporate buyers of green power are unable to make these deals because of the legal and political difficulties of building interstate transmission lines. States retain a veto over transmission siting, and their legal regimes discourage (or outlaw) development of transmission by non-utilities.[35]

In any case, there appears to be a growing momentum for rapid development of cleaner energy sources in the United States. Some of it is coming from the bottom-up in the form of market demand for cheap, clean electricity. Some of it is coming from the top-down in the form of ambitious decarbonisation targets established by left-leaning states.

---

[30] This is true of the plans put forth by Senator Bernie Sanders and Senator Elizabeth Warren. *Ibid*.

[31] See MZ Jacobson et al, 'Low-Cost Solution to the Grid Reliability Problem with 100% Penetration of Intermittent Wind, Water, and Solar for All Purposes' (2015) 112 *Proceedings of the National Academy of Sciences* 15060 (calling for the construction of a continental high-voltage transmission system to connect new and far flung utility-scale renewable generators). Others note that this plan contemplates a level of transmission and generation investment that is 14 times historic annual rates; Clack C et al, 'Evaluation of a Proposal for Reliable Low-Cost Grid Power with 100% Wind, Water and Solar' (2017) 114 *Proceedings of the National Academy of Sciences* 6722.

[32] See J Pyper, 'The Latest Trends in Corporate Renewable Energy Procurement' (*Greentech Media*, 30 June 2017), available at www.greentechmedia.com/articles/read/the-latest-trends-in-corporate-renewable-energy procurement (describing exponential growth in demand recently); D Gardiner and Associates, 'The Growing Demand for Renewable Energy Among Major U.S …' (12 September 2017), available at www.dgardiner.com/wp-content/uploads/2017/09/Renewable-Energy-and-Climate-Commitments-in-the-Manufacturing-Sector_FINAL9.19.2017FINAL.pdf (describing the prevalence of clean energy goals among major manufacturers).

[33] Perhaps the best way to visualise this agenda is to view the map of transmission projects proposed by Clean Line Energy Partners, a merchant transmission company seeking to connect wind farms in the central plains to cities to the East. That map is viewable at: www.cleanlineenergy.com/projects.

[34] The role of the Southern Cross Transmission Project bringing Texas wind power to south-eastern states is explained at the project website, www.southerncrosstransmission.com.

[35] For descriptions of this problem see: R Gold, *Superpower: One Man's Quest to Transform American Energy* (Simon & Schuster, 2019) (telling the story of Clean Line Energy, a failed merchant transmission developer whose business model aimed to support wind energy); DB Spence, 'Naive Energy Markets' (2017) 92 *Notre Dame Law School* 973.

B. Affordability and Reliability Tradeoffs – Are they Real?

If there is to be a rapid transition to drastically lower carbon emissions in the electricity sector, it will require decisions about how managers of the electric grid maintain a reliable supply as intermittent wind and solar generators comprise an ever-larger share of the generation mix. This is an issue that has been plagued by a 'cry wolf' problem in the past. Grid managers have claimed that relatively low penetrations of wind and solar would disrupt the reliability of the energy supply, only to find that the system could accommodate far larger penetrations into the market without jeopardising reliability. Wind and solar generation now regularly exceed 50 per cent of power in parts of the country, sometimes for relatively long stretches of time, without outages. Grid operators have made great strides forecasting wind and adjusting grid management and electricity market institutions to accommodate the unique characteristics of wind power. On the other hand, the variability of wind and solar power do pose new challenges to grid operators. There is *some* level of wind and solar penetration that poses reliability (or cost) problems, in part because the wind sometimes doesn't blow, and the sun doesn't shine.

i. Reliability and Cost in a Mostly Renewables System

In other words, even though integrating renewable power into the electric mix is getting cheaper and easier, we still depend on non-renewable sources when the wind doesn't blow, and the sun doesn't shine at the time and scale required. Without those resources, will the lights remain on? Can we afford to pay for their replacement by zero-carbon generation and storage?

Three rejoinders are often used to assuage this concern. One rejoinder to worries about the cost of a reliable, 100 per cent renewable energy-based system is that the alternative is even more costly. Fossil fuel combustion, and particularly coal combustion, imposes enormous costs on society in the form of premature deaths and other harms to human health and the environment. We have experience valuing those costs, and they are indeed huge.[36] Many analysts conclude that the total costs (including social costs) of a zero emission energy system will be lower than those associated with the current energy mix.[37] But out-of-pocket costs

---

[36] See PR Epstein et al, 'Full Cost Accounting for the Life Cycle of Coal' (2011) 1219 *Annals of the New York Academy of Sciences* 73 (assessing the costs associated with coal production in the hundreds of billions, much of it associated with premature deaths); and NZ Muller, R Mendelsohn and W Nordhaus, 'Environmental Accounting for Pollution in the United States Economy' (2011) 101 *American Economic Review* 1649 (estimating the mortality and morbidity harm associated with coal combustion at more than 50 times that of natural gas combustion); L Chen, SA Miller and BR Ellis, 'Comparative Human Toxicity Impact of Electricity Produced from Shale Gas and Coal' (2017) 51 *Environmental Science & Technology* 13018 (documenting similarly disparate impacts from discharges of toxics over the life cycle of coal and natural gas for use as electricity fuels).

[37] Jacobson et al (n 31).

matter too, because someone must pay for the construction of new infrastructure necessary to make the transition a reality. A greener energy system will impose more out-of-pocket costs than the current system does. Acknowledging that fact and making decisions about how those costs should be distributed, are important elements of a just and reasonable green transition. Hence the enormous price tags attached to proposals like the Green New Deal.[38] Those distributional cost impacts will shape the politics of pursuing a green grid.

A second rejoinder (offered most often by economists) is to say that we can simply let the market make these tradeoffs for us if we get prices right by imposing a carbon tax. This may be conceptually true, and even a modest carbon tax would hasten reductions in carbon emissions from the power sector.[39] However, there is considerable disagreement among policy analysts about the appropriate size of the tax, whether it should be revenue-neutral, and more production vs consumption focused. And like most taxes, carbon taxes are not popular with voters, and the prospects for a national carbon tax appear remote.

A third rejoinder to worries about affordability and reliability is to deny that a green transition poses reliability and affordability tradeoffs in the first place, because renewable power is already less expensive than the alternatives; indeed, cities and companies are already purchasing 100 per cent renewable power. Political jurisdictions[40] and companies[41] that have pledged to consume only renewable energy now or in the future will (with very few exceptions) continue to consume electricity, some of which comes from non-renewable sources, for at least the next several decades. Even though those consumers contract to purchase electricity only from renewable generators (or buy renewable energy credits) in amounts that represent all of their annual consumption, the electricity they take from the grid cannot be directed to specific consumers; nor is there sufficient grid-connected renewable power to serve demand at all times (say, on still nights). In that sense, these 100 per cent renewable consumers effectively rely in part on non-renewable power.[42]

---

[38] Proponents of the Green New Deal overcome cost limitations by assuming that the Federal Government can fund trillions of dollars of spending on a new green grid through a combination of public debt and quantitative easing. A macroeconomic theory called 'modern monetary theory' or 'modern money theory' differs from mainstream macroeconomic theory in its optimism about the ability of the US Government to issue large amounts of additional public debt without significantly chilling demand for that debt, and to increase the money supply without triggering inflation. This is partly why the Sanders campaign proposes federal ownership of most of the new green grid.

[39] D Adelman and D Spence, 'U.S. Climate Policy and the Regional Economics of Electricity Generation' (*Energy Policy*, September 2018), available at www.sciencedirect.com/science/article/pii/S0301421518303112?via%3Dihub.

[40] See Sierra Club's list of '100% renewable' cities at: www.sierraclub.org/ready-for-100/commitments.

[41] An organisation called 'RE100' keeps track of companies that have pledged to secure 100% renewable power. That list can be found at: www.there100.org/companies.

[42] J Rhodes, 'What Does 100% Renewable Energy Really Mean?' (*Forbes*, 22 August 2018), available at www.forbes.com/sites/joshuarhodes/2018/08/21/what-does-100-renewable-energy-really-mean/#50b094fe1ac8.

It is true that renewables are indeed cheapest on a levelised-cost basis: that is, if we assume that generators can sell all the power they generate over the course of their useful life, wind and solar generators can turn a profit at a lower average power price than gas-fired, coal-fired or nuclear generators.[43] However, unlike those other technologies, wind generators cannot be counted upon to back up other wind generators (and other solar generators) because they tend to generate power during the same – or substantially overlapping – subsets of the day and year. Might excess wind and solar power be stored for later use during daily or seasonal wind and solar droughts? The costs of battery storage have been falling, and more 'solar plus storage' projects are being built, financed by long-term power purchase agreements with utilities or other buyers. Given the downward cost trajectory of battery storage, these systems may offer a zero-carbon answer to the daily supply problem (overnight supply).

In traditional, vertically integrated utility systems, these projects can thrive. In competitive markets, they face some challenges. A glut of renewable power at certain times (of the day or year) improves the economics of operating a storage system because it reduces the costs of storage; but it hurts the economics of operating a wind or solar generator because it means that wind and solar farms will either have to pay to 'sell' their power to storage facilities (negative pricing), or will not be able to sell to anyone during glut periods. Either way, this weakens the business case for developing a renewable generation facility in the first place. Stated differently, if the generator must recover its costs of operation from the sale of fewer kilowatt-hours of electricity during its useful life, its levelised costs go up. In lay terms, it must command higher prices for its product.

That seems unlikely in a market in which the spot price is determined by the marginal cost of the last-dispatched generator, and more and more (renewable) generators have zero marginal costs. In traditional markets, IOUs can recover the costs of building (or buying from) a renewable generator; in competitive markets, they cannot. In some competitive wholesale markets, generators can earn capacity payments, but ISOs and RTOs sometimes make it difficult for renewable generators to compete for those payments.[44] In one American market – Texas – regulators use scarcity pricing to incentivise investment in reserve generation capacity. Wholesale prices can rise as high as $9000/mwh there. However, reserve capacity has fallen almost 50 per cent below the regulators' targets there, and it remains to be seen whether scarcity pricing alone will incentivise investment in an adequate supply of reserves there.

Bluntly put, the prospect of having to compete with other renewable generators for scarce buyers during oversupply periods will make these facilities difficult to finance absent very high scarcity prices or some sort of price guarantee from

---

[43] J Lazard, 'Lazard's Levelized Cost of Energy Analysis -Version 12.0' (*Lazard*, November 2018), available at www.lazard.com/media/450784/lazards-levelized-cost-of-energy-version-120-vfinal.pdf.
[44] J Macey and S Salovaara, 'Rate Regulation Redux' (*University of Pennsylvania Law Review*, 2019), available at https://papers.ssrn.com/sol3/papers.cfm?abstract_id=3362920.

government or other market overseers like RTOs and ISOs. Moreover, even if we build a continental grid connecting massive additional numbers of wind and solar generators, that is unlikely to entirely eliminate the need for some form of additional back-up supply to cover rare-but-inevitable long wind or solar droughts.[45] Might storage of renewable power offer a solution to seasonal renewables droughts?

Technologies like pumped storage hydro or compressed air storage have much longer duration, and have lower levelised costs of storage compared to batteries. But they are large capital projects unlikely to be financed absent revenue guarantees that are not yet forthcoming from the market or from governments. Given what we know about wind and solar variability and the current cost of long-term (more than four hours) battery storage, transforming that supplementary power into zero-carbon (emissions) power will require some combination of changing economics and mandates. Without those mandates, conservative Republican states are likely to keep natural gas generators on the grid for back-up supply, because it is more expensive to build a large enough system of (rarely used) wind farms, solar arrays, transmission lines and batteries necessary to ensure a reliable supply. Left-leaning states seem more willing to push the market in that direction. California, for example, is actively pushing to reduce emissions from back-up power supplies. Californians hold more negative attitudes toward natural gas, and the state aggressively subsidises batteries and other kinds of electricity storage in an attempt to lay the foundation for a truly 100 per cent renewable power supply: one that generates renewable energy for direct use now and also stores it for use later when the wind isn't blowing and the sun isn't shining. Presumably those presidential candidates whose plans exclude nuclear and fossil-fuelled generation from the future generation mix assume the existence of an affordable set of storage options for renewable power in the future.[46] That is a big assumption.

A small number of political jurisdictions and firms have access to sufficient amounts of dispatchable renewable resources – like geothermal power or hydroelectric power operated in storage mode – to provide sufficient back-up supply in the face of these short-term weather conditions. Iceland, for example, has ample geothermal and hydroelectric power that is generally dispatchable when needed. In the United States, where wind and solar are the dominant renewable resources, some sort of more traditionally-dispatchable source of power (or electricity storage) is needed to fill in when the wind isn't blowing, and the sun isn't shining. Moreover, building a truly 100 per cent renewable electric grid would require building an enormous amount of mostly-redundant renewable generation to compensate for regional variation in wind and charge electricity storage facilities, as well as much more electricity storage and transmission capacity. Right now,

---

[45] Energy and Environmental Economics, Inc (E3), 'A Study of Policies to Decarbonize the Electric Sector, Pacific NW' (2017), available at www.ethree.com/projects/study-policies-decarbonize-electric-sector-northwest-public-generating-pool-2017-present/. E3, 'Resource Adequacy in the Pacific NW' (2019), available at www.ethree.com/wp-content/uploads/2019/03/E3_Resource_Adequacy_in_the_Pacific-Northwest_March_2019.pdf.

[46] Senator Bernie Sanders' plan is framed this way.

that kind of commitment looks technically possible but politically unrealistic and expensive: a little like jumping off a cliff and hoping to invent a parachute on the way down.

One meta-analysis concludes that including firm low-carbon (but non-renewable) resources is more achievable, less expensive, and yields a more reliable low- or zero-carbon electric system.[47] Some other analyses conclude that the out-of-pocket price of a renewables-only supply is very high. Wood McKenzie puts the cost of such a system at $35,000 per US household.[48] The American Action Forum puts the cost at $5.7 trillion, or $42,000 per household.[49] Others have highlighted a different kind of cost – namely, the magnitude of the scaling problem inherent in a rapid transition, which in turn implicates environmental issues. A massive build-out of wind, solar and batteries consistent with a zero-carbon emission future implies huge increases in world outputs of copper, zinc, aluminum, lead, silver, cadmium, lithium and various other minerals that are used in the production of these forms of energy production and storage. One analysis put the increase in lithium production above current levels at 2700 per cent. Many of these supplies come from countries with lax environmental standards.[50] Thus, the environmental and security-of-supply implications create a separate dilemma and set of externalities that are often under-emphasised or overlooked.

For the time being, it's much cheaper to back up renewable power with non-renewable, firm resources. Perhaps by 2045 that no longer will be true. This reality may explain the difference between presidential candidates' promises to phase out nuclear and gas-fired generators, and state plans' focus on eliminating emissions rather than particular fuels. The plan proposed by Senator Bernie Sanders comes with a $16.3 trillion price tag, some of which may be attributable to the need for a massive build-out of (rarely used) back-up generation, transmission and storage infrastructure. Senator Sanders' energy plan and the Sunrise Movement's Green New Deal have common roots (Sanders calls his plan the 'Green New Deal'), and both are apparently premised on the notion that federal financing of new green infrastructure can be used to avoid imposing costs on ratepayers. Citing a strain

---

[47] JD Jenkins and S Thernstrom, 'Deep Decarbonization of the Electric Power Sector: Insights from the Recent Literature' (*Energy Innovation Reform* Project, March 2017), available at www.innovationreform.org/wp-content/uploads/2018/02/EIRP-Deep-Decarb-Lit-Review-Jenkins-Thernstrom-March-2017.pdf; and NA Sepulveda et al, 'The Role of Firm Low-Carbon Electricity Resources in Deep Decarbonization of Power Generation' (2018) 2 *Joule* 2403.

[48] D Shreve and W Schauer, 'Decarbonisation' (*Decarbonisation*, June 2019), available at www.decarbonisation.think.woodmac.com/; See also I Gheorghiu, 'Transitioning US to 100% Renewables by 2030 Will Cost $4.5 Trillion: Wood Mackenzie' (*Utility Dive*, 28 June 2019), available at www.utilitydive.com/news/transitioning-us-to-100-renewables-by-2030-will-cost-rate-payers-45t-wo/557832/; A Watts and T Benson, 'Analysis: Cost Of U.S. Transition To 100% Renewables – $4.5 Trillion' (*Watts Up With That?*, 9 July 2019), available at www.wattsupwiththat.com/2019/07/09/analysis-cost-of-u-s-transition-to-100-renewables-4-5-trillion.

[49] P Rossetti, 'What It Costs to Go 100 Percent Renewable' (*American Action Forum*, 25 January 2019), available at www.americanactionforum.org/research/what-it-costs-go-100-percent-renewable.

[50] J Hickel, 'The Limits of Clean Energy' (*Foreign Policy*, 6 September 2019), available at www.foreignpolicy.com/2019/09/06/the-path-to-clean-energy-will-be-very-dirty-climate-change-renewables/.

of macroeconomic theory called 'modern monetary theory', proponents of the Green New Deal contend that the Federal Government can pay for it by issuing enough government debt and/or increasing the money supply to cover the tens of trillions of dollars it is estimated to cost without triggering inflation or harming the credit-worthiness of the American Government.[51] This is apparently not a mainstream macroeconomic view, but it is gaining adherents among the American progressive left.

Can some of these tradeoff problems be solved by reducing reliance on the electric grid in the first place, and instead generating energy and using it more efficiently at home, or in local microgrids, ie distributed and decentralised energy systems? Perhaps, if technology improves and becomes less costly. Microgrids and home devices can add resiliency to parts of a system, but right now going completely off the grid means more expensive, less reliable energy in most places. For example, the average cost of generating electricity from rooftop solar units is several times higher than the cost of generating it at utility-scale solar farms and sending it to customers.[52] And owners of rooftop solar units do not merely supply their own homes and businesses with the power they generate; rather, the owner of a rooftop unit typically consumes power from the grid when the sun isn't shining and dispatches excess power to the grid when the sun is shining. Not only do owners of rooftop solar continue to depend upon grid power, they are often compensated for the excess power they sell to the grid more generously than owners of utility-scale solar units. In many jurisdictions, the consumer is compensated at the retail rate (rather than the wholesale rate) for the power it sells to the grid, a practice called 'net metering'. There is considerable disagreement about the appropriate compensation level for that power, but there is no disagreement that this practice tends to shift out-of-pocket grid costs from (relatively wealthy) adopters of solar units to non-adopters.[53]

On the other hand, there are important legal and political obstacles to building the transmission system we need to support the green grid.[54] State vetoes and local opposition make taking advantage of cheaper, more equitably priced utility scale renewable power difficult. If those obstacles cannot be overcome, perhaps a more decentralised (albeit more expensive) system may offer a second-best route to a greener electricity system by avoiding difficult political tradeoffs.

---

[51] S Horsley, 'This Economic Theory Could Be Used To Pay For The Green New Deal' (*NPR*, 17 July 2018), available at www.npr.org/2019/07/17/742255158/this-economic-theory-could-be-used-to-pay-for-the-green-new-deal.

[52] Lazard (n 43).

[53] S Burger, '#16 – The Economics of Rooftop Solar' (*SoundCloud*), available at www.soundcloud.com/mitenergy/the-economics-of-rooftop-solar; and S Burger, 'Rate Design for the 21st Century: Improving Economic Efficiency and Distributional Equity in Electric Rate Design' (Massachusetts Institute of Technology, PhD Dissertation, 9 August, 2019), available at www.dropbox.com/s/gsox-1prub8cj193/190726_Dissertation_Burger_Final.pdf?dl=0.

[54] DB Spence, 'The New Politics of (Energy) Market Entry' (2019) 95 *Notre Dame Law Review* 327.

Green ambitions implicate a number of difficult value and distributional choices – tradeoffs that politicians and policymakers will decide more or less explicitly. Unfortunately, the polarisation and emotional intensity that characterises energy politics in the United States makes it difficult to address those tradeoff questions openly and honestly.

ii. The Politics of Tradeoffs

Two interrelated societal forces seem to be intensifying conflict over energy infrastructure in the twenty-first century. One is the shift of information exchange and policy discussion on to digital platforms, and the other is the well-documented hyper-polarisation of the American polity. At first, scholars treated the rise of digital media and the Internet as a force for social integration. The integration argument sees digital inter-connectedness as likely to expose citizens to a broader set of views, improving civic culture and promoting deliberative democracy.[55] More recent scholarship, however, contradicts that optimistic view and points instead to fragmented internet subcultures and homogenous opinion ecosystems that contribute to ideological polarisation among the politically-active portion of the population, in part by inoculating belief against the effects of new information.[56] These technological changes, in turn, may be both a cause and a consequence of increasing ideological polarisation of American political parties, particularly over the issue of government intervention in the market (regulation), including energy markets.

By any of several measures, Congress is more ideologically polarised than ever before in the modern regulatory era. The parties have grown steadily farther apart ideologically since the 1970s, making bipartisan action to address important problems like climate change much more difficult. A large and growing academic literature has documented this growing polarisation.[57] Keith Poole and Howard

---

[55] P Dahlgren, 'In Search of the Talkative Public: Media, Deliberative Democracy and Civic Culture' (2002) 9 *Javnost-The Public* 5; J Kim, RO Wyatt and E Katz, 'News, Talk, Opinion, Participation: The Part Played by Conversation in Deliberative Democracy' (14 November 2014) 16 *Political Communication* 361; DV Shah et al, 'Information and Expression in a Digital Age' (2005) 32 *Communication Research* 531; and Cramer Walsh K, *Talking About Politics: Informal Groups And Social Identity In American Life* (The University of Chicago Press Books, 2004).

[56] MD Vicario et al, 'The Spreading of Misinformation Online' (2016) 113 *Proceedings of the National Academy of Sciences* 554; MD Vicario et al, 'Mapping Social Dynamics on Facebook: The Brexit Debate' (2017) 50 *Social Networks* 6; M Schudson, 'Why Conversation Is Not the Soul of Democracy' (1997) 14 *Critical Studies in Mass Communication* 297; and DC Mutz, 'Impersonal Influence: How Perceptions Of Mass Collectives Affect Political Attitudes' (1998) 12 *Critical Studies In Mass Communication*.

[57] For a good overview of the various databases and theories of congressional polarisation, and an integration of some of those theories and data, see SM Theriault, *Party Polarization In Congress* (Cambridge University Press, 2008); JH Aldrich, *Why Parties?: The Origin and Transformation of Political Parties in America* (University of Chicago Press, 2007); KT Poole and H Rosenthal, *Ideology & Congress: A Political-Economic History of Roll Call Voting* (Transaction Publishers, 2007); MP Fiorina and SJ Abrams, 'Political Polarization in the American Public' (2008) 11 *Annual Review of Political Science* 563; MP Fiorina, 'Whatever Happened to the Median Voter?' (Midwest Political Science Association Annual Meeting in Chicago, Illinois, 1999).

Rosenthal's DW-NOMINATE dataset places members of Congress on an ideological spectrum based upon voting behaviour.[58] They conclude from their data that polarisation in the US House and Senate are at their highest levels since the end of Reconstruction.[59]

It seems almost self-evident that polarisation would increase the emotional intensity of political conflict, in two ways. First, as the parties' policy agendas grow farther apart ideologically,[60] each agenda appears increasing unacceptable – even alarming – to members of the opposite party, making political victory seem an ever more important moral imperative. If politically active Democrats and liberals see reducing carbon emissions as an urgent national priority requiring government attention, the unwillingness of Republicans and conservatives to support that urgent project seems alarming.[61] At the same time, if increasing numbers of Republicans and conservatives equate unregulated markets (including energy markets) with freedom and the good, see regulators as part of a dangerous and anti-democratic 'deep state', and characterise regulation as antithetical to freedom,[62] then a massive, rapid, government-centred green transition appears to be equally alarming. Second, in Congress,[63] polarisation begets gridlock[64]

---

[58] For a thorough explanation of these data and how they document increasing polarisation in American politics, see KT McCarty, KT Poole and H Rosenthal, Polarized America: *The Dance of Ideology and Unequal Riches* (MIT Press, 2006). For a striking visual illustration of polarisation in Congress, see Keith Poole's web page, available at https://legacy.voteview.com/Polarized_America.htm.

[59] K Poole, 'Voteview web page', available at voteview.com.

[60] The most commonly cited database illustrating ideological polarisation between the congressional parties is the so-called 'DW-NOMINATE' maintained by Keith Poole and others. Analyses of that data indicate that the parties in Congress are farther apart ideologically than at any time after the Second World War, and that 'role of government' issues drive polarisation.

[61] S Macdonald, 'Bill McKibben: Pope's Encyclical Gives Everyone "Marching Orders" on Climate' (National Catholic Reporter, 30 June 2015), available at www.ncronline.org/blogs/eco-catholic/bill-mckibben-pope-s-encyclical-gives-everyone-marching-orders-climate.

[62] Some trace the rise of this view to the funding of academic research by conservative funders, like the Koch Brothers foundations. N Maclean, *Democracy in Chains* (Penguin Random House, 2017). Others trace its origins to the growing influence of Austrian economics and conservative philosophy. See, eg, FA Hayek, *The Road to Serfdom* (Routledge, 1944) (laying out the argument that social welfare is maximised by free exchange in ways we cannot know or estimate ex ante); MN Rothbard, *Man Economy and the State: a Treatise on Economic Principles* (Van Nostrand, 1962) (arguing that democratic governance is coercive, and that social organisation by bilateral bargaining maximises welfare); and R Nozick, Anarchy, *State and Utopia* (Basic Books, 1974) (advancing a case for a minimal state lying somewhere between Hayek and Rothbard).

[63] The causes of congressional polarisation are disputed, but are ascribed by scholars to a variety of factors, most of which fall within either of two categories: one focusing on the increasing ideological homogeneity in congressional districts. B Bishop, *The Big Sort: Why the Clustering of like-Minded America Is Tearing Us Apart* (Mariner Books, 2009); JM Stonecash, MD Brewer and M Mariani, *Diverging Parties: Social Change, Realignment, and Party Polarization* (Westview Press, 2002); JL Carson et al, 'Redistricting and Party Polarization in the U.S. House of Representatives' (2007) 35 *American Politics Research* 878. A second set of diagnoses focus on various kinds of institutional factors that affect how parties manage congressional business. See GC Layman, TM Carsey and JM Horowitz, 'Party Polarization in American Politics: Characteristics, Causes, and Consequences' (2006) 9 *Annual Review of Political Science* 83; RH Pildes, 'Democracy, Anti-Democracy, and the Canon' (2011) 99 *California Law Review* 273.

[64] See S Binder, *Stalemate: Causes and Consequences of Legislative Gridlock* (Brookings Institution Press, 2003).

much of the time, which frustrates the policy agendas of any group seeking policy change. Conservatives have a difficult time repealing regulatory regimes they view as oppressive obstacles to progress, leaving those regimes in place; for their part, liberals cannot legislatively regulate greenhouse gas emissions or establish national standards for renewable energy.[65] In this way, gridlock further increases both groups' frustration.

The presidential election of 2016 revealed another source of centrifugal force in American politics: namely, the ability of interested parties to shape belief, and to mislead, using the tools of modern digital communication.[66] Long before the modern behavioural revolution,[67] political philosophers and psychologists recognised that propagandists can shape belief by playing to the cognitive biases. James Madison's admonition in 'Federalist No. 10' that a person's reason and passion have 'reciprocal effects' on one another is an acknowledgment that emotion feeds bias.[68] Henry Adams' description of politics as the 'systematic organization of hatreds' was a more blunt and condemnatory assessment of the manipulation of biases on American politics.[69] Academic psychologists began to chronicle the idea of biases in the early part of the twentieth century.[70] What *is* new is the speed and effectiveness with which these biases can now be exploited using modern communication tools.

Today, information about energy and environmental policy is transmitted online through news aggregators, or links sent to friends via online social communities. This way of acquiring and digesting (socially) new information tends to skew our understanding of the energy tradeoffs, as algorithms feed us more of what we like and less of what we dislike. Consequently, we form and harden our beliefs much more quickly in the digital environment. In the debate about the green transition, it becomes more difficult to respectfully debate questions associated with tradeoffs, and much easier to ascribe malicious or otherwise nefarious

---

[65] For a description of the failure of carbon regulation at the national level, see B Walsh, 'Why the Climate Bill Died' (*Time*, 26 July 2010), available at www.science.time.com/2010/07/26/why-the-climate-bill-died.

[66] M McKew, 'Did Russia Affect the 2016 Election? It's Now Undeniable' (*Wired*, 17 February 2018), available at www.wired.com/story/did-russia-affect-the-2016-election-its-now-undeniable/; and G O'Connor and A Schneider, 'How Russian Twitter Bots Pumped Out Fake News During The 2016 Election' (*NPR*, 3 April 2017), available at www.npr.org/sections/alltechconsidered/2017/04/03/522503844/how-russian-twitter-bots-pumped-out-fake-news-during-the-2016-election.

[67] For summaries of the Kahneman and Tversky research, see D Kahneman, *Thinking, Fast and Slow* (Farrar, Straus and Giroux, 2013); and D Kahneman and A Tversky (eds), *Choices, Values, and Frames* (Cambridge University Press, 2000).

[68] James Madison, 'The Federalist No. 10' in *The Federalist Papers* (*The Independent Journal*, 1787).

[69] H Adams, 'Chapter One: Quincy' in *The Education of Henry Adams* (1918).

[70] For a history of the idea of confirmation bias, for example, see RS Nickerson, 'Confirmation Bias: A Ubiquitous Phenomenon in Many Guises' (1998) 2 *Review of General Psychology* 175. Confirmation bias applies irrespective of the truth or falsity of the belief. *Ibid* at 188 ('not only can it contribute to the perseverance of unfounded beliefs, but it can help make beliefs for which there is legitimate evidence stronger than the evidence warrants'). Leon Festinger's work on cognitive dissonance and rationalisation dates to the mid-20th century. See L Festinger, *A Theory of Cognitive Dissonance* (Sandford University Press, 1957).

motives to those whose policy preferences or understanding of the issues differs from ours. No doubt these trends are amplified during the ever-lengthening American political campaign season.

More specifically, our reliance on digital communication media creates 'filter bubbles' that limit information flows and homogenise (ideologically) social networks.[71] These are the networks exploited by Russian bots in the 2016 election, and more generally by digital marketers. Where Americans once relied on a few sources of curated news, on the Internet they are now confronted with vast amounts of uncurated information presented as 'news'. Human nature reacts to this not only by selecting information sources that feed our biases; in addition, Twitter, Facebook and other platforms employ algorithms that amplify those biases in ways we never see. In this way, digital communities accelerate the effects of confirmation bias,[72] and feed the increasingly segmented cultural identities that shape our politics and our receptivity to new information about risk.[73] Emotional messages spread faster across social media than factual messages do.[74] Furthermore, if filter bubbles become too insular, false factual beliefs (about climate science, economics, or anything) can persist. For example, Noah Friedkin and Francesco Bullo find that when a false belief about a scientific fact predominates in most groups, the truth can eventually win out 'if any individual who understands the relevant science or mathematics must come to the [truthful] conclusion'; but this finding does not hold 'when social movements or social media elevate the adoption of a particular set of false facts and logic'.[75]

Thus, for example, Trump loyalists and Democratic Party loyalists hold not only different values, but also diametrically opposed beliefs about what is true over a wide variety of subjects – including the drivers and severity of climate change.[76] Online communities reinforce members' outrage about opposition positions and beliefs: 'the right is destroying our home, the earth', and 'the left is destroying our freedom'. The combination of targeted messaging and emotion is a powerful one

---

[71] E Pariser, *The Filter Bubble: How the New Personalized Web Is Changing What We Read and How We Think* (Penguin Books, 2011).

[72] Nickerson (n 70).

[73] See M Douglas and A Wildavsky, *Risk and Culture: An Essay on the Selection of Technical and Environmental Dangers* (University of California Press, 1982); and DM Kahan and D Braman, 'Cultural Cognition and Public Policy' (2006) 24 *Yale Law & Policy Review* 147.

[74] S Stieglitz and L Dang-Xuan, 'Emotions and Information Diffusion in Social Media – Sentiment of Microblogs and Sharing Behavior' (2013) *Journal of Management Information Systems* 217.

[75] NE Friedkin and F Bullo, 'How Truth Wins in Opinion Dynamics along Issue Sequences' (2017) 114 *Proceedings of the National Academy of Science* 11380.

[76] L Griffin and A Neimand, 'Why Each Side of the Partisan Divide Thinks the Other Is Living in an Alternate Reality' (*The Conversation*, 18 May 2019), available at www.theconversation.com/why-each-side-of-the-partisan-divide-thinks-the-other-is-living-in-an-alternate-reality-71458; B Azarian, 'An Analysis of Trump Supporters Has Identified 5 Key Traits' (*Psychology Today*, 31 December 2017), available at www.psychologytoday.com/us/blog/mind-in-the-machine/201712/analysis-trump-supporters-has-identified-5-key-traits (suggesting reasons why Trump voters accept the President's demonstrably false statements).

that marketing professionals have long exploited to their advantage. Policy activists and interest groups on both sides of the ideological divide are now beginning to do so as well: that is, to employ data analytics to take advantage of these characteristics of digital and social media platforms, in order to better test the appeal and effectiveness of political messages to specific audiences.[77] These sophisticated message targeting efforts may explain why voter polarisation apparently increases with voter engagement in politics and policy debate, implying that activists can drive polarisation among the rank-and-file.[78]

All of this makes grappling openly and collaboratively with difficult tradeoffs inherent in a green transition nearly impossible. Proponents of the Green New Deal feature prominently in election fundraising appeals by conservatives, who depict the plan as socialism run amok.[79] Conversely, in the context of intense political conflict there are strategic reasons why progressives may not want to talk openly about tradeoffs either. Discussing the devil-in-the-details can undermine the task of building support for a policy goal. 'Have your cake and eat it' narratives are attractive and easier to sell – for politicians seeking votes, businesses seeking clients, or websites seeking clicks. This may have been part of what former New York Governor, Mario Cuomo, meant when he said that 'you campaign in poetry [but] govern in prose'.[80] So political strategists advise candidates to focus on ends rather than means, to adopt simpler, positive narratives and to avoid uncomfortable truths.[81] That idea may be part of the plan to develop and sell the Green New Deal, which articulates a vision of a desirable future state in which these energy tradeoffs have (somehow) been addressed or resolved.[82]

This strategy seems premised on the idea that the articulation of an inspiring message can generate congressional majorities in support of wholesale change – a premise that seems far from evidently true. It seems just as likely that future left-of-centre majorities in Congress will include a healthy representation of moderate Democrats whose agreement will be required to address climate change

---

[77] David Karpf, *Analytic activism: Digital listening and the new political strategy* (Oxford University Press, 2016).

[78] 'Political Polarization in the American Public' (*Pew Research Center*, 12 June 2014), available at www.people-press.org/2014/06/12/section-1-growing-ideological-consistency/#interactive; See also, GC Layman et al, 'Activists and Conflict Extension in American Party Politics' (2010) 104 *American Political Science Review* 324–27 (describing how party activists play a leading role in moving party rank-and-file away from the ideological middle and toward the poles – a process the authors call 'conflict extension').

[79] Z Hirji, 'Republicans Plan to Wage War against the Green New Deal in 2020' (*Buzzfeed*, 13 February 2019), available at www.buzzfeednews.com/article/zahrahirji/republicans-green-new-deal-2020-elections.

[80] E Kolbert, 'Postscript: Mario Cuomo (1935-2015)' (*The New Yorker*, 1 January 2015), available at www.newyorker.com/news/news-desk/postscript-mario-cuomo.

[81] A Burns, 'Pete Buttigiegs Focus: Storytelling First. Policy Details Later' *The New York Times*, 14 April 2019, available at www.nytimes.com/2019/04/14/us/politics/pete-buttigieg-2020-writing-message.html.

[82] D Roberts, 'The Green New Deal, Explained' (*Vox*, 30 March 2019), available at www.vox.com/energy-and-environment/2018/12/21/18144138/green-new-deal-alexandria-ocasio-cortez.

effectively. In the so-called 'blue wave' election of 2018 (so named because many Democrats supplanted Republicans in the House of Representatives, and also because Democrats in the United States are associated with the colour blue), both moderate Democrats and progressive Democrats claimed victories, but more seats were transferred from Republican to Democrat hands by moderates. As of this writing (2019), among the 235 Democrats in the House of Representatives, 101 are members of the moderate 'New Democrat' caucus, and 95 are members of the Progressive Caucus. There has been tension between the groups over the green transition, with some progressives denouncing moderate Democrats on social media for their failure to support the Green New Deal.[83] The two sides seem to be pursuing separate agendas, with moderates pursuing a climate agenda comprising market-friendly measures that might claim some bipartisan support,[84] and progressives eschewing those kinds of measures as insufficient and endorsing the kind of government-centric redesign of energy markets represented by the Green New Deal.

IV. Conclusion

Regardless of whether the political logic of avoiding discussion of tradeoffs is correct, the question of how best to reach the shared goal of a greener energy mix ought to be debated. As described above, a rapid green transition entails thorny value choices about how to allocate the cost and responsibility for ensuring a reliable energy supply. Increased reliance on wind and solar power will force choices about how to ensure that the lights stay on when the wind and sun are unavailable. Who will make those investments? Who will pay for them ultimately? Should individual consumers bear more responsibility for ensuring (and paying for) a reliable supply of energy, or is this a collective project? How will Democrats, Republicans, liberals, and conservatives come to a consensus (or a durable majority view) on the need to reduce carbon emissions sharply and quickly, and the means to accomplish that task? How will choices about how to manage these reliably and cost tradeoffs figure into that process?

Presumably, a full, public exposition of these issues will promote a better understanding of the truth about these tradeoffs, and a better and more coherent policy response to them in the end. In a hyper-polarised American polity, however, grappling honestly with difficult tradeoffs is uncomfortable. When the politics of a policy discussion are fraught or emotionally-charged, facing the inconvenient

---

[83] H Caygle and S Ferris, 'Do Not Tweet: Pelosi Scolds Progressives in Closed-Door Meeting' (*Politico*, 10 July 2019), available at www.politico.com/story/2019/07/10/pelosi-progressives-twitter-1405763.

[84] JE Peters, 'Rep. Scott Peters Releases "Climate Playbook" as alternative to Green New Deal' *The San Diego Tribune*, 10 April 2019, available at www.sandiegouniontribune.com/news/environment/story/2019-04-10/rep-scott-peters-releases-climate-playbook-as-alternative-to-green-new-deal.

truths associated with the issue is more difficult for all concerned. Social media amplify these problems. The kinds of insulated, parallel narratives that arise in online communities may persuade community members, but they only *educate* those audiences when competing narratives intersect in ways that engage the other's assumptions and arguments fairly. That seems to happen only infrequently in online communities.

Perhaps the energy policy debate in the United States will mature into something more than competing, simple narratives. Maybe the costs of climate change will drive even Republican voters to insist on a national climate policy. Perhaps businesses will add their voice to that chorus, driven by the desire to avoid the costs of climate change in their operations. Perhaps a critical mass of Republicans in Congress will join the vast majority of Democrats in crafting a national green energy transition policy. Perhaps not. Absent a policy push, in more traditionally regulated electricity markets, IOUs continue to earn a return on their fossil-fuelled generators, insulating them from competition from cheaper renewables and slowing the transition to a greener energy mix. In the competitive parts of the American electricity sector, the market will continue to favour inexpensive, zero-marginal cost wind and solar generators for at least as long as new entrants can be assured of selling all the power they can generate to customers. That process will continue to reduce the carbon intensity of the American electric grid for some time. But progress beyond that point will require a policy push. That, in turn, will require policymakers to face the distributional questions described in this chapter, which will be difficult in the polarised, fragmented policy environment that currently dominates American energy politics.

2

The US Gas Supply Boom under Carbon Constraints: Examining the Role of Regulatory Institutions

TADE OYEWUNMI*

I. Introduction

In a functional sense, the process of regulation stems from a framework of statutes, judicial and quasi-judicial decisions, secondary and tertiary rules and policy guidelines which ideally contain prescriptive and descriptive standards of social or economic conduct. The institutions and administrative agencies that carry out regulation in this regard are only as effective as the extent to which the underlying policy objectives are realised.[1] When viewed as a system, energy supply entails the extraction and processing of primary sources such as oil and natural gas, followed by the conversion into a final form thereby creating secondary energy sources such as petrol, diesel oil and electricity, which is then transmitted, transported or distributed (as the case may be) in a useable form to applications in, for example, residential and office buildings, vehicles and industrial complexes. Generally, the policy and legal framework that underpins the supply system aims at:

i. ensuring suppliers and operators earn just and reasonable returns on 'ex ante' investments and affordable prices for consumers;
ii. reliability and security of supply; and
iii. protection of the public from environmental harm and sustainability.

---

*This chapter is part of the 'Energy Industry and Decarbonization' research project, thankfully supported by the Finnish Cultural Foundation, Helsinki, Finland and hosted by the Institute for Energy and the Environment at Vermont Law School, VT, USA. For the working paper of this chapter see Tade Oyewunmi, *Natural Gas in a Carbon-Constrained World: Examining the Role of Institutions in Curbing Methane and Other Fugitive Emissions* (5 March 2020) (forthcoming in *LSU Journal of Energy Law and Resources*, volume IX, 2020), available at https://ssrn.com/abstract=3550292.

[1] Tade Oyewunmi, *Regulating Gas Supply to Power Markets: Transnational Approaches to Competitiveness and Security of Supply* (Wolters Kluwer, 2018) 360, 9–11; Barry Barton et al, *Regulating Energy and Natural Resources* (Oxford University Press, 2006). Scott Hempling, *Preside or Lead? The Attributes and Actions of Effective Regulators*, 2nd edn (Scott Hempling Attorney at Law LLC, 2013).

The first two objectives seemed to have been predominant as the energy industry, especially the conventional systems powered by hydrocarbons, grew and thrived on factors such as economies of scale, reliability and competitiveness of relevant commercial ventures. However, overtime environmental externalities arise from these supply systems such as carbon dioxide and air pollution from (a) burning coal and diesel oil to produce electricity downstream, or (b) gas flaring and venting upstream, or (c) methane leaks from worn-out compressor stations and pneumatic controllers midstream. As knowledge and understanding of these implications developed, so was and still is the need to regulate and develop effective ways to curb or internalise the externalities. Additionally, the growing concerns about climate change mitigation over the past two decades add another layer of complexity to the energy trilemma. Thus, in a carbon-constrained world, energy supply systems are facing increasing scrutiny with increasing calls for operators to be more environmentally responsible and regulators to be more accountable and responsive. In the unfolding contexts, the development of high-quality regulatory frameworks should be a priority. Such a framework should ideally exemplify attributes such as:

a. independence of regulatory institutions from undue political influence and capture;
b. clarity of roles and curtailing information asymmetry between the regulator and the regulated;
c. accountability and transparency;
d. regular stakeholder engagement and regular assessments and performance evaluations.

In a similar vein, it is worth noting Hempling's comments in 'Preside or Lead? the Attributes and Actions of Effective Regulators' that government decision makers, ie regulatory agencies carrying out the dictates of legislation and engaged in balancing private vis-vis public interests should at a minimum be honest, diligent, judicious, objective, competent, purposeful, decisive and independent, etc.

For instance, while industry operators are quick to blame gas flaring and venting on inadequate transmission pipelines or gas gathering capacity or unfavourable downstream gas prices, it does lead to environmental externalities such as carbon dioxide (CO_2), methane and pollutants. Likewise, the burning of coal for heat and electricity leads to pollution (accounting for about 30 per cent of global energy-related CO_2 emissions). Therefore, depending on the specific context, the regulator should be able to make an informed decision without political interference as to when the environmental costs imposed by such activities are impermissible or

---

Such institutions engage in fact-finding, sometimes in a quasi-judicial manner, and have rulemaking and law-implementation responsibilities depending on the particular context, eg energy supply. Regulation in this sense, includes the standard-setting performance based-regulation, the responsive, incentive-based, consensual or market-based models, and not necessarily the traditional command-and-control forms.

technically unavoidable rather than just a question of commercial expediency. In such a situation the regulatory process should facilitate a just and reasonable pathway towards the development of innovative solutions to curb or avoid the emissions.[2]

The idea that natural gas is the 'cleanest' and 'environmentally-friendly' conventional hydrocarbon-based source of energy no longer depends solely on beating the emission(s) performance of other hydrocarbons such as coal and diesel oil. Rather it is more likely to depend on the willingness of the relevant operators and institutions to work together to ensure the emissions attributable to the gas production and supply system is as low as reasonably possible. Operators and suppliers in the gas value chain must be able to compete favourably with the increasing array of net-zero carbon or zero-carbon energy sources such as renewables and electricity produced from cleaner sources or remodel their operations to become 'integrated energy providers' and not just 'resource vendors', as will be discussed further in chapter three.

In the US context, successful decarbonisation of energy systems would require effectiveness in the applicable energy-related air pollution and greenhouse gas regulation framework. The framework comprises of concepts such as the best system of emissions reduction (BSER) and the best available control technology (BACT) under the purview of the US Environmental Protection Agency (EPA) on the one hand, and upscaling investments in the deployment of emerging solutions such as carbon capture storage and utilisation (CCUS), waste-to-energy, biogas/biofuels production and methane reformation.

This chapter aims at examining these issues by highlighting the growing role of natural gas in the evolving energy supply mix of the US following the shale gas revolution. It discusses the imperative of effectively regulating greenhouse gas (GHG) emissions arising from gas supply systems as well as the impact on the interconnected electricity sector in the evolving transitional and carbon-constrained scenarios. This chapter reflects the pivotal role of relevant institutions and the strong influences from politics and interested economic actors. It inter alia concludes that 'over-regulation' is just as bad as 'under-regulation' or a trend of engineering legal and regulatory gaps to foster political and private economic interests. The tendency to 'over-regulate' or otherwise 'under-regulate' at the expense of accountability and innovation or when it is reasonably appropriate simply because of political inclinations hinders progress towards the effective realisation of the three important dimensions of energy law and policy.

---

[2] See the US Environmental Protection Agency (EPA), 'Recommended Technologies to Reduce Methane Emissions under the Natural Gas Star Programme', available at www.epa.gov/natural-gas-star-program/recommended-technologies-reduce-methane-emissions; Heather D Dziedzic and Tade Oyewunmi, 'Decarbonization and the Integration of Renewables in Transitional Energy Markets: Examining the Power to Gas Option in the United States' (2019) *Oil, Gas & Energy Law Intelligence Journal*, available at www.ogel.org/journal-advance-publication-article.asp?key=622.

II. Gas Production Boom and Interconnections with Electricity Supply

Natural gas exploration and production could occur from associated gas fields, ie comprising of reservoirs in which oil is found together with a cap of a mixture of hydrocarbon gases including mostly methane and lesser amounts of ethane, propane, butane, pentane and impurities such as nitrogen and helium.[3] Gas production could also be from non-associated gas fields comprising of reservoirs that contain only the mixture of such hydrocarbon gases and no oil. Advancements in unconventional drilling technologies such as horizontal drilling and hydraulic fracturing allow gas-rich geologic shale rock formations to be fracked thus producing 'shale gas'. The gathering, processing, storage, transmission and/or distribution of gas equally involves a unique set of regulatory and permitting hurdles, contracting with established and creditworthy buyers and planning.[4] In the US, the typical gas supply chain and market, comprises of an unbundled sector in which:

a) upstream exploration and production operations are carried out in a competitive setting by multiple operators pursuant to leases from private landowners or leases from federal government-owned public lands granted by the US Department of Interior's Bureau of Land Management's (BLM) pertaining to onshore lands or the Bureau of Ocean Energy Management (BOEM) pertaining to offshore areas in the Outer Continental Shelf;

b) the midstream segment involves a separate set of pipeline companies and operators now subject to open access and its own unique economic and regulatory framework; and[5]

c) multiple downstream gas distribution networks and operators are supplying gas to residential, industrial and commercial users.[6]

Figure 1 below depicts the typical gas production, commercialisation supply systems involving the markets and networks though which produced gas eventually gets processed, transported, distributed and disposed. Depending on the objectives of the parties involved and consolidated by underlying licences, permits and contractual provisions, the processed gas could be sold to the domestic market

---

[3] Schlumberger Oil Field Glossary on Natural Gas, available at www.glossary.oilfield.slb.com/.

[4] Buford Pollett, 'The Impact of the Interface of Regulatory Jurisdictional Issues on the Life Cycle of Natural Gas Pipelines in the United States of America' (2019) *Oil, Gas and Energy Law Intelligence (OGEL) Journal*, available at www.ogel.org/article.asp?key=3846; Richard Pierce Jr, 'Reconstituting the Natural Gas Industry from Wellhead to Burnertip' (2004) 9 *Energy Law Journal* 57–112; Tade Oyewunmi, 'Examining the Role of Regulation in Restructuring and Development of Gas Supply Markets in the United States and the European Union' (2017) 40 *Houston Journal of International Law* 191–296.

[5] Pollett, *ibid*; Oyewunmi, *ibid*.

[6] International Energy Agency (IEA), 'Energy Policies of IEA Countries: The United States 2019 Review' (2019) 283, 158–63.

in the country where the production took place or exported via liquefied natural gas (LNG) or cross-border pipelines. In the US, the export of gas through LNG is subject, among other things, to the regulatory oversight of the Federal Energy Regulatory Commission (FERC) and includes the assessment of environmental impacts. In a domestic market scenario, gas processing and midstream activities could also be designed to produce natural gas liquids (NGLs) and liquefied petroleum gas (LPG) or cooking gas carried to residential and commercial areas through distribution pipelines and other small-scale systems. In an international context, there is a recent growth in the deployment of offshore floating LNG (FLNG) facilities, while floating storage and regasification units (FSRUs) are now very popular to import LNG and regasify into a usable form in countries with limited access to cross-border pipelines and little or no domestic gas resources.

Figure 1 The Typical Gas Production, Commercialisation Supply Systems

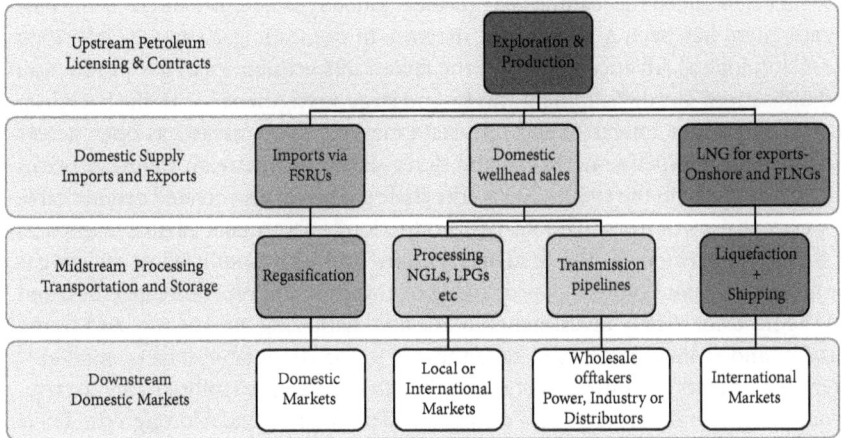

Natural gas has some peculiar features that distinguish it from oil and other hydrocarbons as a primary source of modern energy. For example: (i) its physical properties (ie gas being of a lower density but higher volatility than oil), burning qualities and thermal efficiency (gas is 'cleaner' and advancements in technologies such as combined-cycle turbines makes it more efficient for power generation than coal);[7] and (ii) the requirements for storage and marketing of gas is more complex. This is unlike oil which can be kept in barrels and storage tanks and trucked or shipped around more easily. Natural gas, on the other hand, requires specialised tanks and shipping or pipeline transmission to get to predesignated creditworthy buyers or markets. Without such predesignated arrangements, the upstream producer (which could generally be the private independent producer in Oklahoma or an International Oil Company (IOC) operating together with a

---

[7] IEA, 'Energy, Climate Change and Environment: 2016 Insights' (IEA Publications, 2016).

National Oil Corporation (NOC) in Mexico or Nigeria) would likely flare, vent or keep it in the ground.[8]

Note also that gas storage facilities are relatively more complex and expensive to maintain, requiring further costs in building processing facilities or cryogenic tanks, although operators also use underground storage facilities such as depleted reservoirs, aquifers and salt caverns. In the US for example, there were 388 active storage fields reported with a design storage capacity of 4,791 Billion cubic feet (bcf) by the end of 2017 spread across 30 states.[9] The US natural gas pipeline network ships gas throughout the lower 48 states via an integrated network of interstate and intrastate pipelines.[10] It comprises about 210 natural gas pipeline systems and over 300,000 miles (483 000 kilometres) of transmission pipelines. The state with the most developed natural gas pipelines by far is Texas (58,588 miles); the other five states with the most developed gas pipelines are Louisiana (18,900 miles), Oklahoma (18,539), Kansas (15,386), Illinois (11,900) and California (11,770).[11]

The US has been the leading gas producer globally since 2009 and over the past decade there has been a 29 per cent increase in domestic gas supplies following the technological advancements and the favourable economics of gas production and utilisation. The development was by and large strengthened with the backdrop of the competitive interstate and intrastate markets that emerged as open access to transmission pipeline networks and deregulation of upstream wellhead prices gained a foothold in the 1990s–2000s. The shale gas boom also created a remarkable 40 per cent growth in indigenous gas production.[12] Two major plausible impacts of the boom include: (i) the tendency to flare and vent unutilised or excess gas for lack of adequate gathering, processing or transmission pipeline capacities; and (ii) the need for timely investments in essential gathering, processing, and transmission and storage systems to take the gas to the designated buyers' market.[13] Such investments and infrastructure are key to ensuring reliability in an electricity and energy market that relies significantly on natural gas. Although the US is now a net exporter of natural gas, note that domestic consumption also reached a historic high in 2018, ie an 18 per cent increase in domestic consumption

---

[8] Oyewunmi (n 1).
[9] IEA, 'United States 2019 Review' (n 6) 173.
[10] IEA, 'United States 2019 Review' (n 6) 167–70.
[11] American Gas Association, 'Gas Industry Miles of Pipeline and Main by State and Type, Table 5-3' (2018) www.aga.org/contentassets/71fe352cf6fa4291a29be724ab0622b8/table5-3.pdf.
[12] IEA, 'United States 2019 Review' (n 6) 156–57; Oyewunmi (n 4).
[13] Monika U Ehrman, 'Lights Out in the Bakken: A Review and Analysis of Flaring Regulation and its Potential Effect on North Dakota Shale Oil Production' (2014) 117(2) *West Virginia Law Review* 550–90. Ehrman explains that 'Often used when midstream connections are not available, flaring is common practice in the oil and gas industry. *Operators may employ flaring (1) during flowback, which is the period of time in the hydraulic fracturing operation when the injected slurry of water, proppant, and chemicals flows back through the wellbore or (2) when connection timelines are delayed*-midstream companies can be notoriously uncertain with regards to construction timelines. In lieu of shutting in the well (stopping production), which delays income of saleable and more valuable hydrocarbons, operators instead send these non-connected volumes of gas (often referred to as "waste gas" or "flare gas") up through flare stacks, where those volumes are then ignited and combusted. Ideally the entire

between 2007 to 2017.[14] The electricity sector's demand and gas utilization trend has clearly been a major driving force in this regard. The extensive network of interstate and intrastate gas pipelines and storage systems can be accessed through the US Energy Information Administration (EIA) Energy Mapping System. The networks depict the interconnectedness between gas production, supply and consumption.[15]

In comparison, electricity is a secondary source of energy in an electrical form and is supplied as a current flowing through a network of transformers, cables and wires. It has a unique feature of been difficult and expensive to store as a result of its physical properties. Thus, its generation and supply should ordinarily meet demand and consumption in real-time. If such electricity supply depends on gas-fired generation, then there is no doubting the importance of timely, coordinated, and reliable supplies of sufficient gas volumes to fuel the power generation capacity. Such guaranteed and coordinated supply will also be essential for grid and system reliability as utilities increasingly shut down coal plants and other conventional systems and switch to gas-fired generation. These decisions and choices have considerable implications for the competitiveness, sustainability or decarbonisation and security of energy supply going forward. In facilitating the need for efficient integration and coordination between the wholesale gas and electricity markets as well as interstate network transmission, FERC Order No 809 (2015),[16] Order No 787 (2013)[17] and Order No 757 (2012)[18] respectively exemplify the role of regulation in clarifying and outlining relevant rules.

The EIA opines that electricity generation from both coal and nuclear power is expected to decline in its 2019 outlook to 2050, while the share of natural gas generation rises from 34 per cent in 2018 to 39 per cent in 2050, and the share of renewable generation increases from 18 per cent to 31 per cent due to falling costs, cheaper supplies and preference for cleaner and less-carbon-intensive sources of energy.[19] Thus, gas supply and the affiliated infrastructure network will play

---

volume of flare gas combusts, resulting in the formation of carbon dioxide and water. But inefficient flaring may lead to partial combustion and the consequent exhaust of methane and other toxics into the atmosphere.' (Emphasis added.) Note that the inability of midstream pipeline companies to confirm or guarantee available pipeline capacity or completion of new pipeline projects may be due to other sets of issues such as political conflicts, regulatory bottlenecks, environmental activism against pipelines, etc.

[14] IEA, 'United States 2019 Review' (n 6). The main sectors in the domestic consumption trend as at 2017 were: (i) heat and power generation (37%); (ii) industry (23%); (iii) residential (16%); commercial and others (11%); energy (9%); and transport (3%).

[15] The US EIA Energy Mapping System is available at www.eia.gov/state/maps.php. For more about the US natural gas pipeline network and storage, see US EIA, 'Natural Gas Explained: Natural Gas Pipelines Basics' at www.eia.gov/energyexplained/natural-gas/natural-gas-pipelines.php.

[16] Order No 809 (RM14-2-000) *Coordination of the Scheduling Processes of Interstate Natural Gas Pipelines and Public Utilities* (Final Rule).

[17] Order No 787 (RM13-17-002) *Communication of Operational Information between Natural Gas Pipelines and Electric Transmission Operators* (Final Rule).

[18] Order 757 (RM11-4-000) *Storage Reporting Requirements of Interstate and Intrastate Natural Gas Companies* (Final Rule).

[19] The EIA opines that from a 28% share in 2018, coal generation drops to 17% of total generation by 2050. Nuclear generation expectedly declines from a 19% share of total generation in 2018 to 12% by

a role in evolving projections and transitional scenarios for the energy system.[20] However, there is a need for a coherent, critical and pragmatic consideration of the pathways of controlling the environmental externalities and impact of the evolving systems.

III. Understanding GHG Emissions and Gas Supply Systems

The climate change forcing GHG's greenhouse effect is primarily a function of the concentration of water vapour, carbon dioxide (CO_2), methane (CH_4), nitrous oxide (N_2O), and other trace gases in the atmosphere that absorb the terrestrial radiation leaving the surface of the Earth.[21] While GHGs occur naturally, resulting from water vapour, CO_2, CH_4, N_2O, and ozone (O_3), anthropogenic activities such as the combustion of hydrocarbon, cement production, land-use, land-use change, forestry, agriculture or waste management, lead to the release of additional quantities, thus changing their global average atmospheric concentrations and the natural balance.[22] Although carbon dioxide is the most prevalent GHG,[23] methane (the main component of natural gas) is noted to have 80 times the global warming potential (GWP) of carbon dioxide when considered within a duration of 20 years. Methane, however, remains in the atmosphere for a much shorter period, ie about 12 years, in comparison to carbon dioxide which remains in the atmosphere for 100 years when emitted. Considering the significant role of energy and the combustion of hydrocarbons in the emission and atmospheric concentration of GHGs, growing attention has been focused on reducing or preventing emissions

---

2050. See the US EIA, *Annual Energy Outlook 2019: With Projections to 2050* (AEO2019, January 2019) 83, 21–22.

[20] *Ibid.* The EIA adds that the share of natural gas generation rises from 34% in 2018 to 39% in 2050, and the share of renewable generation increases from 18% to 31%.

[21] See the US EPA, 'Overview of Greenhouse Gases' at www.epa.gov/ghgemissions/overview-greenhouse-gases.

[22] The US EPA, 'Inventory of Greenhouse Gas Emissions and Sinks 1990–2017' (430-R-19-001, 11 April 2019) 10–86, 1–3. The report further states that 'If greenhouse gas concentrations continue to increase, climate models predict that the average temperature at the Earth's surface is likely to increase from 0.5 to 8.6 degrees Fahrenheit above 1986 through 2005 levels by the end of this century, depending on future emissions and the responsiveness of the climate system'.

[23] Carbon dioxide enters the atmosphere among other things through burning fossil fuels (coal, natural gas, and oil), solid waste, trees and other biological materials, and as a result of certain chemical reactions (eg, manufacture of cement). Carbon dioxide is removed from the atmosphere (or 'sequestered') when it is absorbed by plants as part of the biological carbon cycle. The US EPA reports that in 2017 carbon dioxide comprised of 82% of GHGs, while methane was 10%, nitrous oxide (6%) and fluorinated gases (such as hydrofluorocarbons, perfluorocarbons, sulphur hexafluoride, and nitrogen trifluoride are synthetic, powerful GHG that are emitted from a variety of industrial processes) was 3%. See US EPA, 'Overview of Greenhouse Gases' (n 21).

in pathways that would be consistent with 2°C warming scenarios.²⁴ According to the Intergovernmental Panel on Climate Change (IPCC),

> limiting global warming to 1.5°C would require 'rapid and far-reaching' transitions in land, energy, industry, buildings, transport, and cities. Global net human-caused emissions of carbon dioxide (CO_2) would need to fall by about 45 percent from 2010 levels by 2030, reaching 'net zero' around 2050. This means that any remaining emissions would need to be balanced by removing CO_2 from the air.²⁵

The Obama-led US federal administration played an instrumental role in the build-up towards the United Nations Framework Convention on Climate Change (UNFCCC) Conference of Parties (COP) 21 in Paris in December 2015, which lead to the 'Paris Agreement'. Amongs other things, the Agreement aimed to:

i. accelerate and intensify the global actions and investments needed for a sustainable low carbon future;
ii. combat climate change and adapt to its effects; and
iii. drive efforts in keeping global temperature rise this century well below 2 degrees Celsius above pre-industrial levels and to pursue efforts to limit the temperature increase even further to 1.5 degrees Celsius.

However, the current Trump-led administration has since withdrawn the US's role and participation in the Agreement.

A. Developments in the United States and United Kingdom

In the US, energy-related emissions from combustion processes in the power and heat generation, transport, industry, households and commercial sectors are the biggest source of total GHG emissions.²⁶ In 2017, energy-related emissions accounted for 84 per cent of total GHG emissions followed by the agriculture sector (eight per cent), industrial process emissions (six per cent) and the waste sector (two per cent).²⁷ Energy-related emissions include carbon dioxide emissions from fossil fuel combustion, as well as other emissions sources such as methane leakage from natural gas systems.²⁸ There has been a considerable decline in the emissions from energy supply and particularly in the power sector over the past decade. The decline is mostly due to the energy transitions towards fewer carbon

---

²⁴ The Intergovernmental Panel on Climate Change (IPCC), 'Special Report: Global Warming of 1.5°C' (2018), available at www.ipcc.ch/sr15/.
²⁵ *Ibid.*
²⁶ US EPA, 'Inventory of Greenhouse Gas Emissions and Sinks 1990–2017' (n 22); IEA, 'United States 2019 Review' (n 6) 43–45.
²⁷ US EPA, 'Inventory of Greenhouse Gas Emissions and Sinks 1990–2017' (n 22); IEA, 'United States 2019 Review' (n 6) 43–45.
²⁸ US EPA, 'Inventory of Greenhouse Gas Emissions and Sinks 1990–2017' (n 22); IEA, 'United States 2019 Review' (n 6) 43–45.

intensive sources, including energy efficiency and conservation and as the electrification of things gain traction, coal-fired generation is being replaced by gas-fired generation and renewables.[29] Texas for instance has a longstanding reputation as the leading oil and gas producer in the US and the biggest energy-consuming state.[30] However, it could be argued that the market-based paradigm of the Texas gas and electricity markets enabled the development of zero-carbon wind energy to surpass coal-fired and nuclear for power generation.[31] The boom in gas supply, however, had considerable environmental impacts as gas flaring and venting also increased from the Permian Basin.[32]

The UK also witnessed a similar downward trend in energy-related emissions as there was an increasing switch from coal to gas utilisation in the electricity sector.[33] According to the UK's Department for Business, Energy & Industrial Strategy (DBES) report, even though electricity consumption was eight per cent higher in 2018 compared to consumption levels in 1990, overall emissions from power stations were 68 per cent lower in 2018 than in 1990.[34] The decline in emissions is attributed to changes in the mix of power generation fuels, ie the switch from coal to natural gas and growth in the use of renewable energy sources, combined with greater efficiency resulting from improvements in technology and a decline in the relative importance of energy-intensive industries.[35]

The IEA recently reported that about 15 per cent of global energy-related GHG emissions arise from oil and gas exploration, production processes and delivery to

---

[29] US EPA, 'Inventory of Greenhouse Gas Emissions and Sinks 1990-2017' (n 22); IEA, 'United States 2019 Review' (n 6) 43–45.

[30] US EIA, 'Texas State Energy Profile' (16 January 2020), available at www.eia.gov/state/print.php?sid=TX. Texas produces more electricity than any other state, generating almost twice as much as Florida, the second-highest electricity-producing state. It is the largest energy-producing state and the largest energy-consuming state in the nation.

[31] Ibid. Although natural gas-fired power plants supplied almost half of the state's net electricity generation in 2017 and exceeded that share in 2018, more than 5,000 megawatts of Texas coal-fired generating capacity was retired in 2018 alone, while wind-powered generation has rapidly increased in the state since the first reported utility-scale generation in 2010. Thus, Texas currently leads the nation in wind-powered generation and produced one-fourth of all the US wind-powered electricity in 2017. Texas wind turbines have produced more electricity than both of the state's nuclear power plants since 2014.

[32] Flaring and venting of natural gas in the Permian Basin in Texas and New Mexico reached an all-time record high in the third quarter of 2019, averaging more than 750 million cubic feet per day (MMcfd). Increased flaring and venting at the production wellhead is mostly attributed to higher activity levels, more production from areas with less developed gas gathering infrastructure, and Basin-wide takeaway 'pipeline' capacity bottlenecks. See Rystad Energy, 'Permian Gas Flaring Reaches Yet another High' (5 November 2019), available at www.rystadenergy.com/newsevents/news/press-releases/permian-gas-flaring-reaches-yet-another-high/; Rachel Adams-Heard and Catherine Ngai, 'The Permian Gas Problem Is Just Getting Worse' (*Bloomberg Business*, 24 December 2019), available at www.bloomberg.com/news/articles/2019-12-24/permian-gas-problem-just-gets-worse-as-shale-drilling-slows-down.

[33] UK Department for Business, Energy & Industrial Strategy (DBES), '2018 UK Greenhouse Gas Emissions, Provisional Figures – Statistical Release' (London, DBES, March 2019) 1–20, 7–10.

[34] Ibid.

[35] Ibid. In 2018, coal made up only 7% of fuel used for electricity generation in the UK, down from 65% in 1990. Nuclear and renewables, which are net-zero carbon energy sources, accounted for 47% of fuels used for electricity generation in 2018, up from 22% in 1990.

consumers.³⁶ Thus, reducing fugitive emissions and avoidable leaks is key for the industry to bring down these emissions. There are other cost-effective opportunities to bring down the emissions intensity in the oil and gas space. Examples include minimising gas flaring and venting, monitoring and curbing methane emissions, and integrating renewables and low-carbon electricity into new upstream and LNG developments. Other options include investing in carbon removal and recycling technologies,³⁷ CCUS,³⁸ or power-to-gas and hydrogen, methane gathering and reformation, bioenergy systems, etc which will be discussed further in chapter three.³⁹ The oil and gas operators could also transform into 'energy' companies investing in and supplying an increasing amount of zero-carbon secondary or final energy sources.⁴⁰ Some of the identified industry-led approaches to curtailing emissions cost-effectively include detecting and fixing equipment leaks, deploying satellite technologies as recommended by the Oil and Gas Climate Initiative (OGCI),⁴¹ implementing reduced emissions completion technologies ('green completions') for unconventional gas wells, incentivising operators or third-party users to capture gas that would ordinarily be flared or vented as in the case of Nigeria's recent Flare Gas Commercialisation Programme.⁴²

B. To Penalise or Commercialise: The Nigerian Experience with Flaring Regulation

The longstanding approach of issuing penalties alongside a pronouncement of deadlines to stop routine flaring and venting in Nigeria was ineffective due to several regulatory and institutionalised factors.⁴³ First, operators had historically

---

[36] IEA, 'The Oil and Gas Industry in Energy Transitions: World Energy Outlook Special Report' (IEA, 2020).

[37] Wendy B Jacobs and Michael T Craig, 'Carbon Capture and Sequestration' Chapter 28 in Michael B Gerrard and John C Dernbach (eds), *Legal Pathways to Deep Decarbonization in the United States* (Environmental Law Institute, 2019).

[38] See the Oil and Gas Climate Initiative (OGCI), 'Scaling Up Action Aiming for net zero emissions: A Report from the Oil and Gas Climate Initiative' (September 2019); Eli Kintisch, 'Technologies' in Michael B Gerrard and Tracy Hester (eds), *Climate Engineering and the Law Regulation and Liability for Solar Radiation Management and Carbon Dioxide Removal* (Cambridge University Press, 2018) 28–56.

[39] See Dziedzic and Oyewunmi (n 2) See also Donald Zillman, Lee Godden, LeRoy Paddock and Martha Roggenkamp (eds), *Innovation in Energy Law and Technology: Dynamic Solutions for Energy Transitions* (Oxford University Press, 2018); the IEA, 'The Oil and Gas Industry in Energy Transitions' (n 36).

[40] Dieter Helm, *Burn Out: The Endgame for Fossil Fuels* (Yale University Press, 2017).

[41] OGCI, 'The Oil and Gas Climate Initiative Annual Report' (September 2018), available at https://oilandgasclimateinitiative.com/wp-content/uploads/2018/09/OGCI_Report_2018.pdf.

[42] Oluwaseun Oke, 'Gas Flaring in Nigeria and the Flexed Muscles of the 2018 Regulations: Key Implications and Investment Considerations' (2019) *Oil, Gas & Energy Law Journal*, available at www.ogel.org/article.asp?key=3806.

[43] The Associated Gas Re-Injection Act 1979 ('Associated Gas Act') 147 and the Associated Gas Reinjection (Continued Flaring of Gas) Regulations 1984 provided for exemptions to a general legal ban on gas flaring and applicable penalties. See also Yinka Omorogbe, 'Law and Investor Protection in the Nigerian Natural Gas Industry' (1996) 14 *Journal of Energy & Natural Resources Law* 179.

been more interested in oil rather than gas. Although significant commercial interests in gas had grown since the late 1990s as well as domestic gas demand,[44] the domestic price for gas supply to power generators was often not reflective of reasonable and projected costs. As a result, most oil and gas producers found it cheaper to flare and pay penalties rather than invest in new processing and domestic pipelines to supply at below-market prices, although there were some wholesale supply arrangements to domestic industrial users and some power generators.[45] Most of the produced and processed gas was also designed for export projects such as the West African Gas Pipeline and the Nigerian LNG Project.[46] Second, as in most major oil and gas producing countries, Nigeria has a NOC with a local subsidiary responsible for gas transmission and distribution. Entering into joint ventures with the private IOCs in which the Government held majority participating interests under a joint and several liability framework in oil and gas production makes the role of government as the regulator more complex. Hence, the challenge of ending activities like gas flaring and the resulting environmental externalities required an independent and well-equipped, informed agency, which was often not the case.[47] In July 2018, the current Nigerian Federal Government issued the Flare Gas (Prevention of Waste and Pollution) Regulations 2018 ('Flare Gas Regulations'). The Flare Gas Regulations applies to all petroleum leases, licences and marginal fields in Nigeria and provides a framework aimed at:

i. protecting affected communities from the adverse effects of gas flaring;
ii. preventing waste of associated gas; and
iii. creating social and economic benefits by permitting interested third-parties to gain access, capture and utilise gas that would otherwise be flared during oil production operations.[48]

C. The Main Sources of GHG Emissions from Gas Supply Systems

The main component of natural gas is methane, thus, it is useful to highlight gas-related methane emissions. Methane emissions from the gas production and

---

[44] See Rahmat Poudineh and Tade Oyewunmi, 'Natural Gas in Nigeria and Tanzania: Can it Turn on Lights?' (2018) *Oxford Institute for Energy Studies, Electrifying Africa Issue* 115, 14–20. Tade Oyewunmi, 'International Petroleum Transactions and the Development of Gas-to-Power Markets in West Africa' (2019) *Oil, Gas & Energy Law Journal*, www.ogel.org/article.asp?key=3805.
[45] Oyewunmi (n 1) 111–71; Tade Oyewunmi, 'Examining the Legal and Regulatory Framework for Domestic Gas Utilization and Power Generation in Nigeria' (2014) 7 *Journal of World Energy Law & Business* 538–57.
[46] Oyewunmi (n 1) 111–71.
[47] Dickson Omukoro, 'Environmental Degradation in Nigeria: Regulatory Agencies, Conflict of Interest and the use of Unfettered Discretion' (2017) 15 *Oil, Gas & Energy Law Intelligence Journal*, available at www.ogel.org/article.asp?key=3678.
[48] Ọkẹ (n 42). See also the Nigerian Gas Flare Commercialisation Programme at https://ngfcp.dpr.gov.ng/.

supply chain could arise from unanticipated leaks or process-related venting (intentional release of gas) or incomplete flaring (burning off the gas),[49] normal operations, routine maintenance and system disruptions.[50] For example, emissions can result from the venting of gas from compressors or pipelines when they are taken out of service, or from normal operation of natural gas-powered pneumatic devices. Emissions vary from facility to facility, while operators have or should develop specific ways and standards of monitoring, reporting and curtailing emissions. It is largely a function of the types of equipment and systems, operation and maintenance procedures, and equipment conditions, all of which could be specified as much as possible by regulation and relevant guidelines.[51] In the US, the pattern of methane and carbon dioxide emissions related to natural gas systems appears in tandem with the boost in domestic production, especially from associated gas fields over the past decade. Dry gas production in the US witnessed a 53 per cent increase from 1990 to 2017; while methane emissions from production also increased by 62 per cent from 1990 to 2017.[52] The main sources for the emissions are reportedly from pneumatic controllers (due to an increase in the number of controllers required over the period) and increases in emissions from gathering and boosting stations. Most of the carbon dioxide emissions came from routine flaring during oil production when there is limited or no gas gathering, processing and evacuation network and plan in place. Note that flaring is also used to control tank emissions and offshore flaring.[53]

IV. US Institutions and Regulatory Approaches

The governance framework for global efforts to address global warming and climate change is essentially based on the 1992 United Nations Framework Convention on

---

[49] The burning of unwanted gas through a pipe (also called a flare). Flaring is a means of disposal used when there is no economically feasible means or sufficient processing and transmission capacities to transport the gas to market and the operator cannot use the gas for another purpose.

[50] During production operations, gas gathering and boosting stations receive natural gas from well sites and transfer it, via gathering pipelines, to transmission pipelines or processing facilities, gas treatment equipment such as dehydrators and separators.

[51] IEA, *Energy Sector Methane Recovery and use: The Importance of Policy* (IEA Publications, 2009). Some emissions are accidental, for example because of a faulty seal or leaking valve, while others are deliberate, often carried out for safety reasons or due to the design of the facility or equipment.

[52] According to the US EPA, 'Inventory of Greenhouse Gas Emissions and Sinks 1990–2017' (n 22), 'Methane and non-combustion CO_2 emissions from natural gas systems include those resulting from normal operations, routine maintenance, and system upsets. Emissions from normal operations include: natural gas engine and turbine uncombusted exhaust, flaring, and leak emissions from system components. Routine maintenance emissions originate from pipelines, equipment, and wells during repair and maintenance activities. Pressure surge relief systems and accidents can lead to system upset emissions'.

[53] See also US EPA, Inventory of Greenhouse Gas Emissions and Sinks 1990-2017' (n 22) 3–80 and 3–81.

Climate Change (UNFCCC) and subsequent protocols and agreements such as the Kyoto Protocol and Paris Agreement. Previous US federal administrations took some steps which essentially recognised the 'climate change mitigation' issues, for example the Clinton administration signed the 1997 Kyoto Protocol. However, it was the Obama administration's EPA that commenced direct steps to regulate GHGs in the US based on the framework provided under the Clean Air Act (CAA) 1970 as amended.[54] The CAA is a national legislation originally designed to regulate air pollutants regarded as harmful to social health and wellbeing, such as toxic and hazardous air pollutants.[55]

The CAA requires stationary sources of pollution such as power plants to secure a permit from state regulators before emitting criteria pollutants such as lead, carbon monoxide, ozone, sulphur dioxide (SO_2), particulate matter (PM) and nitrogen oxide (NOx). The main objective is to encourage active measures for internalising the environmental costs of the combustion of hydrocarbons by requiring the installation of pollution control facilities. Such permits typically include limits to the emissions and *reflect certain technology-based standards that are defined by the CAA*. The stringency of the limits or standards depends on whether the source is in an area that is in attainment with national ambient air quality standards (NAAQS) for the pollutants in question. If a new or modified major pollution source facility is within the attainment area, then the owner must obtain a Prevention of Significant Deterioration (PSD) permit and the emissions limit must reflect the BACT.[56] In non-attainment areas, the limits must reflect the 'lowest achievable emissions rate' (LAER).[57]

The CAA's framework for prevention and control of air pollution is the primary responsibility of individual states and local governments, even though the Federal Government plays a crucial role. The framework is typically referred to as 'cooperative federalism' in which the Federal Government develops baseline standards that the states individually implement and enforce. The states are allowed to employ standards that are more stringent than those specified by the federal agencies involved in the implementation and rulemaking process. The EPA at the federal-level is responsible for developing acceptable NAAQS, which provides a uniform level of air quality across the US. The specifics of how to meet the NAAQS are left to individual states' regulatory agencies and policymakers. In addition, each state is required to create and submit to an Implementation Plan ('SIP') to the EPA, which outlines the plan for implementation, maintenance and enforcement of NAAQS within the state. After submitting a SIP to the EPA and the latter approves, then its requirements become federal law, and enforceable in federal court.[58]

---

[54] Joel Eisen et al, *Energy, Economics and the Environment, Cases and Materials* 4th edn (University Casebook Series, Foundation Press, 2015) 290–320.

[55] *Ibid*.

[56] 42 United States Code (USC) section 7475 (a)(4).

[57] 42 USC section 7503 (a)(2).

[58] See *Wyoming v Dep't of Interior*, No 2:16-CV-0285-SWS (District of Wyoming (D. Wyo), 16 January 2017).

Notably, states must also regulate all stationary sources located within the areas covered by the SIPs and implement a mandatory permit programme that sets limitations to the amount and types of emissions that each stationary source is allowed to discharge.[59]

The formation of the EPA and the enactment of the CAA has been part of a coherent national-level framework to clean up the air and deal with air pollution in the US since the 1970s.[60] GHGs such as CO_2 and methane are not directly toxic or directly harmful to society, rather it is the cumulative effects of their atmospheric concertation which creates a global warming effect and potential adverse impacts such as rising sea levels, floods, increase in ground-level ozone (smog) and changing weather patterns that could create droughts in some regions. In 1999, some organisations filed a petition requesting that the EPA should issue rules for the regulation of four GHG, including carbon dioxide, emitted from new motor vehicles. Following public comments, the EPA (in the Republican/Bush era) denied the petition in 2003, stating that:

a) it did not have authority under the CAA to issue mandatory regulations to address the global issue of climate change because Congress would have explicitly directed the EPA to do so if Congress so intended. As a result, GHG could not be considered 'air pollutants' under the CAA.
b) even if it did have authority, it would be unwise to set GHG emission standards at this time because:
   i. there was uncertainty regarding the link between GHG and global warming;
   ii. mandatory regulation was a piecemeal approach that would interfere with the President's more comprehensive approach; and
   iii. it might hamper the President's ability to persuade developing countries to limit GHG emissions.[61]

The EPA's decision was challenged by Massachusetts and some other states in the DC Circuit. Consequently, a divided panel upheld the EPA's decision not to dabble with GHG regulation. On appeal, the US Supreme Court in *Massachusetts v EPA* (2007) granted *certiorari* and addressed *among other things* the issue of whether the EPA had statutory authority to regulate GHG emissions from new motor vehicles and if so whether the reason stated for refusing to do so was consistent with

---

[59] *Ibid.*
[60] This era was particularly notorious for air pollution arising from industrial processes and use of fuels such as coal for heat and energy. The burning of coal produces particulate matter (PM) which causes respiratory problems, heart and lung disease. These particulates can also contain mercury – a toxic metal that can enter the food chain through deposition of combustion particulates into waterways. Sulphur dioxide mixes with moisture in the upper atmosphere and forms sulphuric acid which leads to acid rain – damaging vegetation and aquatic environments. Nitrogen oxides are a precursor to acid rain and ground level ozone, ie smog which triggers respiratory problems in some humans.
[61] See US Department of Justice, *Massachusetts v EPA* at www.justice.gov/enrd/massachusetts-v-epa.

the CAA.[62] First, the Supreme Court decided that Massachusetts had standing to seek review of the EPA's denial of the rulemaking petition in light of the harms global warming could cause that state, including submersion of state-owned property on the coast due to an increase in ocean levels. In a majority opinion, the Court then held that under the language of the CAA, the EPA has authority to regulate GHG as 'air pollutants'. The EPA had argued that it lacked authority to regulate because:

i. the US congress was aware of the climate change issue when it did its last comprehensive review of the CAA in 1990 and decided not to adopt a proposed amendment that could have specifically imposed binding limitations. Rather, in its 1990 amendments, the US Congress focused more on pollutants that depleted the ozone layer;
ii. GHGs are not air pollutants as contemplated by Congress under the CAA – arguing that if CO_2 can be considered as an air pollutant the only feasible method was to impose fuel economy standards through the Department of Transport.

In delivering the majority opinion (five justices in support and four dissenting), Justice Stevens stated that the text of the CAA's definition of 'air pollutant' as 'any' air polluting agent or combination of such agents, whether they be physical or chemical substances which are emitted into the air forecloses the EPA's contentions. Thus, given the reference to all airborne compounds, CO_2, methane, nitrous oxide and hydrofluorocarbons are substances that are emitted into the air and are therefore pollutants as contemplated under the CAA.[63] The Court held further that while the Congress at the time of enacting the CAA might not have appreciated the possibility that burning fossil fuels could lead to global warming or expressly provided for the regulation of GHG by the EPA in its 1990 amendments, it did understand that without regulatory flexibility, changing circumstances and scientific developments could eventually render the CAA obsolete. In its majority opinion, the Supreme Court held that:

> EPA's reliance on post enactment congressional actions and deliberations it views as tantamount to a command to refrain from regulating greenhouse gas emissions is unavailing. Even if post enactment legislative history could shed light on the meaning of an otherwise-unambiguous statute, EPA identifies nothing suggesting that Congress meant to curtail EPA's power to treat greenhouse gases as air pollutants. The Court has no difficulty reconciling Congress' various efforts to promote interagency collaboration and research to better understand climate change with the agency's preexisting mandate to regulate 'any air pollutant' that may endanger the public welfare ... Also unpersuasive is EPA's argument that its regulation of motor-vehicle carbon dioxide emissions would require it to tighten mileage standards, a job (according to EPA) that Congress has assigned to the Department of Transportation. The fact that DOT's mandate to promote

---

[62] *Massachusetts v EPA* 549 US 497 (2007); Eisen et al (n 54).
[63] *Massachusetts v EPA, ibid.*

energy efficiency by setting mileage standards may overlap with EPAs environmental responsibilities in no way licenses EPA to shirk its duty to protect the public 'health' and 'welfare,' ... EPA's alternative basis for its decision 'that even if it has statutory authority to regulate greenhouse gases, it would be unwise to do so at this time' rests on reasoning divorced from the statutory text. While the statute conditions EPA action on its formation of a 'judgment' that judgment must relate to whether an air pollutant [such as greenhouse gasses, if they are considered agents of air pollution] 'cause[s], or contribute[s] to, air pollution which may reasonably be anticipated to endanger public health or welfare' ... Under the Act's clear terms, *EPA can avoid promulgating regulations only if it determines that greenhouse gases do not contribute to climate change or if it provides some reasonable explanation as to why it cannot or will not exercise its discretion to determine whether they do.*[64]

With this line of reasoning, the US Supreme Court could be said to have adopted the 'mischief rule' of statutory interpretation by attempting to (i) determine the intention of Congress, finding the defect in a statute that was enacted decades before the science of climate change gained the traction it currently has, and (ii) to implement a remedy in the context of the case under consideration. Consequently, CO_2 and GHGs are now classified as pollutants under the CAA following the *Massachusetts v EPA* case, although the EPA could still decline to regulate under Title II for permissible reasons. In 2009, the Obama-EPA decided that GHGs from cars and trucks 'endanger' public health and welfare. This led to more specific rule-making regarding mobile and stationary sources of GHGs.

Furthermore, the Supreme Court in *American Electric Power Co v Connecticut (AEP)*,[65] unanimously held that the EPA has the authority to regulate GHGs under section 111(b) of the CAA with respect to stationary sources and that the CAA displaced federal common law public nuisance claims related to GHG emissions from power plants because the US Congress had delegated to the EPA the authority to decide whether and how to regulate pollutants such as GHG emissions from power plants under CAA section 111.[66] In *Utility Air Regulatory Group v EPA* (2014)[67] it was held that emissions of GHGs alone from stationary sources could not activate both the PSD programme and Title V permitting requirements under the CAA framework. It is, however, possible to apply the PSD programme's BACT requirement to the emission of GHGs from those sources that emit enough quantities of other pollutants that are or would be ordinarily subject to the PSD framework.[68]

---

[64] *Massachusetts v EPA, ibid* (emphasis added).
[65] *American Electric Power Co v Connecticut (AEP)* 564 US 410 (2011).
[66] *Ibid.*
[67] *Utility Air Regulatory Group v EPA* 134 S Ct 2427 (2014). See also of *Utility Air Regulatory Group v EPA* (2014) Harvard Law Review: Environmental Law, at https://harvardlawreview.org/2014/11/utility-air-regulatory-group-v-epa/.
[68] *Ibid.*

A. Highlighting Federal Agencies and Other Institutions

At least three federal agencies have the statutory authority that is relevant to the regulation of methane emissions in the US, including: (i) the EPA under the CAA; (ii) the BLM under the Mineral Leasing Act of 1920; and (iii) the Pipeline and Hazardous Materials Safety Administration (PHMSA) under several statutes, as well as the Natural Gas Pipeline Safety Act of 1968.

i. The Environmental Protection Agency

The EPA is the Federal Government's principal environmental regulator and has the primary responsibility to 'protect human health and the environment' in the US. It has the statutory authority to maintain and improve the nation's air quality and protect the public from dangerous air pollutants. As discussed earlier, the EPA's regulation of GHGs began following the decision in *Massachusetts v EPA* concluding that GHGs are 'air pollutants' under the CAA.[69] As a result of the obligation to regulate any air pollutants that may 'endanger public health or welfare', the EPA determined that GHGs endanger health and safety.[70] Hence, several rules and regulations have been issued over the years, including ones pertaining to methane emissions, reporting requirements, permitting requirements and performance standards.

a. GHG Reporting Programme

In the FY2008 Consolidated Appropriations Act, Congress directed the EPA to establish the GHG Reporting Programme (GHGRP) to collect annual GHG emission data pursuant to its existing authority under the CAA.[71] The resulting rules require reporting of GHG emissions from all major sectors of the economy.[72] The 'Petroleum and Natural Gas Systems' sector is subject to part 98, subpart W of the rule, and this industry sector provides the most reporters to the programme: 2,253 as of 2018.[73] Subpart W 'requires petroleum and natural gas facilities to report annual methane (CH_4) and carbon dioxide (CO_2) emissions from equipment leaks and venting, and emissions of CO_2, CH_4, and nitrous oxide (N_2O) from flaring' in addition to other emissions, such as those from on-site combustion equipment.

---

[69] *Massachusetts v EPA* (n 62).
[70] The 'endanger public health or welfare' language is found in both CAA section 202(a), which gives the EPA authority over automobiles (the context of the *Massachusetts v EPA* decision) and in CAA section 111, which gives the EPA authority over stationary sources, the source of most methane emissions.
[71] HR 2764, PL 110–161; Richard K Lattanzio, 'Methane and Other Air Pollution Issues in Natural Gas Systems' *Congressional Research Service* (R42986, 5 November 2018) 1–25.
[72] Mandatory Reporting of Greenhouse Gases, 74 Federal Register (Fed. Reg.) 56, 260 (30 October 2009).
[73] EPA, 'GHGRP Reported Data' (12 December 2018), www.epa.gov/ghgreporting/ghgrp-reported-data.

Petroleum and natural gas facilities may also be subject to further reporting under other subparts of the rule.

The data collected through the Reporting Programme contributes to the EPA's *Inventory of US Greenhouse Gas Emissions and Sinks*, which is instrumental in understanding the nature, scope and sources of GHG emissions. In 2019, this report revealed that methane emissions from petroleum and natural gas systems decreased between 1990 and 2017, but these two sectors combined still represented the largest sources of CO_2 and methane emissions in the country. Moreover, due to increases in flaring emissions, CO_2 emissions from the sectors increased by 27 per cent over the same period.[74] It is also important to stress that the combustion of fossil fuels (especially oil and coal for energy, eg for electricity and heat) comprise the main source of energy-related emissions, with CO_2 being the most prevalent GHG.[75]

b. CAA Permitting Requirements

In 2010, the EPA issued a decision that CAA permitting requirements would apply to GHGs when such pollutants become 'subject to regulation' under the Act. Thus, methane and other GHGs would be included in CAA permits when any new regulations controlling GHG emissions took effect.[76] In 2014, the US Supreme Court's decision in *Utility Air Regulatory Group v EPA* modified EPA's interpretation of the permitting requirements,[77] as discussed earlier. Due to the ambiguities and differing interpretations and understanding of the term 'air pollutants' as defined under the CAA and the extent of that interpretation and understanding regarding GHGs; the EPA could not require stationary sources to receive permits solely based on their potential to emit GHGs. Instead, if a source was otherwise required to obtain a CAA permit – based on its emissions of other regulated hazardous or criteria pollutants – then the EPA could include GHGs in its permit.

In general, there are two types of CAA permits. These are preconstruction permits, which are a part of the New Source Review (NSR) programme and operating permits, also known as Title V permits. Any new stationary sources

---

[74] US EPA, 'Inventory of Greenhouse Gas Emissions and Sinks 1990-2017' (n 22) 2-14, 3-1.

[75] US EPA, 'Inventory of Greenhouse Gas Emissions and Sinks 1990-2017' (n 22) 2-14, 3-1. Fossil fuel combustion also leads to emissions of CH_4 and N_2O. Stationary combustion of fossil fuels was the second largest source of N_2O emissions in the US and mobile fossil fuel combustion was the fourth largest source. Energy-related activities other than fuel combustion, such as the production, transmission, storage and distribution of fossil fuels, also emit GHG. These emissions consist primarily of fugitive CH_4 from natural gas systems, coal mining and petroleum systems.

[76] Reconsideration of Interpretation of Regulations That Determine Pollutants Covered by Clean Air Act Permitting Programs, 75 Fed. Reg. 17004 (2 April 2010); see also, Air Quality Policy Division, EPA, 'PSD and Title V Permitting Guidance for Greenhouse Gases', EPA-457/B-11-001 (March 2011) 3, www.epa.gov/sites/production/files/2015-12/documents/ghgpermittingguidance.pdf (hereinafter, 'EPA Permitting Guidance').

[77] *Utility Air Regulatory Group v EPA*, 573 US 302, 331 (2014).

or modifications to existing stationary sources that are considered 'major' must undergo NSR and receive either a PSD permit or a nonattainment NSR (NNSR) permit. Only PSD permits apply to GHGs.[78] Once a major source is subject to PSD, in order to obtain a permit and begin construction the emitter must meet all the requirements of the programme, the most relevant of which is the BACT requirement. A BACT is defined as an emissions limitation that *is based on the maximum possible reduction that is deemed achievable for each facility on a case-by-case basis*, 'taking into account energy, environmental, and economic impacts and other costs'.[79] Accordingly, the PSD permit ensures that any new or modified major sources will reduce their methane and regulated emissions to the greatest extent that is 'technologically feasible' and 'cost-effective' by requiring such devices before construction can begin. Although the GHG mitigation technologies utilised are 'likely to vary based on the type of facility, processes involved, and GHGs being addressed', the devices identified by EPA as suitable for methane reduction – such as thermal oxidisers and the repair of equipment leaks – can be found in the EPA Clean Air Technology Center.[80]

Title V operating permits are required for all major sources and certain other sources under the CAA. Title V permits generally do not add pollution control requirements but rather consolidate all CAA requirements applicable to a particular source and mandate certain procedures be followed. Required procedures include 'providing a review of permits by the EPA, states, and the public, requiring permit holders to track, report and annually certify their compliance status with respect to their permit requirements, and otherwise ensuring that permits contain conditions to assure compliance'.[81] Therefore, the addition of GHGs to Title V permits does not appear to significantly alter their functioning. In relation to methane and other GHGs, Title V permits can be viewed as a way to improve compliance with the CAA by clarifying the exact measures that sources must perform to control GHG pollution.

c. CAA New Source Performance Standards (NSPS) for Oil and Gas Systems

Section 111 of the CAA directs the EPA to regulate emissions of air pollutants from stationary sources. Industries that emit air pollutants are divided into over 70 different source categories and subcategories, such as cement plants, petroleum

---

[78] Different regions of the US are classified as 'attainment areas' or 'nonattainment areas' depending on whether the EPA's established NAAQS are exceeded for that area. The PSD programme applies to attainment areas (areas not exceeding the established NAAQS), while the NNSR permits apply to nonattainment areas. Because NAAQs have not been established for GHGs, the NNSR programme does not apply.

[79] CAA section 169(3), 42 USC section 7479 (3).

[80] EPA Permitting Guidance (n 76) at 28–29; EPA, 'RBLC Basic Search' (Clean Air Technology Center – RACT/BACT/LAER Clearinghouse), available at https://cfpub.epa.gov/rblc/index.cfm?action=Search.BasicSearch&lang=en.

[81] EPA Permitting Guidance (n 76) at 50.

refineries and sewage treatment plants.[82] The EPA included crude oil and natural gas production, transmission and distribution (Subpart OOOO) as a source category for the first time in 2012 (ie the 'NSPS 2012').[83] Hence, as a source category, crude oil and natural gas facilities are now subject to the NSPS, the air pollution emission standards of the CAA for new or modified sources. The NSPS 2012 rule only directly controlled volatile organic compounds (VOC) and SO_2 emissions from the affected facilities;[84] however, the EPA recognised that methane reductions would occur as a co-benefit of the rule.

In 2016, the EPA extended the Subpart OOOO regulations of the oil and natural gas source category by promulgating Subpart OOOOa ('NSPS 2016'), which established the relevant performance standards based on the best system of emissions reduction (BSER) for reducing emissions of greenhouse gases (GHGs), specifically methane.[85] For instance, with regard to fugitive emissions from well sites and compressor stations, the BSER for monitoring and repair was based on semiannual monitoring using optical gas imaging (OGI), while the performance standard required the monitoring and repair of fugitive emission components.[86] The BSER for leaks at gas processing plants and pneumatic controllers in natural gas processing plants was determined to be 'leak detection and repair' and 'instrument air systems' respectively. Leaks from compressor stations and venting from pneumatic controllers are a significant source of methane emissions. Thus, it is interesting to note the specific rules and performance standards being set. Also, it is worth pointing out that during the notice-and-comment period, the EPA received comments pertaining to capturing and control of emissions from pneumatic controllers.[87]

Specifically, there were comments suggesting that pneumatic controllers should be required to capture emissions through a closed vent system and route the captured emissions to a process or a control device, similar to the approach the EPA has taken in its proposed standards for pneumatic pumps and compressors. The commenters cite recent Wyoming proposed rules for existing pneumatic controllers that allow operators of existing high-bleed controllers to route emissions to a process and the California Air Resources Board (CARB) proposed rules which require that operators capture emissions and route to a process control device. Commenters opined that this approach would work for all types

---

[82] Standards of Performance for New Stationary Sources, 40 Code of Federal Regulations (C.F.R.), Part 60.

[83] Oil and Natural Gas Sector: New Source Performance Standards and National Emission Standards for Hazardous Air Pollutants Reviews, 77 Fed. Reg. 49, 490 (16 August 2012).

[84] 40 C.F.R. § 60.5360. The 2012 rule applied to all oil and natural gas facilities that commenced construction, modification or reconstruction after 23 August 2011, and on or before 18 September 2015.

[85] Oil and Natural Gas Sector: Emission Standards for New, Reconstructed, and Modified Sources, 81 Fed. Reg. 35, 824 at 35, 825. This subpart applies to facilities that commence after 18 September 2015.

[86] Ibid.

[87] Ibid.

of pneumatic controllers and it is cost-effective. However, the EPA disregarded the recommendation and decided that

> capturing and routing emissions from pneumatic controllers to a processor control device [would not be] a viable control option under our BSER analysis. While the commenter stated that a few permits in Wyoming indicate that a facility is capturing emissions from controllers and routing to a control device, we believe that there are insufficient information and data available for the EPA to establish the control option as the BSER.[88]

Clearly, there are divergent opinions on the BSER that is aimed at reducing emissions for the sake of the environment but which equally as significant 'cost-efficiency' implications. Perhaps, the comment in this instance could have been better resolved by asking for more data or technical evidence from the industry or further inquiries from advisors knowledgeable about the proposed system.

The EPA's justification for the NSPS 2016 was the need to improve the effectiveness and implementation of the NSPS 2012 rules and specifically provide standards for GHGs. The 2016 rule also covers additional equipment and sources from oil and gas production systems that were not previously covered by the NSPS 2012 rule, such as hydraulically fractured oil wells. The NSPS 2016 rule, among other things, states that:

> While the controls used to meet the VOC standards in the 2012 NSPS also reduce methane emissions incidentally, in light of the current and projected future GHG emissions from the oil and natural gas industry, reducing GHG emissions from this source category should not be treated simply as an incidental benefit to VOC reduction; rather, it is something that should be directly addressed through GHG standards in the form of limits on methane emissions under CAA section 111(b) based on direct evaluation of the extent and impact of GHG emissions from this source category and *the emission reductions that can be achieved through the best system for their reduction* ... the high quantities of methane emissions from the oil and natural gas source category demonstrate that it is rational for the EPA to set methane limitations.[89]

Given the justifications stated by the EPA, some of the key requirements of the 2016 EPA methane rule include the requirements to:

i. locate and repair leaks, also known as 'fugitive emissions';
ii. reduce natural gas venting and flaring;
iii. use reduced emissions completions (RECs, or 'green completions') to capture emissions from hydraulically fractured oil wells;
iv. route methane emissions from a pneumatic diaphragm pump to a control device;
v. continue to follow all requirements of the NSPS 2012 rule, such as limiting emissions from storage tanks; and

---

[88] *Ibid.* Emphasis added.
[89] *Ibid.* Emphasis added.

vi. reduce emissions that occur from the operation of centrifugal compressors and reciprocating compressors, which are used at natural gas compression stations to move natural gas along a pipeline.

The rule includes requirements that apply at every step of the production and transmission process: oil and natural gas well sites, natural gas production gathering and boosting stations, gas processing plants, natural gas transmission compressor stations and storage facilities.[90]

The NSPS 2016 and NSPS 2012 rules were designed to provide a performance-based framework of specific rules and requirements for the operators. To the extent that the rules aim at encouraging and guiding operators to be environmentally responsible and to take active measures to curb emissions without unreasonably hindering lawful operations or impose avoidable costs, then a critical evaluation should not be a question of creating 'unnecessary' regulatory burdens as the current political leaders seem to suggest. Rather it appears to be a justifiable case of setting out clear, comprehensive and coherent rules for guiding expected behaviour. Such coherence and clarity are a hallmark of a good regulatory system. A few months after the current Trump administration resumed, several attempts at deregulation unfolded, most of which commenced with Executive Order 13783 of 28 March 2017, on 'Promoting Energy Independence and Economic Growth' which among other things aimed at the removal of what it refers to as regulatory 'burdens' that *unnecessarily obstruct, delay, curtail, or otherwise impose significant costs on the siting, permitting, production, utilization, transmission, or delivery of energy resources.*[91]

Considering the tenor and rationale of Executive Order 13783, it is useful to take a closer look at the processes and framework established through the rules and regulations issued by the affected agencies under the Obama administration. Clearly, the amendments to NSPS 2012 by the NSPS 2016 rule were well thought out and followed due process. As stated by the EPA, due considerations were given to comments received during the proposal stages, including having a structured engagement process with states and stakeholders. As part of the process, the EPA issued draft white papers addressing various technical issues, including public and expert reviewers' comments. The rules were also designed to complement other federal actions as well as state regulations and the EPA highlights that it worked closely with the US Department of Interior's BLM during the rulemaking process in order to avoid conflicts in requirements between the NSPS and BLM's proposed rulemaking. Thus, the move by the Trump-EPA for a proposed rulemaking on 16 June 2017, with the aim of staying the implementation of the NSPS 2016 rule for two years while it reconsidered the rule, appears to be political or due to a

---

[90] See EPA, 'Final Rules and Draft Information Collection Request Fact Sheet and Presentation' (May 2016), www.epa.gov/stationary-sources-air-pollution/epas-actions-reduce-methane-and-volatile-organic-compound-voc.

[91] Executive Order No 13,783, 82 Fed. Reg. 16,093 (28 March 2017).

preference for a different regulatory approach or a more deregulated paradigm.[92] This was done even though the NSPS 2016 rule included an in-built mechanism through which 'any owner or operator claiming technical infeasibility, nonapplicability, or exemption from the regulation' could seek exemptions or make the claims for reviews.[93]

Following the Trump-EPA's stay decision, the DC Circuit vacated the EPA's administrative stay of the rule because it was unlawful under the CAA.[94] Nonetheless, the Court did emphasise that even though the stay was unlawful, the EPA can still substantially modify the rule via the normal notice-and-comment rulemaking under the Administrative Procedure Act. The Trump-EPA began this process on 15 October 2018, by issuing a proposed rule.[95] The public comment period for this proposal closed on 17 December 2018, and interestingly enough, major oil and gas corporations expressed support for maintaining the key elements of the underlying Obama-EPA NSPS 2016 rule, such as leak detection and repair programmes. However, some operators applauded the Trump-EPA's efforts to make the regulations more cost-effective. Some of the changes proposed by the new Trump-EPA include:

a. weakening of the leak detection and repair rules allowing longer intervals between inspections;
b. a change from requiring that leaks be fixed within 30 days to requiring that a "first attempt at repair" be made within 30 days, with repairs made within 60 days;
c. allowing a broader use of the "technical infeasibility" exception; and
d. allowing in-house engineers to certify system designs and declarations of technical infeasibility.

On 28 August 2019, the EPA signed proposed amendments to the 2012 and 2016 NSPS rules on the basis of removing 'regulatory duplication and save the industry millions of dollars in compliance costs each year, while maintaining health and environmental protection from oil and gas sources that the Agency considers appropriate to regulate'.[96] The 2019 reviews under the current administration aimed among other things at revising the inclusion of sources in transmission and storage as part of the source category and the inclusion of GHG, in the

---

[92] Oil and Natural Gas Sector: Emission Standards for New, Reconstructed, and Modified Sources: Stay of Certain Requirements, 82 Fed. Reg. 27,645 (16 June 2017).
[93] *Ibid*.
[94] *Clean Air Council v Pruitt*, 862 F.3d 1 (DC Cir 2017).
[95] Oil and Natural Gas Sector: Emission Standards for New, Reconstructed, and Modified Sources Reconsideration, 83 Fed. Reg. 52,056 (15 October 2018).
[96] The US EPA, 'Proposed Policy Amendments 2012 and 2016 New Source Performance Standards for the Oil and Natural Gas Industry' (2019) available at www.epa.gov/controlling-air-pollution-oil-and-natural-gas-industry/proposed-policy-amendments-2012-and-2016-new accessed 12.12.29019. See also the US EPA, 'Regulatory Impact Analysis for the Proposed Oil and Natural Gas Sector: Emission Standards for New, Reconstructed, and Modified Sources Review' (EPA-452/R-19-001, August 2019).

form of methane, as a regulated pollutant in NSPS 2016. The Regulatory Impact Assessment of the NSPS 2012 and 2016 that accompanied the 2019 proposed rules suggest that the proposed rules will aim, among other things, at rescinding the requirements of NSPS 2016, ie OOOOa for:

i. sources in the transmission and storage segment; and
ii. methane regulation requirements from sources in the production and processing segments, while leaving VOC regulations in place for the production and processing sources. The alternative co-proposed option considered is to rescind the methane requirements for all affected sources.

The Regulatory Impact Assessment states that as methane control options are redundant or seemingly unnecessary because there are VOC control options, there are thus no expected cost or emissions effects from removing the methane requirements in the production and processing segments. It states further that there are no expected cost or emissions impacts for the alternative co-proposed option for the same reason because methane control options on all sources would be redundant since there are VOC control options already.[97] According to the Trump-EPA, the proposed amendments are estimated to save the oil and gas industry $17 to $19 million a year, for a total of $97 to $123 million from 2019 through to 2025. Hence, a vital question here is – was the objective to save the industry some or a lot of money, ie to be cost-efficient while dealing with emissions, or to reduce 'unnecessary' regulatory burdens? Would such be justifiable enough vis-à-vis the imperative of curbing emissions in a coherent manner and requiring environmentally-responsible action from the industry? It appears that the need to save costs and deregulate even if gaps in regulation are created was prioritised. The current state of affairs shows potential for political and commercial influences and by implication 'regulatory capture' on an agency's ability to independently decide when and how to regulate.

ii. *The Bureau of Land Management*

The Bureau of Land Management (BLM) manages public lands and subsurface estate under its jurisdiction pursuant to the Federal Land Policy and Management Act 1976. Its core mandate relates to conservation and regulation of multiple-use and sustained yield while ensuring an environmentally responsible development of energy resources and mining on Federal lands (comprising about 245 million acres of land and 700 million acres of a mineral estate).[98] The BLM's Waste Prevention, Production Subject to Royalties, and Resource Conservation Rule ('BLM 2016 Rule') was issued pursuant to the Mineral Leasing Act of 1920 (MLA)

---

[97] US EPA, Regulatory Impact Analysis, *ibid*.
[98] The BLM 2016 Rule notes that 'Domestic production from 96,000 Federal onshore oil and gas wells accounts for 11 percent of the Nation's natural gas supply and 5 percent of its oil. In Fiscal Year (FY) 2015, operators produced 183.4 million barrels (bbl) of oil, 2.2 trillion cubic feet (Tcf) of natural

which requires the BLM to ensure that lessees use all reasonable precautions to prevent waste of oil or gas developed in the land.[99] The leases issued by the BLM must ensure that operations are conducted with 'reasonable diligence, skill, and care' and comply with rules for the prevention of undue waste. Accordingly, the main focus for BLM should be on conservation and waste prevention, both in terms of wasting gas as a resource and preventing loss of accruable revenues such as royalties and taxable income arising from such waste through, eg venting and flaring.[100] Thus, BLM is in order when stating its basis for the 2016 Rule to include ensuring operators (a) promote the economical, cost-effective, and reasonable measures to minimise gas waste and (b) enhance the nation's natural gas supplies, boost royalty receipts for American taxpayers, tribes, and states. However, when the BLM begins to dabble in the objective of reducing pollution and preventing climate change, then it raises the question(s) of potential conflicts with the EPA's statutory mandate under the CAA.[101]

It was apt for the Obama administration's BLM to finalise the 2016 Rule with the aim of replacing the decades-old framework for regulating venting, flaring and royalty-free use of gas on Federal Land, ie the 1979 Notice to Lessees and Operators of Onshore Federal and Indian Oil and Gas Leases, Royalty or Compensation for Oil and Gas Lost (NTL-4A). The 2016 Rule inter alia aimed at preventing the 'waste' of natural gas due to venting, flaring and leaks during oil and gas production operations on onshore Federal and Indian (other than Osage Tribe) leases; as well as defining the contexts in which such lost or wasted gas could be subject to royalties or when it would be considered royalty-free on-site. Although the regulations aimed at stopping or reducing 'waste' through flaring, venting and leaks, it would understandably have the indirect impact of reducing the pollution and GHG emissions attributable to such activities. The BLM pointed out the thorough processes and engagements undertaken before issuing the 2016 rule,

---

gas, and 3.3 billion gallons of natural gas liquids (NGLs) from onshore Federal and Indian oil and gas leases. The production value of this oil and gas exceeded $20.9 billion and generated over $2.3 billion in royalties, which were shared with tribes, Indian allottee owners, and States.'

[99] BLM's Waste Prevention, Production Subject to Royalties, and Resource Conservation, 81 Fed. Reg. 83,008, 83013 (18 November 2016) (codified at 43 C.F.R. pts. 3100, 3160 and 3170) ('BLM 2016 Rule').

[100] The Mineral Leasing Act (30 U.S.C. 225) requires that leases granted by the BLM include a provision that such rules for the prevention of undue waste shall be observed.

[101] In the Background Statement to the BLM 2016 Rule it was stated that: 'BLM is not the only regulator with the responsibility to oversee aspects of onshore oil and gas production, and throughout this rulemaking the BLM has focused on potential interactions of this rule with other Federal, State, or tribal regulatory requirements. For example, the U.S. Environmental Protection Agency (EPA) issued rules in 2012 and early 2016 to control emissions of methane and volatile organic compounds (VOCs) from new, modified and reconstructed oil and gas wells and production equipment, and many States and tribes regulate aspects of the oil and gas production process to address safety, waste, production accountability, and/or air quality concerns. *Regulatory agencies often have overlapping authority and may adopt very similar measures to realize those complementary goals, such as improving air quality and reducing waste. For example, measures in this rule that aim to avoid the waste of methane gas through venting or leaks will also reduce methane pollution.*' Emphasis added.

such as (a) carrying out consultations with tribal leaders, state authorities, companies and non-governmental organisations and relevant stakeholders, including public meetings in Colorado, New Mexico, North Dakota and Washington, DC.[102] It received and considered approximately 330,000 public comments on the proposed rule, including approximately 1,000 unique comments.[103] It is therefore interesting to note the different actions taken by the current Trump administration and the 115th Congress to target the BLM 2016 Rule as part of an elaborate deregulatory drive.

a. Dismantling of the 2016 BLM Methane Rule

First, the Rule was slated for revocation by the Congressional Review Act (CRA). Under the CRA, Congress has 60 days to review major regulations before they go into effect; if both houses disapprove of a rule, then it can be repealed by a joint resolution signed by the President.[104] Because a president can simply veto a resolution attempting to overturn a regulation promulgated by his own administration, the CRA is viewed as a protection against 'midnight' legislation by a president about to leave office.[105] Before President Trump, the CRA had only been successfully used once, at the beginning of the Bush presidency in 2001.[106] During the first months of the administration's term, however, Congress considered 33 regulations for repeal under the CRA.[107] The CRA resolution addressing the BLM 2016 Rule narrowly failed in the Senate, losing by only one vote.[108]

After the attempted repeal via the CRA, the BLM issued a postponement of most of the provisions of the rules.[109] However, because the rule had already gone into effect and the BLM did not engage in proper rulemaking, the postponement was vacated following a suit brought by California, New Mexico, and a coalition of 17 conservation and tribal citizen groups against BLM, claiming that the latter violated the Administrative Procedure Act by publishing a notice postponing

---

[102] BLM 2016 Rule (n 99).
[103] BLM 2016 Rule (n 99).
[104] Congressional Review Act (CRA), 5 U.S.C. section 801 *et seq* (2012).
[105] Susan E Dudley, 'Don't Write off the Congressional Review Act Yet' (2017) *Yale Journal on Regulation*: Notice & Comment, yalejreg.com/nc/dont-write-off-the-congressional-review-act-yet-by-susan-e-dudley/.
[106] *Ibid*. However, before Trump's term, Congress had passed five other resolutions of disapproval, but each were vetoed by President Obama. Maeve P Carey, Alissa M Dolan and Christopher M Davis, 'The Congressional Review Act: Frequently Asked Questions' (Congressional Research Service, November 2016).
[107] Eric Lipton and Jasmine C Lee, 'Which Obama-Era Rules Are Being Reversed in the Trump Era' *New York Times*, 18 May 2017, www.nytimes.com/interactive/2017/05/01/us/politics/trump-obama-regulations-reversed.html.
[108] Valerie Volcovici, 'Bid to Revoke Obama Methane Rule Fails in Surprise U.S. Senate Vote (*Reuters*, 10 May 2017), www.reuters.com/article/us-usa-congress/bid-to-revoke-obama-methane-rule-fails-in-surprise-u-s-senate-vote. The resolution failed 49 to 51, but it can be assumed that Vice President Pence would have sided with Trump to break the 50–50 vote in favour of disapproval.
[109] Waste Prevention, Production Subject to Royalties, and Resource Conservation, Postponement of Certain Compliance Dates, 82 Fed. Reg. 27,430 (15 June 2017).

the compliance dates for certain sections of the 2016 Rule.[110] Thus, the BLM 2016 Rule was back in place and thereafter the administration commenced a notice-and-comment rulemaking to suspend the 2016 Rules,[111] but this suspension was also invalidated when it was enjoined by the Court.[112] The same day the suspension rule was enjoined, the Trump-BLM released a Revised Rule, which repealed most of the BLM 2016 Rule.[113] After issuance of the proposed rule, the Wyoming District Court in *Wyoming v US Dep't of Interior* ordered a stay of the implementation of major provisions of the original BLM 2016 Rule, preventing the rule from going into effect.[114] On 28 September 2018, the BLM issued its Final Rule modifying the 2016 Rule, and this new rule went into effect on 27 November 2018.[115] The Wyoming case exemplifies how politics, conflicting economic interest groups and lack of clarity in roles of relevant institutions could lead to controversies at the expense of sound energy policy and regulation.

On 16 January 2017, a Wyoming Federal Court declined to issue a preliminary injunction staying the effective date of the BLM 2016 Rule. In this case, the states of Wyoming, Montana and North Dakota requested that the Court enjoin the Rule before it took effect on 17 January 2017, because according to them, the Rule represented unlawful agency action since it exceeded the BLM's statutory authority and was otherwise arbitrary and capricious.[116] It was held that the petitioners had not shown a 'clear and unequivocal right to relief' because the Court was unable to conclude that the rule's provisions lacked a 'legitimate, independent waste prevention purpose or are otherwise so inconsistent with the [Clean Air Act] as to exceed BLM's authority and usurp that of the EPA, states, and tribes'.[117] Although the Court questioned whether the 'social cost of methane' was an appropriate factor to consider in issuing a 'resource conservation rule' pursuant to the Mineral Leasing Act, the Court said it could not conclude 'at this point' that the rule was arbitrary and capricious.[118]

b. Comparison of BLM's 2016 and 2018 Final Rules

Following the Trump-BLM's 2018 Rule, the following requirements of the 2016 Rule were removed in their entirety: (i) waste minimization plans; (ii) well drilling and completion requirements; (iii) pneumatic controller and diaphragm pump

---

[110] *California, et al, v United States Bureau of Land Management, et al*, 277 F.Supp.3d 1106 (2017).
[111] BLM Suspension Rule, 82 Fed. Reg. 58,050 (8 December 2017).
[112] *California v US BLM*, 286 F. Supp. 3d 1054, 1076 (N.D. Cal. 2018).
[113] BLM Revision Rule, 83 Fed. Reg. 7,924 (22 February 2018) (to be codified at 43 C.F.R. pt. 3160 and 3170).
[114] *Wyoming v U.S. Dep't of Interior*, 2:16-CV-0285-SWS (D. Wyo.) (4 April 2018).
[115] Waste Prevention, Production Subject to Royalties, and Resource Conservation; Rescission or Revision of Certain Requirements, 83 Fed. Reg. 49,184 (28 September 2018).
[116] *Wyoming v U.S. Dep't of Interior*, 2:16-CV-0285-SWS (D. Wyo.) (Order on Motions for Preliminary Injunction, 16 January 2017).
[117] *Ibid.*
[118] *Ibid.*

requirements; (iv) storage vessel requirements; and (v) Leak Detection and Repair requirements. The following requirements of the 2016 Rule were modified and/or replaced:

i. Gas-capture requirement – The BLM will now defer to state or tribal regulations in determining when the flaring of associated gas from oil wells will be royalty-free;
ii. Downhole good maintenance and liquids unloading requirements; and
iii. Measuring and reporting volumes of gas vented and flared.

By and large, the 2018 BLM Methane Rule eliminated key requirements of the 2016 Rule and reinstated the previous regulations, ie the NTL-4A that dates back to the 1970s. The 2016 Rule had applied to both new and existing oil and natural gas activities on federal lands, meaning that it covered some facilities not regulated by the EPA rules, which only cover new and modified sources. Natural gas at oil wells (associated gas) is often vented or flared, resulting in substantial waste, and the 2016 BLM Rule had set 'capture targets' to require producers to capture an increasing percentage of all associated gas: 85 per cent in 2018; up to 98 per cent in 2026. The capture targets have been completely eliminated in the 2018 Final Rule issued by the Trump-BLM, and producers will only be forced to capture associated gas where required by state regulations. Like the EPA requirement, the 2016 regulations required regular inspections for methane leaks and the repair of any leaks detected. However, the 2018 BLM rule also completely rescinded these requirements.

iii. Pipeline and Hazardous Materials Safety Administration

The US Department of Transportation's Pipeline and Hazardous Materials Safety Administration (PHMSA) has the authority to regulate the safety of pipelines and underground natural gas storage facilities. President Obama provided some additional mandates to the agency, including some affecting GHG emissions, when he signed the Pipeline Safety, Regulatory Certainty, and Job Creation Act of 2011 and the Protecting our Infrastructure of Pipelines and Enhancing Safety Act of 2016.[119] In response to Southern California Gas Company's large natural gas leak that remained out of control from October 2015 to February 2016, the PHMSA was authorised to issue safety standards for underground natural gas storage facilities. The PHMSA also has the authority to set standards for the use of pipeline leak detection systems, automatic shut-off valves, and accident notification systems, which can all help to lower methane emissions from the nation's pipeline infrastructure.

---

[119] Lattanzio (n 71) 13–14.

iv. State Actions on Methane Emissions

Most state regulations regarding methane focus on other sources of emissions, such as landfills and local distribution infrastructure.[120] Only about six states (California, Colorado, Ohio, Pennsylvania, Utah and Wyoming) currently have regulations or permit requirements regarding methane or VOC emissions from the oil and gas sector.[121] New Mexico may soon be added to this list, as the Governor has ordered state regulators to develop similar rules.[122] In Pennsylvania, the state Department of Environmental Protection proposed a new rule limiting methane and VOC emissions in April 2019, and the State Senate Democratic Policy Committee was discussing making the regulations even tighter.[123] Colorado has been considered the leader in methane leak reduction because it passed the first regulations in the country requiring producers to routinely check oil and gas wells for methane leaks and to fix leaky equipment. Colorado's regulations in 2014 actually preceded the EPA's 2016 methane standards and were considered to be 'more protective' than the EPA rule. Two years after Colorado's rule went into effect, the Colorado Department of Public Health and Environment announced a 75 per cent drop in oil and gas sites with detected methane leaks.[124]

V. Conclusion

This chapter builds on the premise that in the most ideal scenarios policy and regulatory frameworks should: (i) exemplify coherence rather than uncertainty; (ii) protect regulatory independence and accountability rather than susceptibility to the hidden dictates of various interest groups in the energy spectrum; as well as (iii) support efficient communication and information-sharing between the regulator and industry. In a carbon-constrained world where energy supply systems and markets are facing increasing scrutiny and justifiable calls for greater environmental responsibility and accountability, the development of such high-quality regulatory and policy frameworks should be a priority. Looking forward,

---

[120] National Conference of State Legislatures (NCSL), 'State Methane Policies' (11 February 2014), www.ncsl.org/research/environment-and-natural-resources/state-methane-policies.aspx.

[121] Environmental Defense Fund (EDF), 'Leading Regulatory Practices to Abate Oil and Gas Methane Emissions: Lessons Learned from Mexico' (7 August 2018), www.edf.org/sites/default/files/documents/MX%20Methane%20Regs_FactSheet_English.pdf.

[122] Laila Kearny and Jennifer Hiller, 'New Mexico Governor Moves to Limit Methane Emissions, Combat Climate Change' (*Reuters*, 29 January 2019), www.reuters.com/article/us-new-mexico-regulation-energy/new-mexico-governor-moves-to-limit-methane-emissions-combat-climate-change-idUSKCN1PN35R.

[123] Elizabeth Hardison, 'Environmental Proponents to State Senate Panel: Pa. Needs Better Methane Regulations (Pa. Capital Star, 23 April 2019), www.penncapital-star.com/blog/environmental-proponents-to-state-senate-panel-pa-needs-better-methane-regulations/.

[124] Cathy Proctor, 'EPA Follows Colorado Lead in Targeting Methane Leaks from Oil & Gas' (2016) *Denver Business Journal*, www.bizjournals.com/denver/blog/earth_to_power/2016/05/epa-follows-colorado-lead-in-targeting-methane.html.

the 'cleaner' energy and environmental case for gas compared to other hydrocarbons does not depend on beating the emissions performance of these other carbon-intensive energy sources, rather it is more likely to depend on the willingness of the relevant operators, stakeholders and institutions to work together to ensure the emissions attributable to the gas production and supply chain are as low as practicable or compete favourably with the increasing array of net-zero carbon or zero-carbon sources. This presupposes the development, investments in and implementation of necessary innovations and technologies exemplified in concepts such as the BSER and the BACT and also leading to the large-scale cost-efficient deployment of emissions-removal technologies such as CCUS and methane reformation.

3

Decarbonising Gas and Electricity Systems: An Outlook on Power-to-Gas and other Technology-Based Solutions

TADE OYEWUNMI*

I. Introduction

The conventional approach to energy supply from a systemic standpoint includes: (i) generation of electric energy from primary sources such as hydropower-dams, coal and natural gas; (ii) transmitting the energy through high voltage wires, substations, transformers and other network facilities; and (iii) distribution via local networks to various classes of consumers such as commercial, industrial and residential groups. This energy supply system is typically based on a patchwork of contracts, rules, regulations and policy frameworks involving vertically-integrated utilities, natural monopolies, open and non-discriminatory access to essential networks, property rights, cost-of-service, just and reasonable rate-of-return to utility investors. Increasingly, such policies also include integrated planning by utilities and transmission network operators to balance demand and supply in real-time, while maintaining mid-to-long-term reliability and considering the physical nature of electric currents and power. By and large, energy law and policy initiatives were directed at ensuring security of supply, viable markets and protection of the public and environment for the harmful externalities that arise as a result. As discussed in chapter two, the imperative of curbing energy-related greenhouse gas emissions has become essential. Likewise is the need to ensure reliability, affordable access and security of energy supply to power modern societies and the economy. Given the significant role carbon-intensive sources such as coal and oil have played over the past century, the imperative of carbon-constraints will surely impact on the way and manner in which energy, especially energy derived from conventional hydrocarbon-based sources, is delivered to a growing number of end-users globally.

*This chapter was written as part of the 'Renewable Energy Integration, Decarbonization, and Power-to-Gas' project at the Institute for Energy and the Environment, Vermont Law School, VT, USA.

The IPCC Special Report for Policymakers 2018 provides a useful outlook on the various options and strategic pathways towards effective decarbonisation. The Report agreeably underscores the need for comprehensive policy-driven systemic change and pathways. It is instructive to note the suite of technologies and innovative solutions recommended in this regard. These include energy efficiency, electrification of energy end-use sectors like transportation, renewable energy utilisation, Carbon Dioxide Removal (CDR) options, Carbon Capture and Storage (CCS), deployment of low to net-zero carbon fuels such as hydrogen in key areas. All these options and 'tools' clearly have their own unique features and would require a significant degree of pragmatism by policymakers and stakeholders to be implemented at the right time and scale for them to have any meaningful decarbonisation effect in reality.

For instance, cheap and abundant supply of natural gas and the interconnectedness of gas and electricity networks have grown over the past several decades.[1] Thus, the stakeholders and operators along that value chain can play a significant role in the evolving energy systems, transitional approaches and innovative solutions to meet the challenge of decarbonisation.[2] Some of the key factors driving more or less the evolving transitions include the falling costs of renewables such as wind and solar; progress in energy efficiency and demand side management programmes, electrification of activities previously fuelled by conventional sources such as transportation and manufacturing, etc. As the conventional system of energy supply changes, so also will the 'old guard' of oil and gas industry operators and utilities need to evolve as the energy transitions unfold. The International Energy Agency (IEA) forecasts that renewables will have the fastest growth in the electricity sources globally, meeting almost 30 per cent of power demand in 2023, up from 24 per cent in 2017.[3] In the same vein, renewables are projected to meet more than 70 per cent of global electricity generation 'growth' onwards to 2023, led by solar photovoltaics (PV) and followed by wind, hydropower and bioenergy.

---

[1] In the US, the share of natural gas in power generation increased from about 21% in 2008 to 34% in 2018. Following record domestic production, gas consumption recorded an 18% increase from 2007 to 2017. The main consuming sectors were: (i) transformation (heat and power generation) accounting for 37% of the total US gas consumption in 2017: and (ii) industry accounting for 23% of consumption in 2017. See the International Energy Agency, 'Energy Policies of IEA Countries: The United States 2019 Review' (IEA Publications, 2019) 283, 155–58.

[2] The International Energy Agency (IEA), 'The Oil and Gas Industry in Energy Transitions: World Energy Outlook Special Report' (IEA Publications, 2020) ('IEA Special Report') 164, 10–11; V Masson-Delmotte et al (eds), 'IPCC, 2018: Summary for Policymakers' in: Global Warming of 1.5°C. An IPCC Special Report on the impacts of global warming of 1.5°C above pre-industrial levels and related global greenhouse gas emission pathways, in the context of strengthening the global response to the threat of climate change, sustainable development, and efforts to eradicate poverty' The IPCC (October 2018) ('IPCC Special Report for Policymakers 2018'), available at www.ipcc.ch/sr15/chapter/spm/.

[3] US Energy Information Administration (EIA), 'Annual Energy Outlook 2019 with Projections to 2050' (2019) 1–83 at 22 ('EIA, Annual Energy Outlook'), www.eia.gov/outlooks/aeo/pdf/aeo2019.pdf; the IEA, 'Renewables 2018' (IEA Publications, 2019).

In the US, the Energy Information Administration (EIA) projects that about 21 gigawatts of additional solar PV capacity will be commissioned by 1 January 2024, while new wind capacity will also occur, albeit at a much lower level compared to solar after the Federal production tax credits expire in the early 2020s.[4]

Decarbonisation is a key objective in the push for more renewables in the energy mix of economies that hitherto relied largely on carbon-intensive sources such as oil and coal. However, it is worth pointing out that most of the preferred 'clean' energy sources are intermittent and variable since they significantly depend on factors such as when the sun shines and the wind blows; or geographical location that could impact on energy production intensity and scale of the relevant technology. Considering the intermittency issues and the variability concerns of the fastest growing renewables, ie solar and wind, plus the structural or organisational impact of an increasing array of distributed energy resources, several issues arise from a coherent energy regulation and policy standpoint. One such challenge is illustrated in the 'duck curve', a dilemma in which utilities and transmission operators must balance mismatched supply and demand across a typical day of renewable energy production and consumption. The dilemma is created when solar energy, generated when the sun is shining, exceeds typical demand; and, just as real-time generation drops in the evening, demand increases.[5] Other issues also include long-term planning and risk mitigation,[6] network congestion management and load balancing, the need to curtail energy generation from renewables due to inadequate storage or network connection options, the 'missing money' problem and shirking by investors in traditional energy utilities leading to potential capacity inadequacies.[7] These issues underscore the need for ensuring efficient integration of the growing array of intermittent and decentralised renewable systems with existing networks as well as developing advanced storage and network coupling solutions. Some of the pragmatic ways of facilitating a proper integration of net-zero carbon and renewable energy in conventional gas and electricity markets includes the deployment of advanced energy storage solutions

---

[4] The US EIA's Annual Energy Outlook 2019 reports that based on the current regulatory and legal framework, utility-scale solar plants that are under construction before 1 January 2020, receive a full 30% Investment Tax Credit (ITC), while those under construction before 1 January 2021, receive a 26% ITC and those under construction before 1 January 2022, receive a 22% ITC. Although the commercial solar ITC decreases and the ITC for residential-owned systems expires, the growth in solar PV capacity continues through 2050 for both the utility-scale and small-scale applications because the cost of PV declines throughout the projection.

[5] US Office of Energy Efficiency & Renewable Energy, 'Confronting the Duck Curve: How to Address Over-Generation of Solar Energy' (17 October 2017) at www.energy.gov/eere/articles/confronting-duck-curve-how-address-over-generation-solar-energy.

[6] LeRoy Paddock and Karyan San Martano, 'Energy Supply Planning in a Distributed Energy Resources World' in Donald Zillman et al, (eds), *Innovation in Energy Law and Technology: Dynamic Solutions for Energy Transitions* (Oxford University Press, 2018) 371–89.

[7] Amy L Stein, 'Distributed Reliability' (2016) 87 *University of Colorado Law Review* 887–1008; William Boyd, 'Public Utility and the Low-Carbon Future' 61 (2014) *UCLA Law Review* 1614–1711.

to enhance reliability.[8] Other innovative solutions to some of the regulatory and technical problems include the production of zero-carbon hydrogen or synthetic methane using a power-to-gas (P2G) technology which converts the excess electricity from the growing array of renewable energy systems; or the production of renewable natural gas (RNG) from excess renewable energy or from biomass and waste.

RNG is essentially pipeline compatible gaseous fuel derived from biogenic or other renewable sources that have lower lifecycle carbon dioxide equivalent emissions than geological natural gas. Thus, while helping to solve the storage and intermittency issues with typical renewable energy systems, it could help to allay the fears of stranded assets for energy utilities since it can be made fully interchangeable with natural gas and useable in existing networks. Globally, there are growing interests in RNG fuels such as Biogas produced through processes comprising of anaerobic digestion, thermal gasification and RNG derived from municipal solid wastes. Another emerging technology in this context is the P2G system designed to convert excess renewable energy into pipeline-quality zero-carbon hydrogen. When combined with methanation, the process leads to synthetic methane which could be stored and transported through new-build, project-specific or existing gas supply networks.[9]

This chapter will focus on the potential for RNG, Hydrogen and P2G systems deployment in the US and regulatory issues that could impact such objectives as a means of integrating clean energy sources in Parts II–V. Part VI examines the potential role of carbon capture, utilisation, and storage (CCUS) and other negative emissions technology solutions as options for energy decarbonisation.

II. Climate Change Mitigation and Decarbonisation

If atmospheric concentrations of greenhouse gas (GHG) continue to increase, climate science predicts that the average temperature at the Earth's surface is likely to increase from 0.5 to 8.6 degrees Fahrenheit above 1986 through 2005 levels by the end of the century, 'depending on future emissions and the responsiveness of

---

[8] Kevin B Jones, Benjamin B Jervey and Matthew Roche, *The Electric Battery: Charging Forward to a Low-Carbon Future* (Praeger, 2017) 1–212.

[9] Heather D Dziedzic and Tade Oyewunmi, 'Decarbonization and the Integration of Renewables in Transitional Energy Markets: Examining the Power to Gas Option in the United States' (2019) *Oil, Gas & Energy Law Intelligence (OGEL) Journal*; Martin Lambert, *Power-to-Gas: Linking Electricity and Gas in a Decarbonising World?* (Oxford Institute for Energy Studies (OEIS), OEIS Insight: 39, October 2018); Ruven Fleming and Joshua P Fershee, 'The 'Hydrogen Economy' in the United States and the European Union: Regulating Innovation to Combat Climate Change' in Donald Zillman et al (eds), *Innovation in Energy Law and Technology: Dynamic Solutions for Energy Transitions* (Oxford University Press, 2018) 449 at 137–53.

the climate system'.[10] Such reports and assessments prompted the United Nations Framework Convention on Climate Change (UNFCCC) Conference of Parties (COP) 21 in Paris in December 2015 to reach a significant agreement (ie the 'Paris Agreement'). The aim of the Agreement included: (i) to accelerate and intensify the global actions and investments needed for a sustainable low carbon future; (ii) to combat climate change and adapt to its effects; and (iii) to drive efforts in keeping global temperature rise this century well below 2 degrees Celsius above pre-industrial levels and to pursue efforts to limit the temperature increase even further to 1.5 degrees Celsius. Considering the significant role of energy and the combustion of hydrocarbons in the emission and atmospheric concentration of GHGs, growing attention has been focused on reducing or preventing emissions in pathways that would be consistent with 2°C warming scenarios.

Due to the growing calls to hold the energy, oil and gas industry accountable as a significant contributor, it is imperative to ask whether operators in the energy, oil and gas sector should be viewed as 'the problem', only 'part of the problem', or if they should be considered as an essential 'part of the solution'?[11] A pragmatic response would be to echo that all stakeholders (public and private) are part of the solution for several reasons. Firstly, the atmospheric concentration of GHGs due to anthropogenic activities are not only as a result of hydrocarbon exploration, production and combustion, but rather as a result of almost all activities that could be considered as important to socio-economic development and modernisation such as industry, forestry and agriculture. Secondly, it is essential to carefully consider the pros and cons, cost and benefits, including the opportunity costs of any pathway adopted as well as how such a pathway plays out in reality. Thirdly, climate change mitigation is a complex and multi-dimensional problem that cannot be viewed through a one-dimensional lens, eg of a 'climate scientist' or 'politician' or 'proft-motivated project developer' alone without due regard to the peculiarites of the particular context being considered. For instance, while it is crucial to curb environmental and climatic impacts of conventional energy systems, it is equally important to factor in the requirements of delivering constant, reliable and affordable energy that matches demand in real-time and also considers the broader economic, legal and developmental context within which such objectives take place.

A comprehensive framework of solutions would entail an understanding that there are different facets to such a complex issue. Such facets include engineering, socio-economics and poverty eradication needs in a developing economy for instance, or energy justice versus environmental justice concerns in both developed and developing economy contexts, as well as financing universal access to modern energy services, permanent sovereignty over natural resources, rights to

---

[10] The Intergovernmental Panel on Climate Change (IPCC), 'Summary for Policymakers of IPCC Special Report on Global Warming of 1.5°C Approved by Governments' (2018) (IPCC Special Report), www.ipcc.ch/sr15/.

[11] IEA Special Report (n 2).

economic growth and development, etc. Consequently, mitigation efforts are better considered through the lens of counterbalancing the three cardinal dimensions of energy policy, ie: (i) security and reliability of supply: (ii) affordability, access and reasonable returns on investments: as well as (iii) environmental sustainability and protection from externalities. Some of the ways of addressing the issues in an energy context are fostering an efficient integration of zero-carbon energy sources, as well as innovatively removing or altering the concentration of the 'enemy', ie GHG in the atmosphere.

According to the Intergovernmental Panel on Climate Change (IPCC),[12]

> limiting global warming to 1.5°C would require 'rapid and far-reaching' transitions in land, energy, industry, buildings, transport and cities. Global net human-caused emissions of carbon dioxide (CO_2) would need to fall by about 45 percent from 2010 levels by 2030, reaching 'net zero' around 2050. This means that any remaining emissions would need to be balanced by removing CO_2 from the air ... Allowing the global temperature to temporarily exceed or 'overshoot' 1.5°C would mean a greater reliance on techniques that remove CO_2 from the air to return global temperature to below 1.5°C by 2100.'[13]

While this chapter does not delve into the nitty-gritty of the IPCC report nor examine the economics and calculations informing the recommendations for policymakers provided in the report; it is worth reiterating here that the objective of the chapter is to consider the regulatory and policy issues that arise in some of the options for deploying zero-carbon energy sources, especially renewables via RNG and P2G systems as well as highlighting recent developments in CCUS and negative emissions technologies.

III. Integration of Renewables in Conventional Systems

As stated earlier, renewable energy deployment and distributed energy systems are increasing rapidly in developed economies. The chapters discussing Nigeria, China and Southern Africa also highlight the growing interests in off-grid systems powered by renewables. Thus, low-carbon and net-zero-carbon sources are expected to play a key role in meeting energy demand in the coming decades. The main factors pushing the exponential growth in the utilisation of renewable energy sources comprise climate change mitigation and carbon emission reduction targets, behavioural changes of the twenty-first century consumer, and other initiatives mostly at the state and local level, such as policy-driven electrification and generation standards imposed on utilities to generate and invest in renewables and low-carbon sources. Notwithstanding, there are operational, policy and energy

---

[12] IPCC Special Report (n 10).
[13] IPCC Special Report (n 10).

regulation challenges that arise following such growth and systemic changes. In the US, the electricity sector contributed about 28 per cent of total GHG emissions by economic sector in 2017–2018.[14] As mentioned in chapter two, there has been a gradual decline of emissions particularly due to an increasing switch from carbon-intensive, coal-fired generation to natural gas and more renewables.[15]

Energy sector decarbonisation is a significant pathway towards a future Sustainable Development Scenario (SDS) for energy which is the projected outlook for achieving universal access to energy for all, reduce the severe health impacts of energy-related air pollution and to tackle climate change. Decarbonisation of electricity and other interconnected systems such as gas networks presupposes a need for cross-sectoral coordination to maximise low-carbon pathways across all energy uses, including transportation and space heating. Thus, a more comprehensive approach to energy policymaking is needed, just as a greater understanding of the various sectors, and the peculiar challenges that arise when integrating electric power from distributed systems powered by variable renewable energy (VRE) sources, like solar PVs and wind, with energy markets that rely mostly on conventional energy systems such as gas-to-power utilities.[16] Technologies producing what is now commonly known as RNG, a 'pipeline quality gaseous fuel derived from biomass or other renewable sources',[17] create an avenue for exploring such cross-sectoral alignment and potential. RNG has lower lifecycle GHG emissions compared to conventional (ie, fossil-based) natural gas, due to its ability to capture and condition GHGs, such as methane and carbon dioxide (CO_2), that are emitted from agricultural and other waste management activities.

RNG can also be produced through advanced systems that convert excess electrical energy from renewables into gaseous energy forms. These systems, known as P2G, create carbon-free gaseous fuels in the form of hydrogen, or carbon neutral synthetic methane.[18] Both offer significant reductions in GHG emissions

---

[14] See the US Environmental Protection Agency (US EPA), 'Sources of Greenhouse Gas Emissions' at www.epa.gov/ghgemissions/sources-greenhouse-gas-emissions; the US EPA, 'The Inventory of U.S. Greenhouse Gas Emissions and Sinks: 1990–2017' (2019) at www.epa.gov/ghgemissions/inventory-us-greenhouse-gas-emissions-and-sinks-1990-2017. Transportation, Industry, Commercial & Residential and Agriculture sectors account for about 29%, 22%, 12% and 9% respectively.

[15] EIA, Annual Energy Outlook (n 3) 1–83 at 22; most electric generation capacity retirements occur by 2025 as a result of many regions that have surplus capacity and lower natural gas prices. The retirements reflect both planned and additional projected retirements of coal-fired capacity. On the other hand, new high-efficiency natural gas-fired combined-cycle plants and renewables generating capacity are added steadily through to 2050 to meet growing electricity demand.

[16] For more on the organisational structure of a typical gas-to-power market and value chain, see Tade Oyewunmi, *Regulating Gas Supply to Power Markets: Transnational Approaches to Competitiveness and Security of Supply* (Wolters Kluwer, 2018) 360 at 14–47; Tade Oyewunmi, 'Examining the Role of Regulation in Restructuring and Development of Gas Supply Markets in the United States and the European Union' (2017) 40(1) *Houston Journal of International Law* 191–296.

[17] American Gas Association, 'Securing a Role for Renewable Gas', 2, www.aga.org/sites/default/files/legacy-assets/our-issues/renewable-gas/Documents/AGA_RenewableGas_Summary_3.pdf.

[18] Lambert (n 9); Fleming and Fershee (n 9); Sonal Patel, *Why Power-to-Gas May Flourish in a Renewables-Heavy World* (POWER, 1 December 2019), www.powermag.com/why-power-to-gas-may-flourish-in-a-renewables-heavy-world/.

on their own. Several US states have recognised this benefit and have begun designing policy initiatives around renewable natural gas.[19] Another potential application of P2G is that upon conversion to its gaseous form of hydrogen or synthetic methane, the energy inherent in the excess electricity can be stored or transported to demand centres through existing gas supply networks. Such a development could help allay the fears of stranded assets for extant utilities and network operators in a deep decarbonisation scenario. Arguably, P2G technologies enable and enhance the integration of growing renewable energy generation with the existing electric grid, as well as the natural gas supply system, energy storage and waste reduction objectives while remaining net-carbon neutral.[20]

A. Developing Cleaner Energy Systems in the US

Coal and other carbon-intensive sources have played a major role in the US energy mix over the years, hence the sector's significant contribution to overall GHG emissions. In 2018 alone, the CO_2 emissions from the sector accounted for 1,763 million metric tons (MMmt) of CO_2 or about 33 per cent of total US energy-related CO_2 emissions, arising from coal (65 per cent), gas (33 per cent), petroleum (one per cent) and others.[21] A logical means to reduce energy-related GHG emissions is to incentivise generation of power from net-zero carbon sources, renewables, or less carbon-intensive and more efficient systems such as gas-to-power. In evaluating the overall GHG emissions impact of gas-to-power facilities, some pundits consider the lifecycle impacts attributable to segments such as upstream development and midstream pipeline transportation discussed in chapter two vis-à-vis actual downstream emissions arising from the 'combustion' natural gas as fuel in a gas-to-power facility. However, it is worth clarifying that the various sectors in a typical gas-to-power value chain, ie upstream, midstream and downstream are unique and subject to distinct economic, regulatory and policy dynamics. Thus, it could be misleading to factor in such 'climatic' or lifecycle emissions impacts in a manner that equates the emissions and operational tendencies of an upstream

---

[19] California Bioenergy, Environmental Protection Agency webinar, 'RNG Projects in the Ag Sector' (27 March 2019).

[20] Dziedzic and Oyewunmi (n 9); Paula Schulze, et al, *Power-To-Gas in A Decarbonized European Energy System Based on Renewable Energy Sources* (European Power to Gas Platform/DNV, Norway), www.afhypac.org/documents/European%20Power%20to%20Gas_White%20Paper.pdf.

[21] The US EIA, 'How Much of US Carbon Dioxide Emissions are Associated with Electricity Generation?' Available at www.eia.gov/tools/faqs/faq.php?id=77&t=11; in 2017 the electricity sector accounted for 28% of GHG emissions by sector according to the US EPA on 'Sources of Greenhouse Gas Emissions' at www.epa.gov/ghgemissions/sources-greenhouse-gas-emissions; energy-related CO_2 emissions increased by 2.8% in 2018 but will likely decrease in 2019 and 2020 as more renewables come on line and coal-plants are shut down and replaced by natural gas fired generation. Despite the growing switch from coal-fired electric generating units (EGUs) to gas-fired EGUs, the 2018 increase is the largest in energy-related CO_2 emissions since 2010, perhaps due to weakening regulations, greater economic activities and growing demand and consumption patterns.

producer (which is subject to a different set of technical, organisational and regulatory realities) with that of an energy utility operating a gas-fired power generator (most likely alongside other generating systems such as concentrated solar PVs, wind farms or coal) in the electricity industry.

Burning natural gas instead of coal for electricity in the downstream energy sector reduces the pollution rate from power generation systems and helps to avoid more than half the emissions that would have occurred otherwise with coal-fired generation. In addition, developing innovative policy-driven solutions to capture, store and utilise emissions arising from gas supply systems (on the one hand) and technologies such as P2G which allows for an increasing cross-sectoral coupling between gas and electricity networks with an increasing share of VREs (on the other hand), is arguably a pragmatic pathway to approach energy decarbonisation.

If upstream gas producers on the one hand, and downstream energy utilities operating gas-fired generators due to its reliability, efficiency and lower-emissions advantages (compared to coal-fired generation) on the other hand, can reduce, capture, or innovatively deal with emissions attributable to that value chain,[22] then the credentials of natural gas as being relatively 'cleaner' or 'less-environmentally harmful' could be further validated in the context of decarbonisation.

In the last 25 years, the energy industry in the US has seen a wave of laws and policies seeking to boost electricity generation from renewable sources. Since 1994, about 29 states and the District of Columbia have introduced Renewable Portfolio Standards (RPS), setting both voluntary and mandatory targets for renewable electric generation.[23] These targets have served to increase demand for renewable electric generation, primarily from wind and solar[24] by requiring the overall portfolio of electricity supply from utilities to include specific percentages of renewable energy capacity. It is reported that about half of all growth in US renewable electricity generation and capacity since 2000 is associated with state RPS requirements, though not all of that is strictly attributable to RPS policies.[25]

---

[22] There has been a lot of debate pertaining to emerging technologies such as Carbon Capture Utilization and Storage (CCUS), commercial acceptance of regulations pertaining to methane emissions midstream and prevention of waste and emissions through flaring in the upstream gas sector. See Bradley N Kershaw, 'Flames, Fixes, and the Road Forward: The Waste Prevention Rule and BLM Authority to Regulate Natural Gas Flaring and Venting' (Winter 2018) 29(1) *Colorado Natural Resources, Energy & Environmental Law Review* 115–64; US EPA, 'The Inventory of U.S. Greenhouse Gas Emissions' (n 14), chapter on 'Energy'; Ryan Collins, 'Texas Oil Regulator Shifts Stance as Gas Flaring Hits Record' (*Bloomberg Markets*, 7 August 2019, updated on 8 August 2019).

[23] Barbose, Galen, Lawrence Berkeley National Laboratory, 'U.S. Renewable Portfolio Standards: 2018 Annual Status Report' (November 2018), slide 8.

[24] *Ibid*, slide 15.

[25] See the National Conference of State Legislatures (NCSL), 'State Renewable Portfolio Standards and Goals'; Galen L Barbose, Lawrence Berkeley National Laboratory, 'U.S. Renewables Portfolio Standards: 2019 Annual Status Update' at https://emp.lbl.gov/publications/us-renewables-portfolio-standards-2. Only about 30% of renewable energy generation developments in 2018 was attributable to RPS. The framework continues to play a significant role in particular regions such as the Northeast and Mid-Atlantic regions of the US.

RPS seeks an indirect reduction in GHG emissions, by displacing traditional, carbon-intensive fuels like coal and oil. Furthermore, the Clean Power Plan (CPP) from the Obama era,[26] issued in 2015, sought to tackle the issue head-on, by limiting the emissions from electric generators, in particular emissions from carbon-intensive coal generators.[27]

The CPP was issued by the EPA pursuant to the US Clean Air Act (CAA) section 111(b). It comprised a framework of performance-based standards upon which emissions of CO_2 from affected newly constructed, modified, and reconstructed fossil fuel-fired electric generating units (EGUs) could be curtailed. The Obama-EPA also issued guidelines for states to use in developing plans to limit CO_2 emissions from existing fossil fuel-fired EGUs under the CAA section 111(d). The highlighted regulatory steps aimed at curtailing carbon emissions from hydrocarbon-based EGUs by requiring innovation and active steps from operators. The utilities that failed to innovate or achieve the requisite standards, would have become less competitive when compared to other less carbon-intensive or net-zero carbon sources. Such prospects were essentially obfuscated following the Trump administration's repeal of the CPP. In 2019, following prior stays by the courts,[28] and the proposed Affordable Clean Energy rule, the CPP stands repealed.[29]

To some, this was a setback in climate policy; while others recognise that economics and state-level policies have already driven the electric industry to a 33 per cent reduction in GHG emissions.[30] This surpasses the 32 per cent reduction sought by the CPP and achieves that target a decade early. It also exceeds the initial commitment of the United States to the Paris Climate Agreement, which was a 28 per cent reduction by 2025.[31] These achievements, however opportune they may be, demonstrate the ability of corporate sustainability initiatives, energy markets, state and regional policy, and economic incentives to drive meaningful change in the energy sector and its carbon footprint.

---

[26] US EPA's *Standards of Performance for Greenhouse Gas Emissions from New, Modified, and Reconstructed Stationary Sources: Electric Utility Generating Units* (40 CFR Parts 60, 70, 71, and 98).80 Federal Register ('Fed. Reg.') 64510 (23 October 2015).

[27] Georgetown Climate Center, 'State-by-State Resources to Better Understand EPA's Carbon Pollution Rule' (2 June 2014), www.georgetownclimate.org/articles/state-by-state-resources-to-better-understand-epas-carbon-pollution-rule.html#summary.

[28] Stanford University, Stanford News Service, 'Goodbye, Clean Power Plan: Stanford Researchers Discuss the New Energy Rule' (21 June 2019).

[29] US EPA's *Repeal of the Clean Power Plan; Emission Guidelines for Greenhouse Gas Emissions from Existing Electric Utility Generating Units; Revisions to Emission Guidelines Implementing Regulations* (40 CFR Part 60) 84 Fed. Reg. 32520 (8 July 2019).

[30] Maggie Shober, Southern Alliance for Clean Energy, 'Should We Mourn the Clean Power Plan?' (18 June 2019), https://cleanenergy.org/blog/trump-replacing-clean-power-plan/.

[31] United Nations Framework Convention on Climate Change, Nationally Determined Contributions Registry, available at www4.unfccc.int/sites/NDCStaging/Pages/All.aspx.

B. Energy Assets: Untapped and Under-Utilised Resources

Following the apparent success of RPS implementation, and other economic incentives,[32] renewables-based electric generation has doubled in the US within the last decade, and now provides 17.8 per cent of the country's electricity.[33] Paired with the aforementioned reduction in GHG emissions, there is strong evidence that the energy system is headed in the right direction. But, if the system has already surpassed previous national and international targets for decarbonisation, then where is the next signpost? Industry experts have different visions of the future system, some seeking an electric system powered 100 per cent by wind, solar and hydro.[34] Others have cautioned that this approach, while technically feasible, ignores the political, technical and financial hurdles to achieve such an aggressive target.[35] Instead, analysis of future electric generation seems to have coalesced around a lower target of an 80 per cent penetration rate for renewables-based electricity, at least as a starting point for meaningful modeling.[36] Even at 80 per cent, this target comes with significant challenges considering the nearly five-fold increase of renewables' contribution to the grid. It also confirms the current reliance on the electric grid to do the heavy lifting of decarbonising our society, including powering industrial, transportation, commercial and agricultural activities.

As mentioned earlier, several renewable energy sources that depend on weather and seasonal patterns thus have significant intermittency issues. In other words, energy from such systems like solar PV systems and wind turbines is only available at a specific scale and time, when the sun shines and the wind blows, unless the capacity to adequately store that energy exists at the necessary scale and time. Such 'storage' solutions must also compete with other, existing forms of energy storage such as batteries and pumped-hydro systems, while also meeting the required scale and duration to guarantee reliability, affordability and security of a fully renewable energy supply. Note that unpredictability creates a reasonable risk to long-term and real-time capacity and therefore not a desirable trait in either electric supply or grid management. Reliable energy or the ability to flip the

---

[32] Federal incentives include Production Tax Credits and Investment Tax Credits, United States Energy Information Administration, 'U.S. Renewable Electricity Generation has Doubled Since 2008' (19 March 2019), at www.eia.gov/todayinenergy/detail.php?id=38752.

[33] *Ibid.*

[34] Mark Z Jacobsen, et al, 'Low-cost Solution to the Grid Reliability Problem with 100% Penetration of Intermittent Wind, Water, and Solar for all Purposes' (*Proceedings of the National Academy of Sciences of the United States of America*, 8 December 2015) PNAS, 112 (49) 15060–15065, at www.pnas.org/content/112/49/15060?ijkey=ad4e81fadea8184253ab4229251f1cbac6996abb&keytype2=tf_ipsecsha.

[35] Christopher TM Clack, et al, 'Evaluation of a Proposal for Reliable Low-Cost Grid Power with 100% Wind, Water, and Solar' (*Proceedings of the National Academy of Sciences of the United States of America*, 27 June 2017) PNAS 114 (26) 6722–6727, at www.pnas.org/content/114/26/6722.full.

[36] National Renewable Energy Laboratory, 'Renewable Energy Futures Study: Exploration of High-Penetration Renewable Electricity Futures'. Volume 1, Chapter 3, 3-3, at www.law.berkeley.edu/php-programs/courses/fileDL.php?fID=7308.

switch in our homes and offices and expect the light bulbs or electric cookers or air conditioners and coffee machine to function for example, requires an instantaneous balancing of both supply and demand, something that wind and solar struggle to achieve, depending on the time of the day, season and location.

For grid managers, like Regional Transmission Operators (RTOs) and Independent System Operators (ISOs) (collectively, 'grid operators'), these distributed and variable resources challenge their ability to maintain the grid's stability and reliability. Without examining the detailed engineering principles involved in the electric grid, it's sufficient to note here that balancing supply and demand, while maintaining frequency and voltage are key components of a secure and reliable electricity network.[37] These characteristics are captured in the Ancillary Service markets throughout the country, via the RTOs and ISOs. For the purpose of this evaluation, it must be assumed that as the penetration of intermittent or distributed renewable-based energy increases from 17 per cent to 80 per cent, there will be a growing need for system resources to contribute such ancillary services, which seek to level fluctuations of intermittent supply. Of interest here is the ability of non-traditional, non-electric resources to aid load levelling and energy storage.[38]

Because traditional renewables-based electricity is generated when the fuel (eg, wind, water or sunshine) is available, its contribution to electric supply is naturally less dependent on demand. During times of overproduction, when renewable supply exceeds demand, grid operators must eliminate this imbalance to inter alia: (i) preserve the integrity of the electric system; (ii) prevent network congestion; and (iii) regulate the supply's potential impact on market prices and cost-recovery projections. These issues lead to curtailment, which in essence limits the generation, or output of renewable energy to the grid, thus, decreasing the overall contribution of renewables-based electricity to energy consumption below what is achievable without curtailment.[39] Without significant changes in demand, expansion of transmission resources, or the development of adequate, cost-efficient storage solutions; increasing renewables on the grid will only serve to increase curtailment and redundancy. Curtailment is generally low in terms of percentage of total generation, roughly four per cent of wind supply annually for example.[40] Nevertheless, this curtailment equates to significant energy waste: hundreds of thousands of megawatt-hours (MWh) in each regional market.[41] It is noted that in 2013, the MidContinent Independent System Operator (MISO)

---

[37] New England States Committee on Electricity, 'Electricity Ancillary Services Primer' (August 2017).

[38] Andrew Mazza, et al, 'Applications of Power to Gas Technologies in Emerging Electrical Systems' (September 2008) *Renewable and Sustainable Energy Reviews* Volume 92, 794–806, 3–1.

[39] Lori Bird, et al, 'Wind and Solar Energy Curtailment: Experience and Practices in the United States' (*National Renewable Energy Laboratory*, March 2014).

[40] Lori Bird, et al, 'Wind and Solar Energy Curtailment Practices' (*National Renewable Energy Laboratory*, 17 October 2014), at www.nrel.gov/docs/fy15osti/63054.pdf.

[41] *Ibid.*

curtailed over one million MWh of wind energy.[42] That is enough energy to power nearly 100,000 homes in that region alone, for an entire year.[43]

In addition to curtailment issues, renewable energy faces a continued barrier when trying to move electricity from the point of generation to areas of demand, due to the lack or inadequacy of necessary transmission and distribution networks. With large-scale wind and solar projects sited for optimal production and not necessarily for proximity to transmission, this disparity manifests as a stranded supply.[44] These conditions are known as transmission constraints and are the result of the infrastructure's physical limitations, system design, or reliability rules, any or all limiting cost-efficient and optimised power flow.[45] This limitation of power transmission below levels of market demand leads to 'grid congestion'.

Again, using MISO as an example, there were $1.2 billion of costs associated with grid congestion in 2011, a figure that is increasing.[46] While not the sole indicator of congestion, the US Department of Energy has looked to interconnection queues as a gauge. Midwest interconnection requests totalled over 33 gigawatts (GW), with wind dominating the queue in 2012.[47] Correcting this issue at the transmission level is not as simple as building new infrastructure and high voltage wires. Transmission lines are both expensive and generally unpopular, 'Often it may be easier, cheaper, and environmentally preferable to eliminate or shift demand, or to locate generation strategically than it is to build new lines'.[48] Solutions that help to avoid the challenges of building new transmission networks include providing more on-site, location-specific energy conversion or storage options, like P2G technology.[49] Rather than curtailment, excess energy from renewables can be converted into gaseous forms, such as hydrogen or synthetic methane, and stored in existing or new gas networks and storage facilities.[50]

To the extent that the P2G option utilises surplus renewable energy, results in pipeline quality hydrogen gas or synthetic methane, and the utilisation of existing gas supply network or storage facilities, then it arguably exemplifies a pathway towards: (a) preventing the stranded assets question faced by existing gas industry

---

[42] *Ibid.*
[43] 1,000,000 MWh= 1e+9 kwh. Calculated using 2017 average US household electric consumption of 10,399 kwh/year. US EIA, 'Frequently Asked Questions' (26 October 2018), www.eia.gov/tools/faqs/faq.php?id=97&t=3.
[44] Dziedzic and Oyewunmi (n 9).
[45] US Department of Energy, 'National Electric Transmission Congestion Study' (September 2015) viii, www.energy.gov/sites/prod/files/2015/09/f26/2015%20National%20Electric%20Transmission%20Congestion%20Study_0.pdf.
[46] *Ibid.*
[47] *Ibid*, xiv.
[48] Shelly Welton, 'Non-Transmission Alternatives' (Columbia Law School, Sabin Center for Climate Change Law, September 2014) 2, https://web.law.columbia.edu/sites/default/files/microsites/climate-change/files/Publications/welton_-_non-transmission_alternatives.pdf.
[49] Dziedzic and Oyewunmi (n 9).
[50] Kevin Harrison (National Renewable Energy Laboratory), 'How to Use Utility Pipelines to Store Electric Power: Discussing Power-to-Gas (P2G) & Utility Pipelines as the Better Battery', RNG WORKS Technical Workshop & Trade Expo, Nashville, TN, USA, RNG Coalition, (11 September 2019).

suppliers and utilities in a carbon-constrained world; and (b) supporting the growing net-zero-carbon energy industry by creating options to store excess renewable energy in usable and safe forms within existing supply systems.[51]

Figure 1 below shows the potential uses in which hydrogen or synthetic methane produced from a P2G facility could be deployed (eg in transportation, power generation on-demand and residential uses).[52]

Figure 1 Schematic on the US H2@Scale Concept and Integration of Energy Supply Systems[53]

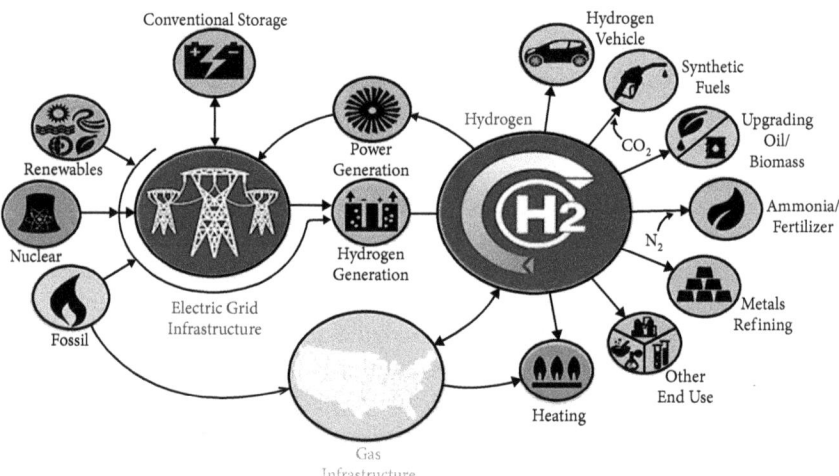

Some options for scaling-up and deploying the clean energy produced via the P2G facility include supplying the produced hydrogen for utilisation in industrial applications such as ammonia, methanol and steel production. Likewise, in transportation, hydrogen can provide a zero-carbon energy source to be used for fuel cell electric vehicles (FCEVs). Currently, shipping and aviation have limited low-carbon fuel options available, thus, these transportation sub-sectors represent an opportunity for hydrogen-based fuels. Hydrogen and synthetic methane could also be supplied to residential and commercial buildings using existing natural gas networks in cities with an already extensive infrastructure base, although this may require further costs and need to retrofit such networks for hydrogen compatibility or ensure safe blending processes with existing gas supplies. In power generation, hydrogen and ammonia can be used in gas turbines to increase power system

---

[51] Dziedzic and Oyewunmi (n 9) ibid.
[52] See also Patel (n 18); Fleming and Fershee (n 9); Lambert (n 9) at 5; International Energy Agency (IEA), 'The Future of Hydrogen Seizing Today's Opportunities' (IEA Publications, Technical Report, June 2020), www.iea.org/reports/the-future-of-hydrogen.
[53] Source: The US Department of Energy-Office of Energy Efficiency and Renewable Energy on the H2@Scale Project at www.energy.gov/eere/fuelcells/h2scale.

flexibility, while ammonia could also be used in coal-fired power plants to reduce emissions.

Currently, a major concern inhibiting the deployment of P2G electrolysers is the absence of a coherent and comprehensive regulatory and policy framework, coupled with necessary incentives to make deployment more cost-efficient compared to other existing options. Also, most P2G projects are in the pilot phase, thus it becomes more of a complex gamble to determine the scale at which investments could become economically feasible depending on the target end-users and the clarity and coherence of applicable policy frameworks. For instance, how much hydrogen and synthetic methane can be reasonably and safely supplied to a residential building or fuel station and to what extent will such end users need to retrofit their facilities to store and utilise hydrogen and synthetic methane? Is there a viable market and sufficient potential demand compared to alternatives such as diesel, gasoline, electric vehicles in transportation sector for example? There are also alternative and perhaps less costly means of producing hydrogen at the moment, ie methane reformation, though the process leads to significant carbon emissions as it relies on hydrocarbons.

Given the declining costs for solar PV and wind generation, building electrolysers at locations with excellent renewable resource conditions could become a low-cost supply option for 'green' hydrogen, even after taking into account the transmission and distribution costs of transporting hydrogen to end-users. Production and supply cost reductions are key factors since hydrogen and synthetic methane would be produced from renewable energy systems that are often located in remote sites or offshore.

i. Gas and Electricity Interconnections and Network Systems

In the US, natural gas accounts for about 31 per cent of total primary energy consumption and 35 per cent of that consumption went into electricity generation.[54] Thus, gas supply networks play a major role in electricity supply. Consequently, when considering national energy reliability, security and competitiveness objectives, one should consider the natural gas transmission and distribution system, as well as the electric transmission system. The nation's electric network is comprised of roughly 240,000 miles of high-voltage transmission lines.[55] There are over 300,000 miles of natural gas transmission pipelines nationwide.[56] One advantage

---

[54] See the US EIA's 'Annual Energy Outlook to 2050' ('AEO 2019') 1–83 at 22, www.eia.gov/outlooks/aeo/pdf/aeo2019.pdf. In its 2050 projections for electricity generation by fuel sources, the US EIA reports that by 2050 39% of electric generation capacity will be fuelled by natural gas (up from 34% in 2018), while renewables will grow from 18% in 2018 to 31% by 2050. Nuclear is expected to decline from 19% in 2018 to 12% by 2050, while coal continues to decline from 28% in 2018 to 17% by 2050.

[55] Edison Electric Institute, 'Transmission', www.eei.org/issuesandpolicy/transmission/Pages/default.aspx.

[56] American Gas Association, 'Gas Industry Miles of Pipeline and Main by State and Type' Table 5-3 (2018), www.aga.org/contentassets/71fe352cf6fa4291a29be724ab0622b8/table5-3.pdf.

that the natural gas value chain has, which is unmatched by the electric sector, is energy storage capacity. There are about 400 active storage facilities spread across 30 states with the capacity to store roughly four trillion cubic feet (Tcf) of natural gas for consumer use in the US.[57] This is enough storage to accommodate 20 per cent of all-natural gas consumed in the US. By comparison, storing 20 per cent of the electricity consumed would require 85 GW of advanced battery storage,[58] more than triple the available electrical energy storage installed in the US to date.[59] The question for future energy policymakers will be whether the vast gas supply networks can efficiently decarbonise and play a key role in the unfolding energy transition and low-carbon future. Over the past two decades, gas supply networks have become increasingly interconnected with the electricity market,[60] while electricity generated from renewables such as solar and wind is expected to gain more market share onwards to 2050.[61]

Notwithstanding the energy storage, reliability, capacity adequacy and intermittency challenges, the utilisation of renewable energy sources such as solar and wind continue to grow due to factors such as the falling costs of installation and project development, concerns relating to decarbonisation and climate change mitigation, demand for new, domestic energy supplies, as well as direct policies such as RPS and federal tax incentives.[62]

IV. US Energy Supply Systems and Operators

The network of electric transmission lines comprises the main part of the complex power supply grid in the US, which is often categorised into three interconnected

---

[57] American Gas Association, 'Reliable Natural Gas', www.aga.org/natural-gas/reliable/.

[58] See the US EIA Electricity End-Use Consumption (Table 7.6) data for the total annual energy consumption figures from 2007–2018 (per Million Kilowatthours (MkwH)) estimated as 4,003,299.07 MkwH as at 2018, while the total sold to consumers via retail as at 2018 was about 3,859,185 MkwH, available in www.eia.gov/totalenergy/data/browser/?tbl=T07.06#/?f=A&start=2007&end=2018&charted=5-6-7.

[59] As of May 2019, the US had over 31.2 GW of rated power in energy storage compared to 1,098 GW of total in service installed generation capacity as of January 2019. See the Center for Sustainable Systems, '2019 U.S. Energy Storage Factsheet' (School for Environment & Sustainability, University of Michigan, Pub. No. CSS15-17, 2019).

[60] See Oyewunmi, *Regulating Gas Supply to Power* (n 16) 85–96. As the markets and organisation of natural gas supply to power developed in the US, the role of gas and network infrastructure has also grown since the 1990s, driven largely by the policy-led restructuring of the interstate gas market, independent economic regulation initiatives, competitiveness and security of supply edge compared to coal and other base load sources, technological advancements and efficiency improvements in gas-to-power facilities, abundance of gas supply from the local shale gas production boom and the attendant effects on reducing the price and costs of gas-to-power, growing fuel-switching patterns from coal to gas for environmental and commercial reasons.

[61] AEO 2019 (n 54).

[62] Troy A Rule, 'Still Growing: How America's Renewable Energy Industry is Surviving in the Trump Era' (2018) *Oil, Gas & Energy Law*, www.ogel.org/article.asp?key=3785.

network systems (ie, the eastern interconnection,[63] the western interconnection,[64] and the Electric Reliability Council of Texas (ERCOT)).[65] Power generation, supply and consumption within these interconnected network systems could be entirely within a state's territory (ie intrastate) or from one state to consumers in another state (ie interstate). Operators in the value chain include an extensive collection of: (i) public, private and cooperative utilities; (ii) over 1,000 independent power generators; (iii) seven ISOs and four RTOs;[66] and (iii) an increasing number of distributed homes and businesses with on-site generating systems.

Wholesale electricity markets formed after the enactment of the Public Utilities Regulation Act 1978 (PURPA)[67] prompted the growth of qualified non-utility generators, including small scale renewables. The Energy Policy Act 1992 (EPAct 1992')[68] facilitated the emergence of wholesale electricity generators in the US.[69] The Federal Energy Regulatory Commission (FERC) also initiated several regulatory actions to introduce unbundling of vertically-integrated monopoly utilities and open access to transmission networks mostly owned and operated by such utilities. Thus, consolidating the competition and market-based approach to supply, pricing and access to interstate transmission networks. Note that the electricity market in some states/regions comprise a hybrid of regulated monopolies and access to existing energy (gas and electricity) networks by non-operating entities and third-party suppliers.[70] Among other things, the EPAct 1992 was implemented pursuant to FERC's (i) Order No 888 of 24 April 1996 for promoting wholesale competition through open access non-discriminatory transmission services by public utilities; recovery of stranded costs by public utilities and transmitting utilities; and (ii) Order No 889 of 24 April 1996 regulating open access same-time information system (formerly real-time information networks) and standards of conduct.

In addition, FERC's Order No 888 provides that public utilities that own or operate interstate transmission facilities are to file non-discriminatory open access

---

[63] Including the region east of the Rockies, excluding most of Texas, but including adjacent Canadian provinces except Québec.
[64] Extending from the Rockies to the Pacific Coast, again including adjacent Canadian provinces.
[65] Covering most of Texas.
[66] See the Federal Energy Regulatory Commission (FERC), *United States Electricity Industry Primer*, Office of Electricity Delivery and Energy Reliability U.S. Department of Energy DOE/OE-0017 (July 2015) 1–92 at 26–28. There are currently seven ISOs within North America, comprising: CAISO – California ISO, NYISO – New York ISO, ERCOT – Electric Reliability Council of Texas; also, a Regional Reliability Council, MISO – Midcontinent Independent System Operator, ISO-NE – ISO New England, AESO – Alberta Electric System Operator, IESO – Independent Electricity System Operator, additionally, there are currently four RTOs within North America: PJM – PJM Interconnection, MISO, SPP – Southwest Power Pool; also a Regional Reliability Council, ISONE – ISO New England; also an RTO.
[67] Public Law (Pub. L.) 95-617, 92 Statutes at Large (Stat.) 3117 (9 November 1978).
[68] Pub. L. 109–58, 119 Stat. 594 (8 August 2005).
[69] Joseph Tomain and Richard Cudahy, *Energy Law in a Nutshell*, 3rd edn (West Publishing Co, 2016) 394–402.
[70] *Ibid* at 402–403.

tariffs outlining the minimum terms and conditions for non-discriminatory service. Order No 888 also requires utilities to 'functionally unbundle' their transmission service from their generation and power marketing functions and to provide unbundled ancillary transmission services. Currently, the traditional wholesale electricity markets exist in the Southeast, Southwest, and Northwest where utilities are responsible for system operations and management while providing power to retail consumers. Such utilities are vertically integrated to the extent that they own the generation, transmission and distribution systems used to serve electricity consumers.[71]

As a result of Order No 888, several transmission network operators and owners formed ISOs from existing power pools, helping to facilitate open access to supply networks for wholesale purposes. Going a step further, in FERC's Order No 2000 of 20 December 1999 on the establishment of Regional Transmission Organisations, the Commission encouraged utilities to join RTOs which, like an ISO, would operate the transmission systems and develop innovative procedures to manage transmission equitably. In essence, newcomers or independent producers should be able to 'ship' and 'transmit' their electrons to designated bulk buyers via the networks of existing transmission network operators (now organised as ISOs/RTOs) without discrimination and access to the same information and pricing fundamentals. Each of the ISOs and RTOs has energy and ancillary services markets in which buyers and sellers could bid for or offer generation, capacity, and other valuable services. The ISOs and RTOs use bid-based markets to determine economic dispatch. While major sections of the country operate under more traditional market structures, two-thirds of the nation's electricity load is served in RTO regions. Notably, FERC's Order No 1000 of 21 July 2011 on transmission planning and cost allocation by transmission owning and operating public utilities had the effect of requiring transmission operators to cooperate with neighbouring systems and to consider state-level policy on such matters as renewable energy, energy efficiency, environmental and land-use regulatory authorities, so far as decisions by those regulatory bodies impact the ability of the transmission operators to accurately assess system reliability.

V. RNG and P2G Systems

RNG comes from three main sources: (a) Anaerobic Digestion, ie biological method using micro-organisms to break down organic matter and produce a mixture called biogas comprising mainly of methane and CO_2; (b) Pyrogasification, ie thermochemical methods for producing synthetic gas (comprising of methane, hydrogen, carbon monoxide and CO_2) from organic matter. The process can be completed

---

[71] Wholesale physical power trade typically occurs through bilateral transactions, and while the industry had historically traded electricity through bilateral transactions and power pool agreements, Order No 888 promoted the concept of ISOs.

by methanation or separation to produce a gas whose thermodynamic properties are equivalent to those of natural gas; and (c) Power-to-gas (P2G) which entails the conversion of renewables-based electricity into synthetic gas through the electrolysis process involving water. It essentially separates the chemical component of water, ie oxygen and hydrogen and releasing the former and capturing the latter hydrogen. It could also include a second step of converting the hydrogen to methane via methanation involving the use of carbon.[72]

The above three sources can be broadly categorised into two main groups for RNG production, which are set out in the following paragraphs.

First, there are gaseous fuels that are created by processes not directly associated with energy production. These include waste gases that are collected from a variety of feedstock, such as wastewater treatment digesters, manure and other agricultural wastes or landfill gases. These waste gases are captured and either used locally for heat or electricity or conditioned further for injection into an existing natural gas pipeline. Most often associated with methane, a potent GHG, these waste gases have a large carbon footprint, and their capture results in carbon-negative fuel supply. This is because methane is 25 times more potent in terms of global warming impact than CO_2, which is the resulting emission from natural gas combustion.[73]

A simple way to visualise this positive environmental attribute is a methane capture equal to −25 plus a combustion emission of +1 is equal to a total greenhouse gas impact of −24.[74] The number of RNG facilities in this category has nearly doubled in the last five years.[75] These facilities have the potential to displace up to 10 per cent of natural gas supplied from traditional, fossil-based sources.[76] Arguably, their positive impact on decarbonisation, by reducing GHGs, far exceeds their impact on natural gas supply, due to the global warming potential of methane mentioned earlier. One study of a southern California gas utility found that replacing 14 per cent of the gas system throughout, for that single utility, could achieve the same GHG reduction as electrifying *all* buildings in California.[77] These environmental benefits have been noted by both regulators and utilities nationwide, and both are moving forward with investments, laws and policies that support further development of these resources.[78] Some states have

---

[72] Dziedzic and Oyewunmi (n 9); the French Environment and Energy Management Agency (ADEME), 'A 100% Renewable Gas Mix in 2050? – Technical/economic Feasibility Study' (ADEME, 2018) 1–24 at 13–14.

[73] US EPA, 'Understanding Global Warming Potentials', www.epa.gov/ghgemissions/understanding-global-warming-potentials.

[74] This does not include upstream impacts associated with potential land use changes.

[75] Alyssa Danigelis, 'Renewable Natural Gas Production Facilities Grow by 85% in Four Years' (*Energy Manager Today*, 20 April 2018), www.energymanagertoday.com/renewable-natural-gas-production-growth-0176212/.

[76] American Gas Foundation, 'The Potential for Renewable Gas' (Sept 2011) 1, www.gasfoundation.org/researchstudies/agf-renewable-gas-assessment-report-110901.pdf.

[77] Navigant Consulting, 'Gas Strategies for a Low-Carbon California Future' (2018) 42.

[78] State of Nevada SB154, www.leg.state.nv.us/Session/80th2019/Bills/SB/SB154.pdf; Oregon SB98, https://olis.leg.state.or.us/liz/2019R1/Downloads/MeasureDocument/SB98/A-Engrossed;and California CA SB605, https://leginfo.legislature.ca.gov/faces/billNavClient.xhtml?bill_id=201320140SB605.

required RNG potential studies and voluntary procurement targets for utilities to further motivate the expansion of this industry.[79] Because these RNG facilities are finding a supportive policy, at least in some states, and because these renewable energy supplies remain isolated within the gas system, this chapter does not evaluate the details of capture-based RNG any further than noted above. There are many opportunities for further studies associated with these fuels, their end-uses, regulatory support and the need for incentives.

Second, there are fuels created out of excess energy production systems such as P2G. Hydrogen produced from P2G systems results from the first of two potential processes: electrolysis. By completing a second step in the process, methanation, a P2G system can also produce synthetic methane. This second step involves the added benefit of 'carbon capture and utilisation', as the chemical conversion of hydrogen to methane requires the addition of a carbon source. In both cases, these systems are categorised as carbon neutral. Hydrogen production and use do not require nor emit GHGs. Methane production in this context requires carbon as an input, which creates a carbon-sink. Methane's end-use, however, involves combustion and release of carbon dioxide, thus the synthetic methane produced by P2G is carbon neutral.[80] These fuels can then be used on-site for heat or electricity or injected into the natural gas pipeline system. Because P2G systems rely on electricity as the primary input, it is important that this energy comes from low-carbon or carbon neutral renewable sources to make an argument for its GHG benefits.[81]

There is now a growing class of energy consumers in an increasingly decentralised electricity value chain as a result of distributed energy systems such as roof top solar PVs with batteries, smart meters and smart mini-grids, etc. With the adoption of ancillary technologies such as net metering and smart meters, electricity supply stakeholders that were primarily consumers can sell excess energy they produce to the conventional grid and also provide essential grid services such as storage, efficiency and demand response. This growing class of electricity sector stakeholders is widely referred to as 'prosumers'.[82] The P2G option and concept align well with the evolving paradigm in which consumers and suppliers of distributed renewable-based electricity are increasingly involved in grid reliability issues, demand response and energy storage.[83] Conversely, it could also be

---

[79] In Oregon, a SB98 for Renewable Natural Gas Bill was recently signed into law which outlines the objectives of adding as much as 30% RNG into the state's pipeline system. The new law sets voluntary RNG goals for Oregon's natural gas utilities. Additionally, it: (i) allows utility investment in the interconnection of renewable natural gas production; (ii) supports targets of 15% by 2030, 20% by 2035 and 30% by 2050; and (iii) provides local communities a potential revenue source to turn their waste into energy.

[80] Evaluation of carbon footprint for P2G systems does not include lifecycle emissions associated with renewable energy production, land use changes, or other potential contributors to GHG emissions such as material or equipment fabrication.

[81] Dziedzic and Oyewunmi (n 9).

[82] Sharon B Jacobs, 'The Energy Prosumer' (1 February 2017) 43(3) *Ecology Law Quarterly* 519–80; Amy L Stein, 'Distributed Reliability' (2016) 87 *University of Colorado Law Review* 887–1008, https://pdfs.semanticscholar.org/a12e/e551544803fd04803c359b2ec9fe4aef6f91.pdf.

[83] Dziedzic and Oyewunmi (n 9).

argued that scaling-up P2G adds additional regulatory complexity to the natural gas and electricity regulatory framework from a legal and institutional perspective. For instance, policymakers would have to consider issues such as: (i) what is/are the most effective approach(es) and rules for access regulation and pricing in shipping or storing hydrogen produced via P2G in existing natural gas systems; and (ii) which institutions (state or federal) will oversee the development of P2G projects and transactions involving interstate or intrastate supply or supplies for bulk 'storage' purposes.[84]

A. Regulatory Oversight of P2G

In order to address the regulatory complexity of P2G systems, it is beneficial to evaluate the dynamics of each sector supply framework separately, before we can understand the interplay between the two. P2G's electric supply can be reasonably procured from a variety of sources and markets and by a diverse number of buyers as shown earlier in Figure 1. Energy can be sourced from three basic categories: Interstate transmission, intrastate transmission and distribution, or local generation. The first two are traditional 'grid' supplies, while the third is most commonly associated with isolated systems such as co-generation or self-generation facilities, where no connection to external grids exists, thus, mostly independent of distribution networks.[85] Another example of this isolated generation could include local microgrids, where energy is physically isolated to local infrastructure.[86] The locational aspect of the sourced energy is key in identifying whether power is purchased in wholesale or retail markets, or outside of existing market structures. The importance of these market differences, if not already apparent, will be detailed further in this section.[87]

In addition to the physical location of energy offtake, power purchasers range from private firms and power marketers to traditional investor-owned electric utilities. Because the ultimate product in most P2G systems is gaseous fuel (ie hydrogen or synthetic gas), there is a high likelihood that gas producers and gas utilities also become power purchasers. Additionally, on the issue of energy purchases, there are notable differences in regulatory oversight when traditionally regulated firms are involved. Gas utilities are typically associated with local distribution networks and are regulated by state Public Utility Commissions and institutions. Such gas utilities could also own and operate interstate pipelines, thus subject to the jurisdiction of the Federal Energy Regulatory Commission.[88]

---

[84] Dziedzic and Oyewunmi (n 9).
[85] Dziedzic and Oyewunmi (n 9).
[86] Dan T Ton and Merrill A Smith, 'The U.S. Department of Energy's Microgrid Initiative' (2012) *The Electricity Journal* 84, www.energy.gov/sites/prod/files/2016/06/f32/The%20US%20Department%20of%20Energy's%20Microgrid%20Initiative.pdf.
[87] Dziedzic and Oyewunmi (n 9).
[88] Federal Energy Regulatory Commission, 'NGPA Section 311 Pipelines', www.ferc.gov/industries/gas/gen-info/intrastate-trans/section-311.asp.

This distinction is significant in determining the applicable regulatory framework affecting P2G systems, their energy supply and their gas production.

The final group of variables that must be considered is the ultimate disposal/offtake of the gas from the P2G system. Here too, we see a wide array of options available to P2G facilities. The first, and by far most simplistic in terms of regulatory obligations, would be consumption. In this case, gas is combusted locally, eliminating the interaction with pipelines or other existing infrastructure. This consumptive use can be expanded to include the broader category of Power-to-Gas-to-Power, where the resulting renewable gas is combusted in a steam turbine system, for electric generation. While arguably the least efficient use of the P2G system, it is a route worth exploring. The more likely scenarios involve existing pipelines and underground storage systems. P2G products could be transported through interstate pipelines, distribution systems, and/or retained in underground storage fields for future use or transport. As detailed above, the energy source, the identity of the P2G developer, and the disposition of gas can each play a pivotal role in the ultimate framework affecting these systems. Figure 2 depicts this intricate relationship.

Figure 2 Power-to-Gas Regulatory Interactions by Power Source and Gas Disposition[89]

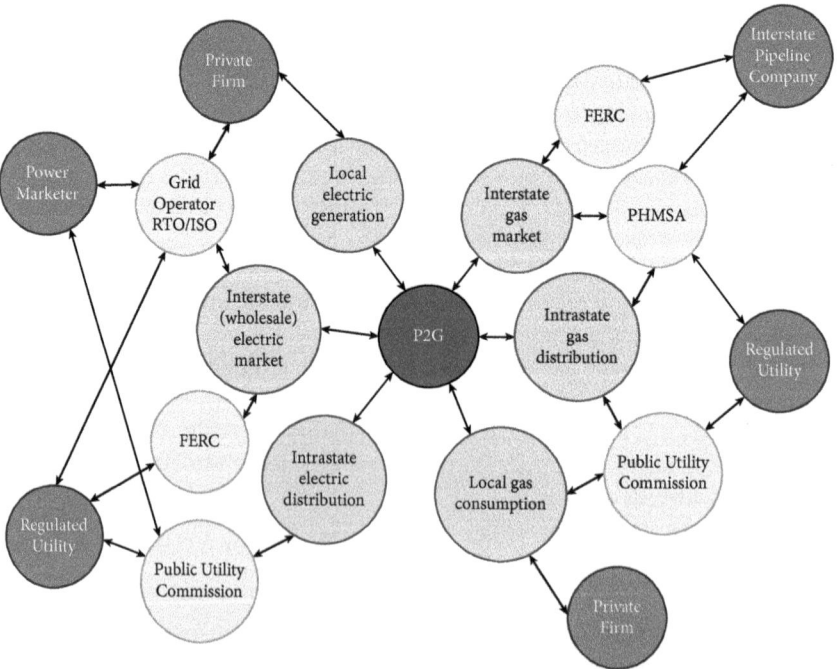

[89] See Dziedzic and Oyewunmi (n 9).

B. Developing an Integrated Policy Framework

The novelty of P2G is the fact that the whole is greater than the sum of its parts. Electric consumption is not created equal, nor is renewable gas production interchangeable with fossil gas development. P2G systems offer opportunities to flatten supply curves, reduce curtailment, alleviate grid congestion and store energy. These benefits allow the electric system to take on greater percentages of intermittent energy resources, like wind and solar, and defer or eliminate costly investments in electric transmission expansions. P2G systems also have the ability to sequester carbon and decarbonise heat and transportation fuels. Several studies and policy initiatives have outlined the importance of the latter, in terms of meeting larger GHG reduction goals.[90] Seeking significant reductions in GHG emissions, or carbon neutral societies will require a major shift in energy system design. The current question among industry analysts and policymakers is whether the electric system alone can supply enough renewable energy, at a swift enough pace, to meet decarbonisation targets, while maintaining energy reliability, the security of supply and environmental sustainability. Recent studies suggest that aggressive electrification models achieve end-use penetration of only 52 per cent by 2050 while continuing to rely on natural gas for electric generation.[91] Such aggressive electrification is expected to double the demand for electric supply by 2050,[92] further stressing current grid infrastructure. In order to accommodate this level of electrification, considerable costs are anticipated to complete necessary upgrades to transportation systems and bolster generation supplies.[93] A 2018 study modelled an aggressive electrification profile, assuming 100 per cent electrification of residential and commercial buildings, in addition to significant electrification of several industrial processes. That study concluded that electrification alone can achieve only a 20 per cent reduction in GHG emissions.[94]

In order to achieve notable reductions, closer to 70 per cent, significant grid decarbonisation must occur, in the form of increased low-carbon supply. The same study assumed 33 per cent of electric supply would come from wind and solar, with an additional 22 per cent from other low-carbon sources like gas with CCS or nuclear.[95] Yet, '… these combined measures … are insufficient to achieve the 2050 emission levels indicated by climate scientists to reduce the most severe impacts

---

[90] Audrey Partridge, 'Decarbonizing Natural Gas End Uses in Minnesota' (e21 Initiative, 11 June 2019); Timme Van Melle, et al, 'Gas for Climate: How Gas can Help to Achieve the Paris Agreement Target in an Affordable Way' (Navigant for Gas for Climate Consortium, 15 February 2018).
[91] Electric Power Research Institute, 'US National Electrification Assessment' (April 2018) 8.
[92] Trieu Mai, et al, 'An Electrified Future: Initial Scenarios and Future Research for US Energy and Electricity Systems' (IEEE Power Magazine, July/August 2018) 35.
[93] Patrick Plas, 'Expediting a Renewable Energy Future with High-Voltage DC Transmission' (*Green Tech Media*, 6 July 2017), www.greentechmedia.com/articles/read/expediting-a-renewable-energy-future-with-high-voltage-dc-transmission#gs.wflqpm.
[94] Mai (n 92) 44.
[95] Mai (n 92) 42.

of climate change'.[96] Since, about 28 per cent of the electric supply in that model is still sourced from natural gas. Therefore, looking at electric supply alone, decarbonisation of gas supply has considerable value. When the end-use of natural gas is added to this system-wide emission profile, we see that low-carbon and carbon neutral RNG has a significant role to play in decarbonising energy supplies.[97]

Some studies from Europe reveal that minimising gas use, often as part of larger, policy-driven electrification process, increases the overall costs of decarbonisation. Alternatively, by utilising existing gas infrastructure to supply renewable natural gas and hydrogen, one study estimated that across all sectors, the European Union can save 217 billion Euros per year, when compared to the 'minimal gas' scenario studied.[98]

Similar conclusions were made in another study, which examined how a fully decarbonised European energy sector can be achieved and what are the 'risks' of precluding options in favour of certain technologies such as gas, hydrogen and CCS, while focusing just on electrification based only on VRE resources through implicit or explicit policy actions.[99] In this regard, Pöyry developed an analytical framework focusing on the EU's power, heat and transport sectors with the aim of quantifying the risks.

Accordingly, a balanced 'Zero-Carbon Gas' pathway in which hydrogen, biomethane and CCS competes fairly with renewables, biomass and nuclear in all sectors were compared to a forced 'All-Electric' pathway which excludes gas infrastructure and technologies that could foster decarbonisation of existing networks as more and more VREs become integrated into the mix. Under the 'Zero Carbon Gas' scenario, economics, costs and policy initiatives influence decarbonisation technologies and the gas industry is allowed to adapt to the necessities of supplying net-zero carbon energy following investments in technologies such as methane reformation, CCS and P2G. While the 'all electric' scenario builds upon the assumption that only electrification can achieve decarbonisation and policies are put in place to prevent the development of 'Zero Carbon Gas' alternatives, while reliance on more VREs and new nuclear and biomass build out.[100] According to the report, the all-electric scenario leads to a substantial surge in demand for electricity compared to the alternative zero-carbon gas pathway. Since such growth in demand would be met mostly by VREs, the costs and requirements for maintaining resilience and capacity adequacy, reliability and storage also makes it a much more expensive pathway compared to the alternative Zero-Carbon Gas scenario.[101]

Such studies of European energy decarbonisation issues provide a reasonable proxy for the United States and other developed economies now facing similar

---

[96] Mai (n 92) 45.
[97] Dziedzic and Oyewunmi (n 9).
[98] Van Melle (n 90) 92.
[99] Pöyry, 'Fully Decarbonising Europe's Energy System by 2050' (*Pöyry*, Point of View Report, May 2018), www.poyry.com/news/articles/fully-decarbonising-europes-energy-system-2050.
[100] *Ibid.*
[101] *Ibid.*

challenges and already locked-in carbon-intensive energy systems or reliance on secure and reliable gas and electricity systems. It is also useful for the increasing array of hydrocarbon and gas-rich developing or emerging economies which are seeking more sustainable pathways to universal energy access and security of energy supply.

i. Proactive, Integrated Policy: Next Steps

The US electric energy landscape, as it exists today, is a complex web of regulated, semi-open and fully open markets.[102] This variability becomes more apparent due to the absence of a national renewable energy standard and the general flexibility granted to the states vis-à-vis the Federal Government's role in recent court decisions.[103] While natural gas markets are generally more streamlined, a patchwork of renewable natural gas laws and regulations has been developed. On the whole, however, the regulation of renewable natural gas has, thus far, mirrored its fossil-based counterpart. Arguably, the legal construct that exists today is capable of regulating P2G facilities.[104] P2G is unique when viewed as a holistic energy system. But, when viewed through the lens of jurisdiction and institutional framework, the system functions as two separate points of regulation: electric consumption and gas production. Power-to-Gas-to-Power systems add a third: electric generation. Undoubtedly, the latter creates another layer of complexity, yet does not stray from the existing framework for such generators.[105] As already outlined above, these systems provide added value above their contribution to their respective, segregated markets, and future regulation must recognise and incentivise these multi-industry benefits to achieve maximum decarbonisation potential.[106]

Existing laws and regulations are agnostic to the benefits P2G systems provide. This approach is by design, where RTO/ISOs are concerned. While neutrality may be appropriate for system operators, it does not satisfy, nor align with the greater policy goals of state and federal lawmakers seeking to decarbonise energy supplies. From the ISO/RTO Council (IRC) report on emerging technologies, several key positions were identified in the pursuit of increased renewable penetration.[107] Two of these positions are especially relevant.

---

[102] Retail Energy Supply Association, 'State-by-State'. Available at www.resausa.org/states.
[103] *Rocky Mountain Farmers Union v Corey*, 730 F.3d 1070 (9th Cir. 2013) at 1089, as referenced in Brannon Denning, 'Environmental Federalism and State Renewable Portfolio Standards' (2014) *Case Western Reserve Law Review* Vol 64, Issue 4, 30. Available at https://scholarlycommons.law.case.edu/cgi/viewcontent.cgi?referer=https://www.google.com/&httpsredir=1&article=1159&context=caselrev.
[104] Dziedzic and Oyewunmi (n 9).
[105] Public Utility Regulatory Policies Act, 16 USC ch 46 § 2601 et seq.
[106] Dziedzic and Oyewunmi (n 9).
[107] ISO/RTO Council, 'Emerging Technologies: How ISOs and RTOs Can Create a More Nimble, Robust Bulk Electricity System' (March 2017) 6. Available at: https://isorto.org/wp-content/uploads/2018/05/PUBLIC_IRC_Emerging_Technologies_Report.pdf.

1. [The IRC] Generally supports policies and positions that recognise the electricity system's ability to reliably and efficiently accommodate large-scale amounts of renewables and realise their growing technological potential.
2. [The IRC] Is agnostic to specific technologies that may be applied to the renewable integration problem while simultaneously ensuring that policies include the greatest possible optionality for new and emerging technologies to be applied to renewable integration.

If the goal of system operators is to integrate as much renewable electricity as possible, while balancing the grid reliability, then P2G is at least an equal competitor with battery storage. Yet, the recent ruling by the FERC relating to energy storage makes no mention of 'gas as an energy storage medium', nor the potential of existing storage assets to play a role in a seasonal capacity.[108] The final rule instead creates a split definition of energy storage that prioritises a storage resource's ability to 'inject electric energy back onto the grid' while remaining neutral on the storage medium:

> The Commission stated that this definition is intended to cover electric storage resources capable of receiving electric energy from the grid and storing it for later injection of electric energy back to the grid, regardless of their storage medium (e.g., batteries, flywheels, compressed air, and pumped-hydro).[109]

This definition is supportive of Power-to-Gas-to-Power systems, as these facilities would be 'physically designed and configured to inject electric energy back onto the grid'.[110] However, FERC Order Nos 841 and 841a do not address energy conversion systems, like P2G, despite the ability to provide analogous grid services, while achieving improved storage capacity.[111]

Furthermore, Order 841 requires RTOs/ISOs to revise tariffs in order to establish a participation model for electric storage resources. One of the requirements of the participation model is that the RTOs 'ensure that a resource using the participation model can be dispatched and can set the wholesale market clearing price as *both* a wholesale seller and wholesale buyer consistent with existing market rules'.[112] This obligation further limits the participation of P2G in storage markets by requiring facilities to be wholesale sellers to the electric market. In order to take full advantage of P2G, it is preferable to move produced gas into other markets in need of decarbonisation, such as heat and transportation. Additionally, hydrogen

---

[108] FERC Order No 841a, Order on Rehearing, *Electric Storage Participation in Markets Operated by Regional Transmission Organizations and Independent System Operators* (2019). Available at: www.ferc.gov/whats-new/comm-meet/2019/051619/E-1.pdf.

[109] FERC Order No 841, as quoted in Order No 841a, *ibid*.

[110] FERC Order No 841a (n 108).

[111] Dziedzic and Oyewunmi (n 9). See also FERC Order 841 on Electric Storage Participation in Markets Operated by Regional Transmission Organizations and Independent System Operators (15 February 2018, updated 28 February 2018).

[112] FERC Order No 841, *ibid* (emphasis added).

can be redirected to energy storage via hydrogen fuel cells.[113] None of these pathways currently qualifies under FERC's rules for electric storage resources. FERC's interpretation of storage resources is decidedly focused on electricity storage, rather than energy storage. The resulting framework, therefore, excludes P2G and any benefits it may bring to the grid. FERC could consider segregating the buyer-side participation from the seller-based obligation, by lifting the dual requirement in Order No 841. This would allow P2G facilities to participate as a storage resource, without the responsibility of returning power to the grid.

Alternatively, because the most significant benefits of P2G occur on the demand-side of the electric market, FERC could also consider P2G as a distributed energy resource (DER). Though traditionally defined as a generation resource on the distribution system, the interpretation has evolved to include a wide variety of resources and interactions with the energy system, depending upon the jurisdiction. Currently, FERC's proposed definition is

> A source or sink of power that is located on the distribution system, any subsystem thereof, or behind a customer meter. These resources may include, but are not limited to, electric storage resources, distributed generation, thermal storage, and electric vehicles and their supply equipment.[114]

This definition continues to exclude non-generation and non-electric resources. A preferred definition and one that is likely to suit P2G applications are from the National Association of Regulated Utility Commissioners (NARUC):

> A resource sited close to customers that can provide all or some of their immediate electric and power needs and can also be used by the system to either reduce demand (such as energy efficiency) or provide supply to satisfy the energy, capacity, or ancillary service needs of the distribution grid. The resources, if providing electricity or thermal energy, are small in scale, connected to the distribution system, and close to load.[115]

By including ancillary services, demand reduction, and thermal energy in its definition, NARUC leaves the door open for novel DERs like P2G systems. If FERC were to adopt a similarly broad definition, then P2G may have access to wholesale markets as DERs as an alternative pathway to storage. At the moment, FERC has not yet issued the long-awaited order on distributed energy resources; therefore, a definitive interpretation of what constitutes a DER does not yet exist.[116]

---

[113] Dziedzic and Oyewunmi (n 9).
[114] Electric Storage Participation in Markets Operated by Regional Transmission Organizations and Independent System Operators, 157 FERC ¶ 61,121, at 1 (2016) as referenced in FERC Staff Report, 'Distributed Energy Resources Technical Considerations for the Bulk Power System' (February 2018) 8, www.ferc.gov/legal/staff-reports/2018/der-report.pdf.
[115] National Association of Regulatory Utility Commissioners, Distributed Electric Resource Manual at p 45, as referenced in *ibid*, p 9.
[116] Dziedzic and Oyewunmi (n 9).

What these two examples demonstrate is a clear focus by FERC on electric energy resources. While not surprising, the scope of FERC's oversight does not preclude them from taking a broader view. In 2012, the Commission issued an Order directing further conferences and reports on the interaction of natural gas and electric industries.[117] While this Order was focused on improving the knowledge and coordination of the sectors as it related to natural gas generation, the same coordination need can be identified for P2G applications. FERC is in a unique position, with authority over both electric and gas interstate transmission assets.[118] By taking an integrated view of both systems, the agency could leverage the assets and capabilities of both to foster a more efficient system, with a higher percentage of renewable energy resources. The regulated states also have this advantage, with public utility commissions retaining authority over both electric and gas distribution systems. Here too, the commissions have the capability to regulate both sectors to maximise the overall efficiency and decarbonisation pathways.[119]

Some preliminary framework already exists in state policy. State regulation of oil and gas development is based in significant part on the concept of waste avoidance, and these policies are generally known as Conservation Regulation.[120] This regulation is meant, traditionally, to prevent the physical waste of valuable oil and gas resources, prevent economic waste, and protect correlative rights.[121] While drafted during the last century, and ever-evolving, these conservation regulations establish a valuable history of regulating for efficiency and waste reduction. In the systems discussed throughout this chapter, it is evident that, across multiple sectors, there are ample opportunities to reduce or avoid waste energy.

Specifically, as already outlined, curtailed renewable energy and vented methane are two readily identifiable sources of waste that could be prevented. In 2018, the federal Bureau of Land Management (BLM) drafted a rule designed to minimise waste associated with oil and gas development on BLM land, and limited venting and flaring of methane.[122] This rule is an expansion of traditional conservation regulation by including vented gas, a byproduct or waste of development. State conservation commissions, or other agencies with authority for such regulations,[123] could reasonably amend conservation regulation to address similar

---

[117] Order Directing Further Conferences and Study, *Coordination Between Natural Gas and Electricity Markets*, 141 FERC ¶ 61,125 (2012), www.ferc.gov/whats-new/comm-meet/2012/111512/M-1.pdf.

[118] See Office of Electricity Delivery and Energy Reliability (US Department of Energy), 'The United States Electricity Industry Primer' (July 2015).

[119] Dziedzic and Oyewunmi (n 9).

[120] Joel Eisen et al, *Energy, Economics and the Environment, Cases and Materials*, 4th edn (University Casebook Series, Foundation Press, 2015) 169–91.

[121] Owen Anderson, 'The Evolution of Oil and Gas Conservation Law and the Rise of Unconventional Hydrocarbon Production' (2015) 68 *Arkansas Law Review* 231–58, 241.

[122] Bureau of Land Management, *Waste Prevention, Production Subject to Royalties, and Resource Conservation; Rescission or Revision of Certain Requirements* (43 CFR Pts 3160 and 3170) 83 Fed. Reg. 49, 184 (28 September 2018), www.govinfo.gov/content/pkg/FR-2018-09-28/pdf/2018-20689.pdf.

[123] Many states have retained specific agencies to oversee oil and gas operations and conservation regulations, including but not limited to Idaho, Wyoming, West Virginia, Colorado and Arizona. Other states, however, have delegated conservation regulation to other agencies. Michigan's conservation

economic and energy waste, depending upon the authority granted each agency under state law. Alternatively, the responsibility for these conservation rules could be shifted to utility commissions, with the intent of managing all energy resources under a single entity. Where this model fails is in deregulated states, where many functions of the utility commissions are no longer relevant and where energy systems are managed primarily by market design. In these states, and as an option in regulated states, new agencies could be created to address energy management in all its forms, regulated and unregulated, gas and electric, with the goal of creating the most efficient, lowest carbon system possible, at a reasonable cost.[124] A drastic shift from business as usual, expanding conservation regulation beyond conventional oil and gas development could provide a route for cross-industry synergies that today are unrealised, such as P2G and RNG.

With this mindset, states also have the opportunity, via legislative action, to expand RPS to gas supply utilities. To date, no state has taken this step and there are no equivalent RPS laws governing natural gas. Similar in function to an RPS, some states have set voluntary targets or study requirements around RNG, but none have set strict limits. For the regulated gas utility, an RPS would provide the same benefit as demonstrated in the electric utility. It would serve to drive demand for RNG and lower technology costs, while providing a mechanism for utilities to invest in these systems. Without this definitive and clarifying legislative solution, regulated utilities are typically unable to pursue such innovative solutions, even if those solutions offer low-carbon options for customers or provide reliability benefits via storage. These are generally not least-cost options and are therefore unlikely to pass the scrutiny of some regulators.[125] However, some progressive states, including North Carolina and California, have recognised the benefits of RNG, primarily biogas, and have begun building frameworks to capture waste from agricultural operations. But, even in states fostering waste reduction, most renewable gas is still routed to electric generation or vented to the atmosphere. A gas RPS would ensure RNG has value as an end-use fuel, without conversion to electricity.[126]

VI. Removing, Storing and Utilising CO_2

Carbon capture, utilisation, and storage (CCUS), often used interchangeably with carbon capture and sequestration or storage (CCS), involves (a) capturing CO_2 that would otherwise be emitted into the atmosphere from combustion sources like refineries, industrial plants, coal and gas-fired power plants, (b) transporting

---

rules are managed by the Department of the Environmental, Great Lakes, and Energy. Texas conservation regulation is managed by the Railroad Commission of Texas.
[124] Dziedzic and Oyewunmi (n 9).
[125] Dziedzic and Oyewunmi (n 9).
[126] Dziedzic and Oyewunmi (n 9).

the captured CO_2 mostly via pipelines, and (c) either reusing or storing it in designated underground sites permanently.[127] The geological formations for storing CO_2 includes oil and gas reservoirs, unmineable coal seams and deep saline reservoirs – structures that have naturally stored crude oil, natural gas, brine and CO_2 over millions of years.[128] In the US, the main industrial facility types that capture CO_2 which is then supplied for other uses include ethanol, natural gas, and ammonia production. The captured CO_2 is commonly used in food and beverage production and enhanced oil recovery processes. The captured CO_2 could also serve as a source of carbon in the production of synthetic methane in an integrated P2G system.

The ability to capture and store carbon emissions from fossil fuel combustion and carbon-intensive energy and industrial processes is an essential element in achieving net-zero emissions globally as well as a just transition to a net-zero to low carbon economies.[129] As of 2018, there were only two large-scale CCUS projects in operation in the power sector globally. Both had a combined capture capacity of 2.4 million tonnes of CO_2 ($MtCO_2$) per year.[130] The current fleet of power generation and industrial sector CCUS projects is reportedly inadequate considering the current scale required to reach the various SDS projections according to the IEA's Tracking Report as at May 2019. Thus, in order to provide the necessary support for the much needed investments and projects, it is essential to make provisions for necessary legal and policy measures such as tax credits, as well as project finance and implementation initiatives aimed at cost reductions and broadening the portfolio of CCUS technologies.

According to the IEA,

> limiting the availability of CO_2 storage would increase the cost of the energy transition. The emissions reduction pathway of the Clean Technology Scenario (CTS) assumes that CO_2 storage is widely available to meet globally-agreed climate goals. It requires an additional investment of USD 9.7 trillion in the power, industrial and fuel transformation sectors, relative to a scenario that includes only current national commitments.

---

[127] See Ashley J Lawson, 'Carbon Capture Versus Direct Air Capture' *Congressional Research Service Report* (IF11501, 6 April 2020) 1–4. Carbon capture technologies involve the use of a facility that can 'grab' CO_2 from or near the source of a CO_2 stream. The captured CO_2 is then released and compressed so that it can be transferred by pipeline to be utilised or stored permanently in suitable underground locations.

[128] Alexandra B Klass and Elizabeth J Wilson, 'Climate Change, Carbon Sequestration, and Property Rights' (2010) 2 *University of Illinois Law Review* 363–428; Peter Folger, 'Carbon Capture and Sequestration (CCS) in the United States' *Congressional Research Service Report* (R44902, 14 November 2017) 1–21.

[129] The Dan Brouillette, 'The Role of Carbon Capture, Utilization, and Storage in Forming a Low-Carbon Economy' (*US Department of Energy*, 21 May 2018), www.energy.gov/articles/role-carbon-capture-utilization-and-storage-forming-low-carbon-economy; Global CCS Institute, 'Global Status of CCS Report' (2019), www.globalccsinstitute.com/resources/global-status-report/.

[130] See the IEA, 'Carbon Capture, Utilisation and Storage', at www.iea.org/fuels-and-technologies/carbon-capture-utilisation-and-storage. See also the IEA's Tracking Power Report (May 2019) at www.iea.org/reports/tracking-power-2019/ccus-in-power#abstract. The IEA's 'Tracking Clean Energy'

Limiting CO_2 storage results in an increase of these additional investments by 40%, to USD 13.7 trillion, relying on more expensive and nascent technologies.[131]

Looking at the long-term scenarios where decarbonised energy systems are prioritised, the IEA also opines that at least an

> additional low-carbon generation capacity of 3 325 GW in 2060 [is required], which is nearly half of the total installed global capacity in 2017. In locations where a rapid scale-up of wind and solar capacity are constrained due to land use or other factors [some of which are discussed in this chapter above], imported hydrogen may become an important alternative.[132]

In a very far-reaching 'all-electric' pathway where zero-carbon energy proponents also push for relying primarily on variable sources of energy such as wind and solar, there will be the need for massive investments and manufacture of advanced battery technologies. Unfortunately, most often than not the supply and environmental risks associated with minerals such as lithium and cobalt and components for battery storage and emerging technologies are often underplayed.[133]

Recently a group of International oil companies (IOCs) launched the Oil and Gas Climate Initiative (OGCI),[134] in which the companies pledge to help facilitate: (i) reductions in methane emissions during the production, delivery, and usage of oil and gas; (ii) reduction in CO_2 emissions by increasing energy efficiency in power, industry, and transport; and (iii) recycling and storage of CO_2 produced during power generation or industrial processes by using it in products or storing it (CCUS).[135] According to the OGCI report, the following pilot projects have been initiated as a means of scaling up investments in recycling and storing CO_2:

a) The Inventys Project: aims to halve the capital cost of carbon capture through its modular, scalable technology, while creating demand for CO_2 on a

---

progress indicator provides a status snapshot of 39 critical energy technologies needed to meet a less than 2°C target under its Sustainable Development Scenario (SDS). Only seven of the technologies assessed are 'on-track'. Critically CCS in power, and in industry and transformation, are 'off-track'. To achieve the levels outlined in the SDS, the number of industrial scale facilities needs to increase a hundredfold, from 19 in operation now to more than 2,000 by 2040.

[131] IEA, 'The Role of CO_2 Storage: Exploring Clean Energy Pathways' Technology Report (IEA Publications, July 2019), www.iea.org/reports/the-role-of-co2-storage.

[132] Ibid.

[133] The world's soaring demand for cobalt is at times met by workers, including children, who labour in harsh and dangerous conditions, mostly in mines located in Congo, Africa. See Amnesty International, 'Democratic Republic of Congo: "This is What We Die For": Human Rights Abuses in the Democratic Republic of the Congo Power the Global Trade in Cobalt' AFR 62/3183/2016 (19 January 2016); Andy Symington, 'Lithium-Ion Batteries: Positive and Negative Rights Impact' (2019) 28 Human Rights Defender 36–37; Lauren Neuhaus, 'The Electrifying Problem of Used Lithium Ion Batteries: Recommendations for Recycling and Disposal' (2018) 42 Environs: Environmental Law and Policy Journal 67–94.

[134] The OGCI, 'At Work: Committed to Climate Action: A Report from the Oil and Gas Climate Initiative' (September 2019), https://oilandgasclimateinitiative.com/annual-report/.

[135] Ibid.

gigatonne scale by building a physical marketplace. It involves operating the 30 tonnes per day carbon capture plant in Canada in conjunction with Husky Energy. It demonstrates the potential for low-cost capture technology for storage in an enhanced oil recovery field.

b) The Solidia Project involves using CO_2 to produce lower-carbon cement.
c) Accelerating decarbonisation in UK energy and industry by investing in a UK-based CCUS hub project that aims to build the world's first commercial abated gas power plant, while providing collective carbon transport and storage infrastructure to enable decarbonisation of the Teesside industrial hub.
d) A project to capture and store CO_2 from Wabash Valley Resources' co-located ammonia plant. This is expected to be the largest carbon storage project to date in the USA and the first ammonia produced with a near-zero carbon footprint.

The US Internal Revenue Code Section 45Q Credits and recent commercialisation focused incentives underscores the important role such policy measures could play in supporting future projects. The Section 45Q provides a tax credit on a per-ton basis for CO_2 that is sequestered. Thus, an incentive of $20 per metric ton for CO_2 geologic storage and $10 per metric ton for CO_2 used for enhanced oil and gas recovery was available between 2008 and 2018. The credit was capped at 75 million tons, while the IRS reported that 35 million tons had already been claimed. Further to the passage of the Bipartisan Budget Act of 2018, the tax credit provisions were updated, thus, approving an increase to $35 per metric ton for EOR and $50 per metric ton for geologic storage by 2026. The $35 tax credit is also available for non-EOR CO_2 utilisation and direct air capture projects. Notably, tax policies adopted by numerous state governments complement these federal tax incentives.[136]

A. Highlights of Legal and Policy Issues for CCUS

Apart from commercial and fiscal incentives to reduce costs and scalability of projects, there are legal and regulatory issues that often arise in the process of considering CCUS projects. First, the idea of storing CO_2 in 'pore spaces' of underground formations or depleted hydrocarbon reservoirs permanently or for hundreds of years creates some land use and property rights challenges depending on the jurisdiction and the applicable legal framework governing such issues. There are also pertinent questions pertaining to the allocation of long-term risks and liability. Second, there are things to consider in transportation of CO_2,

---

[136] Angela C. Jones and Molly F Sherlock, 'The Tax Credit for Carbon Sequestration (Section 45Q)' *Congressional Research Service (CRS) In Focus* (IF11455, 12 March 2020), https://crsreports.congress.gov/product/pdf/IF/IF11455.

especially to offshore sites.¹³⁷ Third, there is the need for an environmental impact assessment of long-term CO_2 storage, reporting standards and maintaining the integrity of the CO_2 storage site. Fourth, property rights in the offshore marine areas are distinct from onshore areas, thus in deciding who owns storage rights below the sea bed, it is important to distinguish between the territorial waters of the country from the high seas which are subject to international law.¹³⁸

In most jurisdictions outside the US, there is a domanial framework placing ownership of land in the Government and also the property in all mineral resources *in situ* in the state as well. Such jurisdictions may find the allocation of licences and permits for access to land and store CO_2 in underground formations less complex and in reality, depends largely on the relevant government's policy and terms of granting such licences or permits under the relevant constitutional, administrative and land use law provisions. However, in the US there is an extensive system of private ownership of land and split interests between such landowners with surface ownership rights and underground mineral interest holders. Additionally, there are questions relating to the use and conservation of public land owned by the Government, thus there are arguably more issues requiring specific legal and policy solutions. For instance, who owns the potential storage pore spaces within the deep underground formations, which are also sometimes in locations crossing or beneath existing oil and gas reservoirs? Are any rights to the pore space vested in the owner of the surface lands above the pore space? What if the mineral rights have been severed and transferred to a third party? Does the Government own the pore space because it is so far beneath the surface that neither the surface owner nor the mineral owner has ever had a reasonable expectation that it would make use of that space? If rights to the pore space are in fact vested in a surface owner or mineral owner, can the Government exercise the power of eminent domain to implement CCS as a 'public use' under the Fifth Amendment to the US Constitution? If so, what constitutes 'just' compensation?¹³⁹ There is arguably enough experience as at today in dealing with some of these issues from public and private sector stakeholders. By and large, policymakers, judges and relevant stakeholders as the case may be would need to agree on the rationale of facilitating CCUS as a key tool towards decarbonisation and also strike a balance between such objectives vis-à-vis the need to protect property rights and allocate risks and liabilities fairly.

---

¹³⁷ Tara K Righetti, 'Siting Carbon Dioxide Pipelines' (2017–2018) 3(4) *Oil and Gas, Natural Resources, and Energy Journal* 907 to 975; Romany Webb and Michael B Gerrard, 'Sequestering Carbon Dioxide Undersea in the Atlantic: Legal Problems and Solutions' (2018) 36(1) *UCLA Journal of Environmental Law and Policy* 1–78.

¹³⁸ Alexandra B Klass and Elizabeth J Wilson, 'Climate Change and Carbon Sequestration: Assessing a Liability Regime for Long-Term Storage of Carbon Dioxide' (2008) 58 *Emory Law Journal* 103–80; Global CCS Institute, 'Property Rights in Relation to CCS', http://www.globalccsinstitute.com/resources/publications-reports-research/property-rights-in-relation-to-ccs/.

¹³⁹ See Klass and Wilson (n 128) for further consideration of these issues.

In the context of storage of CO_2 in depleted hydrocarbon reservoirs in Canada, ownership of the geological formation remains with the owner of the mineral interest after the minerals (oil and gas) have been extracted. While in several states in the US, ownership of the geological formation remains associated with the surface estate, ie landowner. Where the mineral interest is owned by the state, pore space is typically also vested in the state, though this is not always clearly specified by existing laws. In some jurisdictions, legislation has now been passed to clarify that the state owns the pore space, for example, in the Province of Alberta in Canada.[140]

On the issue of liability for CO_2 management, it is important to distinguish and clearly outline the allocation of risks and liabilities arising when capturing CO_2 from the emission source and during the transportation and injection phase of a project, as well as long term liability for stored CO_2. Ordinarily, the rights to the storage plus the stored CO_2 should follow the entity that takes on the long-term stewardship of the storage site, whether it remains with the lessor of the site, a licensed operator or remains vested in the state.[141] It is common to find that long-term liability of the storage operation is transferred to a public body after closure once a series of conditions have been met.[142] Where the pore space was owned or leased by a private entity during the operational phase, the rights to the pore space will have to be transferred to the public body taking on the liability for the site.[143] Given the experiences gathered over the years and with recent and planned projects such as those listed above, one could posit that the issue of 'liability' for stored CO_2 is not a 'showstopper' for feasible CCUS projects.[144] It is clearly possible to develop a commercial and effective approach addressing such risk allocation and liability issues.

Recently, a resolution to a considerable barrier to transporting CO_2 offshore to ideal sites internationally was made by the parties to the Convention on the Prevention of Marine Pollution by Dumping of Wastes and Other Matter 1972 (ie the 'London Protocol'). Inadvertently, Article 6 of the Protocol prevents transboundary transportation of CO_2 for geological storage.[145] The signatories passed an amendment to resolve this issue in 2009, although two thirds of the Protocol's contracting parties must ratify the amendment for it to come into force.[146] The Parties recently allowed provisional application of the 2009 amendment allowing for cross-border transport and export of CO_2 for geological storage in sub-seabed geological formations.

---

[140] Global CCS Institute (n 138).
[141] Global CCS Institute (n 138).
[142] Global CCS Institute (n 138).
[143] Global CCS Institute (n 138).
[144] Global CCS Institute, 'Global Status of CCS Report' (n 129).
[145] *Ibid.*
[146] *Ibid.*

B. Options for Getting Negative Carbon Emissions

There are significant potentials for achieving negative emissions, or CO_2 removal in the path towards decarbonisation of energy systems amongst others.[147] Carbon neutrality, or 'net-zero', implies that any 'CO_2 released into the atmosphere from human activity is balanced by an equivalent amount being removed. Becoming carbon-negative on the other hand requires a company, sector or country to remove more CO_2 from the atmosphere than it emits'.[148] In the energy systems context, such objectives will undeniably require the collaborative understanding and effort of all stakeholders, both private and public. Under the IPCC Special Report on Global Warming of 1.5°C, published in late 2018,[149] almost all the pathways considered relied to some extent on carbon removal approaches in order to achieve net negative emissions after 2050.

Carbon removal technologies can be a significant contributor to both long-term and near-term climate change mitigation and clean energy transitions drive. Such technologies can 'neutralise or offset emissions that are currently technically challenging or prohibitively expensive to address. This includes in some industrial processes, such as steel-making and cement production, and long-distance transport, like shipping and aviation'.[150] These technologies and options can be categorised as including:

 i. nature-based solutions;
 ii. measures that aim to enhance natural processes; and
 iii. technology-based solutions.

The nature-based solutions include the repurposing of land use by growing forests where there was none before (afforestation) or re-establishing a forest where there was one in the past (reforestation). Other nature-based solutions include the restoration of coastal and marine habitats to ensure they continue to draw CO_2 from the air.[151] The enhanced natural processes include land management approaches to increase the carbon content in soil through modern farming methods. This can incorporate the addition of biochar (charcoal produced from biomass) to soils, where the carbon can remain stored for hundreds or thousands of years. Other less developed approaches include enhanced weathering to accelerate natural processes that absorb CO_2 (for example, by adding very fine mineral silicate rocks to soils) or ocean fertilisation in which nutrients are added to the ocean to increase its capacity to absorb CO_2. Enhanced weathering and ocean fertilisation approaches require further research to understand their potential for carbon

---

[147] Sara Budinis, 'Going Carbon Negative: What are the Technology Options?' (*IEA Commentary*, 31 January 2020), www.iea.org/commentaries/going-carbon-negative-what-are-the-technology-options.
[148] *Ibid.*
[149] IPCC Special Report (n 10).
[150] Budinis (n 147).
[151] Budinis (n 147).

removal as well as their costs, risks and tradeoffs.¹⁵² The technology-based solutions include bioenergy with carbon capture and storage (BECCS) and direct air capture,¹⁵³ which – as the name suggests – involves the capture of CO_2 directly from the atmosphere. Both of these solutions rely on the geological storage of CO_2 for large-scale carbon removal and could play an important role in clean energy transitions.¹⁵⁴ It is interesting to note the key messages from a recent report by the Global Carbon Capture and Storage (CCS) Institute, which stated that:

- BECCS requires the wide-scale deployment of CCS.
- Historically, BECCS deployment has been slow; there are few operating facilities.
- Major BECCS technologies are mature; their potential is substantial.
- The availability of land, water and fertiliser to supply biomass is the major constraint on BECCS.
- Most climate change scenarios use negative emissions technologies to draw CO_2 from the atmosphere; of these, BECCS is the best option.
- The scale of BECCS deployment reaches gigatonnes of CO_2 stored per year to meet global warming targets set for the end of the century.¹⁵⁵

In pathways limiting global warming to 1.5°C with limited or no overrun, the IPCC found that agriculture, forestry and land-use measures could remove between one billion and 11 billion tonnes of CO_2 per year by 2050. The potential amount of CO_2 removal from BECCS ranged from zero to eight billion tonnes per year by then. To put this in context, global energy-related CO_2 emissions were 33 billion tonnes in 2018.¹⁵⁶ While these carbon removal technologies should not be adopted as an excuse for a carbon-intensive industry to persist in environmentally irresponsible behaviour, they are worth considering in view of the opportunity costs of doing nothing about curbing emissions. This chapter will not delve into detail on the pros and cons of each technology but outline briefly the main features of each emerging option as part of a potential solution to the climate-energy-economy crisis.

BECCS involves the capture and permanent storage of CO_2 from processes where biomass is burned to generate energy. This can include power plants using biomass (or a mix of biomass and fossil fuels); pulp mills for paper production; lime kilns for cement production; and refineries producing biofuels through fermentation (ethanol) or gasification (biogas) of biomass.¹⁵⁷ BECCS enables carbon removal because biomass absorbs CO_2 as it grows, and this CO_2 is not

---

¹⁵² Budinis (n 147).
¹⁵³ The Global CCS Institute, 'Bioenergy and Carbon Capture and Storage' (14 March 2019), www.globalccsinstitute.com/resources/publications-reports-research/bioenergy-and-carbon-capture-and-storage/.
¹⁵⁴ *Ibid.*
¹⁵⁵ Christopher Consoli, 'Bioenergy and Carbon Capture and Storage: 2019 Perspective' (Global CCS Institute, 14 March 2019).
¹⁵⁶ Budinis (n 147).
¹⁵⁷ Budinis (n 147).

re-released when it is burned. Instead, it is captured and injected into deep geological formations, removing it from the natural carbon cycle.[158] The Illinois Industrial Carbon Capture and Storage project is capturing up to one million tonnes of CO_2 from a bioethanol facility each year and storing it in a dedicated geological site. In the United Kingdom, Drax has begun a pilot project to capture CO_2 from its biomass-fuelled power plant. If the project is successful, it could become the world's first negative emissions power plant.

Direct air capture can enable carbon removal in which CO_2 captured from the atmosphere is permanently stored. The captured CO_2 can also be sold for use, for example, in food and beverage production or for blending with low-carbon hydrogen to make synthetic fuels. But in most cases, the captured CO_2 that is used is re-released into the atmosphere, such as when the fuel is burned.[159] In these cases, the use of the captured CO_2 could still generate climate mitigation benefits, particularly where synthetic fuels are replacing conventional fossil fuels, for example. But this would not result in negative emissions. Due to the low concentration of CO_2 in the atmosphere, direct air capture technologies are currently more energy-intensive and expensive than other carbon capture applications, which draw off more concentrated CO_2 from industrial facilities or power plants. Today, more than 10 direct air capture plants are operating in Europe, the United States, and Canada. Most of these plants are small and sell the captured CO_2 for use – for carbonating drinks, for example. However, the first large-scale direct air capture plant is now being developed in the United States by a partnership between Carbon Engineering and Occidental Petroleum.[160]

VII. Conclusion

P2G, RNG production and negative emissions technologies can form part of a portfolio of technologies to foster a just and less acrimonious energy transition and decarbonisation pathway. It is noted, however, that P2G and RNG fit into the context(s) of facilitating the more efficient and reliable integration of a growing mix of intermittent renewable energy sources. Negative emissions technologies and CCUS pertains mostly to systems that could enhance the direct removal of CO_2 in the atmosphere and storing it safely for future use or permanently. These innovative solutions are evolving and require concerted effort and collaboration from all stakeholders to have any meaningful impact on energy of decarbonisation. Regulatory institutions also need to be prepared, well equipped and supported by providing a more coherent and comprehensive policy and legal framework to deal with the evolving challenge.

---

[158] Budinis (n 147).
[159] Budinis (n 147).
[160] Budinis (n 147).

In order to realise the greatest potential penetration of renewable electricity on the grid, novel technologies like P2G are necessary. Likewise, decarbonising heating and transportation fuels will require equally innovative solutions. While technological advancement and markets would undoubtedly foster innovative solutions such as P2G, it is unlikely this will occur within a relevant timeframe, without a coherent, comprehensive and pragmatic legislative and policy intervention.

4

Economic Waste and Environmental Problems: Natural Gas Flaring in Texas

KIM TALUS AND CHERI R HASZ

I. Introduction

Natural gas 'flaring' is a nasty word in today's international energy and environmental world. Natural gas flaring points to two things: the waste of a valuable commodity and contributor to climate change. Justifiably so, both of these factors are driving down the volumes of natural gas that is flared around the world. National as well as international efforts to curb flaring have been effective and the oil and gas industry flares less and less gas as time goes on. Countries like Nigeria are creating policies to reduce flaring, companies like Exxon are committed to reduce flaring and so on. Despite this, approximately 140 bcm of natural gas was flared in 2017. This corresponds roughly to the gas consumption of the entire African Continent.[1] Flaring is the burning of natural gas at well sites, and produces carbon dioxide, carbon monoxide, sulphur dioxide, nitrogen oxides and other compounds, depending on both the chemical makeup of the natural gas and how well it burns in the flare.[2] Although flaring releases greenhouse gas emissions into the air, it is preferable to venting, which is simply releasing the natural gas into the air.[3] Venting natural gas releases methane, which is a much stronger greenhouse gas, thus raising more emissions than flaring.[4]

While international efforts are directed towards the reduction of flaring where possible, the recent practice of the Texas Railroad Commission (Railroad Commission) offers an alternative scenario. The volumes of gas flared in Texas have grown exponentially over the last several years and the Railroad Commission's

---

[1] See International Energy Agency (IEA), 'Tracking Fuel Supply' Report (*IEA*, November 2019), www.iea.org/reports/tracking-fuel-supply-2019/flaring-emissions.
[2] US Energy Information Administration (eia), 'Natural Gas Explained' (*US Environmental Protection Agency*, April 2019), www.eia.gov/energyexplained/natural-gas/natural-gas-and-the-environment.php.
[3] *Ibid.*
[4] *Ibid.*

relaxed attitude towards the flaring of natural gas has gathered national and international attention.[5] The reason for the increased flaring in Texas is connected with the growth in oil production in the state and the lack of pipeline capacity to transport the associated gas to market. However, behind the increase in flaring is also a regulatory change dating back to 1990.

This chapter will provide an account of the regulatory framework for gas flaring in Texas. It will also examine pre- and post-1990 regulatory practice by the Railroad Commission and seeks to explain some of the causes for the more relaxed approach of the Railroad Commission towards flaring of associated gas.

II. Background to Flaring in the Permian Basin

Petrohawk unlocked the secret of producing directly from the nonconventional formation in the Eagle Ford shale when it employed horizontal drilling and multi-stage hydraulic fracturing techniques in 2008.[6] Following the Eagle Ford field's rush to drill for shale oil, development in the Permian Basin shale oil fields in West Texas followed.[7] The Permian Basin area is many times larger than the Eagle Ford's, and the pipeline infrastructure built decades earlier to carry oil and gas produced from conventional wells simply cannot accommodate the huge volumes of oil and associated gas flowing from the several thousand shale wells drilled there over the last few years.[8] Thus, an extremely large amount of associated gas is flared, placing the United States in the top ten gas-flaring countries globally.[9]

In the years from 2012 to 2017, data analysis from the Environmental Defense Fund (EDF) showed that the state of Texas flared nearly one trillion cubic feet of gas – 'enough to meet the needs of every household in Texas for about 2½ years'.[10] The dramatic increase in flaring has led the Office of the US Department of Energy's Office (DOE) of Fossil Energy (FE) to issue a report informing the states and other important stakeholders on natural gas flaring and venting regulations, with a view that flaring and limited venting may never be entirely eliminated.[11]

---

[5] See, eg, the following news articles: www.reuters.com/article/us-usa-shale-flaring/natural-gas-flaring-hits-record-high-in-first-quarter-in-us-permian-basin-idUSKCN1T5235; https://oilprice.com/Energy/Natural-Gas/Gas-Flaring-Running-Rampant-In-The-Permian.html;andwww.nytimes.com/2019/10/16/climate/natural-gas-flaring-exxon-bp.html.

[6] Bret Wells, 'Please Give Us One More Oil Boom – I Promise Not to Screw It Up this Time: The Broken Promise of Associated Gas Flaring in the Eagle Ford Shale' (2014) 9 *Texas Journal of Oil, Gas & Energy Law* 319, 320.

[7] Ernest E Smith and Jacqueline Lang Weaver, *Texas Law of Oil and Gas* (LexisNexis, 2015) § 10.6, section A.3.

[8] Ibid.

[9] Ibid.

[10] Ibid.

[11] US Department of Energy–Office of Oil and Natural Gas & Office of Fossil Energy, 'Natural Gas Flaring and Venting: State and Federal Regulatory Overview, Trends, and Impacts' (June 2019) ('US Department of Energy Report), www.energy.gov/sites/prod/files/2019/08/f65/Natural%20Gas%20Flaring%20and%20Venting%20Report.pdf.

The report states that both industry and regulators agree 'that there is value in developing and applying technologies and practices to economically recover and limit both practices'.[12]

A. Competency over Flaring: Who Decides?

The Texas Legislature designated oil pipelines as common carriers to prevent abuses in the oil fields, and in 1917, gave jurisdiction to the Texas Railroad Commission – which was already regulating the transportation industry.[13] In 1919, the Railroad Commission was given jurisdiction over oil and gas production;[14] thus, all property in oil and gas production is subject to the Railroad Commission's police powers.[15] The Commission is authorised to act under many statutory provisions and for the flaring of natural gas, these provisions are codified in the Texas Natural Resources Code, which was enacted for the purpose of conserving oil and gas.[16] As such, the Railroad Commission is authorised and empowered to 'make all necessary rules for governing and regulating ... operations that are subject to its jurisdiction' and to make any rules and orders necessary to carry out legislative intent.[17]

The Texas Railroad Commission therefore possesses the authority to both authorise the venting and flaring of associated gas from oil wells, and prevent waste of oil and gas.[18] The statutory framework may disfavour gas flaring; however if no infrastructure is available to capture and market the gas from oil production, the Commission has the authority to permit the flaring via exceptions.[19] No statute *expressly* prohibits escape of associated gas from oil wells; instead, the Natural Resource Code sets out different uses for the associated gas from oil wells, as opposed to from gas wells.[20] There seems to be an implied tradeoff between what constitutes 'waste' and the requirements that the Railroad Commission 'take into consideration and protect the rights and interests of the purchasing and consuming public in oil and all its products'.[21]

On flaring from oil wells, section 86.183 of the Texas Natural Resource Code states that associated gas may be used for 'any beneficial purpose'[22] rather than

---

[12] *Ibid.*
[13] Railroad Commission of Texas, 'Oil and Gas', www.rrc.state.tx.us/about-us/history/informal-history-toc/oil-and-gas/.
[14] *Ibid.*
[15] Francis M Dougherty et al, '§ 738.Generally; authority of Commission' in 56 Tex. Jur. 3d Oil and Gas § 738 (October 2019).
[16] *Ibid.*
[17] *Ibid* and see generally § 735 (expanding on the full scope of the Texas Railroad Commission powers).
[18] Smith and Weaver (n 7) at section A.1.
[19] Smith and Weaver (n 7) at section A.1.
[20] Smith and Weaver (n 7) at section A.1.
[21] Dougherty et al (n 15) § 773 and see generally § 773–§776 (discussing in-depth what constitutes 'waste').
[22] Texas Natural Resource Code ('Tex. Nat. Res. Code Ann.') § 86.183 (West 2019).

the only four lawful uses allowed for gas-well gas in section 86.181.[23] Unsold and unused associated gas *must be flared* for public safety unless the Railroad Commission has granted the well operator an exception.[24] Thus, the Railroad Commission can use its authority to prevent flaring under the statutes when it views the practice as wasteful. Statewide Rule 32 governing the flaring and venting of natural gas was added to the Texas Administrative Code in 1978.[25] Under Rule 32, operators may flare gas 'for a period not to exceed ten producing days after initial completion' of a well.[26] The flared gas must be 'measured ... reported and charged against lease allowable production', but not for the initial ten-day period.[27] If an operator wants to flare beyond the ten-day period, an exception must be requested.[28] The flaring exception for additional time was authorised upon a showing that the exception is a 'necessity'.[29] From its promulgation in 1978 until its amendment in 1990, this 'necessity' meant situations such as '(i) cleaning a well of sand or acid or both following stimulation treatment of a well and (ii) repairing or modifying a gas-gathering system'.[30] The 1990 Amendment to Rule 32 removed this one hurdle to flaring.[31]

B. Obtaining the Exception to Flare

Statewide Rule 32 implements the venting and flaring statutes.[32] It *generally* prohibits escape of gas from any well (gas or oil), gas-gathering system, plant, or other gas-handling equipment; however, the Railroad Commission can grant *exceptions* to this prohibition.[33] Rule 32 also exempts releases of gas that are not readily measured by devices routinely used in the operation of wells, gathering systems and gas plants.[34]

The 1990 Amendment to Rule 32 provides a statutory necessity for flaring associated gas from an oil well beyond the initial ten-day period: a necessity exists whenever there is 'unavailability of a gas pipeline or other marketing facility, or

---

[23] Tex. Nat. Res. Code Ann. § 86.181 (West 2019). The four lawful uses are: 1. Light or fuel; 2. Efficient chemical manufacture; 3. Reinjection; 4. Extraction of natural gasoline when the residue is reinjected.
[24] Tex. Nat. Res. Code Ann. § 88.055 (West 2019).
[25] Wells (n 6) 329.
[26] 16 Texas Administrative Code ('Tex. Admin. Code') §3.32(f)(1)(A) (2019).
[27] 16 Tex. Admin. Code §3.32(f)(1) (2019).
[28] 16 Tex. Admin. Code §3.32(f)(2) (2019).
[29] Wells (n 6) 329.
[30] Wells (n 6) 329.
[31] Wells (n 6) 330.
[32] Wells (n 6) 329.
[33] Smith and Weaver (n 7) section A.2.
[34] 16 Tex. Admin. Code §3.32(d)(1) (2019).

other purposes & uses authorized by law'.[35] The Railroad Commission issues the flare permits (exceptions) for 45 days at a time.[36] This exception allows for an operator to flare natural gas for up to 180 days after the initial ten-day period.[37] Essentially, if no immediately available outlet exists for produced natural gas, then flaring is a necessity.[38] What is notable is what Rule 32 does not require that this necessity to flare is shown.[39] Rule 32 does not require a weighing of the economic benefit of producing oil more quickly versus the economic cost of flaring and wasting natural gas.[40]

Rule 32 now allows the Railroad Commission to grant a flaring exception after the initial 180 days.[41] First, there must be an administrative hearing following the issuance of a final order signed by the Railroad Commission. The only information required for the grant of this exception beyond the 180-day period includes a map showing the nearest pipeline capable of accepting gas, the volume to be flared during the time period requested, and a cost-benefit analysis.[42] Like the exception for the initial 180-day period, what is notable here is what the application does not need to contain.[43] Operators do not need to show that crude oil would be lost if it was not produced immediately, or to otherwise protect their correlative rights by preventing drainage to competing operators.[44] Exceptions here have been granted when gas pipeline connections are within three miles of the new well and scheduled to be completed in a matter of months,[45] and when the operator only needs a few months to remove excessive H[2]S from the gas.[46] These final order issuances are routine as a method to avoid any interruption in oil production.[47]

---

[35] 16 Tex. Admin. Code § 3.32(f)(2)(D) (2019).
[36] US Department of Energy Report (n 11) 22.
[37] Wells (n 6) 330.
[38] Wells (n 6) 331.
[39] Wells (n 6) 330.
[40] Wells (n 6) 330.
[41] 16 Tex. Admin. Code §3.32(h)(4) (2019).
[42] See the Texas Railroad Commission's Statewide Rule 32 Exception Data Sheet, available at www.rrc.state.tx.us/media/8015/swr32datasht.pdf.
[43] Wells (n 6) 331.
[44] Wells (n 6) 331.
[45] See, eg, Texas Railroad Commission, 'The Application of EOG Resources, Inc. for an Exception to Statewide Rule 32 for the Donnell Lowe Pasture Unit, Eagleville (Eagle Ford-1) Field, McMullen County, Texas', Docket No 01-0279308 (6 December 2012), www.rrc.state.tx.us/media/13058/01-79308pfd.pdf (allowing for a flaring exception for the four months during which gas pipelines connecting to EOG's gas gathering lines 2.7 miles away would be completed).
[46] See, eg, Texas Railroad Commission, 'The Application of Talisman Energy USA Income for an Exception to Statewide Rule 32 for the Powers Lease, Well Nos. L1H L3H, and L5H in the Eagleville (Eagle Ford-1) Field, McMullen County, Texas', Docket No 01-0281356 (11 April 2013), www.rrc.state.tx.us/media/13099/01-81355-r32.pdf (allowing for flaring of valuable natural gas even though the operator would have fixed the operational issues and had already flared for 180 days).
[47] Wells (n 6) 332.

i. Reporting Permits Issued

The Railroad Commission allows for industry self-reporting; the Commission then reports the levels of combustion to the US Energy Information Administration (EIA).[48] However, the amount of gas flared in the Permian Basin as reported to the Railroad Commission is two times lower than the analysis by the EDF.[49] These findings are consistent with reports from the S&P Global Market Intelligence that 'showed significant disparities between industry-reported flaring data and satellite data in Texas, North Dakota and New Mexico'.[50] The report noted that operators have 'an incentive to under-report flaring so that they can continue to produce higher-valued oil'.[51] Whether one believes the EIA's figures or the National Oceanic and Atmospheric Administration's (NOAA) figures, both indicate a 'non-trivial level of gas flaring, with 977 Bcf combusted over six years by NOAA data or 516 Bcf according to data from EIA reports'.[52] Furthermore, the DOE has taken notice of this discrepancy, citing both the EDF and the S&P studies.[53]

Figure 1 Volume of Natural Gas Flared, Bcf, Comparison[54]

Year	NOAA data	EIA data
2012	125	48
2013	142	76
2014	182	90
2015	204	114
2016	160	88
2017	163	101

The Texas Railroad Commission (RRC) allows for viewing of total permits issued as well as the permits for flaring exceptions granted on its site:[55]

---

[48] US Department of Energy Report (n 11) 9.
[49] Smith and Weaver (n 7) at section A.3.
[50] Brian Collins, 'Financial Focus: Are Some Shale Producers Under-Reporting Gas Flaring to Keep Oil Flowing?' (S&P Global Market Intelligence, 24 October 2018), https://platform.mi.spglobal.com/web/client?auth=inherit&sf200858251=1#news/article?id=47199929&cdid=A-47199929-12062.
[51] Ibid.
[52] Ibid
[53] US Department of Energy Report (n 11) at 13.
[54] US Department of Energy–Office of Oil and Natural Gas & Office of Fossil Energy, 'Natural Gas Flaring and Venting: State and Federal Regulatory Overview, Trends, and Impacts' (June 2019).
[55] The Texas Railroad Commission, Flaring Regulation (2019), www.rrc.state.tx.us/about-us/resource-center/faqs/oil-gas-faqs/faq-flaring-regulation/.

Figure 2 Venting and Flaring Permit Approval

Fiscal Year	Total Venting and Flaring Permits Approved by RRC
FY 2019	6.972
FY 2018	5,488
FY 2017	3,708
FY 2016	4,870
FY 2015	5,689
FY 2014	5,285
FY 2013	3,092
FY 2012	1,963
FY 2011	651
FY 2010	306
FY 2009	158
FY 2008	107

The dockets for exceptions to Statewide Rule 32 are displayed in full on the Texas Railroad Commission's website. Operators currently do not need to find a way around the flaring regulations; the majority of permit requests are now for flaring associated gas *after* an oil well's completion in Eagle Ford, for example.[56] Analysis from the Railroad Commission regarding how many wells received long-term flaring permits and were currently flaring despite being connected to a gas pipeline, identified 3,073 wells operating under 234 long-term flaring permits (180 days or longer) that were also connected to pipeline systems.[57] This amounts to about one per cent of all the wells currently in production; those wells, in May 2019, flared about 5.4 per cent of the natural gas they produced, compared to a statewide flaring rate of 1.34 per cent for the same month.[58]

However, prior to 1978, the RRC operated quite differently and took a much more active role in restricting natural gas flaring.

C. Going Down Memory Lane: The Pre-1978 Flaring Cases

Before the 1990 Amendment, which 'ushered in the era of routine flaring', the Texas Railroad Commission had a history of successful no-flare orders in oil

---

[56] Wells (n 6) 331.
[57] Kiah Collier, 'Pipeline Giant Sues Railroad Commission, Alleging Law Oversight of Natural Gas Flaring' *Texas Tribune*, 3 December 2019, www.texastribune.org/2019/12/03/railroad-commission-sued-lax-oversight-natural-gas-flaring/.
[58] *Ibid*.

fields starting after the Second World War.[59] The Commission viewed the practice of unitisation as a way to prevent the waste, via flaring, of natural gas. Given that Texas has a voluntary unitisation act, making it difficult in large fields with hundreds of owners to negotiate the necessary agreements, the Commission utilised its power over production to force these owners to cooperate.[60] For example, the Railroad Commission used the 'stick' of 'no-flare' or 'no-waste' order to functionally make unitisation compulsory[61] and employed the 'carrots' of special allowables, like bonus and transfer allowables, to assist in ensuring the profitability of the unitisation operations.[62] The Commission would shut down production to prevent the wasteful practice of flaring natural gas. Several cases from this era demonstrate the Railroad Commission's methodology and purpose in practice; although the fields in these cases involve conventional formations, they clearly define the contours of the Commission's authority to prohibit flaring to prevent waste in the pre-Statewide Rule 32 era.

The first order prohibiting oil and gas production was on 17 March 1947.[63] The Texas Railroad Commission shut down the entire Seeligson field in South Texas until the associated gas from the wells was utilised rather than flared.[64] The Seeligson field wells were oil wells, and at this time, no statute existed which expressly prohibited the flaring of associated gas from oil wells; in fact, the practice had been accepted and was routine in the field since 1941.[65] The operators in the Seeligson field immediately filed and obtained a temporary injunction against enforcement of the Railroad Commission's no-flare order until the final determination of the order's legality.[66] Although the Texas Supreme Court affirmed the injunction against the no-flare order, the Court did find authority to confirm the Commission's authority to issue such orders.[67] The legality of the no-flare order itself would depend on whether it would be reasonably supported by substantial evidence.[68] At this time, no statute allowed operators in oil fields to voluntarily unitise without facing antitrust violations.[69] After this case, Texas passed the 1949 Voluntary Unitisation Act, granting antitrust immunity to operators in oil fields who voluntarily joined in cooperative producing operations.[70] This assisted the operators in decreasing wasteful practices, as regulated by the Texas Railroad Commission.[71]

---

[59] Smith and Weaver (n 7) section A.3.
[60] Smith and Weaver (n 7) section A.1.
[61] Smith and Weaver (n 7) section D.
[62] Smith and Weaver (n 7) section C.
[63] Smith and Weaver (n 7) section B.2.a.
[64] Smith and Weaver (n 7) section B.2.a.
[65] Smith and Weaver (n 7) section B.2.a.
[66] Smith and Weaver (n 7) section B.2.a.
[67] *Texas Railroad Commission v Shell Oil Co*, 206 S.W.2d 235, 240 (1947).
[68] *Ibid* at 242.
[69] Smith and Weaver (n 7) section B.2.a.
[70] Tex. Nat. Res. Code Ann. § 101.001–101.052 (West 2019); See also Smith and Weaver (n 7) § 11.1 (discussing the history of unitisation in Texas).
[71] Smith and Weaver (n 7) § 11.1.

The following year, the Railroad Commission began issuing no-flare orders across Texas to combat waste.[72] In November 1948, the Commission issued no-flare orders for 16 oil fields; the flaring in some of these fields were not of associated gas at the wellhead, but rather the residue plant gas from associated gas plants.[73] Operators in another 26 fields were ordered to 'show cause' as to why they should *not* be given no-flare orders; the reasonableness of these orders was challenged in the Heyser field.[74] In *Railroad Commission v Sterling Oil & Refining Co*, the Texas Supreme Court found that the no-flare order in the Heyser field was reasonable.[75] There, the operators were on notice for three years that flaring was to cease and their resulting delay in settling on marketing facilities, given that pipeline connections would take an additional five months to complete and the resulting shutdown until then would cause 'irreparable damage and loss' to a few wells, led the Court to regard the loss as a problem of the operators' own making.[76]

Even a combined showing of uneconomic practices to prevent waste and economic loss of oil from a shutdown was not enough to hold a no-flare order as unreasonable.[77] In *Railroad Commission v Flour Bluff Oil Corp*, the Court of Civil Appeals of Texas held that the Railroad Commission was an expert body in this field and in preservation and thus its shut down order was 'neither unreasonable nor arbitrary and … supported by substantial evidence'.[78] There, Humble Oil and Refining's petroleum engineer testified that shutdown of the well would cause 270,000 barrels of oil to be lost by driving the oil into sand formerly filled with gas.[79] Not flaring the natural gas would only lead to a gain of 217,000 barrels of oil.[80] Additionally, the engineer stated that it was not 'economically justified' to return the gas to the reservoir;[81] a pipeline connection would also not be complete for another five months.[82] The Court did not dispute Humble Oil's evidence; however, it noted that '[m]any of our laws, such as health and safety regulations, are upheld under police powers of the government although obedience results in financial loss'.[83]

'Conservation laws are similar in nature and noncompliance therewith cannot be justified on economic grounds.'[84] The Courts continued to support the Railroad Commission's waste-prevention orders; even though Texas's unitisation law was

---

[72] Smith and Weaver (n 7) section B.2.b.
[73] Smith and Weaver (n 7) section B.2.b.
[74] Smith and Weaver (n 7) section B.2.b.
[75] *Texas Railroad Commission v Sterling Oil & Refining Co*, 218 S.W.2d 415, 421 (Tex. 1949).
[76] *Ibid* at 421.
[77] Smith and Weaver (n 7) section B.2.b.
[78] *Texas Railroad Commission v Flour Bluff Oil Corp*, 219 S.W.2d 506, 509 (1949).
[79] *Ibid* at 508.
[80] *Ibid*.
[81] *Ibid*.
[82] Smith and Weaver (n 7) section B.2.b.
[83] *Flour Bluff Oil Corp* (n 77) at 508.
[84] *Flour Bluff Oil Corp* (n 77) at 508.

voluntary, the effect of the Railroad Commission's orders were clearly designed to force unitisation, and Texas courts, by not acknowledging the voluntary provisions of the law, were persuasively deterring further lawsuits that questioned the Commission's power to prevent waste.[85]

The Texas Supreme Court continued supporting the no-flare mission of the Railroad Commission in 1953, when it suggested the Commission employ its pro-rationing authority to prevent waste and protect the correlative rights of the flarers.[86] In *Texas Railroad Commission v Rowan Oil Co*, the Court held that the Commission did not have the authority to shut down non-flaring wells that were not producing waste in addition, but could make use of 'administrative devices not available to the courts'.[87] The Railroad Commission had shut down the huge Spraberry field in the Permian Basin – 2400 wells – by an order shutting down all production until facilities became available to market all gas from the wells in the field.[88] However, this was not done solely to prevent waste; the complete shutdown of the field was to prevent the non-flaring wells from 'confiscating part of the oil and gas which would have been produced from the flaring wells but for the shutdown'.[89] This ruling actually increased the power of the Railroad Commission, by stating that the no-flare order in the Spraberry field would be considered reasonable even if the operator had exercised diligence in attempting to make a productive use of the gas, and regardless of the decreased profits and increased problems with creditors to the operators.[90] Although the Texas legislature had never given the Railroad Commission the express authority to prohibit the flaring of associated gas from an oil well, the courts upheld the Commission's ability to do so.[91]

Following the Spraberry decision, many operators subject to similar no-flare or show-cause orders stopped litigating the orders.[92] The Railroad Commission, in each no-flare order, issued the orders for wells that were close to existing pipelines where, in a short time frame, the natural gas could be produced by sound conservation measures and marketing commercially.[93] These no-flare orders actually assisted in preserving the long-term viability of many conventional formations; without the orders, because of the fear of drainage from the fields, many operators would produce oil as quickly as they could, regardless of the effect of this behaviour compounded on the field.[94]

---

[85] Smith and Weaver (n 7) section B.2.b.
[86] Smith and Weaver (n 7) section B.2.c.
[87] *Texas Railroad Commission v Rowan Oil Co*, 259 S.W.2d 173, 177 (1953).
[88] *Ibid* at 175.
[89] *Ibid*.
[90] Smith and Weaver (n 7) section B.2.c.
[91] *Rowan Oil Co* (n 86) at 177.
[92] Smith and Weaver (n 7) section C.
[93] Wells (n 6) 328.
[94] Wells (n 6) 329.

III. Environmental Protection Agency and Flaring

The Environmental Protection Agency (EPA) sets the standards for air quality under the authority of the Clean Air Act (CAA).[95] For most states, the EPA allows them to develop and implement any necessary regulations to meet the federal standard.[96] Currently, 'there are no significant impediments to oil and natural gas production derived from federal regulation on natural gas flaring and venting'.[97]

In 2016, the Obama administration required the oil and gas industry to limit releases of methane and volatile organic compounds (VOCs) at well sites and from other equipment used for the production, storage and transport of fossil fuels.[98] As a first step in implementing this new regulation (which was an update of the EPA's 2012 Oil and Gas New Source Performance Standard, or NSPS), the EPA sent out Information Collection Requests (ICRs) to oil and natural gas companies on their existing oil and gas sources.[99] President Trump took office in late 2016 and promised to rescind the emissions limits for methane across the energy sector.[100] In March 2017, the EPA withdrew the ICRs.[101] In August 2019, the EPA officially rescinded the Obama-era requirements. While methane is a product of venting natural gas, not of flaring, flaring produces CO_2, which would still be covered by the emissions limits of ozone-forming VOCs on equipment to transport and store fossil fuels.[102]

Three major companies have voiced their criticism of the rollback. Exxon, Shell and BP have all invested in equipment that can recapture leaking natural gas at various stages of production, which in turn increases the amount they can sell to power plants.[103] It also hurts the case these companies are trying to make for natural gas as a low-carbon transitions fuel.[104] However, this rollback is beneficial to smaller operators in Texas, because they see the Obama-era regulations as a burden.[105]

The Railroad Commission's aim is to prevent waste of resources; the Texas Commission on Environmental Quality (TCEQ) monitors emissions, and both

---

[95] US Department of Energy Report (n 11) 17.
[96] US Department of Energy Report (n 11) 17.
[97] US Department of Energy Report (n 11) 19.
[98] Kiah Collier, 'Trump Administration Announces Rollback of Obama-Era Methane Regulations' *Texas Tribune*, 29 August 2019, www.texastribune.org/2019/08/29/trump-administration-announces-rollback-obama-era-methane-regulations/.
[99] Linda Tsang, 'EPA's Methane Regulations: Legal Overview' (*Congressional Research Service*, 24 January 2018) 6, https://fas.org/sgp/crs/misc/R44615.pdf.
[100] Collier (n 97).
[101] Collier (n 97).
[102] Collier (n 97).
[103] Amal Ahmed, 'The Environmental Protection Agency Wants to Repeal its Methane Emissions Limits', *Texas Observer*, 30 August 2019, www.texasobserver.org/the-environmental-protection-agency-wants-to-repeal-its-methane-emissions-limits/.
[104] *Ibid.*
[105] *Ibid.*

agencies have a reputation for being lax at enforcing Texas's environmental regulations.[106]

IV. Recent Litigation

Tulsa-based Williams Companies, a pipeline operator, filed a suit against the Texas Railroad Commission in November 2019, alleging that the Commission 'has blatantly disregarded longstanding state law that restricts the controversial and growing practice of burning off natural gas'.[107] In December 2017, Exco Operating Company requested permission from the Railroad Commission to flare excess natural gas from 130 wells in the Eagle Ford Shale and later asked for a two-year extension of this exception.[108] What is unusual about this exception is that the wells in question were already connected to a gathering pipeline system owned by Williams that can transport the natural gas to market.[109] Usually, an exception request is made precisely because there are no gathering pipelines to the wellhead.[110] However, Exco claimed it needed the exception because it did not have a contract with Williams, and even if it did, it could not afford Williams' rates to transport the gas.[111] Historically, Exco stated that Williams could only accept 70 per cent of its gas, so it would still have needed the flaring permit.[112] Given that the price of natural gas has traded in negative territory this year (2019), oil producers have either flared it or paid pipeline operators with spare capacity to take it.[113]

Williams filed a protest with the Railroad Commission in early 2018, arguing that Exco did not have the need to flare because it had the ability to move the gas to market.[114] Furthermore, Williams alleged the cost-benefit analysis required for the exception stated only the revenues from the much cheaper natural gas, and omitted the revenues from oil, in order to convince the Commission that Exco was barely turning a profit.[115] Thus, Williams argued that approving the exception request was a waste of the state's valuable natural resource.[116] Exco countered that without the exception, it would have to shut in the 138 wells, which could cause damage to them and the reservoir, resulting in a waste of hydrocarbons.[117]

---

[106] *Ibid.*
[107] Collier (n 56).
[108] Sergio Chapa, 'Flaring Under Fire: Pipeline Operator Sues Railroad Commission' *Houston Chronicle*, 3 December 2019), www.chron.com/business/energy/article/Flaring-Under-Fire-Pipeline-operator-sues-14879260.php?cmpid=ffcp.
[109] Collier (n 56).
[110] Collier (n 56).
[111] Collier (n 56).
[112] Collier (n 56).
[113] Collier (n 56).
[114] Collier (n 56).
[115] Collier (n 56).
[116] Collier (n 56).
[117] Chapa (n 107).

In August 2019, the Commission voted 2-1 to allow the exception; it reasoned that it was unreasonable for it to rule in a way that would significantly cut into the profits of Exco.[118] Following this decision, Williams filed a lawsuit on 20 November 2019 before Judge Jan Soifer in the 345th State District Court in Austin asking for it to be overturned.[119]

What is notable is the dissenting vote casted by Commission Chairman Wayne Christian. The dispute set off a debate, with all three commissioners acknowledging the legitimate issues it raised; Christian 'rebuked the commission's recent tendency to approve any and all flaring requests and expressed concern over whether it has approved others out of convenience rather than necessity'.[120] While the majority viewed that it was beyond the Railroad Commission's authority to force an agreement to transport the gas, Christian reasoned the loss in profit (Exco claimed $40,000 a month loss in profit if it had to sell the natural gas, against the $98,000 profit a month from selling oil – leaving it with $58,000 in profit) as simply a cost of doing business.[121] This split has given some hope to those urging the Railroad Commission to curb flaring practices in Texas.[122]

V. Private Rights as Measures to Stop Flaring?

While the Texas Railroad Commission has the authority to both prevent and allow flaring of natural gas, any party damaged by the lessee's activities may be able to bring a private cause of action.[123] Regulatory approval of flaring does not take away the rights of private parties to seek redress against operators who breach their contractual duties under the lease or who commit a tort that harms the correlative rights of affected parties.[124] Here, the Railroad Commission has no jurisdiction; ironically, by loosening the standard by which it grants regulatory approval for flaring, the Railroad Commission is allowing a practice that can subject operators to suits by lessors.[125] Three main causes of action exist: breach of implied covenant to administer the leasehold estate; correlative rights harmed by the negligent waste of natural gas; and tort claims for nuisance by surface owners.[126]

The basic premise for breach of implied covenant to administer the leasehold estate is that lessors are harmed when their lessees flare associated gas because this practice destroys a product – natural gas – that should have provided royalties to

---

[118] Collier (n 56).
[119] Chapa (n 107).
[120] Collier (n 56).
[121] Collier (n 56).
[122] Collier (n 56).
[123] Wells (n 6) 334.
[124] Wells (n 6) 334–35.
[125] Wells (n 6) 335.
[126] Wells (n 6) 337, 343, 346.

the lessor.[127] For adjacent landowners, they can claim that the negligent waste of natural gas harms their correlative rights.[128] Here, 'if an operator flares commercially profitable associated gas drained from neighbouring tracts, owners of mineral interests in those tracts have standing to bring an action against that operator on the grounds that such flaring represents an improper and unreasonable practice'.[129] This practice harms their correlative rights in that common reservoir. Lastly, surface owners can bring a tort claim for nuisance if 'an operator's activities substantially interfere with the use and enjoyment of another's land'.[130]

The biggest landowners in the Permian Basin and Eagle Ford Shale are either industry-friendly, or industry-owned. Although there is considerable case law covering the rights of private landowners against the waste of natural gas, it has not affected the practice of flaring, given that the power-players do not follow suit.[131] Texas Pacific Land Trust, based in Dallas, has a perpetual oil and gas royalty interest in 900,000 acres in West Texas.[132] EOG Resources is the largest acreage holder in the Eagle Ford Shale.[133] However, despite of a lack of action, the potential for private action remains.

VI. Conclusion

This chapter has examined gas flaring in Texas and the practice of the Texas Railroad Commission. It has been explained that the increase in flaring in Texas is connected to two primary issues: the rapid increase in associated gas through increase in shale oil production and a regulatory change that took place in 1990. This development is regrettable as it leads to economic waste and contributes to climate change. Natural gas has economic value for the producer, even for the oil producer that has to deal with associated gas. Natural gas is also valuable to the individual landowner, perhaps even more so as the landowner is unlikely to have a large portfolio of producing properties. Flaring of natural gas is a waste of a valuable commodity. It prevents the landowner from attracting the maximum return for its assets prior to depletion. It also reduces the maximum return available for the investor. Of course, there is the aspect of time-value for money: money today might be more valuable than money tomorrow. The same applies to oil that is

---

[127] Wells (n 6) at 355.
[128] Wells (n 6) 343.
[129] Wells (n 6) 344.
[130] Wells (n 6) 346.
[131] Wells (n 6) 334–54.
[132] Mitchell Schnurman, 'Texas Pacific Land Trust Has Sky-High Returns in the Permian. Why Isn't That Enough?' *The Dallas Morning News*, 3 May 2019, www.dallasnews.com/opinion/commentary/2019/05/03/texas-pacific-land-trust-has-sky-high-returns-in-the-permian-why-isn-t-that-enough/.
[133] EOG Resources, Premium Combination: High Return Organic Growth (1Q 2019), http://investors.eogresources.com/Cache/1500119996.PDF?O=PDF&T=&Y=&D=&FID=1500119996&iid=4075407.

being produced, and it has a higher value than natural gas. However, the value of oil depends on the market prices and oil produced tomorrow may be substantially more valuable than today. Of course, the opposite might also be true. Of course, gas pipeline development is not always possible, this holds particularly true for remote and offshore areas, but in areas like Permian, this lack of pipeline capacity is more difficult to accept.

As with all polluting economic activities, there is a need to balance potential economic gains to pertinent and urgent climate considerations. More and more, this balance needs to tilt towards climate considerations. This is particularly so, where pipelines can be built and landowner and producer may maximise their economic return, albeit it maybe come with a small delay.

5
Global Governance Networks for Climate Change and Energy Investments

FRÉDÉRIC GILLES SOURGENS

As earlier chapters have already amply shown, it is impossible to consider 'decarbonisation' without also considering 'climate change'. The terms 'decarbonisation' and 'climate change' are flip sides of the same coin: anthropogenic climate change is driven by the emission of greenhouse gases (GHGs).[1] Far and away the most important GHG is carbon dioxide (CO_2).[2] In fact, when policymakers address GHG in general, they do so in a measure that reflects the relative importance of CO_2 – the measure of atmospheric GHGs emissions is a volume expressed in the newly created unit or 'carbon dioxide equivalent' or CO_{2e}.[3]

The equation of slowing climate change is maddeningly simple. It requires a net reduction of CO_{2e} emissions to zero. This can be achieved in one of two ways. First, it is possible to reduce or 'mitigate' CO_{2e} emissions themselves.[4] Second, and somewhat more complicatedly, it is also possible to increase GHG sinks that naturally (or not so naturally) remove GHGs from the atmosphere. Chapter three highlights the various technological options developed to increase sinks – that is the technology to optimise Carbon Capture Utilisation and Storage (CCUS).[5] When CO_{2e} emitted minus CO_{2e} removed by means of sinks equals less than zero, we are slowing climate change.

---

[1] Intergovernmental Panel on Climate Change (IPCC), 'Special Report, Global Warming of 1.5⁰ C' (2019) ('IPCC 2019') at 59, www.ipcc.ch/site/assets/uploads/sites/2/2019/05/SR15_Chapter1_Low_Res.pdf.
[2] *Ibid* at 54.
[3] 'What are CO_2e and Global Warming Potential (GWP)?' *The Guardian*, 27 April 2011, www.theguardian.com/environment/2011/apr/27/co2e-global-warming-potential.
[4] See Daniel Bodansky, 'The United Nations Framework Convention on Climate Change: A Commentary' (1993) 18 *Yale Journal of International Law* 451, 533–34.
[5] See chapter 4; see also Frédéric G Sourgens, 'Geo-Markets' (forthcoming, June 2020) 38 *Virginia Environmental Law Journal*.

The equation to halting or reversing climate change is only slightly more complicated. Climate change is not only an emissions problem. It is a 'stock problem' – that is GHGs contribute to climate change so long as they are in the atmosphere.[6] Some GHGs like methane have a relatively short atmospheric lifespan.[7] But others – most centrally CO_2 – have a very long atmospheric lifespan.[8] To halt climate change therefore not only requires halting the 'flow' of emissions, but also requires one to return to what is deemed an acceptable CO_{2e} concentration.[9] This means that it will be necessary to continue operating at a net negative carbon flow for a period of time equivalent to the target CO_{2e} stock reduction to effectively halt and reverse climate change.[10]

As maddeningly simple the equations outlined in the last two paragraphs appear to be, designing and implementing the policies that can make these equations work is anything but. In the first place, no one actor, no matter how powerful, can balance the CO_{2e} equation alone.[11] It takes a concerted international effort to do this.[12] What is more, balancing the equation likely requires a massive overhaul of energy infrastructures on a global scale. Such an effort is very expensive – or 'highly capital intensive' to use jargon.[13] To combat climate change, that is to decarbonise the energy industry, is only possible through massive energy investments on a global scale. How, then, should the process of combating climate change be governed?

This chapter submits that the very task of decarbonisation governance cannot be monolithic. It cannot look to a single actor to bring about the desired result. It is instead made up of interweaving, intercommunicating and frequently competing governance networks.[14] This chapter outlines what governance networks are involved in the decarbonisation process. The chapter further explains how these networks interact with each other so as to (hopefully) balance the maddeningly simple carbon equation of less out than in.

---

[6] Daniel Bodansky, Jutta Brunée and Lavanya Rajamani, *International Climate Change Law* (Oxford University Press, 2017) 125.
[7] IPCC 2019 (n 1) at 64.
[8] IPCC 2019 (n 1) at 51.
[9] Bodansky et al (n 6) at 125.
[10] For full discussion, see Sourgens (n 5).
[11] United Nations Framework Convention on Climate Change (UNFCCC), 'Fact Sheet: The Need for Strong Global Action on Climate Change' (November 2010), https://unfccc.int/files/press/fact_sheets/application/pdf/fact_sheet_climate_deal.pdf.
[12] *Ibid*.
[13] Jake Frankenfield, 'Capital Intensive' (*Investopedia*, 12 August 2019), www.investopedia.com/terms/c/capitalintensive.asp; see also London School of Economics, 'How Much Will It Cost to Cut Global Greenhouse Gas Emissions?' (*LSE*, 8 May 2018), www.lse.ac.uk/GranthamInstitute/faqs/how-much-will-it-cost-to-cut-global-greenhouse-gas-emissions/.
[14] For a full discussion of governance networks in the climate context, see Frédéric G Sourgens, 'The Paris Paradigm' (2019) *University of Illinois Law Review* 1637, 1641–43; see also Anne Marie Slaughter, 'The Paris Approach to Global Governance' (*Project Syndicate*, 28 December 2015), https://scholar.princeton.edu/sites/default/files/slaughter/files/projectsyndicate12.28.2015.pdf.

I. But First, History

When most lawyers and lay people think of climate change governance, they typically default to considering diplomatic conferences. To younger lawyers, this understanding of climate change governance perhaps evokes the pictures of an exuberant throng of delegates celebrating together in Paris at the conclusion of the 2015 Paris Agreement.[15] To more experienced lawyers, it might be pictures from the 1992 Earth Summit in Rio de Janeiro and the opening for signature of the United Nations Framework Convention on Climate Change (UNFCCC) that anchor this understanding of climate change governance.[16]

This common perception of how governance processes came about – or what makes them tick – is frequently historically inaccurate. This inaccuracy typically is the result of a kind of hindsight bias. We have a certain view of how climate change governance works because we had the Paris Agreement and the Rio Summit, the UNFCCC and its Kyoto Protocol. But the fact that diplomatic conferences ultimately negotiated these framework agreements does not mean that these framework agreements began as governmental priorities or as foreign policy initiatives. To view them exclusively in this light therefore is to make an important mistake in understanding the organic nature of how climate governance came into being in the first place – and what currents continue to shape it today beneath the choppy seas of head of state diplomacy.[17]

Climate change initiatives were first and foremost the brain child of scientists.[18] A group of scientists sought to draw attention to the problem of climate change in the late 1980s.[19] At that time, scientists first began to understand the complex processes of manmade climate change – the effect of rising CO_{2e} emissions on the energy budget.[20] These scientists did not yet, however, have much political traction.[21] They operated at the outskirts of ordinary domestic policy processes, engaging instead other scientists and, with the help of the press, civil society at large.[22]

In fact, it took the successful scientific press campaign to make the world aware of the depletion of the ozone layer to get traction for climate change policies.[23] Similar networks of scientists to those working on global warming had warned of

---

[15] Coral Davenport, 'Nations Approve Landmark Climate Accord in Paris' *The New York Times*, 12 December 2015, www.nytimes.com/2015/12/13/world/europe/climate-change-accord-paris.html.
[16] Bodansky (n 4).
[17] For a discussion of the early development of climate change law, see Bodansky et al (n 6) at 96–102. For a discussion of current broader trends in climate change law, see Frédéric G Sourgens, 'States of Resistance' (2019) 14 *Duke Journal of Constitutional Law & Public Policy* 91.
[18] Bodansky et al (n 6) at 96–102.
[19] Bodansky et al (n 6) at 96–102.
[20] Bodansky et al (n 6) at 96–102.
[21] Bodansky et al (n 6) at 96–102.
[22] Philippe Sands and Jacqueline Peel, *Principles of International Environmental Law*, 4th edn (Cambridge University Press, 2018) 276–77.
[23] *Ibid.*

the risks of the depletion of the ozone layer.[24] They managed to communicate their findings that human emissions were responsible for a dramatic shrinking of the ozone layer with great effect – in part because they were able to conjure horrors of what would happen if the problem continued on unaddressed.[25] With mounting popular pressure, the issue became a pressing diplomatic issue, leading to the conclusion of two treaties, the 1985 Vienna Convention and the 1987 Montreal Protocol.[26] These treaties were wildly successful at reducing ozone depleting emissions and thus restoring the ozone layer.[27]

It was this success which permitted scientists to press on and include climate change on the broader diplomatic agenda. The key questions of where climate change policy originated, who shaped the early discussions, and how we got to where we are today thus does not point back to the room full of diplomatic delegates. It points in quite a different direction. It highlights the contributions of members of the scientific community, the press and civic society. It also casts the heads of state and government we associate with climate change negotiations distinctly in the role of historical followers, rather than historical leaders.

It is of course important not to overstate the point. The core multilateral climate change conventions are of tremendous importance for the global governance of climate change and (carbon-neutral or carbon-negative) energy investments. They in fact will take pride of place in anchoring the discussions of global governance networks in the next section. History just reminds us to be careful not to over-read their importance as more than first among equals – and not to view them as causes but rather as symptoms of larger constitutive processes of global climate governance that are on the whole more complex than even the Byzantine diplomatic conferences that gave us the Paris Agreement.

II. The Constitutive Processes of Decarbonisation Governance

The global governance of climate change and energy investment – or decarbonisation – is a process. The choice of 'governance' to describe the management of global decarbonisation already implies as much. As one commentator recently put it, 'whatever definition of governance we take, it centres on the idea of what we may loosely indicate as "shaping the market and society [and science ...] into a desired form".[28] Such 'shaping' is continuous engagement

---

[24] Bodansky et al (n 6) at 98.
[25] Bodansky et al (n 6) at 98.
[26] Sands & Peel (n 22) at 276–90.
[27] Sands & Peel (n 22) at 276–90.
[28] John Grin, 'Reflexive Modernization as a Governance Issue, or: Designing and Shaping Re-structuration' in Jan-Peter Voss et al (eds), *Reflexive Governance for Sustainable Development* (Edward Elgar, 2006) 57.

to bring about a particular result – decarbonisation. The first step therefore is to understand the features that render decarbonisation not the accidental result of 'occasional choices, but as a *continuous process* of authoritative decision, both maintaining the constitutive features by which it is established and projecting a flow of public order decisions [specific regulations] for the shaping and sharing of community values'.[29]

This section seeks to set out the core features of this process. It tries to identify the players involved, the values which they seek to implement, and the manner in which they implement these values into specific rules and regulations. As this section will show, one of the key features of decarbonisation governance is that it is not subject to a single such formal process, but sits between different, overlapping processes each of which interact with the others in a myriad of ways.

A. The Climate Process

Despite the observation that one must view climate diplomatic conferences in context, the climate process remains far and away the most visible and the most important process when considering climate change governance. This process took definitive shape with the Rio de Janeiro Earth Summit.[30] The Rio de Janeiro Earth Summit took place in 1992 under the auspices of the United Nations, with the official name of the United Nations Conference on Environment and Development.[31]

One of the central treaties opened for signature at the Rio Summit was the United Nations Framework Convention on Climate Change, or UNFCCC.[32] The UNFCCC, as the name already suggests, sets the principle framework for the community of states to respond to climate change.[33] Article 2 states the overall goal of the UNFCCC, 'stabilization of greenhouse gas concentrations in the atmosphere at a level that would prevent dangerous anthropogenic interference with the climate system'.[34] The UNFCCC did not on its face agree to any substantive binding commitments.[35] Rather, it established certain principles and procedures that would guide future commitments to address climate change.[36]

Despite the lack of substantive climate mitigation commitments, the UNFCCC made three early and defining contributions to global climate change governance.

---

[29] W Michael Reisman, Siegfried Wiessner and Andrew Willard, 'The New Haven School: A Brief Introduction' (2007) 32 *Yale Journal of International Law* 575, 580.
[30] Benoit Mayer, *The International Law on Climate Change* (Cambridge University Press, 2018) 33–37.
[31] Bodansky et al (n 6) at 100–101.
[32] Bodansky et al (n 6) at 100–101.
[33] Bodansky et al (n 6) at 100–101.
[34] UN Framework Convention on Climate Change (UNFCCC), Art 2, 9 May 1992, S Treaty Doc No 102-38, 1771 U.N.T.S. 165, 166, 170.
[35] Bodansky et al (n 6) at 104–105.
[36] Bodansky et al (n 6) at 104–105.

First, it set out that climate change was itself a central global governance problem in need of robust action.[37] This step in its own right created an independent climate discourse. This independent climate discourse remained closely tied to the broader environmental discourse encapsulated by the Rio Declaration.[38] But it also gained a certain form of legal independence as a separate and independent problem for global action.[39]

Second, the UNFCCC drew 143 UN Member States to the final negotiating session.[40] This underscores the global nature of the climate change problem. There are no 'persistent objectors' to climate change.[41] Rather, the universal adoption of the UNFCCC signals that the entire international community is in fact united in seeing climate change as a global and existential threat for mankind. The UNFCCC thus obviates any need to ask whether global climate governance is necessary, etc. For 20 years, there has been universal global agreement that it is.

Third, the UNFCCC created the procedural framework in which future global climate change governance would principally be developed. Most importantly, it set up a process of regular, high level meetings known as the Conference of the Parties.[42] This Conference of the Parties mechanism is at the centre of global climate change governance today.[43] The UNFCCC also set up a secretariat to guide those deliberations.[44] Finally, the UNFCCC mandated that this secretariat would cooperate closely with one of the leading scientific bodies involved in global climate change governance, and discussed in its own right below, the Intergovernmental Panel on Climate Change.[45]

i. Rio – The Conflicting Values of Decarbonisation

To understand the current impasses and opportunities in decarbonisation governance, it is first important to understand the underlying values which the governance process seeks to implement. A key issue informing decarbonisation governance is that it is in fact driven by attempts to balance fundamentally inconsistent values. This inconsistency is at the heart of many of the political and global governance debates surrounding decarbonisation to this day. The values informing decarbonisation efforts through at least 2009 – and arguably through today – were set

---

[37] Sands & Peel (n 22) at 299–300.
[38] Sands & Peel (n 22) at 299–300.
[39] For that reason, climate change is treated separately from atmospheric protection in the Sands and Peel's standard work on international environmental law. Sands & Peel (n 22) at 253.
[40] Sands & Peel (n 22) at 299.
[41] For a discussion of this issue in the development of customary international law on climate change, see Frédéric G Sourgens, 'Climate Commons Law: The Transformative Force of the Paris Agreement' (2017) 50 *New York University Journal of International Law and Politics* 885, 974–76.
[42] UNFCCC (n 34) at Art 2.
[43] UNFCCC (n 34) at Art 7.
[44] UNFCCC (n 34) at Art 8. The secretariat at first was an interim secretariat.
[45] UNFCCC (n 34) at Art 21(2).

out at Rio.⁴⁶ The Rio de Janeiro Earth Summit concluded with a declaration of 27 principles, known as the Rio Declaration.⁴⁷ Many, if not all of these principles, continue to shape climate governance.

These principles can be grouped into three sets of potentially conflicting values. Central to decarbonisation, the Rio Declaration placed a significant emphasis on environmental protection. Centrally:

- Principle 4: Sustainable development mandates environmental protection as an integral part of economic policy;⁴⁸
- Principle 11: A duty for states to 'enact effective environmental legislation';⁴⁹
- Principle 15: The precautionary principle requiring that in the face of threats of serious or irreversible damage, lack of full scientific certainty shall not be used as a reason for postponing cost-effective measures to prevent environmental degradation.⁵⁰

In direct conflict with these principles, the Rio Declaration also insisted on developmental goals. Principle 2 insisted upon the sovereignty of each state to exploit resources and promulgate environmental regulation is limited by the obligation not to cause transboundary harm.⁵¹ Principle 5 codified a duty to cooperate towards the eradication of poverty.⁵² These principles pull in the opposite direction of decarbonisation – the insistence on sovereign rights to exploit resources developed predominantly in the oil and gas context.⁵³ Similarly, the eradication of poverty depends, in part at least, upon industrialisation driven by cheap energy.⁵⁴ Both of those principles thus create a value conflict with the environmental values expressed in principles 4, 11, and 15 to be managed by decarbonisation processes.

Finally, the Rio Declaration also included a principle seeking to address thorny issues of responsibility. It included as Principle 16 that 'the polluter should, in principle, bear the cost of pollution, with due regard to the public interest and without distorting international trade and investment'.⁵⁵ Potentially more controversially still, it sought to apply this principle to industrialised nations in the climate change context.⁵⁶ Principle 7 states that the duties of states are 'differentiated'.⁵⁷ Countries which had not yet fully industrialised at the signing

---

⁴⁶ Sands & Peel (n 22) at 41–43.
⁴⁷ Conference on Environment and Development, Rio Declaration on Environment and Development, A/CONF.151/26 (Vol 1) (12 August 1992) ('Rio Declaration').
⁴⁸ *Ibid* at Principle 4.
⁴⁹ *Ibid* at Principle 11.
⁵⁰ *Ibid* at Principle 15.
⁵¹ *Ibid* at Principle 2.
⁵² *Ibid* at Principle 5.
⁵³ See Sands & Peel (n 22) at 41.
⁵⁴ See Sands & Peel (n 22) at 41.
⁵⁵ Rio Declaration (n 47) at Principle 16.
⁵⁶ Mayer (n 30) at 74–75.
⁵⁷ Rio Declaration (n 47) at Principle 7.

of the UNFCCC insisted that it was the industrialisation by the global North, which was principally to blame for climate change.[58] They thus insisted that it was the obligation of these states, and these states alone, to fix the problem – and pay for their GHG pollution. Industrialised states, naturally enough, disagreed with this interpretation but were willing to concede that pre-industrialised states would be less able to address climate change and therefore would be exempted from responsibility for doing so.[59] In a rushed effort, the UNFCCC therefore put states into three categories to give effect to Rio Principle 7: Annex I countries with mitigation obligations; as well as Annex II parties with additional financial obligations;[60] and countries not listed on either Annex I or II that did not have any such obligations.[61]

The Rio Declaration sought to overcome this value conflict by imposing procedural obligations. These procedural obligations required states to cooperate 'to strengthen endogenous capacity-building for sustainable development by improving scientific understanding through exchanges of scientific and technological knowledge, and by enhancing the development, adaptation, diffusion and transfer of technologies, including new and innovative technologies'.[62] Further, and centrally, the Rio Declaration closes with a duty of states *and people* to cooperate in good faith and in a spirit of partnership.[63] It is this process of cooperation and exchange that it was hoped would overcome the inherent inconsistencies in value set out in the Rio Declaration and incorporated in the UNFCCC.

ii. *The Conference of the Parties (COP) Process*

The UNFCCC set up one of the central governance processes that still shapes climate governance today – the Conference of the Parties, or COP process, to implement Rio Principle 27.[64] This COP process is akin to a traditional diplomatic conference.[65] It brings together high-level representatives from all UNFCCC parties.[66] These high-level representatives frequently include heads of state, heads of government, or both, thus underscoring the global governance importance.[67]

The COP process sadly suffers from many of the governance drawbacks that come with international diplomatic conferences.[68] First, diplomatic conferences

---

[58] Bodansky et al (n 6) at 127–28. The discussion typically takes place in the context of the concept of common but differentiated responsibility.
[59] See Bodansky et al (n 6) at 127–28.
[60] UNFCCC (n 34) at Arts 4(2), 4(3).
[61] Bodansky et al (n 6) at 130.
[62] Rio Declaration (n 47) at Principle 9.
[63] Rio Declaration (n 47) at Principle 27.
[64] UNFCCC (n 34) at Art 7.
[65] See UNFCCC (n 34) at Art 7.
[66] Harold H Koh, 'Triptych's End: A Better Framework To Evaluate 21st Century International Lawmaking' (2017) 126 *Yale Law Journal Forum* 338.
[67] *Ibid* at 360.
[68] See Leila Nadya Sadat, 'Crimes Against Humanity in the Modern Age' (2013) 107 *American Journal of International Law* 334, 352 (discussing the functioning of diplomatic conferences).

are hard to move.[69] They are not staffed by expert administrators with a common interest in solving a shared problem.[70] They are instead staffed by diplomats seeking to advance broader diplomatic objectives.[71]

The UNFCCC process is particularly hard to move as it operates effectively by consensus. The COP was supposed to set its own rules of voting procedure at the first meeting.[72] It however failed to be able to do so.[73] It thus was 'stuck' to operating under the preliminary rules of procedure requiring decision by consensus.[74] Such a consensus is notoriously difficult to build, particularly in the context of diplomacy that, even if it is guided only by the Rio principles rather than extraneous geo-political concerns, is still subject to inconsistent value commitments as outlined in the last section.

Second, diplomatic conferences respond to traditional diplomatic pressures that may be unrelated to the subject matter of the diplomatic conference itself. Thus, diplomatic conferences are frequently subject to extraneous geo-political concerns rather than just the goal of finding the 'best' solution to the problem set for the diplomatic conference.[75] Who emerges as a 'leader' and who is in which camp decidedly matters in conference diplomacy.

The UNFCCC process in its infancy has played host to several exchanges that mirror traditional north-south dynamics. For example, the questions of differentiation and responsibility have shaped discussions at COPs in the past.[76] Some of these exchanges continued debates from other fora that had reasonably little to do with the UNFCCC process.[77] And finally, diplomatic conferences hold on to diplomatic victories won at earlier conferences with an unrivaled tenacity, creating roadblocks to needed reform. Again, differentiation is a key example of this phenomenon at the UNFCCC.[78] The Annexes created as part of the UNFCCC to distinguish between parties with mitigation responsibilities and those without such responsibilities were in principle intended to be open to change. Yet, diplomatic practice has prevented such change.[79] Even when Kazakhstan sought to move from the status of a 'developing state' and voluntarily assume responsibility for climate change mitigation, it was prevented from doing so.[80] The concern

---

[69] See *ibid*.
[70] See Timothy Meyer, 'From Contract to Legislation: The Logic of Modern Lawmaking' (2014) 14 *Chicago Journal of International Law* 559, 568–69.
[71] See *ibid* (noting also that legal expertise may at times be consulted by these diplomats).
[72] UNFCCC (n 34) at Art 7(3).
[73] Bodansky et al (n 6) at 143.
[74] Bodansky et al (n 6) at 143.
[75] For a discussion of such geo-politics in climate negotiations, see Nick Mabey, 'The Geo-Politics of the Paris Talks, The Web of Alliances Behind the Climate Deal' (*Foreign Affairs*, 13 December 2015), www.foreignaffairs.com/articles/2015-12-13/geopolitics-paris-talks.
[76] Mayer (n 30) at 37.
[77] Jack Schick, 'Climate Diplomacy: A Mismatch between Science and Politics' (2018) *SAIS Review of International Affairs*, www.saisreview.org/2018/11/12/climate-diplomacy-a-mismatch-between-science-and-politics/.
[78] UNFCCC (n 34) at Arts 3(1), 4(2), 4(3).
[79] Bodansky et al (n 6) at 123.
[80] Bodansky et al (n 6) at 123.

was that any such move would be inconsistent with the broader fault lines drawn by industrialising states regarding the responsibility of industrialised nations for climate change.[81] It would instead suggest that differentiation was a developmental (as opposed to a responsibility-based) criterion. On that basis, Kazakhstan was prevented from voluntarily assuming international climate change mitigation obligations – something that is clearly at odds with the overall decarbonisation objectives of the UNFCCC.[82]

On the flipside, the COP process also has the key governance advantages of a traditional conference of the parties. The high-level governmental participation by such a large number of states endows the agreements reached by COPs with a unique kind of authority.[83] Due to the fact that such high-level stakeholders have jointly agreed on a course of action, the decisions of a COP typically benefit from significant political advantages both domestically and internationally. Domestically, a COP decision indicates the highest level of policy priority given the involvement of the highest ranking government officials in their promulgation. As these high-level officials frequently have to give personal assurances to achieve agreement, they are likely invested in the domestic implementation of the compromises so brokered. This provides COP decisions with significant staying power.[84]

At the international level, similarly, the fact that a critical mass of high-level government officials have agreed on a decision by consensus provides the decision with a kind of diplomatic (if not always legal) imprimatur.[85] That is to say, even when those decisions are pronouncement of principle rather than the development of a legally binding rule, the fact that the principle was adopted by consensus at the highest level of state will make deviating from these principles a diplomatic nightmare. The principles agreed upon at COPs are therefore part of the authoritative language of diplomatic praise and rebuke driving the ordinary course of affairs of state.

iii. The Kyoto Setback

Climate governance took a significant setback during the negotiations of what was supposedly a crowning achievement of the international community in the fight against climate change – the Kyoto Protocol.[86] The Kyoto Protocol sought to negotiate firm GHG mitigation obligations and then provide a robust mechanism to secure compliance with these obligations.[87] This approach, had

---

[81] Bodansky et al (n 6) at 123.
[82] Bodansky et al (n 6) at 123.
[83] Koh (n 66).
[84] Koh (n 66).
[85] Koh (n 66).
[86] Kyoto Protocol to the United Nations Framework Convention on Climate Change, 10 December 1997, 37 I.L.M. 22 (1998) ('Kyoto Protocol').
[87] Bodansky et al (n 6) at 150.

it fully succeeded, would have created a close to uniform global administration of climate change response processes in the institutions created by the Kyoto Protocol under the auspices of the UNFCCC. Had the Kyoto Protocol succeeded, in other words, this chapter would be devoted to detailing the functioning of the Kyoto machinery.

The Kyoto Protocol in fact did create an impressive array of mechanisms to secure compliance with the negotiated GHG mitigation obligations mandated by the agreement.[88] The Kyoto Protocol set up mechanisms for states transparently to estimate and report their emissions.[89] The Kyoto Protocol further set up a market mechanism and a mechanism to achieve additional GHG emission reductions in third states where reductions could more efficiently be achieved.[90] The Kyoto Protocol further set up two different compliance mechanisms, a Facilitative Branch and an Enforcement Branch to assist states in complying with their obligations to the extent that a failure to comply looked likely and to impose sanctions on states by excluding them from the market mechanisms should they in fact fail to meet their targets.[91]

This Kyoto machinery was, however, stillborn. The reasons for the failure of the Kyoto approach can be debated and are debated. The indication by the United States Senate in a unanimous resolution that it would not ratify the Kyoto Protocol because of its commitment to the principle of differentiation was a serious blow.[92] One might further argue that the top down approach adopted by Kyoto is inimical to state diplomatic behaviour to the point that even a grudging US participation may not have saved the agreement. Finally, one might submit that a top down approach with such deep repercussions for the respective economies of even developed countries would become politically untenable over the long haul as the Kyoto process itself would lack democratic legitimacy and yet have a close to dispositive hand in economic development policies by controlling energy generation and energy markets.

Each of these factors doubtlessly contributed to the failure of the Kyoto mechanism to become the blueprint for a scaled global response to climate change. While much of the global North continued to participate in the Kyoto Protocol following the withdrawal of the United States, this commitment never reached the critical mass needed to change the trajectory of climate change. In fact, Canada, when faced with the potential for a finding of non-compliance, left the Protocol.[93]

---

[88] Bodansky et al (n 6) at 160–208.
[89] Kyoto Protocol (n 86) at Arts 5, 7.
[90] Kyoto Protocol (n 86) at Art 17.
[91] Kyoto Protocol (n 86) at Art 18. For a discussion of the dispute resolution mechanism, see Sands & Peel (n 22) at 173–76.
[92] See Cass R Sunstein, 'Of Montreal and Kyoto: A Tale of Two Protocols' (2008) 38 *Environmental Law Reporter News & Analysis* 10566, 10568.
[93] 'Canada Pulls out of Kyoto Protocol' *The Guardian*, 12 December 2011), www.theguardian.com/environment/2011/dec/13/canada-pulls-out-kyoto-protocol.

It thus became a reasonably toothless mechanism – it never built up the needed political capital to move the world energy markets towards decarbonisation.

iv. The Copenhagen Shift

The failure of the Kyoto model overlapped with the tenure of George W Bush as US President. Under President Bush's leadership, the United States Federal Government was a detractor from serious climate change efforts.[94] The period in question therefore was an ill-timed and ironic ice age for climate diplomacy, moving at a glacial pace when the climate change it was supposed to regulate was picking up an alarming rate of speed with the roaring industrialisation in China on the heels of economic globalisation.[95]

To say that the world community therefore set high hopes in a renewed vigour for climate diplomacy following the election of President Barak Obama is an understatement.[96] The 2009 UNFCCC COP meeting to take place in Copenhagen was billed as the last clear change to avoid the catastrophic effects of climate change.[97] Decarbonisation, the scientific community warned, would be successful only if the world acted immediately, having lost almost a decade to political inaction.[98]

The Copenhagen COP proved to be one of the most enigmatic events in climate diplomacy. On its face, the meeting was a colossal failure.[99] The UNFCCC parties could reach no legally binding agreement, at all.[100] In fact, it even rejected the non-binding political accord brokered at the last minute by President Obama in an attempt to save face and live to fight another day.[101] From a contemporaneous perspective, the Copenhagen COP, without hyperbole, looked like the end of the world.[102]

---

[94] Clive Hamilton, *Earthmasters, The Dawn of the Age of Climate Engineering* (Yale University Press, 2013) 87.

[95] See Bodansky et al (n 6) at 161 (discussing the slow pace of climate change law in the Bush administration); see also Climate Change Tracker, 'Country Summary China' (2 December 2019) https://climateactiontracker.org/countries/china/ (showing an increase from 5000 $MtCO_2e$/a to 10920 from 2000 to 2010).

[96] Suzanne Goldenberg, 'Obama's Arrival Expected to Inject Fresh Momentum into Copenhagen Talks' *The Guardian*, 17 December 2009, www.theguardian.com/environment/2009/dec/17/barack-obama-copenhagen-hillary-clinton.

[97] See Douglas Fischer, 'What Would Failure at Copenhagen Mean for Climate Change?' (*Scientific American*, 10 November 2009), www.scientificamerican.com/article/copenhagen-climate-talks-consequences/. (Copenhagen 'talks are, in other words, the last, best chance to change course before chaos descends.')

[98] *Ibid*.

[99] John Vidal et al, 'Low Targets, Goals Dropped: Copenhagen Ends in Failure' *The Guardian*, 18 December 2009, www.theguardian.com/environment/2009/dec/18/copenhagen-deal.

[100] Bodansky et al (n 6) at 110.

[101] Bodansky et al (n 6) at 112 (the COP only took note of the Accord as opposed to endorsing or adopting it).

[102] See Hamilton (n 94) at 8–9.

And yet, with the benefit of a decade's worth of hindsight, the Copenhagen COP revolutionised and reinvigorated climate governance by creating the global climate governance networks. The reason for this success is that the political Copenhagen Accord brokered by President Obama proved to have been more than an apparent face-saving measure. It completely changed the dynamic of climate governance.[103]

The first and most important substantive success of the Copenhagen Accord significantly weakened the principle of differentiation.[104] The principle of differentiation as it was applied in the context of the Kyoto Protocol would have exempted the rapidly industrialising states like China and India from responsibility for climate change mitigation. This would have made it close to impossible to fashion a credible climate change policy.

This substantive change had significant procedural repercussions. The most important of these repercussions is the role of China in climate diplomacy. In the pre-Copenhagen paradigm of differentiation, China would have had no role in decarbonisation. As it is not an Annex I or II party to the UNFCCC, it was exempted from decarbonisation obligations.[105] And a voluntary move to Annex I or II for most of the states not included in Annexes I and II was out of the question for the reasons discussed above.[106] The Copenhagen Accord opened the door to Chinese leadership without the double-edged sword of differentiation.[107] From the vantage point of the second year of Donald Trump's presidency, this change was hugely impactful: it opened the door for China to take on a leadership role in climate change at a time of US hesitation – though it is a door that China has not embraced walking through to date.[108]

Second, the Copenhagen Accord also set the stage for a move away from classic COP diplomacy. It put climate governance on the path to networked, coordinative governance outside of the traditional scope of international governmental organisations governed by multilateral treaties.[109] It chose a softer governance approach that intended to build upon mutual reliance and trust building between states as they faced the daunting challenges of climate change mitigation and adaptation together.[110] This governance approach was by definition bottom up, 'soft' in the

---

[103] Bodansky et al (n 6) at 111; Koh (n 66).
[104] See Copenhagen Accord ¶ 5, Copenhagen Accord (18 December 2009) in UNFCCC, Report of the Conference of the Parties on Its Fifteenth Session, Addendum, UN Doc FCCC/CP/2009/L.7 (18 December 2009), https://unfccc.int/resource/docs/2009/cop15/eng/l07.pdf at 5 ('Non-Annex I Parties to the Convention will implement mitigation actions'). For a fuller discussion of the Copenhagen Accord, see Daniel Bodansky, 'The Copenhagen Climate Change Conference: A Postmortem' (2010) 104 *American Journal of International Law* 230.
[105] See UNFCCC (n 34) at Annex I, II; China UNFCCC Status, https://unfccc.int/node/180417.
[106] Bodansky et al (n 6) at 123.
[107] On this shift in Chinese assertiveness at Copenhagen in particular, see Bodansky et al (n 6) at 110.
[108] See Matt McGrath, 'Climate Change: China Coal Surge Threatens Paris Targets' (*BBC*, 20 November 2019), www.bbc.com/news/science-environment-50474824.
[109] For a discussion of this change in governance approach after Copenhagen, see Koh (n 66).
[110] Koh (n 66).

sense of avoiding the structured commands of a multilateral regime, and inclusive of all manner of actors on the international stage including sub-national governments and non-state actors.[111]

Copenhagen therefore completely changed the trajectory of decarbonisation. It thus ended up meeting the moment in bringing a new governance approach to climate change that could replace the stagnating Kyoto mechanism. Whether it ended up mastering the challenge of decarbonisation remains to be seen. The largest deficit of the Copenhagen approach is that the organic growth of governance networks takes time. While it has the potential to deliver far more meaningful results by leveraging full internalisation of shared goals, it does so at an initially slower pace than traditional diplomatic conferences. In light of the potential for climate tipping points in the near future, the question will remain whether the Copenhagen approach was indeed the right tool to use to re-launch the climate governance process on its new trajectory.

v. The Paris Paradigm

The Paris Agreement of 2015 arguably fully implemented the governance shift, which was first sketched out at Copenhagen.[112] It agrees on a clear target of '[h]olding the increase in the global average temperature to well below 2°C above pre-industrial levels and pursuing efforts to limit the temperature increase to 1.5°C above pre-industrial levels'.[113] It further significantly weakens the concept of differentiation so as to remove it as an obstacle to truly global action to address climate change in line with the Copenhagen shift.[114]

The Paris Agreement is a master study in network-building and leveraging of international regulatory coordination. This master study relied upon the inverse of the Kyoto Protocol approach in two important respects. First, the Paris Agreement champions a radical bottom up rather than top down approach.[115] This bottom up approach asks each Paris Agreement Member State to make nationally determined contributions that the Member State independently set.[116] The nationally determined contribution is not a negotiated commitment that is bargained for and in exchange for the commitment of other Member States.[117] Rather, the nationally determined contribution reflects the domestically achievable level of ambition to mitigate climate change.[118] It thus seeks to harness the authority

---

[111] Koh (n 66).
[112] Paris Agreement (13 December 2015) in UNFCCC, Rep. of the Conference of the Parties on its Twenty-First Session, UN Doc FCCC/CP/2015/10/Add.1 (29 January 2016) Addendum at 21 ('Paris Agreement').
[113] Ibid at Art 2(1)(a).
[114] Ibid at Arts 4(2),(3).
[115] Bodansky et al (n 6) at 231.
[116] Paris Agreement (n 112) at Art 4(2).
[117] Paris Agreement (n 112) at Art 4(2).
[118] Paris Agreement (n 112) at Art 4(2).

lent to domestic regulatory action that is not subject to the legitimacy deficits of international interventions in the core functions of domestic economies.[119]

Second, the Paris Agreement's bottom up approach does not even make the nationally determined contributions communicated by Member States binding on those Member States as a matter of the Paris Agreement itself.[120] The Paris Agreement therefore leaves compliance with the nationally determined contributions, and the mechanisms a state wants to make available to secure compliance, to that state itself. In other words, the Paris Agreement steps back from any form of a multilateral command energy economy. It rather gives ample room for organic growth of networked coordination through exchange and trust built through mutual compliance with nationally determined contributions as the way to answer climate change.

The Paris paradigm is a master class in network-building because it makes a conscious bet on the power of reliance and path dependence cemented by reliance. Symptomatically for this approach, the United States sought to coordinate the communication of its nationally determined contribution with important partners in fighting climate change.[121] The United States' intended nationally determined contribution included its full throated commitment to the Clean Power Plan – an initiative aimed at significantly decarbonising electricity generation in the United States by requiring states effectively to move inefficient coal-fired powerplants from the grid and replace them with low emission and alternative energy generation capacity.[122] It further included flaring and methane capture rules for oil and gas development to address non-carbon dioxide (CO_2) GHG.[123] The United States and China exchanged their intended nationally determined contribution prior to their ultimate release.[124] The United States and Canada likewise coordinated their policy initiatives.[125] This coordination is not just a trust-building exercise. It is a tool to shape engagement and heighten ambition, as well as consult on available policy toolkits to improve mitigation techniques.[126]

The Paris paradigm further sets the climate governance network on a distinct path by two related strategies. First, it creates increased opportunities for engagement and exchange of data.[127] This exchange both forces transparency and creates synergies across regulatory agencies. These agencies are now more likely to network with each other to increase their respective efficiencies in achieving

---

[119] For a full discussion, see Sourgens (n 14).
[120] Bodansky et al (n 6) at 231.
[121] See, eg, Joint Statement, 'The White House, U.S.-China Joint Announcement on Climate Change' (11 November 2014).
[122] *Ibid.*
[123] *Ibid.*
[124] *Ibid.*
[125] National Archives, 'Joint Statement by President Obama and Prime Minister Justin P.J. Trudeau of Canada on Climate, Energy, and Arctic Leadership' (Daily Compilation of Presidential Documents, 10 March 2016).
[126] For a full discussion, see Sourgens (n 41) at 928–44.
[127] See, eg, Paris Agreement (n 112) at Arts 4(12), 9(5), 14.

firmly shared goals as evidenced by shared and transparently communicated data. Second, the Paris paradigm in one of the few mandatory provisions of the Paris Agreement requires increased ambition once a party has set out on a mitigation path.[128] This, too, creates the institutional conditions to further coordinate across international agencies to find ways to copy or jointly design mitigation responses.

One might be excused for thinking that the Paris paradigm and its strategic use of reliance follows the classic soft law governance playbook. Eyal Benvenisti points out that this playbook frequently relies upon networking and informal standard setting that then is implemented on the back of regulatory coordination, public and private market access restrictions and private 'voluntary' standard-setting required to be adhered to by all market leaders.[129] Such structures, Professor Benvenisti points out, are at the heart of global governance techniques of the global elite to maintain maximum control over policy processes all the while leveraging optimum global compliance and outcomes.[130] Professor Benvenisti does not make this observation from a perspective of decrying current global governance models – governance, he submits, is needed. Yet, he does point out that this global governance model comes with significant design imperfections for affected parties not sufficiently represented in 'the room where it happens'.[131]

However, it is also possible to take a slightly less suspicious perspective of the Paris paradigm. This perspective looks not to the governance aspect of the current network but to its legal consequences. Reliance has legal significance even when it is the result of unilateral state action – or more precisely, state action that is not bargained for and in exchange but seeks to induce action or forbearance through leading by example.[132] Such reliance creates international legal obligations for the states that induced it to come through in the law of unilateral acts.[133] Premised on the principle of good faith, this part of international law requires states to follow through on commitments made in a public forum with the intent to induce reliance if such reliance either was or could reasonably have been forthcoming.[134]

The Paris paradigm was revolutionary precisely because it harnessed this legal power of reliance. The exchange of intended nationally determined contributions between the United States and China indicated that both states sought to induce the other and were induced in turn by the actions proposed by their counterparty. The exchange of information and attempt to cajole and lead others by both of these

---

[128] Paris Agreement (n 112) at Art 4(3).
[129] Eyal Benvenisti, *The Law of Global Governance* (Brill, 2014) 37–42.
[130] *Ibid.*
[131] *Ibid* at 210–15.
[132] For a full discussion, see Sourgens (n 14).
[133] For a discussion of unilateral acts in climate law, see Sourgens (n 41). For a support for a unilateral act view of the Paris Agreement, see also Mayer (n 30) at 119.
[134] See Sourgens (n 41).

carbon superpowers had the (likely intended) consequence to put these carbon superpowers on the legal hook for their commitments. This asymmetry of leadership in this case also implied the rare asymmetry of obligation. Or to borrow an over-quoted phrase from comic book lore, it is the rare instance in which two superpowers impose upon themselves the adage that 'with great power comes great responsibility'.[135]

III. The Climate Institutions

The networked solution of the Paris paradigm reserves a different role for multilateral institutions than would otherwise be typical for international organisations. A key reason that states seek to avoid the creation of international institutions is that they fear that these institutions, once created, will 'mission creep' and assume an ever greater amount of power and competence.[136] This increased power and competence in turn will lead to the loss of autonomy by the states creating the institution in the first place.[137] This being very much against the interest of most states, there is thus a certain hesitation in the competence that is given to international institutions.

The institutions outlined below should be seen through this prism. As it stands, the Paris paradigm has sought to create truly facilitative international institutions. It did not seek to create the kinds of institutions that would have the power to hamper the organic growth of networked solutions by asserting traditional administrative powers. These institutions are thus important players for the functioning of global climate governance networks. But they are not traditional international administrators as one might have expected to find in a Kyoto solution to climate governance.

A. The Secretariat

The UNFCCC in its Article 8 set up a secretariat.[138] The UNFCCC operates as the secretariat for the Paris Agreement by virtue of Article 17 of the Paris Agreement.[139] The establishment of a secretariat for the UNFCCC was itself contentious.[140]

---

[135] See Maya Rhodan, 'The Supreme Court Just Quoted Spider-Man' (*Time*, 22 June 2015), https://time.com/3930115/supreme-court-spiderman/.
[136] See Jessica Einhorn, 'The World Bank's Mission Creep' (*Foreign Affairs*, September/October 2001), www.foreignaffairs.com/articles/2001-09-01/world-banks-mission-creep (discussing perceived mission creep at the World Bank).
[137] Benvenisti (n 129) at 42.
[138] UNFCCC (n 34) at Art 8.
[139] Paris Agreement (n 112) at Art 17.
[140] Bodansky et al (n 6) at 143–44.

Several states were concerned about the kind of mission creep discussed above.[141] For this reason, the role of the secretariat under the UNFCCC was largely facilitative and administrative in nature.[142] The secretariat would receive and disseminate information by compiling and transmitting reports,[143] to facilitate assistance to the parties in complying with duties to compile and submit information under the UNFCCC,[144] to coordinate with secretariats of other intergovernmental organisations,[145] and provide administrative assistance to the parties.[146] In addition, the secretariat further has the responsibility to compile reports as required by the work of the UNFCCC.[147]

The secretariat further serves as repository under the Paris Agreement. Its duties as repository require parties to file nationally determined contributions,[148] any agreement of parties jointly reducing emissions under the Paris Agreement market mechanism,[149] and communications about adaptation priorities.[150]

The secretariat fulfills an important facilitative function. The transparent communication of information is of tantamount importance for the functioning of the Paris paradigm. The secretariat otherwise has reasonably limited powers. That is not to say that one should under-estimate the powers still ceded to the secretariat under the UNFCCC and Paris Agreement respectively. The secretariat is tasked with writing of reports.[151] In a Paris paradigm essentially built upon mutual trust and growing reliance, such reports are of particular significance in setting agendas and reinforcing a sense of shared purpose.[152] The role of the secretariat therefore remains central to the functioning of the climate network as a conduit through which information flows and the manner in which information is digested and disseminated to the parties and the public at large.

B. The IPCC

The historical introduction to climate networks already mentioned the importance of scientific discourse to climate change policy. The key international driver of this scientific engagement in global climate change governance is the

---

[141] Bodansky et al (n 6) at 143–44.
[142] Bodansky et al (n 6) at 143–44.
[143] UNFCCC (n 34) at Art 8(2)(b).
[144] UNFCCC (n 34) at Art 8(2)(c).
[145] UNFCCC (n 34) at Art 8(2)(e).
[146] UNFCCC (n 34) at Art 8(2)(a), (f).
[147] UNFCCC (n 34) at Art 8(2)(d).
[148] Paris Agreement (n 112) at Art 4(12).
[149] Paris Agreement (n 112) at Art 4(16).
[150] Paris Agreement (n 112) at Art 7(12).
[151] UNFCCC (n 34) at Art 8(2)(b), (d); Paris Agreement (n 112) at Art 17.
[152] See Gralf-Peter Calliess and Peer Zumbansen, *Rough Consensus, Running Code, A Theory of Transnational Private Law* (Hart, 2010) 135–36 (discussing the role of the working group chair in proposing rules in internet governance and its analogous role in transnational private law making).

Intergovernmental Panel on Climate Change (IPCC).[153] The IPCC is responsible for determining the current state of knowledge on climate change.[154] It is thus responsible for validating and disseminating the best available scientific understanding of the trajectory of climate science. This body works in close collaboration with, but remains independent from, the UNFCCC and the Paris Agreement.[155]

In the current environment, it is difficult to overstate the importance of the IPCC. The IPCC in 2018 and again in 2019 published an update on the best available science on the climate change trajectory.[156] Its warning was dire.[157] It projected that according to the best modelling of climate change, the Paris Agreement target limit for an increase in global temperatures above pre-industrial levels will be breached by 2030.[158] This report was received by the press with the ominous, if largely correct, headline 'We have 12 years to limit climate change catastrophe'.[159] Such communications are central to the functioning of the Paris paradigm and should further spur action.

Importantly for decarbonisation, the same IPCC reports contained projected pathways to respond to the climate change modelling. Its recommendation is a 45 per cent cut of CO_{2e} emissions by 2030 and it warns of the necessity to cut at least 20 per cent of CO_{2e} emissions in the same timeframe to avoid calamitous consequences.[160] The IPCC further projects that net CO_{2e} emissions should be reduced to zero by 2050 and must be reduced to zero by 2070 to avoid the most catastrophic consequences of climate change.[161]

The IPCC benchmarked its projections against the Paris Agreement goals of keeping temperature 'to well below 2°C above pre-industrial levels and pursuing efforts to limit the temperature increase to 1.5°C above pre-industrial levels'.[162] It warns that the 1.5°C level from a scientific perspective is a clear threshold level as further temperature increases exponentially increase the effects of climate change on needed biodiversity to maintain the ecosystem.[163] The IPCC concluded its report with the catastrophic assessment that current climate change governance efforts would likely lead to a rise in temperature well in excess of current targets, at levels that would have a massive impact on climate systems.[164]

---

[153] Mayer (n 30) at 5–6; Bodansky et al (n 6) at 98–99.
[154] Mayer (n 30) at 5–6; Bodansky et al (n 6) at 98–99.
[155] IPCC, 'Principles Governing IPCC Work' (1–3 October 1998) Art 1, www.ipcc.ch/site/assets/uploads/2018/09/ipcc-principles.pdf.
[156] *Ibid* at Art 2.
[157] *Ibid* at Art 1; UNFCCC (n 34) at Art 21; Paris Agreement (n 112) at Art 7(a).
[158] IPCC 2019 (n 1).
[159] Jonathan Watts, 'We Have 12 Years to Limit Climate Change Catastrophe, Warns UN' *The Guardian*, 8 October 2018, www.theguardian.com/environment/2018/oct/08/global-warming-must-not-exceed-15c-warns-landmark-un-report.
[160] IPCC 2019 (n 1) at 12, 129.
[161] IPCC 2019 (n 1) at 13.
[162] IPCC 2019 (n 1) at 5, 137.
[163] IPCC 2019 (n 1) at 8.
[164] IPCC 2019 (n 1) at 126.

This and other IPCC reports are significant in setting the stage for climate governance and decarbonisation. As it stands, it is highly unlikely that the IPCC's recommendations will be heeded. Without massive strides in carbon capture technology, it is currently not realistic to believe that a 45 per cent cut in CO_{2e} emissions by 2030 is possible.[165] Nor does it appear likely that mitigation alone will be able to achieve a net zero carbon economy by 2050.[166] Such efforts would require a near complete overhaul of existing grid and physical infrastructure. For comparison, the construction of a GHG emission-free nuclear powerplant (not counting regulatory approvals, etc) is around 80 months in Germany, France and Russia.[167] A recent US nuclear powerplant reportedly had a 20-year delay.[168] This is broadly consistent with the time for construction of a single hydroelectric powerplant (four to seven years).[169] These timeframes would thus put the world on the brink of the 2030 timeframe if there was a will to replace coal and gas-fired powerplants with nuclear power or hydroelectric power. Further, while incentives for solar and wind energy have significantly increased the representation of renewables in the energy mix, this increase alone will have difficulty in making up baseload in time, due in part to intermittency problems.[170] While these problems can be resolved, the IPCC report has presented one of the hardest problems for policy makers to resolve – and has not been able to provide a feasible policy or engineering solution to meet the needs in question. Further, recent efforts by EU Member States to subsidise solar power in particular only to scale down subsidies ahead of the projected date creates significant trust issues whether the EU would even be willing to invest the money needed to make solar or wind energy a fast and meaningful alternative to existing coal-fired powerplants such as the one current supplying Munich with power.[171]

C. Climate Finance

Climate governance networks will have to make available robust climate finance to meet the challenge. As Alexander Zahar has pointed out, the rise of climate

---

[165] IPCC 2019 (n 1) at 32.
[166] IPCC 2019 (n 1) at 102 (outlining pathways).
[167] Pedro Carajilescov and João ML Moreira, 'Construction Time of PWRs' (2011 International Nuclear Atlantic Conference – INAC 2011), available at https://inis.iaea.org/collection/NCLCollectionStore/_Public/42/105/42105221.pdf.
[168] 'Power Plant Construction Costs' (*ProEst*, 6 August 2018), https://www.proest.com/power-plant-construction-costs/.
[169] 'How Long Does it Take to Build a Hydroelectric Power Station? (*AQPER*), available at www.aqper.com/en/how-long-does-it-take-to-build-a-hydroelectric-power-station.
[170] See Earl Richie, 'Managing Wind and Solar Intermittency in Current and Future Systems' (*Forbes*, 27 February 2017), www.forbes.com/sites/uhenergy/2017/02/27/managing-wind-and-solar-intermittency-in-current-and-future-systems/#58ab93ed3c5d.
[171] Pia Ratzesberger and Kassian Stroh, 'Zu relevant zum Abschalten' (*Süddeutsche Zeitung*, 1 November 2019), www.sueddeutsche.de/muenchen/heizkraftwerk-muenchen-nord-zu-relevant-zum-abschalten-1.4664081.

finance is intimately tied to the Copenhagen shift.[172] The Copenhagen shift imposed an obligation on the entire world community to participate in decarbonisation and climate change mitigation efforts.[173] Such an effort would not be possible for many industrialising countries to shoulder on their own.[174] Many of these countries see their policy goals as more tied to bringing a reasonable share of economic prosperity to their population and thus create conditions for economic growth as opposed to securing environmental protection. As the case of China should suggest, there is an inflection point when states do begin to care about the long-term sustainability of their development policies for the simple reason that current policies are killing swaths of the population in leading urban centres (probably literally, in the case of Beijing).[175] Disappointingly, that inflection point apparently has not yet been reached.[176]

In order to permit industrialising states to continue along the path to secure a reasonable share of prosperity for a larger proportion of their population, it is necessary to assist these states financially in their efforts to decarbonise. Decarbonisation is capital intensive. Industrialising countries frequently do not have the capital to spare to invest in short-term, more expensive technology. This obligation is a matter of self-interest – without the participation of industrialising states, it will be difficult to meet the steep challenges outlined in the most recent IPCC report. But this obligation is also a matter of other regarding global stewardship. Part of the reason that current industrialisation strategies are not available to these industrialising countries is that other countries utilised them first, frequently climbing on the backs of the very industrialising countries in question to achieve their own industrial growth. It is therefore a matter of basic fairness to assist these states with their own industrialisation efforts in a sustainable manner.

The UNFCCC and Paris Agreement structures have already set up various financing mechanisms in principle to assist with climate finance. The current goal is to obtain approximately $100 billion in climate finance per annum. This goal may well be insufficient to meet the challenges ahead. But it is a start. The available climate finance facilities will be disbursed through four predominant funds.[177] These funds are the Global Environment Facility,[178] the Climate Investment Fund,[179] the Clean Technology Fund[180] and the Strategic Climate Fund.[181]

---

[172] Alexander Zahar, *Climate Change Finance and International Law* (Routledge, 2017) 17–19.
[173] *Ibid* at 10.
[174] *Ibid* at 85–86.
[175] See David Pilling, *The Growth Delusion, Wealth, Poverty and the Well-Being of Nations* (Tim Duggan Books, 2018) 137.
[176] Jillian Ambrose, 'China's Appetite for Coal Power Returns Despite Climate Pledge' *The Guardian*, 20 November 2019, www.theguardian.com/world/2019/nov/20/china-appetite-for-coal-power-stations-returns-despite-climate-pledge-capacity.
[177] Zahar (n 172) at 38.
[178] Zahar (n 172).
[179] Zahar (n 172) at 39.
[180] Zahar (n 172) at 39.
[181] Zahar (n 172) at 39.

Three of these funds are administered by Bretton Woods institutions.[182] A further important arrival on the scene is the Green Climate Fund.[183]

Even with this change to financing mechanisms, it should be pointed out that adaptation finance is one of the least developed areas of climate finance. Adaptation – the retrofitting of infrastructure for climate change – will be inevitable.[184] It is also very expensive.[185] Climate finance instruments in principle should be available for mitigation and adaptation purposes.[186] Perhaps reflecting the concern of industrialising countries, the financial facilities are focused on mitigation rather than adaptation.[187] They thus focus on efforts that will benefit both the state that adopts mitigation strategies, as well as the larger world community by removing CO_{2e} emissions from the global GHG flow.[188] Adaptation on its face does not create such immediate benefits for third states – adaptation simply 'climatises' existing infrastructure. It is thus less in the interest of third states to support. (Notably, this calculus does not take climate refugees into account – an error that may well have significant political repercussions when considering that the populist revivals in Western democracies tracked the refugee crises created by the Yugoslav and Syrian civil wars in Europe, Central American climate and political instabilities in the Americas.)[189]

As is, climate finance funds and institutions are a constitutive part of global climate governance and decarbonisation regulation. They are central decision-makers on what technology will get funded and how. They will thus have the power of the purse in influencing both technological standards and energy policy on a global scale. Any actor interested in studying, affecting or benefiting from global climate governance would therefore do well to look in detail at climate finance facilities.

D. Other Relevant International Regimes

The climate process is not the only constitutive global governance network responsible for climate change. Other regimes are similarly relevant for the articulation of climate change governance norms. This section very briefly identifies potential processes that will affect climate change governance.

---

[182] Zahar (n 172) at 39.
[183] Zahar (n 172) at 41.
[184] See IPCC 2019 (n 1) at 110.
[185] IPCC 2019 (n 1) at 110.
[186] Zahar (n 172) at 105–11.
[187] Zahar (n 172) 38–39.
[188] Zahar (n 172) 38–39.
[189] See Jane McAdam, *Climate Change, Forced Migration and International Law* (Oxford University Press, 2012); Shadi Hamid, 'The Role of Islam in European Populism: How Refugee Flows and Fear of Muslims Drive Right-Wing Support' (*Brookings*, February 2019), www.brookings.edu/research/the-role-of-islam-in-european-populism-how-refugee-flows-and-fear-of-muslims-drive-right-wing-support/.

i. Bio-Diversity

An obvious process that will affect the global governance of climate change and energy markets is the bio-diversity governance process.[190] Climate change has the regrettable effect of significantly reducing bio-diversity.[191] Further, several mitigation or removal approaches, as well as other geo-engineering approaches, have potential negative impacts on bio-diversity themselves.[192] The protection of bio-diversity is a central international environmental law priority. International environmental law guides bio-diversity governance through the 1992 Convention on Biological Diversity, as well as the Nagoya Protocol.[193]

It is therefore unsurprising that the bio-diversity process – also organised under a conference of the parties process under the 1992 Convention – has taken an interest in climate change regulation.[194] The bio-diversity and the climate network themselves have together formed a 'network of networks' that jointly govern overlapping aspects of climate change mitigation.[195]

ii. Law of the Sea

The law of the sea is yet another area of international law that is affected by climate change. The law of the sea is governed principally by the UN Convention on the Law of the Sea.[196] The UN Convention on the Law of Sea and the various authorities it created, such as the International Tribunal on the Law of the Sea and the Seabed Authority, are likely to have regulatory authority over parts of climate change and energy governance, particularly as oil and gas reserves in the Arctic become commercially viable.[197] Further, decarbonisation itself will likely make relevant various international legal regimes pertaining to the law of the sea. Thus, offshore wind platforms may well require the transport of hydrogen generated through electrolysis to shore through pipeline networks.[198] Any governance of climate change and energy resources will therefore need to take into account the law of the sea as well as the bio-diversity and climate change networks.

---

[190] Sands & Peel (n 22) at 384–450.
[191] IPCC 2019 (n 1) at 8.
[192] IPCC 2019 (n 1) at 12–13.
[193] Sands & Peel (n 22) at 388–408.
[194] Bodansky et al (n 6) at 32.
[195] Bodansky et al (n 6) at 32.
[196] Sands & Peel (n 22) at 462–64.
[197] Mayer (n 30) at 242–43.
[198] See Benjamin Wehrmann, 'UK and Germany Mull Boosting Cooperation on Hydrogen Production with Offshore Wind' (*CleanEnergyWire.org*, 21 November 2019), www.cleanenergywire.org/news/uk-and-germany-mull-boosting-cooperation-hydrogen-production-offshore-wind/.

IV. Non-Climate International Governance Networks

In addition to other environmental networks, global governance of climate change and energy investments also draws on other global governance networks. A full discussion of these networks is beyond the scope of this chapter. One network that materially affects climate and energy investment governance is international economic law, and particularly international investment law.[199] International energy investments are protected by a significant network of international investment treaties.[200] These treaties provide recourse to international arbitration to international energy investors to pursue claims against the host state of their investments for expropriations, as well as arbitrary or unfair treatment.[201] These treaties protect both renewable and traditional fossil fuel-based energy producers.[202] This network therefore provides both a backstop for promises made by states to incentivise investments in the renewable energy sector and to provide a level of protection to existing traditional energy investors. The influence of international investment law on decarbonisation governance is discussed in full in a later chapter.

The need for large scale energy investment further makes relevant international trade law. International trade law is governed by a network of international free trade agreements.[203] The predominant international trade agreement is the set of agreements constituting the World Trade Organisation.[204] These agreements create their own governance network policing the maintenance of liberal free trade policies around the world. To the extent that the intense focus on energy investments made necessary by the climate network would create incentives for states to act in a protectionist manner, the trade governance network would be implicated and could trigger a review of the underlying domestic policy initiatives as potential violations of free trade commitments.

Decarbonisation and climate change further make relevant international human rights governance networks. The Dutch Supreme Court in the *Urgenda* case upheld a judgment that the Netherlands' lack of climate action constituted a violation of the European Convention on Human Rights.[205] Similarly, the Inter-American Court of Human Rights recently addressed the impact of global CO_2 emissions as a human rights violation.[206] The judgment was remarkable in that

---

[199] See chapter 6.
[200] *Ibid.*
[201] *Ibid.*
[202] Bodansky et al (n 6) at 327–47.
[203] Bodansky et al (n 6) at 327–47.
[204] Bodansky et al (n 6) at 327–47.
[205] See 'Landmark Decision by Dutch Supreme Court' (*Urgenda.nl*, 2019), www.urgenda.nl/en/themas/climate-case/ (linking to all relevant case documents).
[206] See Giovanny Vega-Barbosa and Lorraine Aboagye, 'Human Rights and the Protection of the Environment: The Advisory Opinion of the Inter-American Court of Human Rights' (*EJILTalk!*, 26 February 2018), www.ejiltalk.org/human-rights-and-the-protection-of-the-environment-the-advisory-opinion-of-the-inter-american-court-of-human-rights/.

it did not focus purely on the domestic, territorial CO_2 emissions, but also considered the extraterritorial effect of such emissions and their impact on human rights of persons living in third countries.[207] As climate change begins to threaten the right to life, as well as other rights to a dignified life, it is likely that human rights governance networks will be implicated immediately in climate change governance.[208] Further, the responses to climate change will in and of themselves implicate human rights governance networks, as well. Thus, the failure to adequately adapt to climate change is likely going to give rise to additional human rights claims above and beyond claims that arise out of CO_{2e} emissions. Further, mitigation measures themselves might give rise to human rights claims depending upon how they are implemented. Currently, the use of carbon taxes in France and Canada has proved hugely unpopular.[209] In France, it has led to protests that border on riots.[210] The public response to such riots obviously implicates human rights.[211] Further, the very political mechanisms used to institute climate change mitigation policies might themselves implicate human rights concerns to the extent that they would deprive people of a right to political freedoms. In other words, climate governance makes relevant a significant number of human rights concerns at every level of governmental action or inaction.

Finally, it is important to mention indigenous rights networks. Climate change threatens indigenous rights by threatening ecosystems of spiritual and social significance to indigenous groups.[212] Indigenous groups have begun to lodge claims asserting their rights under indigenous rights treaties and decisions.[213] Further, as new energy projects are licensed by the state that is host to an indigenous population, indigenous peoples are likely going to assert their position that such projects require the free, prior, and informed consent of the indigenous group precisely because of the climate change implications for indigenous groups.[214] This would certainly be applicable to the development of traditional energy investment that might themselves fuel more climate change (say, the licensing of

---

[207] Ibid.

[208] Stephen Humphreys, 'Competing Claims: Human Rights and Climate Harms' in Stephen Humphreys (ed), *Human Rights and Climate Change* (Cambridge University Press, 2010) 37.

[209] Alissa J Rubin and Somini Sengupta, '"Yellow Vest" Protests Shake France. Here's the Lesson for Climate Change' *New York Times*, 6 December 2018, www.nytimes.com/2018/12/06/world/europe/france-fuel-carbon-tax.html; Graeme Gordon, 'Most Canadians Unwilling to Pay Much for Carbon Tax: Poll' (*Toronto Sun*, 29 June 2019), https://torontosun.com/news/national/most-canadians-unwilling-to-pay-much-for-carbon-tax-poll.

[210] Rubin & Sengupta, *ibid*.

[211] 'Rights of "Gilets Jaunes" Protesters in France, "Disproportionately Curtailed", say UN Independent Experts' (*UN News*, 14 February 2019), https://news.un.org/en/story/2019/02/1032741.

[212] M Alexander Pearl, 'Human Rights, Indigenous Peoples, and the Global Climate Crisis' (2018) 53 *Wake Forest Law Review* 713.

[213] Jeffrey Williamson, 'As Climate Lawsuits Grow Worldwide, Legal Strategies Evolve Too' (*ClimateLiabilityNews.org*, 26 December 2018), www.climateliabilitynews.org/2018/12/26/legal-strategy-climate-lawsuits/.

[214] International Labour Organisation (ILO), Indigenous and Tribal Peoples Convention, ILO Convention No 169 (27 June 1989).

a new coal-fired powerplant in a state that is host to an indigenous population).[215] But indigenous rights would also be applicable to the development of alternative energy projects. Most intuitively, the use of nuclear energy is likely to face indigenous peoples' rights scrutiny.[216] But less intuitively, renewables may also face such scrutiny. Thus, the use of hydropower may pose significant issues due to the spiritual and social importance of waterways.[217] Further, even wind and solar projects could be implemented in a manner that would raise indigenous peoples' rights concerns.[218] International indigenous rights governance networks therefore also must be borne in mind when considering climate change and energy investment governance.

V. Non-State Responses

Climate change and energy investment governance extends significantly beyond the state. The governance networks discussed so far focus in one way or another on the state. The climate governance networks discussed so far, for instance, focus on the traditional state-based climate change governance responses. Global governance networks, including climate and energy networks, have extended significantly below the classic state-to-state paradigm of international law and diplomacy. Global governance networks also have extended beyond the realm of public organs and include private institutions as well as public institutions.

The non-state participation in climate governance became manifest when President Trump expressed his intention to withdraw the United States from the Paris Agreement.[219] Immediately, US states such as California and Washington and cities such as New York stepped up to promise to continue to meet the nationally determined contributions set out by the Paris Agreement by whatever means are at their disposal.[220] States like California have entered into sub-national arrangements

---

[215] See Noni Austin, 'Indigenous Australians Take Fight Against Giant Coal Mine to the United Nations' (*EarthJustice.org*, 15 August 2018), https://earthjustice.org/blog/2018-august/indigenous-australians-take-fight-against-giant-coal-mine-to-the-united-nations.

[216] 'Indigenous Peoples Condemn Nuclear Colonialism on "Columbus" Day' (*IndigenousAction.org*, 14 October 2016), www.indigenousaction.org/indigenous-peoples-condemn-nuclear-colonialism-on-columbus-day/.

[217] Stephen R Munzer, 'Dam(n) Displacement: Compensation, Resettlement, Indigeneity' (2019) 51 *Cornell International Law Journal* 823.

[218] Justine Calma, 'Renewable Energy is Violating Human Rights as much as Fossil Fuels have for Decades' (*Quartz*, 25 November 2016), https://qz.com/845206/renewable-energy-human-rights-violations/.

[219] Michael D Shear, 'Trump Will Withdraw U.S. From Paris Climate Agreement' *The New York Times*, 1 June 2017, www.nytimes.com/2017/06/01/climate/trump-paris-climate-agreement.html.

[220] For a full discussion, see Sourgens (n 17). The initiative at issue is the United States Climate Alliance. Its goal is to limit GHG emissions on a state and territory level to assure US Paris compliance. Further, the Alliance also creates reporting capabilities to track progress and exerts pressure on the Federal Government to limit GHG emissions. For a full list of activities and reports, see the United States Climate Alliance website at www.usclimatealliance.org.

with other foreign provinces to create carbon markets.²²¹ These efforts are likely to grow. They are further likely to impact climate governance.

Similarly, the question of what new energy infrastructure will be licensed where is not just subject to national regulation. It is also subject to various levels of federal and municipal oversight depending on the constitutional nature of the state developing the energy investment in question.²²² Important federal states and cities will therefore likely have an important voice in energy governance as the world is considering decarbonisation measures.

At the same time, much of global climate and energy governance also looks to self-regulation and private sources of regulation. Carbon credits, for instance, are subject to various self-regulatory standards.²²³ As decarbonisation intensifies, these self-regulatory or private institution governance mechanisms are likely to grow in importance. One of the institutions to single out as a potential first among equals is the International Organization for Standardization (ISO).²²⁴ The ISO already offers 'principles, requirements and guidelines for the quantification and reporting of the carbon footprint of a product (CFP), in a manner consistent with International Standards on life cycle assessment'²²⁵ and 'standards for greenhouse gas accounting and verification'.²²⁶ Such private standard-setting efforts will only continue to grow in importance as climate change governance networks continue their push towards to decarbonisation.

A. Networked Decision-Making

To understand how global governance is likely to operate in the climate and energy investment regulatory space in the near future, one must make sense of the fact how such disparate governance processes interact with each other. As is clear by now, no one set of actors or processes alone will guide the governance of decarbonisation and energy investments going forward. Rather, a highly diverse set of actors will set potentially inconsistent standards, all of which will have to be taken into account by regulators and energy investors alike. This begs the question – how can such governance lead to anything but chaos?

The answer to this question lies in a networked approach to governance. This chapter is emphatically about climate governance *networks*.²²⁷ The chapter takes

---

[221] Sourgens (n 17).
[222] Sourgens (n 17).
[223] Elizabeth Gasiorowski-Denis, 'Raising New ISO Standards for Saving the Planet' (*ISO*, 16 April 2019), www.iso.org/news/ref2384.html.
[224] *Ibid*.
[225] ISO Standard 14067:2018, ISO, www.iso.org/standard/71206.html.
[226] Chan Kook Weng and Kevin Boehmer, 'Launching of ISO 14064 for Greenhouse Gas Accounting and Verification' (*ISO Management Systems*, March/ April 2006), www.iso.org/files/live/sites/isoorg/files/archive/pdf/en/greenhouse.pdf.
[227] Anne-Marie Slaughter, *A New World Order* (Princeton University Press, 2005).

this term seriously. And this again takes the discussion a little afield from the traditional understanding of a more hierarchical understanding of regulation.

To highlight the point, it is important to highlight what is not a network. For example, an army is not a network. An army in principle is an integrated structure. The more integrated the structure, and better it is at obeying commands coming from the top and implementing them throughout the army ranks, the more effective it becomes. The benefit of such a structure is that it is highly centralised and thus can act and achieve what appear to be super-human feats with breath-taking alacrity. One still hears the disbelief in the retelling of the bridging of the straights between Europe and Asia by the Persians in Greek tragedy.[228] The same awe underlies the retelling of the crossing of the Rhine by Roman troops under Caesar.[229] These feats were possible because of the structure inherent in army discipline.

Networks are in many ways the opposite of such structures. It is almost impossible to get anyone to obey the command of any one person in a network. Think of the Internet as the quintessential network. Controlling the Internet is such a difficult task because it is networked and gives independent authority to a large group of participants.[230] This makes networks significantly more resilient – but it also comes at a cost of speed.[231]

Climate change governance, for good or for ill, is not a structure like an army. It operates as a network like the Internet. That climate change governance is networked rather than structured is readily observable when comparing the approach by the parties to the Kyoto Protocol (and the relative lack of success it had in achieving broad subscription) to the approach by the parties to the Paris Agreement (and the relative success in achieving broad subscription for the Paris Agreement) outlined above. Even just the Paris Agreement part of global climate governance operates from the bottom up and seeks to connect regulators with each other to increase decarbonisation ambition through mutual trust and reliance. This feature of even the central process of climate change governance – the Paris Agreement – shows that climate governance is principally networked rather than principally structured.[232] It relies upon the communication of voluntary commitments.[233] This communication of voluntary commitments then supports further commitments through the operation of networked transnational legal processes.[234]

The discussion so far in this chapter has shown that there is more than one governance network responsible for climate change and energy investment.

---

[228] Aeschylus, 'Persians' (translated by James Romm) in Mary Lefkowitz and James Romm (eds), *The Greek Plays* (Modern Library, 2017) 9, 33.
[229] Gaius Iulius Caesar, 'Gallic War' in Robert B Strassler (ed), *The Landmark Julius Caesar* (Pantheon, 2017) 1, 117.
[230] Calliess & Zumbansen (n 152) at 135–36.
[231] Calliess & Zumbansen (n 152) at 135–36.
[232] For a full discussion, see Sourgens (n 14).
[233] Sourgens (n 14).
[234] Sourgens (n 14).

Rather, there are multiple such governance networks that overlap. This means that governance increases in complexity from a network to a network of networks.

Anne Marie Slaughter has theorised the development of both networks and networks of networks.[235] The global governance regime for climate change and energy investments follows the blueprint she has set out. Slaughter distinguishes between different levels of formality.[236] She notes that global governance networks can form from the very informal setting of exchanges between like-minded regulators discussion shared problems to the highly formal setting of exchanges taking place under the auspices of an international treaty.[237] She further theorised that networks themselves will begin to network with each other as different networks of regulators find that other regulators domestically (and internationally) have begun to address a shared problem.[238] When this occurs, the dialogue between these different regulators at the domestic and at the international level joins the networks together, that is, it creates links between two previously independent networks.[239] These links share information between networks and start to create regulatory friction between the networks to determine how to overcome the effects of potentially inconsistent approaches to regulation.[240]

Each engagement within and between networks follows what Harold Koh calls a transnational legal process.[241] Each engagement between network participants involves a communication that expresses a governance demand.[242] This governance demand is then interpreted by the participant receiving it in terms of her own governance experience.[243] In interpreting the governance demand, the participant translates it into her own idiom.[244] As the governance demand is translated, it is integrated into the broader governance framework as a possible solution to a governance problem by the recipient of the governance demand.[245] Conversations in transnational legal processes are not one way streets.[246] They involve a constant back and forth through the global governance networks of governance demands and interpretations of governance demands. In this manner, the networks create a resilient means of communication across national barriers that continually strengthen the value demand.[247]

---

[235] Slaughter (n 227).
[236] Slaughter (n 227) at 48–49.
[237] Slaughter (n 227) at 63–64.
[238] Slaughter (n 227) at 48–49.
[239] Slaughter (n 227) at 48–49.
[240] Slaughter (n 227) at 48–49.
[241] Harold Koh, 'Tryptich's End: A Better Framework to Evaluate 21st Century Lawmaking' (2017) 126 *Yale Law Journal Forum* 338, 364.
[242] Harold Hongju Koh, 'Transnational Legal Process' (1996) 75 *Nebraska Law Review* 181, 194–207.
[243] *Ibid.*
[244] *Ibid.*
[245] *Ibid.*
[246] *Ibid.*
[247] *Ibid.*

This process looks very much like the bottom up, Copenhagen shift of climate governance.[248] This is not coincidental. Two of the leading advisers to the US delegation at Copenhagen were Harold Koh in his capacity as legal adviser to the US State Department and Anne Marie Slaughter in her capacity as director of Policy Planning for the United States Department of State.[249]

The important question then is what happens when governance networks collide with each other. In principle, the same transnational legal process logic is then applied to itself. That is, different governance networks are going to communicate their respective governance demands to each other. This will create a significant amount of friction between the governance networks. This friction will cause both networks to interpret, translate and internalise the governance demands from the respective other network. This, however, will not occur immediately but rather will take time as interpretation, translation and internalisation work themselves through the communicative engagement between the networks.[250]

This lag has the effect of creating a sense of legal fragmentation.[251] There is no uniform governance network that governs any one area of human endeavour.[252] There are always multiple networks that communicate and compete with each other.[253] This sense of fragmentation evokes a certain feeling of chaos.[254] It is not always clear what one is to do in a given situation – what governance demand to follow and what governance demand to ignore.

The literature on fragmentation and governance suggests that part of the answer to this conundrum comes from the manner in which parties navigate the networks.[255] The invocation of one or another network is likely to result in a different governance result – that is, the human rights answer is not going to be the climate change governance answer to any particular problem that might arise in the context of a proposed energy investment.[256] This gives the energy investor a potential advantage of choosing which governance network to approach in what order so as to benefit from the path dependence advantage of framing the regulatory conversation. Networks would then respond to this choice by creating incentives for different participants to select their network over others to get a relative advantage in the ongoing transnational legal exchange between the

---

[248] Bodansky et al (n 6) at 214.
[249] See Harold Hongju Koh, 'The Obama Administration and International Law' (US State Department, 25 March 2010), https://2009-2017.state.gov/s/l/releases/remarks/139119.htm.
[250] Sourgens (n 17).
[251] See Harro van Asselt, 'Managing the Fragmentation of International Environmental Law: Forests at the Intersection of the Climate and Biodiversity Regimes' (2008) 44 *New York University Journal of International Law and Politics* 1205 (discussing the fragmentation of even international environmental law).
[252] Andreas Fischer Lescano and Gunther Teubner, 'Regime-Collisions: The Vain Search for Legal Unity in the Fragmentation of Global Law' (2004) 25 *Michigan Journal of International Law* 999.
[253] *Ibid* at 1005.
[254] *Ibid* at 1022–23.
[255] *Ibid* at 1022–23.
[256] *Ibid* at 1022–23.

potentially applicable networks in question. This, one might theorise, would lead to a governance race to the bottom.

While a full answer to this problem is beyond the scope of this chapter, transnational legal processes should intuitively appear more resilient than the fragmentation sceptics might first suggest. While there are competitive pressures between networks, and while these competitive pressures can be skillfully navigated by experienced lawyers, these pressures tend to resolve problems through broader based governance rather than through less governance. That is, as networks connect with other networks and compete with other networks for regulatory competence, they communicate their regulatory demands to each other. This communication is not principally driven by the logic of market competition, as some critics have suggested. Rather, it is driven by the logic of transnational legal processes to understand the normative demands made by other networks and to convince the other regulator that she is wrong in her concerns. This transnational legal process over the long-term will affect the governance networks on both sides of the communication by incorporating the results of the communication with the respective other network into the network's own understanding of the regulation it promulgates. The exchange therefore is more likely to provide alternative rationales for action than competing rationales for action.

This is not to say that such processes are fast. Governance networks follow their own logic. This logic is inherently difficult to move. Governance networks therefore will resist change – they will argue back that they have the better answer to the underlying regulatory problem, presumably because the value the governance network serves will appear the more important within the network itself. It is this resistance, this arguing back, which creates a sense of inconsistency and fragmentation. And this resistance, this arguing back, is a necessary feature of governance networks as without it, the very mechanism of transnational legal process would cease to function. Transnational legal process depends upon friction, engagement and disagreement in order to slowly move the conversation of its participants.

This feature of global governance networks will create issues already hinted at earlier in this chapter. Climate change is upon us. It will create the need for energy, economic and regulatory responses that will strain the capacity of markets, investors and regulators alike. An inherently slow process therefore may create governance issues. One might expect that the appearance of fragmentation will dramatically increase as climate change responses and decarbonisation pick up speed. One would therefore do well to lay the groundwork now to increase the intensity of regulatory and market dialogue about decarbonisation and create stronger conduits between these different networks. As Eyal Benvenisti would point out, this goes against the diplomatic grain of states, which purposefully avoided creating umbrella networks. In this case, one can hope that the logic of transnational legal process and governance networks themselves – the logic of reliance – will help overcome this last but lasting global governance barrier.

VI. Conclusion

This chapter has outlined the key global governance networks involved in climate change mitigation and energy investment. It has shown that there are a large number of networks with competence over the regulatory enterprise. It has further sought to demonstrate that climate change and energy governance has taken a bottom up approach. This bottom up approach relies heavily upon the networked approach to problem solving – that is the creation of trust and reliance interests that become legally cognisable in their own right. Once these reliance interests have matured, it is then possible to communicate across governance networks to improve and broaden the authority of governance demands. This chapter hoped to show that the processes constituting global climate governance are both more complex than might at first appear and more flexible and resilient than one might have imagined. For good or ill, these processes will guide one of the most fundamental energy transformations since the industrial revolution. They will have to do what even the oil and gas boom of the second half of the twentieth century and beginning of the twenty-first century was unable to achieve – fully displace coal as the engine of industrialisation and energy markets.

What does provide more than just a little hope in this regard is that one can see a convergence of different governance regimes towards this goal. Climate change governance is currently not at odds with human rights and indigenous rights networks. Quite to the contrary, human rights networks have taken the first steps towards enforcing climate change obligations. Further, some of the largest energy companies in the world like ExxonMobil are themselves participants in the current energy transformation. Maligned though he was by environmental activists, former Exxon CEO and then Secretary of State Rex Tillerson was a voice counselling against a US departure from the Paris Agreement.[257] Exxon today invests in solar energy and is installing solar energy panels next to its developments in the largest oil and gas deposit in the United States – the Permian basin in Texas and New Mexico.[258] Shell, another major oil and gas company, is investing in wind power.[259] Chevron, similarly, is strongly committed to climate change response.[260] When climate change governance, human rights regimes, and oil and

---

[257] Timothy Cama, 'Tillerson: "My View Didn't Change" on Paris Climate Agreement' (*The Hill*, 13 June 2017), https://thehill.com/policy/energy-environment/337578-tillerson-my-view-didnt-change-on-paris-climate-agreement.

[258] Velda Addison, 'ExxonMobil Turns to Solar, Wind for Power in Permian' (*Hart Energy*, 29 November 2018), www.hartenergy.com/exclusives/exxonmobil-turns-solar-wind-power-permian-31640.

[259] Julia Pyper, 'Shell Brings Deep-Water Expertise to Boston to Capitalize on US Offshore Wind Boom' (*GreenTechMedia*, 17 June 2019), www.greentechmedia.com/articles/read/shell-brings-deep-water-expertise-to-boston-us-offshore-wind.

[260] Chevron, 'Climate Change', available at www.chevron.com/corporate-responsibility/climate-change.

gas supermajors are beginning to move in the same direction, something is afoot. As the rest of this volume will showcase, this something may well be the successful decarbonisation of the energy industry through a combination of all the different engineering tools at our disposal. If climate change is an engineering problem, as Rex Tillerson once noted, we may finally have come upon the governance mechanisms that will help us design and implement it.

6

Investment Law and Decarbonisation

DIANE DESIERTO AND FRÉDÉRIC GILLES SOURGENS

I. Introduction

International investment law has attracted its share of controversial criticism,[1] particularly against the general backdrop of populist challenges to international legal processes.[2] For the critics, investment law invites controversy from its inherent nature of protecting foreign investments – that is the property invested by foreign investors[3] – lending itself to speculation that the system is captured and designed to the advantage of large corporate investors.[4] When corporate actors object to the impacts of new governmental regulations, critics argue that governmental responsibilities to enact protective policies are eroded, if not wholly thwarted.[5]

This linear depiction of international investment law, in our view, raises significant obstacles to the kinds of decarbonisation and climate change adaptation and mitigation initiatives outlined elsewhere in this volume. If the narratives of international investment law were simply reduced to the protection of large corporate investors such as large multinational, oil, or gas companies,[6] these narratives would obscure the real nature of complex relationships between states and the private sector towards devising and implementing clean energy reforms to

---

[1] Elizabeth Warren, 'The Trans-Pacific Partnership Clause Everyone Should Oppose' *Washington Post*, 25 February 2015), www.washingtonpost.com/opinions/kill-the-dispute-settlement-language-in-the-trans-pacific-partnership/2015/02/25/ec7705a2-bd1e-11e4-b274-e5209a3bc9a9_story.html.

[2] Eric A Posner, 'Liberal Internationalism and the Populist Backlash' (2017) 49 *Arizona State Law Journal* 795.

[3] Malcolm Langford, Daniel Behn and Ole Kristian Fauchald, 'Backlash and State Strategies in International Investment Law' in *The Changing Practices of International Law: Sovereignty, Law and Politics in a Globalising World* (Cambridge University Press, 2019), available at https://papers.ssrn.com/sol3/papers.cfm?abstract_id=2704344.

[4] *Ibid.*

[5] See Gus Van Harten, *Investment Treaty Arbitration and Public Law* (Oxford University Press, 2007).

[6] See Giuseppe Bellantuono, 'Legal Pathways of Decarbonization in the EU: The Case of Coal Phase Out' (2019) 17 *Oil Gas & Energy Law Intelligence* 1, 20, available at https://papers.ssrn.com/sol3/papers.cfm?abstract_id=3411986.

realise the desired deep structural decarbonisation of 'green economies'.[7] Taking the reductionist narrative to its (il)logical extreme, international investment law would have to be dismantled swiftly so as not to impede efforts to avoid a global climate disaster – which, ironically, would be inevitable by 2030 if massive decarbonisation efforts prove unsuccessful.[8]

As this chapter will outline, such a crude portrayal of international investment law unfortunately misses the mark in many important respects. It does not appropriately understand how international investment law operates – what it protects, why, and how. This misunderstanding of the constitutive processes involved is significant because it focuses only on part of the overall investment law framework.[9] That is, it looks only at claims raised by investors as opposed to the overall context in which these claims are being raised. This context includes, among other things, that the foreign company in question made the investment in the first place.[10] It further misses that the investment law framework is typically bi-directional in that it allows for a host state to raise counterclaims or invoke considerable jurisdictional defences that, in turn, could incentivise stronger corporate governance towards environmental and social protections.[11] Finally, international investment law adjudicates claims asserted with arguments, as opposed to outcomes achieved in actuality.[12] The crude portrayal of international investment law would ultimately generalise that any justice system is somehow 'dangerous' because parties can freely avail themselves of it to commence questionable claims, occluding what that justice system does to winnow out, dismiss and filter such claims. In our view, one has to look at the full mass of all empirical results over time as they are achieved through investment law as a system, rather than rushing to generalise from one-sided static narratives of specific international investment law disputes.

Our analysis in this chapter begins with an initial important question for any study on decarbonisation and investment law: What is the relationship between investment protection and human development? It would be too facile to answer

---

[7] See David G Victor, 'Deep Decarbonization: A Realistic Way Forward on Climate Change' (*Yale Environment 360*, 28 January 2020) at https://e360.yale.edu/features/deep-decarbonization-a-realistic-way-forward-on-climate-change.

[8] For a discussion of the Intergovernmental Panel on Climate Change (IPCC) report in question, see Frederic G Sourgens, 'Geo-Markets' (forthcoming, April 2020) 38 *Virginia Environmental Law Journal*.

[9] Diane A Desierto, 'Public Policy in International Investment and Trade Law: Community Expectations and Functional Decisionmaking' (2014) 26 *Florida Journal of International Law* 51, 72, 84–99, 107–17; see also Diane A Desierto, *Public Policy in International Economic Law: The ICESCR in Trade, Finance, and Investment* (Oxford University Press, 2015).

[10] Jeswald W Salacuse and Nicholas P Sullivan, 'Do BITs Really Work?: An Evaluation of Bilateral Investment Treaties and their Grand Bargain' (2005) 46 *Harvard International Law Journal* 67. For a summary of contrary views, see Jason W Yackee, 'Political Risk and International Investment Law' (2014) 24 *Duke Journal of Comparative & International Law* 477, 492–93.

[11] Frederic G Sourgens, 'Supranational Law' (2016) 50 *Vanderbilt Journal of Transnational Law* 155, 195–206.

[12] Matthew Rimmer, 'The Chilling Effect: Investor-State Dispute Settlement, Graphic Health Warnings, the Plain Packaging of Tobacco Products and the Trans-Pacific Partnership' (2017) 7 *Victoria University Law & Justice Journal*. 96.

this question in purely economic, growth centred terms. We draw from the 1986 UN Declaration on the Right to Development's definition of development, to argue that an investment law regime should strive to act as a catalyst for human development rather than simply as an aggregator of economic growth.

Against this yardstick, we then appraise the role of investment law in global policy processes aimed at decarbonisation, beginning with the often-overlooked necessity for investment law protections to instantiate, establish and entrench green energy development. One of the leading areas of development in international investment law is the use of investment protection to bind states to their promises to incentivise 'green' energy generation capacity such as solar power or renewable energies.[13] In this context, the availability of investment law has proved a potential backstop against states shirking from their climate change commitments, such as by promising meaningful changes in energy infrastructure all the while moving the bill for these changes purely on to the investors in these ventures.[14] Following the adage of 'fool me once, shame on me', if such a policy backsliding could not effectively be stopped, the cost of the so-called green energy revolution would increase significantly.

Thereafter, we turn to a significant design problem. Energy projects have a long life. Problematically, it is the older generation of energy projects which create the greatest difficulty for decarbonisation because these projects are responsible for such large GHG emissions.[15] Does investment law allow investors in the older powerplants to stand in the way of policy initiatives to drive these projects from the grid? We identify relevant criteria against which an investment law tribunal would have to make its determination.

Even assuming for the sake of argument that investment law does in fact *systemically* hamper policy space, we argue that, from a human development perspective, there are also regulatory contexts in which the slowing down of policy initiatives would in fact be salutary, if not necessary. Conversely, we enumerate instances in which such a slowing down of policy or regulatory reforms would also be outright problematic.

The last section of this chapter will suggest proposals for how international investment law instruments might be changed so as to provide for stronger policy tools in support of current decarbonisation efforts. Specifically, the current paradigm is insufficiently sensitive to the negative impacts host state policymakers may have on their own populations' expectations of decarbonisation, environmental

---

[13] See Deyan Dragiev, 'Legitimate Expectations in Renewable Energy Treaty Arbitrations: The Lessons So Far' (*Kluwer Arbitration Blog*, 22 March 2018), http://arbitrationblog.kluwerarbitration.com/2018/03/22/legitimate-expectations-renewable-energy-treaty-arbitrations-lessons-far/ (detailing the first generation of investment arbitrations concerning renewable energy).
[14] *Ibid.*
[15] See Carnegie Mellon University, 'Aging U.S. Power Plants Provide Risks and Opportunities' (*Science Daily*, 19 July 2017), www.sciencedaily.com/releases/2017/07/170719113334.htm (discussing the conflicting trend lines for decarbonisation of retiring old coal-fired powerplants versus retiring aging nuclear powerplants).

measures and climate change protections. The chapter therefore will note how this negative impact might be subsumed into the existing investment law paradigm and recommend the system's reinforcement to ensure the fullest protection of host state populations' broader environmental, climate change and decarbonisation interests.

II. The Investment Law Infrastructure

To speak of international investment 'law' is as popular as it is a misnomer.[16] There is no multilateral investment agreement that would provide the framework for the substantive development of 'investment law' in the way of a General Agreement on Tariffs and Trade or World Trade Organisation (WTO) agreement.[17] Rather, what is lumped together under the heading of international investment law is the result of several thousand bilateral investment treaties, as well as certain specialised multilateral treaties.[18] These treaties can have wildly different terms. In fact, they extend protections to vastly different persons.[19] They then provide meaningfully different protections to each other even should they agree on the 'who' and 'what' is covered.[20] Finally, they may even differ as to what remedy is available to an aggrieved party.[21]

---

[16] See Christoph Schreuer and Rudolf Dolzer, *Principles of International Investment Law*, 2nd edn (Oxford University Press, 2012) 19 ('Today, it remains a matter of semantics whether it is appropriate to speak of the existence of a separate category of "principles of foreign investment law", given their strong links to international economic law in general. But there is no doubt that the international law of foreign investment has become a specialized area of the legal profession and that special courses are offered on the subject in universities worldwide. The common usage and parlance in the terminology of international law has always been to single out and to designate distinct fields, such as the "laws of war", or the "law of the sea", whenever the body of rules in any one area has become extensive and dense enough to justify special attention and study.').

[17] *Ibid* at 12.

[18] *Ibid* at 13.

[19] See Campbell McLachlan et al, *International Investment Arbitration: Substantive Principles*, 2nd edn (Oxford University Press, 2017) 176–78 (discussing differences in corporate nationality in BIT definitions of investors protected by respective treaty programmes).

[20] See Patrick Dumberry, *Fair and Equitable Treatment: Its Interaction with the Minimum Standard and Its Customary Status* (Brill, 2017) (discussing the absence of the core fair and equitable treatment provision in some early treaty programmes).

[21] See Thomas W Wälde and Borzu Sabahi, 'Compensation, Damages & Valuation' in Peter Muchlinski et al (eds), *The Oxford Handbook of International Investment Law* (Oxford University Press, 2008) 1049, 1069 (noting differences in compensation language in Bilateral Investment Treaties and allowing '[w]hatever one makes of differences in language it seems that currently the overwhelming state practice in concluding investment treaties has outweighed the challenge to customary international law in the NIEO period'). A different question arises whether different BITs allow – or do not allow – non-compensatory remedies. This question similarly is dealt with differently in different BITs. Compare, eg, Agreement between the Federal Republic of Germany and the Argentine Republic on the promotion and reciprocal protection of investments art 10(5), 9 April 1991, 171 UNTS 1910 ('The arbitral tribunal shall issue its ruling in accordance with the provisions of this Treaty, with those of other treaties existing between the Parties, with the laws in force in the Contracting Party in which the investments were made, including its rules of private international law, and with the general principles of international law.') *with* Agreement between the Government of the Republic of Korea and the Government of the Union of Soviet Socialist Republics for the Promotion and Reciprocal Protection of Investments art 9, 10 July 1991, IC-BT 1970 (1990) (limiting dispute resolution to compensation for expropriation or violation of free transfer provisions).

Why then do general commentators, lawyers practising in the field, and academics studying the field refer to 'investment law'? The answer to this question lies in the unique, and largely consistent, dispute resolution mechanism included in this web of treaties. First, this mechanism allows an investor to bring an international legal claim against the host state directly.[22] It does not need to proceed under the mantle of its home state (this latter type of proceeding is in fact a defining characteristic of the WTO dispute settlement understanding).[23] Second, the treaties almost universally agree on a form of international arbitration as a mechanism pursuant to which the investor seeks to hold the state to account.[24] Third, these arbitrations are subject to a reasonably narrow and reasonably consistent means to find facts, determine applicable law and then apply law to facts.[25]

International investment law is not a 'system of law' in the classical sense; it is more a process of decision-making.[26] This process of decision-making is largely uniform, even if the substantive norms applied through this process are anything but uniform.

This clarification speaks to criticisms of international investment law. The *substantive* criticism of 'international investment law', in a nutshell, asserts that the norms applied through the investment process are the wrong norms to apply internationally. Responses to this type of criticism focus on changing the *norms* that the process of decision-making would, or should, apply to any set of circumstances in investment disputes.[27]

Alternatively, the criticism could go deeper. It could assert that no matter what norm the process of decision-making would apply, it would also do harm just by its very existence and availability. That is to say, the focus of criticism is the *process* itself not the law it ends up applying. This criticism is significantly more far reaching. And it is this criticism that political foes of investment protection are advancing and on which so many current reform efforts are premised.[28]

This focus of the critics suggests that there is something in how the current process of investment protection applies norms that are contentious. To understand this criticism, it is briefly necessary to explain this process. Due to space constraints, the chapter will focus on the key features of how one particular

---

[22] Schreuer and Dolzer (n 16) 236–37.
[23] Schreuer and Dolzer (n 16) at 233.
[24] Schreuer and Dolzer (n 16) at 236–37.
[25] Schreuer and Dolzer (n 16) at 238–43.
[26] See Diane A Desierto, 'Rawlsian Fairness and International Arbitration' (2015) 36 *University of Pennsylvania Journal of International Law* 939; Frederic G Sourgens, *A Nascent Common Law: The Process of Decisionmaking in International Legal Disputes Between States and Foreign Investors* (Brill, 2014) 284–325.
[27] This arguably underpinned the re-interpretation of the fair and equitable treatment standard in the North American Free Trade Agreement (NAFTA) by the NAFTA parties. See Todd Weiler, *The Interpretation of International Investment Law, Equality, Discrimination and the Minimum Standard of Treatment in Historical Context* (Brill, 2013) 242–87.
[28] See generally Sergio Puig and Gregory Shaffer, 'Imperfect Alternatives: Institutional Choice and the Reform of Investment Law' (2018) 112 *American Journal of International Law* 361.

provision contained in varying formulae in investment treaties has been applied by tribunals. The point, however, is not the 'what' of the protection in question. It is the 'how' it has been divined and applied by investment tribunals.

The core protection at issue in a plurality, if not majority, of investment arbitrations is a protection that a state extends fair and equitable treatment to the investor's investment at all times.[29] How does an investment tribunal establish what this provision means? And how does it then apply this provision to the facts at bar?

The 'what' question appears deceptively simple. The protection is applicable in most investment arbitrations because two states included the provision in a bilateral investment treaty.[30] The law of treaties governs how treaties are to be interpreted.[31] The law of treaties provides that treaties are to be interpreted so as to give meaning to the ordinary meaning of their terms as viewed in the context in which these words appear and in light of the object and purpose for which the words have been included.[32] One would thus need to look at the various gradations of fair and equitable treatment provisions in order to establish the meaning of each provision as compelled by the specific treaty language used in a particular context.[33]

Tribunals in fact appear to follow this approach. That is, most investor-state decisions make reference to the fact that the protection in question is contained in a treaty.[34] They then dutifully note that the question of treaty interpretation is governed by the law of treaties.[35] They then duly mention the rules of interpretation at international law.[36]

Surprisingly, however, tribunals do not in fact determine that the fair and equitable treatment protections vary significantly from treaty to treaty. Quite the opposite is true.[37] It has focused on a set of common elements such as whether reasonable expectations have been frustrated or decisions have been made on patently pre-textual bases.[38] Some tribunals candidly rejected textualist arguments as irrelevant in this context, as one tribunal did in *Paushok v Mongolia* in which the underlying treaty did not include one of the traditional elements of the fair and equitable treatment formula.[39]

---

[29] Jeswald W Salacuse, *The Law of Investment Treaties* (Oxford University Press, 2015) 242.
[30] Ibid.
[31] See Richard K Gardiner, *Treaty Interpretation*, 2nd edn (Oxford University Press, 2015) 30–40.
[32] Vienna Convention on the Law of Treaties, 23 May 1969, 1155 U.N.T.S. 331, art 31.
[33] McLachlan et al (n 19) 291–95.
[34] Ibid 295–96.
[35] See, eg, *Blue Bank International & Trust (Barbados) v Venezuela*, ICSID Case No ARB/12/20, award (26 April 2017) ¶ 118; *İçkale İnşaat Limited Şirketi v Turkmenistan*, ICSID Case No ARB/10/24, award (8 March 2016) ¶ 195; *Rawat v Mauritius*, PCA Case No 2016-20, award (6 April 2018), ¶¶ 168–71.
[36] See decisions cited in n 35.
[37] Rudolf Dolzer, 'Fair and Equitable Treatment: Today's Contours' (2014) 12 *Santa Clara Journal of International Law* 7, 15.
[38] Ibid at 18, 31–32.
[39] *Paushok v Mongolia*, UNCITRAL jurisdiction and liability (28 April 2011) ¶¶ 250–55.

The 'how' of applying this provision is just as perplexing. An international treaty on its face would only apply international legal obligations on the state.[40] It would thus not look to the conduct of the investor all things considered. That is, to the extent the state acted in response to investor conduct, the question would be the reasonableness of the response by the *state* to the stimulus it received.[41]

Again, investment tribunals surprise. They very much look to circumstances beyond the treaty to apply the legal obligations contained in treaties. And the circumstances include the conduct of the investor in its own right.[42] That is, in applying fair and equitable treatment obligations, investment tribunals are not content to establish whether the state violated a norm of public international law contained in a treaty when it responded to a specific factual predicate in a certain manner. Investment tribunals instead look at whether the investor itself acted in a reasonable fashion, quite apart from what was known to the state.[43]

What explains this process? Though a full explanation of this process is beyond the scope of this chapter, one might intuit that tribunals weigh the relative actions and omissions of state and investor in applying norms that are heavily tinged by notions of reasonable reciprocal reliance. In doctrinal terms, investor-state tribunals take good faith as a substantive *Grundnorm* for their mission as a process of decision-making.[44] And it views this *Grundnorm* as reflecting a balancing task in which the reasonable relative interests of the parties, as well as the strategies chosen and not chosen, feature as prominently as the treaty language to be applied in a certain case.[45]

As a matter of result, it is perhaps unsurprising that such a more searching analysis will be less inclined to find state liability. If the analysis looks only to the reasonableness of state conduct, liability will lie if the state over-reacted to what it knew.[46] If the analysis looks to the substance of investor conduct, the investor may well lose out in certain circumstances even though the state may have over-reacted in its own right.[47] This means that the recovery achieved by claimants in investor-state proceedings frequently lags far behind what claimants have sought.[48] And it means that many claims are dismissed in their entirety or lead to a truly negligible

---

[40] Vaughan Lowe, 'The Law of Treaties or Should This Book Exist?' in Christian J Tams et al (eds), *Research Handbook on the Law of Treaties* (Edward Elgar, 2014) 3, 3.
[41] Ibid.
[42] For a full discussion, see Sourgens (n 11).
[43] *MTD Equity Sdn Bhd v Chile*, ICSID Case No ARB/01/7, award (25 May 2004), ¶ 176.
[44] See Dolzer (n 37) at 16–17.
[45] For a full discussion of good faith in the application of the fair and equitable treatment standard, see Emily Sipiorski, *Good Faith in International Investment Arbitration* (2019) 177–86.
[46] For further discussion, see N Jansen Calmita, 'The Principle of Proportionality and the Problem of Indeterminacy in International Investment Treaties' in Karl Sauvant (ed), *Yearbook on International Investment Law and Policy 2013-2014* (Oxford University Press, 2015) 157–200.
[47] See *Occidental Petroleum Corp v Ecuador*, ICSID Arb. 06/11, award (5 October 2012) ¶ 825.
[48] See Susan D Franck, 'Empirically Evaluating Claims about Investment Treaty Arbitration' (2007) 86 *North Carolina Law Review* 1, 59. The observation still holds true slightly less than 15 years later.

damages award even if one might muse that in the abstract, the state may well have acted unreasonably.[49] Context helps states.

Further, this approach has led tribunals to be willing to impose significant liability on investors either directly by finding in favour of counterclaims or indirectly by way of set off.[50] These counterclaims are generally permissible under the arbitral rules to which the parties consented to submit the main dispute.[51] They frequently are also permissible under the actual words of consent in the investment treaty.[52] Such counterclaims can lead to significant exposure on the part of the investor.[53] And even when such counterclaims are not directly heeded, the reduction in damages discussed in the last section is functionally consistent with a set off from damages owed to the investor of harm suffered by the state. It is thus stealthily present in almost any arbitration proceeding (or at least, almost any arbitration proceeding involving competent counsel for the respondent host state). Variances as to tribunal practices on counterclaims and damages, in this respect, do not diminish the value of the actual availability of these mechanisms in the first place to address investor liability.

To advance a critique that the process of decision-making – 'investment law' – is corrupt, or must be replaced, or represents a threat to decarbonisation (or for that matter supports decarbonisation) must be viewed through this lens. What is at stake is a certain form of process of decision-making. This process of decision-making takes into account the reasonable reliance interests of investors and the reasonable reliance interests of states.[54] This process is more opaque in taking into account the interests of third parties. The question thus becomes whether a process of decision that privileges the reasonable reliance interests of these actors vis-à-vis each other by imposing robust good faith requirements is compatible with decarbonisation.

III. Investment and Development

One further preliminary thought is needed before one can address this broader question head on. And it is a question that is important for decarbonisation more generally. What is the relationship between investment, investment law, and development?

A standard answer may well be that investment and investment protection is good for development so long as it supports economic growth.[55] This perspective

---

[49] *Ibid* at 5559.
[50] For a discussion, see Sourgens (n 11) at 195–206.
[51] International Centre for Settlement of Investment Disputes (ICSID) Convention Ar. 46; 2010 United Nations Commission on International Trade Law (UNCITRAL) Arbitration Rules, Article 21(3).
[52] *Saluka Investment BV v. Czech Republic*, counterclaim (7 May 2004) ¶ 76.
[53] For a discussion, see Sourgens (n 11) at 195–206.
[54] *Ibid*.
[55] See Matthew McCartney, *Economic Growth and Development, A Comparative Introduction* (Red Globe Press, 2015) 4 (discussing sustained economic growth and its impact on development).

would equate economic growth and development. Unsurprisingly, such a perspective would almost critically proclaim that more investment protection is good for growth for instance because it removes uncertainty from capital investments. This argument would thus largely reprise the arguments for deregulation as chief arguments in favour of investment protection.

This answer is both too facile and dangerous. It is too facile because it does not take seriously the question whether growth is always the answer.[56] The reason to ask the question is to have doubts that growth in fact always provides for salutary development. To refer back to growth is therefore not an answer to the question. It is also a dangerous path to take, all things considered. The question whether all growth leads to salutary development is politicised. One would expect 'fiscal conservatives' or 'libertarians' or 'classic liberals' all to agree and 'social democrats' or 'liberals' or 'socialists' to disagree. To hitch one's wagon to a pure growth dynamic therefore would be to limit the role of investment to a certain political outlook. This is dangerous as 'investment' as such is not a political or partisan activity, and establishing an ideological nexus to foreign investment requires actual and empirical substantiation. (Thus, a social democrat may well lose from view that certain kinds of investment allow the Government to achieve important policy goals – such as when an investor provides the capital needed for shifting to renewable energies or providing investment financing for green infrastructure and technologies. A libertarian on the other hand could lose from view that certain investors are corrupt actors who undermine efficient markets rather than supporting the development of such markets through their investment.)

In order to escape this facile and dangerous rubric, it is helpful to look not to growth as the measure of development but to take a broader, human development perspective. Nobel Prize winning economist Amartya Sen introduced such a broader human development perspective from an economics perspective.[57] Kyoto and Berggruen Prize winning philosopher Martha Nussbaum further developed this approach from a philosophical perspective, linking it to her understanding of human capabilities as anchored in ethics.[58] The United Nations Development Programme, in turn, has used a human development approach to measure development by means of a measure other than growth.[59]

The United Nations Development Programme summarises the approach in the following terms: 'human development focuses on improving the lives

---

[56] See David Pilling, *The Growth Delusion, Wealth, Poverty, and the Well-Being of Nations* (Tim Duggan Books, 2018).

[57] Amartya Sen, *Development as Freedom* (Anchor, 1999); Amartya Sen, *The Idea of Justice* (Harvard University Press, 2009).

[58] Martha Nussbaum, *Creating Capabilities* (Harvard University Press, 2011).

[59] Mozaffar Qizilbash, 'Amartya Sen's Capability View: Insightful Sketch or Distorted Picture?' in Flavio Comim, et al (eds), *The Capability Approach, Concepts Measures, Applications* (Cambridge University Press, 2008) 53, 65 (discussing the relationship of Sen's work to the United Nations Development Programme's work and the reduction of development to a single indexing number over Sen's objections). Arguably, the reduction of capabilities to a single number misses the philosophical point of the human capabilities approach, as Nussbaum in particular would submit that human good is

people lead rather than assuming that economic growth will lead, automatically, to greater wellbeing for all. Income growth is seen as a means to development, rather than an end in itself'.[60] It goes on that '[h]uman development is about giving people more freedom to live lives they value. In effect this means developing people's abilities and giving them a chance to use them'.[61] It submits that '[t]hree foundations for human development are to live a long, healthy and creative life, to be knowledgeable, and to have access to resources needed for a decent standard of living'.[62] This broader compass of human development reflects essential elements of the emerging right to development, as articulated in Article 1 of the 1986 UN Declaration on the Right to Development,[63] and the current Draft Convention on the Right to Development.[64] Under both these instruments, the human right to development enables all persons and peoples to participate, contribute and enjoy economic, social, cultural and political development, including the right to self-determination, on the premise that development is anchored on respect for, protection of, and fulfilment of, all human rights and fundamental freedoms.

It is thus at least helpful to measure the investment law paradigm against these broader goals. Before making a more forceful claim about the value of investment law for human development, one should begin from a weaker – and less controversial – starting point. Thus, investment law does not, all things considered, create an *obstacle* to human development. Investment law does not deprive human beings in the host country or anywhere else on the planet of the ability to live lives they value. Importantly, international investment tribunals do not extend the protections of investment law to investments that have been procured by corruption.[65] International investment law also requires the investor to live up to the fundamental requirements of international public policy for these investments to enjoy protection.[66] To choose an extreme example, it is highly unlikely that a supplier of poisons used in the execution of prisoners would have an investment claim against a state that chose to execute prisoners in a more 'humane' manner in violation of a contractual arrangement with the supplier – it is just as unlikely that the investor would have a reasonable claim if the state embraced the value of the sanctity of the dignity of human life and abolished the death penalty altogether. Finally,

---

precisely not reducible to a single measure or number. See Martha Nussbaum, *The Fragility of Goodness: Luck and Ethics in Greek Tragedy and Philosophy* (Cambridge University Press, 2001).

[60] UN Development Programme, Human Development Reports, 'About Human Development' (2019), http://hdr.undp.org/en/humandev.

[61] *Ibid.*

[62] *Ibid.*

[63] 1986 UN Declaration on the Right to Development, full text at www.ohchr.org/en/professionalinterest/pages/righttodevelopment.aspx.

[64] Draft Convention on the Right to Development, full text at www.ohchr.org/Documents/Issues/Development/Session21/3_A_HRC_WG.2_21_2_AdvanceEditedVersion.pdf.

[65] *World Duty Free Co v Kenya*, ICSID Case No ARB/00/7, award (4 October 2006).

[66] For an interesting discussion, see Cameron Miles, 'Corruption, Jurisdiction and Admissibility in International Investment Claims' (2012) 3 *Journal of International Dispute Settlement* 329.

investment law does not protect investments that have been procured in violation of host state law.[67] Nor does it protect investments against the imposition of reasonable health and safety regulations such as plain packaging rules to prevent the marketing of cigarettes to minors.[68]

The notion that investment law does not impose an obstacle to human development should not be revolutionary or controversial. Investment law therefore is at least neutral on broader human development questions. In other words, investment does not drive policy goals; it merely is a means to meet them. Investment law therefore does not pre-determine permissible policies. It is structurally designed to ensure protection only to those investors that seek to meet existing state-policies in good faith.

As it is currently being applied, investment law further does more than simply doing no harm. Investment law is a means to achieve beneficial human development goals in its own right. Thus, in the first place, human development goals crucially depend upon the available of access to justice for all and a means to review and shine a light on both economic and regulatory practices.[69] Investment law is a key international means to shed a light on both. Investors who make claims against host states expose the latter's regulatory practices and operational activities to transparent global scrutiny. Hugo Perezcano, one of the leading international economic lawyers in Mexican government service at the time of Mexico's signing and implementation of international investment agreements, noted that this transparency and international scrutiny was a benefit for state and investors alike.[70] It created a forum in which uncomfortable questions could be asked of both states and investors. It also provided a much needed backstop against arbitrary regulatory practices that would not only affect foreign investors covered by investment treaties but also the citizenry of the host state itself against depredatory political acts of politicians and regulators.

Further, international investment law provides an additional reason for transnational commercial actors to act with restraint and respect. Investment law provides a powerful tool for potential review and recovery against the state. But the availability of this tool is, in turn, concomitantly contingent upon the good faith conduct of the investor towards the state and its population.[71] An investor that wishes to maintain a potential claim if arbitrary government conduct would impair its investment is, therefore, well-served to act consistently not only with

---

[67] *Inceysa Vallisoletana SL v Republic of El Salvador*, ICSID Case No ARB/03/26, award (2 August 2006); *Plama Consortium Ltd v Republic of Bulgaria*, ICSID Case No ARB/03/24, award (27 August 2008).

[68] *Philip Morris Brands SARL v Uruguay*, ICSID Case No ARB/10/7, award (8 July 2016) ¶¶ 391–92.

[69] United Nations Development Programme, UN Development Report 2016, 'Human Development for Everyone' (2016) 16–17.

[70] See Hugo Perezcano Díaz, 'Enhancing the Dispute Settlement System or Much Ado About Nothing' in Ian Laird, et al (eds), *Investment Treaty Arbitration and International Law* (Juris Publishing, 2013) 6.

[71] *Fraport AG Frankfurt Airport Services Worldwide v The Republic of the Philippines*, ICSID Case No ARB/03/25, award (16 August 2007) ¶ 402.

domestic law in the host state, but also to act consistently with international best practices, for instance in interacting with indigenous peoples affected by the investment.[72]

This second aspect of human development – and the impact of investment on human development – is extensively explored in the literature on the social licence to operate in the international mining sector.[73] Recent scholarship has extended this discussion beyond the mining sector to economic activity as a whole.[74] Importantly, this social licence to operate and cognate concepts of corporate social responsibility do not function in a vacuum. They require international fora in which they can meaningfully make a difference for international businesses seeking to be both responsible global actors and protect their bottom lines for shareholders.

International investment law is not the only means by which social licences to operate can become internationally meaningful in a tangible sense.[75] But international investment law is a meaningful component of the broader economic and regulatory processes in which social licences to operate are embedded and in which corporate social responsibility can make a tangible difference. Thus, international investment tribunals will not only look to the investor's social licence to operate in extreme cases such as corruption. International investment tribunals are conscious of the fact whether investors were broadly responsible actors for their host societies.[76]

This positive role at one point had a contentious doctrinal anchor. The very concept of investment was defined – and continues to be defined by some – to require that the investment make a positive impact on the development of the host state.[77] This definitional statement may well be overbroad.[78] It would require tribunals to make thorny abstract judgments about the value of an investor's conduct without looking at the overall merits of the claim in which they are embedded. Tribunals that do not consider the question of contributions to host

---

[72] See *ibid*.
[73] For a discussion of the literature see Andrea Bjorklund, Georgios Petrochilos, Stephan Schill and Diane Desierto, 'Investment at the Crossroads' in Reinisch et al (eds), *International Law and ... Select Proceedings of the European Society of International Law* (Hart Publishing, 2016) 151, 158.
[74] *Ibid*.
[75] Diane Desierto, 'Why Arbitrate Business and Human Rights Disputes? Public Consultation Period Open for the Draft Hague Rules on Business and Human Rights Arbitration' (*EJILTalk!*, 12 July 2019), www.ejiltalk.org/public-consultation-period-until-august-25-for-the-draft-hague-rules-on-business-and-human-rights-arbitration/.
[76] For a full discussion, see Sourgens (n 11).
[77] *Fedax NV v Venezuela*, ICSID Case No ARB/96/3, jurisdiction (11 July 1997) ¶ 43; *Fakes v Turkey*, ICSID Case No ARB/07/20, award (14 July 2010) ¶ 111 ('Such development is an expected consequence, not a separate requirement, of the investment projects carried out by a number of investors in the aggregate.').
[78] On the development of this feature of the meaning of investment, see Katia Yannaca-Small and Dimitrios Katsikis, 'The Meaning of "Investment"' in Katia Yannaca-Small (ed), *Investment Treaty Arbitration, Arbitration Under International Investment Agreements: A Guide to the Key Issues*, 2nd edn (Oxford University Press, 2018) 266, 293.

state development as a matter of the very definition of investment typically do consider such a contribution, or the lack thereof, in the context of applying the most basic protection enshrined in almost all investment treaties – the obligation to treat the investment fairly and equitably. This analysis almost always looks to investor conduct as well as state conduct to determine whether or not the investor has a meritorious claim.[79] And in this context, a social licence to operate can make the difference between a claim that has merit and one that does not – and between a claim for which significant compensation is granted and one for which almost no compensation is granted.

IV. Investment Law as a Catalyst for Green Development

How then does investment law support human development in the context of decarbonisation? One of the often overlooked factors in the context of the debate about the role of investment law in decarbonisation is that decarbonisation itself cannot be achieved by the community of states alone. For example, decarbonisation requires a significant shift in energy infrastructure away from particularly coal-burning powerplants and towards non-fossil fuel burning powerplants.[80] The existing legal infrastructure for the construction and operation of powerplants in many countries requires long-term private investment.[81] Should one wish to decarbonise based on existing legal and economic models, one therefore needs investment to bring about the shift in energy landscapes.

In the context of decarbonisation, it is further not feasible for almost any state to carry the burden of capital investment needed to change the domestic energy infrastructure upfront and on its own. The costs involved are staggering with renewable sources of energy at the upper end of the cost scale.[82] The expertise required is complex. It therefore becomes all the more necessary for the state to rely upon foreign investment to achieve this goal. The state will need help. In the global community, that need for help is all the more staggering. The global community consists not just of economic powerhouses like the United States.

---

[79] See Sourgens (n 11).
[80] John P Banks, Tim Boersma and Charles K Ebinger, 'Does Decarbonization Mean De-coalification? Discussing Carbon Reduction Policies' (*Brookings*, 2 November 2015), www.brookings.edu/articles/does-decarbonization-mean-de-coalification-discussing-carbon-reduction-policies/. ('The experts presenting to the Task Force agreed that research to date largely indicates that carbon reduction policies, regardless of the type, will significantly and negatively impact coal. In the words of one participant, "de-carbonization means de-coalification".)
[81] Kfir Abutbul, 'Private Equity Investment in Power Infrastructure Looks Bright' (2019) *The Texas Lawyer*, available at www.paulhastings.com/publications-items/details/?id=0471796c-2334-6428-811c-ff00004cbded (altering clients to private equity investment opportunities in power and their regulatory environment).
[82] 'Basic Economics of Power Generation, Transmission and Distribution' (PennState College of Earth and Mineral Sciences), www.e-education.psu.edu/eme801/node/530.

It also consists of many transitional economies. These transitional economies need to decarbonise just as much as the leading economies to meet climate goals.[83]

Importantly, this decarbonisation in transitional economies presents a particular human development problem. Thus, access to affordable energy is one of the key requirements for life in the modern global economy. But the existing energy infrastructure frequently does not allow transitioning economies to provide affordable energy that does not create significant air pollution or generate significant greenhouse gases. To achieve this additional goal, governments will thus not only need investment – they will in all likelihood need foreign investment and capital.[84]

The problem of foreign investment in affordable, clean, non-fossil energy is the risks involved. Thus, even facially rich developed countries such as Italy and Spain rolled out renewable energy programmes to entice investment in solar energy only to renege on their promises to investors in renewable energy projects following the 2008 financial crisis.[85] The investment in renewable energy projects therefore involves significant risk of a regulatory about face even in EU countries. This risk is not lessened when investing in industrialising economies.

How then does investment law assist in overcoming this regulatory obstacle? The claims by international investors in solar energy projects against EU countries provide a blueprint to answer this question. These claims fundamentally arose because the subsidies codified in the law of EU states were phased out following the financial crisis.[86] Investors brought claims that states such as Spain and Italy violated their investment treaty commitments when these countries changed the regulatory structure providing the original investment incentives and subsidies.[87]

Centrally, the resulting investment arbitrations have yielded mixed results. Some tribunals noted that investors were not directly promised a stable price environment.[88] These tribunals focused on the inherent business risk involved in investing in energy markets – and the potential for regulatory change in those markets.[89] Yet, other tribunals focused on the cumulative representations made by the state to specific investors and focused on the particular economic commitments made by these investors.[90] This analysis led some tribunals to conclude that the specific impairment of investments making investments completely unprofitable despite reasonable *ex ante* diligence and conduct by the investor did lead to treaty breaches.

While a more detailed analysis of these cases is beyond the scope of the present chapter, it does provide a helpful blueprint for how investment law does in fact support and foster the *right kind of investment in renewable energy*, in turn

---

[83] For a discussion of differentiated responsibility in the post-Copenhagen climate world, see Alexander Zahar, *Climate Change Finance and International Law* (Routledge, 2016).
[84] See ibid.
[85] For a discussion see Graham Coop and Isabella Seif, 'ECT and States' Right to Regulate' in Maxi Scherer (ed), *International Arbitration in the Energy Sector* (Oxford University Press, 2018) 222–23.
[86] Ibid.
[87] Ibid.
[88] See, eg, *Charenne BV v Spain*, SCC Case No V 062/2012, award (21 January 2016) ¶ 503.
[89] Ibid.
[90] See *OperaFund Eco-Invest SICAV PLC v Spain*, ICSID Case No ARB/15/36, award (6 September 2019) ¶ 484 (discussing stabilisation promises in the specific case at bar).

embracing human development. Investment law requires investors to act with diligence when making renewable energy investments in order to benefit from investment protections should the regulatory landscape drastically change to make their investments unprofitable. It further requires that investors act reasonably and operate reasonably in the environment as they find it. They cannot rely upon governmental handouts but must in fact do their part to operate in a manner consistent with current conditions. One can assume that the social licence to operate would be an additional factor taken into account as and when it is relevant to the dispute.

This means that investment law can in fact act as a catalyst for investment in renewables by removing or limiting political risk factors that particularly affect industrialising economies with volatile or unpredictable regulatory track records. Investment law requires investors to act reasonably *ex ante* and to make available needed, 'clean' (that is, non-polluting and carbon-neutral) energy consistent with their social licence to operate. What investment law adds is that it allows investors to hold states to their word once investors have held up their end of the bargain. This legal certainty therefore provides a significant boon for achieving policies of rapid decarbonisation and thus is a net benefit to global energy policy.

In other words, international investment law is a powerful pre-commitment device.[91] It binds states to hold the course they have struck and allows foreign investors to commit significant capital to bring about the desired decarbonisation policy goals. It further allows this to happen in an industry-wide setting without requiring cumbersome contractual negotiations on an ad hoc basis. This is not an insignificant benefit. Energy policy is becoming an increasingly important and contentious part of electoral politics around the world.[92] As it stands, any election risks toppling existing decarbonisation policies. Creating meaningful pre-commitment devices in this political environment is a necessary condition for decarbonisation to progress apace. Investment law is a means to do so without the need for significant institutional reform. It is therefore a net plus for decarbonisation efforts and the human development results that depend upon it.

V. Investment Law as a Brake on Decarbonisation – Developmental Implications

The previous section has shown that investment law is a meaningful pre-commitment device for energy policy. Problematically, pre-commitment devices

---

[91] Craig Martin, 'Binding the Dogs of War: Japan and the Constitutionalizing of Jus Ad Bellum' (2008) 30 *University of Pennsylvania Journal of International Law* 267 (discussing the pre-commitment device literature).

[92] 'Why is there a Backlash against Climate Policies?' (*BBC*, 2019), www.bbc.co.uk/programmes/w3csyth0.

are precisely blind to changed policy appetites. They thus protect *any* energy investment alike, whether we currently consider this investment to be in a desirable technology or not. This creates the thorny issue as to whether international investment law is a potential brake on decarbonisation because any such effort would seriously upset existing energy infrastructures.

The risk is a serious one in concept. Thus, a policy that is serious about decarbonisation would likely force an acceleration in shutting down coal-fired powerplants.[93] This was one of the intended results of policy initiatives such as the Clean Power Plan in the United States.[94] Without an acceleration of a phase out of coal-fired powerplants, it is reasonably unlikely that current mitigation goals could be met.

As coal-fired powerplants benefit just as much from investment law as renewable projects, one might therefore ask – to what extent are coal-fired powerplant operators protected by international investment law and how much of a brake will this create for a quick switch away from coal? The answer to this question is complicated but on the whole, particularly recently approved coal-fired power projects have a reasonable prospect of investment law protection. Is this, then, a reason to doubt the overall developmental benefit of international investment law?

Even in this context, one should proceed carefully. The neutrality of international investment law presents one of its key benefits from a human development perspective. Investment law does not make the choice for states as to what energy solutions they should choose for themselves. It honours and protects the choice made by states once they have embarked on it. Of course, this means that investment law will enforce the result of 'bad' choices on the polities that made them. A diligent coal investor is just as worthy of protection as a diligent solar investor. Both make available needed electricity to support human development. While both choose different means of generating electricity, both contribute to development – be it in different ways, at different price points, with different externalities, and implying different supply chains and economic partners. The fact that investment law protects both equally alike therefore is a logical consequence of the underlying value of investment law of deferring in the first place to the local policy processes and value goals of the host state, rather than imposing independent policy and value goals of their own.

Importantly, this problem is lessened somewhat by the fact that a significant portion of coal-fired generating capacity worldwide is in fact aging.[95] The reasonableness of investment expectations regarding these older plants is significantly more doubtful. Echoing the solar power cases, certainly coal-fired power plant

---

[93] Banks et al (n 80).

[94] 'The Clean Power Plan, EPA Interprets the Clean Air Act to Allow Regulation of Carbon Dioxide Emissions from Existing Power Plants' (2016) 129 *Harvard Law Review* 1152.

[95] Taylor Kuykendall Krizka and Danielle Del Rosario, 'Coal's "Aging Out" Problem: Most US Customers Operating Older Power Plants' (*S&P Global Market Intelligence*, 30 January 2018), www.spglobal.com/marketintelligence/en/news-insights/trending/c-mlubpvfukfng57myl_za2.

investors should have expected shifts in energy policy at some point.[96] Technical reports from industry experts,[97] including the International Renewable Energy Agency,[98] increasingly estimate a much faster rate of obsolescence and phasing out of traditional energy sources and a much more rapid expansion of renewable energy supplies. The older the plant, the less reasonable the expectation that business as usual will continue to prevail. For those older plants, it would thus take an extraordinary circumstance for a meritorious investment claim to ripen from *bona fide* decarbonisation policies and an even more extraordinary circumstance for such a meritorious claim to somehow lead to significant compensatory recovery.

In sum, even when investment law serves as a possible brake on decarbonisation, it does so for reasons that are on the whole consistent with human development goals. It protects freedom of choice and freedom of action for host states, as well as their citizens. This freedom of political choice is one of the essential functions and elements of human development. The fact that this freedom has consequences – that commitments made through the legislative and regulatory process are not 'free' when others rely upon the commitments made – may have negative ramifications. One may wish that past generations had made different policy choices. But the responsibility that comes with having to 'buy out' those who reasonably relied upon earlier commitments, while pragmatically problematic, is little reason for questioning the system that gives effect to those earlier decisions.

VI. The Need for Limited but Important Reform

This is not to say that the current investment law paradigm is perfect. The current investment law paradigm as it is currently used is lagging behind the need for *ex ante* transparency and clarity and *ex post* remedies for affected communities that similarly suffered from the negative consequences of investment treaty violations on the one hand or energy investor malfeasance on the other. There is thus a reasonable need for continued reform efforts to further improve the usefulness of investment treaties for the future of decarbonisation.

In the first place, the newest model international investment agreements are more express about the role of environmental legislation in the overall policy

---

[96] See *Charenne BV v Spain*, SCC Case No V 062/2012, award (21 January 2016) ¶ 503.
[97] Jillian Ambrose, 'Renewable Energy to Expand by 50% in Next Five Years – Report' *The Guardian*, 21 October 2019, www.theguardian.com/environment/2019/oct/21/renewable-energy-to-expand-by-50-in-next-five-years-report.
[98] International Renewable Energy Agency (IRENA), 'Global Energy Transformation: A Roadmap to 2050', 2019 edition (*IRENA*, 2019) at www.irena.org/-/media/Files/IRENA/Agency/Publication/2019/Apr/IRENA_Global_Energy_Transformation_2019.pdf.

process.⁹⁹ They provide meaningful exclusions from treaty protection to the extent that the state is responding in good faith to environmental needs.¹⁰⁰ Investment treaties could be further reformed to provide greater transparency for investors in this regard and to provide for a greater dialogue between investors and their regulators so as to limit the need for unforeseen environmental intervention in the energy sector in the first place.

One of the key features of the regulatory process in transitional economies in particular is that there is a reasonable lack of regulatory expertise. This lack of regulatory expertise means that the structure for energy projects is frequently borrowed from other states and borrowed imperfectly by failing to embed the new structure in the peculiarities of local law. This creates significant problems for both the host state and the investor with regard to the implementation of any given project.

From the state's perspective, it is reasonably possible for investors to achieve bargains that the host state did not fully intend because it did not fully understand the repercussions of project structures and project commitments. This means that many states will find that their regulatory responses can only mature as they learn in practice. This in turn means that there is a significant need for regulatory adjustments once the full repercussions of given project structures become apparent to the state. These adjustments can in fact lead to treaty claims – and successful treaty claims, as ignorance of law is no defence even for states.

From the investor's perspective, the regulatory uncertainty in energy projects is similarly undesirable. It presents opportunities for costly misunderstandings that project companies would rather avoid, as no investor enters an energy market only to prosecute an investment treaty claim against the state. Rather, investors typically wish to have certainty and transparency as to the regulatory environment at the front end.

The needs of both states and investors could meaningfully be addressed by requiring pre-investment communications and diligence for investors to be granted certain safe-harbour protections from environmental exclusions codified in current generation international treaties. Thus, to the extent that project investors conduct certain kinds of environmental and social impact assessments, educate the state about their results, and collaborate with the state to re-structure the project to avoid potential environmental and social risks, investors should be insulated from regulatory responses that should have been included by the state in this process.

This approach would apply something akin to good faith. It would facially require states to make their policy elections at the front end before the investor incurs meaningful expenses to perform an agreed upon bargain. But for this good faith obligation to vest, the investor would have to show that the state in fact made a relevant policy election at the time – meaning that state and investor are

---

⁹⁹ Anna Aseeva and Tatiana Beketova, 'Sustainability Provisions in Canadian Investment Agreements with African LDCs: A Social Licence to Operate?' (2019) *Oil, Gas & Energy Law*, www.ogel.org/news.asp?key=571.
¹⁰⁰ *Ibid.*

encouraged to communicate fully at the outset of the investment before capital has been committed, rather than at a later point in time.

A second key point of potential reform is the serious under-compensation available in international investment treaties for affected communities. The failure of a state to live up to its decarbonisation commitments to an investor has negative consequences for the investor in the form of lost profits or lost opportunities, as well as loss of capital investments. The failure of the state also has significant repercussions for affected communities: they will need to adapt to the environmental and climate impact to which the state's policy contributed. The current investment treaty structure appears to allow only for the first of these losses to be compensated. Further, to the extent that remedial theories could be developed to broaden the scope of available relief from the state for affected communities, investment treaties currently do not provide for guidance as to how such remedies should be awarded or administered. The most glaring gap in investment law thus far is in its current inability to provide direct redress for affected communities against both host state governments' misfeasances towards communities with respect to decarbonisation commitments, and foreign investors that do not operate according to the host state's decarbonisation commitments.

In addition, while many investment treaty claims give rise to a reasonable right to counterclaim in the state, the remedy that the state could achieve again does not inure to the benefit of the affected communities that suffered harm from the investor's misconduct. The state's counterclaim is typically brought on behalf of a community that suffered environmental or other harm due to the investor's conduct. If the counterclaim is granted, the natural result is either a setoff of the investor's claim or a monetary award to the host state. This result obviously does not aid the affected community. In the case of a setoff, it is reasonably clear that the state will not use the equivalent of the setoff amount to benefit the affected communities which suffered the loss in the first place. Further, even in the case of a monetary award on a counterclaim, there is no guarantee that the state will in fact use the funds ordered to address the harm done by an investor.

Investment treaties therefore would do well to provide clear guidance regarding the power of tribunals to award remedies that flow directly from the harm done to local communities. Current treaty structures are silent on these issues. This is a significant blind spot in investment treaties, given the significant costs that climate change adaptation will bring with it and the need to use funds to investment in adaptation locally to protect affected communities rather than nationally to ease the burden on the state budget.

VII. Conclusion

International investment law is a key part of the global legal infrastructure to affect decarbonisation efforts. As discussed in this chapter, investment law as a whole has both helpful and harmful effects for decarbonisation. But as this chapter also discussed, to the extent investment law has problematic effects from a decarbonisation perspective, these effects are not due to investment law processes but to the underlying policy decisions preceding an investment claim.

This chapter has discussed that investment law can be one of the chief pillars upon which states could anchor their commitments to decarbonise. Thus, one of the problems of current climate policy is the significant political volatility of energy policy resulting from climate concerns. This volatility significantly obstructs the efficient deployment of urgently needed private capital to support decarbonisation and green economy transformation efforts. Investment law can reduce the risk of political volatility by providing remedies for conscientious investors operating energy infrastructure-supporting decarbonisation efforts in a socially responsible manner. This benefit is not to be underestimated.

As it stands, the current investment infrastructure however does too little to foster communication between investor and state concerning energy projects and too little to help affected communities suffering from a failure to decarbonise. There is thus significant room for improvement as treaty-drafting becomes ever more conscious of the need to support state energy and climate policy. The most important of these improvements concerns the ability of tribunals transparently and effectively to award compensation to affected communities to aid in their adaptation to climate change and other systemic policy problems flowing from an investment dispute.

7

Private Mineral Rights and Africa's Shale Gas

EMEKA DURUIGBO*

I. Introduction

Africa is endowed with significant quantities of natural gas in conventional fields as well as unconventional fields, particularly shale rock formations. Developing Africa's shale gas, as expected in other places, will promote energy security,[1] offer environmental gains[2] and enhance the economic fortunes of the producing countries.[3] Additionally, it will improve global energy access in line with the United Nations' Sustainable Energy for All (SEFA) initiative.[4] There are, however, a number of legal, geological, political and economic obstacles to shale gas development.

This chapter addresses the legal aspect of the impediments, primarily the absence of the United States' system of private ownership of mineral rights *in situ* in most parts of the world. This absence has occasioned resistance from surface owners, engendered a lack of motivation to innovate and forestalled the cooperation between mineral owners and energy companies that contributed significantly to the American Shale Revolution. In that light, this chapter examines the role played by private mineral ownership in the Shale Revolution. It argues that the absence

---

* A version of this work was presented at the Inaugural Environmental Works-in-Progress Roundtable at the University of Houston Law Centre on 7 December 2018. Many thanks to the organisers and participants at the workshop for their helpful comments. Special thanks to former acting Dean Gary Bledsoe and Associate Dean L Darnell Weeden for financial support through the Thurgood Marshall Summer Stipend programme in 2019 that made completion of this chapter possible. I am grateful to my students Katelyn Logie (JD 2019), Connor Smith (JD 2020) and Juana Eburi (JD 2020) for excellent research and editorial assistance.
[1] Gina Tincher, 'The Unconventional Gas Technical Engagement Program: How to Ensure the United States Shares its Experience in a Socially and Environmentally Responsible Manner' (2015) 36 *Energy Law Journal* 113, 114.
[2] *Ibid* at 119.
[3] *Ibid* at 118; Justin P Atkins, 'Hydraulic Fracturing in Poland: A Regulatory Analysis' (2013) 12 Washington University *Global Studies Law Review* 339, 341–42.
[4] International Energy Agency, 'Modern Energy For All', www.iea.org/energyaccess/modernenergyforall/.

of private ownership is an obstacle that needs to be overcome for shale gas development to thrive abroad. Nevertheless, the problem is not insurmountable. Policy makers simply need to consider private ownership of minerals or introduce effective substitutes to overcome the impediment, facilitate development of these resources and reap the expected gains for the economy and environment. This chapter proposes one such substitute, namely civic shares. These shares will provide ownership interests in energy development projects, thereby providing an incentive for, and reducing resistance to, shale development in countries outside the United States.

This discussion is particularly pertinent for Africa. The continent suffers from energy poverty in the form of limited access to modern energy services. At the same time, it is home to substantial natural gas deposits. Two African countries, Algeria and South Africa, are poised to develop their shale gas reserves. It is important to understand what lies ahead as these countries explore the possibilities.

Section II of this chapter presents the rationale for increased natural gas development. Section III focuses on shale deposits in Africa. Section IV discusses impediments to shale gas development generally. Section V closely examines the impediment of sovereign ownership or absence of private ownership of subsoil resources in virtually every country that holds substantial shale reserves. Section VI proposes a substitute for private ownership, in the form of civic shares, as a mechanism for addressing this impediment and facilitating the development of the shale resources. Section VII presents a critical appraisal of the proposal by considering potential objections to it. The chapter concludes by stating that developing the vast quantities of shale resources in Africa and around the world is a net positive development for humanity and should receive all the needed legal, technical and economic support to make it a reality.

II. The Natural Gas Rationale

Natural gas can play an important role in addressing the problem of energy poverty that plagues a significant portion of the world population. Energy is needed for economic development and social progress. Natural gas can satisfy substantial energy demands in a relatively cleaner way.

A. Sustainable Energy for All

Modern economic development is virtually impossible without access to modern energy services, including electricity and clean cooking facilities.[5] Demonstrable

---

[5] Adrian J Bradbrook, Judith G Gardam and Monique Cormier, 'A Human Dimension to the Energy Debate: Access to Modern Energy Services' (2008) 26 No 4 *Journal of Energy & Natural Resources Law* 526, 526–28; Raffaella Centurelli, 'Energy Poverty: Can We Make Modern Energy Access Universal? Focus On Financing Appropriate Sustainable Energy Technologies' (2011) 22 *Colorado Journal of*

economic growth is thus linked to energy consumption.[6] The path to poverty alleviation goes through energy access.[7] Indeed, to function successfully on this earth, human beings need energy.[8] In recognition of these facts of life, the United Nations launched SEFA.[9] In 2010, the UN General Assembly (UNGA) issued a declaration designating 2012 as 'International Year of Sustainable Energy for All'.[10] Acting under the request of UNGA, then UN Secretary General, Mr Ban Ki Moon, introduced the SEFA initiative in 2011. The SEFA initiative is a multi-stakeholder endeavour that aims to attract worldwide attention and public and private commitments to meeting three objectives by 2030, including ensuring universal access to modern energy services, accelerating the rate of improvement in energy efficiency two-fold and increasing the share of renewable energy in the global energy mix to double its present size. In 2012, UNGA intensified efforts in this regard by declaring 2014–2024 as the United Nations Decade of Sustainable Energy for All.[11] In 2015, UNGA adopted the Sustainable Development Goals (SDGs), with Goal 7 targeting the provision of access to affordable, reliable, sustainable and modern energy for all.[12]

Energy access is a critical component of SEFA.[13] Access includes availability, portability and affordability. The importance of energy access cannot be

---

International Environmental Law & Policy 219, 221; International Energy Agency (n 4) ('Energy is a critical enabler. Every advanced economy has required secure access to modern sources of energy to underpin its development and growing prosperity.'); Steven Ferrey, 'Law of Independent Power' (2015) 1 *Law of Independent Power* § 2:1 ('Electricity has made possible a high-energy modern society.').

[6] Stuart Bruce, 'Climate Change Mitigation through Energy Efficiency Laws: From International Obligations to Domestic Regulation' (2013) 31 *Journal of Energy & Natural Resources Law* 313, 320 (restating the generally accepted view that energy consumption and economic growth are positively correlated).

[7] Adrian J Bradbrook, 'Sustainable Energy Law: The Past and the Future' (2012) 30 *Journal of Energy & Natural Resources Law* 511, 512 ('The crucial role of energy in alleviating poverty in developing nations has been belatedly recognized. It appears to be now settled that there can be no escape from poverty without universal access to energy services.').

[8] Stuart Bruce, 'International Law and Renewable Energy: Facilitating Sustainable Energy for All?' (2013) 14 *Melbourne Journal of International Law* 18, 19 ('Energy use is indispensable to human life.').

[9] Nadia B Ahmad, '"Turn on the Lights"--Sustainable Energy Investment and Regulatory Policy: Charting the Hydrokinetic Path for Pakistan' (2013) 5 *Washington & Lee Journal of Energy, Climate, & the Environment* 165, 217 ('The Sustainable Energy for All initiative realizes the central role energy plays in development.').

[10] See *International Year of Sustainable Energy for All* UN Doc A/RES/65/151 (February 2011) 2 para 1; Heather Leibowitz, 'Harmony with Nature and Genetically Modified Seeds: A Contradictory Concept in the United States and Brazil?' (2013) 30 *Pace Environmental Law Review* 558, 559.

[11] See United Nations Department of Public Information, 'United Nations General Assembly Declares 2014-24 Decade of Sustainable Energy for All' (Press Release, GA/11333 EN/274, 21 December 2012).

[12] General Assembly (GA) Resolution 70/1, 'Transforming our World: The 2030 Agenda for Sustainable Development' (21 October 2015) at 1; Julia Chen, 'Financing the Sustainable Development Goals: The Role of African Sovereign Wealth Funds' (2019) 51 *New York University Journal of International Law and Politics* 1259, 1264.

[13] American Bar Association (ABA), 'ABA Environment, Energy, and Resources Law: The Year in Review 2012' (2012); ABA, 'ABA Environment, Energy, and Resources Law The Year in Review 2013 (2013) 313, 318; Todd Moss, Roger Pielke, Jr and Morgan Bazilian, 'Balancing Energy Access and Environmental Goals in Development Finance: The Case of the OPIC Carbon Cap' (Center for Global Development Policy Paper 038, 2014) 1, 2 (stating that the provision of universal access to modern

over-emphasised.[14] As Pielke points out, 'Access to energy is one of the big global issues that has hovered around the fringes of international policy discussions such as the Millennium Development Goals or climate policy, but which has been getting more attention in recent years'.[15] Indeed, access to energy has achieved such a level of significance that some scholars view it as an existing or emerging human right.[16] There are also national security and foreign policy implications of minimal energy access in a country, such as socio-economic and political instability that could spill across borders.[17] Little wonder that this global push for energy access attracted the attention of the White House, being an issue that touches many angles. In June 2013, then US President Barack Obama launched 'Power Africa', a significant initiative that aimed to use a host of US government agencies to double energy access within five years in six target countries in Africa, namely Ghana, Kenya, Nigeria, Tanzania, Ethiopia and Liberia. Over the years, Power Africa has expanded its activities and locations of operations across all of sub-Saharan Africa, including Ethiopia, Ghana, Guinea, Kenya, Liberia, Malawi, Nigeria, Rwanda, Senegal, Sierra Leone, South Africa, Tanzania, Uganda and Zambia.[18]

The various initiatives to increase energy access are of critical importance in view of the dire situation that exists in many countries as a result of energy poverty. It is estimated that more than 1.6 billion people, living mainly in sub-Saharan Africa and South Asia, lack access to modern energy services.[19] One can put the figures in context to demonstrate the stark contrast and the gloom it portends:

> Residential electricity consumption in Sub-Saharan Africa, excluding South Africa, is roughly equivalent to consumption in New York. In other words, the 19.5 million inhabitants of New York consume in a year roughly the same quantity of electricity, 40 TWh, as the 791 million people of Sub-Saharan Africa.[20]

In addition, a large proportion of the global population, representing about 40 per cent of the population and numbering about 2.7 billion people, do their

---

energy services is '[t]he "principal" goal (as first among equals of three goals)' of the Sustainable Energy for All initiative.)

[14] Moss et al, *ibid*, at 2 (asserting 'that energy access will remain a high-profile objective on the international development agenda for the foreseeable future.'); Centurelli (n 5) at 221.

[15] Roger Pielke, Jr, 'Against "Modern Energy Access"' (*Blog Spot*, 28 November 2012), http://rogerpielkejr.blogspot.com/2012/11/against-modern-energy-access.html.

[16] See Jenny Sin-hang Ngai, 'Energy as a Human Right in Armed Conflict: A Question of Universal Need, Survival, and Human Dignity' (2012) 37 *Brooklyn Journal of International Law* 579, 605–16; Stephen R Tully, 'The Contribution of Human Rights to Universal Energy Access' (2006) 4 *North Western Law Journal of International Human Rights* 518, 531.

[17] See Morgan D Bazilian, 'Power to the Poor: Provide Energy to Fight Poverty' (*Foreign Affairs*, March/April 2015), www.foreignaffairs.com/articles/africa/2015-02-16/power-poor ('The issue also reaches beyond the bounds of poverty to foreign policy, since a lack of energy access can foster instability.').

[18] USAID, 'Where We Work: Power Africa Works in all of Sub-Saharan Africa' (*USAID*, 7 February 2018), www.usaid.gov/powerafrica/wherewework.

[19] Bradbrook (n 7) at 520.

[20] Centurelli (n 5) at 221.

cooking through traditional use of biomass.²¹ Using inefficient devices, these biomass users cook with wood, charcoal, leaves falling or removed from trees, residue from crops and dung from animals.²²

The lack of access to electricity and modern cooking facilities

> entrenches poverty, causes respiratory diseases owing to indoor air pollution resulting from the burning of wood and animal dung for cooking, makes medical care difficult owing to the lack of refrigeration and renders schooling difficult because of the lack of electric light.²³

Improved access will engender enhanced progress socially and economically in developing countries. The circumstances under which women operated a century ago in the United States unfortunately parallels the condition of life in some regions of the world today with little or no access to electricity.²⁴ On that note, it should be mentioned that the challenge of energy access is not limited to developing countries. There are many people in the developed world who have limited access to energy services because of their inability to pay for the costs of these services.²⁵

B. Shale Gas and Energy Access

Energy access and indeed sustainable energy for all can be boosted through a replication of the Shale Revolution in other countries outside of the United States. The Shale Revolution refers to the phenomenon ushered in through the extraction of huge volumes of hitherto trapped oil and gas from shale and tight rock formations in the US using horizontal drilling and hydraulic fracturing ('fracking') – a process that consists of fluid injection into a well to cause the fracture of subsurface formations and consequent escape of natural gas into a production channel.²⁶ Shale gas development through fracking and horizontal drilling has had a positive effect on access to modern energy services by providing an additional supply of natural gas for electricity generation in the US.²⁷ The resulting low price of natural gas

---

[21] Centurelli (n 5) at 221.
[22] Centurelli (n 5) at 230.
[23] Bradbrook (n 7) at 520.
[24] See Jude Clemente, 'Lighting Up The World' (2011) 149 No 7 *Public Utilities Fortnightly*. 56, 60–61; Centurelli (n 5) at 227.
[25] Ngai (n 16) at 580 (stating that energy services to underprivileged persons are frequently disconnected because they cannot afford the bills for these services).
[26] *Mason v Range Resources-Appalachia LLC*, 120 F.Supp.3d 425 (2015) (US District Court, W.D. Pennsylvania, 2015) 428, fn 2.
[27] It should be pointed out that while gas production increase has led to reduced carbon emissions as coal use for electricity has been significantly replaced with natural gas, regulators in the US are still grappling with environmental issues linked to natural gas, notably gas flaring, methane emissions, greenhouse gas (GHG) emissions and Volatile Organic Compounds. See Linda Tsang, 'EPA's Methane Regulations: Legal Overview' (Congressional Research Service, R44615, 24 January 2018) 1–26; Monika U Ehrman, 'Lights Out in the Bakken: A Review and Analysis of Flaring Regulation and Its Potential Effect on North Dakota Shale Oil Production' (2014) 117(2) *West Virginia Law Review* 549–92; David B Spence, 'Responsible Shale Gas Production: Moral Outrage vs. Cool Analysis' (2013) 25(1) *Fordham Environmental Law Review* 141–90.

orchestrated by fracking has ensured a lower cost of electricity delivery to residential, commercial and industrial consumers than would have been the case without this additional source of supply. Increased petroleum production in the US, including those from shale formations, catapulted the US to the position of the No 1 oil and gas producer in the world.[28] With growth in the level of production, the US is poised to become a major exporter of crude oil, after becoming a net exporter of natural gas.

III. Shale Gas Resources in Africa

Technically or economically recoverable unconventional oil and gas reserves exist in many countries in the world.[29] Countries outside the United States with appreciable volume of technically recoverable shale gas deposits include China, Argentina, Algeria, Canada, Mexico, Australia, South Africa, Russia, Brazil and Poland.[30] A range of operations have commenced in some countries with sizeable shale deposits. Wells have been drilled in shale formations in Argentina, China, Mexico and Poland which have 'helped to clarify their geologic properties and productive potential.'[31]

The US Energy Information Administration and Advanced Resources International (EIA/ARI) state that Algeria's '[p]roved natural gas reserves totaled 159 trillion cubic feet (Tcf) in 2014, with an additional 49 Tcf of undiscovered natural gas resources estimated by USGS and more than 700 Tcf of technically recoverable shale gas resources estimated by EIA/ARI.'[32] Algeria is estimated to hold 'the biggest shale gas deposits in the world after those of China and Argentina.'[33] Sensing the country's potentials, some energy companies, including ENI, Shell and Talisman signed exploration agreements.[34] ENI commenced

---

[28] Matt Egan, 'America is now the World's Largest Oil Producer' (*CNN.com*, 12 September 2018), https://money.cnn.com/2018/09/12/investing/us-oil-production-russia-saudi-arabia/index.html; 'The U.S. Leads Global Petroleum and Natural Gas Production with Record Growth in 2018' (US Energy Information Administration, 20 August 2019), www.eia.gov/todayinenergy/detail.php?id=40973.; Rania El Gamal and Dmittry Zhdannikov, 'Upset by Trumps Iran Waivers, Saudis Push for Deep Oil Output Cut' (*Reuters*, 6 November 2018), www.reuters.com/article/us-oil-opec-saudi/upset-by-trumps-iran-waivers-saudis-push-for-deep-oil-output-cut-idUSKCN1NK20S.

[29] For the distinction between technically recoverable reserves and economically recoverable reserves, see US Energy Information Administration (EIA), 'Technically Recoverable Shale Oil and Shale Gas Resources: An Assessment of 137 Shale Formation in 41 Countries Outside the United States' (US Department of Energy, 2013) 10 www.eia.gov/analysis/studies/worldshalegas/pdf/fullreport.pdf.

[30] *Ibid*; Atkins (n 3) at 340.

[31] US EIA (n 29) at 12.

[32] US EIA, 'Algeria is Reforming its Laws to Attract Foreign Investment in Hydrocarbons' (*EIA*, 4 August 2015), www.eia.gov/todayinenergy/detail.php?id=22352.

[33] Kieran Cooke, 'Algeria's Shale Gas Dreams are a Nightmare for Locals' (*Middle East Eye*, 5 March 2017), www.middleeasteye.net/opinion/algerias-shale-gas-dreams-are-nightmare-locals.

[34] African Development Bank, 'Shale Gas and its Implications for Africa and the African Development Bank' (*African Development Bank Group*, 17 October 2013), www.afdb.org/en/documents/document/shale-gas-and-its-implications-for-africa-and-the-african-development-bank-33878.

exploration while Sonatrach, Algeria's national oil company, drilled its first shale wells in 2011.[35] Sonatrach drilled two exploratory shale gas wells near the desert town of In Salah in 2014.[36] The African Development Bank views Algeria as 'a likely place for shale gas production to develop'.[37] A number of factors underlie this assessment:

> First, although the country is currently a major gas exporter, local demand is growing to the extent that conventional gas exports are likely to decrease. Because Algeria is heavily dependent on gas for export revenue (90% of which comes from hydrocarbons), extra gas reserves would enable exports to keep fueling the country's development. Second, Algeria is a longtime major gas producer and has both the infrastructure and technical expertise to manage a substantial expansion in the scale of the sector. It has a regional natural gas pipeline, as well as international export pipelines and an LNG terminal, demonstrating the established nature of its domestic and export markets. Algeria, with its lengthy history of gas production and export, is likely to be regarded as an attractive environment by potential investors, and this is reflected in the interest major companies are already showing in its shale gas reserves.[38]

South Africa's shale gas reserves are located within the Karoo Basin, an expansive area that covers nearly two-thirds of the country.[39] Estimates of South Africa's recoverable gas reserves have varied over the years. Estimates have been as high as 390 Tcf of technically recoverable shale gas resources, according to a June 2013 report released by the US EIA.[40] A more recent estimate put the recoverable shale gas reserves in Karoo Basin at about 40 Tcf, which is still a substantial number.[41] Yet another estimate from 2017 put the shale gas reserves estimates at 13 Tcf.[42] The Government of South Africa has kept a close eye on fracking, imposing a moratorium on exploring drilling in 2011 so that it could study issues arising from fracking and lifting the moratorium the following year to allow exploration, but not fracking itself.[43] In the past few years, some companies, including Shell and Falcon, applied for technical cooperation permits.[44]

The African Development Bank assesses South Africa's gas consumption and development future in the following words:

> South Africa consumed about 180 bcf of gas in 2011, of which one-quarter was domestically produced and the rest imported by pipeline from Mozambique for use in a

---

[35] *Ibid.*
[36] Cooke (n 33).
[37] African Development Bank (n 34).
[38] African Development Bank (n 34).
[39] African Development Bank (n 34).
[40] Vinson & Elkins, 'Shale & Fracking Tracker – Global Fracking Resources – South Africa' (*Vinson & Elkins*, September 2018), www.velaw.com/Shale---Fracking-Tracker/Global-Fracking-Resources/South-Africa/.
[41] *Ibid.*
[42] Ed Stoddard, 'South Africa Karoo Shale Gas Deposits Seen Less Than Earlier Estimates' (*Reuters*, 28 September 2017), www.reuters.com/article/safrica-shalegas/south-africa-karoo-shale-gas-deposits-seen-less-than-earlier-estimates-idUSL8N1M92P3.
[43] African Development Bank (n 34).
[44] African Development Bank (n 34).

gas-to-liquids (GTL) plant. The dominant source of energy is coal, of which the country has very large reserves. Coal accounted for more than 90% of electricity generation in 2009, and is a major feedstock for the synthetic coal-to-liquids program. Although the overall electrification rate is 75%, almost half of rural households are still not connected to the grid, and as the economy continues to grow, rolling blackouts are imposed at times. However, the possibility of large domestic gas supplies adds a new factor to the country's energy equation. ... Gas infrastructure and domestic production are limited, but South Africa, although not a major hydrocarbon producer, has some experience in this sector and would be capable of ramping up the level of technical expertise required to manage the creation of a domestic gas industry.[45]

The Government of South Africa, after a period of strident debate and speculation, formally approved the development of shale gas in the Karoo region in March 2017.[46]

There are also shale gas deposits in varying quantities in other African countries, including Nigeria, Tunisia, Libya and Morocco.[47] Current and future studies may reveal the presence or otherwise of reserves in other places on the continent.[48] While activities toward development of shale gas deposits have commenced in some countries, within and outside of Africa, we are yet to see a replication of the US shale gas revolution.[49] This state of affairs is not unconnected to impediments to a robust development of the resources.

There are geological, political, economic, environmental, social and legal impediments to developing shale oil and gas resources abroad. While shale gas development across the world could deliver social, economic, environmental and geopolitical[50] benefits, judging by the experience in the United States, the challenge lies not necessarily in repeating the American results but in replicating the development model. Experts have identified a number of factors that facilitated shale development in the United States, assessing the impediments that other countries face in the absence or limited presence of these facilitating factors.[51] Some authors have summarised these factors into eight measurable variables, including private ownership of subsurface mineral rights; independent gas companies that had the requisite technical knowledge and the incentive to deploy

---

[45] African Development Bank (n 34).

[46] Ken Fullerton, 'South African Government Supports Fracking in the Karoo' (*Sense & Sustainability*, 28 August 2018), www.senseandsustainability.net/2018/08/28/south-african-government-supports-fracking-in-the-karoo/.

[47] Ibid.

[48] Ibid.

[49] One African country that has attracted recent interest by investors is Namibia because of its Kavango Basin, 'a 6.3-million-acre basin that potentially holds undeveloped shale and conventional plays'. Meredith Taylor, 'Is this the Next Great Oil Frontier?' (*Oilprice.com*, 2 January 2020), https://oilprice.com/Energy/Energy-General/Is-This-The-Next-Great-Oil-Frontier.html.

[50] John Siciliano, 'Poland Inks Huge Natural Gas Deal with US, Becoming Less Reliant on Russia' (*Washington Examiner*, 8 November 2018), www.washingtonexaminer.com/policy/energy/poland-inks-huge-natural-gas-deal-with-us-becoming-less-reliant-on-russia.

[51] Peter Cameron et al, 'Across the Universe of Shale Resources – A Comparative Assessment of the Emerging Legal Foundations for Unconventional Energy' (2018) 11 *Journal of World Energy Law & Business* 283.

or develop it; available pipeline infrastructure and capacity; presence of large volumes of water; low population density that reduced opportunities for public resistance; rich capital markets; appreciable natural gas prices and gas demand; and royalties and taxes.[52]

IV. Impediments to Shale Development Outside the United States

The low level of development of shale gas reserves in several regions of the world is attributable to a plethora of impediments to extracting the resources. First, there is the political impediment.[53] Fracking abroad has been greeted with a range of reactions from outright hostility to warm embrace with a dose of caution sprinkled in the middle.[54] Fracking has got off to a slow start in other places partly because political leaders are responding to the concerns of their citizens about fracking or intense lobbying against it. Political instability in some countries can also constitute an aspect of political impediment. For example, Exxon had plans to partner with Sonatrach to develop a field in South-western Ahnet Basin, in Algeria, but halted these plans in response to political protests against the Algerian President's 20-year rule. The protests frustrated the partnership and Algeria's development of shale resources.[55]

There is also the geological impediment. Shale deposits abroad may be found in formations that are not always as auspicious for development as many of the formations in the United States. For instance, many of the shale fields in China are hobbled by bad geology.[56] In addition, there are resource impediments, especially the availability of water that would be used in the fracking process. Not only are there challenges regarding sufficient quantities of water in a drilling area or country to support fracking, but there are also concerns about water contamination as a result of fracking.[57]

---

[52] *Ibid* at 287–88.
[53] Lauren Karam, 'Fracking across the Globe: The Debate in the United States and Europe and the Role of Federal, State, and Local Regulations' (2018) 41 *Suffolk Transnational Law Review* 173.
[54] Tincher (n 1) at 114.
[55] Lamine Chikhi, Dmitry Zhdannikov and Ron Bousso, 'Exxon's Talks to Tap Algeria Shale Gas Falter Due to Unrest – Sources' (*Reuters*, 20 March 2019) www.reuters.com/article/us-algeria-protests-exxon-mobil/exxons-talks-to-tap-algeria-shale-gas-falter-due-to-unrest-sources-idUSKCN1R11G8.
[56] David Sandalow et al, 'Meeting China's Shale Gas Goals' (*Center on Global Energy Policy, Columbia University*, September 2014) 14, https://energypolicy.columbia.edu/sites/default/files/China%20Shale%20Gas_WORKING%20DRAFT_Sept%2011_0.pdf.
[57] Tincher (n 1) at 129 (stating that India would suffer if fracking were to adversely affect the availability or quality of water in the country in view of its population density). Drought and the possibility of bore water contamination are real concerns in Australia where two of the most resource rich states currently have fracking moratoria. See generally 'Fracking Policies are Wildly Inconsistent across Australia, from Gung-ho Development to Total Bans' (*The Conversation*, 3 December 2018), http://theconversation.com/fracking-policies-are-wildly-inconsistent-across-australia-from-gung-ho-development-to-total-bans-108039.

Closely related to geological and resource constraints are technological impediments. The technology for unlocking shale deposits is highly sophisticated and not cheaply available outside the US. As a result, there have been efforts by business and governmental interests to find solutions to the problem, primarily through technology transfer. The United States Government introduced the Unconventional Gas Technical Engagement Program that has attracted the participation of a number of foreign governments.[58] Foreign and American energy companies have also been entering into joint ventures, with technology transfer as part of the objectives for the commercial relationships.

Another factor is the economic impediment. Developing these resources entails enormous capital investments by private, foreign investors in the face of limited financial capability of national governments that may be willing to see the exploration and production of shale gas in their territory. Moreover, the current environment of lower prices for crude oil and natural gas militate against proceeding with contemplated projects or envisioning brand new ones.[59]

Finally, there is the legal impediment relating to the ownership of minerals under the laws and constitutions of countries with recoverable shale reserves. There are two major mineral ownership systems in the world: sovereign or state ownership which vests all rights to minerals *in situ* in the sovereign and private ownership which permits private interests to own rights to minerals *in situ*. Private rights are recognised primarily in Canada and the United States, while the rest of the world vastly embraces sovereign ownership.[60] Private rights provide an incredible incentive for a country to seek efficient means of production based on a competitive market model.[61] Thus, a lack of private rights is an impediment to replicating the shale gas revolution abroad because these other countries lack this unique feature of American law and society. In the absence of private rights, opposition to fracking finds a fertile ground, conflicts arise, decision-making is either not streamlined or is further complicated, and accountability structures are not robust. For instance, commentators 'have hypothesized that the degree

---

[58] For a detailed description of the programme and analysis of its potentials, see Tincher (n 1) at 120–37.

[59] See eg Arthur Nelsen, 'Polish Shale Industry Collapsing as Number of Licenses Nearly Halves' *The Guardian*, 9 October 2015 (discussing collapse of shale gas projects in Poland and noting that exploratory drilling was decreasing in Poland partly due to low global oil prices), www.theguardian.com/environment/2015/oct/09/polish-shale-industry-collapsing-as-number-of-licenses-nearly-halves.

[60] Fred Bosselman et al, *Energy, Economics and the Environment: Cases and Materials*, 3rd edn (United States: Foundation Press, 2010) 353 ('The United States and Canada are virtually the only countries on earth where minerals can be owned privately.'); AN Kleit and DR Cahoy, 'Contingent Efficiency In Natural Gas Leases' (2016) 11 *Texas Journal of Oil, Gas & Energy Law* 89, 91 ('Unlike most countries, mineral rights in the United States are commonly privately owned.').

[61] Nonetheless, private ownership can also generate inefficiencies because when multiple owners own the same resource, the rule of capture applies, which may result in sub-optimal tapping of reservoirs. In response, the rule of capture has been modified, in large part, by federal and state conservation legislation that aims to control waste and protect correlative rights of mineral owners. See Keith B Hall, 'Single Well Spacing and Pooling: State Spacing and Jurisdiction over Conservation' (2019) No 6 *Rocky Mountain Mineral Law Foundation-Institute* 12.

of opposition to hydraulic fracturing in South Africa may be driven in part by the government's sole ownership of mineral rights; thus, local communities see little direct incentive, economic or otherwise, to support shale development'.[62] Section V below describes the American ownership system and how it helped birth the fracking revolution.

V. The Sovereign Ownership Impediment

A. Mineral Ownership in the United States and Other Countries

In the United States, the owner of land also owns the mineral resources under the land, as encapsulated in the maxim *cujus est solum, ejus est usque ad coelum et ad inferos*.[63] The owner may be an individual, corporate entity, state government, federal government or any other institution.[64] It is also not uncommon to have cases of split estates in which the surface estate is severed from the mineral estate.[65] In that situation, the minerals belong to the owner of the mineral estate, who may or may not be the landowner prior to the severance. The mineral estate has an implied easement to use the surface estate reasonably for the exploration and production of the minerals.[66]

Most countries in the world follow the option of exclusive state ownership of mineral resources, if not all forms of natural resources.[67] In state ownership,

---

[62] Vinson & Elkins (n 40).

[63] 'To whomever the soil belongs, he owns also to the sky and to the depths'. This doctrine is also known as the 'heaven to hell' principle. See OL Anderson et al, *Oil and Gas Law and Taxation* (St. Paul, Minnesota, West Academic Publishing, 2017) 3, fn 16. The doctrine is subject to some well-recognised exceptions, including airspace, groundwater, wild animals and oil and gas where the rule of capture assigns true ownership to the person that extracts them legitimately. See generally John S Lowe et al, *Cases and Materials on Oil and Gas Law*, 7th edn (St Paul, Minnesota, West Academic, 2018) 57–67.

[64] H Philip (Flip) Whitworth, 'Leasing and Operating State-Owned Lands for Oil and Gas Development' (1985) 16 *Texas Tech Law Review* 673–723 at 680; SP Otillar et al, 'Private Equity in Upstream Oil & Gas Transactions: The Evolution of Purchase and Sale Agreements', Paper presented at the Institute for Energy Law's 70th Annual Oil & Gas Law Conference (Houston, Texas, 21–22 February 2019) 1–35 at 1 (stating that the federal government is '[t]he largest mineral rights owner in the U.S.').

[65] See Alexandra B Klass and Hannah J Wiseman, *Energy Law* (United States: Foundation Press, 2017) 54 ('[T]he mineral portion of a property may be severed from the surface and sold separately, and minerals in many states have been severed from the surface.').

[66] See, eg, *Hunt Oil Co v Kerbaugh*, 283 N.W.2d 131 (N.D. 1979); *Getty Oil Co v Jones*, 470 S.W.2d 618 (Tex. 1971).

[67] Mark Bowler-Smith, 'Rethinking the Taxation of (Large) Corporates' (2017) 27 *New Zealand Universities Law Review* 744–66 at 746 (stating that 'most countries regard subsoil assets as the state's inalienable property'); Ricardo Pereira and Orla Gough, 'Permanent Sovereignty over Natural Resources in the 21St Century: Natural Resource Governance and the Right to Self-Determination of Indigenous Peoples under International Law' (2013) 14 *Melbourne Journal of International Law* 451, 475, fn 18 ('In most legal systems, ownership over subsoil natural resources such as oil and gas is vested in the state.').

the state owns natural resources, especially oil, gas and solid minerals. For some of the countries that follow state ownership, this feature was passed down from colonial rule.[68] The United Kingdom and many civil law countries follow the option of sole government ownership of some specific minerals such as oil and gas.[69]

Through the Mineral & Petroleum Resources Development Act, No 28 of 2002, South Africa abolished private ownership of mineral resources and vested the resources in the state.[70] Similar legal provisions exist in other African countries. For instance, in Egypt, all minerals, including petroleum, existing mines and quarries in the country, including the territorial waters, and in the seabed subject to its jurisdiction and extending beyond the territorial waters, belong to the state.[71]

A number of arguments have been advanced to support or reject public and private ownership systems.[72] Public ownership is favoured, among other reasons, because it presents less of a negotiation nightmare to a foreign investor. As Filho states:

> Without addressing academic and historical debates regarding the permanent sovereignty over natural resources, it actually seems to make more sense – from an investor's perspective – to have to deal with one single owner (i.e. the federal government) than with a number of them (provinces, federalised states or private owners).[73]

Due to mismanagement of public resources, however, calls for private ownership of oil, gas and mineral resources have gained traction in some quarters.[74]

---

[68] Patrick Wieland, 'Going Beyond Panaceas: Escaping Mining Conflicts in Resource-Rich Countries through Middle-Ground Policies' (2013) 20 *New York University Environmental Law Journal* 199, 208.

[69] James G Stewart, *Corporate War Crimes: Prosecuting the Pillage of Natural Resources*, 2nd edn (Open Society Foundations, 2011) 40; Pereira and Gough (n 67) at 455, fn 17.

> Most civil law countries vest ownership of subsoil resources in the surface landowner, though an exception is usually made for energy resources such as oil, gas and coal, which are subject to state ownership. The Netherlands, Norway, Poland and Spain as well as the United Kingdom (which is not a civil law country) follow this model.

Meri-Katriina Pyhäranta, 'State Ownership of Petroleum Resources: An Obstacle to Shale Gas Development in the UK?' (2017) 10 *Journal of World Energy Law & Business* 358, 360 (stating that in the UK, ownership of petroleum, gold and silver are vested in the state and these minerals are exceptions to the general rule that confers the right to subsurface minerals and everything in, on or over the land to the landowner); *R v Earl of Northumberland (Case of Mines)* (1568) 1 Plowden 310; 75 ER 472 (holding that gold and silver within the realm belong to the Queen).

[70] See *Agri South Africa v Minister for Minerals and Energy* [2013] ZACC 9; Lael K Weis, 'Resources and the Property Rights Curse' (2015) 28 *Canadian Journal of Law & Jurisprudence* 209, 220, fn 37.

[71] Mining and Quarries Law No 66 (1953).

[72] For extensive discussion of the rationale and complaints about public and private ownerships, see Emeka Duruigbo, 'The Global Energy Challenge and Nigeria's Emergence as a Major Gas Power: Promise, Peril, or Paradox of Plenty' (2009) 21 *Georgetown International Environmental Law Review* 39, 440–44.

[73] Carlos Vilhena Filho, 'Security of Tenure in Brazil' [2005] No 9C(2) *Rocky Mountain Mineral Law Foundation-Institute*.

[74] Emeka Duruigbo, 'Realizing the People's Right to Natural Resources' (2011) 12 *Whitehead Journal of Diplomacy & International Relations* 111, 115.

B. The Role of Private Mineral Ownership in US Shale Development

Among other factors, private ownership of mineral rights has contributed significantly to the Shale Revolution in the United States.[75] That it has played a pivotal role cannot be over-emphasised, as the following observation illustrates:

> None of this could have happened without the United States' unique legal framework. It grants landowners the rights not only to the surface of their property but also to everything below – all the way, theoretically, to the center of the earth. In the rest of the world, these mineral rights are virtually all owned, or strictly controlled, by sovereign governments. In the United States, any company can strike a deal with a willing landowner to lease the rights to the oil and gas beneath his land and start drilling, a setup that has spawned Darwinian competition among entrepreneurs in order to survive and grow. And so the United States boasts more than 6,000 independent oil and gas companies and an equal number of associated service companies, compared with the handful of independents and service companies that exist overseas.[76]

In other words, private mineral ownership triggers a number of outcomes that facilitated the shale gas revolution. Some of these factors are discussed below.

i. Innovation and Risk Taking

At a forum at Harvard University's Kennedy School of Government, a noted oil entrepreneur, Robert A Hefner III made reference to the innovative character of private ownership of mineral rights. According to a report from the event:

> Hefner agreed that the United States has some unique conditions that have encouraged the natural gas boom. Especially, he said, the U.S. legal principle in which property owners also own the mineral rights below their land has driven the huge market growth here. In the United States, 'we're all entrepreneurs and we're all innovators, and that's what makes America different, particularly in this industry, than any other place in the world. That's what brought the shale gas revolution around … It was all of us that were in the independent sector innovating every day to try and make a buck,' Hefner said.[77]

The opportunity and ability to innovate clearly played a vital role. There are also other factors stemming from private ownership that made innovation and experimentation possible.

---

[75] US EIA (n 29) at 11 ('Key positive above-the-ground advantages in the United States and Canada that may not apply in other locations include private ownership of subsurface rights that provide a strong incentive for development …').

[76] Robert A Hefner III, 'The United States of Gas: Why the Shale Revolution Could Have Happened Only in America' (*Foreign Affairs*, May/June 2014) 9–14, www.foreignaffairs.com/articles/united-states/2014-04-17/united-states-gas.

[77] Dominic Contreras, 'Natural Gas as a Bridge to the Future' (*Harvard Kennedy School, Belfer Center for Science and International Affairs*, 11 April 2012),.

ii. Decentralised Decision-Making

In the US system of private ownership, there are tens of thousands of owners of mineral rights, who are in a position to permit oil and gas drilling. That means that there are thousands of final decision-makers who can respectively make quick decisions to grant access to oil and gas developers to begin exploration and development activities on their land. This process is much faster than decision-making by bureaucrats under the sovereign ownership model.[78] With quick decision-making, experimenting with innovative drilling technology became an easier journey to take.

iii. Economic Incentive

It is likely that many private mineral owners have been inclined to give fracking a chance because of the potential to receive economic benefits (eg through rents and royalties) should the drilling efforts prove successful. Besides, mineral owners receive economic benefits at the time of permitting development through bonuses paid by energy developers, without regard to the success or failure of the project.[79] This penchant for personal wealth accumulation, sometimes pejoratively referred to as greed, motivated early fracking efforts and sustains interest in developing subsequent projects.[80] Oil and gas entrepreneur Hefner captures this point and the contrast with other countries as follows:

> And because governments in other countries own or control virtually all the underground resource rights, landowners have no skin in the game. Receiving none of the economic benefits and facing only the downsides of intrusive projects in their own backyards, they justifiably tend to resist drilling projects.[81]

The mineral owner's incentive to be open to fracking is further understood from the perspective that if the mineral owner owns only a severed interest (and thus does not own the surface) he will be reaping economic gains without being concerned about the lessee's surface use or generally about the environmental impacts of petroleum development.[82] Surface owners, who ordinarily in such circumstances

---

[78] Thomas W Merrill, 'Four Questions About Fracking' [2013] 63 *Case Western Reserve Law Review* 971:

> In a country like the United States that follows the ad coelum rule, ownership and hence control over subsurface minerals is fragmented among tens of thousands of separate owners. A production company that wants to experiment with an innovative technology can always find an owner sufficiently willing to take risks – or if you are more cynical, sufficiently ignorant of the risks – to convey the required rights. When mineral rights are owned by the government, access is necessarily controlled by a centralized bureaucracy. Bureaucracies tend to be slow and cautious. Promoting innovative extraction technologies that could easily end up a bust is difficult to explain to the boss.

Ibid at 978.
[79] Nancy Saint-Paul, *Summers Oil and Gas*, Chapter 31 (October 2019) § 31:1 (3rd edn).
[80] Merrill (n 78) at 977–78.
[81] Hefner (n 76).
[82] Owen L Anderson, 'Shale Revolution or Evolution: Opportunities and Challenges for Europe' (2013) 4 *Global Business Law Review* 1, 24.

would oppose oil and gas development projects that do not inure to their benefit, often receive financial compensation from oil and gas companies either voluntarily or as mandated by statute, which further demonstrates the importance of economic incentives.[83]

iv. Cooperation

For oil and gas development to proceed smoothly, if at all, it is imperative to secure the cooperation of all relevant stakeholders. In some places around the world, development efforts are stymied because landowners complain about unjust treatment or inadequate financial attention.[84] Sabotage or physical damage to oil and gas facilities and operations becomes an avenue for frustrating development projects.[85] With private ownership and the built-in incentive structure, cooperation is elicited more easily. The role of cooperation is paramount when considering that we were dealing with the experimental application of techniques, the potential for harm or failure of which was largely unknown.

v. Financing Mechanism

Pioneers of shale gas fracking engaged in the acquisition of vast acreages of land that contained minerals and selling those properties at an opportune time. As Wang and Krupnick stated:

> This mechanism – leasing land at low prices early and selling at a higher price later – overcomes the difficulty of monetizing most technology innovations and know-how in the industry. This mechanism is made possible by the private land and mineral rights ownership system in the United States.[86]

Without the value associated with those mineral interests, they would have taken longer to reap returns from their investments and might have found it difficult to raise the huge amounts of money needed to fund subsequent fracking operations, especially when alternative or traditional funding sources were not available.[87]

---

[83] See *ibid*.
[84] US EIA Report on Nigeria (6 May 2016), www.eia.gov/beta/international/analysis.php?iso=NGA.
[85] *Ibid*.
[86] Zhongmin Wang and Alan Krupnick, 'A Retrospective Review of Shale Gas Development in the United States What Led to the Boom?' (Resources for the Future, 2013) 4.
[87] For further discussion of this mechanism, see *ibid* at 30:

> Shale gas development in the United States has essentially taken place in areas with private land and minerals ownership. Private land ownership contributed to the development of shale gas in that it offered entrepreneurial natural gas firms a method of obtaining reasonable returns from their early investments in technology innovations necessary for developing a new shale play. Early movers found that they could lease large tracts of land at low prices, and the leases became more valuable as the cost of extracting gas decreased. It is through land acquisition, not innovations per se, that early movers obtained their financial returns for their early investments.

VI. Civic Shares: A Substitute to Overcome Sovereign Ownership Impediment

A. Overview

Introducing meaningful mechanisms to placate surface rights owners in order to facilitate oil and gas development is not a new phenomenon. When surface owners resisted production of state-owned oil and gas under their land, the State of Texas introduced the Relinquishment Act regime that is still in place today. Under the Relinquishment Act, as interpreted by the Texas Supreme Court, and applied by the State of Texas, surface owners in certain tracts of land who received their land with the state's mineral reservation are entitled to at least half of the royalties and other lease benefits when the mineral interests are leased for development.[88] The surface owner is designated the state's agent and, in that capacity, arranges for the lease between the lessee and the state.[89]

Canada addressed the surface-owner challenge decades ago through surface rights legislation adopted in various provinces, including Alberta, British Columbia and Saskatchewan.[90] Surface rights statutes require the oil and gas producer to obtain the permission or cooperation of the landowner prior to drilling on the land and to pay compensation to the landowner. If the landowner and the producer cannot come to an agreement, the Surface Rights Board is empowered to impose a surface lease on the landowner.[91] In some oil-producing states in the United States, there are also surface damage statutes to protect landowners and smoothen the relationship between landowners and oil and gas companies.[92]

It is beyond question that countries that want to achieve meaningful progress in developing their shale resources need to be creative in overcoming obstacles confronting any significant step in that direction. For instance, then British Prime Minister, Theresa May, proposed a system of 'Disruption Payments' to provide incentives to individual property owners in neighbourhoods that would host fracking operations and hopefully reduce resistance to the development of shale

---

[88] Emeka Duruigbo, 'Oil, Turmoil and a Texas Export for Energy Security' (2012) 37 *Thurgood Marshall Law Review* 231.

[89] *Ibid.*

[90] Surface Rights Act: Revised Statutes of Alberta 2000, c S-24. Surface Rights Acquisition and Compensation Act (Saskatchewan) RSS 1978, c 65; Petroleum and Natural Gas Act (British Columbia) RSBC 1996, c 361.

[91] Sarah Nykolaishen and Nigel Bankes, 'The Jurisdiction of the Alberta Surface Rights Board under Section 30 of the Surface Rights Act' [2011] 49 *Alberta Law Review* 1; David Ukrainetz, 'The Surface Rights Acquisition and Compensation Act- Current Saskatchewan Framework' (*McKercher*, 11 February 2019), www.mckercher.ca/resources/the-surface-rights-acquisition-and-compensation-act-current-saskatchewan-framework.

[92] Christopher S Kulander, 'Common Law Aspects of Shale Oil and Gas Development' (2013) 49 *Idaho Law Review* 367, 371 (stating that such statutes exist in at least ten states).

resources in their area.⁹³ This section proposes a creative tool in the form of civic shares. Under this arrangement, equity stakes in businesses or projects may be offered to relevant communities and individual or corporate landowners.

B. Civic Shares

Civic shares may be defined as financial instruments issued by companies to individuals or groups in communities hosting the companies' projects.⁹⁴ They are a part of a broader movement on the part of resource companies to go beyond the hitherto prevalent quasi-philanthropic approach to distributing benefits to communities.⁹⁵ Instead, these companies now deploy corporate social investments 'more strategically to mitigate social risk, protect their corporate social licence to operate, and address growing societal expectations'.⁹⁶ While corporate social investment historically has been voluntary, there is a growing trend of state intervention to pressure or require businesses to embark on measures that exceed such regular requirements or expectations, such as payment of taxes and royalties or creation of employment by companies.⁹⁷

Shares represent an ownership interest in the company. Companies issuing civic shares will provide shareholders with an ownership interest in the commercial enterprise undertaking the mineral development. Shareholders will receive dividends from the profits of the venture. The civic shares will be structured in a hybrid form. One part of it will guarantee a percentage of revenue from production to the shareholders, without regard to whether the venture is profitable or not. In essence, this component will take the form of royalty payments, which are paid 'off the top' without deducting expenses.⁹⁸ A second component will enable shareholders to share in the profits of the venture. This aspect will resemble shareholder

---

⁹³ For an extensive discussion of former Prime Minister May's proposal and disruption payments generally, see Emeka Duruigbo, 'Fracking and the NIMBY Syndrome' (2018) 26 *New York University Environmental Law Journal* 227.

⁹⁴ Companies may also issue civic bonds. While shares are a form of ownership interest, bonds are debt obligations secured by some asset. On the bond-share distinction, see generally PM Vasudev, 'Law, Economics, and Beyond: A Case for Retheorizing the Business Corporation' (2010) 55 *McGill Law Journal* 911, 940; Adam Feibelman, 'Commercial Lending and the Separation of Banking and Commerce' (2007) 75 *University of Cincinnati Law Review* 943, 948.

⁹⁵ Karen McNab, et al, 'Beyond Voluntarism: The Changing Role of Corporate Social Investment in the Extractives Sector' (Centre for Social Responsibility in Mining, The University of Queensland, 2012) 2.

⁹⁶ Ibid.

⁹⁷ Ibid at 2–3:

> Progressive resource companies continue to make substantial voluntary social investments but this is increasingly occurring in a context in which the State is also an active player. In a growing number of jurisdictions, companies are being required, or pressured, to contribute to the social and economic development of impacted communities and broader society.

⁹⁸ Monika U Ehrman, 'A Call for Energy Realism: When Immanuel Kant Met the Keep It in the Ground Movement' (2019) *Utah Law Review* 435, 463 ('The royalty – here the lessor's royalty – is a cost-free share of production paid to the lessor out of the stream of production.').

treatment in the corporate sense. The prospect of economic benefit offered by shares presents an incentive similar to the one enjoyed by private mineral owners in the US that made it easier for them to accept fracking on their land.

A characteristic of shareholding is risk-bearing. Shareholders bear the risk of corporate failure. By accepting civic shares, property owners are taking a risk that the adventure will turn out well. The risk-taking and entrepreneurial spirit that aided shale gas development in the US is reflected in this feature as both the civic share owners and oil and gas operators engage in risky moves that they hope will pay off handsomely.[99]

Shareholding aligns incentives of the various participants in the business venture. Because shareholders know that their financial returns are tied to the company's wellbeing, they will be motivated to cooperate with the resource developer. Again, cooperation is an offshoot of private mineral ownership that worked to the advantage of mineral development.

C. Experience with Shares in Other Mineral Settings

The use of equity for investment promotion and risk management in other mining settings can provide valuable lessons for countries considering fracking, especially where resistance is anticipated or already present.

Papua New Guinea (PNG) presents one such example. PNG is a country blessed with an abundance of mineral resources, including copper and gold.[100] Modern exploration for minerals in the country commenced in the 1960s, zeroing in on copper and nickel deposits.[101] The minerals sector policy contains such features as state ownership of minerals, the reliance on foreign investment for the development of mineral deposits where internal capital, technology and expertise are in short supply locally, and a focus on raising government revenue from the sector and then utilising the money raised for broader economic development within the country.[102] In the course of time, the minerals sector policy has undergone some transformation, with the placement of greater emphasis on landowner rights and community development.[103] To ensure an orderly environment for development, revenue distribution and compensation arrangements have included, among other things, equity participation by landowners.[104] A report prepared for the World Bank stated the following about PNG:

> Since the late 1980s, landowners have taken direct equity in major mining projects. At Porgera, the Enga provincial government and landowners each hold 2.5 percent

---

[99] See Merrill (n 78) at 978 (stating that private owner's willingness to take risks may have played a role in facilitating shale gas development).
[100] Environmental Resources Management, 'Mining Community Development Agreements – Practical Experiences and Field Studies' (June 2010) 33.
[101] Ibid at 34.
[102] Ibid at 37–38.
[103] Ibid at 38.
[104] Ibid at 43–44.

equity in the Porgera mine; Lihir landowners hold a 6.8 percent stake in Lihir Gold Ltd through an entity called Mineral Resources Lihir. Dividends generated can take some time to become significant but ultimately can be substantial, and may even dwarf the amounts paid in royalties.[105]

While it is the case that the resources sector in PNG is one of the most corrupt and conflict-ridden in the world, it is hoped that the use of equity participation may ultimately prove effective.

Equity arrangements can also be found in other countries. In South Africa, the Royal Bafokeng Nation holds shares of Implats which is the company developing the substantial platinum reserves in the ethnic homeland.[106] In Zimbabwe, the Indigenisation and Economic Empowerment Act 2007 provides for Community share ownership trusts.[107] The community share ownership portion of the indigenisation programme 'involves vesting equity (10% in some cases) in community trusts specifically for the social development of communities in mining areas'.[108] Any payment is made to the community trust, which also has responsibility for managing the funds.[109]

VII. Potential Objections to Proposals and Responses to Them

A. Environmental Challenges

Fracking has been associated with a host of environmental concerns, including water availability, water contamination, air pollution and exposure to earthquakes.[110] While some of these concerns remain in the realm of possible risks, as proof of causation is largely absent, the accompanying fear is real, leading to opposition to fracking in some parts of the United States and in several countries across the world.[111] Opposition to fracking in South Africa has been based partly on environmental grounds with environmental groups 'raising questions about the advisability of allowing fracking in an area where water is in short supply

---

[105] *Ibid* at 44.
[106] For extensive discussion of this project or arrangement, see Emeka Duruigbo, 'Community Equity Participation in African Petroleum Ventures: Path to Economic Growth?' (2013) 35 *North Carolina Central Law Review* 111.
[107] McNab (n 95) at 15.
[108] McNab (n 95) at 15.
[109] McNab (n 95) at 15.
[110] Wang and Krupnick (n 86) at 5 ('The environmental impact of shale gas development has been a highly controversial subject, has raised difficult public policy issues, and has affected the pace of development in some areas.'); Anderson (n 82) at 9–10, 16.
[111] Noah Rothman, 'The Fracking Decade' (*Commentary Magazine*, January 2020), www.commentarymagazine.com/articles/the-fracking-decade/; Anderson (n 82) at 16.

and where there would be competition for its use'.¹¹² With regard to Algeria, the African Development Bank has observed:

> The one unfamiliar aspect of the development of shale gas will be the various environmental risks associated with its production. The need for large quantities of water for fracking, in areas where water supplies are scarce, is likely to be a major concern.¹¹³

There are also questions about whether the private ownership framework will exacerbate environmental risks by undermining public protections that may exist where the state is the owner of resources.

While the various shades of environmental objection are not peculiar to private ownership of minerals, it is nevertheless germane to the discussion as general opposition to fracking would translate into a rejection of any proposal, including the one in this chapter, which seeks to advance it.¹¹⁴ In November 2019, The UK banned fracking, citing new scientific analysis that it was impossible, with current technology, 'to accurately predict the probability or magnitude of earthquakes linked to fracking operations'.¹¹⁵ A press release in that regard stated in part: 'On the basis of the disturbance caused to residents living near Cuadrilla's Preston New Road site in Lancashire and this latest scientific analysis, the government has announced a moratorium on fracking until compelling new evidence is provided.'¹¹⁶

Environmental risks should not be minimised.¹¹⁷ Yet it may be argued that shale gas development presents net environmental gains. For one, increased use of natural gas for electricity generation displaces or reduces the use of coal for that purpose.¹¹⁸ Since natural gas is a cleaner burning fuel than coal, this movement helps in the fight against climate change.¹¹⁹ Shale gas development in other countries will lessen coal consumption in those countries, such as South Africa, leading to gains for the global environment.¹²⁰ Besides, environmental laws should not apply with less force where private rights are recognised, as is the case in the United States and Canada.

---

[112] African Development Bank (n 34).
[113] African Development Bank (n 34).
[114] Rothman (n 111) ('Revolutionary technological advances are often accompanied by a popular backlash, and fracking is no exception. Germany, France, Holland, the UK, and Bulgaria have effectively banned it ... In March 2019, Israel's environmental ministry placed a hold on all domestic fracking projects.').
[115] Press Release, 'Government Ends Support for Fracking' (*GOV.UK*, 2 November 2019), www.gov.uk/government/news/government-ends-support-for-fracking.
[116] *Ibid*; see also Andrew Critchlow, 'UK Bans Fracking in Blow to Onshore Gas Production Hopes (S&P Global, 2 November 2019), www.spglobal.com/platts/en/market-insights/latest-news/natural-gas/110219-uk-bans-fracking-in-blow-to-onshore-gas-production-hopes.
[117] See generally Jonathan Verschuuren, 'Hydraulic Fracturing and Environmental Concerns: The Role of Local Government' (2015) 27 *Journal of Environmental Law* 431.
[118] Nathanael Johnson, 'Despite Everything, U.S. Emissions Dipped in 2019' (*GRIST*, 7 January 2020), https://grist.org/energy/despite-everything-us-emissions-dipped-in-2019/.
[119] *Ibid* ('Surging natural gas was the biggest reason for coal's demise. Gas comes with its own problems for the climate – burning it releases carbon, and leaks release methane – but replacing coal with gas led to a decline in globe-warming gases ...'); Rothman (n 111).
[120] See Merrill (n 78) at 991–92.

B. Effect on Renewable Energy Transition

An emphasis on natural gas production could be viewed as an additional roadblock in the journey toward transiting to renewable energy forms, such as wind and solar, which are known to be cleaner and more environment-friendly. It is the case that 'the environmental community is very concerned that shale gas will displace renewables such as wind and solar that emit no greenhouse gases'.[121]

A quick response to this objection is one that has been made on many occasions by scholars and political leaders, which is that natural gas is considered a bridge fuel that could prove useful as the world makes a full transition from fossil fuels to renewable energy.[122] The point here is that natural gas is a cleaner source of energy than its other fossil fuel relatives – coal and oil.[123] The 'bridge fuel' argument does not enjoy universal acclaim and has been assailed by those who do not consider natural gas as sufficiently clean to stem the dangers of climate change,[124] or who highlight the dangers posed by methane that is released during the fracking process. Indeed for idealists looking for a perfect solution to an imperiled planet, natural gas is not a panacea. However, when we look at the reality that renewables are not ready to completely replace fossil fuels as energy sources, a more realistic option should not be discarded or disregarded with ease.[125]

Regarding the release of methane, the scientific response is that in the long term, methane does less damage to the atmosphere than carbon dioxide because methane stays in the atmosphere for about 12 years, while carbon dioxide lingers for much longer.[126] Further, there is ongoing research to figure out ways of reducing the greenhouse gas emissions that result from releasing methane in the course of fracking operations.[127] Further, there is the realisation by

---

[121] Anderson (n 82) at 10.

[122] See Contreras (n 77); Tincher (n 1) at 116 (stating that the Obama administration takes this position).

[123] Kate Yoder, 'Gas and Oil Will Save us All, say Oil and Gas Companies' (*GRIST*, 9 January 2020) ('It's true that natural gas is generally cleaner than other fossil fuels.'), https://grist.org/energy/gas-and-oil-will-save-us-all-say-oil-and-gas-companies/.

[124] Tincher (n 1) at 116, fn 21 (referencing a statement by a climate scientist that high levels of carbon dioxide, melting ice caps and oceans that are acidified would remain with us in a world where natural gas use continues, even as a bridge fuel).

[125] For competing viewpoints on this issue, see Jody Freeman, 'A Critical Look at "The Moral Case for Fossil Fuels"' (2015) (36) *Energy Law Journal* 327.

[126] Isabelle Smith, 'Legislating a Net-Zero Emissions Future' (2019) (1) *Georgetown Environmental Law Review Online*, www.law.georgetown.edu/environmental-law-review/blog/legislating-a-net-zero-emissions-future/ (stating that 'carbon dioxide remain[s] in the atmosphere for hundreds of years and methane ha[s] a comparatively short-life cycle of about 12 years ...'). This truth should not obscure other facts about methane. See United Nations Framework Convention on Climate Change (INFCCC), 'Why Methane Matters' (INFCCC, 7 August 2014) ('Methane is particularly problematic as its impact is 34 times greater than CO_2 over a 100-year period, according to the latest IPCC Assessment Report.'), https://unfccc.int/news/new-methane-signs-underline-urgency-to-reverse-emissions.

[127] Tincher (n 1) at 133.

governments and development agencies that achieving universal energy access might go beyond natural gas, to include dirtier fossil fuels, especially coal.[128] Some scholars have summarised the current understanding as follows:

> The United Nations, the multilateral development banks, and the U.S. Obama Administration have thus all broadly agreed in principle (albeit with different emphasis) to balance energy access and environmental goals in a similar manner: invest in clean energy, allow countries and their unique circumstances to determine their energy pathways, seek alternatives to fossil-fuel investment where possible, but ultimately do not restrict demand for electricity services in developing countries, while honoring countries' individual plans and decisions.[129]

The central message from the foregoing is to intensify efforts toward addressing energy issues through renewable energy but with the understanding that even if progress is somewhat slow, if it is steady and sustained the goal is likely to be attained.

C. Relative Weakness of Minority Civic Shareholders

Since the civic shareholders will own only a small percentage of the total number of shares in the company, their power to influence corporate policy may be very limited and the oil and gas operator that owns the majority of shares can frustrate the civic shareholder's expectations. For instance, the majority, through its control of the board of directors, may choose not to declare dividends on profits and thus deprive the minority community of income. It is unlikely that any prudent operator will resort to such means, considering that the minority can deploy some tactics within and outside corporate law to make it harder for the company to continue to operate profitably in the area. More importantly, as discussed earlier, the civic share arrangement will be structured in such a way that does not leave the company an option regarding payment of royalties and dividends to the shareholders. That is, payments are guaranteed when production commences and additionally when the venture becomes profitable. In view of that, the chances of the shareholders being placed in financial jeopardy because of their minority status is largely non-existent.

VIII. Conclusion

Extending the Shale Revolution beyond the United States can assist in achieving the international community's goal of universal energy access and to liberate many of the world's poor from the shackles of energy poverty. Lack of access to modern

---

[128] Moss et al (n 13) at 4–6.
[129] Moss et al (n 13) at 6.

energy services leads to poor economic outcomes. Gathering of biomass is an unhealthy, time-consuming and hard task, involving long walks carrying heavy loads in all kinds of weather. Tasks take several times longer than would be the case with modern energy. In such places, health services are poor, and schools, where they exist, function at very rudimentary levels. Thus, without modern energy, poor communities have greatly reduced productivity with fewer opportunities for economic growth and social advancement. These citizens simply find it difficult to break away from the prevailing cycle of poverty.

While it is desirable that the goal of energy access be accomplished through the use of renewable energy, it is not realistic to expect the immediate attainment of this goal. The availability of gas from shale formations will provide relatively clean energy while the transition to renewable energy continues. Apart from energy access, shale gas development also offers economic, environmental, national security, geopolitical benefits and social advancement. Yet, shale resources face enormous impediments to development, one of which is sovereign ownership of mineral resources. In the United States, where private ownership of subsoil resources is permitted, this factor has made it possible to utilise the techniques of hydraulic fracturing and horizontal drilling to produce shale oil and gas. This chapter has proposed civic shares as a substitute for countries outside the US that do not permit private ownership of minerals. This tool will address most of the problems associated with lack of private ownership and has a strong potential for success.

8
International Oil and Gas Operators and Decarbonisation

PETER KAYODE ONIEMOLA

I. Introduction

Decarbonisation is having an impact on international oil and gas transactions. International oil and gas operators have shown a huge dominance in the development of oil and gas in most resource rich countries.[1] The quest for energy transition is now charting new courses for a shift in fossil fuel production and consumption patterns.[2] Oil and gas resources contribute to the rate of global emission,[3] whilst remaining a major source of export earnings for oil rich countries.[4]

Transitioning from low carbon pathways has been a major concern, given the role played by oil and gas in the international energy markets and as a source of foreign exchange to oil rich countries. Decarbonisation of the oil and gas sector has been on the cards for a while with the international measures put in place. International oil and gas companies are also putting in place different initiatives to promote decarbonisation in their operations.[5]

---

[1] Most oil and gas countries generally lack the sufficient resources to engage in exploration and production activities, which are very high risk. Therefore, turning to multinational oil companies for development purposes has been a major consideration for these countries. See Raymond F Mikesell, *Foreign Investment in the Petroleum and Mineral Industries: Case Studies of Investor-Host Country Relations* (RFF Press, 2011) 20.

[2] J Rogelj, G Luderer, RC Pietzcker, E Kriegler, M Schaeffer, V Krey and K Riahi, 'Energy System Transformations for Limiting End-of-Century Warming to Below 1.5 °C' (2015) 5(6) *Nature Climate Change* 519–27.

[3] Intergovernmental Panel on Climate Change (IPCC), *Climate Change 2014: Mitigation of Climate Change-Contribution of Working Group III to the Fifth Assessment Report of the Intergovernmental Panel on Climate Change* (Cambridge University Press, 2014) 536.

[4] John Mitchell and Beth Mitchell, 'Paris Mismatches: The Impact of the COP21 Climate Change Negotiations on the Oil and Gas Industries' (Chatham House Research Paper, August 2016), www.chathamhouse.org/sites/default/files/publications/research/2016-08-11-paris-mismatches-climate-change-oil-gas-industries-mitchell-mitchell.pdf.

[5] Oil and Gas Climate Initiative, 'Scaling up Action: Aiming for Net Zero Emissions-A Report from the Oil and Gas Climate Initiative' (September 2019), https://oilandgasclimateinitiative.com/wp-content/uploads/2019/10/OGCI-Annual-Report-2019.pdf.

The rise in oil prices and the role played by the Organisation of Petroleum Exporting Countries (OPEC) and the other oil rich countries in the geopolitics of energy set the process for decarbonisation to enhance energy security through alternative sources of energy other than from fossil fuel.[6] This development has been on the increase, with the attention of the world now focused on addressing the impact of global warming which is attributed to the anthropogenic activities of oil exploration, production and consumption.

International oil and gas operators have played a leading role in the development of the oil and gas sector and have expanded their operational bases. The oil and gas sector carries out a series of activities from exploration and production to the various value chains of the sector, (upstream), transportation, storage and refining (midstream) and distribution and retail (downstream),[7] leading to the release of greenhouse gases (GHGs) in the atmosphere. The emissions of the GHGs are largely associated with high emissions in the atmosphere. However, the rise in domestic and international actions to check the activities leading to the release of GHGs in the atmosphere is being intensified. Thus, via the United Nations Framework Convention on Climate Change (UNFCCC), the United Nations has developed a series of sustainable energy initiatives which, through various domestic legal and policy measures, is creating a new impetus for promoting decarbonisation. This therefore, among other implications, raises legal questions on continued exploration and production activities carried out by oil and gas companies that do not take into consideration the call for decarbonisation.

This chapter will critically examine the development of the oil and gas sector where the sector has contributed to an increase in the level of GHGs in the atmosphere. The international climate change regime and steps taken to reduce the climate change phenomenon through the promotion of decarbonisation will be discussed. This is followed by a review of the relevant soft laws that have improved the development of low carbon management. It looks further at what the international legal regime on climate change can offer in the development of a regime which supports clean energy technologies through the sustainable development and market-based options that can be used under the Paris Agreement. It discusses the trends in decarbonisation and how international oil and gas operators are affected. It examines measures to prepare states and the international oil and gas operators in the push for decarbonisation and concludes on the need to follow decarbonisation paths. The chapter concludes that international oil and gas operators will need to continue to assess their business and operation models and ensure that they comply with domestic and international legal response seeking to address decarbonisation.

---

[6] The emergence of the International Energy Agency (IEA) was motivated by the need to promote energy security and develop alternative energy pathways. These alternative energy sources are largely in the form of decarbonised energy sources such as nuclear, biomass, geothermal, hydro, wind energy, solar, etc.

[7] Tade Oyewunmi, 'International Petroleum Transactions and the Development of Gas-to-Power Markets in West Africa' (2019) 1 *Oil, Gas and Energy Law*, www.ogel.org/article.asp?key=3805.

II. Climate Change Issues in Exploration and Production Activities

Since the first discovery of oil in the 1850s in the US, companies mostly from the US and Europe have expanded their operations vertically and horizontally globally, by acquiring exploration and production concessions and interests in various regions such as the Middle East and West Africa. Such global expansions led to strategic partnerships, albeit sometimes controversial ones, with various host governments thus leading to the formation of national oil corporations, ministries and governmental departments in charge of petroleum regulation, international organisations such as OPEC and the International Energy Agency.[8]

Different forms of international oil and gas transactions have therefore over the years been conceived and expressed in obligations in contracts with host states such as concessions/licensee, service contracts, joint venture agreements, production sharing contracts and other forms of hybrid arrangements.[9] Private investors in oil and gas exploration and production are involved in a wide range of contracts that may take the form of Confidentiality Agreements, Letters of Intent, Joint Bidding Agreements, Farm-in/Farm-out Agreements, Joint Operating Agreements (JOA), Production Sharing Contracts (PSC), Marketing Agreements/Lifting Agreements, Unitisation Agreements and a host of other service agreements.[10] This has further necessitated intricate funding arrangements from the domestic and international money and capital markets, given the huge capital-intensive nature of oil and gas exploration and production. The upstream oil and gas sector were dominated by the oil majors that wielded much influence in the countries where they operated. Today the number of multinational oil corporations has increased, leading to more competition and the possibility of carrying out exploration activities in countries considered to have oil and gas discovery potential. Even national oil companies which were previously conceived to enhance the local participation in the domestic sector have now moved beyond their country of operation to participate in the international upstream oil and gas sector.[11] Consequently, countries which hitherto have in the past not been considered to offer viable opportunities for exploration and production, such as Ghana, Mozambique and Uganda, are

---

[8] Tade Oyewunmi, *Regulating Gas Supply to Power Markets: Transnational Approaches to Competitiveness and Security of Supply* (Wolters Kluwer, 2018) 360 at 15–20; Luis E Cuervo, 'OPEC: From Myth to Reality' (March 2008) 30(2) *Houston Journal of International Law* 433–615.

[9] For an appreciation of these agreements, see Y Omorogbe and PK Oniemola, 'Property Rights in Oil and Gas under Domanial Regimes' in A McHarg, DN Zillman, C Redgwell, YO Omorogbe and LK Barrera-Hernandez (eds), *Property and the Law in Energy and Natural Resources* (Oxford University Press, 2010) 124–31.

[10] K Talus, S Looper and S Otillar, 'Lex Petrolea and the Internationalisation of Petroleum Agreements: Focus on Host Government Contracts' (2012) 5(3) *Journal of World Energy Law & Business* 181, 182.

[11] Examples include Equinor of Norway, Petrobras of Brazil, Chinese National Petroleum Corporation, etc.

now oil rich countries or considered as potential places for future exploration and production activities.

Rising climate change and energy security concerns have, however, given impetus to the shift towards decarbonisation. The rate of pollution in the environment has led to a serious release of GHGs. The increment in the release of GHGs has been found to be associated with exploration and production and other anthropogenic activities.[12] The GHGs in the oil and gas sector include carbon monoxide, carbon dioxide and sulphur.

With the rise in public interest litigation and level of support received through environmentalists and civil societies, actions are now being directed at challenging unsustainable practices by oil and gas companies. For example, one area that has received attention is public interest-motivated litigation, which can be seen in cases whereby the court has been approached to make pronouncements and compel oil and gas companies to engage in practices that promote decarbonisation. Examples of such cases are *Kivalina v ExxonMobil Corporation & Ors*,[13] where the Plaintiff contended that they were adversely affected by the climate change resulting from the activities of the defendants and *Comer v Murphy Oil USA Inc*,[14] where they argued that the defendants' activities contributed to Hurricane Katrina.[15] Therefore, using the instrumentalities of international law and domestic law, most especially human rights law, the continuous use of fossil fuel or failure to control emissions is being questioned and challenged before the courts. The trend in climate change litigation is gaining much momentum.[16] In 2018, New York filed a case challenging oil majors BP, Chevron Corporation, ConocoPhillips, Exxon Mobil Corporation and Royal Dutch Shell Plc in the case of *City of New York v BP and Ors*.[17]

In another case, the courts in the Netherlands have appeared to approve the need for the country to observe the obligations of cutting its greenhouse emission level. In the case of *Urgenda Foundation v The Netherlands*,[18] the Plaintiff, consisting of Urgendra Foundation and 900 persons, brought an action challenging the Netherlands' commitments to reduce GHGs on the grounds that it breached the right to life and private family life under the provisions of Articles 2 and 8 of the European Convention on Human Rights and Article 21 of the Dutch Constitution, as well as the duty of care provided for under the Dutch Civil Code. The District Court, however, only found that the breach was in regards to the duty of care requiring the taking of precautionary measures that check against

---

[12] IEA, 'Global Energy & CO_2 Status Report 2019', www.iea.org/reports/global-energy-and-co2-status-report-2019

[13] *Kivalina v ExxonMobil Corporation & Ors* 2012 WL 4215921 (9th Cir 2012) 849.

[14] *Comer v Murphy Oil USA Inc* 607 F.3d 1049 (5th Cir 2010).

[15] Geetanjali Ganguly, Joana Setzer and Veerle Heyvaert, 'If at First You Don't Succeed: Suing Corporations for Climate Change' (2018) 38(4) *Oxford Journal of Legal Studies* 841, 846–47.

[16] See Joana Setzer and Mook Bangalore, 'Regulating Climate Change in the Courts' in A Averchenkova, S Fankhauser and M Nachmany (eds), *Trends in Climate Change Legislation* (Edward Elgar, 2017) 175–92.

[17] *City of New York v BP and Ors*, Case No 18 Civ. 182 (JFK).

[18] *Urgenda Foundation v The Netherlands* [2015] HAZA C/09/00456689 (24 June 2015).

hazardous impacts. The Government was therefore found to be negligent in failing to meet the target, which was to reduce CO_2 emissions to 25% below 1990s levels by 2020, finding the Government's 17% pledge insufficient. A further appeal to the Court of Appeals in the Hague upheld the decision of the District Court and also held that there was a breach of the provisions of the European Convention on Human Rights.[19]

III. Conscious Measures and Policy Push Towards Decarbonisation

Nations are taking measures towards the development of the oil and gas sector. Countries are putting in place strategic plans to integrate a climate change agenda into their economy through measures such as green growth plans.[20] There have been many obvious policies directed and targeted at ensuring that fossil fuel is phased out.

The promotion of electric vehicle use is now occasioned by laws and policies directed at climate change mitigation.[21] The promotion of environmental sustainability through the control of vehicular emissions has received much attention. Vehicular emissions are one of the key contributors of the release of GHGs in the atmosphere. In the nationally determined contributions that were submitted to the UNFCCC in furtherance of the obligations under the Paris Agreement, GHGs reduction measures focusing on transportation were identified in 119 countries.[22] Some examples of this can be seen with the policies that are directed towards the shift from fossil fuel-powered vehicles to hybrid or electric vehicles. Technological advancement and research and development are being coordinated to promote the development of electric cars.[23] There has been a conscious and

---

[19] *Urgenda Foundation v The Netherlands* C/09/456689/ HA ZA 13-1396 (9 October 2018). For further appreciation of the arguments in the case, see Petra Minnerop, 'Integrating the "Duty of Care" under the European Convention on Human Rights and the Science and Law of Climate Change: The Decision of the Hague Court of Appeal in the Urgenda Case' (2019) 37(2) *Journal of Energy & Natural Resources Law* 149, 149–79.

[20] See Alina Averchenkova, Sam Fankhauser and Michal Nachmany, 'Introduction' in Alina Averchenkova, Sam Fankhauser and Michal Nachmany (eds), *Trends in Climate Change Legislation* (Edward Elgar Publishing, 2017) 5.

[21] See Barry Barton and Peter Schütte, 'Electric Vehicle Law and Policy: A Comparative Analysis' (2017) 35(2) *Journal of Energy & Natural Resources Law* 147, 147–70.

[22] E Löhr, N Perera, N Hill, D Bongardt and U Eichhorst, *Transport in Nationally Determined Contributions (NDCs): Lessons learnt from case studies of rapidly motorising countries: Synthesis Report* (Deutsche Gesellschaft für Internationale Zusammenarbeit (GIZ) GmbH, Bonn, 2017) 9.

[23] Since the recorded success in 1997 of the introduction of the hybrid electric vehicle in Japan, known as the Toyota Prius, the rate of advancement in the promotion of electric vehicles has been promising. See Jeffrey Sachs, 'Electric Cars are Driving the Transition to Sustainable Technologies' *The Guardian*, 21 September 2009, www.theguardian.com/environment/cif-green/2009/sep/21/electric-cars-sustainable-technology.

gradual deployment of electric vehicles worldwide which are aimed at reducing the rate of use of petroleum products. The technological innovation occasioned by the use of electric mobility will affect oil and gas suppliers, among others.[24] The implication of such development and progress made in the deployment of electric vehicles will be a cut in the consumption of petroleum products which are used for powering vehicles.

The European Union has developed a policy agenda to put in place a framework in order to be carbon neutral by 2050.[25] The oil majors are now taking measures to ensure that they would remain profitable if they found themselves in a situation where oil and gas was no longer in such high demand. They are therefore pushing to diversify their energy investment portfolio through investment in renewable energy and sustainable energy is increasing. The World Bank Resolution to stop the funding of fossil fuel and the further commitments to support the promotion of decarbonisation within the framework of the Paris Agreement is also another source of concern for oil and gas companies. The World Bank has confirmed that it would be meeting its targets of '28% of its lending going to climate action by 2020 and to meeting the goals of its Climate Change Action Plan – developed following the Paris Agreement'.[26] It will also support and invest U$325 million in the Green Cornerstone Bond Fund, which is targeted at attracting an investment worth U$2 billion.[27]

It is widely acknowledged that soft laws such as declarations, resolutions and guidelines issued by international organisations, non-governmental international organisations and a good number of those issued within the United Nations, are not regarded as binding in international law. These soft law instruments largely contain customary international law and established principles of international law that are enshrined in international treaties. Their enforcements on the other hand cannot be. Decarbonisation has also not been limited to the possible use of binding international law treaties, particularly those that are related to climate change.[28] Soft law provisions have been quite instructive on the ways in which multinational oil companies can be regulated and made to take commitments on decarbonisation.

For example, it will be of great importance for the international effort towards decarbonisation if oil and gas operators are made to take targets and move towards clean energy development; targets seen in the United Nations Declaration on

---

[24] See Christoph Mazura, Marcello Contestabile, Gregory J Offer, NP Brandona, 'Assessing and Comparing German and UK Transition Policies for Electric Mobility' (2015) 14 *Environmental Innovation and Societal Transitions* 84, 86.

[25] European Commission, 'Going Climate-Neutral by 2050: A Strategic Long-term Vision for a Prosperous, Modern, Competitive and Climate-Neutral EU Economy' (16 July 2019), https://op.europa.eu/en/publication-detail/-/publication/92f6d5bc-76bc-11e9-9f05-01aa75ed71a1/language-en/format-PDF/source-101373850.

[26] World Bank, World Bank Group Announcements.

[27] *Ibid.*

[28] For eg, it has been argued that the Copenhagen Accord on climate change passed by virtue of the United Nations Resolution amounted to a statement of intent of the parties that signed as it lacked the essentials of a binding international law instrument.

Environment and Development (Stockholm Declaration), Rio Declaration, the United Nations Declaration on Sustainable Energy for All, among many other guidelines issued by the organisations within the United Nations system. The World Bank Equator Principles for example seeks to promote sustainability and it will be important that they are developed and implemented. In the past, the World Bank Group has supported the development of the upstream oil and gas industry through offering robust finance facilities and guarantees. Examples of such facilities offered by the World Bank are those made through the International Finance Corporation (IFC) and Multilateral Investment Guarantee Agency (MIGA), which have extensively supported the development of the oil and gas industry in the past.[29] The trend is changing as over the years the World Bank has been subjected to criticism for funding projects that do not achieve sustainable development.[30] The World Bank has been previously attacked for supporting unsustainable energy development and has even announced that it would stop financing upstream oil and gas projects by 2019.[31] Due to worries over public opinion, the World Bank has also been very conscious about the nature of investments it is venturing into or supporting, which led it to develop practices that support sustainability.[32] Therefore, part of the World Bank initiative was to offer and develop carbon support schemes. Some projects have benefitted under the scheme but turn out to have contributed to the problem of climate change. Generally, financial development institutions have evolved the practices of ensuring that they fund projects that promote sustainability.

Financial institutions are also responding to climate change in varied ways. The landscape of financial reporting is changing as the trend now is to make financial institutions report their funding to carbon intensive companies.[33] The managers of the Norwegian Sovereign Wealth Fund (Government Pension Fund Global), developed by Norway, has taken a new approach regarding the nature of investments in carbon intensive sectors such as oil and gas.[34]

---

[29] On support offered by the MIGA, see MIGA, 'MIGA: Securing Oil and Gas Investments', www.miga.org/documents/oil-gas-brief.pdf.

[30] For eg, the World Bank's involvement in the funding of oil and gas projects in Chad was criticised as falling short of social, environmental and other benefits. See Stephen V Arbogast, 'Project Financing & Political Risk Mitigation: The Singular Case of the Chad-Cameroon Pipeline' (2009) 4 *Texas Journal of Oil, Gas, and Energy Law* 284.

[31] However, the Bank noted that it will only in exceptional circumstances consider 'financing upstream gas in the poorest countries where there is a clear benefit in terms of energy access for the poor and the project fits within the countries' Paris Agreement commitments'. See World Bank Group, 'World Bank Group Announcements at One Planet Summit' (Press Release, 12 December 2017), www.worldbank.org/en/news/press-release/2017/12/12/world-bank-group-announcements-at-one-planet-summit.

[32] World Bank, 'Where Does the World Stand in Reaching Sustainable Energy Objectives?', www.worldbank.org/en/news/feature/2015/05/18/where-does-the-world-stand-in-reaching-sustainable-energy-objectives.

[33] Zachary Folger-Laronde and Olaf Weber, 'Climate Change Disclosure of the Financial Sector' CIGI Papers No 190 – September 2018 (Centre for International Governance Innovation, 2018) www.cigionline.org/sites/default/files/documents/Paper%20no.190.pdf.

[34] Norges Bank Investment Management, Responsible Investment 2017: Government Pension Fund Global Annual Report, 2018, www.nbim.no/contentassets/02bfbbef416f4014b043e74b8405fa97/annual-report-2018-government-pension-fund-global.pdf.

It has reassessed its position regarding participation in unsustainable practices. Its Regulation requires that sustainability should be at its fore and the financing of oil and gas projects and ventures will be required.[35]

The Sovereign Wealth Fund, for example, will be such that it should not engage in any form of investment that does not promote a change or improvement in the problem of climate change. It has been investigating countries and even placed some on a watch list. It placed Shell Nigeria on a watch list, for example, due to its activities in the Niger Delta region of Nigeria. It promotes investments in the oil and gas sector. Therefore, much will need to be done within the UN process to engage financial institutions so that they do not participate in the funding of projects that are contributing to the problems of climate change. Therefore, steps will be expected to be taken to ensure that funds support low carbon development or the transition to less carbon development. The pace of decarbonisation has been seen to be gradually having an impact on the investment topography of international oil and gas transactions.[36] It is recorded that there is now divestiture of assets in upstream transactions. Some companies are therefore pulling off their assets and venturing into other low carbon technologies or investments. There is likely going to be the gradual rise in the number of stranded assets as oil and gas companies may be unable to maintain some of their assets leading to them being abandoned. The nature of project financing for the oil and gas sector will invariably continue to change given the risks that are associated with the move towards decarbonisation.[37]

Further opportunities in regards to the development of low carbon transition can be seen from the proponents for sustainability as evidenced by the move towards sustainable development within the UN systems and the declaration of the Decade of Sustainable Energy for All.[38] The various energy components of the

---

[35] This is by virtue of the Guidelines for the Observation and Exclusion of Companies from the Government Pension Fund Global's Investment Universe which was adopted by the Ministry of Finance on 1 March 2010 in pursuance of section 7 of Act No 123 of 21 December 2005 relating to the Government Pension Fund. See Council on Ethics for the Government Pension Fund Global, '2014 Annual Report' (31 December 2014), www.banktrack.org/download/council_on_ethics_2014_annual_report_pdf/councilonethics2014annualreport.pdf.

[36] Romain Debarre, Tancrede Fulop and Bruno Lajoie, 'Consequences of COP21 for the Oil and Gas Industry: GHG Targets and Possible Outcomes' (*Accenture*, 2016), www.accenture.com/t00010101T000000__w__/br-pt/_acnmedia/PDF-11/Accenture-Strategy-Energy-Perspectives-Consequences-COP21.pdf.

[37] It is argued that with the waning reserves in the North Sea in the 1990s, project financing was considered by oil majors as a means of increasing and meeting the demands. With many discoveries being made and the potential risks associated with the fight against climate change and the move towards decarbonisation, project financing arrangements are likely to change with a number of innovations introduced as a means of responding to these risks.

[38] United Nations General Assembly Declaration of 2014-2024 as a decade of Sustainable Energy for All is to underscore 'the importance of energy issues for sustainable development and for the elaboration of the post-2015 development agenda'. See United Nations, 'United Nations General Assembly Declares 2014-2024 Decade of Sustainable Energy for All', www.un.org/press/en/2012/ga11333.doc.htm.

sustainable development goals are further pointers that engage the international oil and gas companies to be part of the process. Other considerations which oil companies are signing up to includes the Natural Resource Charter,[39] which has developed some principles and best practices to promote sustainability. Soft law instruments therefore are impacting on the need to promote decarbonisation of the operations of oil and gas companies. To therefore build their reputation and demonstrate their involvement in decarbonisation, they are signing up to observing these soft laws and even putting in place policies to show their commitment to such soft law initiatives.

International oil and gas operators such as Shell, ExxonMobil among others are feeling the heat under a huge level of criticism. More actions are being directed towards the fight against climate change through efforts that will de-emphasise carbon intensive paths to development. Much has therefore been advocated in favour of movement towards a greener economy by organisations such as Friends of the Earth and Greenpeace. Civil society organisations are at the forefront in challenging actions that they consider to promote the utilisation of fossil fuel. They are becoming more emboldened in continuing to explore avenues to compel oil and gas companies to reduce their emission levels. For example, the *Lofoten Declaration* of 2017 was signed by about 500 non-governmental organisations with the focus on promoting the management of the decline in the production of fossil sources of oil, gas and coal.[40] It therefore calls for the reduction of fossil fuel demand which requires immediate action and calls further for ambitious actions to 'stop exploration and expansion of fossil fuel projects and manage the decline of existing production in line with what is necessary to achieve the Paris climate goals'.[41] The Declaration stressed that there 'is the urgent responsibility and moral obligation of wealthy fossil fuel producers to lead in putting an end to fossil fuel development and to manage the decline of existing production'.[42] Oil majors have come under severe criticism for actions that are inimical to the fight against climate change. For instance, Exxon Mobil was revealed to have had close engagements with climate deniers. There are even allegations against it that it has suppressed information regarding its rate of emissions.[43]

---

[39] The Charter is an initiative seeking to ensure the promotion of natural resources wealth sustainable utilisation in countries rich in non-renewable energy sources. Precept 11 of the Charter enjoins that 'Companies should commit to the highest environmental, social and human rights standards, and to sustainable development'. See Natural Resource Charter (Second Edition, 2014), https://resourcegovernance.org/sites/default/files/documents/nrcj1193_natural_resource_charter_19.6.14.pdf.

[40] Lofoten Declaration, www.lofotendeclaration.org/#read.

[41] *Ibid.*

[42] *Ibid.*

[43] Geoffrey Supran and Naomi Oreskes, 'Assessing ExxonMobil's Climate Change Communications (1977–2014)' (2017) 12 *Environmental Research Letters*.

IV. Regulating Oil and Gas Operations and Commitments by Host States

The implementation of international commitments in treaties largely lies with state party compliance. Depending on the legal system, states may be required to pass laws in order to implement international commitments. The legal regimes in the state parties should be supportive of such and not operate as a barrier to effective implementation.[44] For the developed countries, the question of regulation for climate change by decarbonisation may not be as complicated as seen in the developing countries with very rich petroleum resources. Apart from the existence of the international regime, the domestic laws have been quite proactive. Take for example, the coordination taking place under the auspices of the European Union. The European Union adopts the EU type target and through the directives and communications of the European Parliament has considerably sought to promote climate change mitigation in accordance with the environmental objectives of the EU Treaty. Thus, the EU has shown much directional leadership in its quest to cushion the effects of anthropogenic emission. The US regulation shows to some extent that whilst it may not have taken binding targets and has been quite deviant in the climate change regime since the Kyoto Era to date, we have seen a commendable effort within the framework of its domestic laws that could have far reaching consequences on decarbonisation. The desire to reduce climate change mitigation in Africa and ensure that the problem is addressed has some major consequences for consideration in the penalisation of emitters of oil and gas. A look at the experience from the spill in the Gulf of Mexico showed the ability of developed countries to arrest the situation.[45] However, the case is different from most developing countries that will find it difficult to regulate or control the emissions that are being released in the atmosphere. These are serious questions that they may find very difficult to address due to economic reasons. Therefore, there is the question which developing countries will have to address of whether it is feasible that companies face sanctions for environmental pollution. The Environmental Court sitting in Paris imposed a heavy fine on Total for the sinking of the Erika Ship which led to the pollution of water around the shores of Brittany, France.[46]

---

[44] The Vienna Convention on the Law of Treaties 1969 enjoins countries to ensure that domestic laws do not operate as a barrier to the implementation of a treaty. Article 26 provides that: 'Every treaty in force is binding upon the parties to it and must be performed by them in good faith'.

[45] The notable cases that emanated out of the spill leading to compensation being paid include *United States v BP Exploration & Production Inc* (No. 10-4536 in MDL 2179 (E.D. La.)); *State of Alabama v BP* (Case No 2:10-CV-04182 (E.D. La.)); *State of Florida v BP Exploration & Production Inc Case No.* 5:13-cv-00123 (N.D. Fla.); *State of Louisiana v BP Exploration & Production, Inc* (Case Nos. 11-cv-0516 and 10-cv-03059 in MDL 2179 (E.D. La.)); *State of Texas v BP Exploration & Production Inc* (Case No. 13-cv-4677 (E.D. La.)); and *Hood v BP Exploration & Production, Inc* (Case No 1:13-cv-00158 (S.D. Miss.)).

[46] Wang Hui, *Civil Liability for Marine Oil Pollution Damage: A Comparative and Economic Study of International, US and Chinese Compensation Regime* (Kluwer Law International, 2011) 361–65.

The oil rich countries that fall within the global South can be rated as some of the least developed countries. They may be referred to as major pollution havens. Nigeria for example has the Associated Gas Reinjection Act 1979 which was passed into law to control gas flaring. However, Nigeria has not been able to effectively regulate the sector to address the problem of gas flaring. Shell was discovered to have flared gas with impunity as indicated in a 2015 report of the Nigerian Extractive Industry Transparency Initiative (NEITI).[47] A similar occurrence was recorded in Ghana where Kosmo Energy polluted the land with discharge of muds that contained poisonous substances. The company was fined by the Ministry of Environment, Science and Technology but the company however maintained that it was not in breach of any law as there was no law disallowing them from such practices.[48]

In the United Kingdom the case is different, as carbon intensive companies are taxed through the Climate Change Levy which aims to increase energy efficiency and reduce carbon emissions.[49] Ghana, on the other hand, saw a case of pollution with tar muds where fines imposed on a company, Kosmo Energy, were not considered by the company as binding on it. It even went as far to claim that there was no law preventing it from pollution. The United States has witnessed a plethora of cases arising from the implementation and compliance with the provisions of the Clean Air Act 1970. For example, in the case of *Massachusetts v Environmental Protection Agency (EPA)*,[50] the US Supreme Court was of the view that regulatory authorities must give an informed judgment on the adverse impact of carbon dioxide emission. It held that the broad definition of air under the Clean Air Act cover pollutants such as GHGs, which cause climate change. The Supreme Court also confirmed that if the EPA makes a so-called 'endangerment finding', and concludes that GHGs pose a danger to human health or the environment; it must act to reduce such emissions. In 2009, the EPA issued an Endangerment Finding covering carbon dioxide and other GHGs, requiring the agency to develop a plan to reduce GHG emissions.[51] In the case of *Coalition for Responsible Regulation v EPA*,[52] the US Court of Appeal of the State for the District of Columbia Circuit, confirmed the power of the EPA to make an endangerment finding. Thus, the aftermath of the judgment led the EPA to develop several rules and regulations to regulate emissions from oil and gas systems.[53]

---

[47] Friends of the Earth, 'Shell's Big Dirty Secret Insight into the World's most Carbon Intensive Oil Company and the Legacy of CEO Jeroen van der Veer', www.foei.org/wp-content/uploads/2014/08/shellbigdirtysecret_June09.pdf.

[48] The development led to the passage of the Petroleum (Exploration and Production) Act 2016.

[49] See Peter Kayode Oniemola, 'Taxation of Fossil Fuel Electricity Generation in Favour of Renewables: Lessons for other Countries from the UK Climate Change Levy Scheme' (2016) 14(4) *Oil, Gas and Energy Law Intelligence Journal* 1, 1–11.

[50] *Massachusetts v Environmental Protection Agency (EPA)* 549 US 497 (2007).

[51] See Francis Choi, 'Coalition for Responsible Regulation v. EPA: An Analysis of Judicial Deference and Regulatory Discretion' (2013) 40 *Ecology Law Quarterly* 525, 525–32.

[52] *Coalition for Responsible Regulation v EPA* No 09-1322 (Decided 26 June 2012).

[53] *Ibid*.

Generally, domestic laws have a major role to play in the determination of the extent to which international oil and gas operators will continue to observe practices that favour decarbonisation. Whilst the international law instruments will largely be considered as prescriptive and could lack the apparatus to fully enforce decarbonisation, the domestic and international law instruments play a central role. Therefore, the preparedness of the state parties signing up to the treaties and other best practices will be an important consideration for the success of ensuring that international oil and gas companies are liable.

The preparedness for climate change will need to be backed by a well-conditioned mechanism that promotes enforcement. One of such practices will be seen in the development of transparency in monitoring, reporting and verification (MRV) within the Paris Agreement.[54] Much will need to be done at the domestic level to set and put in place sufficient legal measures that enhance effective reporting of decarbonisation measures by oil and gas companies in a way that is more transparent. Translating this into the decarbonisation agenda of the world, will mean that oil and gas companies will be made to report their levels of emissions in countries where they are still not under any obligation to do so.

One area which the Paris Agreement on climate change has built upon is the promotion of transparency in MRV. The Paris Agreement has therefore envisioned a detailed framework on reporting for mitigation outcomes. Effort towards ensuring that domestic legal measures are deployed for the realisation of such transparency may be grounds to challenge companies not reporting their emissions appropriately. Further, the implication is that oil and gas companies will be made to account for their emissions and the proper implementation of the Paris transparency rules will expose oil and gas companies that don't play by the rules.

States are usually the subjects of international law and are required to observe all commitments they make to keep the emission of GHGs under control. The Kyoto Protocol set the agenda for international climate change mitigation. The Paris Agreement built on this development and it is expected that nations will set in place measures to support climate change mitigation. The international legal regime committed nations to take targets which can be utilised. The provisions of the Paris Agreement will require nations to take action. Countries have made commitments under the climate change regime. In particular, there is the requirement for companies to enter into nationally determined contributions. Initially, countries developed their own nationally determined contributions.

Norway has committed to reduce its GHGs by 40 per cent by 2030 in comparison with the 1990 levels.[55] Even new producer Ghana indicated that it would commit to a reduction of GHG emission by 15 per cent by 2030 and would conditionally reduce the same by 45 per cent where there exists external support in

---

[54] Paris Agreement (United Nations, 2015), Art 13.
[55] 'Submission by Norway to the ADP: Norway's Intended Nationally Determined Contribution', www4.unfccc.int/sites/submissions/INDC/Published%20Documents/Norway/1/Norway%20INDC%2026MAR2015.pdf.

the form of finance, technology transfer and capacity building.[56] Saudi Arabia has committed to reduce its carbon dioxide equivalent emissions by 130 million tons annually till 2030.[57] These countries are rich in oil and gas and these commitments could be a way forward if strictly implemented, even though much is expected to be done beyond these commitments. On the other hand, whilst the quest for the development of renewable energy could be considered as suspicious or curious in the Middle East given the abundant oil and gas deposits and operations carried out by the multinational oil and gas companies, these measures are gradually changing the game. It is possible for oil and gas operators to take targets towards decarbonisation. Strictly speaking, treaty commitments can usually be seen as binding on states. However, companies can voluntarily sign up to initiatives that are directed towards the promotion of decarbonisation. Therefore, taking a cue from such development, international climate change cooperation will be required to move the process of engaging oil and gas companies. Companies are taking measures that require them to observe international standards promoting mitigation.

A look at the climate change debate further raises issues with oil rich developing countries getting involved in climate change mitigation. For example, while it may be viewed that the developing countries perceive the fight of climate change with much suspicion, their engagements have been pushed further through bringing them into the heart of negotiation, particularly in the course of the post-2012 negotiation process.[58] There is an ethical question about the activities of the international oil and gas operators and their commitments towards sustainable energy development. A further question is how auspicious it would be for oil revenue to be utilised to fund alternative energy sources that enhance decarbonisation. The question on whether a polluter will continue to develop measures that seek to bring about a reduction in the release of GHGs in the atmosphere remains critical. How realistic will it be for the multinational oil corporation to be willing to forego its investment choice in furtherance of technologies that are propelled by clean energy?

More so, oil and gas resources are one of the major sources of energy in the world and the idea of a total displacement may not auger well with the oil and gas companies. The competition across countries for maximising the exploration and production opportunities continues to grow and for the very least developed

---

[56] Republic of Ghana, 'Ghana's Intended Nationally Determined Contribution (INDC) and Accompanying Explanatory Note' (September 2015), www4.unfccc.int/sites/submissions/INDC/Published%20Documents/Ghana/1/GH_INDC_2392015.pdf.

[57] See 'The Intended Nationally Determined Contribution of the Kingdom of Saudi Arabia under the UNFCCC' (Riyadh, November 2015), www4.unfccc.int/sites/ndcstaging/PublishedDocuments/Saudi%20Arabia%20First/KSA-INDCs%20English.pdf.

[58] The overriding arguments of developing countries in the negotiations leading to the Post Kyoto Agreement was that the developed countries should take more targets and commitments towards climate change mitigation because historically they have been the main emitters. See Peter Kayode Oniemola, 'Reflections on the Copenhagen Accord and Divergent Poles in International Climate Law Negotiations' (2012) 7 *University of Ibadan Journal of Private and Business Law* 124–30.

countries it will be an opportunity for them to make revenue from oil and gas.[59] By the same token, emerging oil and gas producers continue to expand their operational base. National oil companies for example have expanded their bases across their countries and a good number of them operate transnationally. Equinor (formerly Statoil) of Norway has expanded its operations beyond Norway to countries such as Nigeria. Likewise, Petrobras of Brazil has operational bases in Nigeria and Ghana. The Chinese National Petroleum Corporation is similarly playing a lead role in the North Sea and Nigeria.

It appears that corporate social responsibility is playing a role in changing the attitude of multinational oil companies. Reports from these companies show that they are also taking measures that seek to address climate change concerns and mainstreaming sustainable practices in their operations.[60] Going beyond corporate social responsibility commitments, opportunities may be keyed into the process whereby obligation can be created for the polluters to support the development of projects that enhance decarbonisation. Ultimately, the oil and gas companies are chief polluters of the release of GHGs in the atmosphere. They should therefore pay for decarbonisation through the creation of a legal responsibility that will mandate them to take mitigation measures beyond promotion of energy efficiency to even participate in the development of renewable energy projects as alternatives.

V. Changes in Energy Mix and Structure of Supply

The configurations for energy and its demands are leading to changes in energy choices.[61] Therefore, there is a trend towards changes in energy mix and the structure of the energy supply network into decentralised and distributed suppliers. This is a departure from the traditional structure, which places reliance on centralised, vertically integrated utilities with significant monopoly and state-control. The EU in its directives on renewable energy provides a framework upon which

---

[59] This will have impacts on companies that have fully engaged in oil and gas and economies seeing their discoveries as opportunities to make additional revenue from exploration and production. See Cleo Verkuijl, Georgia Piggot, Michael Lazarus, Harro van Asselt and Peter Erickson, 'Aligning Fossil Fuel Production with the Paris Agreement: Insights for the UNFCCC Talanoa Dialogue' (Stockholm Environment Institute, March 2018), https://unfccc.int/sites/default/files/resource/11_12_13__SEI_Talanoa_Fossil_Fuels_0.pdf.

[60] ExxonMobil, '2020 Energy & Carbon Summary', https://corporate.exxonmobil.com/-/media/Global/Files/energy-and-carbon-summary/Energy-and-carbon-summary.pdf; Shell, 'Shell Energy Transition Report', www.shell.com/energy-and-innovation/the-energy-future/shell-energy-transition-report.html.

[61] See Rosemary Lyster, 'The Implications of Electricity Restructuring for Sustainable Energy Framework: What Law got to do with it' in Adrian J Bradbrook, Rosemary Lyster, Richard L Ottinger and Wang Xi (eds), *The Law of Energy for Sustainable Development* (Cambridge University Press, 2012) 415–48.

Member States can promote the development of renewable energy between the EU states and third countries.[62] The directives provide joint development of projects which could change the pattern of trade in electricity.

For example, even the least developed economies that have not been able to make progress in the discovery of oil and gas are also in the race for the shift towards decarbonisation through tapping of the available energy resources such as renewable energy. Kenya has considered exploring the development of its abundant renewable energy sources to power the nation. It has successfully implemented a policy and legal regime that promotes investment in renewable energy sources in the country. The investment in renewable energy in Kenya has even received support from financial development institutions. The 20 million Euro Partial Risk Guarantee programme supporting the deployment of renewable electricity in Kenya has been considered as a positive development for decarbonisation. The project, the Lake Turkana Wind Power Project, is the largest in Africa aimed at the construction of a 300 MW and 33kV electrical network.[63] Another area that has contributed in changing the global energy system is the gradual competitiveness of energy sources such as renewable energy.[64]

VI. Changing Patterns of Energy Disputes and Decarbonisation

International investment treaties are further creating obligations requiring that environmental considerations are given to investments. The issues of regulatory chill in investment promotion or ensuring that clean technologies are promoted or encouraged may not be considered to be a way of restricting the role of investment. Therefore, international investment tribunals have been holding in favour of sustainability in investment by showing that such measures in place are in furtherance of a legitimate purpose, which in the context of this chapter includes climate change mitigation through decarbonisation. Therefore, the new generation bilateral investment treaties (BITs) are recognising the role of sustainability and are

---

[62] See Directive 2009/28/EC of the European Parliament and of the Council of 23 April 2009 on the promotion of the use of energy from renewable sources and amending and subsequently repealing Directives 2001/77/EC and 2003/30/EC [2009] OJ L140/16–62, Art 9 and Directive 2018/2001 of the European Parliament and of the Council of 11 December 2018 on the Promotion of the use of Energy from Renewable Sources [2018] OJ L328/82.

[63] Emeka Oragunye, 'First ADF Partial Risk Guarantee Approved in Kenya for Largest African Wind Power Project' (2 October 2013), www.afdb.org/en/news-and-events/first-adf-partial-risk-guarantee-approved-in-kenya-for-largest-african-wind-power-project-12324.

[64] See Simone Tagliapietra, 'The Impact of Global Decarbonization Policies and Technological Improvements on Oil and Gas Producing Countries in the Middle East and North Africa' (IEMed Mediterranean Yearbook, 2018).

promoting socially responsible investments that meet environmental sustainability. For example the Netherlands-United Arab Emirates BIT provides that:

> Contracting Parties recognize the right of each Contracting Party to establish its own level of domestic environmental protection and its own sustainable development policy and priorities, and to adopt or modify its environmental laws and regulations and shall strive as far as possible to continue to improve their laws and regulations.[65]

Environmental objectives are considered to be one of the objectives set for exploration and production of petroleum resources.[66] This will therefore offer a buffer for the question of regulatory chill. Investors would have in the ordinary course of things to question effort or regulatory commitments of states to the matters relating to decarbonisation through the invocation of the various protective standards such as fair and equitable treatment, unlawful expropriation, full protection and security, umbrella clauses and arbitral proceedings.[67] In the wake of the exercise of states' sovereign rights, there was a rise in international oil and gas disputes, occasioned by nationalisation of assets of the multinational corporations. There have been disputes also connected to changes in the fiscal regime and unilateral alternations of terms of contractual obligations in connection with the government's stake in the oil.[68] The push for sustainable energy, such as renewable energy, takes a different path.[69] Recently, there also appears to have been a diversion of attention in international investment disputes in the oil and gas sector to the renewable energy subsector.[70] Thus, issues regarding environmental regulation, renewable energy and energy efficiency have exponentially increased.[71] Therefore, sustainable energy has experienced a series of disputes arising under BITs, the North American Free Trade Agreement and Energy Charter Treaty

---

[65] Preamble to the Netherlands-United Arab Emirates BIT 2013.

[66] K Tienhaara, *The Expropriation of Environmental Governance: Protecting Foreign Investors at the Expense of Public Policy* (Cambridge University Press, 2009) 102–103.

[67] For an insightful appreciation of the above proposition, see A Boute, 'Improving the Climate for European Investments in the Russian Electricity Production Sector: (I) The Role of Investment Protection Law' (2008) 26 (2) *Journal of Energy and Natural Resources Law* 267, 284–85; Nigel Bankes, 'Decarbonising the Economy and International Investment Law' (2012) 30(4) *Journal of Energy & Natural Resources Law* 497–510; Nigel Bankes, Anatole Boute, Steve Charnovitz, Shi-Ling Hsu, Sarah Mccalla, Nicholas Rivers and Elizabeth Whitsitt, 'International Trade and Investment Law and Carbon Management Technologies' (2013) 53 *Natural Resources Journal* 285, 285–324.

[68] See generally A Kolo, 'Fat Cats and "Windfall" Taxes in the Natural Resources Industry: Legal and Policy Analysis in the Light of Modern Investment Treaties' in Jacques Werner and Arif Hyder Ali (eds), *A Liber Amicorum: Thomas Wälde – Law Beyond Conventional Thought* (CMP Publishing Ltd, 2009).

[69] Kim Talus, 'Introduction – Renewable Energy Disputes in the Europe and Beyond: An Overview of Current Cases' (2015) 13(3) *Oil, Gas and Energy Law* 1, 16.

[70] See Peter Kayode Oniemola, 'Investment in Renewable Energy in Nigeria and the Snags of Regulatory Risks' (2016) 14 *Nigerian Juridical Review* 35, 35–66.

[71] Jorge E Vanuales, 'Foreign Investment and the Environment in International Law: Current Trends' in Kate Miles (ed), *Research Handbook on Environment and Investment Law* (Edward Elgar Publishing Ltd, 2019) 19–25.

claims. For example, the floodgates of arbitration were opened in Spain owing to changes in its support for renewable energy.[72]

It is reported that disputes have been filed before the International Centre for Settlement of Investment Disputes, all arising from the renewable energy sector. The commitments to oil and gas contracts entered into by host states may not be kept, because the state considers them to be no longer convenient.[73] Therefore in the bid to support sustainable energy development or achieve the goals of decarbonisation, states may find it unfashionable to keep to the terms of the contracts. Similarly, the trade in renewable energy goods and services has resulted in a series of disputes within the World Trade Organisation's (WTO) dispute settlement system.[74] Particularly the provisions of some agreements annexed to the WTO Agreement such as the General Agreement on Tariffs and Trade (GATT), Technical Barriers to Trade Agreement and Agreement on Subsidies and Countervailing Measures have been subjected to analyis before the WTO dispute settlement system. The trends have been ongoing within the WTO jurisprudence.[75] Notable cases include *Canada–Renewable Energy/Feed-In Tariff*[76] where the support for renewable energy through local content measures by the Province of Ontario under the Green Energy Act was challenged by Japan and the EU for breaching the provisions of the GATT and the Agreement on Trade-Related Investment Measures.

VII. The Legal Preparedness of States and Oil and Gas Operators for Decarbonisation under the Paris Agreement

The Paris Agreement came into force on 4 November 2016, 30 days after at least 55 parties deposited their instruments of ratification, acceptance, approval or accession at the designated depository. It has therefore been ratified by 187 states.[77] The Paris Agreement is the development of the international

---

[72] Carmen Otero García-Castrillón, 'Spain and Investment Arbitration: The Renewable Energy Explosion' (Investor-State Arbitration Series Paper No 17, November 2016), www.cigionline.org/sites/default/files/documents/ISA%20Paper%20No.17.pdf.

[73] F Solimene, 'Political Risk in the Oil and Gas Industry and Legal Tools for Mitigation' (2014) 2 *International Energy Law Review* 81, 82.

[74] See Jenya Grigorova, 'EU's Renewable Energy Directive saved by GATT Art. XX?' (2013) 13(3) *Oil, Gas and Energy Law* 1–21.

[75] Debra P Steger, 'Green Energy Programs and the WTO Agreement on Subsidies and Countervailing Measures: A Good FIT?' (2015) 13(3) *Oil, Gas and Energy Law* 1, 1–14.

[76] WTO, *Canada–Certain Measures Affecting the Renewable Energy Generation Sector/Canada–Measures Relating to the Feed-In Tariff Program* (Appellate Body Reports) WT/DS412/AB/R and WT/DS426/AB/R.

[77] UNFCCC, 'Paris Agreement – Status of Ratification', https://unfccc.int/process/the-paris-agreement/status-of-ratification.

framework. The development of a domestic regime complementing the Paris Agreement becomes very important in the emergence of a robust decarbonisation plan coordinated within the scheme of things offered by the Paris Agreement. As may be seen, the treaty process could take the form of dualism or monism.[78] Some states have their treaties coming into force upon it being ratified to or acceded and deposited at the designated repository. On the other hand, other states will require further steps to be taken on the treaty which will include further ratification of such treaty by the legislative arm of government. The oil and gas companies are therefore subjects of the state in which they operate and become automatically bound to continue to observe the laws of the state.

The grant of oil and gas licences takes different forms, in particular where an oil exploration and production licence/lease is granted by a state to the international oil and gas operators. Typical conditions have been made to make licence-holders commit themselves to environmental management plans or measures that reduce environmental degradation.[79] The conditions for grant can be utilised to set major benchmarks for climate change by ensuring that exploration and production companies deploy carbon management technologies in their operations. For example, the generation of electricity for renewable energy in respect to certain appliances on site or in use will be another way to encourage the development of low carbon technologies. The development of clean energy technologies by compelling oil-producing companies to engage in production of clean energy sources within certain areas of their operations may not be out of place. This could be incentivised through tax rebates and other waivers.

The trend in corporate governance is to mainstream risks as part of areas which are required to be addressed in codes of corporate governance. Oil and gas companies have been adopting corporate governance codes and strategies in their businesses globally. One area is in relation to corporate disclosures. Climate change has associated risks which could take the form of legal and regulatory risk; it could even be in relation to commercial risk. Legal risks will therefore lead to a change in the regulatory regime, making it challenging for upstream investments in oil and gas.

The commercial risks could be seen in the shift from petroleum resources to renewable energy, thereby leading to a shortage in demand for petroleum

---

[78] Similarly, some countries operate a system of government whereby the laws are centralised with no powers for the regions to be able to make laws, while some may give leeway for regions to make laws, in which case there will be regional laws in addition to the central law for the country. A question may arise whether states are bound to observe the provisions of international law. See arguments offered by David R Hodas, 'State Law Responses to Global Warming: Is It Constitutional to Think Globally and Act Locally' (2003) 21 *Pace Environmental Law Review* 53.

[79] For eg, the grant of oil production licences in the UK will require that the licence-holder should demonstrate that it has the technical and financial ability to effectively carry out environmental remediation. GW Gordon, 'Production Licensing on the UK Continental Shelf: Ministerial Powers and Controls' (2015) 4(1) *LSU Journal of Energy Law and Resources* 75, 79–80.

products. The development of these risk portfolio analyses within the codes could take into consideration the risks associated with climate change. Taking the duration and buy-back period for oil and gas projects, there is the likely risk that the investments may end up locked in should a country stick to its decarbonisation commitments.[80] On the face of it, companies are developing policies that may be considered to be suitable for the promotion of decarbonisation. However, it is equally important to assess whether the companies are true to their word when it comes to decarbonisation measures.

It is expected that the Paris Agreement will open up new opportunities for oil and gas operators to participate in decarbonisation activities. The options available will include utilising the carbon markets and the sustainable development mechanism developed under the Paris Agreement. Therefore, oil and gas operators should key into the opportunities. In particular, it is the oil and gas operators that will substantially determine how the sector will be regulated for the promotion of climate change mitigation. The upstream and midstream sectors of the oil and gas industry release a high amount of GHGs. Many projects have been developed and promoted through the Kyoto Protocol market mechanisms. The prominent mechanisms include the Clean Development Mechanism (CDM),[81] Joint Implementation,[82] and Emission Trading Scheme.[83] The CDM as operated under the Kyoto Protocol requires that developed countries initiate projects for sponsorship in developing countries. The participants have largely been part of the international gas operators that develop projects to meet their obligations. Evidence abounds on the existence of these projects that have been initiated to promote decarbonisation in developing countries rich in oil and gas. The projects were required to demonstrate that without their existence, there would have been no change.

The Paris Agreement seeks to put in place two main mechanisms that could lead to the creation of decarbonisation projects. These are the sustainable development mechanism and the market-based mechanism. The sustainable development mechanism is not envisioned to be a market-based instrument unlike the market-based mechanism which would operate as a form of crediting mechanism known as the internationally transferred mitigation outcomes.[84] International oil and gas operators will therefore be part of the process and will be expected to engage in a series of transactions under the schemes.

---

[80] It has been argued that it would be difficult for gas companies to convince the Government that 'coal to gas switching and backing up renewables' would contribute in meeting decarbonisation targets in Europe for 2030. See Jonathan Stern, 'Narratives for Natural Gas in Decarbonising European Energy Markets' (Oxford Institute for Energy Studies, February 2019), www.oxfordenergy.org/wpcms/wp-content/uploads/2019/02/Narratives-for-Natural-Gas-in-a-Decarbonisinf-European-Energy-Market-NG141.pdf.
[81] See Kyoto Protocol, Art 12.
[82] *Ibid*, Art 6.
[83] *Ibid*, Art 16.
[84] See generally, Paris Agreement, Art 6.

VIII. Conclusion

The oil and gas sector attracts huge investment. Exploration and production are among the major anthropogenic activities that contribute to global climate change concerns. International oil and gas operators are responsible for making huge investments in different countries that ultimately lead to the release of GHGs in the atmosphere. The fight to cushion the effect of climate change has been ongoing, with the Paris Agreement committing nations to take steps to control their emission levels. These commitments, among other national policy and regulatory efforts, have largely impacted the nature of investment in the oil and gas sector. Therefore, the dominance of oil and gas as energy sources has seen the gradual promotion of other sources considered to lead to zero or less emissions.

Whilst oil and gas continues to play a major role in the international energy market and remains the main source of energy and foreign exchange-earning for resource rich countries, the trends within the decarbonisation web appear to be gradually catching up with the oil and gas companies. Whether companies pursue the agenda for decarbonisation with honesty or not, the atmosphere of support towards decarbonisation requires that they brace themselves for future challenges. Evidence abounds that suggests that most countries are considering the decarbonisation option through legal measures and the development of technologies that harness energy in a more sustainable manner. Investment options supporting the deployment of clean energy technologies are changing energy mix and demand. It is therefore crucial that international oil and gas operators continue to devise ways to live up to expectations as they are much more likely to be faced by investment and legal risks if they fail to follow a development path that ensures the mitigation of climate change. Whether fossil fuel will be completely displaced for sustainable energy sources or not is a question to be determined in future. Decision-making and projections by international oil and gas companies should always seek to explore the trend and base their future investments on a scenario that gives them room to diversify and continue to explore technologies that promote decarbonisation. The dictates of international and domestic law and policy will continue to shape the commitments and actions taken by international oil and gas operators towards decarbonisation.

9

The Carbon Taxation Conundrum

FRÉDÉRIC GILLES SOURGENS AND LORI A McMILLAN

I. Introduction

Taxation has long been a device used to achieve social and economic policies, through various incentives and disincentives embedded in tax systems. As a regulatory tool, it aims at issues that are important to society; both the figurative carrot and stick are used. A carbon tax is a charge levied on the production, distribution and/or use of various fossil fuels based on the carbon produced by their combustion. The tax, or 'price' is set per ton on this carbon produced, and this is applied to make things like electricity, oil, and natural gas more expensive in correlation to their carbon-intensity. The goal of this tax is pretty clear – it is meant to reduce pollution, both by discouraging the consumption of fossil fuels, as well as by encouraging the development of other types of zero-carbon or low-carbon 'non-fossil' fuels to meet humanity's voracious appetite for energy. But tax provisions should also be judged not just on their goal(s), but on whether they achieve their goal, and do so in an efficient manner. In short, it isn't good enough to have a laudable goal, but the goal must be attained, and in a desirable way.

Carbon taxation goes hand in hand with cap-and-trade schemes, as both are a market-based attempt to tackle the problem of polluting emissions. Cap-and-trade targets greenhouse gas emissions such as carbon dioxide (CO_2), by the relevant overseeing body setting a cap on the amount of allowable emissions, thereafter, emissions within the range of allowances, ie the allowances under this cap are certified under a scheme of tradeable permits thereafter traded or auctioned off to businesses or other players in the market who would need to meet there own emissions reduction goals.[1] Players and operators that emit more than their allowance have the option of either reducing their output, or buying the excess allowance of another player. A market is thus created, and players with excess allowance can sell them, or save them for their own use later. The idea is that the players will have incentive to reduce their emissions, whether to avoid the penalty for excess,

---

[1] Environmental Protection Agency, 'Cap and Trade', www.epa.gov/airmarkets/cap-trade/index.html.

or to ensure that they have spare capacity that they might sell to others. The value of the cap is, obviously, key. If the cap is too high, then no reductions in emissions will occur, as no incentive will exist to decrease them, nor will the value of excess allowances be high enough to command a price on the market sufficient to encourage the creation of the excess. If the cap is too low, then a market distortion occurs by inflating the value of the allowances and creating a situation of scarcity. Similar to cap-and-trade allowances, credits can also be used.

A. Why have a Carbon Tax?

The issue of pollution, specifically with regard to fossil fuels, is not a new one, and with global warming increasingly in the spotlight it does not appear that it will abate soon. The idea of negative externalities drives this endeavour, as much of our legal system is geared toward forcing the people who create unexpected costs that are borne by others to be responsible for those costs. However, a negative externality is more than just a cost, it is a cost that results from but is not priced in the particular transaction that generates it, and as a general idea it is desirable for these types of costs to be internalised by those who create them. From an economic perspective, internalisation of these costs more accurately reflects the true cost of the 'pollution creating' transaction. When negative externalities are not accounted for in the price of a good, efficient equilibrium is not achieved, and excess production is the result, as the producer of the goods does not bear all the costs associated with production. Specifically, with regard to pollution, if polluters do not internalise the costs of their pollution, then the costs associated with this pollution are not borne by the manufacturers or uses of their products, but rather by society at large, whether directly or indirectly.

As stated above, it is not enough that a goal is identified for policy and law to achieve – even if it is a laudable goal with a large consensus behind it. Care must be taken that the legislation – in this case a tax provision – is sufficiently well-crafted to ensure that the goal is in fact reached in a just, fair and reasonable way, ie it does so in the least harmful manner. In short, tax policy requires us to test that the tax does in fact do what the hype promises – in this case, bring about a reduction in carbon emissions and attendant pollution, or at the very least force polluters to internalise the negative externalities they are creating. However, consideration must also be given to who actually bears the incidence of the tax, and whether there are consequences aside from the policy goal itself. In short, all sides must be identified and weighed when crafting a response to a problem such as what we see in carbon taxation.

B. The Important Questions

Decarbonisation is a matter not just of technology and law. When the veneer of policy proposals and legal arguments is stripped away, what remains are principally three questions of economics writ large. These questions are, first, is decarbonisation feasible in any real-world sense? If the answer to the first question is 'yes', we then need to ask how do we pay for this transition? Finally, once we have a proposal of how we can pay for decarbonisation, we must ask: does decarbonisation disproportionately affect any one group or set of groups?

The first two questions are purely a matter of economics. They are not a question of desiderata of what we wished the world might look like. They go to the dollars and cents of what would need to be done in order to achieve the desiderata. It is one thing to desire a world in which deep decarbonisation has already happened. It is another to establish whether that world is achievable and in what timeframe and at what cost and who bears the cost. It is one thing to say that it is technologically feasible to replace the world's entire energy infrastructure and to forego carbon intensive luxuries. It is another to provide a blueprint of the economic effects of such a blueprint on world society.[2] To say that something is technologically possible, in other words, does not mean that we can afford it.

C. Identified Costs

A complete infrastructure overhaul intuitively is an expensive proposition. It must swap out a core feature of daily life. One estimate as to a complete US grid replacement alone is $5 trillion.[3] This swap must happen not just in one place but everywhere. And it must happen everywhere reasonably at once to be successful (imagine what would happen if cars and trucks from the Eastern part of the United States could not be fuelled or maintained in the West of the Mississippi and vice versa).

Such an infrastructure overhaul in economic terms costs more than the cost of removal of the prior infrastructure and replacement of that infrastructure with new physical structures. The cost of an infrastructure overhaul radiates and permeates through the entire society as businesses have made significant capital investments relying on the current energy infrastructure.[4] Thus, if internal combustion engines were prohibited, this would certainly affect oil and gas

---

[2] For one such leading blueprint, see International Energy Agency (IEA), 'World Energy Outlook 2018' (2018). The IEA's work has found significant industry acceptance. See, eg, Chevron, 'Climate Change Resilience, A Framework for Decision Making' (March 2018), www.chevron.com/-/media/shared-media/documents/climate-change-resilience.pdf.

[3] Joshua Rhodes, 'The Old, Dirty, Creaky US Electric Grid would Cost $5 trillion to Replace. Where Should Infrastructure Spending Go? (*The Conversation*, 16 March 2017), http://theconversation.com/the-old-dirty-creaky-us-electric-grid-would-cost-5-trillion-to-replace-where-should-infrastructure-spending-go-68290.

[4] This phenomenon is known as path dependence. For a discussion of path dependence, see Roger Fouquet, 'Path Dependence in Energy Systems and Economic Development' (*Nature*, 11 July 2016), www.nature.com/articles/nenergy201698.

companies that provided the fuel for these engines to run. While comparison might be made to the makers of the buggy whip, and the role of government in protecting industries from inevitable progress might be debated, it is worth noting that the sheer size and scope of the industries involved preclude facile comparisons. Such a prohibition would also affect entire supply chains that build and service these engines, provide parts and services to those companies, and so on. This supply chain effect of fossil fuels has been noted in a different – and highly critical context – in the literature.[5] The flipside, however, is also true – if, as the literature shows, the current energy infrastructure is deeply entangled in supply chains, it is very difficult and cost intensive to undo these entanglements given the cost of path dependence.

Though they sound abstract, these concepts have very real-life consequences. For example, radical decarbonisation would affect every person that currently owns a vehicle with an internal combustion engine – it would require everyone to buy a new vehicle. And barring buying a new vehicle, people would have to consider whether their work, their children's school, etc is accessible without one. If not, it would require considerations of switching jobs to be able to make life work without a vehicle with an internal combustion engine or to move. But moving would be complicated by the fact that there is as of yet no fleet of vehicles that could physically move one to a new location. Further, once such infrastructure were to exist, the price of real estate around those new hubs would significantly increase (consider the price of housing around subway access points in New York).[6] Further, switching jobs to jobs that are more readily accessible from one's current location would be complicated by the fact that a significant number of people would be looking for work at exactly the same time, given the policy switch away from internal combustion engines. If the dominoes fall incorrectly, it is not difficult to see how such a policy shift would bring about not only an economic contraction, but also cause the kind of personal costs most recently seen by the Great Recession and before that in the Great Depression.

D. Distribution of Costs

Technological change, even though desirable, always comes at a cost. This cost is always borne by someone, and ultimately the true incidence of this cost must be ascertained. This therefore leads to the third question as to how the high cost of any infrastructure swap will be distributed across society. Are there people who would disproportionately bear the brunt of the cost? If so, how high is

---

[5] Carol Olson and Frank Lenzmann, 'The Social and Economic Consequences of the Fossil Fuel Supply Chain' (2016) *MRS Energy & Sustainability: A Review Journal*.
[6] Noah Manskar, 'Home Prices Skyrocket Near These Subway Stations, Study Shows' (*Patch.com*, 2 October 2019), https://patch.com/new-york/new-york-city/home-prices-skyrocket-near-these-subway-stations-study-shows.

that cost? Does the cost stem from an adjustment of lifestyle away from luxuries to a more frugal life, or is it an adjustment that harbours existential perils?[7] It is only once these economic questions have been answered that it is possible to answer the policy question whether such a world is 'just'. In other words, it is only when the winners and losers – and the respective distribution of winnings and losses – are accounted for that it is possible to ask whether this distribution is efficient and just in the sense of utility maximisation, fair and just in the sense of protecting the worst-off groups best, or pragmatically sustainable in the sense that it will not bring about a collapse of the very effort at infrastructure overhaul that started it all.[8]

These appear to be reasonably lofty questions. How are they related to carbon tax efforts? Carbon taxes are policy tools that are brought to bear in order to answer all three questions.[9] In other words, carbon taxes assume that it is economically feasible to decarbonise without bringing about the collapse of the political economy engaged in decarbonisation. And carbon taxes assume that it is possible to do so by internalising the costs of decarbonisation in the consumption of carbon.[10] By pricing carbon we affect the economic behaviour of market participants away from carbon consumption towards alternatives. This switch in behaviour will create the demand for a new infrastructure.[11] The revenues raised from carbon taxes, meanwhile, provide the financial wherewithal to support the infrastructure overhaul through governmental subsidies paid for by carbon consumption.[12] Carbon taxes thus bet that they can be instrumental in bringing about the desired goal of deep decarbonisation through affecting market mechanisms and making carbon consumption expensive.

It turns out that this bet may well beg the question if one does not independently assess the three economic questions outlined above. As this chapter will discuss, carbon taxation certainly has much to commend itself. But it will also highlight that carbon taxation has significant difficulties as a modelling matter to account for the deep disruptions that pricing carbon through taxation brings with it. Carbon taxation assumes economic efficiencies that do not currently exist, including the assumption that the market is able to bring about the desired result of decarbonisation in an efficient manner once people are forced to make choices internalising the cost of carbon emission. Carbon taxation further assumes

---

[7] A leading climate change philosopher suggests that the issue is one of insistence on luxuries. Stephen M Gardiner, *A Perfect Moral Storm: The Ethical Tragedy of Climate Change* (Oxford University Press, 2006).

[8] The principle at issue is known as the maximin principle. For the principle, see John Rawls, *A Theory of Justice, The Original Edition* (2009) 154. For a discussion of the maximin principle and its alternatives in the climate context, see Lauren Hartzell-Nichols, *A Climate of Risk, Precautionary Principles, Catastrophes and Climate Change* (Routledge, 2017) 69.

[9] Gilbert E Metcalf, *Paying for Pollution: Why a Carbon Tax Is Good for America* (Oxford University Press, 2019) 45.

[10] *Ibid.*
[11] *Ibid.*
[12] *Ibid.*

technological efficiencies that do not currently exist. As it stands, even the most aggressive decarbonisation plans rely upon fossil fuels as one of the greatest – if not the greatest single part – of the energy mix.[13] Further, there is currently no viable removal technology that could be paid through carbon taxation. Carbon taxes therefore 'bank' money and impose hardships that cannot deploy a corresponding benefit either as economic or as a technological matter.

This chapter will outline these challenges and sketch how carbon taxation models have run into significant difficulties. The chapter concludes that carbon taxation on its own is not currently an effective policy tool to support the decarbonisation effort.

II. The Feasibility of Decarbonisation

A. Carbon Tax Assumptions

Carbon taxes in principle have many advantages from an economic perspective. These advantages are particularly pronounced when carbon tax approaches are compared to an alternative means of managing decarbonisation, cap-and-trade regimes. This section outlines the conceptual attractiveness of carbon taxation, exploring advantages of carbon tax over cap-and-trade approaches. It finally addresses the feasibility of assumptions that underlie the arguments in support of carbon taxation.

i. The Conceptual Case for Carbon Taxation

Carbon taxes have much to recommend them in theory. Thus, as Nancy Shurtz recently noted, '[e]conomists favor taxes because "they provide the clearest price signal, unencumbered by factors like baselines, allowance allocation, and use of credits"'.[14] She explains that '[p]rice instruments are thought to perform better under uncertainty, to raise valuable revenues and to avoid transaction costs'.[15]

The central benefit of such a pricing mechanism is that it is not premised upon central planning. Rather, it assigns a price to carbon. This price acts as a signal which will in turn be internalised by economic actors across markets. Economic actors will seek to find ways to adapt their behaviour either by reducing their use of carbon emissions or finding alternative means to achieve the same tasks that were previously carbon intensive in a less carbon intensive manner.

---

[13] IEA, 'World Energy Outlook 2016' (2016).
[14] Nancy Shurtz, 'Carbon Pricing in Initiatives in Western North America: Blueprint for Global Climate Policy' (2016) 7 *San Diego Journal of Climate & Energy Law* 61, 89.
[15] *Ibid.*

The key benefit of carbon taxation therefore is that it is fundamentally a market mechanism.[16] Rather than dictate behaviour, carbon taxation uses pricing mechanisms in order to allow the market and relevant operators to respond of their own accord to the new variable. The carbon taxation regime therefore fundamentally rests upon individual choices by businesses and consumers alike instead of the Government's command or restraint.

In principle, what carbon taxes achieve is to internalise the costs of carbon emissions rather than externalise these costs.[17] Costs are externalised when actors offload what is known as negative externalities to society at large or the host community of their operations.[18] A negative externality is a cost suffered by an affected third party that does not directly participate in a given transaction.[19]

As it currently stands, the costs of climate change brought about by carbon emissions is not something for which economic actors or consumers pay as part of their day-to-day transactions.[20] The cost of climate change is simply offloaded, slowly, to world society at large.[21] Somewhat simplistically, carbon emissions cause and accelerate climate change.[22] Climate change causes sea levels to rise, for example, through melting polar ice.[23] This sea level rise threatens to submerge low lying islands in the Pacific Ocean.[24] The inhabitants who will be displaced by rising sea levels did not themselves cause any meaningful share of the carbon emissions that brought about their own precarious position.[25] These inhabitants suffer a negative externality of energy consumption around the world because they are third parties to these transactions or behaviours of consumption and nevertheless suffer significant economic consequences.

By pricing carbon emissions, carbon taxes have the potential to change the equation. The costs of carbon emissions are no longer pushed off to society at large. Rather, they are made part and parcel of every transaction and thus bring market forces to bear to change behaviour and thus limit or even eliminate the negative effects of noxious behaviour.

---

[16] Metcalf (n 9) 45.
[17] Metcalf (n 9) 45.
[18] For a discussion of negative externalities, and the conceptual difficulty of treating externalities as negative or their inverse as a positive, see Lisa Grow Sun and Brigham Daniels, 'Mirrored Externalities' (2014) 90 *Notre Dame Law Review* 135; Lisa Grow Sun and Brigham Daniels, 'Externality Entrepreneurism' (2016) 50 *University of California Davis Law Review* 321 (2016).
[19] Grow Sun and Daniels, Mirrored Externalities, *ibid* 135, 137.
[20] Grow Sun and Daniels, 'Externality Entrepreneurism' (n 18) 321, 371.
[21] Grow Sun and Daniels, 'Externality Entrepreneurism' (n 18) 321, 371.
[22] The Intergovernmental Panel on Climate Change (IPCC), 'Special Report: 'Global Warming of 1.5 C' (IPCC, 2019), www.ipcc.ch/sr15/.
[23] *Ibid* at 4.
[24] IPCC, 'Special Report: Special Report on the Ocean and Cryosphere in a Changing Climate', 4–10, https://report.ipcc.ch/srocc/pdf/SROCC_FinalDraft_Chapter4.pdf.
[25] See www.ipcc.ch/site/assets/uploads/2018/02/WGIIAR5-Chap29_FINAL.pdf.

ii. Carbon Tax versus Cap-and-Trade Regimes

The discussion of the conceptual advantages of carbon pricing already outline the key benefit of a carbon tax approach over a cap-and-trade approach. A carbon tax approach in principle does not depend upon an *ex ante* determination of how much carbon emissions a particular economy can feasibly cut in any given period of time. Rather, it theoretically creates economic incentives for a fast but 'organic' decrease in carbon emissions and the replacement of carbon intensive infrastructure with carbon-neutral infrastructure.

This is not the case in the context of cap-and-trade approaches. Rather, the approach of cap-and-trade assumes and requires baselines to be set *ex ante* so as to provide the 'goods' or 'services' to be traded.[26] In the cap-and-trade context, actual emissions that are permitted as allowances are traded.[27] These emissions allowances are valuable because they are scarce.[28] That means that there must be yearly emissions targets against which trading will occur.

The disadvantage of a cap-and-trade approach over a carbon pricing approach therefore is readily apparent. The market for cap-and-trade is forced in a manner that carbon pricing, correctly done, is not.[29] Cap-and-trade regimes assume that they can set realistic targets on a yearly basis at the front end without the benefit of understanding or knowing the actual realities and market reactions, thus handicapped by incomplete information. It thus risks setting unrealistic expectations of what carbon emissions reductions are realistic in a given timeframe. Despite their hybrid market structure, cap-and-trade regimes therefore still introduce the risks of command economy into a reasonably uncertain environment – that is, it is currently unclear what reductions can be accomplished by the private sector in any given yearly timeframe. This means that setting the baselines is simply not possible under current circumstances.

The advantage of carbon pricing – and carbon taxation models – is that these approaches do not set fixed timeframes but leave it to the market to adjust to the newly internalised cost of carbon emissions based on the perceived urgency generated by the financial penalty.[30] This means that there is less forcing of the market from the outside. This in turn should yield far more efficient outcomes both in managing the transition to a decarbonised economy by allowing the market to catch up to the new carbon price gradually and by setting reduction goals organically as a result of market response to costs as opposed to setting reduction goals by a command-and-control approach to rules and regulation.

---

[26] For a discussion of cap-and-trade programmes, see, eg, Ann Carlson, 'Designing Effective Climate Policy: Cap-and-Trade and Complementary Policies' (2012) 49 *Harvard Journal on Legislation* 207.
[27] *Ibid* at 209.
[28] See *ibid*.
[29] Shurtz (n 14) 61, 89.
[30] Shurtz (n 14) 61, 89.

iii. The Underlying Assumptions of the Conceptual Case

The underlying assumption of the carbon tax case is that it is possible to appropriately price carbon by means of a tax and thereby regulate the conduct of potential emitters and consumers of carbon-intensive goods and services. Thus, the carbon tax model does not internalise the cost of carbon emissions on a *true* market basis. Rather, the carbon tax model assumes that the price for carbon will be set by the government.[31] This means that the advantages outlined in the prior sections is only truly available to the extent that the carbon tax set by the Government can reflect the true cost of carbon emissions. Also, it assumes that any future carbon price fluctuations that happen after the price is established will be accurately reflected.

Importantly, this is not an on-off switch. Thus, government A may come closer to the true price of carbon emissions in its carbon tax regime than government B. The pricing of government A therefore will be more efficient than that of government B. The effectiveness of carbon taxation therefore is inherently tied to the means used to implement it, which is problematic given that multiple governments have to coordinate while responding in a manner they each deem most appropriate, and consensus is highly unlikely. 'Climate change affects people differently in terms of location, age and income …'[32] and this is true of countries, not just individuals, and highlights the challenge of getting groups with disparate interests and impacts to agree to adhere to a solution, including the price to pay for this solution. This is especially problematic given the fact that pollution does not respect borders, nor does climate change, and there is incentive to engage in rent-seeking behaviours if all governments do not appropriately price carbon emissions. Without symmetrical responses by all affected governments, the effectiveness of carbon taxation is severely compromised.

This sliding scale of carbon taxation efficiency has significant repercussions for the comparison of carbon tax models to cap-and-trade models, as well. It may be true that the carbon taxation model chosen by government B would be as inefficient as a particular cap-and-trade model, for example, because it sets the price of carbon emissions too high or too low. In the context of carbon taxation, it is therefore dangerous to make broad general statements about all carbon taxation models as such or to compare carbon taxation as such to other means of addressing carbon pricing and decarbonisation.[33]

---

[31] David M Driesen, 'Putting a Price on Carbon: The Metaphor' (2014) 44 *Environmental Law* 695, 703 ('any approach that requires a political body to establish a price as a means of meeting an environmental goal constitutes a pricing mechanism. By contrast, any approach that requires the regulator to establish the quantity of pollution reductions demanded constitutes a quantity mechanism.').

[32] Frank B Friedman and David A Giannotti; updated by Frank B Friedman, 'International Environmental Law: A Global Audit/Assessment' (2019) 1 *Law of Environmental Protection* §8:48 at 38.

[33] For a similar critique of over-ideological uses of cap-and-trade or carbon taxation, see Driesen (n 31).

This is not to say that carbon taxation is immune from a general conceptual critique. Rather, this critique should focus on the question about how carbon pricing relates to carbon taxation and to what extent carbon pricing under current circumstances is in itself feasible. The sections below outline the challenges inherent in any carbon pricing mechanisms underlying the carbon taxation model. As the sections below will show, it is inherently difficult currently to price carbon emissions accurately. Any such attempt would need to establish the direct costs of decarbonisation to be internalised through a carbon tax. But at the same time, it would need to understand the externalities that decarbonisation itself creates through the indirect costs that decarbonisation inherently brings with it. This difficulty in setting an appropriate price for carbon emissions creates significant conceptual issues that all carbon tax regimes share, which will have to be addressed in turn. This is especially true given that no price stays static, and this would be equally true of carbon, so mechanisms for the set carbon price to adjust over time must be made if the true cost reflection is the goal.

B. Direct Costs of Decarbonisation

There are broadly three ways to measure the cost of decarbonisation. Each of these is complementary rather than exclusive and each should be borne in mind when setting a price for carbon emissions. These three ways look to the cost of emission reduction (or mitigation), the cost of carbon removal, and the cost of adaptation to the effects of climate change.

i. Mitigation Costs

Carbon emission mitigation costs are one key measure to establish the price of carbon. In this context, the overarching question is 'how much does it cost to replace existing energy or transportation infrastructure?' Once the price of this infrastructure replacement is established, the next question is the size of the carbon emitting infrastructure to be replaced. With the carbon emitting infrastructure to be replaced established, it is then possible to attribute a price for carbon that is the pro-rated share of emissions over a fixed period of time to pay for the replacement cost.

By way of example, the US electrical grid currently consists of 23.5 per cent coal, 38.4 per cent gas, 1.3 per cent other fossil fuel-based generation, 17.5 per cent renewables and 19.7 per cent nuclear.[34] This means that as it currently stands, 62.7 per cent of US electricity generation is from fossil fuels.[35] In theory, it is

---

[34] The US Energy Information Administration, 'What is U.S. Electricity Generation by Energy Source?', www.eia.gov/tools/faqs/faq.php?id=427&t=3.
[35] *Ibid.*

possible to calculate the cost of mitigating greenhouse gas emissions by calculating the cost of replacing fossil fuel with non-fossil fuel-burning generation capacity – and one such estimate suggests a cost of $5 trillion to do so.[36] One can then amortise the cost of carbon to take into account the time when payments will need to be deployed to build the replacement infrastructure.

In broad strokes, many of the policy initiatives like the Green New Deal in the US, the Green Deal in the EU and similar initiatives worldwide could in principle be supported by a carbon tax.[37] The cost of the programme could be funded in significant part through carbon taxation.[38] To the extent that carbon taxation would raise less revenue than anticipated, market mechanisms would have reduced carbon emissions faster than the government programme. This would mean that market mechanisms would do a better job than the government programme in fighting climate change, all things considered. To the extent that carbon pricing does not reduce carbon emissions, on the other hand, government programmes would replace carbon intensive infrastructure and thus reduce emissions in this manner.

ii. Removal Costs

An alternative or additional measure to price carbon is to price it at the cost removal. At the time of writing, there is not yet a scalable technology for carbon removal. That being said, well-funded research companies have announced technological advances that would suggest that removal prices of $100 per ton of carbon would in principle be achievable. Assuming that this price is in fact borne out by further testing and research, there would be a straightforward means to price carbon – the cost to remove it from the atmosphere.[39]

A removal measure may be an additional rather than alternative measure for carbon taxation. First, pricing carbon by reference to carbon removal does not affect the underlying energy infrastructure. It would thus not decarbonise at the emission source but would decarbonise after emissions have already occurred. Second, this price is significantly higher than current tax models. In Canada, for example, the nationwide carbon tax implemented in 2019 saw pricing between $20 and $50 per ton. This suggests that a removal measure would currently be too high to serve as a policy justification in its own right for carbon taxation (with the exception of economic activity that is truly a luxury, such as the flying of private jets for personal travel, etc).

---

[36] Rhodes (n 3).
[37] Carbon Tax Center, 'Green New Deal', www.carbontax.org/green-new-deal/; Mehreen Khan, 'EU Unveils "Green Deal" Plan to Get Europe Carbon Neutral by 2050' *Financial Times*, 11 December 2019, https://insideclimatenews.org/news/11122019/europe-green-deal-plan-carbon-neutral-2050-border-adjustment-tax-just-transition (Green Deal includes climate border tax adjustment).
[38] Green New Deal, *ibid* and Khan, *ibid*.
[39] For a full discussion of the removal cost metric, see Frédéric G Sourgens, 'Geo-Markets' (forthcoming 2020) 38 *Virginia Environmental Law Journal*.

iii. Adaptation Costs

A final measure for pricing carbon is not to look to the cost of replacing energy infrastructure but at the cost of building infrastructure necessary to protect vulnerable communities against the effects of climate change. For instance, the building of seawalls would protect communities against rising sea levels. In the US, the cost of such seawalls has been estimated at $416 billion by 2040.[40] Other disaster preparedness measures may address the risk of severe weather, such as increased frequencies and intensities of hurricanes and tornadoes, etc.

To truly address all negative externalities, such prices could not only look to local adaptation. Rather, it would need to fund global adaptation in communities affected by climate change that did not themselves significantly contribute to it. Thus, carbon pricing under the adaptation model cannot be exclusively national. It needs to allocate the burden of foreign adaption finance to greenhouse gas emitting countries pro rata.

iv. Conclusion

The three measures of setting potential carbon prices all reasonably show that carbon prices are not cheap. At $100 a ton, the removal of all carbon emissions per annum (not historical emissions) would be $3.62 trillion (36.2 gigatons emitted in 2017. A gigaton is a billion tons. 36.2 gigatons = 36.2 billion tons. 36.2 billion* $100 = $3.62 trillion. By reference, the world economy in 2017 equalled some $80.27 trillion.).[41] That means that the price of carbon would be slightly less than five per cent of the value of the global economy. This price does not yet directly support government expenditure on a shift in energy infrastructure. Nor does this price include the cost of adaptation. A true cost of carbon per ton therefore is higher and not lower than $100 per ton (ie, the cost of removal, plus cost of adaptation, if one assumes that at $100 per ton of carbon, private financing will be available for infrastructure replacement).

The problem with a price that is significantly less than this cost measure is that it cannot possibly achieve the necessary goals of decarbonisation it sets out to meet. It would create externalities of its own without absorbing the externalities of carbon emissions.

C. Indirect Costs of Decarbonisation

There are significant indirect costs of decarbonisation. As discussed in the Introduction, there are significant reliance interests that have matured throughout

---

[40] Emily Holden, 'Seawalls to Protect US against Rising Oceans Could Cost $416bn by 2040, *The Guardian*, 20 June 2019), www.theguardian.com/environment/2019/jun/20/us-rising-seas-defense-seawalls-cost-report.

[41] For a full discussion of the removal cost metric, see Sourgens (n 39).

world society in the existing energy infrastructure.[42] Decoupling the world economy from this mode of energy generation, even if it is technologically feasible, involves significant costs. It undoes settled economic assumptions that are at the core of many economic sectors.

It is this cost of decoupling that explains the reaction from two opposite sides of the economic spectrum to current decarbonisation efforts. Predictably, industry interests point out the immediate economic costs of a reduction in fossil fuel reliance. These costs include not only economic contractions due to loss of revenue in fossil fuel-producing companies. It will lead to a significant loss of economic productivity throughout the economy during decoupling efforts. Companies that need energy will need to pay more for it. This increased cost will depress economic output as companies cannot afford to pay the increases in costs. This in turn will lead to a decrease of demand as fewer people have money to spend, and so on in a potentially economic vicious cycle. Not only that, it can further lead to a loss of essential services during this period, if decarbonisation is taken to an extreme (think horse-drawn ambulances).

Less predictably, these efforts also led to sustained resistance from poorer segments of the population. An example of this was the yellow vest protests in France. These yellow vest protests were in part a response to French carbon pricing initiatives. These protests were carried out by farming communities in the first place. After that, these protests also carried many disaffected poorer voters into the fray.

These protests show the dangers of decoupling. The loss from decoupling is frequently borne first by the weakest members of society with the thinnest economic margins. These groups are hit from two different directions by higher energy prices and less available energy. On the one hand, they need to pay for these rising energy prices. If they are unable to do so, they will need to make drastic changes to their lifestyles. These changes will not involve the loss of luxuries. Rather, it will likely need to tradeoff necessities and essentials against each other. On the other hand, they are also the most vulnerable population in regards to disappearing profitability margins at the industry level. As industry loses profitability, it will need to either pay each worker less or employ fewer workers. Either option will leave the weakest members of society in the perilous position of losing their livelihoods. It is thus on the whole unsurprising that right-wing populism has successfully used anti-climate change policies as a wedge issue with poorer voters that previously voted with centre-left and left-of-centre parties.

D. Timelines

The problem for carbon tax approaches are exacerbated by current scientific estimates. Current climate change estimates are beyond alarming. They predict

---

[42] Olson and Lenzmann (n 5).

catastrophe with near certainty if action is not taken immediately. This immediate need for action significantly reduces timelines for a soft economic landing. It requires a higher price for carbon as more infrastructure is needed more quickly to combat climate change at the same time as removal, so carbon will become an absolute necessity, even at these higher prices.

This timeline also exacerbates the indirect costs from decoupling from carbon-based energy infrastructures. A higher price for carbon will have a more immediate and potentially catastrophic impact on global economies. It thus presents policymakers with significant design problems which are not alleviated by choosing carbon taxation as a means of addressing the problem.

E. Checking the Carbon Tax Assumptions

The assumptions underlying carbon taxation and carbon pricing come under considerable strain when one contemplates the factors discussed above. To begin with, there is no clear way to price carbon emissions. There are different approaches that could be used in order to set a price, such as financing the construction of a renewable energy infrastructure, the removal of carbon emissions, or the construction of a new physical infrastructure to help society adapt to the consequences of climate change through carbon taxation. This price would further have to set a target timeline during which the new renewable energy infrastructure or physical infrastructure should be built. Currently, these timelines are impossibly short given the dire predictions made by the Intergovernmental Panel on Climate Change.

This means that the assumptions underpinning carbon taxation come under significant strain. Thus, one of the key benefits of carbon taxation is that it would internalise costs and thereby gradually change behaviour and create new market-based solutions to a previously underpriced problem. The problem is that this requires time for organic adjustments to work their way through the economy and lead to gradual adjustment. This timeline is not currently available.

Accurately and honestly pricing carbon would lead to a sort of economic shock therapy that would require a massive cost that was previously externalised to be internalised all at once. Past experiences with economic shock therapy in the context of the transition from command to market economies in the post-Soviet context have been rather dire. There is no reason to believe that shock therapy in the current context would have any better result. To the contrary, shock therapy in both instances is potentially devastating because it fails to account for the reliance interests destroyed by a decoupling from economic realities from previous deep structures conditioning economic life. In the context of the post-Soviet reconstruction, there was no legal and social infrastructure and no market that could step in and organise social and economic life. Depriving social and economic life of existing legal and social infrastructure to grow the new market-based economies precisely showed the cost of radical breaks with settled reliance interests.

In the context of carbon pricing, the switch in infrastructure concerns one of the most fundamental backbones of any modern economy – energy supply. A complete and fast reversal with regard to this infrastructure will lead to significant disruption that risks mirroring the post-Soviet shock scenario. The disruption of economic, social and legal reliance interests is similarly elemental in both instances. Perhaps the one saving grace of a switch in energy infrastructures as opposed to legal infrastructures is that markets are currently available to guide the transaction. Yet this is reasonably feeble comfort given that markets themselves are path dependent and therefore cannot adapt immediately to new fundamental circumstances.

This leaves carbon taxation with the uneasy problem of setting a price that will not in and of itself achieve the goals that it aims to bring about. That is, one cannot set a carbon tax at the price of carbon – doing so risks massive harm. This means that carbon taxation can only partially internalise the costs of carbon emissions. This partial internalisation will still do significant economic harm – but, problematically, it will not raise the means to overcome the current impasse. It will not provide the funds needed to build a new energy infrastructure, remove carbon from the atmosphere or adapt to new climate conditions. This means that it will cause significant disruption without itself offering a feasible way out of the carbon emission conundrum.

Carbon taxation thus assumes that which it cannot: that an efficient market to which energy infrastructures can transition already exists. It does not fully take into account the transitional period – or at least not a transitional period that is as short as the one currently faced by the world community. Carbon taxation therefore can only be one of the levers that can be used to support decarbonisation efforts. It cannot be the exclusive lever, nor does it currently look likely to be an appropriate principal lever.

III. Modality of Payment for Decarbonisation

This section briefly demonstrates that existing carbon taxation approaches do all suffer in one way or another from the fundamental problems outlined in the previous section, by examining highlights of the Canadian and French carbon taxation systems.

A. Canada

Canada introduced a federal carbon tax in 2018, with two parts: a fuel charge on fossil fuels used for combustion and a pollution price for industry known as the Output-Based Pricing System (OBPS).[43] The legislation is structured to allow each

---

[43] The Greenhouse Gas Pollution Pricing Act, S.C. 2018, c.12, s 186. For further details, see www.nytimes.com/interactive/2019/04/02/climate/pricing-carbon-emissions.html.

subnational jurisdiction to make decisions on implementation, while establishing certain minimum conditions. Each province or territory can put into place its own system that meets or exceeds the federal benchmarks, otherwise the federal benchmark requirements apply.

The OBPS prices carbon pollution for industrial facilities that emit at least 50,000 tonnes per year, and is optional for facilities in certain sectors that emit 10,000 or more tonnes per year to address competitiveness concerns. The OBPS sets a level for greenhouse gas emissions per unit of output for each sector, and facilities that exceed the emissions level must pay for the excess emissions. The facilities that have emissions below the standard get credits that may be saved for later use or sold, giving a financial incentive for facilities to reduce their carbon pollution. In 2018, CO_2 was priced at $10 per tonne, increasing by $10 annually until 2022 when it will reach $50 per tonne. Some of the revenue generated must be returned to taxpayers, in an effort to address the regressive nature of the tax. The jurisdictions that adopt the federal carbon tax system will have all tax revenues returned to the subnational level of government, while the remaining jurisdictions will receive most of the direct revenues, with the remainder going to municipalities, small and medium-sized businesses, schools, hospitals, post-secondary institutions, non-profit organisations, and First Nations communities.

There are a number of problems with the Canadian approach, including the fact that the carbon price is not set to capture the precise level of the externality carbon pollution creates, but rather is an arbitrary amount. It is supposed to be revenue neutral, meaning that it is not intended as an actual revenue raiser for government to offset some of the costs of pollution, but rather is an exercise in moving money around to different taxpayers. Having part of the system be voluntary also undercuts its effectiveness. In addition, it is still a regressive tax, despite the attempts to mitigate the regressive nature. Lower income taxpayers will still bear the incidence of the tax, which will be reflected in the daily goods they consume, and any attempts to reduce this either overshoot the mark and end up as a naked wealth transfer to the poor, or do not pay for the full amount of taxes being paid.[44] Timing differences between paying the tax and getting whatever rebate the taxpayer may be entitled to receive will also matter to lower income taxpayers. In short, the offsets are estimates, which are imperfect at best, and will have a less-than-targeted impact as an incentive to change behaviour, and will have concerning distributional impacts. If the goal is to truly price the externalities of the carbon being consumed, then inexact rebates or credits should not be part of

---

[44] For example, the taxes collected will be returned to the subnational government from which they were collected, which will then rebate the vast majority of these to individual taxpayers. However, '[t]he rebates are anticipated to exceed the increased energy costs for about 70% of Canadian households'. See www.theguardian.com/environment/climate-consensus-97-per-cent/2018/oct/26/canada-passed-a-carbon-tax-that-will-give-most-canadians-more-money.

the system, or at least not in excess of the costs being borne by the end consumer. Also, with the United States sharing a vast border with Canada, the fact that the United States does not participate in any large scale carbon reduction scheme will likely temper Canadian successes with pollution reduction initiatives.

B. France

France has had a difficult time implementing and maintaining its carbon tax. After an attempt to levy a carbon tax in 2009 was blocked on the basis that it was too ineffective, *la taxe carbone* was implemented in 2014. Households and businesses pay an excise duty at the time of purchase on carbon, natural gas and energy products. This national carbon tax is in addition to a cap and trade system in the European Union.

The carbon tax was set at €7 per tonne in 2014, hit €44.60 per tonne in 2018, and was set to increase annually to reach €86.20 per tonne in 2022. The first years of this tax were projected to generate 1 million tonnes of CO_2 reductions in road transportation emissions, with an additional 2 million tonnes reduced in housing, but the projections did not happen; global oil prices in this initial period fell to a 10-year low, which resulted in little price difference to the consumer to prod consumption changes. This tax generated billions in revenue, but instead of investment in renewable resources infrastructure, or mitigating the impact of the tax on the poor or those unable to significantly change their carbon emissions for structural reasons, this revenue was used as a general revenue item to pay down the budgetary deficit.

Planned increases to the carbon tax price in 2018 were met with protests, as the regressive nature of the tax was challenged and vilified. These *Gilets Jaune* protests (yellow vests) demonstrated that political unrest can result when higher prices are seen as a result of a carbon tax, which can completely undermine the goals of the tax in the first place; billions of dollars of tax cuts were implemented in order to appease the protestors, and the tax has since remained at €44.60.[45] In addition to this arbitrary price, set by political expediency, a large number of exemptions are built into the tax, as national, international and European Union rules exempt various sectors entirely. The static price does not reflect the level needed to internalise the costs imposed by carbon pollution, and is a weakness in the structure and effectiveness of the French tax. In addition, the numerous exemptions built into the French system impose costs, reduce its efficiency, and create significant equity concerns by cherry-pickers who will be bearing the incidence of the tax.

---

[45] See www.bloomberg.com/news/articles/2020-02-04/carbon-taxes-may-not-be-the-economic-gamble-governments-fear.

IV. Disparate Impact of Carbon Taxation

The upshot from the discussion in section II is that carbon taxation creates significant design problems. As outlined in the Introduction, the assumptions underlying carbon pricing and carbon taxation are themselves strained in light of the current climate crisis. The cost of carbon emissions is so high, and replacement of the underlying energy infrastructure is so time- and cost-intensive that passing it on is potentially economically devastating.

Section II has also shown that there is a further problem of the carbon taxation models deployed so far. All of these models are essentially regressive in nature. A tax is regressive when the tax is applied uniformly irrespective of income. An example of such a regressive tax is sales tax. Sales taxes are applied uniformly to each transaction. Sales tax is blind to who is buying the goods in question.

Carbon taxation similarly in principle applies to carbon emissions uniformly. The point is to internalise, wholly or in part, the costs of carbon emissions. This cost of carbon emissions per ton does not change based on who does the emitting. Climate change does not take into account the income level of the carbon emitter. Rather, each ton of carbon will have an income-independent impact on climate change.[46]

This leads to significant problems in application. As with sales tax, regressive taxation can have at least two separate yet aggregating disparate impacts on poorer members of society. The first of these is straightforward. If two people, A and B, use the same amount of energy to heat and cool their home, cook, run the television, and drive to and from work, they will both be subject to the same carbon tax levels. Assume for argument's sake that the tax amounts to $10,000. If A earns $100,000 and B earns $50,000, then B's proportionate share of the tax in terms of B's income will be double that of A's. That is, the poorer person pays what amounts to a carbon tax of 20 per cent of their income and the better-off person pays a carbon tax of 10 per cent of their income. When using ability-to-pay as a metric for what constitutes a good tax provision, typically taxing a poorer person at a higher effective rate than a wealthy person is frowned upon when spreading the burden of a tax across society.

The second one of these is less straightforward and yet similarly intuitive. It is more likely that the taxes from the poorer person often goes to fund basic and public necessities than taxes paid by the rich and upper class. The bulk of the energy use of a person earning $50,000 is more likely to concern basics needed for survival in a market economy – food, warmth, transportation to work, etc. The higher the income, the more likely some energy use will be for luxuries

---

[46] This is not to say that each ton of carbon emissions will have exactly the same impact on climate systems – it does not as climate systems are not linear by any stretch of the imagination. Rather, it is to say that the impact of carbon emissions in climate systems will be completely independent of the identity and financial wherewithal of the emitter.

(a trip to a Caribbean resort, etc). Treating both sets of emissions in the same way to internalise the cost of carbon is problematic because it disproportionately taxes the lower income-earning taxpayer for transactions needed to survive.

The problem is that this second problem is not easily avoidable. Much of the world's carbon emissions come from basic energy infrastructure – that is electricity generation. Further, much of transportation, too, tends to be for essential commuting purposes, thus presenting a further carbon emissions problem. That is, to internalise the cost of carbon emissions means to penalise people for the ordinary use of existing energy infrastructures. This will hit the poorer sections of society more heavily and for more essential items in order to yield the desired effect.

Obviously, the perversity of this outcome was not lost on states that did implement carbon tax regimes. Rather, tax regimes should address these problems through exemptions, deductions, and allowances, etc so as to minimise the impact of carbon taxation on the most economically vulnerable. This design approach has two fundamental problems in turn. Most obviously, there is the significant potential for abuse.

Less obviously, exempting the transactions for which legislatures are granting relief is undermining the very point of carbon taxation. The point of carbon taxation is to internalise costs so as to drive consumer preferences and thus create markets. If the baseload of transactions is exempted, no such market incentive will form. There will be insufficient customers to support the new products. Renewable energy will be a luxury item in the way that rooftop solar panels are luxury items – they require that a person own their home, and have the financial ability to pay for the solar panels in the first place. This will not apply to the majority of most industrial societies – never mind industrialising societies. Consequently, carbon taxation would create a new market for luxury goods rather than for basic infrastructure. This obviously is beside the point.

V. Conclusion

As outlined in this chapter, carbon taxation faces significant difficulties. Carbon taxation is premised upon the idea of carbon pricing. Carbon pricing is currently difficult to do as there is no removal market and no clear means to attribute the damage done globally to any one ton of carbon emissions. More worryingly still, to function properly carbon taxation must create incentives to establish large markets for non-fossil fuel energy. This means that carbon taxation will always be regressive to a certain point to meet this ambition as any other approach would merely create a small 'luxury' market for non-fossil fuel energy.

Where does this leave us? The first point is one that is difficult to hear in the context of decarbonisation efforts. Fossil fuel-based energy is here to stay for the foreseeable future. Decoupling from fossil fuels is a gradual process. Any decoupling by shock therapy, even if it were technologically feasible, would bring about significant amounts of suffering. Decoupling by anything less than shock therapy means that a gradual decline in fossil fuel use prioritising coal-fired powerplants in the first instance is a more realistic approach to use. In this scenario, it is unclear how carbon taxation would help internalise the remaining costs of carbon emissions.

For carbon taxation to work, it is abundantly clear that governments and non-governmental actors alike must create a market first in which carbon pricing makes sense. Carbon pricing of its own accord will not create a market that is capable of overcoming the imminent and catastrophic dangers of climate change. There is no effective way to spend the money fast enough to make up for the economic disruption created by pricing carbon. That means that carbon taxation is dead on arrival as a political matter. It cannot be sustained – and cannot be sustained for the reasons outlined in this chapter.

If governmental and non-governmental actors must first create markets so as to meaningfully employ carbon taxation as a tool to drive consumers to those markets, how should those markets be built? A full answer to this question is beyond the scope of this chapter. A sketch, however, is not.

First, as concerns mitigation a far better way to use tax and spending powers is to subsidise carbon-neutral means of generating energy. These subsidies can help industries such as the renewable energy industry to gain a foothold and develop technology to produce at cheaper prices and thus become a more competitive part of the energy mix. One example of such a potentially successful use of subsidies is the development of offshore wind in the UK. The use of subsidies helped the industry get off the ground. Commentary on the current 2019 bidding round for offshore wind facilities noted that producers had become so efficient that the need for government subsidies might well be obviated in the next bidding round.

Once these markets have been established, and once they are robust enough to allow customers to buy energy from these markets, it might make sense to use carbon taxation as a means to subsidise further development of the new market through additional subsidies paid through carbon taxation. At this stage, carbon taxation could be used as a further subsidy for the new markets. That is, rather than paying a subsidy to ongoing generation past a certain threshold performance through spending powers, the state could direct customers to the new market by making it comparatively more price competitive by means of targeted carbon taxes. This approach would both potentially raise revenue for the state from the carbon tax during a decoupling phase and support the newly created market with new customers without additional governmental spending.

Second, as concerns removal, the Government can create a market for the production of CO_2 by promising to purchase CO_2 at a set price upon the performance of certain benchmarks. The Government would then use its general taxation and spending power to pay for CO_2 removal, thus avoiding the regressive nature of carbon taxes while also creating a market that could eventually provide a cheap enough carbon removal technology that it could be fully supported through carbon taxation.

Third, as concerns adaptation, the costs of adapting to climate change are so enormous that they are likely beyond the scope of governments to bear alone. A means to address these costs is to create a market for private-public partnerships to provide the necessary infrastructure and the necessary services to adapt to new climate conditions. Some of these public-private partnerships will take on familiar forms as public-private partnerships are already an integral part of infrastructure development around the world. The use of public-private partnerships to build climate resilient infrastructure therefore is not a significant extension. In other contexts, new partnerships may well have to be formed, for example in the context of seawalls or other infrastructure that is intended to address the effects of sea-level rise. These new public-private partnerships could partially be funded by carbon taxation initiatives so as to pay for the costs of the new infrastructure.

In each of these markets, carbon taxation could continue to play an important role to internalise costs. But carbon taxation would do so in tandem with markets in which such an internalisation makes sense and in which the payment made for carbon can actually buy something that is a meaningful way to fight climate change. Carbon taxation cannot create these markets alone. It is thus not a panacea but rather only one tool that should be used judiciously to achieve clearly demarcated targets.

In closing, one might wonder why carbon taxation does not appear to live up to its underlying and significant promise. The answer to this question lies not in any failing of planners who designed carbon taxation. Rather, the problem is one of timing. Carbon taxation assumes that pricing carbon at an economically sustainable price can reduce the shocks of decoupling to tolerable levels and create the incentives for a market-based alternative to fossil fuel use. Current science does not permit this assumption. The timeline is too short for a carbon taxation approach to work in this manner. There is thus no way to avoid a more interventionist approach to the climate crisis. If such an interventionist approach continues to lean on market forces – as well it should, given the massive need for capital to stave off disaster – carbon taxation will continue to have a role to play. But it will be a secondary tool rather than a principal device to organise the global response to the climate threat.

PART II

Energy Transitions: Law and Regulation in Selected Countries and Regions

10

A Primer on United States Energy and Decarbonisation Policy

TROY A RULE

The United States is an indispensable player in the global movement to reduce carbon dioxide emissions and combat climate change. Of course, America's immense influence on global decarbonisation efforts is hardly surprising. Most of the innovations that define the world's modern energy markets trace their origins to American soil, and US energy policies have long had major impacts extending far beyond the country's borders. From the light bulb to hydraulic fracturing, energy technologies first developed in America have upgraded living standards for billions of people living in all corners of the globe. Along the way, American energy innovation has also generated tremendous wealth and political power for the US and its many private energy stakeholders. However, as the adverse consequences of the past century of lucrative US energy industry activity become increasingly apparent across today's planet, America's carbon-heavy economy is facing unprecedented pressures to change. With much at stake, the country continues to exert outsized influence – for good and ill – in the burgeoning worldwide movement to shift modern energy practices onto a more sustainable course. Given America's enduring role in the global energy industry, a solid grasp of energy law and regulation in the US is essential for anyone throughout the world involved in policy efforts aimed at helping to decarbonise the planet's energy system. This chapter provides that foundation by succinctly describing the basic history and features of US energy markets and of the laws and regulations that govern them and then highlighting the uneven and unreliable nature of today's US energy policy.

As highlighted in this chapter, there are plenty of reasons to be optimistic about the future of decarbonisation efforts in the US. Despite waning federal government support, the US renewable energy industry continues to mature and to become increasingly cost-competitive with conventional energy strategies. At last, the industry seems to be approaching a tipping point at which the low cost of renewables will allow market forces to supplant policy incentives as the primary drivers of decarbonisation in the US and beyond.

On the other hand, the growing competitiveness of renewable energy technologies has caused some incumbent energy industry stakeholders within the

US to view renewables and decarbonisation policies as credible threats to their profitability. Some of these private stakeholders have responded by pressuring governments to protect the old-guard energy interests and hinder renewable energy growth. This industry opposition, together with inertia problems resulting from a century of heavy reliance on conventional energy sources, has erected significant obstacles to rapid decarbonisation in the US today. Fortunately, unprecedented efforts by state governments, cities and private corporations across the US are boldly confronting these challenges and are beginning to find some success despite tepid support at the federal government level. This grassroots policy activity provides much-needed hope that the US will eventually develop into a reliable global leader in sustainable energy policy.

I. A Century of World Energy Leadership

For most of the past century, US energy policies have helped to guide development of energy markets and energy regulation throughout the world. As mentioned above, America's large role in shaping global energy policies has been mainly due to the country's exceptional track record of energy innovation and to its abundance of natural energy resources. Levering these advantages and the nation's political power, the US has been highly effective at spreading energy technologies across the globe, while simultaneously generating energy industry jobs and profits within the US. However, as concerns about climate change and other environmental impacts of fossil fuels have intensified in recent years, America's contributions to these problems have also drawn increasing criticism within the country and on the world stage.

A. Impactful Technologies and Abundant Energy Resources

Many of humankind's most significant energy technology advancements and resource development activities over the past 150 years have occurred within US borders, giving American companies first-mover advantages in the formation and expansion of markets built around those resources and technologies. One example of this is Americans' role in the development of coal-fired electricity generation technologies, which have been modern society's predominant generating strategy for over a century. As of 2019, almost 40 per cent of all electricity generated across the globe was from coal – far more than any other resource.[1]

---

[1] See International Energy Agency, 'Coal 2019: Analysis and Forecasts to 2024' (December 2019), www.iea.org/reports/coal-2019.

Of course, many of the greatest pioneers in the early development of coal-fired electricity technologies were Americans. Chief among them was Thomas Edison, who generated the world's first kilowatt hour (kWh) of coal-fired electricity and then leveraged the technologies he had developed to open the Pearl Street Power Station in New York City in 1882.[2]

Several decades later, American researchers from the US state of Idaho became the first to produce electricity from nuclear energy in 1951 – a breakthrough that led to construction of the world's first nuclear energy generating facility in the US state of Pennsylvania in 1957. Pennsylvania was also the site of the planet's first manmade oil well, which launched an enormous worldwide industry that now extracts tens of billions of barrels of oil per day.[3] Even more recently, George Mitchell's drilling experiments in Texas' Barnett Shale formation led to the optimisation of hydraulic fracturing techniques that have since opened up countless new areas to oil and gas extraction across the world.[4] In all of the aforementioned examples, US companies profited from being among the first to develop important new energy technologies that ultimately proliferated and transformed energy markets across the planet. Regulatory structures and initiatives developed within the US to govern these new energy technologies have likewise served as models for numerous other countries over the years.

Another factor that has long enabled the US to heavily impact the global energy sector for decades is the nation's rich abundance of natural energy resources. The US has more known coal reserves than any other country on earth.[5] With the advent of unconventional oil extraction techniques, the US likewise now has more recoverable oil reserves than any other nation.[6] And the US is even in the top five globally in terms of proven natural gas reserves.[7] This wealth of fossil fuel energy resources has understandably incentivised the United States to invest heavily in the development of pipelines, electricity transmission and distribution lines, roads, railroads, ports, and other infrastructure improvements that have enabled the country to better leverage its natural energy assets for economic growth. In addition to these resource-specific advantages, the United States' global status as a political and economic superpower has also helped the country for decades to shape and profit from emerging energy markets around the world.

---

[2] See Troy A Rule, *Renewable Energy: Law, Policy and Practice* (West Academic Publishing, 2018) 12.
[3] See *ibid*.
[4] See Russell Gold, 'The Texas Well that Started the Fracking Revolution' *The Wall Street Journal*, 29 June 2018, www.wsj.com/articles/the-texas-well-that-started-a-revolution-1530270010.
[5] See US Energy Information Administration, 'United States Leads World in Coal Reserves' (2 September 2011), www.eia.gov/todayinenergy/detail.php?id=2930#.
[6] Per Mangus Nysveen, 'U.S. Holds Most Recoverable Oil Reserves' (*The American Oil & Gas Reporter*, 17 April 2019), www.aogr.com/web-exclusives/exclusive-story/u.s.-holds-most-recoverable-oil-reserves.
[7] See 'The World's Biggest Natural Gas Reserves' (*Hydrocarbons-Technology.com*, 11 November 2013), www.hydrocarbons-technology.com/features/feature-the-worlds-biggest-natural-gas-reserves/.

B. Energy Regulation at Three Government Levels

American energy policy is largely decentralised, emanating from activities at the federal, state and local government levels. Authority to regulate certain aspects of the US energy system having nationwide significance has long resided at the federal government level. First established under the 1938 Federal Power Act, a federal agency now known as the Federal Energy Regulatory Commission (FERC) regulates the US transmission and sale of 'wholesale' electricity – electricity generated at large electric generating facilities and sold to electric utilities for resale in retail electricity markets. FERC also oversees several other electricity-related activities involving interstate or national interests, such as the licensing of hydropower and nuclear energy projects.

In addition to FERC, various other federal government agencies regulate other important elements of the US energy industry. For instance, the US Environmental Protection Agency regulates certain emissions from power plants and also regulates automobile tailpipe emissions and fuel economy standards. The US Department of the Interior and subsidiary agencies within that department oversee most aspects of the leasing of offshore areas and public lands for oil and gas extraction, wind and solar energy projects, pipelines, transmission lines and other types of energy development. And federal entities such as the Bonneville Power Administration in the northwestern US and the Tennessee Valley Authority in the southeastern US control and operate extensive networks of hydropower facilities and supporting infrastructure in those regions.

All 50 US state governments also actively regulate important aspects of the nation's energy industry. Most notably, state public utility commissions (PUCs) in a majority of states heavily regulate the activities of most electric utilities within their state boundaries. Typically, PUCs designate an exclusive territory for each state-chartered electric utility. Within the boundaries of that territory, the utility has a duty to distribute electric power throughout the area but is usually also protected from competition from other potential power providers. PUCs also heavily regulate utilities' expenditures and the rates utilities charge to retail customers for electric power. Generally, PUCs assure that such rates are reasonable yet allow utilities to earn a fair return on their investments in power plants, distribution lines, substations and other capital infrastructure. Historically, most electric utilities in the US were 'vertically integrated'. Vertically integrated utilities generally own, control and operate the vast majority of the electric generation, transmission and distribution facilities required for them to supply power to homes and businesses within their territory. Although most electric utilities across the country are still vertically integrated, some states have deregulated their markets for electricity generation and other states are actively considering such deregulation.[8]

---

[8] As of August 2019, deregulation of electricity generation markets was under active consideration in at least three US states. See Millicent Dent, 'Arizona May Have the Best Chance of Breaking up Power Monopolies' (*Bloomberg*, 7 August 2019), www.bloomberg.com/news/articles/2019-08-07/in-battle-to-break-up-utilities-arizona-steps-to-the-front-line (describing ongoing electricity generation deregulation discussions in Arizona, Florida and Virginia).

In deregulated states such as Texas, independently-owned electricity generators compete with each other in the production of electricity. There are ongoing debates within the US over whether deregulating electricity generation markets results in lower electricity rates and better customer service.

Although state PUCs are the primary regulators of electric utilities within their jurisdictions, numerous other state government agencies have regulatory authority over energy-related activities as well. For instance, state laws govern much of the oil and gas extraction process on private land. Unlike landowners in many other countries across the world, owners of land in the US often hold private property interests in coal, oil, gas or other energy resources situated directly below or directly above their parcels.[9] Accordingly, developers of coal- or gas-fired power plants or of wind or solar energy projects typically must seek a long list of permits and approvals from state agencies in connection with their projects. State regulators likewise have some regulatory power over certain aspects of natural gas pipeline siting within their jurisdictions. In fact, regulators in a few states are increasingly restricting pipeline development as part of their decarbonisation efforts.[10]

State governments also possess significant authority over the siting of electric transmission lines within their state boundaries, including interstate lines. This reservation of interstate transmission line siting authority to individual states was probably justifiable in the early days of the electricity industry, when most transmission lines were contained within individual states. However, vesting each state with significant power over transmission line siting decisions is arguably a far less workable or defensible approach given the characteristics of today's expansive US electricity grid, which nearly always stretches across state lines. Because they essentially give individual states veto power over line siting, these rules have made it much more difficult to build out the nation's transmission infrastructure to facilitate greater use of its wind energy resources. As of yet, states and the federal government have yet to find a workable solution to this problem.[11] Despite the disadvantages of affording considerable energy regulatory authority to subnational states, the perceived benefits of this approach have led many other nations to follow suit. Several other countries have followed America's lead and given comparable power to their own subnational governments over the years.

---

[9] The common law's *ad coelum* doctrine, which gives rise to private energy resource rights in the US, clearly has many limitations. For a more detailed discussion of the *ad coelum* doctrine in the context of energy law, see generally Troy A Rule, 'Property Rights and Modern Energy' (2013) 20 *George Mason Law Review* 803, 806–807.

[10] New York regulators' growing restrictions on natural gas pipeline development in that state exemplify this trend. See, eg, Vivian Wang and Michael Adno, 'New York Rejects Keystone-Like Pipeline in Fierce Battle Over the State's Energy Future' *The New York Times*, 15 May 2019, www.nytimes.com/2019/05/15/nyregion/williams-pipeline-gas-energy.html.

[11] For a more detailed discussion of these challenges, see Troy A Rule, *Solar, Wind, and Land: Conflicts in Renewable Energy Development* (Routledge-Earthscan, 2014) 147–55.

Even local governments in the US exercise some regulatory authority over the energy industry. Among other things, most cities and counties have land use planning and zoning power and use it to restrict the locations and features of new energy generation, transmission or distribution facilities. Municipal governments often also have some regulatory jurisdiction over oil and gas well siting, although a growing number of state-level statutes now pre-empt local government restrictions on hydraulic fracturing and certain other extraction-related activities.[12]

Some municipalities even operate their own electric distribution utilities, which affords them additional influence over a wide range of energy policy decisions within their jurisdictions. In fact, more and more cities today are seeking to 'municipalise' or acquire ownership and control of electric utility assets within their boundaries to capture these potential benefits.[13] For obvious reasons, the private utility companies that presently supply grid-delivered power within these cities tend to resist such proposals. Still, regardless of whether they have municipally-owned electric utilities, cities across the US have experimented with various energy policies over the years and developed numerous innovative policy strategies that have spread to other cities around the world.

II. A Wavering Commitment to Decarbonisation

Although the US Federal Government served as a global energy policy leader and driver of progressive energy policy innovation over much of the past century, those leadership qualities have grown less consistent and waned considerably in recent years. In particular, the US Federal Government has increasingly vacillated in its commitments to decarbonisation and sustainable energy. This wavering approach has infused uncertainty into energy regulatory structures within and outside the US, hindering the global transition to a cleaner, more sustainable energy industry.

Throughout much of the twentieth century, Americans were instrumental in helping to form the technological and legal foundations of today's global sustainable energy movement. For example, researchers at Bell Laboratories in New Jersey were pioneers in the development of silicon photovoltaic (PV) solar cells in the 1950s, which served as precursors to today's solar panels. Certain US federal and state government policies enacted in the twentieth century likewise assisted

---

[12] See, eg, Lori Riverston-Newell, 'The Rise of State Preemption Laws in Response to Local Policy Innovation' (2017) 47 *Publius: The Journal of Federalism* 3 (noting that, as of 2017, more than 530 municipalities had adopted restrictions on hydraulic fracturing and that a handful of state legislatures had enacted statutes pre-empting those local restrictions).

[13] For an excellent discussion of issues related to municipalities' efforts to municipalise electric utilities within their jurisdictions, see generally Shelley Welton, 'Public Energy' (2017) 92 *New York University Law Review* 267.

then-fledgling renewable energy markets on the policy side in ways that eventually helped lay the groundwork for rapid growth in today's global wind and solar energy markets. For instance, the federal Public Utility Regulatory Policies Act of 1978[14] helped to provide guaranteed markets for renewable energy producers by requiring utilities to purchase power from qualifying independent electricity producers or 'qualifying facilities'. Tax credit provisions in Congress' Energy Policy Act of 1992[15] likewise incentivised substantial early private investments in wind and solar energy that helped to drive down per-unit production costs to unleash the exponential growth rates that characterise today's global renewable energy industry.

Sadly, over the past couple of decades as climate change concerns have intensified, the US has attracted growing scrutiny over what some have perceived as weak leadership on international climate change and sustainable energy policy issues. The US has emitted more climate change-promoting carbon dioxide into the atmosphere over the past 150 years than any other country on earth, placing the country in a complicated position on the global energy policy stage.[16] With their gas-guzzling sport utility vehicles, oversized air-conditioned homes and countless appliances, Americans have come to rely on massive amounts of inexpensive energy to support their lifestyles. Because of this reliance, most American voters have been reluctant to prioritise climate change mitigation or sustainable energy initiatives in national elections and have generally devoted greater attention to other policy issues such as general economic policies, health care and immigration laws.[17] American voters' hesitancy to engage in global sustainable energy and climate change mitigation efforts first drew considerable international attention in 1997 when the US withdrew from the Kyoto Protocol – an important early international agreement aimed at reducing global greenhouse gas emissions.[18] The US Federal Government achieved some noteworthy advancements in renewable energy policy during Barack Obama's presidency between 2009 and 2016, but its overall trend on decarbonisation issues over the past two decades has been toward decline.

American voters' general ambivalence toward energy issues in national elections has not only slowed the growth of renewables in the US; it has also enabled fossil fuel stakeholders in the country to disproportionately influence federal energy policymaking. For instance, in the 2016 US election cycle

---

[14] Public Law (Pub. L.) No 95–617, 92 Statutes at Large (Stat.) 3117 (9 November 1978).
[15] Pub. L. No 102–486, 106 Stat. 2776 (24 October 1992).
[16] See Justin Gillis and Nadja Popovich, 'The US Is the Biggest Carbon Polluter in History. It Just Walked Away from the Paris Climate Deal' *The New York Times*, 1 June 2017, www.nytimes.com/interactive/2017/06/01/climate/us-biggest-carbon-polluter-in-history-will-it-walk-away-from-the-paris-climate-deal.html.
[17] See Frank Newport, 'Top Issues for Voters: Healthcare, Economy, Immigration' (*Gallup*, 2 November 2018), https://news.gallup.com/poll/244367/top-issues-voters-healthcare-economy-immigration.aspx.
[18] See Frank E Loy, 'The United States Policy on the Kyoto Protocol and Climate Change' (2001) 15 *Natural Resources & Environment* 152, 154.

a whopping eight per cent of all funds spent on the ten most critical Senate elections came from the Koch network,[19] a consortium of nonprofits funded primarily by the Koch brothers that has notoriously championed its fossil fuel interests.[20] Well-heeled fossil fuel stakeholders have long been major supporters of Donald Trump,[21] and the impacts of that support on White House policy-making have been visible throughout Trump's presidency. Trump initiated the country's withdrawal from the United Nations Paris Accord within six months of taking office.[22] He has also repeatedly vowed to restore the nation's coal industry, tweeted skepticism about climate change, and heavily criticised existing renewable energy strategies.[23] The Trump administration's Environmental Protection Agency (EPA) has even rolled back some existing environmental restrictions on coal-fired power plants, resulting in a lawsuit brought by more than two dozen US states.[24] These and other recent federal government actions have tarnished America's reputation as an energy policy leader and drawn denigration from the political leaders of other countries around the world.[25] However, as highlighted in more detail below, renewable energy development continues at a relatively steady pace in the US in spite of these challenges.[26] State governments, municipalities and private businesses throughout the country have shown impressive resolve to press forward and continue to decarbonise in the absence of federal government leadership.

---

[19] See Ian Vandewalker, 'Election Spending 2016: Post-Election Update' (*Brennan Center for Justice*, 23 November 2016), at www.brennancenter.org/blog/election-spending-2016-post-election-update.

[20] See Nathan Reiff, '7 Companies Owned by the Koch Brothers' (*Investopedia.com*, 29 Sept 2019), www.investopedia.com/insights/companies-owned-koch-brothers/; see also Editorial Board, 'The Koch Attack on Solar Energy' *The New York Times*, 26 April 2014.

[21] See, eg, Lisa Friedman, 'How a Coal Baron's Wish List Became President Trump's To-Do List' *New York Times*, 9 January 2018, www.nytimes.com/2018/01/09/climate/coal-murray-trump-memo.html (describing coal company Murray Energy's sizable donation to Donald Trump's inauguration and the Trump administration's efforts to implement policies requested by the company).

[22] See Gillis and Popovich (n 16).

[23] See, eg, Dylan Mathews, 'Donald Trump has Tweeted Climate Change Skepticism 115 Times. Here's all of it' (*Vox.com*, 1 June 2017), www.vox.com/policy-and-politics/2017/6/1/15726472/trump-tweets-global-warming-paris-climate-agreement; see also Michael Collins, 'President Trump has yet to Save the Struggling Coal Industry, Numbers Show (*USA Today*, 4 April 2018), www.usatoday.com/story/news/politics/2018/04/04/president-trump-has-yet-save-struggling-coal-industry-numbers-show/479587002/; Peter Fairley, 'Trump's Impact on Clean-Energy Businesses' (*MIT Technology Review*, 14 November 2016), www.technologyreview.com/s/602833/trumps-impact-on-clean-energy-businesses/ (quoting President Trump as claiming that solar energy is 'very, very expensive' and that wind energy is 'killing all the eagles') (cited in Troy A Rule, 'Still Growing: How America's Renewable Energy Industry is Surviving the Trump Era' (2018) 16 *Oil, Gas & Energy Law Journal* 4, www.ogel.org/article.asp?key=3785).

[24] See Lisa Friedman, 'States Sue Trump Administration Over Rollback of Obama-Era Climate Rule' *New York Times*, 13 August 2019 A11.

[25] See, eg, Ben Doherty, 'US Accused of Obstructing Talks at UN Climate Change Summit' *The Guardian*, 11 December 2018, www.theguardian.com/environment/2018/dec/11/us-accused-of-obstructing-talks-at-un-climate-change-summit (describing the Vanuatu foreign minister's harsh criticism of US actions affecting United Nations climate change negotiations).

[26] See text accompanying nn 61–69.

III. Evaporating Renewable Energy Incentives

The United States' diminishing reputation as a leader in decarbonisation policy is at least partly attributable to the gradual erosion of government support for renewable energy over the past several years. Many US renewable energy initiatives and programmes have been enormously successful, enabling the US to trail only China in cumulative installed renewable energy generating capacity as of 2017.[27] However, the US remains one of the world's highest carbon dioxide emitters and has increasingly been reducing its policy support for renewable energy, even though the country still has a long way to go before transforming the US into a low-carbon economy. The following paragraphs describe several existing state and federal decarbonisation policies in the US, highlight the strengths and shortcomings of each, and describe how many of these policies are being phased or stalled.

A. The Phasing Out of Federal Renewable Energy Tax Credits

The US Federal Government has done much over the past quarter century to drive private investment and growth in low-carbon energy strategies, but its interest in continuing many of its most successful strategies appears to be waning. Federal tax credits, grants and other programmes that have attracted billions of dollars in private investment into renewable energy project development and research over that period and accelerated the world's shift toward clean energy are increasingly appearing on the chopping block.

Arguably the most influential federal renewable energy policies in the US over the past few decades have been the Production Tax Credit (PTC) and the Investment Tax Credit (ITC). Congress established the PTC under provisions in the Energy Policy Act of 1992.[28] The PTC is a per-kWh income tax credit on the generation and sale of electricity from wind energy, geothermal energy and certain other qualifying renewable energy sources. The amount of the PTC was $0.015 per kWh at the time of its creation in 1992 but is tied to inflation and had increased to about $0.023 per kWh by 2016.[29] The PTC's greatest impact has been in the US wind energy market, where the credit has made wind energy far more price-competitive with electricity generated from coal, natural gas or nuclear energy. In part because of the PTC, as of 2018 the US had roughly 96 gigawatts

---

[27] See International Renewable Energy Agency, 'Renewable Capacity Statistics 2020' (March 2020) 2–4, www.irena.org/-/media/Files/IRENA/Agency/Publication/2020/Mar/IRENA_RE_Capacity_Statistics_2020.pdf.
[28] See Energy Policy Act of 1992 (n 15).
[29] See US Energy Information Administration. 'Wind and Solar Data and Projections from the US Energy Information Administration: Past Performance and Ongoing Enhancements' (March 2016) 27, www.eia.gov/outlooks/aeo/supplement/renewable/pdf/projections.pdf.

(GW) of wind energy generating capacity – more than any country in the world other than China.[30] Unfortunately, in 2015, Congress placed the credit on a phase-out schedule that gradually reduced the credit amount and would have completely eliminated it for projects commenced after 31 December 2019.[31] Congress did extend the credit one additional year in late 2020, but as of April 2020 the credit was again only months away from extinction.[32]

Unlike the PTC, the ITC is a tax credit whose amount is based on a taxpayer's expenditure of private funds on qualifying renewable energy generating facilities and devices. First established by Congress under the Energy Tax Act of 1978,[33] the ITC applies primarily to private investments in solar energy, small wind energy and fuel cell projects and equipment. The amount of the ITC was 30 per cent as of 2018 but, like the PTC, the ITC is on a phase-out schedule. Under the schedule, qualifying projects commenced after 31 December 2021 will qualify for a tax credit of just 10 per cent.[34] Certain other renewable energy investments qualify for lesser credit amounts.[35] The ITC's most significant impact has been on US solar energy markets, which have grown exponentially over the past decade and also trail only China's with more than 64 GW of installed generating capacity.[36] However, the phasing out of the ITC and the Trump administration's sizable tariffs on Chinese imported solar PV panels have clearly slowed the pace of US solar development.

In addition to the ITC and PTC, a handful of other federal policies and programmes have done much to promote renewable energy development in the US over the past several years. One such programme is the US Department of Energy's SunShot Initiative, which has sought to incentivise public and private research on strategies for reducing per-kWh costs of solar energy.[37] A federal Loan Guarantee Program for renewable energy established under section 1705 of the American Recovery and Reinvestment Act of 2009[38] has also helped to drive renewable energy investment in the US. By providing federal government guarantees for approved private renewable energy financings, the Loan Guarantee Program made it easier and less expensive for renewable energy developers and entrepreneurs to borrow capital for their projects and businesses. Even special provisions added

---

[30] See Jack Unwin, 'The Top 10 Countries in the World by Wind Energy Capacity' (*Power Technology*, 14 March 2019), www.power-technology.com/features/wind-energy-by-country/.
[31] See *ibid*.
[32] Molly F Sherlock, 'The Renewable Electricity Production Tax Credit: In Brief' (Congressional Research Service, April 2019), https://fas.org/sgp/crs/misc/R43453.pdf.
[33] See Pub. L. No 95-618, 92 Stat. 3174 (9 November 1978).
[34] See US Department of Energy, 'Business Energy Investment Tax Credit' (*programs.dsireusa.org*), http://programs.dsireusa.org/system/program/detail/658.
[35] For eg, geothermal systems have long qualified for a 10% ITC. See *ibid*.
[36] See Solar Energy Industries Association, 'U.S. Solar Market Insight' (19 March 2019), www.seia.org/us-solar-market-insight.
[37] For more information about the SunShot Initiative, visit the Initiative's homepage, www.energy.gov/eere/solar/sunshot-initiative.
[38] Pub. L. No 111–5, 123 Stat. 115 (17 February 2009).

to the Internal Revenue Code in 2015 and expanded in early 2018 further helped incentivise investment in solar energy by allowing bonus depreciation for qualifying commercial solar energy projects.[39] Regrettably, most of the federal renewable energy initiatives and policies that have been most impactful are gradually disappearing and renewable energy industry stakeholders are increasingly having to survive without them.

B. Hit-and-Miss State Renewable Energy Policies

At the state level, there is tremendous variation in the nature and progressiveness of decarbonisation policies in the US. Many US states have been far more aggressive than the Federal Government in embracing policies to promote renewable energy development over the past couple of decades, while other states have done surprisingly little to promote renewable energy in their jurisdictions.

The most impactful state-level renewable energy policies in the past 20 years have been renewable portfolio standards (RPSs) or goals. As of 2019, 29 states and the District of Columbia had RPS policies.[40] RPS policies require that electric utilities source certain minimum percentages of the power they provide to customers from qualifying renewable energy resources before one or more specific dates. Another eight US states have non-binding renewable portfolio 'goals' that operate similarly but generally do not impose penalties on utilities for non-compliance.[41] RPS legislation in many states allows for utilities to comply by purchasing tradable renewable energy credits from others, helping to improve the overall efficiency of these programmes.[42] RPS standards and goals promote renewable energy growth by creating additional demand for renewable electricity projects capable of supplying qualifying electricity to help utilities meet the standards.

As utilities across the country have begun meeting their states' RPS standards, a few state legislatures have increased the standards to require that utilities work to source even more of their electricity from renewables. For example, Hawaii, California, Washington DC and Puerto Rico now have RPS policies requiring utilities in those jurisdictions to eventually source 100 per cent of their power from renewables.[43] However, most states with RPS standards have not legislated such

---

[39] For a detailed discussion of these tax benefits, see Samuel Adeyemo, 'New Tax Bill Offers Unexpected Benefits to Commercial Solar Installations' (*greentechmedia.com*, 3 January 2018), www.greentechmedia.com/articles/read/new-tax-bill-offers-unexpected-benefits-to-commercial-solar-installations#gs.6rpgcf.
[40] See National Conference of State Legislatures, 'State Renewable Portfolio Standards and Goals' (17 April 2020), www.ncsl.org/research/energy/renewable-portfolio-standards.aspx.
[41] See *ibid*.
[42] See *ibid*.
[43] See Iulia Gheorghiu, 'Puerto Rico Passes 100% Renewable Energy Bill as it Aims for Storm Resilience' (*UtilityDive.com*, 26 March 2019), www.utilitydive.com/news/puerto-rico-passes-100-renewable-energy-bill-as-it-aims-for-storm-resilien/551303/.

increases and the policies' impacts are consequently declining in those states.[44] Unless more states become active in updating their RPS standards, the aggregate impact of these policies on renewable energy growth in the US could diminish over the next decade.

Net metering programmes have arguably been the most controversial state-level renewable energy policies in the US during the past ten years. Net metering programmes require utilities to credit retail electricity customers with distributed energy systems for any excess power they generate and do not use onsite. For instance, if a residential landowner is not using very much electricity at her home on a sunny day and her rooftop solar panels are generating more power than she needs, the excess power is typically fed onto the electric grid for use by neighbours. Under a pure retail net metering policy, such a landowner would receive a one-for-one credit on her electricity bill (equal to her own retail electricity rate) for each kWh fed onto the grid during the billing period. These credits offset customers' electricity use at night and at other periods when their solar panels are producing less electricity than they need.

Over the past several years, electric utilities have grown increasingly resistant to retail net metering mandates, arguing that they overcompensate customers for their solar-generated power and prevent such customers from paying their fair share of the utility's cost of building and maintaining the electric distribution grid.[45] However, concerns about their own long-term market position are likely the primary driver of most utilities' opposition to net metering. By making rooftop solar energy systems more economically rewarding, net metering policies also increase retail demand for rooftop solar installations and ultimately reduce the amount of electricity demanded from a utility's customer base. These declines in aggregate electricity demand can ultimately create 'stranded cost' problems for utilities – situations in which utilities find it increasingly difficult to recoup their prior investments in fossil fuel-powered generating facilities.[46] To combat these risks, many electric utilities have lobbied to state legislators and state PUCs for modifications to net metering policies or to electricity rate designs that reduce the financial benefits of rooftop solar systems. These conflicts between electric utilities and the rooftop solar industry over net metering and retail electricity rate design, continues today in states throughout the US.[47]

---

[44] See Megan Cleveland, 'States' Renewable Energy Ambitions' (*National Conference of State Legislators*, 4 February 2019), www.ncsl.org/research/energy/states-renewable-energy-ambitions.aspx (noting that the role of RPS standards as a driver of renewable energy growth has 'diminished in recent years, accounting for only 34 percent of renewable energy capacity additions in 2017').

[45] For a thorough discussion of utilities primary arguments against net metering and some potential rebuttals to these arguments, see generally Troy A Rule, 'Solar Energy, Utilities, and Fairness' (2015) 6 *San Diego Journal of Climate & Energy Law* 115.

[46] See generally Emily Hammond and Jim Rossi, 'Stranded Costs and Grid Decarbonization' (2017) 82 *Brooklyn Law Review* 645, 646–47.

[47] See Rule (n 2) at 406–410 (describing net metering caps, reductions in net metering credits, solar fees and other types of net metering reforms).

In addition to RPS policies and net metering programmes, there are numerous other innovative US state laws and initiatives aimed at promoting renewable energy and decarbonisation. For instance, the California Energy Commission and California Building Standards Commission adopted regulations in 2018 requiring nearly all new homes in the state to have rooftop solar power starting in the year 2020.[48] Minnesota's Community Solar Program has multiple unique features that have enabled the state to become one of the nation's leaders in solar PV installations in recent years, despite the state's mediocre natural solar resources.[49] Further, New York's ambitious Renewable Energy Vision (REV) Connect initiative seeks, among other things, to use shared savings programmes and other policies to drive energy efficiency investment as part of broader plans to greatly reduce greenhouse gas emissions in that state.[50] Through these types of programmes, some state governments continue to be major drivers of decarbonisation policymaking within the US. In contrast, several other US states have taken relatively little action to promote decarbonisation and have seen far more tepid renewable energy growth within their jurisdictions.

IV. Major Obstacles to Future US Decarbonisation Efforts

Although US decarbonisation efforts overall have made some impressive advances in recent years, significant challenges lie ahead. Among them is the fact that many incumbent energy industry stakeholders in the country increasingly view renewable energy and related technologies as significant market threats and are thus lobbying governments to take actions that slow their adoption. Innovation and production economies of scale have rapidly driven down per-unit prices for these technologies over the past two decades, making them increasingly price-competitive with coal- and gas-fired electricity.[51] Although these changes have helped to drive exponential market growth in the US wind and solar energy industries, they have also accelerated the pace of coal-fired power plant retirements across the country.[52]

---

[48] See Julia Pyper, 'California's Rooftop Solar Mandate Wins Final Approval' (*GreenTechMedia.com*, 5 December 2018), www.greentechmedia.com/articles/read/california-solar-roof-mandate-wins-final-approval#gs.6s1g5o.

[49] See, eg, Catherine Morehouse, 'Minnesota Community Solar Hits 400 MW' (*UtilityDive.com*, 30 August 2018) (describing Minnesota's community solar programme and its successes).

[50] For introductory information about REV Connect in New York, visit the initiative's website at https://nyrevconnect.com/innovation-opportunities-older/energy-efficiency/.

[51] PV solar module costs have fallen an astounding 99% since 1980. See Jason Deign, 'Why PV Costs Have Fallen So Far – and Will Fall Further' (*GreenTechMedia.com*, 14 December 2018), www.greentechmedia.com/articles/read/why-pv-costs-have-fallen-so-far-and-will-fall-further#gs.7r4hyp. Further, the average cost of wind energy has declined from about seven cents per kWh in 2009 to less than two cents per kWh by the end of 2018. 'Wind Technologies Market Report' (*Berkeley Lab* 2019), https://emp.lbl.gov/wind-technologies-market-report/.

[52] See, eg, 'S&P: Another 8GW of Coal Capacity Due to go Offline in 2019 (*Institute for Energy Economics & Financial Analysis*, 18 January 2019), http://ieefa.org/sp-another-8gw-of-coal-capacity-due-to-

Meanwhile, rooftop solar energy growth is dampening the aggregate demand for grid-supplied electricity and complicating grid load management in some markets, provoking increasing resistance from investor-owned electric utilities. These shifts have prompted many coal industry stakeholders and utilities to seek to influence policymaking in ways that would better protect them against these new competitive threats within their markets.

A series of federal campaign finance law cases decided in the US over the past several years has unquestionably made it easier for opposition groups to hinder the nation's decarbonisation efforts. Most notably, the US Supreme Court held in *Citizens United v Federal Election Commission* in 2010 that US corporations possessed first amendment rights to express their political views by making unlimited and undisclosed 'dark money' donations through non-profit political entities to indirectly fund election campaigns.[53] At the federal government level, campaign finance laws have helped coal and oil industry stakeholders to wield significant influence in recent years – a reality that is visible in President Trump's declared affection for 'beautiful clean coal' and his open hostility toward renewable energy strategies.[54] Meanwhile, as of late 2019, 21 states were suing the Trump EPA for favouring coal interests by rolling back regulations aimed at limiting the environmental costs of coal-fired power.[55] At the state government level, investor-owned utilities in some states have used dark money channels to funnel tens of millions of dollars to favoured candidates for state utility commissions or for campaigns against renewable energy policies.[56] To the extent they continue, these types of political activities could significantly impede renewable energy growth in the US in the coming years.

In addition to political obstacles, today's US renewable energy industry is facing significant practical challenges that could slow its future expansion. One such challenge is the reality that developers have already developed many of the nation's best renewable energy resources. Accordingly, developers are increasingly having to consider second-best project sites. Such sites are often less desirable

---

go-offline-in-2019/ (noting that coal-fired electricity generation facilities account for 68% of all scheduled generating capacity retirements in 2019 and that wind energy accounts for about 45% of all generating capacity additions).

[53] See *Citizens United v Federal Election Commission* 558 US 310, 339–40 (2010).

[54] See Christina Zhao, 'Donald Trump says Wind Turbines are Bird Killers as he Tries to Revive Coal Industry' (*Newsweek*, 20 August 2018), www.newsweek.com/donald-trump-says-windmills-are-bird-killers-he-tries-revive-coal-industry-1079910.

[55] See Don Thompson and Adam Beam, '21 States Sue Trump Administration over New Coal Rules' (*Associated Press*, 13 August 2019), www.apnews.com/dfd2bf676f89490390e9ee073f86849a.

[56] See, eg, Troy A Rule, 'Buying Power: Utility Dark Money and the Battle over Rooftop Solar' (2017) 5 *LSU Journal of Energy Law and Resources* 1. See also Ryan Randazzo, 'APS Acknowledges Spending Millions to Elect Corporation Commission Members, after Years of Questions' (*Arizona Republic*, 29 March 2019), www.azcentral.com/story/money/business/energy/2019/03/29/arizona-public-service-admits-spending-millions-2014-corporation-commission-races/3317121002/ (describing how the investor-owned utility Arizona Public Service Co used dark money channels to contribute $10.7 million to groups supporting specific Arizona Corporation Commission candidates in 2014).

because of their lower-quality energy resources, their distance from transmission lines with available capacity, or their proximity to military activities, critical wildlife habitats or cultural resources.[57] Until energy storage technologies mature and become more affordable, the intermittent nature of wind and solar energy resources could also slow renewable energy growth because of the continued need for reliable baseload power to balance grid loads. And advancements in shale drilling technologies have unlocked trillions of cubic feet of natural gas reserves,[58] lowering natural gas prices and making it more difficult for cleaner renewables to compete in much of the country, especially in regions with existing extensive networks of interconnected gas pipelines and electricity supply systems.[59] In short, in the US there are still plenty of hurdles for the renewable energy industry to clear before it can become the nation's predominant source of electric power.

V. A (Potentially) Bright Future

Despite the numerous roadblocks facing today's US renewable energy markets and the Federal Government's history of wavering support for decarbonisation, the nation is still likely to be an important leader in the global transition to clean, sustainable energy in the long run. It's doubtful that bold federal decarbonisation approaches like the 'Green New Deal' touted by US Senator Ed Markey and Representative Alexandria Ocasio-Cortez in early 2019 will become law any time soon.[60] As of mid-2020, the prospects for wide-reaching federal decarbonisation legislation remained weak even though some economists were advocating such legislation as a means of resuscitating the nation's pandemic-ravaged economy.[61] Still, regardless of whether consistent federal-level leadership on renewable energy policy ever emerges in the US, the country's state governments, municipalities and corporate giants still seem poised to play major roles in the future reshaping of the global renewable energy landscape.

---

[57] For a detailed examination of the most common conflicts arising in the context of renewable energy development, see generally Rule (n 11).
[58] For example, the Barnett Shale Formation alone has more than 50 trillion cubic feet of natural gas reserves. See United States Geological Survey, 'USGS Estimates 53 Trillion Cubic Feet of Gas Resources in Barnett Shale' (17 December 2015), www.usgs.gov/news/usgs-estimates-53-trillion-cubic-feet-gas-resources-barnett-shale.
[59] See Ariel Cohen, 'The EIA's July Energy Report In Pictures' (*Forbes*, 24 July 2019), www.forbes.com/sites/arielcohen/2019/07/24/the-eias-july-energy-report-in-pictures/#3282f2e72675 (reporting that 'record-low natural gas prices' are leading to sharp increases in natural gas-fired electricity generation in the US and noting that the country's renewable energy industry 'must contend with a booming natural gas market and low electricity prices').
[60] For details on the Green New Deal, see generally David Roberts, 'The Green New Deal, Explained' (*vox.com*, 30 March 2019), www.vox.com/energy-and-environment/2018/12/21/18144138/green-new-deal-alexandria-ocasio-cortez.
[61] See, eg, Matthew Green, 'Green Recovery can Revive Virus-Hit Economies and Tackle Climate Change, Study Says' (*Reuters*, 4 May 2020), www.reuters.com/article/us-health-coronavirus-economy-idUSKBN22G2Z7.

A. Continued Policy Progress at the State and Local Levels

As mentioned briefly above, numerous state and local governments in the US are increasingly embracing decarbonisation measures and offering hope that renewable energy policy will continue to advance throughout much of the country. At the state government level, a handful of states are pursuing aggressive decarbonisation agendas that could ultimately have major impacts on the country's aggregate carbon emissions. Most other states have been less ambitious but are still making steady progress. For instance, at least 1,200 renewable energy-related bills were considered or enacted in state legislatures throughout the country in 2020 alone.[62] State governors and legislatures across the nation are likewise making aggressive voluntary commitments to dramatically reduce their states' use of fossil fuel electricity. At least 11 states, Washington DC and Puerto Rico have made formal commitments to transition to 100 per cent clean or renewable power by 2050 or sooner.[63] Several state governments are also proactively encouraging private investment in energy storage technologies,[64] promoting energy efficiency,[65] or requiring newly-built homes to have rooftop solar panels.[66]

Adding to state governments' renewable energy policy efforts are hundreds of municipal ordinances and programmes across the US that are further targeting carbon emissions in innovative ways. As of early 2020, more than 150 US cities had committed to transition to 100 per cent renewable power by 2050 and at least a half dozen cities had already achieved that goal.[67] Some major cities are likewise considering aggressive building energy efficiency policies as a way to reduce their overall carbon emissions. For example, New York City adopted an ordinance in 2019 requiring the city's larger buildings to reduce their carbon emissions by at least 40 per cent by 2030.[68] As cities continue to creatively legislate towards

---

[62] See National Conference of State Legislatures, 'Energy State Bill Tracking Database' (23 April 2020), www.ncsl.org/research/energy/energy-legislation-tracking-database.aspx#chart.

[63] See Julia Pyper, 'Tracking Progress on 100% Clean Energy Targets' (*greentechmedia.com*, 12 November 2019), www.greentechmedia.com/articles/read/tracking-progress-on-100-clean-energy-targets.

[64] See Michael Grunwald, 'An Unexpected Current That's Remaking American Politics' (*Politico*, 29 April 2019) (noting that 'more than 20 states have changed laws or regulations to make storage more feasible in the past two years').

[65] See Robert Walton, 'States Spent $400M More Last Year on Energy Efficiency, ACEEE Finds' (*UtilityDive.com*, 5 October 2018), www.utilitydive.com/news/states-spent-400m-more-last-year-on-energy-efficiency-aceee-finds/538927/ (reporting that '[s]tates are ramping up efforts to grow energy efficiency … with greater spending and a broad array of strategies').

[66] See Jeff Daniels, 'California Officially becomes First in Nation Mandating Solar Power for New Homes' (*The Orange County Register*, 7 December 2018), www.ocregister.com/2018/12/05/california-officially-adopts-solar-requirement-for-new-homes-built-in-2020-or-later/ (describing new California legislation requiring most new residential homes to have distributed solar energy systems).

[67] See Sierra Club, '100% Commitments in Cities, Counties, & States', www.sierraclub.org/ready-for-100/commitments (listing 157 cities with 100% renewables goals, including six cities that had already reached their goals).

[68] See Daniel Geiger, 'Emissions Cap has Landlords Scrambling for Clean Energy' (*Crain's New York Business*, 29 April 2019), describing a recently-adopted New York City ordinance imposing caps on building greenhouse gas emissions within the city).

B. Corporate America's Growing Energy Policy Role

In the absence of strong federal government leadership, private corporations are increasingly driving renewable energy growth in the US as well. With numerous large US corporations now pursuing their own renewable energy commitments, demand for corporate renewable energy 'procurements' is skyrocketing. Sustainability-conscious companies have been installing solar panels on their buildings or purchasing renewable energy credits on open markets for several years. However, corporations engaging in renewable energy procurement take a somewhat different approach, contracting with developers to build offsite large wind or solar energy projects that the corporation intends to own. Behemoth US companies such as Amazon, Apple, Facebook and AT&T have led the way in this trend, which is already accelerating the pace of the country's renewable energy development.[69] Meanwhile, smaller companies are increasingly banding together to negotiate their own renewable energy procurement deals, further bolstering renewable energy demand.[70]

VI. Conclusion

Across the US, decarbonisation policy is trudging forwards despite near-constant opposition from inside and outside of government. The real-life impacts of the past century's unprecedented global greenhouse gas emissions levels are increasingly apparent throughout the country and beginning to prompt Americans to take notice. Although it's impossible to accurately measure how much of Hurricane Harvey's severe inland flooding of Houston in 2017, California's 2018 wildfire damage, or the devastating Midwest flooding in 2019 were attributable to climate change, Americans' losses from such events are undeniably growing and

---

[69] See Julia Pyper, 'Corporate Renewable Energy Deals Smash Records in 2018' (*greentechmedia.com*, 18 October 2018), www.greentechmedia.com/articles/read/corporate-renewable-energy-deals-smash-record-2018#gs.8roorw (noting that corporate renewable energy procurements in 2018 had set a record by October of that year). See also Katherine Tweed, 'Which State Leads in Corporate Renewable Offtake Deals? Hint: It's Not California' (*greentechmedia.com*, 11 April 2019), www.greentechmedia.com/articles/read/which-state-leads-in-corporate-renewable-offtake-deals-its-not-california#gs.8rskxc (reporting that, as of April 2019, 22 US states had at least 50 megawatts of renewable energy projects 'operating or in development with corporate offtakers').

[70] See Sarah Golden, 'Clean Energy Deal Tracker: Utilities Want in on Growing Demand for Renewables' (*greenbiz.com*, 18 April 2019), www.greenbiz.com/article/clean-energy-deal-tracker-utilities-want-growing-demand-renewables (describing how the company LevelTen helped to aggregate renewable energy demand for five smaller companies to procure a North Carolina solar energy project).

are beginning to convince more Americans of the need to take action on decarbonisation. On the other hand, American innovators, landowners and businesses that have profited greatly for more than a century from their heavy involvement in the proliferation of fossil fuel energy technologies and resources across the planet are resisting changes to the status quo. Having benefitted tremendously from their role in creating and fuelling the world's carbon-intensive energy systems, these stakeholders could potentially lose the most from a transition to a cleaner, more sustainable energy industry and are likely to continue to fight such changes. As sustainable energy technologies become more cost-competitive, the tension between incumbent energy interests and disruptive energy innovators in the US grows more and more palpable. How well Americans and their government institutions succeed in managing that tension and facilitating a swift decarbonisation of the US economy will have profound long-term ramifications for the nation and for the world.

Until recently, politically powerful fossil fuel companies and other incumbent energy industry stakeholders had been fairly effective at protecting their own interests and limiting renewable energy policy support at the federal level. However, unprecedented policy activity among states and local governments and within corporate America is beginning to drive decarbonisation forward in the US in spite of lackluster federal support. And as the costs of renewables and energy storage continue to fall, market forces could increasingly be the primary drivers of renewable energy development and unleash even faster rates of growth. These trends provide some optimism that the US will still ultimately become a true positive leader in humankind's march toward a sustainable, low-carbon future.

11

The Integration of Renewable Energy Sources in the EU Electricity Grid: Adapting Current Market Rules to 'New Market Realities'

SIRJA-LEENA PENTTINEN AND LEONIE REINS

I. Introduction

The European Union ('EU') has been hailed as the success story in adopting policies to stimulate investments in renewable energy and advance their market uptake.[1] Indeed, in volume terms the policy choice of subsidy spurred renewable energy production in the EU has been a remarkable story; the quantity of renewable energy produced within the EU-28 increased by 64 per cent between 2007 and 2017.[2]

Despite the growth in renewable energy power production in the EU, challenges in the transition to a low-carbon energy system remain.[3] One of these is introducing the 'next piece to the puzzle', ie how to integrate increasing amounts of variable renewable energy into the power system while maintaining economic and reliable operation of the grid ('power system flexibility'). The traditional, centralised electricity market model has been forced to give way to changes, prompted in particular by the envisaged transition to a low carbon economy.

---

[1] It was however surpassed by China in 2013. See also European Environment Agency (EEA), 'Renewable Energy in Europe 2017 – Recent Growth and Knock-On Effects (EEA, 2017) at 40.
[2] Eurostat, 'Renewable Energy Statistics', available at https://ec.europa.eu/eurostat/statistics-explained/index.php/Renewable_energy_statistics#Renewable_energy_produced_in_the_EU_increased_by_two_thirds_in_2007-2017.
[3] See also H Lindquist, 'The Journey of Reinventing the European Electricity Landscape – Challenges and Pioneers' in L Jones (ed), *Renewable Energy Integration: Practical Management of Variability, Uncertainty and Flexibility in Power Grids* (Academic Press, 2014) 3–12, at 3.

In this regard, the rules provided in the Third Energy Package[4] are mostly outdated and can no longer accommodate the changes required by this transition.[5]

In December 2018 the EU legislator – the European Parliament and the Council – and the Commission reached a political agreement on the conclusion of the so-called 'Clean Energy for All Europeans' legislative package, proposed by the European Commission in November 2016.[6] The Commission's proposals focused especially on reforming the legislative framework in a way to provide for more flexibility to accommodate an increasing share of renewable energy in the energy system. The EU has been one of the forerunners globally in increasing the share of renewable energy in its energy mix, especially with the help of public support policies at Member State level, such as financial incentives for the deployment of solar parks and wind farms.[7] However, the new electricity market design aims to adapt the current market rules to new market realities with a view to introduce tools to solve the power system flexibility challenge.[8] To this end, the recently adopted revised legislation introduces provisions concerning both supply as well as demand-side issues.

The package is a step towards the creation of the Energy Union 'with a forward-looking climate change policy',[9] as well as delivering on the EU's commitments adopted under the Paris Agreement.[10] In particular, the legislative package aims at 'giving European access to secure, affordable and climate-friendly energy and making the European Union world leader in renewable energy'.[11] To this end, the package introduces a legislative revision, which is aimed at facilitating the transition towards the dominance of clean energy sources in the electricity mix.

---

[4] Consisting of, amongst others, Directive 2009/73/EC of the European Parliament and of the Council of 13 July 2009 concerning common rules for the internal market in natural gas and repealing Directive 2003/55/EC [2009] OJ L211/94–136 and Directive 2009/72/EC of the European Parliament and of the Council of 13 July 2009 concerning common rules for the internal market in electricity and repealing Directive 2003/54/EC [2009] OJ L211/ 55–93.

[5] A Marhold, 'The Interplay between Liberalization and Decarbonization in the European Internal Energy Market for Electricity' in K Mathis and B Huber (eds), *Energy Law and Economics*, 1st edn (Springer International Publishing, 2018) Vol 5, 59–75.

[6] Commission Communication, *Clean Energy For All Europeans* COM(2016) 860 (Brussels, 30 November 2016).

[7] For an overview, see SL Penttinen, 'The First Examples of Designing the National Renewable Energy Support Schemes under the Revised EU State Aid Guidelines' (2016) 37 (2) *European Competition Law Review* 77–83.

[8] European Commission Press Release, 'Commission Welcomes Political Agreement on Conclusion of the Clean Energy for All Europeans Package' IP/18/6870 (Brussels, 18 December 2018).

[9] Communication from the Commission to the European Parliament, the Council, the European Economic and Social Committee, the Committee of the Regions and the European Investment Bank, *A Framework Strategy for a Resilient Energy Union with a Forward-Looking Climate Change Policy* COM(2015) 80 final (Brussels, 25 February 2015).

[10] Paris Agreement to the United Nations Framework Convention on Climate Change, T.I.A.S. No. 16-1104 (12 December 2015).

[11] European Commission Press Release, 'Commission Welcomes European Parliament Adoption of Key Files of the Clean Energy for All Europeans Package' IP/18/6383 (Brussels, 13 November 2018).

In total, the package consists of eight pieces of legislation, adopted in 2018 and 2019:

1. Directive (EU) 2018/844 on the energy performance of buildings and Directive 2012/27/EU on energy efficiency ('Energy Performance of Buildings Directive').[12]
2. Directive (EU) 2018/2001 on the promotion of the use of energy from renewable sources ('Renewable Energy Directive').[13]
3. Directive (EU) 2018/2002 amending Directive 2012/27/EU on energy efficiency.[14]
4. Regulation (EU) 2018/1999 on the Governance of the Energy Union and Climate Action.[15]
5. Regulation (EU) 2019/941 on Risk-Preparedness in the Electricity Sector.[16]
6. Regulation (EU) 2019/942 establishing a European Union Agency for the Cooperation of Energy Regulators (ACER).[17]
7. Directive (EU) 2019/944 on common rules for the internal market for electricity and amending Directive 2012/27/EU ('Electricity Market Directive').[18]
8. Regulation (EU) 2019/943 on the Internal Market for Electricity ('Electricity Market Regulation').[19]

This chapter focuses on the EU's approach to introducing flexibility to the grid given the increasing share of renewable energy in the EU's energy mix. First, it presents an overview of the current state of renewable energy production and grid integration in the EU with some remarks considered to be necessary regarding the division of competences and legislative processes in the EU. Second, it

---

[12] Directive (EU) 2018/844 of the European Parliament and of the Council of 30 May 2018 amending Directive 2010/31/EU on the energy performance of buildings and Directive 2012/27/EU on energy efficiency [2018] OJ L156/75–91.

[13] Directive (EU) 2018/2001 of the European Parliament and of the Council of 11 December 2018 on the promotion of the use of energy from renewable sources [2018] OJ L328/82–209.

[14] Directive (EU) 2018/2002 of the European Parliament and of the Council of 11 December 2018 amending Directive 2012/27/EU on energy efficiency [2018] OJ L328/210–30.

[15] Regulation (EU) 2018/1999 of the European Parliament and of the Council of 11 December 2018 on the Governance of the Energy Union and Climate Action, amending Regulations (EC) No 663/2009 and (EC) No 715/2009 of the European Parliament and of the Council, Directives 94/22/EC, 98/70/EC, 2009/31/EC, 2009/73/EC, 2010/31/EU, 2012/27/EU and 2013/30/EU of the European Parliament and of the Council, Council Directives 2009/119/EC and (EU) 2015/652 and repealing Regulation (EU) No 525/2013 of the European Parliament and of the Council [2018] OJ L328/1–77.

[16] Regulation (EU) 2019/941 of the European Parliament and of the Council of 5 June 2019 on risk-preparedness in the electricity sector and repealing Directive 2005/89/EC [2019] OJ L158/1–21.

[17] Regulation (EU) 2019/942 of the European Parliament and of the Council of 5 June 2019 establishing a European Union Agency for the Cooperation of Energy Regulators [2019] OJ L158/22–53.

[18] Directive (EU) 2019/944 of the European Parliament and of the Council of 5 June 2019 on common rules for the internal market for electricity and amending Directive 2012/27/EU [2019] OJ L158/125–99.

[19] Regulation (EU) 2019/943 of the European Parliament and of the Council of 5 June 2019 on the internal market for electricity [2019] OJ L158/54–124.

examines the recently adopted revised legislative framework from the viewpoint of renewable energy grid integration. Most importantly, the article examines how the recently adopted legislative framework addresses the issue of integration of renewable energy into the grid and focuses on the key provisions concerning one of the priorities in the Clean Energy Package; that of introducing a harmonised framework for increasing system flexibility. The tools to introduce power system flexibility have not been harmonised at EU level prior to the issuance of the Clean Energy Package. In this regard, it should be noted that the flexibility needs are different in each EU Member State depending on multiple factors, such as the potential for renewable energy power production and energy mix in general, such as dispatchable generation resources and existing (cross-border) interconnections. In this context, ACER, the coordinating entity of the national regulatory authorities ('NRAs') of the EU's Member States, may play an important role in further developing and implementing EU energy law, taking into account decentralised energy markets and Renewable Energy Sources (RES) integration.[20] Under the Clean Energy Package, ACER has been assigned new competences in areas where the absence of coordination in the decisions of EU Member States with cross-border relevance could have an impact on the effective operation of the internal electricity market. Under the new ACER Regulation, ACER acquires responsibility over, inter alia, the EU Distribution System Operator (DSO) entity. In addition, ACER's involvement extends to developing network codes, guidelines and methodologies, as well as in the implementation thereof.

This chapter argues that whilst the need to support the integration of energy from renewable sources into the transmission and distribution grid is explicitly recognised in the Renewable Energy Directive, there is still a long way to go to ensure effective integration. Finally, some concluding remarks are presented.

II. An Overview of the State of Play of Renewable Energy in the EU

The state of play of renewable energy in the EU Member States is the result of a relatively stable political framework that has been implemented at a legislative level. The backbone of the EU's energy and climate policy framework is formed by the so-called 20-20-20: targets set for greenhouse gas emissions, renewable energy and energy savings.[21]

---

[20] SACM Lavrijssen, 'Independence, Regulatory Competences and the Accountability of National Regulatory Authorities in the EU' (2019) *Oil, Gas & Energy Law* 1, www.ogel.org/article.asp?key=3802.

[21] The EU has set itself three targets to be attained by 2020, these being 20% reduction of greenhouse gas emissions (from 1990 levels), increasing the share of renewable energy to 20% in the EU's energy mix and 20% improvements in energy efficiency; see Communication from the Commission to the European Parliament, the Council, the European Economic and Social Committee and the Committee of the Regions, *20 20 by 2020, Europe's Climate Change Opportunity*' COM(2008) 30 final (23 January 2008).

This policy framework is reflected in various legislative acts adopted at EU level such as the Renewable Energy Directive of 2009[22] which sets a binding target of 20 per cent final energy consumption from renewable sources by 2020,[23] which in turn has been translated into binding Member State specific national targets.[24] In June 2018, the Commission, the Parliament and the Council reached a political agreement on the revision of the Renewable Energy Directive. The new legislative framework includes a binding renewable energy target for the EU for 2030 of 32 per cent, with an upwards revision clause by 2023.[25] In the revised Renewable Energy Directive the EU level target has not been transposed into Member State specific targets, although the current 2020 national targets are maintained as a 'minimum baseline' for individual Member States from 2021 onwards.

Reaching the targets set has been dependent on Member State specific regulatory frameworks or other supporting policies. In particular, the possibility provided by the Renewable Energy Directive of 2009 for Member States to operate different kinds of support schemes to promote investments in renewable energy have been considered particularly relevant in directing steady investment flows to renewable energy. The current legislative framework – as will its successor – leaves quite a lot of leeway for Member States to adopt and apply different mechanisms to support renewable energy production.[26] This is essential in the EU on the one hand because of the Member States' varying natural endowments and climatic conditions, but on the other hand also a necessity due to the division of competences in European energy law and policy. Both 'energy' and the 'environment' are 'shared competences'[27] meaning that 'the Member States shall exercise their competence to the extent that the Union has not exercised its competence'.[28] Moreover, Article 194(1) of the Treaty on the Functioning of the EU (TFEU) states that Union energy policy shall aim to '(a) ensure the functioning of the energy market; (b) ensure security of energy supply in the Union;

---

[22] Directive 2009/28/EC of the European Parliament and of the Council of 23 April 2009 on the promotion of the use of energy from renewable sources and amending and subsequently repealing Directives 2001/77/EC and 2003/30/EC [2009] OJ L140/16–62. The legal instruments that may be adopted under EU law can be broadly characterised as Regulations and Directives. A 'directive' is a legislative act that sets out a goal that all EU Member States must achieve. However, it remains up to them to devise their own laws on how to reach these goals. Directives must always be incorporated into national law by Member States. Regulations, on the other hand, are binding legislative acts that must be applied in their entirety across the EU with no discretion for EU Member States. EU Member States are under an obligation to comply with the provisions of Directives and Regulations.

[23] In 2017 the share of renewable energy represented 17.5% of energy consumed in the EU, see Eurostat (n 2). Whether the EU will meet its 2020 goal, depends largely on the progress of Member States, see, eg, P Teffer, 'Renewables Roll-Out Needs Faster Pace to Reach EU Goal' (*EU Observer*, 12 February 2019), https://euobserver.com/energy/144149.

[24] Annex I of the Directive 2009/28/EC (n 22).

[25] For an analysis on the revised Directive, see SL Penttinen, 'The Gradual Hardening of Soft Law: The Renewable Energy Support Schemes and the Renewable Energy Directive under Revision' (2018) 22(2) *Utilities Law Review* 61–67.

[26] Lindquist (n 3) 3–12, at 8.

[27] Article 4(2)(e) and (i) TFEU.

[28] Article 2(2) TFEU.

(c) promote [...] the development of new and renewable forms of energy [...]'. Paragraph 2 of the same provision however clarifies that 'such measures shall not affect a Member State's right to determine the conditions for exploiting its energy resources, its choice between different energy sources and the general structure of its energy supply'. Consequently, the leeway of the Member States to support renewable energy production described above is necessary in order to not interfere with the Member States' right to determine their own energy mix.[29]

In this regard it should be noted that seven of the eight legislative instruments that comprise the Clean Energy for All European package were adopted solely on the basis of the aforementioned Article 194(2) TFEU. Only for Regulation 2018/1999[30] was a dual legal basis used, as it is based on Article 192(1) as well as Article 194(2) of the TFEU. Regulation 2018/1999 is therefore based on the EU's competences for the Environment as well as those for Energy. Three of the eight instruments were adopted with all 28 EU Member States voting in favour: the Electricity Market Directive,[31] the Regulation on Risk-Preparedness in the Electricity Sector[32] and Regulation 2018/1999 on the Governance of the Energy Union and Climate Action.[33] The other five instruments attracted at least 24 votes of EU Member States in favour, with only Germany abstaining from the vote on Regulation 2019/942 establishing a European Union Agency for the Cooperation of Energy Regulators.[34]

The fact that EU renewable energy policy has to cater for the factual situation in the 28 Member States adds to the complexity and makes it difficult to reach a 'one-size-fits-all' model of regulation. In addition, the renewable energy shares vary widely between Member States. While the Nordic countries have already reached their targets, led by Sweden with the highest share of renewable energy in its energy mix (54.5 per cent), some Member States are still striving to achieve their targets, while others lag far behind. For example, Germany's share of renewables in the final energy consumption rose to 16.6 per cent in 2018, bringing it close to the targeted 18 per cent by 2020. The Netherlands however had only a share

---

[29] For a more detailed discussion, see also Leonie Reins, 'The European Union's Framework for FDI Screening: Towards an Ever More Growing Competence over Energy Policy? (2019) 128 *Energy Policy* 665–72, https://doi.org/10.1016/j.enpol.2019.01.029.

[30] Regulation (EU) 2018/1999 (n 15).

[31] Council of the European Union, *Interinstitutional File:2016/0380 (COD)* (Brussels, 22 May 2019, 9582/19) available at https://eur-lex.europa.eu/legal-content/EN/TXT/PDF/?uri=CONSIL:ST_9582_2019_INIT&from=EN.

[32] Council of the European Union, *Interinstitutional File:2016/0377 (COD)* (Brussels, 22 May 2019, 9585/19) available at https://eur-lex.europa.eu/legal-content/EN/TXT/PDF/?uri=CONSIL:ST_9585_2019_INIT&from=EN.

[33] Council of the European Union, *Interinstitutional File:2016/0375 (COD)* (Brussels, 5 December 2018, 14999/18) available at https://eur-lex.europa.eu/legal-content/EN/TXT/PDF/?uri=CONSIL:ST_14999_2018_INIT&from=EN.

[34] Council of the European Union, *Interinstitutional File:2016/0378 (COD)* (Brussels, 22 May 2019, 9584/19) available at https://eur-lex.europa.eu/legal-content/EN/TXT/PDF/?uri=CONSIL:ST_9584_2019_INIT&from=EN.

of 6.6 per cent renewable energy in its energy mix in 2017, while its target for 2020 is 14 per cent.[35]

The fact that the energy mix in different EU Member States differs, inevitably also means that the requirements for 'power system flexibility' are different. The problem with regard to power system flexibility stems from the fact that two of the 'mainstreaming' renewable energy technologies in the EU are variable: wind and solar photovoltaic (solar PV). Furthermore, decentralised power production with multiple new actors connected to the grid similarly puts stress on grid balancing. Due to these developments, grid balancing – ensuring that demand and supply are always balanced in the grid – has become less predictable.

The objective of integrating energy from renewable sources into the transmission and distribution grid is explicitly recognised in the Renewable Energy Directive (Recast). Recital (60) provides (emphasis added):

> (60) There is **a need to support the integration of energy from renewable sources into the transmission and distribution grid** and the use of energy storage systems for integrated variable production of energy from renewable sources, in particular as regards the rules regulating dispatch and access to the grid. The framework for the integration of renewable electricity is provided for in other Union law relating to the **internal electricity market**. However, that framework does not include provisions on the **integration of gas from renewable sources** into the gas grid. It is therefore necessary to include such provisions in this Directive.

This objective should be attained through an enabling framework at EU level, as per Article 3(5) (emphasis added):

> 5. The Commission shall support the high ambition of Member States through an enabling framework comprising the enhanced use of Union funds, including additional funds to facilitate a just transition of carbon intensive regions towards increased shares of renewable energy, in particular financial instruments, especially for the following purposes:
>
> (a) **reducing the cost of capital for renewable energy projects**;
> (b) **developing projects and programmes for integrating renewable sources into the energy system**, for increasing flexibility of the energy system, for maintaining grid stability and for managing grid congestions;
> (c) **developing transmission and distribution grid infrastructure, intelligent networks, storage facilities and interconnections, with the objective of arriving at a 15 % electricity interconnection target by 2030**, in order to increase the technically feasible and economically affordable level of renewable energy in the electricity system;
> (d) **enhancing regional cooperation between Member States and between Member States and third countries**, through joint projects, joint support schemes and the opening of support schemes for renewable electricity to producers located in other Member States.

---

[35] Commission Communication, *Renewable Energy Progress Report* COM(2019) 225 (Brussels, 9 April 2019) at 5f.

Whilst the Renewable Energy Directive (Recast) thus explicitly mentions the need to integrate gas from renewable sources, the objective equally applies to electricity.

Currently, there are an increasing number of options available for system operators and utilities to accommodate the growing share of renewable power generation while maintaining reliability.[36] These options range from operational changes to new possibilities that become available due to technological innovations. In order to maintain grid stability under these changes and flexible conditions, a regulatory framework that allows and integrates these types of activities is essential. Whether the European legislator has managed to provide the basis for such a framework through its 'Clean Energy for All' legislative package will be discussed in the following sections.

III. From Passive to Active Grids and from Passive Consumers to Active Participants in the Energy Market

The transition to an energy system with a major share of renewables is characterised by a transition from a centralised energy system[37] to a more decentralised (also referred to as distributed or district) energy system.[38] The EU Member States' national markets have long been relying on centralised energy systems, where

---

[36] For an overview, refer to Iñigo Del Guayo Castiella, 'Support for Renewable Energies and the Creation of a Truly Competitive Electricity Market: The Case of the European Union' in Donald Zillman, Lee Godden, LeRoy Paddock, and Martha Roggenkamp (eds), *Innovation in Energy Law and Technology: Dynamic Solutions for Energy Transitions*, (Oxford University Press, 2018) 305–20 and 308–13.

[37] 'Centralised energy system' refers to large-scale energy generation units often located far from the point of use that deliver energy via a vast transmission and distribution network, see C Vezzoli et al, *Designing Sustainable Energy for All: Sustainable Product-Service System Design Applied to Distributed Renewable Energy* (Springer, 2018) 25. For more information refer also to Donna Peng and Rahamat Poudineh, 'Electricity Market Design for a Decarbonised Future: An Integrated Approach' (Oxford Institute for Energy Studies Paper EL-26, October 2017), www.oxfordenergy.org/publications/electricity-market-design-decarbonised-future-integrated-approach/?v=7516fd43adaa; and Tade Oyewunmi, 'Examining the Role of Regulation in Restructuring and Development of Gas Supply Markets in the United States and the European Union' (2017) 40(1) *Houston Journal of International Law* 191–296 (for a discussion on centralised systems in a gas-to-power context).

[38] There is no definition of the concept as such included in the new Directives. However, the new Electricity Directive defines distributed generation in Article 2(32) as 'generating installations connected to the distribution system'; the latter meaning the 'transport of electricity on high-voltage, medium-voltage and low-voltage distribution systems with a view to its delivery to customers, but does not include supply' (Article 2(28)). For the purpose of this chapter, a decentralised energy system can be characterised as being the opposite of a centralised system, meaning that it refers to small-scale energy generation units often located close to the point of use which delivers energy via low-voltage distribution lines at times directly to the consumer. On the definition of distributed generation, refer also to M Altmann et al, 'Decentralized Energy Systems' (European Parliament, June 2010) 19, www.europarl.europa.eu/document/activities/cont/201106/20110629ATT22897/20110629ATT22897EN.pdf.

large-scale electric generation facilities – often state-owned or at least closely state controlled entities – were in charge of the operation of the whole energy supply chain from production to final end-user distribution. In particular, this type of organisational and operational structure was considered to be the best option to ensure security of electricity supply.[39]

Fossil fuel-based electricity generation in particular lends itself to centralised power systems. It requires long supply lines to provide a constant supply of fuel and significant economies of scale in thermal energy production and high-voltage transmission lines to transmit and distribute the electricity through the power grid to multiple end-users. This industry structure explains to a great extent the twentieth century electricity system. Already the first efforts to liberalise the national energy markets in EU Member States' questioned this approach by introducing the idea of a breaking down or 'unbundling' of the Member States' historical monopoly companies.[40]

The introduction of renewable energy-based power generation is likely to change the traditional centralised energy systems. This is, however, nothing new. In the early days of the electrical revolution, the first power plants only supplied connected customers with what can be described as the microgrid within their vicinity. As the first electrical grids were Direct Current (DC) based, the supply voltage was limited as the distance covered between generator and consumer had to be rather short. Technical innovations that emerged later led to the introduction of the Alternating Current (AC) grids, which enabled the transportation of electricity over long distances with high voltages and lower losses. Furthermore, economies of scale in electricity generation led to an increase in the power output of the generation units. These technical developments resulted in the construction of large-scale interconnected electricity systems, supplied by large central generation plants operated by mostly vertically-integrated utilities that invested in generation of power, from traditional sources such as coal, gas and hydro, and then supplied the electrical energy through transmission and distribution networks that they own and operate.[41] Security of supply was often guaranteed by significant excess capacity.[42]

In the last decade(s), the traditional centralised energy system has been the prevalent model for the organisation of the energy markets. However, with the need to reduce greenhouse gas emissions and extend energy access as well as in response to new opportunities provided in particular by new technological

---

[39] Although it should be noted that there was a similar arrangement in place in regards to gas supply.

[40] For a historical overview of the legislative developments in the EU, see LS Reins, 'Developments in Downstream Energy Regulation in the EU: Accommodating the Changing Role of Energy Consumers' (2018) 16(3) *Oil, Gas and Energy Law Journal Special Issue on International Energy Law* 5–12, www.ogel.org/article.asp?key=3769.

[41] TJ Hammons, 'Integrating Renewable Energy Source into European Grids' (2008) 30(8) *International Journal of Electrical Power & Energy Systems* 462.

[42] See, eg, DR Helm, 'European Energy Policy' in E Jones, A Menon and S Weatherill, *The Oxford Handbook of the European Union* (Oxford University Press, 2012) 557–67.

innovations providing more flexibility to different segments of the market, a more diverse and complex system with multiple actors with changing but also new roles is slowly emerging.[43] The traditional power system and market model was not designed for decentralised market actors, eg several consumers with rooftop solar PVs now becoming potential suppliers of energy produced in excess from their distributed systems to the traditional grid.

The new legislative package is aimed to introduce tools to reach this end; 'to adapt the current market rules to new market realities'.[44] It aims to introduce a new electricity market design that is better adapted to the clean energy transition with new, in particular renewable, energy producers, and enabling full participation of consumers in the market. With the revised EU renewable energy target of 32 per cent by 2030 (with the upwards revision clause in 2023), system flexibility becomes key in integrating the variable renewable energy sources to the grid. The key flexibility options are dispatchable power plants, up-to-date (interconnected) transmission and distribution grids, demand-side management, storage technologies, as well as the integration of the power, heat and transport sectors.[45]

The Energy Union Strategy, adopted in February 2015, is based on a goal to give consumers secure, competitive and affordable energy. It emphasises five mutually supporting dimensions; boosting energy security; creating a fully integrated internal energy market; improving energy efficiency; decarbonising the economy; and supporting research, innovation and competitiveness.[46] To reach these objectives, the Energy Union calls for a 'fundamental transformation of Europe's energy system' by, inter alia, ensuring the cost-efficient integration of renewables to the energy system. Furthermore, the Energy Union Strategy envisages active consumer participation in the market by empowering consumers through providing them with information, choice and through creating flexibility to manage demand as well as supply.

In the transition to a clean energy system, conventional back-up power sources are not envisaged, although market distortions are being created by the introduction of capacity mechanisms that remunerate conventional power production facilities for their availability or 'readiness' to generate electricity in situations where energy from variable renewable energy sources such as solar and wind is inadequate due to the sun not shining enough when demand is high or the wind's seasonal patterns. As such, this contribution focuses on the regulation of flexible solutions to inflexible generation capacity, while keeping in mind the objective of transitioning towards a greener energy portfolio.

---

[43] See Del Guayo Castiella (n 36).
[44] European Commission, *Proposal for a Regulation of the European Parliament and of the Council on the internal market for electricity (recast)* COM(2016) 861 final (Brussels, 30 November 2016) 3.
[45] For an overview, see, eg, International Renewable Energy Agency (IRENA), 'Power System Flexibility for the Energy Transition, Part I: Overview for Policy Makers (*IRENA*, 2018) 24–34.
[46] Communication from the Commission (n 9).

IV. Flexible Solutions to Inflexible Generation Capacities: EU Electricity Market Reform Addressing System Flexibility

A. The Role of the Consumers

The Energy Union Strategy underlines the changing role of the consumers, whether industrial, commercial or residential. Instead of being passive users, consumers should be provided with information and possibilities to play a more active role in the energy market as 'active consumers'.[47] Currently the Member States' regulatory frameworks are not (fully) aligned to support different activities the consumers can introduce and benefit from, such as net metering for example.[48] The Clean Energy for All Europeans Package aims to introduce a harmonised level-playing field to engage consumers as active participants in the energy markets. From the flexibility point of view, consumers are envisaged to trade their flexibility and self-generated electricity in the energy markets:

> [c]onsumers are essential to achieving the flexibility necessary to adapt the electricity system to variable and distributed renewable generation ... [b]y empowering consumers and providing them with the tools to participate in the energy market more, and participate in new ways, citizens should benefit from the internal market in electricity and the Union's renewable targets should be attained.[49]

In essence, the consumers should be able to participate directly in the market, either individually or through aggregators and/or other 'community initiatives' and either by selling self-generated electricity, through self-storage or by adjusting their consumption[50] according to market signals and in return benefit from lower electricity prices or other incentive payments.[51] This requires smart metering systems as well as a dynamic electricity pricing contract that would 'reward' those consumers providing flexibility services by reducing their electricity bills. The Electricity Market Directive requires Member States to ensure that final customers

---

[47] See Article 2(6) for the definition of an active consumer. According to the definition, active customers mean a *final* customer. On the active role of the consumer in European Energy Law, see also S Lavrijssen, 'Power to the Energy Consumers' (2017) 26(6) *European Energy and Environmental Law Review* 172–86, as well as SACM Lavrijssen, 'The Right to Participation for Consumers in the Energy Transition' (2016) 25(5) *European Energy and Environmental Law Review* 152–71.

[48] See, eg, SL Penttinen and L Reins, 'System Boundaries of Nearly Zero-Energy Buildings in the European Union – Rethinking the Legal Framework for Active Consumer Participation (2019) 37(4) *Journal of Energy and Natural Resources Law* 37, 3.

[49] Preamble of the Electricity Market Directive (n 18) para 8.

[50] Direct access to retail markets is prohibited; active consumers cannot sell their excess self-generated electricity directly to end-users. Instead, this can only be done through the use of aggregators, see Article 2(14) of the Electricity Market Directive (n 18).

[51] Article 15 of the Electricity Market Directive (n 18).

who have a smart meter installed can request to conclude a dynamic electricity price contract from a) at least one supplier and b) from every supplier that has more than 200,000 final customers.[52] Real-time pricing is essential in encouraging consumers to react to price signals and for them to benefit from participating in demand-side response.

However, as the household loads are generally smaller, the Electricity Market Directive requires Member States to allow and foster participation in demand response through aggregation. What this essentially means, is to pool the smaller demand response resources together. The new electricity market design introduces the concept of 'aggregations', which means 'a function taken by a natural or legal person that combines multiple customer loads or generated electricity for sale, for purchase or auction in any electricity market'.[53] Following an agreement between customers and an aggregator, the aggregator can temporarily reduce their electricity consumption when there is high demand for electricity. The reduced consumption provides flexibility and available energy which can be in turn sold in the market by the aggregator.

While access to markets has typically been possible only for the largest industrial consumers, aggregation service providers enable the participation of consumers through demand response measures. A harmonised approach adopted at EU level is considered to be necessary given that there are still Member States in which regulatory barriers exist; demand response is either not accepted as a resource to some market segments or is still limited to specific areas within the ancillary services.[54] According to the Electricity Market Directive, final customers must be allowed to participate alongside electricity generators in all electricity markets, as well as ancillary services and capacity markets in a non-discriminatory manner.[55] This underlines the equal treatment of supply-side and demand-side resources in the evolving markets. Furthermore, the Electricity Market Directive requires Member States to allow independent aggregators, ie a market participant who is not affiliated to its customer's supplier,[56] to fulfil this role. Member States' regulatory frameworks should enable customers to enter into an agreement with an aggregator directly, without the prior consent of the energy supplier.

In addition, the Electricity Market Directive introduces a new concept of 'Citizens Energy Communities'.[57] Citizens energy communities are for example consumers living in the same neighbourhood or a building who can be engaged

---

[52] Article 11 of the Electricity Market Directive (n 18).
[53] Article 2(14) of the Electricity Market Directive (n 18).
[54] See, eg, Smart Energy Demand Coalition (SEDC), 'Explicit Demand Response in Europe: Mapping the Markets 2017' (SEDC, 2017) 198.
[55] Article 17(1-2) of the Electricity Market Directive (n 18). See also the Preamble to the Directive, para 26.
[56] Article 2(15) of the Electricity Market Directive (n 18).
[57] See Article 2(7) of the Electricity Market Directive (n 18).

in electricity generation, distribution and supply, consumption, aggregation, storage or energy efficiency services, generation of renewable electricity, charging services for electric vehicles or provide other energy services to its shareholders or members. As such, energy communities can participate in all segments of the value chain. While the Commission's original proposal introduced 'local energy communities', the EU legislators renamed them as 'citizens energy communities', underlining their more autonomous character as an element to distinguish energy communities from traditional energy companies. This is further emphasised in the rules concerning the citizens energy communities' governance, as the decision-making powers within an energy community should be limited to those members or shareholders that are not engaged in large scale commercial activity and for which the energy sector does not constitute a primary area of economic activity.

Article 16 of the Electricity Market Directive requires Member States to set up an enabling regulatory framework that ensures the open and voluntary participation in a citizens energy community, certain rights for its members and the respective roles between the citizens energy communities and DSOs, as well as certain procedural rules. In addition, Member States may provide the possibility for the energy communities in their regulatory frameworks to be open to cross-border participation as well as provide for the right to own, manage, establish, purchase or lease the distribution network in their area of operation according to the Electricity Market Directive's provisions concerning DSOs.

In addition to citizens energy communities, the revised Renewable Energy Directive lays down rules for 'renewable energy communities'. Renewable energy communities serve as a subcategory of citizens energy communities. According to Article 2(16), 'renewable energy community' means a legal entity:

a) which, in accordance with the applicable national law, is based on open and voluntary participation, is autonomous, and is effectively controlled by shareholders or members that are located in the proximity of the renewable energy projects that are owned and developed by that legal entity;
b) the shareholders or members of which are natural persons, SMEs or local authorities, including municipalities;
c) the primary purpose of which is to provide environmental, economic or social community benefits for its shareholders or members or for the local areas where it operates, rather than financial profits.

As such, while citizens energy communities encompass all activities of the value chain, renewable energy communities focus on production and supply of energy from renewable energy sources.

Member States must also ensure in their regulatory frameworks the possibility for renewable energy communities to participate, eg, in tendering procedures of available support schemes. Furthermore, the participation should not be hindered due to unnecessarily complex administrative procedures; instead, Member States should simplify administrative barriers that currently exist in many Member States.

B. Storage

The legislative framework on the electricity market in particular aims to facilitate the integration of more flexibility to the conventional grid. Energy storage offers one possibility to do this. While traditional pumped-storage hydro has been dominating the storage technologies, battery storage technologies in particular are growing rapidly especially due to declining technology costs. Prior to the Clean Energy Package, the EU legislative framework on incorporating storage in distribution grids did not exist.[58] The rules on storage contained in the Clean Energy Package aim to remove the regulatory barriers to unlock their potential in the market and provide a harmonised level-playing field for the deployment of storage in the EU Member States.[59] Article 3 of the Electricity Market Regulation underlines this by stating that all generation – including storage and demand resources – shall participate on an *equal footing* in the market. This creates both rights and obligations to market players.[60]

In particular, a level of uncertainty has surrounded the interpretation and application of certain rules on energy storage that the revised legislative framework aims to address. These are especially the rules concerning ownership rights as well as the 'nature' of energy storage – the latter in particular has proved to be a controversial issue in those Member States that employ storage technologies in the energy system.

Due to the lack of a harmonised approach adopted at the EU level concerning specifically storage, the EU Member States have thus far applied the existing legal concepts to energy storage, despite the fact that these might not be fit for purpose.[61] For example, energy storage has been viewed both as production and consumption of capacity at the same time, which has led, inter alia, to the application of double tariff use and/or taxation. There is also the question of how to classify excess renewable energy stored in gaseous forms such as hydrogen in a power-to-gas system.[62] The lack of classification and the diverse interpretation

---

[58] See also M Van Leeuwen and M Roggenkamp, 'Regulating Electricity Storage in the European Union How to Balance Technical and Legal Innovation' in Donald Zillman et al (n 36) 154–171 at 164.
[59] Ibid.
[60] For eg, while the revised legislative framework includes market rules adjusted to provide more of a level playing field for flexible resources (see, eg, Article 7(3) of the Electricity Market Regulation (n 19)), they at the same time set more stringent obligations such as balancing responsibilities for all market participants (Article 4 of the Electricity Market Regulation (n 19)). Nevertheless, in particular with regard to certain small-scale generation exceptions from the participation to the system responsibility are provided.
[61] See, eg, D Haverbeke, W Vandorpe and R Callaerts, 'Energy Demand Response and Energy Storage as Sources of Flexibility: Which Role for Regulatory Authorities?' (2019) 17(1) *Oil, Gas and Energy Law Journal Special Issue on 'Energy Law and Regulation in Low-carbon and Transitional Energy Markets'* 19, www.ogel.org/article.asp?key=3803.
[62] As was the case, for eg, in Belgium. See *ibid* 19.

among Member States has been identified as being one of the main barriers in energy storage deployment.[63]

The revised Electricity Market Directive defined, for the first time, the concept of 'energy storage' at EU level. According to the Directive, energy storage means, within the context of the electricity system,

> deferring the final use of electricity to a later moment than when it was generated or the conversion of electrical energy into a form of energy which can be stored, the storing of that energy, and the subsequent reconversion of that energy back into electrical energy or use as another energy carrier.[64]

Furthermore, an energy storage facility in the electricity system is defined as a facility where energy storage occurs.[65] The definitions are technology neutral, thus providing a wider level-playing field for all storage technologies and applications.

Article 16 of the Electricity Market Regulation addresses the double tariff use problem with regard to storage. It provides that network operators shall not discriminate against energy storage and shall not create disincentives for participation in demand response. Nevertheless, this provision applies only to network tariffs and, at least so far, the issue of possible double taxation remains unaddressed[66] as it falls under the competence of the Member States.[67] However, the Commission recently carried out the evaluation of the Energy Taxation Directive currently in force,[68] which can be expected to shed light on the taxation of storage capacity as well.[69] In some Member States, such as in Finland, the double taxation issue of energy storage has already been addressed.[70]

When it comes to the interpretation of unbundling rules with regard to storage technologies, the revised Electricity Market Directive provides as a general rule that DSOs are not allowed to own, develop, manage or operate energy storage facilities.[71] Nevertheless, derogating from the main rule is possible in a situation where in an open tender procedure, subject to review and approval by the

---

[63] See, eg, Commission Staff Working Document, *Energy Storage – the Role of Electricity* SWD(2017) 61 final (Brussels, 1 February 2017) 17; G Castagneto Gissey, PE Dodds and J Radcliffe, 'Market and Regulatory Barriers to Electrical Energy Storage Innovation' (2018) 82 *Renewable and Sustainable Energy Reviews* 788.

[64] Article 2(47) of the Electricity Market Directive (n 18).

[65] Article 2(47a) of the Electricity Market Directive (n 18).

[66] Also recently noted in the Commission Staff Working Document on the evaluation of Council Directive 2003/96/EC of 27 October 2003 *Restructuring the Community framework for the taxation of energy products and electricity* SWD(2019) 329 (Brussels, 11 September 2019) 36.

[67] See also Van Leeuwen and Roggenkamp (n 58) 154–71 at 165.

[68] Council Directive 2003/96/EC of 27 October 2003 restructuring the Community framework for the taxation of energy products and electricity [2003] OJ L283/51–70.

[69] See https://ec.europa.eu/info/consultations/evaluation-eu-framework-taxation-energy-products-and-electricity_en#about-this-consultation.

[70] 1226/2018 Laki sahkon ja eraiden polttoaineiden valmisteverosta annetun lain muuttamisesta (in Finnish only).

[71] Article 36 of the Electricity Market Directive (n 18).

regulatory authority, no other party has expressed interest in engaging in such activity, and such storage facilities are necessary for the DSOs to fulfil their obligations stemming from the Directive for the efficient, reliable and secure operation of the distribution system. Regulatory authorities must regularly reassess the potential interest of other parties to enter the market. Similar rules apply to Transmission System Operators (TSOs), provided in Article 54 of the Electricity Market Directive.

C. Sector-Coupling: Combining Electricity with Other Forms of Energy

Sector-coupling has traditionally referred only to electrification of end-use sectors such as heating and transport, whereas more recently the concept has broadened to encompass also supply-sector coupling, such as different power-to-applications. Sector-coupling can provide flexibility to the energy system by coupling energy demand for heat, fuels and mobility by using power-to-heat, power-to-gas and power-to-mobility technologies. Prior to the adoption of the Clean Energy Package, these types of cross-sector energy combinations were not addressed at the EU level.

However, the revised regulatory framework cannot be characterised as being too ambitious in regulating such cross-sector activities.

First, the new market design addresses the rules concerning electric vehicles. Article 33 of the Electricity Directive merely notes that Member States must 'provide the necessary regulatory framework to facilitate the connection of publicly accessible and private recharging points to the distribution networks'. In line with the principles of unbundling of integrated companies in the energy sector, and in order to prevent a monopoly of distribution networks and charging points by DSOs, DSOs are prevented from owning, developing, managing or operating recharging points for electric vehicles, with the exception of DSOs' own, private recharging points. Furthermore, the revised Energy Performance of Buildings Directive[72] aims to facilitate the roll-out of electro-mobility by pre-equipping buildings with electric vehicle infrastructure. Nevertheless, the development remains rather modest in this respect, as the Energy Performance of Buildings Directive only requires the installation of at least one charge point with regard to new large, non-residential buildings and non-residential buildings undergoing major renovation.[73] With regard to existing buildings, Member States are competent to decide the minimum number of recharging points for all non-residential

---

[72] Energy Performance of Buildings Directive (n 12).
[73] Article 8 of the Energy Performance of Buildings Directive (n 12).

buildings with more than 20 parking spaces, but only as of 2025. Similarly, according to Article 8, Member States must

> provide for measures in order to simplify the deployment of recharging points in new and existing residential and non-residential buildings and address possible regulatory barriers, including permitting and approval procedures, without prejudice to the property and tenancy law of the Member States.

As can be clearly seen, a lot of discretion is left for Member States in implementing the measures.

Second, the revised Renewable Energy Directive provides a first-ever target for renewable heating and cooling in Europe. According to Article 23, Member States must increase their proportion of renewable energy-based heat by 1.3 per cent each year up to 2030. Waste heat and cold can contribute up to 40 per cent to the target, whereas district heating and cooling will have to contribute to this sub-target by at least a one percentage point annual average increase in renewables. Renewable electricity used in heating does not, however, count towards the indicative target of heating and cooling.

The target – as well as other related provisions on renewable heating and cooling – reflect a compromise between the legislators and Member States. For example converting district heating from mostly coal- or gas powered production to renewables is an area where Member States have very different potentials. Nevertheless, the target is envisaged to spur more efforts to this particular sector that consumes roughly half of the EU's energy, especially in the winter season. A tool to this end is the National Energy and Climate Plans that Member States are required to draft under the Energy Union Governance Framework.

Despite the provisions being similarly modest in respect of heating and cooling, heating and cooling has been characterised as being 'the Cinderella of energy policy, so having it written into legislation like this will only be good'.[74]

D. The Role of the DSOs and System Operators' Enhanced Cooperation

The envisaged shift from the traditional centralised energy system to a more distributed or decentralised energy system with multiple actors, increasing share of renewable energy sources and flexibility of demand requires an enhanced coordination between market parties in order to ensure reliable energy supply.

---

[74] S Morgan, 'IEA Analysts: A Heating and Cooling Target "Could Make a Big Difference"' (*Euractiv*, 27 March 2018), www.euractiv.com/section/energy/interview/iea-analyst-a-heating-and-cooling-target-could-make-a-big-difference/.

Three distinct areas of action have been identified that are traditionally considered to impact the activities of distribution system operators. These are:

1) core activities, such as planning, developing and maintaining the network, connecting the users to the grid, managing technical data and network losses;
2) prohibited activities such as electricity generation; and
3) certain 'grey areas of action' such as infrastructure for electric vehicles and ownership of flexibility assets.[75]

Both the Electricity Market Directive and the Electricity Market Regulation aim to strengthen and/or clarify the different activities of DSOs, in particular given the evolving and more decentralised system structure.

It is acknowledged that allowing DSOs to manage some of the challenges that are associated with variable electricity generation locally, could lead to reduction of network costs.[76] Nevertheless, given that many of the DSOs are part of vertically integrated companies active in the supply side; the regulatory framework should address DSOs' neutrality in the new activities DSOs can and/or should participate in. In particular, Article 32 of the Electricity Market Directive provides for incentives for the use of flexibility in distribution networks. According to this provision, Member States must adopt a regulatory framework that not only allows but also incentivises DSOs to procure flexibility services, including congestion management in their area, in order to improve efficiencies in the operation and development of the distribution system:

> [i]n particular, regulatory frameworks shall ensure that distribution system operators to procure services from resources such as distributed generation, demand response or storage and consider energy efficiency measures, when such services cost-effectively supplant the need to upgrade or replace electricity capacity and which support the efficient and secure operation of the distribution system.[77]

By continuing to underline the equal role of flexibility resources in addition to traditional supply side resources, the Electricity Market Regulation states that disproportionate grid infrastructure should not be built where other alternatives provide a better economic option. Such options include storage and demand response measures.

Further, the Clean Energy Package abolished the priority access rules which were previously included in Article 16 of the Renewable Energy Directive. In the past this measure was introduced as an assurance to 'generators of electricity from renewable energy sources that they will be able to sell and transmit the electricity from renewable energy sources in accordance with connection rules at all times, whenever the source becomes available'.[78] The Electricity Market Regulation

---

[75] See, eg, Council of European Energy Regulators, 'The Future Role of DSOs, a CEER Conclusions Paper' (13 July 2015) 10.
[76] See European Commission (n 44) 5.
[77] Article 32(1) of the Electricity Market Directive (n 18).
[78] Recital 60 of the Renewable Energy Directive (n 22).

provides that the dispatching of all power-generating facilities shall generally be market-based (Article 12(1)) and only a 'light' priority system is included under Article 12(2-6) and Article 16 for small renewable installations at least until 2026. In particular, this should enable feeding the (excess) electricity into the grid by community-owned, small-scale generation and thus facilitate more decentralisation and consumer empowerment.[79]

With regard to the first two categories in the adaptation to the decentralisation of the power system, the DSOs' roles should be strengthened, whereas the respective role(s) of the DSOs in terms of the grey areas of action, where DSOs may participate in the activities but where there might be concerns over the extent of such participation should in turn be clarified. In this respect, a need for regulatory control and/or unbundling has been identified.[80] This is addressed in Article 35 of the Electricity Market Directive that requires both electric vehicle infrastructure and storage to be operated by 'at least' legally unbundled entities.

V. Conclusion

The Clean Energy for All Europeans legislative package is groundbreaking from the viewpoint that it clearly aims to facilitate the shift from the traditional, centralised energy system to a decentralised, low-carbon energy system within a regulatory framework. One instrument that is part of the package, the Renewable Energy Directive, explicitly recognises the need to support the integration of energy from renewable sources into the transmission and distribution grid. While it should be noted that many provisions are more or less general due to the need to find a level of consensus among Member States and relevant institutions during the decision-making, the package nevertheless addresses several issues that the 'new market reality' that has emerged since the adoption of the Third Energy Package has prompted. This in turn provides (legal) certainty for investors and new market players when engaging in new activities. In this respect, the revised regulatory framework creates a level-playing field for the transition to a more decentralised model, in particular by attributing value to demand-side activities as well.

In order to encourage customers to a behavioural change and incentivise demand-side measures providing flexibility to the system, the rules on dynamic pricing schemes and market signals are a step forward given that in many Member States dynamic pricing is still lacking. Citizens energy communities should be granted the right to similar 'regulatory treatment' as that accorded to larger, 'more traditional' market actors. Furthermore, the activities energy communities can introduce should be supported within national legislative frameworks.

---

[79] Article 11 of the Electricity Market Regulation (n 19).
[80] Council of European Energy Regulators (n 75).

The provisions should be transposed into national legislation with certain exceptions by 2021. The Clean Energy Package is underlined as promising a 'new deal' for consumers and 'clean energy for all Europeans'. The shift from the traditional centralised power system to a more decentralised power system is reflected in the package, and in this respect marks a new era in the EU energy landscape, also from the regulatory perspective. Nevertheless, while the Clean Energy Package is successful in updating the outdated rules of the Third Energy Package to reflect the changes taking place in the power sector, it is still only the first step. Much of the success of the Clean Energy Package, in particular in removing the regulatory barriers that have been hampering the realisation of a more consumer-centric energy (electricity) market, depends on the effective implementation of the rules included in the Clean Energy Package to national laws and regulations.

12

Regulating Energy Supply in China

PHILIP ANDREWS-SPEED

I. Introduction

Since the early years of this century, China has made astonishing progress in decarbonising and generally cleaning up its energy sector. After the Communist Party took power in 1949, the country relied heavily on its domestic resources of coal to fuel its industrialisation and economic development. The share of coal in primary energy supply was consistently about 75 per cent. Between 1980 and 1996, annual coal consumption doubled from 600 million tonnes to more than 1,300 million tonnes. Following the 1997 Asian Financial Crisis, the economy picked up again, taking annual coal consumption to 3,000 million tonnes in 2007. China by 2007 accounted for 45 per cent of total global consumption of coal and was clearly the largest emitter of carbon dioxide emissions, well ahead of the USA.[1]

By this time, China's government was already battling with a domestic energy supply crisis as well as rising air pollution. It put in place tough measures to enhance energy efficiency, but also realised that renewable energy of all types could help address the combined challenges of security of energy supply, carbon emission reduction and air pollution mitigation. Further, the leadership recognised that it could turn this crisis into an opportunity for the country to become a major international player in the clean energy industries.

In addressing these challenges, China has built the world's largest installed capacity of hydroelectricity, wind power and solar energy, as well as the fastest growing fleet of nuclear power plants. The Government has combined massive investment in clean energy infrastructure with measures to constrain the production and consumption of coal and to drive down energy intensity. The simultaneous slowing and rebalancing of the national economy led to a temporary peaking of coal consumption and carbon emissions over the years 2013 and 2014. Though coal consumption has since picked up, the country's carbon dioxide emissions from energy are expected to reach a peak by 2030. Furthermore, Chinese manufacturers

---

[1] BP, 'Statistical Review of World Energy 2019' (June 2019), available at www.bp.com/en/global/corporate/energy-economics/statistical-review-of-world-energy.html.

have taken the world by storm to become the largest suppliers of renewable energy equipment, notably solar photovoltaic (PV) equipment. This rapid expansion of manufacturing capacity has been a key factor in driving down the cost of solar PV equipment across the world.

China's legal traditions date back more than 2,000 years and have diverse sources.[2] The result is a legal regime that is quite distinct from those of a European heritage. The combination of a unique legal system and a one-party authoritarian polity results in distinctive governance practices that apply to the energy sector as much as to other fields. The aim of this chapter is to examine the role of law and other policy instruments in the ambitious programme to decarbonise China's energy sector. Section II provides an overview of the political, legal and economic dimensions of state governance in China. Section III identifies the general features of energy sector governance, describing the actors and structures, the energy policy paradigm, the roles of plans and laws, the range of policy instruments, and the challenges of policy implementation. The final section examines in more detail three fields of policy related to decarbonisation: energy efficiency, renewable energy and the substitution of coal by natural gas.

II. The Political, Legal and Economic Dimensions of Governance

A. The Political Context

The formal sources of political power and authority in China lie principally in the Communist Party of China (CPC) and, secondarily, in the Government and the National People's Congress (NPC). The CPC stands at the core of the political system and President Xi Jinping has further enhanced its authority over policy-making since he took office as Party Chairman in 2012. Three bodies stand at the apex of the CPC: the Central Committee with about 200 members, the Politburo with 25 members and the Politburo Standing Committee of just seven individuals.[3]

Central Leading Groups (sometimes referred to as Leading Small Groups) are key coordinating bodies that exist in both the CPC and the Government. The former are more powerful. Xi Jinping has been heading at least five CPC Leading Groups, in addition to his roles as CPC General Secretary, President of the People's Republic of China and Chair of the two Central Military Commissions and of the National Security Committee. The most important of these Leading Groups for the economy is the Central Leading Group for Comprehensively

---

[2] W Chang, *In Search of the Way. Legal Philosophy of the Classic Chinese Thinkers* (EdinburghEdinburgh University Press, 2016) 510.
[3] C Li, *Chinese Politics in the Xi Jinping Era. Reassessing Collective Leadership* (Washington DC, Brookings Institution Press, 2016) 42.

Deepening Reforms. This includes the Premier, two or three members of the Politburo Standing Committee, a number of others from the Politburo and selected Ministers. In March 2018, this Group was recast as a Central Leading Committee, thus enhancing its status. One of the six groups reporting to this Committee addresses economic reform and ecological civilisation. On the Government side, one of the Leading Groups is focused on climate change and is chaired by Premier Li Keqiang.

Although formally a unitary state, de facto authority lies at three main levels of government: central, provincial or municipal, and city or county. Prefectures exist between provincial and county levels but have little authority. Likewise, townships and villages lie beneath the county level. The State Council lies at the apex of the three and resembles a cabinet. All ministers and chairs of national commissions are members of the State Council. However, real authority lies with the Standing Committee of the State Council, which has a membership of ten. The Premier chairs the Standing Committee, which comprises the Vice-Premiers and State Councillors. The number of ministries and commissions has declined over time from 52 in 1981 to 26 in 2018. Nevertheless, the multiplicity of ministries and levels of government results in a complex matrix that is the source of the term 'fragmented authoritarianism', devised to describe the nature of government in China.[4]

It was with the aim of rationalising this matrix muddle that President Xi pushed through a set of radical reforms at the First Session of the 19th NPC in March 2018. These measures had four main effects:

1. The number of ministerial level organisations declined by eight as previously dispersed responsibilities were consolidated.
2. A number of ministries were given enhanced authority over their offices at sub-national level.
3. A new market regulator was created to regulate product quality and safety, and to reduce market entry barriers, including the power of monopolies.
4. A new National Supervision Commission was established, reporting to the CPC, to oversee the performance of government agencies.

Through these changes, the national leadership hopes to gain greater control over national governance.

According to the Constitution, the NPC is the highest organ of state power. The nearly 3,000 delegates are mainly CPC members chosen through restricted election processes at different levels of government across the country.[5] The full NPC meets once a year and is supported during the intervening periods by a standing committee and a permanent staff. Although the NPC has extensive formal

---

[4] KG Lieberthal and M Oksenberg, *Policy Making in China. Leaders, Structures and* Processes (Princeton, Princeton University Press, 1988).
[5] Li (n 3) 46.

powers over law-making, the State Council together with relevant ministries plays the leading role in preparing initial drafts of bills.[6] The State Council also oversees the inter-agency bargaining that can delay a bill for several years.[7]

B. The Traditions and Evolution of the Legal System

China's legal system has several unique features that distinguish it from those in other countries, whether they be authoritarian regimes with rule by law, western democracies practising the rule of law, or other types of mixed or immature legal systems.[8] The approach to law throughout the more than 2,000 years of Imperial China arose from an amalgamation of ideas from several schools of thought, among which the Legalist and Confucian schools were prominent.[9] The result was a system of law-making, laws, regulations and courts that was directed at promoting and protecting the interests of the state. The law provided no formal constraints on the ruler and no protection for the individual. Instead, the legal system viewed the family as the basic unit of society, not the individual. No separation of powers existed, and the legal system was largely a political and administrative device to be managed by the government bureaucracy in support of the state. It was not seen as a reflection of the moral order in society, as in much of Western law, neither did it aim to achieve an abstract goal of social justice. A separate moral code with a Confucian origin existed and was enforced by society itself.[10]

The aim of law was purely pragmatic. State law existed for the Government itself and the role of the general legal code was to protect the state from threats to its authority. Civil law addressed only a limited range of issues relating to property, contract and inheritance. Citizens could gain access to the law, but this involved cost and risk, and might well have required bribes. Because of this, citizens preferred the private ordering of disputes rather than submitting to the courts.[11] Knowledge and intellectual property were considered as public goods and were not subject to any law.[12]

---

[6] JM Otto, 'Conclusion: A Comparativist's Outlook on Law-Making in China' in JM Otto, MV Polak, J Chen and Y Li (eds) *Law-Making in the People's Republic of China* (The Hague, Kluwer Law International, 2000).

[7] MS Tanner, *The Politics of Lawmaking in China. Institutions, Processes, and Democratic Prospects* (Oxford, Clarendon Press, 1999) 127.

[8] MM Siems, 'Varieties of Legal Systems: Towards a New Global Taxonomy' (2016) 12 *Journal of Institutional Economics* 579.

[9] Chang (n 2).

[10] F Michael, 'The Role of the Law' in William T Liu (ed), *Chinese Society under Communism: A Reader* (New York, John Wiley, 1967); J Chen, *Chinese Law. Towards an Understanding of Chinese Law, Its Nature and Development* (The Hague, Kluwer Law International, 1999) 16; W Li, 'China's Road to Rechtsstaat: Rule of Law, Constitutional Democracy and Institutional Change' in X Huang (ed), *The Institutional Dynamics of China's Great Transformation* (London, Routledge, 2012); Chang (n 2) 487.

[11] Michael, *ibid*; R Peerenboom, *China's Long March toward the Rule of Law* (Cambridge, Cambridge University Press, 2002) 38; J Teufel Dreyer, *China's Political System. Modernization and Tradition* (New York, Longman, 2010) 37.

[12] Chang (n 2) 485.

The last years of the Qing dynasty saw the start of an attempt to reform the legal system and to adopt attributes of systems from abroad, especially Germany and Japan. The Nationalists, who preferred a more traditional approach to the role of law, halted these efforts. The first 30 years of Communist rule was characterised by an almost complete lack of interest in the law.[13]

Since the introduction of economic reforms in the late 1970s, the Government has taken great strides to draft new laws and regulations, to create a new cadre of professional lawyers and judges, and to spread understanding of the importance of the law. In pushing forward these reforms, China has drawn extensively on international examples, especially in the realm of economic law.[14] Law-making through the National People's Congress has become more transparent and involves seeking suggestions from the public by placing drafts on the Internet. Further, the Government has passed a number of administrative laws that seek to enhance the accountability, transparency and effectiveness of government itself, though the results vary greatly across the country.[15]

Constraints to the pace and development of legal reform include the close relationship between the courts and both Communist Party and local governments, for the courts are directly responsible to the Government and Party at the level at which they operate.[16] More fundamentally, the overall approach to the law continues to bear a striking resemblance to that of Imperial times. The law is still seen as an instrument of Government and the CPC, to be deployed to retain power, maintain social order and promote economic development.[17]

In terms of the role of law in economic activity, two important features deserve emphasising. First, the law in China is notorious for failing to provide formally secure property rights and government agencies at all levels of government exercise their right to transfer rights with little due process. Within this context, many enterprises have been very successful at enhancing the degree of protection of their property rights through the building of networks and the use of personal connections involving both public and private sectors.[18] Second, citizens, enterprises and

---

[13] Chen (n 10) 36; Peerenboom (n 11) 43.
[14] WC Jones, 'Trying to Understand the Current Chinese Legal System' in CS Hsu (ed), *Understanding China's Legal System. Essays in Honor of Jerome A. Cohen* (New York, New York University Press, 2003); S Zhu, 'Reforming State Institutions: Privatizing the Lawyers' System in J Howell (ed), *Governance in China* (Lanham, Rowman & Littlefield, 2004); DC Clarke, 'Legislating for a Market Economy' (2007) 191 *The China Quarterly* 567; J Garrick, 'Conclusion: Law and Policy for 'Opening Up' [*kaifang*] and 'Going Out' [*zou chu qu*]' in J Garrick (ed), *Law and Policy for China's Market Socialism* (London, Routledge, 2012).
[15] J Horsley, 'The Rule of Law: Pushing the Limits of Party Rule' in J Fewsmith (ed), *China Today, China Tomorrow. Domestic Politics, Economy, and Society* (Lanham, Rowman & Littlefield, 2010).
[16] DC Clarke, 'The Chinese Legal System since 1995. Steady Development and Striking Continuities' (2007) *The China Quarterly* 555; BL Liebman, 'China's Courts: Restricted Reform' (2007) 191 *The China Quarterly* 620.
[17] F Zhang, *The Institutional Evolution of China. Government vs Market* (Cheltenham, Edward Elgar, 2018) 238.
[18] DL Wank, 'Producing Property Rights: Strategies, Networks, and Efficiency in Urban China's Nonstate Firms' in JC Oi and AG Walder (eds), *Property Rights and Economic Reform in China*

public agencies continue to prefer to settle civil disputes through private ordering rather than going through the court system.[19]

Since coming to power, Xi Jinping has emphasised the need to reform the legal system and enhance the role of the courts, thereby building an economy based on the rule of law.[20] Key measures have been to reduce the influence of local governments over local courts by centralising authority at provincial levels and to build on earlier efforts to professionalise the judiciary.[21] The motives for the reforms are clearly instrumental and directed at underpinning economic development and social stability, not least by seeking to enforce property rights and protect citizens from abusive behaviour by local government officials.[22] Further, the supremacy of the Communist Party over the legal system and the judiciary has been maintained[23] and may even be enhanced by the new National Supervision Commission. In this way, the leadership has ensured that the legal system remains a servant of the regime.[24]

C. Economic Governance

China's economy has undergone an almost complete transformation since Deng Xiaoping began his strategy of progressive liberalisation in 1978. Before that time, the central Government, through the State Planning Commission, planned, or rather claimed to plan, all production and consumption. By 2013, its successor, the National Development and Reform Commission (NDRC) retained direct control over few aspects of the economy, either because the activity was no longer subject to planning or approval, or because authority had been delegated to lower levels of government.

Despite the widespread decline of state ownership of industrial enterprises, the Government has kept control of a small number of sectors that it perceives as having strategic economic importance.[25] These include banking,

---

(Stanford, Stanford University Press, 1999); B Krug and H Hendrischke, 'China's Institutional Architecture: A New Institutional Economics and Organization Theory Perspective on the Links between Local Governance and Local Enterprises' ERIM Report Series (2008) *Research in Management*, papers.ssrn.com/sol3/papers.cfm?abstract_id=1131026.

[19] R Peerenboom, *China Modernizes. Threat to the West, or Model for the Rest?* (New York, Oxford University Press, 2007) 228.

[20] C Minzner, 'Legal Reform in the Xi Jinping Era' (2015) 20 *Asia Policy* 4.

[21] AHF Li, 'Centralisation of Power in the Pursuit of Law-Based Governance. Legal Reform in China under the Xi Administration' (2016) 2 *China Perspectives* 63.

[22] J DeLisle, 'Law in the China Model 2.0: Legality, Developmentalism and Leninism under Xi Jinping' (2017) 103 *Journal of Contemporary China* 68.

[23] DL Yang, 'China's Troubled Quest for Order: Leadership, Organization and the Contradictions of the Stability Maintenance Regime' (2017) 103 *Journal of Contemporary China* 35.

[24] BL Liebman, 'Legal Reform: China's Law-Stability Paradox' (2014) 143 (2) *Daedalus, The Journal of the American Academy of Arts & Sciences* 96.

[25] C Li, *China's Centralized Industrial Order. Industrial Reform and the Rise of Centrally Controlled Big Business* (London, Routledge, 2015).

energy, telecommunications, mining, metallurgy, chemicals and railways. In the 1990s, the Government defined these as pillar industries, not just for the domestic economy but also as potential international players. A substantial majority of enterprises in these sectors remain in total or majority state ownership, at either central or local government levels. The steady reform of the state-owned enterprises (SOEs) has allowed them to grow in terms of asset value and revenues as well as presence on the international stage. At the same time, their origins as government ministries have permitted them to retain a close relationship with the Government. In some cases, SOE Chairmen and Chief Executives Officers (CEOs) have been promoted into government.[26] However, the costs of SOE dominance have included the squeezing out of private and foreign enterprises in these industries, abuse of market power, corruption, highly variable profitability, rising indebtedness and a low level of innovation.[27]

Technological innovation has become an increasingly important part of economic policy as the Government seeks to upgrade the nation's domestic technology and industrial production base. The Medium and Long-Term Plan for the Development of Science and Technology (2006–2020)[28] expounded this strategy, which was reinforced by the Made in China 2025 policy issued by the State Council in 2015. These directives have been supported by sector-specific plans and generous state funding.

The ability of the Government to provide generous financial support to favoured entities and activities derives from the continuing state control of banking. Recent examples include the massive surge of money that flowed into the economy after the global financial crisis in 2008, financial support for state-owned enterprises, generous funding of technological research and development, and a range of financial instruments to assist the internationalisation of Chinese companies.

Despite the prevalence of state ownership in certain sectors, progressive decentralisation of authority, combined with liberalisation and privatisation in other sectors have created a regulatory challenge. Not only does the Government often have weak control over policy implementation, but the regulation of such matters as service standards, product quality and environmental and safety performance also frequently encounters severe constraints.

From these observations and the previous section, it is evident that dramatic changes have taken place since 1978 through the co-evolution of politics and economics.[29] By the early years of this century, this had resulted in widening freedoms in both arenas. However, Xi Jinping has reversed these trends. Not only

---

[26] W Leutert, 'The Political Mobility of China's Central State-Owned Enterprise Leaders' (2018) 233 *The China Quarterly* 1.
[27] H Yu, 'The Ascendancy of State-owned Enterprises in China' (2014) 85 *Journal of Contemporary China* 161.
[28] For a summary in English, see www.itu.int/en/ITU-D/Cybersecurity/Documents/National_Strategies_Repository/China_2006.pdf.
[29] L Chen and B Naughton, 'A Dynamic China Model: The Co-Evolution of Economics and Politics in China' (2017) 103 *Journal of Contemporary China* 18.

has he concentrated political power in the Party elite, but he has also re-established the primacy of the state over the market.[30]

III. Overview of Energy Sector Governance

The governance of the energy sector today has its origins in the Marxist-Leninist system put in place by Mao after 1949. At that time, the state took full control of the sector through the planning of production and consumption, ownership of the main energy producing and consuming enterprises, and control over producer and consumer prices.[31] The processes of enterprise privatisation and market liberalisation in the energy sector have been slow and hesitant, with decisive steps being taken only in the period 1997–2003[32] and more recently under Xi Jinping.

A. Actors and Structures

As in many countries, the number of actors involved in China's energy supply chain is very large, but most of them are linked to the state either directly or indirectly. In the days of economic planning, the old State Planning Commission was responsible for planning energy supply and demand, as well as investment, and for setting all energy prices. As of 2019, the NDRC, in part through its subordinate National Energy Administration (NEA), continues to produce five-year energy plans, though it no longer controls supply and demand. It retains oversight of investment in the energy sector, though considerable authority has been delegated to the provinces. It still sets some energy prices, and retains the role of formulating and overseeing the implementation of key energy policy initiatives.

Several other agencies have also been involved in the governance of the energy sector, notably the Ministries of Finance, of Industry and Information Technology, of Commerce, of Land and Resources, of Water Resources, and of the Environment, and the State-owned Assets Supervision and Administration Commission. A National Energy Commission was created in 2010 but is deemed to have been largely ineffective.[33] Some level of coordination is provided by Leading Groups within the State Council that are chaired by the Prime Minister of the day: the Leading Group on Energy was chaired by Wen Jiabao and its

---

[30] Y Zheng and Y Huang, *Market in State. The Political Economy of Domination in China* (Cambridge, Cambridge University Press, 2018) 425; Zhang (n 17) 249.

[31] P Andrews-Speed, *Energy Policy and Regulation in the People's Republic of China* (London, Kluwer Law International, 2004) 61; T Kambara and C Howe, *China and the Global Energy Crisis. Development and Prospects for China's Oil and Natural Gas* (Cheltenham, Edward Elgar, 2007) 10.

[32] P Andrews-Speed, *The Governance of Energy in China. Transition to a Low-Carbon Economy* (Basingstoke, Palgrave Macmillan, 2012) 160.

[33] N Grunberg, 'Revisiting Fragmented Authoritarianism in China's Central Energy Administration' in KE Brodsgaard (ed), *Chinese Politics as Fragmented Authoritarianism. Earthquakes, Energy and Environment* (London, Routledge, 2017).

successor, the Leading Group on Climate Change, Energy Saving and Emission Reduction, is chaired by Li Keqiang. Despite these moves and the growing role of the Communist Party's Leading Small Groups, the governance of energy remains fragmented.[34] At the same time, there is little separation of policy-making, design, planning and implementation.[35] The NDRC, the NEA, and these various agencies all have equivalent bureaus at provincial and lower levels of government that are charged with adopting, adapting and implementing central government policies.

The government reforms announced in March 2018 appear to have slightly reduced the central role of the NDRC and NEA in the governance of the energy sector (Figure 1). The creation of a new Ministry of Ecology and Environment is particularly significant as it has centralised from several different agencies functional responsibility for a variety of environmental issues. The new Ministry of Natural Resources combines the roles of the previous Ministries of Land and Resources and of Water Resources, and has authority over the extraction of oil, gas and coal, and over water and land rights.

Figure 1 Simplified Scheme Showing the Main Energy-Related Organisations and Enterprises at Central Government Level after March 2018

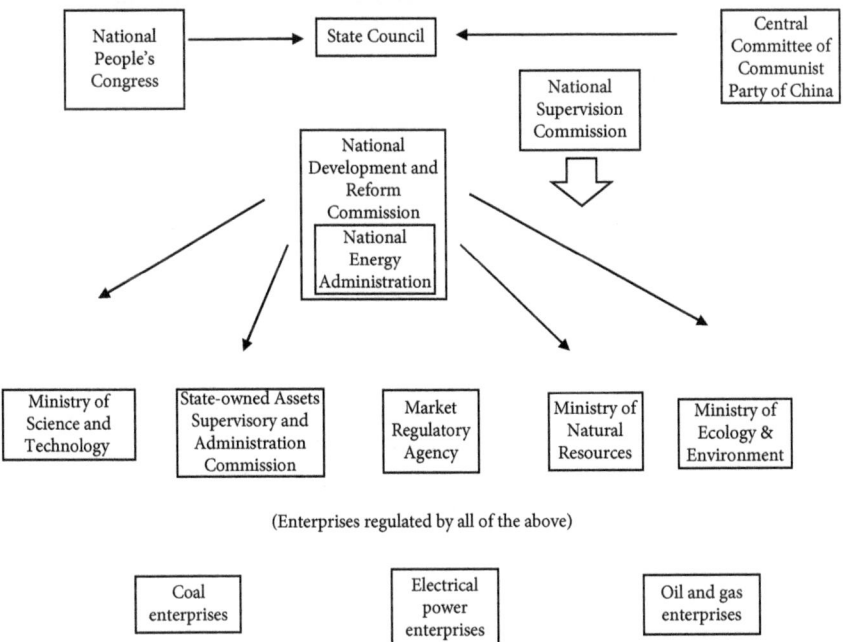

Note: All organisations have local bureaus or subsidiaries at provincial, prefecture and county levels.

---

[34] *Ibid.*
[35] MR Davidson, F Kahrl, and VJ Karplus, 'Towards a Political Economy Framework for Wind Power: Does China Break the Mould?' in D Arent, C Arndt, M Miller, F Tarp and O Zinaman (eds), *The Political Economy of Clean Energy Transitions* (Oxford, Oxford University Press, 2017) 250–70.

The SOEs in the coal, electricity and oil and gas industries are key economic actors in the energy sector. Each of these industries originated as central government ministries with bureaus at the various lower levels of government. Gradual structural reforms initiated in the 1980s led to a progressive process of corporatisation, structural unbundling and adjustment, forced mergers, commercialisation and partial privatisation. Despite listing through initial public offerings, these enterprises retain close links with government and the Party at either central or local government levels.[36] In the past, the Chairmen and CEOs of the largest energy SOEs could aspire to senior government or party positions.[37] However, the new CPC Central Committee announced in October 2017 for the first time did not include any CEOs of SOEs.

The end-users of energy include industrial and commercial enterprises, the agricultural sector, as well as households and individuals. The historic importance of the energy-intensive, heavy industries, such as steel, non-ferrous metals, chemicals and cement, has meant that the Government has traditionally taken into account their interests, most notably by keeping their energy tariffs at relatively low levels. This has changed since 2004 because of efforts to reduce national energy intensity. Nevertheless, the Government has continued to pander to the interests of the selected energy-intensive industries, the agricultural sector and households by keeping electricity tariffs low, despite the introduction of tiered tariffs for households. A new document issued by the NDRC in July 2018 indicated that this approach may be about to change.[38] However, the panned changes may be delayed in the light of the need to support the economy, food production and employment in response to COVID-19.

B. Energy Policy Paradigm

Security of energy supply and self-sufficiency have been and continue to be key components of the policy paradigm for the sector, along with the desire to provide widespread access to energy at affordable prices. This explains the strong and enduring influence of the central Government over the energy sector. Today, this is expressed through state ownership of most of the large enterprises involved in the production and transformation of energy as well as the continuing control of some energy prices. The push for self-sufficiency and the abundance of the resource endowment has supported the long-standing dominance of coal in the primary energy mix, and, in the past, the prevalence of small-scale coal mines across the country to provide local self-sufficiency. The abundance of cheap domestic coal

---

[36] Andrews-Speed (n 32) 173.
[37] Leutert (n 26).
[38] National Development and Reform Commission, 'Opinions on Innovation and Improvement of the Price Mechanisms for Promoting Green Development' (21 June 2018), www.ndrc.gov.cn/zcfb/gfxwj/201806/t20180629_891044.html (in Chinese).

resources allowed the Government to set energy tariffs at low levels, especially for energy-intensive industries and households.[39]

In the past, the Government's strategy for supply security was directed mainly at raising supply rather than constraining demand and promoting efficiency.[40] At the same time, inadequate attention was paid to the environmental consequences of energy production, transformation and end use, notably air and water pollution, and greenhouse gas emissions.[41] Since the beginning of the twenty-first century, the emphasis has steadily shifted to constraining the rise of energy demand and greenhouse gases and reducing pollution from the energy sector. Since 2005, the environment has become an increasingly important topic of public debate and focus of official pronouncements as both global climate change and domestic environmental degradation became seen as threats to national security and societal wellbeing.[42] The leadership now fully recognises the need for China to undergo a transition to a low-carbon energy economy and to reduce all forms of pollution relating to energy. This has been expressed through slogans such as 'Scientific Development' and 'Ecological Civilisation'.

The idea that market forces should play a decisive role in the energy sector remains highly contentious and has still to be accepted by China's leadership. Nevertheless, since the mid-1980s, the Government has taken incremental steps to introduce market forces to the pricing of certain forms of energy, notably coal and, later, oil, as well as gradually subjecting the state-owned energy companies to greater commercial pressure. The last period of major reform took place between 1997 and 2003, when the entire energy sector was restructured, along with the relevant government departments.[43]

Between 2004 and 2013, the Government made only incremental adjustments as the key priorities were, in succession, to alleviate a massive shortage of energy and to mitigate the effects of the global financial crisis.[44] With these two challenges addressed, the Xi Jinping's administration has revitalised the programme of energy sector reform. These measures have been most pronounced in the electricity industry where competition is being introduced in both generation and retail. In addition, the Government is planning to launch a national carbon trading market that will initially involve only the electricity industry. Further planned moves include the unbundling of the vertically-integrated oil and gas industry and enforcement of third-party access.

---

[39] Andrews-Speed (n 31) 267.
[40] Kambara and Howe (n 31) 17; Andrews-Speed (n 32) 20.
[41] E Economy, *The River Runs Black. The Environmental Challenge to China's Future* (Ithaca, NY, Cornell University Press, 2004); CO Delang, *China's Air Pollution Problems* (London, Routledge, 2016).
[42] J Nyman and J Zeng, 'Securitization in Chinese Climate and Energy Politics' (2006) 7 *WIRES Climate Change* 301; M Schroder, 'Supporting China's Green Leap Forward: Political Strategies for China's Climate Policies' in I Bailey and H Compston (eds), *Feeling the Heat. The Politics of Climate Policy in Rapidly Industrializing Countries* (Basingstoke, Palgrave, 2012).
[43] Andrews-Speed (n 31) 169.
[44] Andrews-Speed (n 32) 171.

C. Plans and Laws: The Sources of Energy Policy

Energy policy derives from economic policy, and the key sources of government policy on the economy are the Five-Year Plans for National Economic and Social Development. These broad plans build on the goals for each sector and then form the basis for ministries and agencies to draw up detailed sector plans. Whilst economic reform has been a key focus for recent Five-Year Plans, the text tends to contain vague and contradictory statements. For example, Chapter 45 of the Twelfth Five-Year Plan (2011–2015)[45] called for public ownership to continue playing a leading role in the economy, whilst also promoting the non-public sector. Chapter 49 addressed very briefly the need for natural resource prices to reflect supply and demand scarcity and environmental cost, but with very little guidance on how such a difficult challenge is to be addressed. The Thirteenth Five-Year Plan (2016–2020)[46] reiterated the need to do more to ensure that resource prices reflect market conditions, undertake market reforms of key sectors and ensure that only the most efficient enterprises survive. Yet, these exhortations were made in the context of a socialist market economy under the leadership of the Communist Party.

The sector-specific plans, such as those for energy, contain a large amount of detail and numerous quantitative targets, but generally fail to provide an underlying philosophy or framework that could provide overall coherence as well guidance as to how objectives are to be reached. In addition to the Five-Year Plans for Energy Development, equivalent plans are also being produced for related or subordinate domains such as technology and renewable energy. The NDRC and other ministries also occasionally publish White Papers and Medium- and Long-Term Plans.

A key factor in the rapid growth of China's clean energy sector has been its support for research, development and manufacturing. The Medium and Long-Term Plan for Science and Technology (2006–2020) gave top priority to developing technologies related to energy. Consistent with this plan, the Eleventh Five-Year Plan for Science and Technology (2006–2010) listed energy technologies as a key area. Specifically, this plan highlighted three key clean energy technologies, namely, high power wind turbine units and energy conservation technologies for buildings. The importance of clean and efficient energy technologies of all kinds was reinforced by succeeding plans directed solely at the energy sector: Twelfth Five-Year Plan for Energy Science and Technology Development (2011–2015) and the Thirteenth Five-Year Plan for Energy Technology Innovation (2016–2020). The publication of the latter coincided with the Made in China 2025 strategy.

The formal legal framework governing the energy sector is characterised by laws addressing specific aspects of the sector. Whilst being broadly consistent with

---

[45] For an unofficial English translation, see https://cbi.typepad.com/china_direct/2011/05/chinas-twelfth-five-new-plan-the-full-english-version.html.
[46] For official English translation, see https://en.ndrc.gov.cn/policyrelease_8233/201612/P020191101482242850325.pdf.

the Five-Year Plans, they tend to be promulgated at times of strategic change or when there is a need to reinforce a specific policy priority such as energy conservation or renewable energy. The laws themselves are generally quite vague and tend to indicate general policy directions. They provide for neither rights nor obligations. Further, the rigour and timing of implementation of a law are highly variable. Examples of laws relevant to the energy sector include:

- The Mineral Resources Law of 1986, amended in 1996.
- The Electric Power Law of 1995.
- The Coal Law of 1996.
- The Energy Conservation Law of 1997, amended in 2007.
- The Renewable Energy Law of 2005, amended in 2009.
- The Pricing Law of 1997.
- The Environmental Protection Law of 1989, amended in 2014.
- The Environmental Protection Tax Law of 2016.
- The Nuclear Safety Law of 2017.

In addition, a draft Energy Law was drawn up in 2007 and a draft Law on Addressing Climate Change in 2012. As of 2018, the NPC has enacted neither law, though it issued a new draft Energy Law for public comment in April 2020.[47] The need for an Atomic Energy Law was first identified in 1984, a few years after the decision to develop a civil nuclear power programme. Although the law was included in the National People's Congress Standing Committee Legislative Plan (2013–2018),[48] it is still not yet enacted. Also notable is the absence of any law governing the oil and gas sectors, other than the Mineral Resources Law. Likewise, there is no law governing the recent introduction of market mechanisms in the electricity industry, nor the planned national carbon market.

D. Energy Policy Instruments and Implementation

The plans and laws set the overall policy direction and targets for the energy sector, and are supported by numerous regulations, rules, guidelines and decrees issued variously by Ministries, Commissions and the State Council, as well as by local governments. Many executive orders are issued without any governing law, drawing their authority from a Five-Year Plan or from the need to address an emerging problem.

---

[47] X Chen, L Zeng and Y Lu, 'New Draft Law Puts Clean Power at the Forefront of Chin'as Energy Policy' (*Caixin*, 13 April 2020), www.caixinglobal.com/2020-04-13/new-draft-law-puts-clean-power-at-the-forefront-of-chinas-energy-policy-101542115.html.
[48] See https://npcobserver.com/12th-npcsc-legislative-plan/.

The policy instruments deployed by China's Government in the energy sector can be classified using the scheme of Howlett and Ramesh:[49]

- Nodality: for example, through information or exhortation.
- Authority: for example, through command and control regulation, or standard setting.
- Treasure: for example, through grants, loans, subsidies, user charges or taxes.
- Organisation: for example, through direct provision by government or state-owned enterprises, or by the creation of markets.

The Chinese Government's choice of policy instruments for the energy sector reflects the prevailing policy paradigm and the current state-dominated character of the sector. The preference has long been to combine authority with treasure. Authority takes the form of obligations and targets directed at different levels of government, at an entire industry or at companies within a particular energy-producing or energy-consuming industry. Standard setting has been applied to energy appliances and pollutant emissions, among others. Treasure, in the form of grants and loans from the state, has played a central role in promoting technological advance in the nation's energy industries. User charges and taxes have been deployed only rarely.

As described above, the production and transformation of energy continues to be dominated by enterprises owned by the state at national or local levels. Most energy-intensive industries such as steel, chemicals and cement are also state-owned. State ownership allows the Government to use the enterprises for non-commercial objectives such as the direct provision of preferred forms of energy or other commodities. For these reasons, the Government has introduced market mechanisms to the energy sector only gradually. Through its control of the press and other media, the Government is able to provide information and exhortation on the pressing issues of the day, notably on air pollution in recent years.

A large proportion of the resulting energy policy initiatives have had certain features in common: they have drawn mainly on well-tested administrative instruments; they have preferred major investment in new capacity and thus required substantial finance from the Government or state-owned banks; and they have tended to favour the incumbent, large SOEs rather than smaller enterprises.

Policy implementation in China's energy sector progresses smoothly if there is a relative absence of powerful opposition from parties which might lose from such policies[50] and when funds are available from state banks to support the massive level of investment required. In contrast, policies resulting in short-term economic losses for parties that have a political voice or can undermine policy

---

[49] M Howlett and M Ramesh, *Studying Public Policy. Policy Cycles and Policy Subsystems*, 2nd edn (Oxford, Oxford University Press, 2003).

[50] B Kong, 'China's Energy Decision-Making: Becoming More Like the United States' (2009) 62 *Journal of Contemporary China* 789.

implementation require a major political campaign by the Government to achieve even a modest degree of success.

A longstanding feature of governance in China is the ability of local governments and energy companies, acting separately or in partnership, to undermine central government policies that threaten their short-term interests. Their methods include ignoring or countermanding orders from above, as well as false reporting and feigned compliance, all practices that date back centuries.[51] This requires intense vigilance from the central Government in its efforts to monitor and evaluate policy implementation, a task rendered particularly challenging by the large size and diversity of the country. Despite the growing effectiveness of the press, the courts, non-governmental organisations and individual citizens, the CPC and the Government continue to depend on inspection teams dispatched from Beijing or lower levels of government to bring to light abuses and failures.[52]

The central Government has shown itself to be relatively effective at policy learning and nimble at reacting to policy failures, at addressing risks arising from current policies, and at adjusting policies in response to ongoing experiments. In its haste to launch new initiatives, the Government sometimes creates unanticipated problems. Yet it has been able to modify these policies when they encounter strong resistance or generate undesirable side-effects. Efforts to encourage the preferential dispatch of renewable energy continue to be obstructed by local governments. The latest initiative involves imposing renewable energy obligations on provinces. The rush to convert heating systems in north-east China from coal to gas in the winter of 2017/18 caused some communities to lack sufficient heating as the gas infrastructure could not be delivered until long after the coal-based systems had been demolished. As a result of these and other difficulties, the push to promote clean energy and abate pollution continues to test the patience and resourcefulness of the central Government.

IV. The Regulation of Energy in Practice

A. Energy Efficiency

Energy efficiency and energy conservation have formed a significant component of China's national energy policy since the late 1970s. National energy intensity declined by about 40 per cent during the 1980s. This was a result of a combination of energy quotas, rising energy prices, improved technologies and the gradual marketisation of the economy. The decline of national energy intensity continued

---

[51] LW Pye, *The Spirit of Chinese Politics* (Cambridge Massachusetts, Harvard University Press, 1992) 237.
[52] JH Chung, 'China's Local Governance in Perspective: Instruments of Central Government Control' (2015) 75 *The China Journal* 38.

throughout the 1990s, supported by the continued reform of energy prices and the promulgation of an Energy Conservation Law in 1997.[53] This Law included a number of important provisions relating to investment planning, efficient energy use, technical standards and labelling. However, there was never much follow through on this law at the time.[54] Instead, it has been argued that efficiency improvements were stimulated as much by efforts to improve overall productivity in response to the gradual marketisation of the economy, including the higher energy prices, as by the specific energy efficiency policies.[55]

The years 2002 to 2005 were marked by a boom in economic growth and a rise in the output of heavy industry. Energy intensity rose and the surge in demand for energy was not matched by the supply. Therefore, large areas of the country faced shortages of electrical power and oil products. The electricity supply crisis triggered a succession of measures to curb energy consumption across the economy, with a particular emphasis on heavy industry including the power sector. These included the Medium and Long-Term Energy Conservation Plan (2004),[56] the Top-1000 Energy Consuming Enterprises Programme (2006) and the National Programme for Medium and Long-Term Scientific and Technological Development (2006–2010). These supported an overall objective of reducing national energy intensity by 20 per cent between 2005 and 2010 and by a further 16 per cent by 2015. Further, these measures aimed at reducing the intensity of carbon dioxide emissions by 40–45 per cent between 2005 and 2020. This concerted effort to manage energy consumption more effectively was the first time that provisions of the 1997 Energy Conservation Law were implemented robustly.

This Energy Conservation Plan and subsequent documents set targets for energy consumption per unit of output for the years 2010 and 2020 for individual energy intensive industries and for all provincial and lower level governments. Energy intensity became a measure of performance for the CEOs of SOEs and for government officials. The Plan also provided proposals for technological, process or management improvements needed to achieve these targets. A further key measure was to close outdated and inefficient plants. By 2010, standards for major energy using appliances were to be raised to international levels, and the systems for policy, regulation and technical support for energy conservation were to be dramatically improved. Many of the same targets, objectives and policies appear both in the Eleventh Five-Year Plan for Energy Development (2006–2010) and in the China National Climate Change Programme, both published in 2007. In addition, a revised Energy Conservation Law was issued in October 2007.

---

[53] M Yang, Z Hu and J Yuan, 'The Recent History and Successes of China's Energy Efficiency Policy' (2016) 5 *Wires Energy & Environment* 715.

[54] M Wang, 'China's Plight in Moving Towards a Low-Carbon Future: Analysis from the Perspective of Energy Law' in DN Zilman, C Redgwell, YO Omorogbe and LK Barrera-Hernandez (eds), *Beyond the Carbon Economy. Energy Law in Transition* (Oxford, Oxford University Press, 2008).

[55] K Fisher-Vanden, GH Jefferson, H Liu and Q Tao, 'What is Driving China's Decline in Energy Intensity?' (2004) 26 *Resource and Energy Economics* 77.

[56] For unofficial English translation, see http://fourfact.com/images/uploads/China_Energy_Saving_Plan.pdf.

These key policy and legal documents were supported by a significant increase in financial support. Investment in energy efficiency by the central Government was planned to rise to 21.3 billion RMB in 2007, which was 13 times the level in 2006.[57] Total government expenditure on clean energy and energy efficiency during the Eleventh Five-Year Plan period (2006–2010) is estimated to have been between two and three trillion RMB (US$ 300–450 billion).[58]

The Twelfth Five-Year Plan for Energy Development (2011–2015) continued these strategies with a new set of administrative measures that encompassed a wider range of energy users. This involved the Ten Thousand Enterprise Programme that covered about 16,000 enterprises. At the same time, the energy intensity reduction target for the period was reduced from 20 per cent to 16 per cent, reflecting greater understanding of the challenges faced in the previous five years.[59] The energy consumption per unit of gross domestic product (GDP) decreased by 18.4 per cent between 2011 and 2015, and the intensity of carbon dioxide emissions fell by more than 20 per cent, exceeding the planned target. The subsequent Thirteenth Five-Year Plan for Energy Development (2016–2020) set a target of 15 per cent for the reduction of energy intensity and a cap on total energy consumption of five billion tonnes of coal equivalent. These twin goals relied on the continuation and intensification of existing policy instruments, but with progressively wider application.

The mix of policy instruments deployed by the Government has drawn on the historical experience from when the energy sector was subject to central planning. Even though the role of planning had diminished substantially by the early 2000s, the success of the measures introduced in the Eleventh Five-Year Plan (2006–2010) can be attributed to a combination of the authority and treasure directed at a relatively small number of targeted enterprises. In other words, the traditional policy instruments were successful in that part of the energy sector that is dominated by the state and has changed the least. As the number and diversity of targeted industrial entities has increased since 2010, the efficacy of these administrative instruments has declined.[60] Longstanding challenges persist in the building sector where the effectiveness of energy service companies remains weak.[61] Finally, efforts to constrain household energy use will require a more complex combination of policy instruments.[62]

---

[57] Xinhua News Agency, 'China Earmarks 1.33 bn Dollars for Energy Efficiency, Discharge Reduction' (*Xinhua News Agency Beijing*, 27 July 2007).

[58] SO Ladislaw and J Nakano, *China – Leader or Laggard on the Path to a Secure, Low-Carbon Energy Future* (Washington DC, Center for Strategic and International Studies, 2011).

[59] K Lo and MY Wang, 'Energy Conservation in China's Twelfth Five-Year Plan Period: Continuation or Paradigm Shift' (2013) 18 *Renewable and Sustainable Energy Reviews* 499.

[60] F Zhang and K Huang, 'The Role of Government in Industrial Energy Conservation in China: Lessons From the Iron and Steel Industry' (2017) 39 *Energy for Sustainable Development* 101.

[61] M Zhang, M Wang, W Jin and C Xia-Bauer, 'Managing Energy Efficiency of Buildings in China: A Survey of Energy Performance Contracting (EPC) in Building Sector' (2018) 114 *Energy Policy* 13.

[62] P Andrews-Speed and G Ma, 'Household Energy Saving in China: The Challenge of Changing Behaviour' in B Su and E Thomson (eds), *China's Energy Efficiency and Conservation. Household Behaviour, Legislation, Regional Analysis and Impacts* (Singapore, Springer, 2016).

B. Wind and Solar Energy

In contrast to the case of energy efficiency, formal law seems to have played a significant role in the promotion of renewable energy. China is endowed with rich wind and solar energy resources, but most are concentrated in the north and west of the country, far from the main centres of demand in the east. The initial motivations for supporting the development of wind and solar energy in the 1980s were rural electrification and poverty alleviation.[63] The growing recognition of the health consequences of coal combustion led to environmental concerns becoming a more significant driver in the 1990s. By the early years of the twenty-first century, further impetus came from the desire to develop domestic manufacturing capacity in wind and solar energy.[64] As a result, national research and development agencies started to direct significant funding to wind energy and solar PV manufacturing from 2001 onwards.[65]

The period from 2004 saw a sustained effort by the central Government to promote the deployment of wind and solar PV infrastructure. The motivations included boosting total electricity supply, increasing the share of clean energy, encouraging technological development and exports, and supporting local development and employment. The Renewable Energy Law of 2005 marked a turning point for China's renewable energy industry. The new law was reinforced by a number of subsequent policies such as the establishment of a Special Fund for Renewable Energy Development, successive five-year plans for renewable energy development with targets for capacity, the Medium and Long-Term Plan for Renewable Energy Development (2007)[66] and an update of the Catalogue of Chinese High-Technology Products for Export.[67] Together, these and other policies provided a wide range of incentives for actors along the full supply chains for wind energy and solar PV.[68]

The Renewable Energy Law of 2005 was remarkable in regards to the speed with which it was passed.[69] This suggests strong leadership from the State Council and very little opposition from government ministries. The law introduced the

---

[63] J Pan, W Peng, M Li, X Wu, L Wan, H Zerriffi, B Elias, C Zhang and D Victor, 'Rural Electrification in China 1950–2004. Historical Forces and Key Driving Processes', Program on Energy and Sustainable Development, Working Paper No 60 (Stanford University, 2006).

[64] S Zhang, X Zhao, P Andrews-Speed and Y He, 'The Development Trajectories of Wind Power and Solar PV Power in China: A Comparison and Policy Recommendations (2013) 26 *Renewable and Sustainable Energy Reviews* 322.

[65] P Andrews-Speed and S Zhang, 'Renewable Energy Finance in China' in CW Donovan (ed), *Renewable Energy Finance* (London, Imperial College Press, 2015).

[66] For unofficial English translation, see www.china.org.cn/e-news/news070904-11.htm.

[67] Zhang et al (n 64).

[68] Zhang et al (n 64); Andrews-Speed and Zhang (n 65).

[69] 'China Passes Renewable Energy Law' (*Renewable Energy World*, 9 March 2005), www.renewable-energyworld.com/articles/2005/03/china-passes-renewable-energy-law-23531.html.

concept of mandatory market share for renewable energy for that applied to any generating company with more than 5 gigawatt (GW) of total capacity. The law obliged grid companies to provide wind power and solar PV access to the grid, not just connection but also dispatch and ancillary services. The initial scheme for on-grid tariffs allowed the tariffs to set by the NDRC or through concession bidding. This approach was modified by the revised Renewable Energy Law of 2009, which introduced feed-in-tariffs for the first time. Finally, this period saw an increasing use of the Clean Development Mechanism (CDM), as China was an Annex 1 Party to the Kyoto Protocol. The CDM had been applied to 568 wind power projects in China by the end of 2010.[70]

Together these measures made China a world leader in the deployment and use of wind and solar energy. A combination of subsidies and protectionist measures also allowed it to build a prominent position in the manufacturing output of these technologies. Installed capacity of wind power rose from 2.1 GW in 2006 to 185 GW by the end of 2018, representing about 33 per cent of total installed capacity of wind power around the world. The introduction of feed-in-tariffs for solar PV permitted by the Renewable Energy Law in 2009 boosted the installed capacity from 1.0 GW in 2010 to 175 GW by 2018, some 36 per cent of global capacity. As a result, the share of wind and solar energy in China's electricity mix rose from 0.4 per cent in 2008 to 6.6 per cent in 2018.[71]

The sources of this success lay in the relatively good alignment of interests among the small number of powerful actors involved, and the alignment of policies supporting such investment. However, this approach has been less successful in other respects. Undue haste has led to problems for intermittent renewable energy projects. Poor planning and coordination as well as a failure to address the legitimate interests of the grid company have caused delays in grid connection and poor siting of some projects.[72] Intense price competition and weak government oversight of technical standards has undermined the performance of wind power projects. At the same time, the extraordinarily rapid rate of construction of utility-scale solar PV and wind power projects triggered by excessively generous subsidies resulted in the funding mechanism going into deficit.[73]

The greatest challenges have arisen from the inability of the power system to integrate intermittent renewable energy. In addition to effective planning and coordination at the construction stage, this requires flexibility of infrastructure and institutions. Both forms of flexibility are weak in China's power sector. In the case of infrastructure, the share of gas-fired generation and pumped-storage hydro

---

[70] Z Zhang, *Energy and Environmental Policy in China. Towards a Low-Carbon Economy* (Cheltenham, Edward Elgar, 2011) 132.
[71] BP, *Statistical Review* (n 1).
[72] Davidson et al (n 35).
[73] H Zhang, 'Cao Renxian: The Renewable Energy Subsidy Gap is over 100 billion Yuan' (12 March 2018). http://finance.jrj.com.cn/2018/03/12043124223546.shtml (in Chinese).

is too low, and the incentives for coal-fired plants to invest in greater flexibility are weak.[74] The sources of institutional inflexibility are numerous and include the system for allocating hours to generators, the relatively small balancing areas, the underdeveloped regime for ancillary services, and the immature systems for demand-side response. These deficiencies have been aggravated by the poor alignment of local interests that has resulted in some local governments supporting the dispatch of thermal plants over intermittent renewable energy.[75]

In its endeavour to address the underuse of renewable energy capacity, the Government has taken a number of major policy initiatives in recent years. Prominent among these are the pilot carbon trading markets[76] and the gradual introduction of market mechanisms to electricity supply, including for ancillary services.[77] In 2018, the NDRC launched a scheme that switched the renewable energy obligation from the generators to the grid companies and power retailers, though the details were only finalised in 2019.[78]

C. Substituting Gas for Coal

Natural gas has a potentially important role to play in China's clean energy strategy. In replacing coal, it would reduce both air pollution and carbon emissions. The Government's success in raising the status of natural gas from being a marginal fuel to providing a significant share of the nation's primary energy supply owes much to direct provision by the national oil companies (NOCs) and city gas companies.

Until the mid-1990s, natural gas played little part in China's national energy policy. The discovery of large reserves in north-central and north-western parts of the country triggered a radical change in policy, with the growing need to reduce air pollution. The Government charged the NOCs with developing the production capacity and investing in pipeline capacity. At the same time, city gas companies had to modernise and increase their distribution networks. Exploration boosted China's estimated recoverable reserves of natural gas from 1.4 tcm in 2000 to 6.1 tcm in 2018, and annual production reached 161 bcm in 2018. Annual consumption

---

[74] S Zhang, P Andrews-Speed and P Perera, 'The Evolving Policy Regime for Pumped Storage Hydroelectricity in China: A Key Support for Low-Carbon Energy' (2015) 150 *Applied Energy* 15; S Yin, S Zhang, P Andrews-Speed and W Li, 'Economic and Environmental Effects of Peak Regulation Using Coal-Fired Power for the Priority Dispatch of Wind Power in China' (2017) 162 *Journal of Cleaner Production* 361.

[75] Davidson et al (n 35).

[76] S Zhang, Y Jiao and W Chen, 'Demand-Side Management in the Context of China's Ongoing Power Sector Reform' (2017) 100 *Energy Policy* 1.

[77] M Dupuy, *China Power Sector Reform: Key Issues for the World's Largest Power Sector* (Beijing, Regulatory Assistance Project, 2016).

[78] National Development and Reform Commission, 'Notice Establishing a Mandatory Renewable Energy Consumption Mechanism' (*NDRC Energy*, 10 May 2019) 807 (in Chinese), www.ndrc.gov.cn/gzdt/201905/t20190515_936194.html.

of natural gas has risen more than tenfold since 1999 to 283 bcm in 2017, with a surge of 43 bcm in 2018 alone.[79]

In order to fill the gap between domestic supply and demand, China has had to import gas supplies through pipelines and as liquefied natural gas (LNG). Total imports of natural gas have risen from 1 bcm in 2006 to 121 bcm in 2018. All this has required sustained investment in infrastructure for the production, long-distance transportation and import of natural gas by the NOCs. Despite this rapid rise in consumption, natural gas only contributed 7.4 per cent of primary energy consumption in 2018 on account of the sustained growth of total energy demand, and only 3.0 per cent of electricity generation.[80]

The top priority from the late 1990s was the provision of city gas for residential and commercial use.[81] Successive five-year plans set targets for the production of natural gas. Seeking to boost consumption, the NDRC issued a Natural Gas Utilization Policy in 2012 that encouraged the use of gas for power generation and in industry, and identified the need to construct natural gas storage facilities with emergency and peaking functions. The most recent plan, the Thirteenth Five-Year Plan for Energy Development (2016–2020) set the target of boosting the share of gas in total primary energy consumption from 5.9 per cent in 2015 to 10 per cent in 2020.

Despite this policy drive, efforts to raise the domestic production and consumption of natural gas has faced two major institutional challenges, namely pricing and the strong market position of the NOCs. Little of China's domestic gas resources are cheap to deliver to the end-user, because of either difficult geology or remote location. The growing production of shale gas and coalbed methane will only add to these costs. The price of imported gas depends on the contractual terms and can fluctuate with market conditions. Nevertheless, little if any of this domestic or imported gas can compete with coal on the basis of price.[82]

In order to stimulate the production of gas and the construction of pipelines, the wellhead price and the transmission tariffs must be sufficiently high to encourage investment by the NOCs. At the same time, end-user prices must be sufficiently low to encourage use in the commercial, industrial and power sectors, and to be acceptable to household users. Despite repeated reforms, the pricing system remains unsatisfactory.[83] At the same time, the NOCs' dominance of the natural gas market through their control of most of the reserves and pipelines constrains the emergence of new actors and supplies. As of July 2019, plans are in

---

[79] BP, *Statistical Review* (n 1).
[80] BP, *Statistical Review* (n 1).
[81] T Houser and B Bo, *Charting China's Natural Gas Future* (James A. Baker III Institute for Public Policy, Rice University, 2013).
[82] Y Qin, F Tong, G Yang and D Mauzerall, 'Challenges of Using Natural Gas as a Carbon Mitigation Option in China' (2018) 117 *Energy Policy* 457.
[83] X Dong, G Pi, Z Ma and C Dong, 'The Reform of the Natural Gas Industry in the PR of China' (2017) 73 *Renewable and Sustainable Energy Reviews* 582.

progress to separate the pipelines into a new company and to enforce third-party access.

The challenge of promoting natural gas use was illustrated in the months leading into the winter of 2017/2018. This was a critical time for assessing the achievements of the National Action Plan on Air Pollution Control issued in 2013 that set a number of quantitative targets for the end of 2017. In late August 2017, the Ministry of Environmental Protection was obliged to issue a 143-page plan for the urgent reduction of air emissions across 28 major cities in preparation for the coming winter heating season.

A key element of this strategy was to accelerate the conversion of industrial plants and household appliances from coal to natural gas in northern China. The Government aimed to convert the heating systems of up to four million households to natural gas or electricity in 2017. At the same time, some 44,000 coal-fired boilers were to be scrapped and the sale of coal in the selected towns and villages banned. However, the construction of the necessary pipelines and storage tanks to support this dash for gas was an immense task with a cost of billions of RMB and was not completed in time.[84]

Although meeting with considerable success, the impetuous nature of this short-term gasification plan produced undesirable consequences. First, although natural gas is more convenient and cleaner for families, it is more expensive than coal. Northern China is home to large numbers of low-income families and the high price of natural gas led many households to reduce their use of heating. To alleviate such hardship, the Government provided a certain quantity of gas at subsidised prices. Second, many coal-fired heating systems that were decommissioned had not been replaced by gas-fired ones by the onset of winter, leaving households without any heating at all.

V. Conclusions

The distinctiveness of China's political and legal regimes results in a style of governance in which the role of formal law is not always pre-eminent. This is especially true of the energy sector, which is dominated by state interests due to its perceived strategic importance. Civil law was weakly developed in traditional Chinese law, including in the economic sphere. Instead, the principal role of law was to protect state interests. This only started to change after 1978 when the country began to open up its economy and gradually introduce market forces. The Government took systematic steps to build a body of modern economic law, drawing in part on western models. Nevertheless, the role of formal laws remains ambiguous, not

---

[84] D Sandalow, A Losz, and S Yang, 'A Natural Gas Giant Awakens: China's Quest for Blue Skies Shapes Global Markets' (*China Natural Gas Commentary*, Columbia SIPA, Center on Global Energy Policy, 2018).

least because most laws fail to provide for unambiguous rights and obligations. Even if they do, implementation is subject to bureaucratic or political discretion.

Laws have rarely played a central role in driving forward energy policy. Rather, policies are laid out in five-year plans of different types, and underpinned by regulations, decrees and other executive orders. These instruments then cascade down to lower levels of government or to SOEs. Applying the terminology of Howlett and Ramesh,[85] the main policy instrument deployed is that of direct authority, which may be supported treasure of different types. On occasions, direct provision is supplied by state-owned enterprises.

The three strands of energy policy described in this chapter illustrate the varying role laws can play. In the case of energy efficiency, the Energy Conservation Law of 1997 was overtaken by events. The 1997 Asian Crisis led to an economic slowdown and a surplus of energy supply over demand. As a result, the leadership exerted little effort in implementing the law. The domestic energy supply crisis that began in 2003 triggered a raft of administrative measures to constrain energy demand, but these were only encapsulated in a revised Energy Conservation Law in 2007. In contrast, the Renewable Energy Law of 2005 stimulated a surge in the deployment of wind energy infrastructure. The revised Renewable Energy Law of 2009 achieved the same for solar energy. Finally, the measures to enforce the switch from coal to gas are not supported by any formal law at all.

[85] Howlett and Ramesh (n 49).

13

Energy Law and Regulation in Nigeria – Prospects for Reliable Electricity Supply

TADE OYEWUNMI AND IVIE EHANMO

I. Introduction

This chapter provides an overview of the regulatory framework governing the Nigerian Electricity Supply Industry (NESI) with particular emphasis on the evolution of the on-grid and off-grid electricity systems and the increasing role of renewable energy in a developing economy that is equally rich in hydrocarbons and thus rely considerably on natural gas for electricity generation. It goes on to discuss the challenges with on-grid electricity supply and the increasing role of off-grid power supply in ensuring reliable access to electricity supply.

Nigeria is the most populous country in Africa and currently has the biggest economy on the continent based on gross domestic product (GDP). Nigeria's petroleum industry has been the mainstay of its economy since 1970s.[1] Revenues from oil and gas exports typically constitute about 75 per cent of government revenue and about 90–95 per cent of total export revenue annually. There has been sustained economic growth and an annual average real GDP growth of about seven per per cent within the past ten years, primarily due to developments in the non-oil sector.[2] The primary energy resources in Nigeria include crude oil and natural gas, coal, tar sands, etc. There are also renewable energy resources such as hydro, fuelwood, solar, wind and biomass. According to the Energy Commission of Nigeria (ECN), fuelwood and charcoal account for 60 per cent of the total primary energy consumption (TPEC) as at 2017, largely due to the constraints for low-income consumers in rural areas to afford or gain reliable

---

[1] Tade Oyewunmi, 'Nigeria: Energy Policy' in Günter Tiess, Tapan Majumder and Peter Cameron (eds), *Encyclopaedia of Mineral and Energy Policy* (Springer, November 2017) DOI: https://doi.org/10.1007/978-3-642-40871-7_158-1.

[2] *Ibid.* The services industries such as telecommunications and financial services contributed about 57% of the growth, while manufacturing and agriculture contributed about 9% and 21% respectively. See also the African Development Bank Group (AfDB), 'Country Notes on Nigeria' in *African Economic Outlook 2020*, 173 at www.afdb.org/en/documents/african-economic-outlook-2020.

access to substitutes such as kerosene, cooking gas and grid-based electricity.[3] The US Energy Information Administration (EIA) estimates the TPEC level in Nigeria as of 2012 to be about 4.5 quadrillion British thermal units (Btu). In this regard, traditional biomass and waste (ie wood, charcoal, manure and crop residues) accounted for 80 per cent of the TPEC, oil was 13 per cent, while natural gas and hydro were estimated to account for six per cent and one per cent respectively. Thus, the country is an example of where the evolving global energy transitions could have an impact as a resource-rich but developing economy. However, such a transition to less carbon-intensive and efficient energy systems needs to be fair, just, affordable and pragmatic.

Section II of this chapter provides a brief overview of the NESI and the evolution of the institutional framework, while section III discusses the outlook for the nation's energy mix, including specific issues relating to generation, transmission and distribution of electricity in Nigeria. It highlights the relevant efforts being made to resolve the issues. Section IV considers the role played by the relevant regulatory institutions. Section V highlights the state of the grid-based energy supply networks in Nigeria, while section VI examines the evolving role for off-grid energy systems, in particular renewables. Section VII considers the future outlook and recent development aimed at securing energy supply from both the grid-based and off-grid systems to guarantee reliable access to electricity and energy supply.

II. Overview and Regulatory Developments in the Nigerian Power Sector

The first power-generating plant in Nigeria dates back to 1886 and in 1946 the Nigerian Government established an arm of the Public Works Department dealing with electricity supply in Lagos, while the Electricity Corporation of Nigeria (ECN) was established in 1951.[4] Generation, transmission and distribution gradually evolved as a public service and managed by the Government. In 1962, the Niger Dams Authority (NDA) was established which had the responsibility of constructing dams and developing the hydropower potentials of the country. In 1972, the ECN and NDA were merged to form the National Electric Power Authority (NEPA) with a monopoly over electricity generation, transmission

---

[3] *Ibid.* See also the International Energy Agency (IEA), *Nigeria Energy Outlook*, (IEA, Publications, 2019) at www.iea.org/articles/nigeria-energy-outlook. IEA notes that provided that reliability and supply improve, the grid could become the optimal solution to provide almost 60% of people with access to electricity. Also, Nigeria could achieve universal access by stepping up efforts towards off-grid solutions, connections to distribution gas networks and LPG in the main cities, and to improved cookstoves in rural areas for clean cooking.
[4] The Nigerian Electricity Regulatory Commission, *Power Generation in Nigeria*, (2020) at https://nerc.gov.ng/index.php/home/nesi/403-generation.

and supply.⁵ The gradual liberalisation of the sector began in the late 1980s and the first Independent Power projects started to develop in the 1990s. The National Electric Power Policy (NEPP), 2001 aimed at the fostering liberalisation, competition and private-sector-led growth in the power sector and was consolidated by the enactment of the Electric Power Sector Reform Act (EPSRA) 2005. It laid the foundation for the privatisation and unbundling of NEPA, which was corporatised and unbundled into six generation companies, 11 distribution companies and a national transmission company. The successor generation and distribution companies were eventually privatised in 2013 based on the provisions of NEPP and EPSRA 2005.⁶ In line with the provisions of EPSRA, the Nigerian Electricity Regulatory Commission (NERC) was established as the principal independent regulatory authority for the sector. Since then, NERC has issued several regulations, guidelines and orders to govern the activities of operators within various segments of the electricity market.⁷

III. The Energy Supply Systems

A. The Energy Mix in Nigeria

Sources of energy can be grouped as renewable or non-renewable, in which the non-renewable fuel sources for power generation include natural gas, coal and liquid fuels from crude oil.⁸ Some of the renewable fuel sources include solar, wind, biomass, geothermal, wave/tidal and hydro energy.⁹ The generation of electricity in Nigeria is dominated by two sources – non-renewable thermal (natural gas) and renewable (hydropower).

Electricity generation for Nigeria's grid is largely thermal-based, which means that about 80 per cent of the power plants in Nigeria are fuelled by gas.¹⁰ Currently, electricity generated from solar, wind, biomass and geothermal are not fed into the

---

⁵ Tade Oyewunmi, 'International Best Practices and Participation in a Private Sector Driven Electricity Industry in Nigeria: Recent Regulatory Developments' (2013) (8) *International Energy Law Review* 306–14.
⁶ *Ibid*; the Bureau of Public Enterprises/CPCS (2013) The Nigeria Electricity Privatisation Project. See sections 1–10 of EPSRA. The privatisation involved a process of divestiture and concession in which 51% equity was taken up by private investors in the distribution companies and thermal generation companies on the one hand and the award of a 20–25 year concession in two hydropower generation companies on the other. The Transmission Company of Nigeria is still owned by the Government, but managed by a private company under a management contract.
⁷ Tade Oyewunmi, *Regulating Gas Supply to Power Markets: Transnational Approaches to Competitiveness and Security of Supply* (Wolters Kluwer, 2018) 111–71.
⁸ CO Osueke and CA Ezugwu, 'Study of Nigeria Energy Resources and its Consumption' (2011) Volume 2, Issue 12 *International Journal of Scientific & Engineering Research* 2, www.ijser.org/research-paper/Study-of-Nigeria-Energy-Resources-and-Its-Consumption.pdf.
⁹ *Ibid*.
¹⁰ Nigeria Power Baseline Report (August 2015), https://mypower.ng/wp-content/uploads/2018/01/Baseline-Report.pdf.

grid but are mostly utilised in rural areas and underserved/unserved areas with limited access to electricity.

Although there is an installed generation capacity of about 12,910 megawatts (MW), the country only generates about 4,000 MW; which is less than the 8,400 MW projection for 2018 in the Multi-Year Tariff Order (MYTO).[11] The current generation level is grossly inadequate to cater for the growing demand which should ordinarily be met with at least 200,000 MW of electricity, given the current estimated population of 200 million.[12] Several factors have been blamed for the current shortages; the main issues were the inadequacy of gas supply to a large fleet of gas-fired power plants, liquidity issues and creditworthiness of the NESI operators and years of underinvestment in essential networks pre-privatisation.[13]

Currently, about 55 per cent of Nigerians do not have access to grid-based electricity supply, while power generation falls far short of demand. The necessary infrastructure to guarantee needed access remains inadequate and has been poorly maintained before the liberalisation and privatisation reforms. Consequently, a great deal of load-shedding and blackouts occur, while households and businesses rely to a large extent on private petrol and diesel generators.[14] Although the annual total consumption of electricity has risen very rapidly over the last three decades due to the increase in rural-urban migration, there remains a very high level of suppressed demand. In 2015, power supply in Nigeria averaged 3.1 gigawatts, which is estimated to be only a third of the country's minimum demand.[15] As aptly stated by CPCS Transcom, electricity demand in Nigeria far outstrips supply, and furthermore:

> [C]ompared to smaller economies such as Algeria with 11,000 MW of capacity or comparably sized economies such as Egypt with 24,000 MW of capacity, Nigeria trails far behind, with estimates of available generation capacity of between 3,000 to 4,000 MW; and about 7,500 MW of installed grid capacity. Nigeria's electricity consumption on a per capita basis is among the lowest in the world. A Nigerian citizen consumes 7% of

---

[11] Nigeria Electricity System Operator, 2019, 'Daily Operational Report – 2019/07/28', www.nsong.org/Library.aspx.

[12] The rule of thumb for electricity consumption is 1000 MW to one million households.

[13] Between January and August 2015, Nigeria's power generation firms sent out an average 3,317 MWh/h of electricity daily from 25 grid-connected generators with a total installed capacity of 12,522 MW. These generation plants include the recently privatised Gencos, the National Independent Power Project (NIPP) generators and independent power producers (IPPs). Currently, gas-fired thermal power plants generate about 85% of the installed capacity, while hydroelectric power plants generate the remaining 15%. See Rahmat Poudineh and Tade Oyewunmi, 'Natural Gas in Nigeria and Tanzania: Can it Turn on Lights?' Oxford Institute for Energy Studies (September 2018) *Oxford Energy Forum- Electrifying Africa Issue 115* 14–20.

[14] ECN, The Revised Draft National Energy Policy 2013, available at www.energy.gov.ng/index.php?option=com_docman&task=doc_download&gid=107&Itemid=49 or www.energy.gov.ng. The rate at which private generators are being used is reported to be about 80% of the installed capacity of the national grid.

[15] PWC, 'Powering Nigeria for the Future' (PWC Nigeria, July 2016) 2–34 at 6–7, www.pwc.com/gx/en/growth-markets-centre/assets/pdf/powering-nigeria-future.pdf.

the electricity of that of a Brazilian and 3% of that of a South African. More than half of the population has no connection to the grid whatsoever ...[16]

As in the case of most countries and societies with epileptic and unreliable power supply with no ideal off-grid solutions, the use of private diesel and petrol generators is the prevailing means of energy supply in urban areas. In Nigeria, such carbon-intensive and air polluting petrol and diesel generators is estimated at 6,000 MW, approximately twice the capacity of grid-connected generators. Furthermore, such individual generators cost NGN 50–70/kWh; compared to the regulated price of NGN 8.5/kWh price for grid-supplied power. Thus, the average Nigerian spends between five to ten times as much on self-generated electricity as they do on grid-supplied electricity. To address electricity shortages in Nigeria, the immediate past government set a target of 20,000 MW of generation capacity by 2020, while the current Government is pursuing incremental additions to grid-based and off-grid generation capacity. NERC's regulations and guidelines for captive power generation, embedded generation, and independent distribution networks, mini-grid permits, and renewable-energy-sourced electricity help to outline a cognisable framework for much-needed capacity additions, including off-grid systems.[17]

B. The Electricity Value Chain

The NESI comprises Gas producers, Generation Companies and Independent Power Producers, the Transmission Company of Nigeria, the Nigerian Bulk Electricity Trading Company Plc, Distribution Companies and Customers/End-Users. The value chain is structured to be linked back to back by contracts, which mirror each other to ensure industry liquidity and sustainability.[18] The revenue structure (as shown in Figure 1 below) is facilitated by a reverse payment system commencing from the distribution companies expecting to collect 100 per cent of the revenue from tariffs charged to end-users and remit a portion following deductions to the transmission/wholesale and generation segments of the value chain and feedstock producers.[19]

---

[16] CPCS Transcom, *Privatisation of PHCN Successor Companies Information Memorandum Volume 1* (CPCS 2011, Information Memorandum prepared for the Nigerian Bureau of Public Enterprises, 2011) 1–123, 17.

[17] Poudineh and Oyewunmi (n 13).

[18] Ivie Ehanmo 'Introduction to the Nigerian Electricity Supply Industry' (Presentation delivered to the staff of the legal department of an electricity distribution company and counsel at George Etomi & Partners in 2017).

[19] Nifemi Aluko, 'Power and Utilities in Nigeria: General Overview and Opportunities' (*Spotlight*, June 2018), https://kpakpakpa.com/spotlight/power-and-utilities-in-nigeria/.

Figure 1 Income and Revenue Allocation Structure[20]

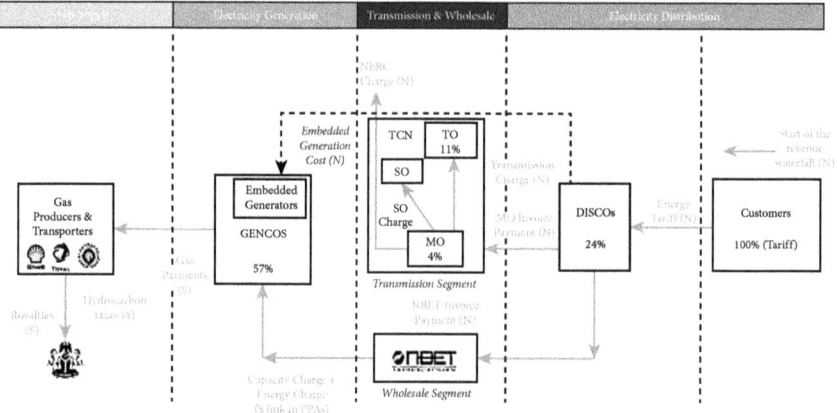

The role of each market participant in the value chain is enumerated below.

i. **Gas Producers**: The gas producers comprise mainly international and local oil and gas companies. Arrangements between gas producers and power generators are typically consolidated by Gas Sales Agreements (GSAs) for the sale of natural gas as a feedstock for power generation and Gas Transportation Agreements (GTAs) to secure the delivery of fuel (gas) to the gas-fired power plant.[21]

ii. **Generation Companies (GenCos) and Independent Power Producers (IPPs)**: GenCos and IPPs generate electricity and sell to the Nigerian Bulk Electricity Trading Company Plc (NBET) and/or other eligible customers. Eligible Customers are a class of buyers whose monthly electricity consumption is a minimum of 2 MW and meets the eligibility requirements under the Eligible Customer Regulation, 2017. The NERC reports that, as of June 2018, only five power purchase agreements (PPAs) were fully active, and only three GSAs were fully active, out of which two were self-suppliers, ie Shell Petroleum Development Company of Nigeria (SPDC)'s AFAM VI, and Okpai IPP, owned by the Nigerian National Petroleum Corporation (NNPC)/Agip Joint Venture.[22]

iii. **Transmission Company of Nigeria (TCN)**: The TCN is responsible for the transmission of electricity from the GenCos to the Distribution Companies. It is also responsible for managing the grid network and is solely owned by the Federal Government of Nigeria.[23] TCN is made up of three major departments: System Operator (SO), Market Operator (MO) and Transmission Service Provider (TSP). The SO is primarily responsible for the planning, dispatch, and operation of the transmission system. The MO is responsible

---

[20] Source: Energy Market and Regulatory Consultants (EMRC).
[21] Tade Oyewunmi, 'Examining the Legal and Regulatory Framework for Domestic Gas Utilization and Power Generation in Nigeria' (2014) 7(6) *Journal of World Energy Law and Business* 538–57.
[22] Poudineh and Oyewunmi (n 13).
[23] Nigerian Electricity Regulation Commission, 'Transmission', https://nerc.gov.ng/index.php/home/nesi/404-transmission.

for the operation of the electricity market and commercial arrangements and also administering the wholesale electricity market. The TSP is charged with improving the reliability, stability and efficiency of the network and expanding and maintaining the network.[24]

iv. **Nigerian Bulk Electricity Trading Company Plc (NBET):** NBET is established in line with the provisions of the EPSRA as the licensed bulk trader for the NESI.[25] NBET engages in the purchase of electricity and Ancillary Services (from IPPs, National Independent Power Projects, and successor GenCos) and subsequent resale to Distribution Companies (DicCos) and eligible consumers. NBET is responsible for providing credit enhancement by backstopping the payment obligations of the DisCos to the GenCos.[26] NBET typically executes a PPA with the GenCos and a Vesting Contract with the DisCos.[27] EPSRA in section 26(1)(a) envisages that NBET's role will cease when the Electricity Market becomes competitive and the DisCos become financially viable to efficiently remit receipts (monies obtained for the end-users) in the NESI.[28]

v. **DisCos:** The DisCos receive electric power allocated to their network (based on an energy allocation percentage per DisCo) for onward supply to the end-users. The DisCos are required to remit receipts to keep the entire value chain of the NESI viable.[29]

Despite the capacity and generation shortages from the grid-based supply systems, several off-grid initiatives are being developed.[30] These initiatives will be highlighted in subsequent sections of the chapter.

i. Electricity Generation

The guiding principle for the regulation of the generation segment is to foster competition and ensure the efficient use of the generation technologies in the system. For instance, the Azura gas-to-power project signifies a growing trend in private sector participation in power generation.[31] The total generation capacity of a power system is a crucial determinant of the ratio of access to electricity within the system. Generally, one measures energy access based on 1 MW to 1,000 homes,

---

[24] Ivie Ehanmo, 'The Legal and Regulatory Context of the Nigerian Power Sector' (Presentation delivered to the staff of the legal department of an electricity distribution company and counsel at George Etomi & Partners in 2017).

[25] Section 25(a) of the EPSRA 2005.

[26] Doing Business in Nigeria: A Guide for Foreign Investors, 'Power Sector' (*George Etomi & Partners*, April 2018), www.geplaw.com/wp-content/uploads/2018/04/pdfresizer.com-pdf-resize.pdf.

[27] Ibid.

[28] Ibid.

[29] Ibid.

[30] Femi Asu, 'Nigerian Firm, USADFT Promote Off Grid Energy Projects' (*Punch*, October 2018) https://punchng.com/nigerian-firm-usadf-promote-off-grid-energy-projects/.

[31] The Azura-Edo IPP is a 450 MW open cycle gas turbine power station and the first phase of a 2,000 MW project. The relevant parties reached financial closure on 28 December 2015 and construction started on 5 January 2016. See the World Bank Group, 'Financial Solutions Brief: Nigeria Azura-Edo IPP' (World Bank, 2018) available at http://pubdocs.worldbank.org/en/629011518200593880/Briefs-Guarantees-NigeriaAzuraEdo.pdf.

which implies that 1,000 consumers can be effectively supplied with a 1 MW generation plant.[32] Considering this premise, it is apparent that energy access in Nigeria is still a far cry from the expected goal with the installed, available and average generation capacity hovering around 13,000 MW, 7,652.6 MW and 4000 MW respectively. This is clearly insufficient to cater for the ever-increasing population currently estimated at 200 million and growing rural-urban migration rates.[33]

The available generation capacity has however increased significantly since 2013 when the sector was privatised. This is especially given the fact that the bids for the generation companies at the time of privatisation were based on the capacity recovery plan of the respective bidders in addition to the standard highest bid value. Thus, the minimum performance target of the generation companies as enshrined in the Performance Agreement (which formed part of the transaction documents at the time of privatisation) was based on capacity improvement. Although available generation capacity has increased incrementally since 2013 following privatisation, average generation capacity has not witnessed an equal increase as expected, which means that the generation companies are not fully dispatched. According to industry best practice in critically underserved countries, available generation capacity should be equal to the average generation, but this has not been the case in Nigeria.[34]

Figure 2 NESI Generation Capacity versus Actual Generation (2012–2019)[35]

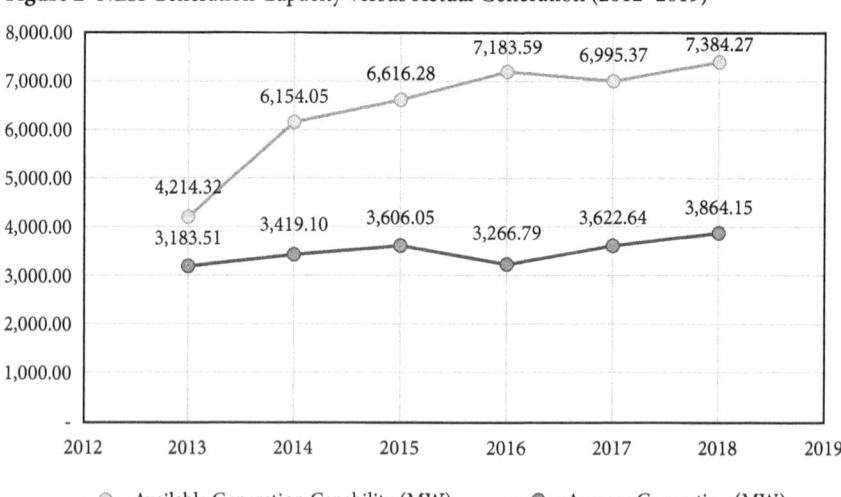

[32] Zach Hagadone, 'Megawhat? How Many Homes Can You Power with a Single Megawatt?' (*Boise weekly*, March 2015).
[33] Nigeria Electricity System Operator, 2019 (n 11).
[34] Association of Power Generation Companies (APGC) 'Gencos Perspective on NESI's Challenges and Way Forward' (Presentation delivered at the PIP (Performance Improvement Plan) Event on the 18th June 2019).
[35] *Ibid.*

From Figure 2, in 2018, out of 7384.27 MW average daily available generation capability, the GenCos were only allowed to generate an average of 3864.15 MW, thus the GenCos lost about 3,520.12 MW daily.

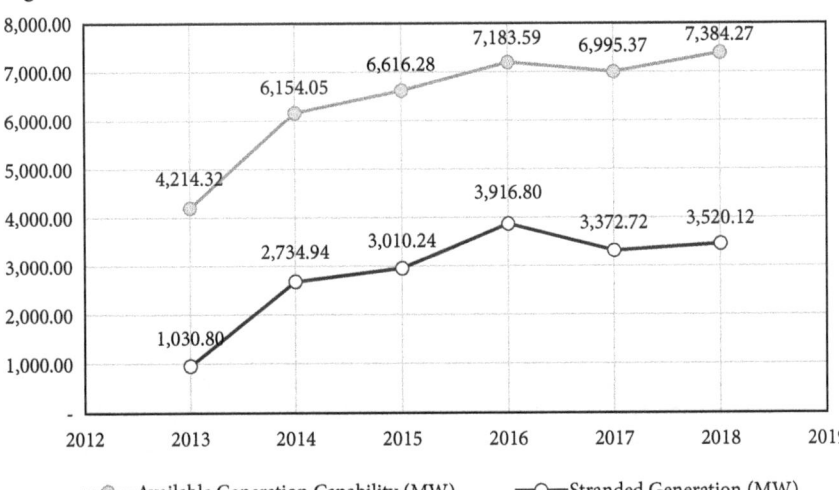

Figure 3 NESI Available Generation versus Stranded Generation (2012–2019)[36]

Furthermore, as seen in Figure 3, there has been an increase in stranded generation, peaking in 2016 where about 54.52 per cent (3,916.80 MW) of GenCos' available generation capacity was stranded daily and not paid for. Thus, GenCos' increased available generation capacity has not translated to a corresponding increase in power supply to consumers, hence, consumers generally believe the entire sector has failed following privatisation.[37]

Other specific challenges associated with the generation segment include:

a) Thermal and Hydropower plants designed to operate optimally and efficiently at baseload operate outside baseload with the attendant reduction in efficiency and implications for increased consumption of gas for thermal plants, considering massive fixed charges incurred to keep such units available.

b) Frequency deviations out of tolerable zones which damage the units as well as increase the maintenance costs close to three times above regular maintenance costs, the effect of which distorts the wholesale price and the cumulative effect is not recognised by the MYTO.

c) System imbalance affects power generators significantly by depriving them of the ability to sell the output of their plants, thus inhibiting investments to

---

[36] *Ibid.*
[37] *Ibid.*

increase the capacity of power plants or contracting for more gas when what is available is not optimally deployed due to transmission network constraints. This translates to increased risks in terms of machine breakdown, maintenance and repair costs or Take-Or-Pay obligations and stranded capacity.

d) Debts incurred by thermal GenCos due to take-or-pay risk for fuel (gas) supply, escalation factors in the GSA and GTAs in addition to the obnoxious efficiency factor imposed on them by NBET.

e) Lack of effective payment security and a guarantee from the Federal Government (NBET) in line with the PPAs to backstop payments due under the PPA, resulting in huge debts on the balance sheet of the GenCos, and their incapacity to service and repay loans and credit facilities.

f) Frequent grid collapses due to lack of spinning reserves and tools to manage the grid.

g) Ancillary service rates are not comparable to market tariff rates, therefore GenCos are not incentivised to put turbines on ancillary services and there is no contract for the procurement of spinning reserve. Tariffs associated with Black Start ancillary services are not commensurate with operational realities.

h) Market performance challenge in terms of low remittance across the value chain with GenCos being owed a significant portion of their invoiced amounts.

i) Communication challenges arising from the non-implementation of Supervisory Control and Data Acquisition (SCADA) systems. The SO still uses radio and telephone communication systems to control the grid network. Poor communication has led to incessant system outages which take a devastating toll on the GenCos which are not considered for the associated deemed capacity.

j) Non-implementation of the Generation Dispatch Tool by the National Control Centre which if deployed can enhance clear communication in real-time as well as record processes and instructions the SO issues to the GenCos.

k) Gas pipeline constraints which significantly affects the gas-to-power value chain, etc.[38]

However, through regulation, various initiatives are being put in place to increase generation capacity in order to achieve a reliable power system that incorporates and accommodates newer and efficient technologies for system expansion goals.

Development of Independent Power Projects has enhanced increases in generation capacity.[39] Also, a framework defining 'Eligible Customer regime' to foster the direct sale of power by the GenCos to off-takers for increased competition and

---

[38] Oyewunmi (n 7), 111–31.
[39] Philips Agboola, 'Independent Power Producer (IPP) Participation: Solution to Nigeria Power Generation Problem' (2011) *World Congress on Engineering* Vol 3, www.iaeng.org/publication/WCE2011/WCE2011_pp2084-2087.pdf.

ultimately promote the rapid expansion of generation capacity is a welcome development as it seeks to enhance the stability and operational efficiency of GenCos which would result in improved quality of supply. A notable initiative to address bottlenecks in the generation segment of the value chain is the recent Nigerian Electrification Roadmap for the strengthening of the transmission and distribution network and increase in the generation capacity which is a partnership between the Nigerian Government and the German Government. The Roadmap is in addition to the World Bank Power Sector Recovery Plan (PSRP)[40] currently being implemented to ensure the stability of the grid.

ii. Electricity Transmission

Generally, the transmission segment exists for efficiency and ease in the wheeling of electricity through to the distribution networks. Within the network, the sub-transmission network is a medium to high-voltage network with the purpose of transporting power over shorter distances, from bulk power substations to distribution substations. These segments comprise the transmission aspect of the typical power generation and transmission to distribution networks value chain.[41] The transmission and sub-transmission systems are meshed networks with a multiple-path structure so that more than one path exists from one point to another to increase the reliability of the system.[42] This is done through circuit breakers, relays, and communication and control mechanisms.[43] The transmission segment may be a natural monopoly, but various power systems have adopted the model which is inclusive of independent TSPs. The transmission segment is basically operated by the SO which is responsible for planning, dispatch, and operation of the power system, as well as the implementation of open access and new connections of generation plants or distribution loads to the transmission line. Where the electricity market is not operated on a bilateral basis between the distribution and generation companies, the market is administered by a MO. In Nigeria where it is applicable, the roles of the MO include the administration of market settlement system, commercial metering system, payment and commercial arrangements, in addition to ensuring market participants' compliance with the Market Rules and Grid Code.[44]

---

[40] The PSRP was conceived by the Federal Government in partnership with other facilitators as a set of policy actions, operational and financial interventions in the NESI. This forms the framework for the provision of government interventions and funding to market participants.

[41] See the Office of Electricity Delivery and Energy Reliability (US Department of Energy), 'The United States Electricity Industry Primer' (July 2015) 1–94 at 13.

[42] Mulukutla Sarma, *Introduction to Electrical Engineering* (Oxford University Press, 2001) 460.

[43] *Ibid*.

[44] Nigerian Electricity Regulatory Commission, 'Nigerian Electricity Supply Industry – Transmission', www.nercng.org/index.php/home/nesi/404-transmission.

The transmission network is managed by the TCN. The TCN's core mandate broadly covers the operation and management of high voltage (330/132kV) transmission system assets, generation dispatch functions (system operations) and provision of open access transmission services on the regulated tariff. The TCN, through the MO, is also responsible for managing the electricity market settlement system based on a set of Market Rules. TCN is run by two departments, ie the TSP and the SO.

The Nigerian transmission segment has encountered drawbacks and bottlenecks that have hindered any form of significant investment for several years. These issues can be broadly classified into management issues, system improvement, expansion funding issues and allowed revenue recovery issues.[45] The transmission network is made up of around 6,680 km of 330 kV lines 7,780 km of 132 kV lines, 330/132 kV substations with installed transformation capacity of 10,166 MVA and 132/32/11 kV substations with installed transformation capacity of 11,660 MVA. TCN is still plagued with high non-technical loss and low infrastructure coverage of the country. Less than 40 per cent of the country is covered by the existing transmission infrastructure.[46] The observed wheeling capacity of the transmission has been around 5,000 MW for some time due to: aging network; obsolete substation equipment; reactive power issues due to long and weak transmission lines in the North, leading to constant under-frequency and voltage collapse; forced outages; overloading of certain corridors and load flow balance of the network due to poor planning of the network; high technical and non-technical losses; incidences of vandalism; radial lines with no redundancies; community and right of way issues during project execution; lack of effectiveness in managing system reliability and inability to perform real-time operations, etc. Other factors hindering investment in transmission include the current liquidity situation in the power sector, etc.[47]

However, there are ongoing reinforcements of the existing 330 kV and 132 kV lines and substations to enable the efficient wheeling of more electricity across Nigeria. A notable initiative to address bottlenecks in the transmission segment of the value chain is the recent Nigerian Electrification Roadmap for the strengthening of the transmission and distribution network and an increase in the generation capacity.

iii. Electricity Distribution

The distribution process entails the conduct of electricity received from the transmission companies to the end-users at a lower voltage of 11 kV or 33 kV.

---

[45] Ivie Ehanmo, 'Private Investment in Electricity Transmission in Nigeria: Barriers to Network Investment and the Way Forward' (*Linkedin*, 4 August 2017), www.linkedin.com/pulse/private-investment-electricity-transmission-nigeria-barriers-ehanmo/.
[46] Ibid.
[47] Ibid.

Other distribution activities include billing, revenue collection, metering and customer services. As electricity markets progress, the distribution functions become further decentralised to include the retail service providers that assume some of the functions of the distribution companies.[48]

The regulation and operation of the distribution segment are critical to the liquidity of the entire sector and this is due to the important role of revenue collection from the consumers. Revenue collection is equally tied to the existence and implementation of cost-reflective tariffs, which will allow DisCos to recover their allowable revenue to invest in the network to meet customer demands while also providing efficient service delivery. In Nigeria, the distribution segment of the value chain has been plagued with a plethora of challenges following the privatisation of the sector. Highlights of the challenges include:

a) Lack of cost-reflective tariffs due to the mismatch of assumptions for tariff computation in the MYTO against market realities. This has resulted in a shortfall accumulating on the books of the DisCos as the industry collection agents and also occasioned by the sculpted nature of the tariffs that allows for under-recovery in the early years and over-recovery in later years, with little or no means to finance the shortfall gap.[49] This has hindered the ability of the DisCos to meet their market obligations and has occasioned shortfalls and liquidity challenges in the sector.[50]
b) Limited Capital Expenditure (CAPEX) allowance in the MYTO which in effect limits the ability of the DisCos to invest in the network(s), giving rise to increased ATC&C (Aggregate Technical, Commercial and Collection) losses.[51]
c) Electricity theft which increases commercial losses.[52]
d) Removal of debts owed by the Ministries, Departments and Agencies (MDAs) from the collection loss component of the ATC&C losses with no mechanism to recover the debts from the MDAs.[53]
e) Foreign exchange pass-through costs following the Central Bank of Nigeria's (CBN) decision to float the Naira against the dollar which is at variance with cost recovery in the MYTO in terms of recovery timelines, etc.[54]

Despite the challenges, various initiatives are being put in place to resolve the bottlenecks in the distribution segment. A notable initiative includes the recent

---

[48] Business Day, 'NERC Consultation Paper on the Development of a Regulatory Framework for Electricity Distribution Franchising in Nigeria' (*PressReader*, June 2019), www.pressreader.com › nigeria › business-day-nigeria.

[49] Ivie Ehanmo, 'Fundamentals of the Nigerian Electricity Supply Industry' (Presentation delivered to industry participants and stakeholders at the George Etomi & Partners Power Masterclass in 2019).

[50] *Ibid*; Poudineh and Oyewunmi (n 13). Note that the recent Order No: NERC/198/2020 of March 2020 on 'the Transition to Cost Reflective Tariffs in the Nigerian Electricity Supply Industry' creates a framework for DisCos to implement 'Service Reflective Tariffs', identify different customer categories and charge end-users based on the service delivery levels.

[51] Ehanmo (n 49).
[52] Ibid.
[53] Ibid.
[54] Ibid.

Nigerian Electrification Roadmap for the strengthening of the transmission and distribution network and an increase in the generation capacity. Notably, the distribution grid's nature is evolving to accommodate off-grid and independent power distribution models.[55] There have been significant investments towards procuring more efficient models of service delivery to the consumers such as Distributed Generation, Mini-Grids, and Independent Distribution Network Operators, etc.

IV. Regulating NESI – The Regulatory Framework

The Regulatory framework governing NESI is made up of primary and secondary legislation. NESI is regulated by various institutions and agencies. The primary legislation for the sector is the EPSRA which sets out the policy principles for the regulation of the sector. Secondary legislation and regulatory instruments are issued by NERC as the primary industry regulator pursuant to the EPSRA, which includes permits, licences, orders, guidelines, regulations, etc. In this regard, an evolving set of regulatory instruments issued by NERC include:

a) NERC Regulation for the Procurement of Generation Capacity 2014;
b) NERC Embedded Generation Regulations 2012;
c) NERC Eligible Customer Regulation 2017;
d) NERC Regulation for Mini-Grids 2016;
e) NERC Regulation for Captive Power Generation 2008;
f) NERC Independent Electricity Distribution Networks Regulations 2012; and
g) NERC Investment in Electricity Networks Regulation 2015, etc.

Other institutions involved directly or indirectly in policy-making and regulation of the NESI includes:

i. **Ministry of Power**: The Ministry through the Minister of Power has the responsibility of providing policy guidance for the NESI to ensure the provision of adequate and reliable power supply in Nigeria. The Ministry's policy development is guided by the 2010 Roadmap for Power Sector Reform, the 2001 National Electric Power Policy, the 2005 Electric Power Sector Reforms Act and the Nigerian Federal Government's Transformation Agenda on Power.

ii. **NERC:** This is the primary regulator for the NESI established by virtue of section 31 (1) and (2) of EPSRA and headquartered in Abuja. It has the main responsibility of licensing and regulating persons engaged in the generation, transmission, system operation, distribution, and trading of electricity in Nigeria.[56] Other duties of the Commission include: to protect consumers' interests; to establish and approve adequate operating codes, as well as security,

---
[55] Oyewunmi (n 5).
[56] Ibid.

reliability, safety and quality standards; to establish and review electricity tariffs (MYTO II – The Order and Model), and; to promote competition and private sector participation in the market where feasible.[57]

iii. **NBET:** The NBET, established in line with the provisions of the EPSRA, is an electricity trading licensee that engages in the purchase of electrical power and ancillary services (from independent power producers and the successor generation companies) and subsequent resale to distribution companies and eligible consumers.[58] The role of NBET is essentially to give credit enhancement to the NESI by the execution of bankable PPAs with the GenCos and IPPs.[59] It is currently the sole electricity buyer, however, it is envisaged that the distribution companies upon attaining commercial viability, will also be able to procure power directly from the generation companies.

iv. **Rural Electrification Agency (REA):** This agency was set up pursuant to section 88 (1) of the EPSRA to administer the Rural Electrification Fund, which is a designated fund to promote, support and provide rural electrification programmes through public and private sector participation in order to achieve more equitable regional access to electricity, maximise the economic, social and environmental benefits of rural electrification subsidies, promote expansion of the grid and development of off-grid electrification and stimulate innovative approaches to rural electrification.[60]

v. **Operator of the Nigerian Electricity Market (ONEM):** This institution is licensed to function as the MO of the wholesale electricity market of the NESI and is a semi-autonomous body under the TCN. It is responsible for the operation of the electricity market and settlement arrangements.[61]

vi. **Nigeria Electricity System Operator (NESO):** This is a semi-autonomous body under the TCN, to provide system operation services to the NESI. The NESO is primarily responsible for the planning, dispatch, and operation of the transmission system. It is also responsible for the security and reliability of the electricity network grid.[62]

vii. **The National Power Training Institute of Nigeria (NAPTIN):** This body was established in 2009 to serve as a focal point for human resource development and workforce capacity-building, and act as a research centre on matters relating to power in Nigeria. A key objective of the Institute is to design, develop and deliver a wide variety of training courses that will enhance the skills and capacity of both technical and non-technical power utility personnel.[63]

---

[57] Section 32 EPSRA.
[58] Nigerian Bulk Electricity Trading Plc, https://nbet.com.ng/about-us/what-we-do/.
[59] *Ibid.*
[60] Rural Electrification Agencyhttp://rea.gov.ng/theagency/.
[61] Operator of the Nigerian Electricity Market, http://www.onemnigeria.org/.
[62] Nigerian Electricity System Operator, www.nsong.org/.
[63] National Power Training Institute of Nigeria, www.naptin.gov.ng/about-us.

viii. **ECN:** The ECN is tasked with the strategic planning and coordination of national energy policies.
ix. **Presidential Task Force on Power (PTFP):** The PTFP is tasked with the goal to ensure the realisation of the reform of the Nigerian power sector.

V. Challenges with On-Grid Electricity Supply in Nigeria

The supply of electricity via the national grid has several constraints, some of which are identified below in this section. Beyond the challenges associated with generation as identified in previous sections, the weak state of the transmission and distribution (T&D) network is primarily responsible for the inability of the grid to supply more than 4000 MW of electricity on the average. The TCN has made several investments towards improving its network capacity to about 8,100 MW[64] and in recent times, it aims at increasing the capacity to 10,000 MW.[65] However, the gains are yet to be felt because the distribution network is lacking in similar capacity. Over 55 per cent of Nigeria's population lacks electricity access[66] and going by the rule of thumb, Nigeria needs over 200,000 MW to attain a full electricity access rate. Recently however, as earlier indicated, the Nigerian Government has entered into a partnership with the German Government for the strengthening of the T&D network and increase in the generation capacity.[67]

Beyond the network challenges, the current state of sector liquidity dilemma has reduced investor-appetite in the sector. The funding and liquidity issues can be attributed to several factors such as:

- The mismatch between the MYTO (the tariff setting framework) and market and operating realities. For example, the MYTO uses an exchange rate of NGN 198 to a US$ in computing tariffs, amongst other parameters. Utilities, however, are billed for energy received from the Bulk Trader on the basis of an exchange rate of NGN 305 to a US$ based on contractual terms between the Bulk Trader and Generating Companies. MYTO tariffs were expected to be

---

[64]'TCN Announces New National Peak of 5,375MW' (Transmission Company of Nigeria, February 2018), https://tcn.org.ng/blog_post_sidebar31.php#.

[65]'TCN Targets 10,000MW with Seven Critical Investment in Transmission Lines Soon' (*Transmission Company of Nigeria*, 16 August 2019), https://tcn.org.ng/blog_post_sidebar48.php.

[66]A Aliyu, A Ramli and M Saleh, 'Nigeria Electricity Crisis: Power Generation Capacity Expansion and Environmental Ramifications' (2013) *Energy* 61, 354–67, cited in PE Akhator, AI Obanor and EG Sadjere, 'Electricity Situation and Potential Development in Nigeria using Off-Grid Green Energy Solutions' (2019) *Ajol* Vol 23(3) 527–37, www.ajol.info/index.php/jasem/article/viewFile/185438/174751.

[67]'Nigeria, Siemens Sign Electricity Agreement to Generate 11,000MW by 2023' (*Premium Times*, 22 July 2019), www.premiumtimesng.com/news/top-news/342295-nigeria-siemens-sign-electricity-agreement-to-generate-11000mw-by-2023.html.

trued up since the privatisation of the sector in 2013 to reflect the true level of ATC&C losses which would determine the Performance Targets and tariffs to be charged by the utilities to end-users for revenue recovery to enable them to achieve assigned targets as enshrined in the Performance Agreement(s). Other assumptions expected but not trued up include: generation; foreign exchange; customer numbers/base growth rates; gas prices; inflation (US and NGN). Therefore, tariff assumptions may not reflect market realities, thus occasioning revenue shortfalls caused by the non-payment of cost-reflective tariffs by consumers. This has in effect hindered access to funding and investments in the sector.[68]

- Acute shortage of generation in comparison to the assumptions in the MYTO due to gas and transmission constraints. Incorporating current generation levels in tariffs would require around a 50 per cent increase in tariffs, which could be higher with adjustments to inflation and forex.[69]

- Inconsistencies in power pricing and cost recovery in a contract-based market. There are instances of mismatch between the contractual terms of the PPAs between the GenCos and the NBET or Bulk Trader and the operation of the MYTO which determines customer tariffs. Generation costs are adjusted by NBET on a monthly basis as a result of the changes in indices and indexations in the PPAs (eg Forex, fuel prices which affect energy and capacity prices), but DisCos are unable to pass on the adjusted generation costs to customers and recover the costs as the six monthly tariff reviews are not reliably implemented.[70]

- Misalignment of contract structures and regulation, eg the MYTO targets are in some cases at odds with the targets stipulated in the Performance Agreement which formed the basis of investors bids during the privatisation process.[71]

- Increased debts from the MDAs not recognised in tariffs and thus resulting in higher losses;[72]

- The lack of cost-reflective tariffs has occasioned a rippling effect across the value chain as market participants are unable to cover costs, earn the allowed revenue and meet their market obligations. The DisCos are heavily indebted to NBET, which in turn are in debt to the GenCos, which are then unable to pay the gas producers.

The market design and regulatory issues in the sector have occasioned several *force majeure* declarations from investors, the initiation of court cases, etc; thus transmitting the wrong investment signals to the regional and international investment community. The poor state of the grid has given rise to the development and

---

[68] Ivie Ehanmo, 'The Regulation of the Nigerian Power Sector' (Presentation delivered at the Florence School of Regulation Special Live Session in 2019).
[69] Ibid.
[70] Ibid.
[71] Ibid.
[72] Ibid.

implementation of several off-grid structures though currently at a nascent stage, to increase access to energy in the country especially in unserved and underserved areas within Nigeria.

VI. The Rise of the Under-Grid and Off-Grid Solutions

The term 'off grid' here refers generally to systems developed in areas that are too far away to connect to the national electrical grid without significant additional investments, while the 'under grid' implies systems that are in areas close enough to connect to a low-voltage line at a relatively low cost. In terms of access to electricity, Nigeria has been classified, in a study conducted by the World Bank, as the third ranking country out of five with rural access of 41 per cent. Nigeria's performance against other countries (Mexico and four other sub-Saharan countries: Kenya, Uganda, Tanzania and Ghana) was measured in the area of off-grid energy access and this was hinged on certain parameters (ie Access, Reliability and Quality, Efficiency and Affordability). In terms of Reliability and Quality, based on a citizen's poll, Nigeria ranked the worst out of the five countries. In terms of Efficiency, the analysis showed that Nigeria would be 80 per cent more efficient when compared to the other five countries, where transmission or distribution losses are eliminated. Regarding Affordability, Nigeria ranked third out of the five countries.[73] Lee et al point out that about 95 million people live in the 'under grid' areas in Nigeria, Kenya, Tanzania, Ghana and Liberia and agreeably opine that if governments wish to leverage existing grid infrastructure, subsidies and new approaches to financing are necessary, while for areas yet to build out 'grid' or 'off-grid' infrastructure, it is important to consider household and business demand for connections, as well as potential economies of scale in costs.

Access to 'modern energy services' entails

> the benefits to be derived by people from an energy system, which itself comprises an energy supply sector and the end-use technologies that convert the energy derived from the particular energy carrier ... Energy services include modern cooking fuels, improved cookstoves, electricity, and mechanical power ... for doing work in agricultural, industrial, and other sectors ...[74]

---

[73] Wayne Energy Consult, 'Off-Grid Renewable Energy Sector Deep-Dive' for the World Bank Group (July 2019). See also Kenneth Lee et al, 'Electrification for "Under Grid" households in Rural Kenya' (2016) 1 *Development Engineering* 26–35; and Destenie Nock et al., 'Changing the policy paradigm: A benefit maximization approach to electricity planning in developing countries' (2020) 264 *Applied Energy* 114583 on the various pathways to addressing the network planning and energy access issues that seem common to developing countries in the region.

[74] Yinka Omorogbe, 'Universal Access to Modern Energy Services: The Centrality of the Law' in Yinka Omorogbe and Ada Okoye Ordor (eds), *Ending Africa's Energy Deficit and the Law: Achieving Sustainable Energy for all in Africa* (Oxford University Press, 2018). World Energy Outlook 2012 defines energy access as a household having reliable and affordable access to clean cooking facilities and a first electric supply connection, with a minimum level of consumption of 250 kilowatt hours (kWh) per year for a rural household and 500kWh per year for an urban household.

As posited by Omorogbe,

> [m]ost electricity grids in Africa cover less than half of the respective countries, and poor communities are the proposed beneficiaries, expensive grid extensions are unlikely to be viable alternatives. The solution is off-grid decentralized energy powered by renewable energy in all areas that are not in petroleum producing areas such as the Nigerian Niger delta or Angola. Apart from the need to combat climate change, promoting the use of renewables leads to cleaner cities and urban environments. The quality of life in cities such as Lagos, which suffer from the problems of epileptic power supply and atmospheric pollution from millions of generators in use whenever the regular blackouts occur, can only improve if there are cleaner forms of energy in use. The challenges are to create structures that promote the use of renewables as an alternative to hydrocarbons for the various self-generation efforts and to stimulate the use of low-cost financing and grants that promote socio-economic objectives such as modern energy access for poor communities.[75]

Before exploring the nitty-gritty of the regulatory framework for off-grid solutions, it is useful to briefly highlight the potentials for sourcing such off-grid solutions from renewable sources.

A. Renewables, Nuclear Energy and Electricity

Nigeria's annual average solar radiation ranges from 3.5 kWh/m^2 in the South to 7.0 kWh/m^2 in the northern arid regions. Wind speed ranges from a low 1.4–3.0 m/s in the South to 4.0–5.12 m/s in the extreme North.[76] The Nigerian Renewable Energy Master Plan 2011 (REMP) suggests a strategy to increase the share of renewable sources in electricity from 13 per cent in 2015 to 23 per cent by 2025 and 36 per cent by 2030.[77] The REMP also outlines relevant fiscal and market incentives to support renewable energy deployments such as a moratorium on import duties for renewable energy technologies and the establishment of further tax credits, capital incentives and preferential loan opportunities for renewable energy projects.[78] On nuclear energy, it is noted that uranium-rich pyrochlore was discovered in significant quantities in the North Central Jos Plateau region in 1947, although there is currently no commercial extraction programme for the uranium. Two nuclear research centres were established in the 1970s and another nuclear science and technology centre was also established in 1993. Some considerable efforts have been made by the Government in establishing the needed institutional and international co-operation framework for developing nuclear energy for electricity generation in the mid to long-term.[79]

---

[75] Ibid.
[76] ECN (2014) Draft National Renewable Energy & Energy Efficiency Policy 1–47.
[77] The International Energy Agency (IEA), 'Nigeria Renewable Energy Master Plan 2011' (IEA/IRENA Joint Policies and Measures Database), www.iea.org/policiesandmeasures/pams/nigeria/name-24808-en.php.
[78] Ibid.
[79] Ibid.

B. Policy and Regulatory Framework for Off-Grid Power Supply

The policy and regulatory framework underpinning the off-grid power supply in Nigeria is primarily steered by NERC. The Federal Government has outlined its commitment and approach to rural electrification in several official policies and plans, as outlined in the timeline table below in Figure 4.

Figure 4 Nigerian Approach to Rural Electrification[80]

2001	2005	2015	2016	2017	2017	2017
National Electric Power Policy (NEPP)	Electric Power Sector Reform Act (EPSRA)	Nigerian Renewable Energy & Efficiency Policy (NREEEP)	Rural Electrification Strategy and Implementation Plan (RESIP)	Power Sector Recovery Programme (PSRP)	NERC Mini-Grid Regulation	Rural Electrification Fund Operational Guidelines (REFOG)
Provides for the structuring and privatisation of the electricity market. Provides for a Rural Electrification Policy and targets as well as the Rural Electrification Fund. Promotes research and development in the power sector	Unbundles and privatises the Nigerian electricity market. Develops a competitive electricity market. Establishes NERC and REA. Consumer protection, licences and tariffs	Develops renewable energy and energy efficiency (RE & EE) targets and action plans. Power roadmap and support for electricity market reforms. Promoted off-grid renewables development and financing. Recommends additional regulations and economic instruments. Research development and training. Requires bilateral and regional cooperation. Implements existing planning policy	Coordinates and implements Nigeria's rural electrification policies, target and strategies. Administers the Rural Electrification Fund. Promotes low-cost technologies and private sector participation	Increases electricity access by implementing off-grid renewable solutions. Establishes data driven processes for decision making across the sector. Develops and implements a foreign exchange policy for the power sector. Makes electricity market effective and ensures cost reflective tariffs	Provides definition, registration and grant of permit for mini-grid systems. Develops contract templates and enforcement of electricity contracts between all parties concerned. Describes operations of the mini-grids including technical specifications. Proposes commercial arrangement including tariff setting. Establishes framework for investor and consumer protection	Provides capital subsidies/grants and technical support to developers of rural electrification projects. Establishes the investor eligibility and the project selection criteria under REF. Outlines the sources and allocations of REF resources. Develops a database of possible locations to be targeted by the REF. Develops a database of possible locations to be targeted by REF. Outlines the REF grant award process, monitoring and evaluation of projects

i. Government and Regulatory Agencies

The key regulatory and government agencies which are responsible for the development of the off-grid sub-sector are the NERC and the REA. The REA is essential for the main agency responsible for the development of off-grid power supply solutions facilitated by the Government. These off-grid projects are renewable-energy based, given that renewable energy has been adopted as the primary energy source for off-grid projects. The REA is charged with the electrification of rural areas and administering the REF. Potential investors looking to venture into mini-grid projects would have to adhere to certain criteria or eligibility requirements proposed by the REA to benefit from the Rural Electrification Fund (REF) which provides capital grants of up to 75 per cent of project costs, including technical

---

[80] Source: Rocky Mountain Institute, 2018.

support to rural electrification.[81] The following regulations are applicable to the off-grid projects:

- **Captive Power Regulations 2008:**[82] Captive power generation is one of the most widely used forms of off-grid structures in Nigeria, deployed by companies and large organisations in driving industrial processes. The Regulations define captive power generation as 'generation of electricity exceeding 1 MW for the purpose of consumption by the generator, and which is consumed by the generator itself, and not sold to a third-party'.[83] In this regard, power generation is intended for self-consumption and would not be distributed through the grid. The Regulations also provide for permitting requirements to be adhered to by an intending captive power operator. Where the captive plant operator intends to supply power in excess of over 1MW to a third party, the licensing requirements state that a generation licence must be obtained.[84]

- **Eligible Customer Regulations 2017:**[85] An eligible customer is described under section 100 of the EPSRA as 'a customer that is eligible, pursuant to a directive or directives issued by the Minister, to purchase power from a licensee other than a distribution licensee'. The Eligible Customer Regulation provides for four categories of customers who can declare eligibility in the sector through the procurement of power directly from the generation companies instead of the distribution companies. However, only one class of the customer classification applies to the off-grid power sector: 'Customers who consume more than 2 MWh/hr over the course of one month and have a direct metered connection to the generation licensee's facility'.[86]

    This creates the framework for the existing generation companies, IPPs and prospective licensees to sell power directly to underserved customers with the requisite monthly consumption threshold under the 'willing-buyer willing-seller' arrangement. Thus, the parties can enter into an agreement for the supply of power from the generation plant directly to the customer's facility via an Independent Distribution Network, without connection through the national transmission grid.

- **Mini-Grid Regulations 2016:**[87] The Mini-Grid Regulation provides an off-grid framework that provides streams of investment and solutions to the challenges

---

[81] Rural Electrification Agency, http://rea.gov.ng/rural-electrification-fund/.
[82] Regulation No NERC-R-0108, Nigerian Electricity Regulatory Commission, https://nerc.gov.ng/index.php/library/documents/Regulations.
[83] Section 2(1) of the Captive Power Regulations.
[84] Section 8(b) of the Captive Power Regulations.
[85] Regulation No NERC-R-111, Nigerian Electricity Regulatory Commission, https://nerc.gov.ng/index.php/library/documents/Regulations.
[86] Section 5(4) of the Eligible Customer Regulations.
[87] Regulation No NER/-R-110/17, Nigerian Electricity Regulatory Commission, https://nerc.gov.ng/index.php/library/documents/Regulations.

of the on-grid electricity supply in the NESI. It provides a clear investment pathway that can be exploited by existing and prospective generation licensees in the industry. A Mini-Grid is defined as an electricity supply system with its own power generation capacity, supplying electricity to more than one customer and can operate in isolation from or be connected to a Distribution Licensee's network.[88] The Mini-Grid must have a generating capacity that ranges between 0 kW and 1 MW. The Regulation aims to boost investments in off-grid rural and urban electrification infrastructure investments, as well as renewable photovoltaic (PV) power by creating a hybrid of the generation capacity of Mini-Grids.

- **MYTO Mini-Grid Model 2015:** Mini-Grid projects are governed by the tariff methodology set out in the MYTO Mini-Grid model.[89] The applicable tariff for grid supply is the Multi-Year Tariff Order (MYTO) 2015 while the tariff for off-grid supply through the Mini-Grid Regulations will be determined by the Mini-Grid model, subject to the negotiations of parties to the project. Outside the mini-grid structure, tariffs for off-grid projects are determined by parties on a willing-buyer, willing-seller basis.

C. Challenges with Off-Grid Power Supply

The market potential of Nigeria for off-grid solutions was adjudged to be one of the best in Africa due to customer willingness and ability to pay. However, some barriers exist which have been credited for the relatively slow uptake of decentralised renewable energy and off-grid solutions.[90] The following points are highlights of the identified challenges:

i. Limited access to affordable project finance by investors and renewable energy developers.[91] Generally, this is a result of a lack of scalable business models given that each off-grid success story is backed by tailor-made solutions to the specific project, limited availability of data for the assessment of demand which usually leads to inaccurate customer enumeration and consumption growth projections.[92] There is also the challenge of foreign exchange risk, given the disparity between the cost of equipment importation, feedstock production and cost of service delivery.

---

[88] Section 3(1) of the Mini-Grid Regulations.
[89] MYTO Mini-Grid Model, https://nerc.gov.ng/index.php/library/documents/Regulations.
[90] Wayne Energy Consult (n 73).
[91] Wayne Energy Consult (n 73).
[92] Nigerian Electrification Project (P161885), The World Bank, p 10, http://documents.worldbank.org/curated/en/367411530329645409/pdf/Nigeria-Electrification-PAD2524-06052018.pdf.

ii. Renewable energy-based off-grid projects are generally known for their high initial cost structure which would eventually be passed on to the customers via a cost-reflective tariff. The high project cost for the developer and affordability by the customer is a challenge, leading to buy-in by only a small fraction of customers.[93]
iii. The current import policy of the Government is another challenge.[94] There is no exemption from duty taxes on imported equipment, machinery, spares and consumables.[95] Also, for solar-powered off-grid projects, 25 per cent combined import duties and value-added tax (VAT) is charged on imported solar components[96] (only solar panels are import-duty exempt). These undesirable policies do not engender fast-paced growth in the sector.
iv. Grid expansion policies do not provide for clear, adequate compensation of mini-grid developers in the event of national grid expansion. This poses a significant threat to investment in mini-grid projects since on-grid electricity provides a subsidised cost of electricity to the consumer and a switch to grid supply will result in a loss to the developer.[97]
v. Inadequate technical expertise and experience across the various relevant stakeholders has hindered the growth of off-grid solutions in Nigeria.
vi. Lack of consumer awareness and trust. The limited number of Nigerians who are aware of off-grid solutions often have a deep sense of distrust for solar technologies linked to a precedent of failed government-sponsored programmes and the low-quality solar products flooding the market.[98]

VII. Future Outlook – Balancing the Grid for Reliable Electricity Supply

Despite the apparent challenges with grid electricity supply and off-grid electricity supply, the Government is taking strides to balance the grid in ensuring increased access to electricity across the country. In a bid to support and augment the efforts of the Nigerian Government and the private sector, international development finance institutions (DFIs) such as the United States Agency for International Development (USAID), the UK Department for International Development (DFID) and the German Corporation for International Cooperation under its

---

[93] Wayne Energy Consult (n 73).
[94] Wayne Energy Consult (n 73).
[95] Wayne Energy Consult (n 73).
[96] Wayne Energy Consult (n 73).
[97] Wayne Energy Consult (n 73).
[98] Wayne Energy Consult (n 73).

Nigeria Energy Support Program (NESP), have contributed to the growth of energy development in Nigeria. The ongoing initiatives are listed in the following subsections:

A. Eligible Customer Regime

This policy which was released in 2017 was followed by the NERC Eligible Customer Regulations. The Regulations set out the classes of customers which may declare eligibility as follows:[99]

i. Customers with at least 2 MWhr/h consumption connected to the metered 11 kV or 33 kV delivery point through the DisCos' network.
ii. Customers with at least 2 MWhr/h consumption connected to a metered 132 kV or 330 kV delivery point on through the TCN's network.
iii. Customers with at least 2 MWhr/h consumption connected directly to the metered 33 kV delivery point on TCN's network to be supplied through the DisCos' network.
iv. Customers with at least 2 MWhr/h consumption directly connected to a GenCo to be supplied through a DisCo's network.

The Eligible Customer Regulation seeks to engender competition in the NESI through the declaration of eligibility by large residential, commercial and industrial electricity consumers. Under this regime, the declaration entails that these strategic customers leverage on the opportunity to receive reliable power supply from GenCos and IPPs. Although the DisCos may become participants under certain categories, the consequence of the regime is that the 'Eligible Customers' are permitted to bypass the DisCos and resort to the GenCos and IPPs for the provision of improved power supply services. The steady growth in businesses in the country coupled with the present challenges of grid supply will essentially foster increased participation of customers, GenCos and DisCos in this regime. The introduction of the policy presumes that the power sector will transition from a monopoly to a fairly competitive industry that would spearhead economic growth.

B. Electricity Distribution Franchising

NERC has proposed electricity distribution franchising as a novel commercial framework for addressing the challenges in the NESI. The commercial arrangement between investors and DisCos will be governed by a franchising regulation and in

---

[99] Section 5 of the NERC Eligible Customer Regulations, 2017.

this regard, NERC had commenced a consultation process with stakeholders.[100] The term 'Electricity Distribution Franchise' refers to a franchise business model operated by a DisCo and a third-party investor (Franchisee) where the Franchisee, acting as the representative of the DisCo, provides electricity distribution and retail services to customers within the DisCo's franchise area at a stipulated tariff. In effect, NERC envisages the augmentation of the quality of service delivery to customers by the Franchisees operating on behalf of the DisCo. The objective is to address challenges in funding and infrastructure gaps, power supply deficit, low customer satisfaction and technological deficiencies within each DisCo's network area.[101]

As a novel concept in the NESI, interested investors may undertake single functions or the entire distribution function under any of the following business models: (a) Metering; Billing and Collection; (b) Total Management of Electricity Distribution Function; and (c) Distributed Generation.[102] Thus, a DisCo may franchise out the entire management of its distribution function in a given area within its franchise area or it may only franchise specific retail or distribution functions to the Franchisee. The Franchisee will in turn, pay the DisCo a franchise fee for its commercial operations within the DisCo's franchise area. While the consultation paper suggests several potential business models for distribution franchising, the distributed generation (DG) based model is particularly relevant for promoting increased energy access. The DG model enables a franchisee to deploy additional generation supply to meet an electricity deficit at the local distribution network level in addition to managing the network's distribution function and metering, billing and collection operations.[103]

Where the regulatory framework for franchising is approved and executed, the NESI will witness significant changes in the operations of the distribution segment of the value chain. Improved power supply, strong network equipment, quality service delivery and enhanced effectiveness at cost-reflective rates can be expected. It is noteworthy that the present challenges which are low-hanging fruits including cost-reflective tariffs, the security of supply and the contractual framework of the market should be addressed prior to the implementation of the regulation.

---

[100] Nigerian Electricity Regulatory Commission, 'Public Consultations on Capping of Estimated Billing and Distribution Franchising', https://nerc.gov.ng/index.php/library/documents/Advertisements/Public-Consultations-on-Capping-of-Estimated-Billing-and-Distribution-Franchising.

[101] Nigerian Electricity Regulatory Commission, 'Consultation Paper on Electricity Distribution Franchising, April 2019', https://nerc.gov.ng/index.php/library/documents/Consultation-Papers/Consultation-Paper-on-Electricity-Distribiution-Franchising-April-2019/.

[102] *Ibid.*

[103] Rocky Mountain Institute, Energy Markets and Regulatory Consultants, Clean Tech Incubation and Acceleration Foundation and Power for All (with funding support from All On) 'Business Models for Undergrid Minigrids' August 2019.

C. Renewable Energy Policies, Regulations and Initiatives

NERC employs the use of policies and regulations to drive investment in electricity generation from renewable energy sources. The Federal Government in 2015 approved the National Renewable Energy and Energy Efficiency Policy (NREEEP) as well as the National Determined Contribution (NDC) 2015 which established Nigeria's commitment to reducing greenhouse gas emissions. The objective of NREEEP is the share increase of on-grid renewable energy in the total electricity supply from 1.3 per cent as of 2015 to 16 per cent in 2030. However, the approval of the National Renewable Energy Action Plan (NREAP) 2016 saw the review of the target to 30 per cent renewable energy by 2030.[104]

The NERC Feed-in Tariffs Regulation 2015 was released in furtherance to the NREEEP and it aims to stimulate investment in power generation from renewable energy sources.[105] The aim is to deploy large-scale renewable energy for the reduction of carbon dioxide (CO_2) emissions. The Regulation will distinguish between small and large renewable energy projects and aims to supplement an additional 2,000 MW to the national grid supply by 2020. It provides that the DisCos and NBET will procure 50 per cent of the total projected energy demand from renewable sources.[106] The Mini-Grid Regulation, 2016 seeks to drive investments in power generation and supply via mini-grids at unserved and underserved locations through a combination of fossil fuel-based technologies and renewable energy technologies.

The NERC Mini-Grid Regulation provides that a mini-grid applies only to any isolated or interconnected network between 0 KW and I MW. Pursuant to the Regulation and in order for both mini-grid developers and DisCos to take maximum advantage of the business opportunities presented therein, interconnected mini-grids exist as a strategic investment vehicle. As an integrated local generation and distribution system, an interconnected mini-grid helps provide blended, consistent and affordable electricity to unserved or underserved areas, thus having the potential to contribute significantly to the improvement of electricity supply in NESI.

D. Rural Electrification Agency Projects

i. Energising Projects

The Energising Projects are the interventions of the Rural Electrification Agency (REA) for the provision of increased electricity access to rural communities in

---

[104] Federal Republic of Nigeria, 'Sustainable Energy For All Action Agenda' (July 2016).
[105] Nigerian Electricity Regulatory Commission, 'Renewable Energy Sourced Electricity', https://nerc.gov.ng/index.php/home/operators/renewable-energy.
[106] Nigerian Electricity Regulatory Commission, 'NERC's Regulation Envisages 2,000MW of Renewable Sourced Electricity by 2020', https://nerc.gov.ng/index.php/media-library/press-releases/315-nerc-s-regulation-envisages-2-000mw-of-renewable-sourced-electricity-by-2020.

Nigeria. The interventions are expressed through the Energising Economies Initiative (EEI) and the Energising Education Programme (EEP). The EEI targets micro, small and medium customers (MSMEs) in economic clusters, while the objective of the EEP is the provision of reliable and stable electricity supply to target federal universities and university teaching hospitals.

ii. Nigerian Electrification Project

In the fourth quarter of 2018, the World Bank, in collaboration with the Federal Government and the REA, commenced the Nigerian Electrification Project (NEP). The project is a US$350 million facility from the World Bank to the Nigerian Government for off-grid development, with the objective of increasing electricity access for households, for MSMEs, and for students and patients at federal universities and university teaching hospitals throughout Nigeria. NEP has four components: solar hybrid mini-grids for rural economic development; stand-alone solar systems for homes, farms and enterprises; power systems for public universities and teaching hospitals; and technical assistance.

E. Government Funded Schemes for Off-Grid Financing

Recently, the Federal Ministry of Power (FMoP) undertook a pilot scheme tagged 3D 24/7 to power an unserved community in Sokoto State. The initiative was undertaken to create a prototype that the FMoP believes can be replicated with the aim of increasing rural electrification rates. The financing for this project came from the proceeds of the green bond employed for the purpose of the project and the Energising Education project of the REA. The community also contributed to the project by donating the land needed for the solar plant to the project developer.

The Lagos State Government (LASG) under the Rural Electrification scheme and Light Up Lagos Project has provided community and state agency electrification, as well as street lighting initiatives. This was procured under the Public-Private Partnership. Financing for the plants was undertaken by the local lenders and financiers of the private developers but with payment assurance guarantees which are backed by the LASG. The Government also simplified the process of land acquisition and encourages private citizens who can afford the same to adopt a streetlight and benefit from concessions on the land use charge. Additionally, the Kaduna Government developed an off-grid approach to increase electricity access across the state to boost Agriculture and Textile. The strategy focused on policy, identification and prioritisation of projects and its implementation which will translate to government support. Notably, renewable energy solutions providers have recently developed various mini-grid solutions across Nigeria. Some of its mini-grid solutions have received state government funding support to ensure the viability of the project.

F. Donor Funded Initiatives

i. Solar Nigeria Programme

The Solar Nigeria Programme, undertaken by the Nigerian Government in collaboration with DFID, was put in place in 2014 to provide solar power to public health and education facilities. The Programme provides credit facilities, grants and technical assistance to companies operating in the solar market.

ii. USAID Nigeria Power Sector Programme

USAID is currently implementing the Nigeria Power Sector Programme NPSP, a five-year programme with the main objective of increasing electricity availability and access by strengthening the enabling environment for private sector investment in the power sector, including the development of business and consumer markets for off-grid solutions, with particular focus on solar home systems, mini-grids and micro-grids.

iii. Nigeria Energy Support Programme

The European Union and the German Government, through the NESP (implemented by GIZ in collaboration with the Federal Ministry of Power, Works and Housing), support the development of solar mini-grid projects in Nigeria. The first phase of the NESP took place between 2013 and 2017, while the second phase commenced in January 2019.

VIII. Conclusion

The NESI represents an interconnected network of diverse operations, which when properly harnessed will deliver excellent value to the Nigerian populace in terms of increased affordable supply and access to energy. The privatisation of the NESI was a step in the right direction, regardless of the present challenges highlighted above. The culmination of several factors will deliver the value required to make the power sector thrive, some of which include: implementation of cost-reflective tariffs across the value chain to guarantee investors a clear sight of investment recovery; increased investments in the generation, transmission and distribution networks; increased investments by DisCos in their networks; regulatory certainty and stability; alignment of contract structures and regulation; consistency in power pricing and cost recovery; privatisation of the transmission segment of the value chain, etc. The effective implementation of the above factors will give credence to the ongoing initiatives and investments currently being undertaken in the sector in order to guarantee improved energy access and reliability of electricity supply in the country.

In an energy transition context there is the need to balance the requirement for reliable and secure energy supplies with affordability and viability of the energy markets alongside supplying sustainable and clean decarbonised energy. The evolving off-grid policy framework and innovations promoting the deployment of renewable energy solutions are promising. As stated in the Introduction, the Nigerian context exemplifies how the peculiar challenges and outlook for a typical developing economy with a significant proportion of its energy derived from traditional carbon-intensive sources, significant rural-urban migration and inadequate electrification and access rates can reasonably transition. As the above discussion highlights, the leading drive of energy policy over the past several decades has evolved from expanding access to regulation and centralised control by relevant government institutions for secure, affordable and reliable supply of modern electricity services mostly in urban areas, to fostering a liberalised and private sector-driven NESI and then more recently to expanding rural off-grid solutions powered primarily by renewable energy sources. As the global drive towards decarbonisation and sustainability moves the energy transition forward, it is important from a developing economy standpoint not to downplay the importance of ensuring universal access to modern energy systems and services. Any global decarbonisation pathway that jeopardises universal access to modern energy services to developing countries cannot be said to be just and fair.

14
Australian Electricity Law and Policy in a Time of Energy Market Transition, National Emergency and Climate Crisis

PENELOPE CROSSLEY

Author postscript: This chapter was originally going to focus on the fraught history of Australia's energy law during the energy market transition given its position as the world's third largest energy exporter. However, while I was revising the chapter, Australia experienced its worst bushfire season on record, largely due to a prolonged period of severe drought and extreme temperatures.[1] As a result, it became evident that this chapter would also have to address the continued failure of the Australian Government to integrate climate policy with energy policy and the National Electricity Law. Indeed, the energy and climate debate in Australia is so politicised, that Australia has been described by Dr Fatih Birol, Executive Director of the International Energy Agency, as 'one of the top three countries in the world where the energy debate is off the rails.'[2]

I. Introduction

Australia is currently experiencing a one in two hundred years transition within its energy sector, as the country moves from its traditional mix of predominantly coal-fired generation to one which incorporates more renewable energy and energy storage. However, the transition has been made difficult due to Australia's

---

[1] Bureau of Meteorology, 'Australia's Warmest Year on Record; Marked by Severe, Protracted Drought' (*Annual Climate Statement 2019*, 9 January 2020), www.bom.gov.au/climate/current/annual/aus/#tabs=Overview (last accessed 14 April 2020).

[2] Bevan Shields, 'Too Emotional, too Hot': World's Top Energy Chief Laments Australia's Climate Debate' *The Sydney Morning Herald*, Sydney, 20 December 2019, www.smh.com.au/world/europe/too-emotional-too-hot-world-s-top-energy-chief-laments-australia-s-climate-debate-20191219-p53lp0.html (last accessed 14 April 2020).

position as the world's largest exporter of coal and liquefied natural gas (LNG) and a significant exporter of uranium. These fossil fuel exports have traditionally represented a pivotal component of the Australian economy, accounting for almost a third of national commodities and goods exports. At the same time, Australia also has a natural abundance of renewable energy sources, with excellent solar and wind resources widespread across the continent and a large hot dry rock geothermal energy potential. These factors, coupled with extremely high electricity prices and a strong desire among segments of the Australian populace to exert more control over their personal energy usage has seen a marked shift towards renewable energy.[3] Indeed, Australia now has the highest penetration of residential photovoltaic solar energy per capita in the world and a significant share of the global battery storage market.

In many jurisdictions around the world, integrated approaches to energy and climate law act as a key driver of the energy transition within the electricity sector. This is particularly important in emission intensive economies such as Australia, which ranks seventh globally for greenhouse gas emissions per capita and for whom the electricity sector is the largest contributor.[4] Despite the importance of a nationally integrated approach, this has never occurred within Australia. This chapter will discuss the conflicting objectives of Australia's approach to energy, the implications of the failure to integrate energy and climate law and how the worst drought and bushfires in Australia's history[5] may change future regulation of the energy sector and Australia's approach to climate change. The chapter will begin with a discussion of how the size and location of the Australian continent impact on the provision of electricity, before moving in section III to a discussion of the shifting energy mix within the National Electricity Market (NEM). Section IV of the chapter will discuss Australia's national approach to regulating energy, with a particular focus on electricity, as the main source of greenhouse gas emissions. Section V will examine the continued failure of the Federal Government to integrate energy and climate law. In section VI the chapter then gives an analysis of the likely changes to energy and climate law following the worst drought and bushfires in Australia's history. Section VII then concludes.

II. The Impact of Australia's Geography on the Provision of Electricity

Australia is an island nation. Other than Antarctica, Australia is the driest and the least populated continent on earth. It is also the second hottest continent. It has

---

[3] Australian Energy Regulator, 'State of the Energy Market 2018' (Australian Competition and Consumer Commission, 2018) ('AER Report') 74.
[4] Ross Garnaut, 'The Garnaut Climate Change Review' (Final Report, Cambridge University Press, 2008) 156.
[5] Bureau of Meteorology, 'Rainfall Deficiencies and Water Availability' (*Drought*, 7 January 2020), www.bom.gov.au/climate/drought/#tabs2=Rainfall-deficiencies (last accessed 14 April 2020).

a population that is heavily concentrated on the east coast of the country, with other parts of the country very sparsely populated. This population distribution can largely be attributed to the climatic conditions in central Australia, which are some of the most hostile on earth. This means that while Australia is the sixth largest country in the world, it also has one of the lowest population densities, with only 3.24 people per km^2.[6] These geographic features make the provision of energy, and in particular, electricity, to the Australian population challenging.

Due to its remote location, Australia has a true internationally 'islanded' grid, with no electricity interconnectors with any other country that can be used to offset supply shortages or to assist in managing a stable voltage. Electricity generated in the eastern and southern regions in Australia is traded through the National Electricity Market, which is one of the longest and stringiest interconnected power systems in the world.[7] This feature of the NEM, also makes it vulnerable in times of extreme climatic conditions or natural disasters such as bushfires and floods, as discussed in more detail below.

Ironically, the NEM is in fact not a national market, with the Northern Territory, Western Australia and other outlying islands not connected to it.[8] This can be explained by the long distances between these regions and the rest of the NEM, and their exceptionally low population densities, which make transporting electricity from the NEM to these regions uneconomic. This has meant that historically, most Australians were served by large-scale fossil fuel fired electricity generators, located relatively close to the point of usage to minimise load losses.

As will be discussed in the section below, the Australian energy mix is now beginning to change with the imminent retirement of aging coal-fired power stations, the rapid uptake of renewable energy sources of generation and increasing use of battery storage. These changes pose new challenges both from a technical perspective, but also a legal and policy perspective.

III. The Australian Energy Mix within the NEM

A. Fossil Fuel Generation

The Australian energy mix reflects the legacy of its indigenous fossil fuel sources, with a heavy dependence on coal-fired generation. In 2018–19, black and brown coal generators accounted for 38 per cent of registered capacity within the NEM,

---

[6] Australian Bureau of Statistics, 'Population Density' (*Regional Population Growth, Australia, 2016–17*, 26 March 2019), www.abs.gov.au/AUSSTATS/abs@.nsf/Previousproducts/3218.0Main%20Features702016-17?opendocument&tabname=Summary&prodno=3218.0&issue=2016-17&num=&view= (last accessed 14 April 2020).

[7] Australian Energy Market Commission, 'National Electricity Market', www.aemc.gov.au/energy-system/electricity/electricity-system/national-electricity-market (last accessed 14 April 2020).

[8] *Ibid.*

but supplied 71 per cent of output.[9] Gas powered generators accounted for 20 per cent of registered capacity, but only supplied eight per cent of output.[10] Thus in 2018–19, 79 per cent of electricity output in the NEM came from fossil fuel sources.[11] While these figures are undoubtedly high, the overall output of fossil fuel generation within the NEM registered a decline over the past 12 months of 3.5 per cent on 2017–18 figures, and over the past ten years there has been a decline of 14.1 per cent.[12] This is predicted to accelerate over the next five to ten years, with an additional 2547MW of the aging coal-fired generators scheduled to retire, and no new coal-fired generation currently planned.[13]

B. Renewable Generation

The most significant source of renewable generation capacity within the NEM has historically been hydroelectricity. In 2018–19, hydroelectric generators accounted for 13 per cent of registered generation, but only supplied seven per cent of output.[14] This output figure was down from the 9.5 per cent of output in 2017–18, which can be attributed to the impact of the worst drought in Australian history. Wind energy accounted for ten per cent of registered capacity but only eight per cent of output.[15] Large-scale concentrated solar and photovoltaic (PV) solar farms meanwhile accounted for five per cent of registered capacity but only two per cent of output.[16]

A recent addition to the Australian NEM statistics is rooftop solar, which now accounts for 13 per cent of registered capacity, but only four per cent of output. However, this later statistic is deceptive as it does not reflect the true level of self-generation, only the volumes of electricity exported to the NEM. Over two million households in Australia (or one in five homes), currently have rooftop solar installed.[17] This means that Australia now has the highest penetration of rooftop solar per capita in the world. Given the exceptionally high electricity prices paid by Australian energy consumers, rooftop solar PV technology is cost competitive throughout Australia, with repayment periods in some regions of just two to three years compared to an expected lifespan of 15 years.[18] This reflects a profound

---

[9] Australian Energy Regulator, 'Data Update – Chapter 2 National Electricity Market – November 2019' (*State of the Energy Market*, 27 November 2019) ('AER Data Update'), www.aer.gov.au/publications/state-of-the-energy-market-reports/state-of-the-energy-market---data-update-november-2019 (last accessed 14 April 2020).
[10] Ibid.
[11] Calculations on differences are the author's own.
[12] AER Data Update (n 10).
[13] AER Report (n 3) 98.
[14] AER Data Update (n 10).
[15] AER Data Update (n 10).
[16] AER Data Update (n 10).
[17] Alison Potter, 'Solar Panel Payback Time' (*Choice*, 10 July 2018), www.choice.com.au/home-improvement/energy-saving/solar/articles/solar-panel-payback-times (last accessed 14 April 2020).
[18] Ibid.

shift within the Australian energy market, and has also impacted on other technologies such as battery storage, energy management systems and other distributed energy resources. In 2019, Australian consumers are predicted to purchase over 30 per cent of the global battery storage market in 2019.[19] Further, it appears that many emerging energy technology innovators globally are using Australia as an international test market due to its islanded grid, high electricity prices and consumer willingness to adopt new technologies.

One of the challenges with increasing the volume of renewable generation in the NEM, and the retirement of aging coal-fired generators is that system balancing and the provision of other ancillary services including frequency support becomes more difficult. In recent years there have been growing concerns expressed about how Australia will secure supplies of baseload and instantaneously dispatchable power. At a recent International Energy Agency/Energy Security Board forum, some of the leading energy policymakers in Australia questioned how capacity will be secured in a variable, and at times, zero marginal cost, environment. At that forum this author argued that going forward, in the absence of other incentives, short-term wholesale electricity prices would be unlikely to provide an adequate long-term signal to attract capital investments in the 'right' mix of generation, the 'right' infrastructure and in the 'right' locations to continue the optimal functioning of the NEM. At the same time, any policy utilising incentives to attract investment need to ensure that competition within the NEM is maintained, or ideally enhanced, and that the policy does not support the continuation of the status quo to the detriment of the adoption of new innovative technologies. This is not an easy task given the potential for self-generation, competition between generation and network investment, the advent of customer provision of ancillary services (eg from smart devices and electric vehicles (EVs)), and the growth of embedded networks and peer-to-peer electricity trading.

Ultimately, any regulatory or policy levers to support the energy transition must be underpinned by a stable, transparent and predictable regulatory framework that operates in the long-term interests of consumers. As will be shown in the next section, this is difficult to achieve given the constitutional settlement that determines the governance of the Australian energy sector.

IV. The Legal Framework Governing the NEM

A. The Constitutional Settlement with Respect to Electricity

Many of the current issues with the Australian energy sector can be traced back to the debates in the Australasian Federation Conference, which took place

---

[19] BloombergNEF, 'Australia to Be Largest Residential Storage Market in 2019' (22 January 2019), https://about.bnef.com/blog/australia-largest-residential-storage-market-2019/ (last accessed 14 April 2020).

between 1890 and 1898. The purpose of the Australasian Federation Conference was to negotiate a draft Constitution under which the six Australian colonies and New Zealand could federate into a new nation. In this regard, the Conference was a success, with the six Australian colonies (minus New Zealand) federated as a Commonwealth of States on 1 January 1901. However, what is striking for a modern reader of the debates and proceedings of the Conference is that while the words 'energy' and 'electricity' are used throughout the debates as a means of signalling 'spirit', 'force' or 'innovation', nowhere is there a discussion of whether energy or electricity should be governed by the new Federal Parliament or the states. In many respects, this is not surprising, while Australia had had electricity supply since the 1880s, it was commonly supplied by local municipalities on a socialised basis. Indeed, the first interstate interconnector was not established until 1959.[20] As such, during the constitutional conventions, it was not viewed as necessary for nation building for the power to legislate the generation and supply of electricity to be vested in the Commonwealth. As a result, the Australian Constitution is silent on the subject and the residual power to legislate was vested in each state.

B. The Historical Background

Since Federation in 1901, there have been three significant transformations in the organisation of the Australian electricity sector:

i. 1920s – The Creation of Vertically Integrated State Government-Owned Monopolies

The first transformation began in the 1920s, with the shift from the municipal and regional provision of energy to vertically integrated state government-owned monopolies which provided all aspects of electricity supply including generation, transmission, distribution and retail services to customers. During this period, each state had its own agencies responsible for planning, developing, commissioning and operating their own electricity supply system, with only limited interconnection between the states.[21]

This means that historically, energy law and policy in Australia, at least as it applied to the electricity sector, developed in a piecemeal fashion, with different states and territories each developing their own laws and policies.

---

[20] Firecone, 'The Evolution of Transmission Planning Arrangements in Australia' (Report, October 2007) 15, www.aemc.gov.au/sites/default/files/content/de879761-9ae6-443f-89b8-bae55028ff1f/Firecone-Report-The-Evolution-of-Transmission-Planning-Arrangements-in-Australia.pdf (last accessed 14 April 2020).
[21] Mike Roarty, 'Electricity Industry Restructuring: The State of Play' (Department of the Parliamentary Library, Research Paper 14, 25 May 1998) 1.

ii. 1990s – The Introduction of Market Competition

The second transformation was prompted by several reviews of the electricity sector in the early 1990s, which found that the existing market structure was inefficient, with low productivity and high barriers to entry.[22] This prompted negotiations between the Commonwealth, states and territories about the future governance of the electricity sector and the need to implement market competition. The product of these negotiations formed the National Electricity Market Legislation Agreement (NEMLA),[23] which sought to introduce a uniform single wholesale electricity market across eastern and southern Australia and harmonise the laws and regulations governing electricity supply in participating jurisdictions. These reforms were designed to facilitate interstate trade, lower barriers to competition, increase regulatory certainty and improve productivity within the electricity sector as it transitioned from being dominated by large unbundled state-owned monopolies to privatised corporations.

a. The Enactment of the National Electricity Law

In 1996, the National Electricity Law (NEL)[24] was enacted, which in its own right was a major achievement, being only the second time cooperative legislation had been agreed to and passed by the jurisdictions.[25] The NEL established the legal framework associated with electricity supply in the NEM. The objective of the NEL is the National Electricity Objective (NEO), contained in Section 7, which states:

> The objective of this Law is to promote efficient investment in, and efficient operation and use of, electricity services for the long term interests of consumers of electricity with respect to-
> (a) price, quality, safety, reliability and security of supply of electricity; and
> (b) the reliability, safety and security of the national electricity system.[26]

The NEO has long been criticised,[27] with questions increasingly being asked about whether it is still fit for purpose. In particular, concerns have been expressed that its narrow focus on the economic interests of consumers limits the ability

---

[22] Ann Rann, 'Electricity Industry Restructuring – A Chronology' (Department of the Parliamentary Library, Background Paper 21, 30 June 1998) 1–3.

[23] In 2004, the Commonwealth, state and territory governments replaced the NEMLA with the Australian Energy Market Agreement (AEMA). This Agreement sets the ongoing agenda for a transition from standalone electricity systems to national energy regulation. The AEMA also aims to '... promote the long term interests of consumers with regard to the price, quality and reliability of electricity and gas services'.

[24] Schedule 1 to the National Electricity (South Australia) Act 1996 (as amended).

[25] Australian Energy Market Commission, 'National Electricity Market: A Case Study in Successful Microeconomic Reform' (*KPMG*, 2013) 31, www.aemc.gov.au/sites/default/files/content/The-National-Electricity-Market-A-case-study-in-microeconomic-reform.PDF (last accessed 14 April 2020).

[26] National Electricity (South Australia) Act 1996, sch 1, s 7.

[27] See, eg, Penelope Crossley, 'Review of the Institutional Governance Arrangements for the National Electricity Market' (Report for the Public Interest Advocacy Centre, 2015).

of the Australian energy market institutions to adequately plan for the long-term future of the electricity sector, especially in relation to growing environmental and climate change concerns and sustainability.[28]

While the NEL was designed with harmonisation in mind, state and territory governments continued to be able to exert significant control over the subsequent development of the NEM and amendments to the NEL. This pressure is applied through the entity responsible for national energy policy, the Council of Australian Governments (COAG) Energy Council,[29] which is made up of the 'ministers from the Commonwealth, each state and territory, and New Zealand, with portfolio responsibility for energy and resources'.[1] Due to the cooperative nature of the NEL, most decisions are made between the participating governments on a consensus basis, which enables individual governments to employ more influence by holding out on agreeing.

b. The Creation of the NEM

The NEM was established by the Commonwealth Government, Queensland, New South Wales, Victoria, South Australia, Tasmania and the Australian Capital Territory and commenced operations in 1998. At its inception, a significant majority of generation and transmission assets were operated by state-owned corporations. This meant that prior to the partial privatisation or full privatisation of state-owned electricity assets, virtually every decision of the COAG Energy Council had significant financial implications on the capacity of the state governments to raise revenue. This clear conflict of interest explains the parochial approach taken by some state and territory governments to the regulatory environment through COAG.

A further challenge to the efforts to affect a nationally consistent approach to the regulation of the electricity sector, has been that a number of important areas of regulatory competence in relation to the NEM were preserved within state and territory legislatures.[30] These areas include:

- The provision of state-based subsidies and other incentives.
- Consumer protections for residential consumers and small business owners through Ombudsman Schemes.

---

[28] This may be contrasted with the position of the EU and China, which both include a focus on sustainability within their equivalent provisions.

[29] The original form of the COAG Energy Council was the Ministerial Council on Energy (MCE), which was established on 8 June 2001. It was designed to be the forum through which the Commonwealth, State and Territory Ministers having primary responsibility for energy matters could meet to formulate national energy policy. The role of the MCE is described in cl 4 of the Australian Energy Markets Agreement (AEMA) (as amended on 9 December 2013). Over the past 14 years, three institutions have held these legally enduring roles and powers:

1. the MCE from 8 June 2001–16 September 2011;
2. the Standing Council on Energy and Resources (SCER) from 17 September 2011–12 December 2013; and
3. the COAG Energy Council from 13 December 2013 to the present day.

[30] Crossley (n 28) 65.

- Energy efficiency standards.
- Environmental regulation.
- Distribution and retail service areas, including the specification of geographic areas in which responsibilities/obligations apply.
- Electrical safety standards.

These reserved areas of regulatory competence within the energy sector had implications for the early development of regulations governing greenhouse gas mitigation, which in the absence of a national approach were driven by the states.

The NEM is currently supported by the six inter-state interconnectors which link the transmission lines between the states and territories, with a number of other inter-state interconnectors planned or under construction.[31] Arguably, given how interconnected the generation and transmission infrastructure is across the NEM, the ongoing presence of divergent regulation across the NEM acts as a significant barrier to its efficient and effective operation. Unfortunately, there is little prospect of successfully amending the Australian Constitution to enable the legislative power to vest solely in the Commonwealth. Since Federation, there have been 44 national referendums submitted to Australian voters, only eight of which have ever been approved and none since 1977. Any such effort by the Commonwealth to amend the Constitution in order to be given these legislative powers is likely to be thwarted by the states forcefully campaigning against any such move, with energy law and policy viewed as critical to state development. The inability of the Commonwealth to amend the Constitution means that if such an approach were to be pursued it would have to be done through another constitutional head of power that currently vests in the Commonwealth. There are a number of heads which could potentially be used for this purpose, including the External Affairs power,[32] or the Trading and Financial Corporations power.[33] While this approach is potentially legally feasible, it would be highly politically unpopular and would cause significant ructions in the Commonwealth–State relations. For these reasons, in the absence of a significant shift in both Australia's approach to cooperative federalism and national energy policy, it is not reasonably foreseeable that the current constitutional settlement will change.

iii. 2000 Onwards – The Growth of Renewable Energy and Distributed Energy Sources

The third transformation of the Australian energy sector is the current shift in the generation mix from fossil fuels to renewable energy, and the greater adoption

---

[31] Australian Energy Council, 'Which Way is the NEM's Energy Flowing?' (*Analysis*, 28 July 2018), www.energycouncil.com.au/analysis/which-way-is-the-nem-s-energy-flowing/ (last accessed 14 April 2020).
[32] Commonwealth of Australia Constitution Act 1901 (Cth) s 51(xxix).
[33] *Ibid* s 51(xx).

of decentralised and distributed supply. As shown in Figure 1, the growth of particularly solar energy in Australia began in earnest after the enactment of the Renewable Energy (Electricity) Act 2000 (Cth).

Figure 1 Australian Electricity Generation from Renewable Sources

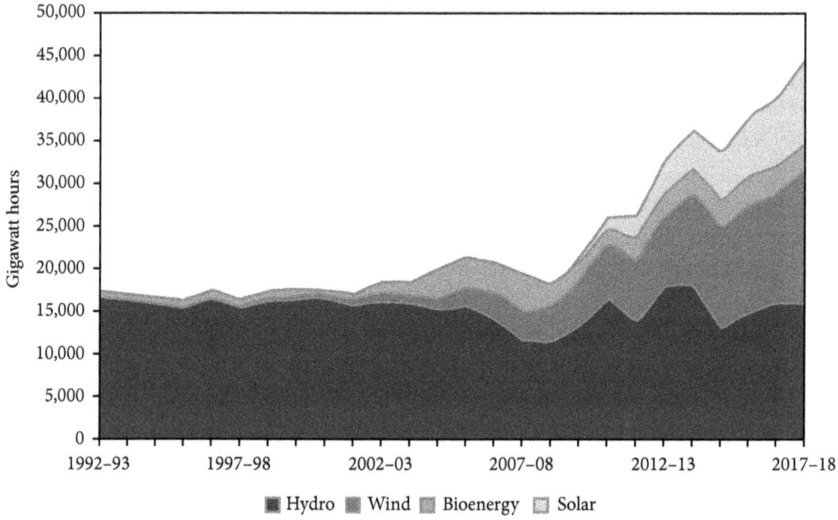

Source: Department of the Environment and Energy (2019) *Australian Energy Statistics*, Table O.

The Act was enacted by the conservative Liberal Government in an attempt to help mitigate Australia's greenhouse gas emissions. This is clearly evident from the objectives located in section 3 of the Act, which are:

a) to encourage the additional generation of electricity from renewable sources;
b) to reduce emissions of greenhouse gases in the electricity sector; and
c) to ensure that renewable energy sources are ecologically sustainable.

The legislation also introduced one of the first Renewable Energy Targets (RETs) in the world, and has proved to be a highly successful means of both increasing renewable generation and reducing greenhouse gas emissions. Under its original design, the RET was 'projected to reduce emissions by about 200 Mt CO_2e (cumulatively) between 2015 and 2030'.[34] It acted as a 'technology pull' quota obligation scheme that requires liable entities to buy renewable energy certificates to meet their RET liability.

---

[34] Australian Government Climate Change Authority, 'Towards a Climate Policy Toolkit: Special Review on Australia's Climate Goals and Policies' (August 2016) 45, http://climatechangeauthority.gov.au/sites/prod.climatechangeauthority.gov.au/files/files/Special%20review%20Report%203/Climate%20Change%20Authority%20Special%20Review%20Report%20Three.pdf (last accessed 14 April 2020).

V. The Lack of Interaction between Energy Law and Climate Policy in Australia

Despite the shift towards renewable generation described above, this transition has not been a smooth one. Two features of Australian energy law and policy are particularly striking. The first is that there has been an ongoing failure to integrate energy law and climate policy over the years. The second is that the fossil fuel industry in Australia fighting both any attempt to increase the amount of renewable energy in the generation mix and, with some segments also challenging efforts to reduce national greenhouse gas emissions.

Indeed, since the introduction of the Renewable Energy (Electricity) Act in 2000, the legislation has been reviewed on no less than six separate occasions.[35] While the Rudd Government Review in 2009 led to a significant expansion of the Scheme increasing the RET and extending the policy to 2020, subsequent reviews arguably increased uncertainty within the sector. In particular, the 2014 Warburton Review, chaired by the former Chairman of Caltex Oil in Australia,[36] has been viewed as particularly damaging to the energy transition in Australia by the renewable energy sector. This Review was initiated by the Coalition Government following their election in 2013 on a platform which included repealing a number of laws and policies supportive of renewable energy and climate change mitigation.

The Warburton Review was launched after concerns were raised by the fossil fuel electricity generators that the RET was increasing renewable energy by squeezing out other sources of generation. In particular, in the context of greater energy efficiency and reduced demand for electricity, the volumetric requirement of the large-scale renewable energy target (LRET) of 41,000GWH of electricity coming from large-scale renewable energy by 2020 meant that approximately 27 per cent of electricity generation had to come from renewable energy sources.[37] This was significantly higher than the 20 per cent that had originally been intended when the RET scheme was designed. The Review found the RET had led to the abatement of 20 million tonnes of carbon emissions and, if left in place, would abate a further 20 million tonnes of emissions per year from 2015 to 2030 – almost 10 per cent of electricity sector emissions.[38]

Despite also finding that the cumulative impact on household energy bills over the period of the RET was likely to be small, the Warburton Review further found

---

[35] These include the Tambling Review in 2003; the Rudd Commonwealth Government in 2009; twice by the Climate Change Authority in 2012 and 2014; the Warburton Renewable Energy Target Expert Review Panel in 2014 and, most recently, also considered by the Australian Competition and Consumer Commission's (ACCC's) Retail Electricity Pricing Inquiry in 2018.

[36] Dick Warburton and others, 'Renewable Energy Target Scheme: Report of the Expert Panel' (Commonwealth of Australia, 2014), https://apo.org.au/sites/default/files/resource-files/2014-08/apo-nid41058.pdf ('Warburton Review').

[37] Ibid 120.

[38] Ibid 60.

that the RET was 'an expensive emissions abatement tool that subsidises renewable generation at the expense of coal fired electricity generation'.[39] As a result, to protect existing fossil fuel generators, the Review recommended removing the existing volumetric target. Instead, it argued that it should be replaced with a revised 'true 20 per cent target' for large-scale renewable generation (equivalent to approximately 33,000GWh) to be achieved through a series of yearly targets, set one year in advance, corresponding to 50 per cent of growth in electricity demand.[40] On 23 June 2015, these changes were adopted through legislative amendments to the existing scheme.[41]

Over the same period as the Warburton Review was recommending reductions be made to the LRET, the Coalition Government also repealed the Clean Energy Act 2011 (Cth). This legislation, which had been introduced by the Gillard Labor Government, created a national Carbon Pollution Reduction Scheme (CPRS), which set an effective price on carbon of $AUD 23 per tonne.[42] This Scheme was designed to shift from a fixed to a floating carbon price under an Emissions Trading Scheme after three years. The repeal of this law, which made Australia the first country in the world to repeal a national carbon tax, occurred despite it proving highly successful in reducing carbon emissions. Indeed, the Australian Energy Regulator reported that:

> Over the two years of the scheme's operation, output from brown coal fired generators declined by 16 per cent (with plant use dropping from 85 per cent to 75 per cent), and output from black coal generators declined by 9 per cent. Coal generation's market share fell to an historical low of 73.6 per cent of NEM output in 2013–14. Overall, these changes contributed to the emissions intensity of NEM generation falling by 4.7 per cent. This fall, combined with lower NEM demand, led to a 10.3 per cent fall in emissions from electricity generation over the two years that carbon pricing was in place.[43]

Following the repeal, this law was replaced by a 'Direct Action' Policy and an Emissions Reduction Fund (ERF). However, for the first few years of the ERF, participation by the electricity sector was voluntary and thus the sector generally just refused to participate. Meanwhile, the Direct Action scheme was shown to be inefficient and largely ineffectual when compared to the CPRS. As a result, subsequent to the repeal of the Clean Energy Act 2011, Australia's carbon emissions have increased every year.[44]

There have subsequently been other attempts to address Australia's growing emissions profile, including the proposed introduction of an Emissions Reduction Obligation (ERO) under the National Energy Guarantee (NEG). The ERO was

---

[39] *Ibid* 18.
[40] *Ibid* iii–iv.
[41] Renewable Energy (Electricity) Amendment Act 2015 (Cth).
[42] Clean Energy Act 2011 (Cth) s 100.
[43] Australian Energy Regulator, 'State of the Energy Market 2015' ('AER 2015').
[44] Department of Environment and Energy, 'Quarterly Update of Australia's National Greenhouse Gas Inventory: March 2019' (Commonwealth of Australia, 2019) 56.

proposed by the Finkel Review, following a large-scale blackout in South Australia in 2016, along with a Retailer Reliability Obligation (RRO) under the guide of the NEG. The NEG was developed as a mechanism to ensure security and reliability, restore investor confidence and address affordability, all while lowering emissions in the electricity sector.[45] The ERO would have effectively operated as a privately-run Emissions Trading Scheme and operating only in NEM jurisdictions would have not applied nationally or operated outside of the energy sector. As it was, despite achieving bipartisan support in the Parliament, the Coalition Government were unable to achieve sufficient internal party room support and the proposed ERO was subsequently withdrawn with only the RRO being subsequently implemented. This again represented a failure to integrate energy and climate law and policy, making it appear increasingly unlikely that this will be achieved in the short to medium term due to a lack of political will on the part of some Australian political parties. Indeed, the current Commonwealth Minister for Energy and Emissions Reductions called in 2019 for existing coal and gas fired generators to continue operating 'flat out'.[46]

As a signatory of the Paris Agreement, Australia has agreed to reduce its emissions in the form of an Intended Nationally Determined Contribution of 26 to 28 per cent of 2005 levels by 2030.[47] However, in the absence of an ETS or any effective national plan to comprehensively reduce emissions within the energy sector and integrate national energy and climate law, reducing carbon emissions to these levels may prove difficult. At present, the Coalition Government is stating that they believe that Australia's Paris Agreements will be achieved through the use of 'Kyoto carry-over credits', ie, the amount by which Australia overachieved its Kyoto targets. However, this approach has not received broad international acceptance and is viewed by segments of both the Australian and international communities as being disingenuous and not in the spirit of the Paris Commitments.

VI. Regulating for Extremes: The Worst Drought in Australia's History and the 2019–2020 Bushfire Crisis

It has often been said that it would take a significant event to occur before Australia's energy and climate laws would ever be integrated due to the need to

---

[45] Kerry Schott, 'Letter from the Board of the Energy Security Board to the Ministers of the COAG Energy Council on the High Level Design of the National Energy Guarantee' (13 April 2018), www.coagenergycouncil.gov.au/sites/prod.energycouncil/files/publications/documents/ESB%20Letter%20to%20Ministers_High-level%20design%20document.pdf (last accessed 14 April 2020).

[46] Steve Price, Interview with Angus Taylor, Commonwealth Minister for Energy and Emissions Reduction (Gladstone, Queensland, 22 August 2019).

[47] Climate Change Authority, 'Towards a Climate Policy Toolkit: Special Review on Australia's Climate Goals and Policies' (Commonwealth of Australia (Climate Change Authority) 2016) 41.

shift the political discourse on the subject. Many critics have argued that the worst drought in Australia's history and the catastrophic 2019–2020 bushfire crisis ought to be the events that fundamentally change the Australian Government's approach to energy and climate law. 2019 saw Australia's hottest and driest year on record, exacerbating a drought that has exceeded the Federation Drought, the Second World War Drought and the Millennium Drought in terms of its severity on the Murray Darling Basin.[48] Combined with persistent hot, dry conditions and strong winds, it has created perfect conditions for bushfires to spread across the country, causing widespread damage. The fires have torched over 10.7 million hectares of land, burnt over 1,700 homes in New South Wales, Victoria and South Australia and a loss of over one billion animals has been estimated.[49] The economic cost of the bushfires is set to exceed a record $4.4 billion set by the Black Saturday bushfires of 2009.[50]

Both of these events have highlighted the greater risk of natural disasters than had previously been predicted and the vulnerability of Australia to climate change.[51] Australia is sometimes referred to as 'the canary in the coal mine' in respect to the dangers of climate change. These disasters have further shown that much of the national emergency response capability is reliant on infrastructure, and in particular energy infrastructure, which has been struck by both reliability and security concerns throughout these disasters. For example, there have been numerous examples of national emergency broadcast communications failing due to local substations and transmission and distribution lines burning down, meaning that affected local communities lose all access to telecommunications such as phone and internet connections, as well as TV and radio broadcasts.[52] There have also been instances of the inter-state interconnectors needed to maintain the

---

[48] Kate Doyle, 'Murray-Darling Basin in "Most Severe" Two-to-Three Year Drought Conditions in 120 Years of Records, BOM Says' *ABC News*, Sydney, 19 July 2019, www.abc.net.au/news/2019-07-19/most-severe-recorded-drought-across-the-murray-darling/11325216 (last accessed 14 April 2020).

[49] Nick Evershed, Andy Ball and Naaman Zhou, 'How Big are the Fires Burning in Australia? Interactive Map' *The Guardian*, Sydney, 8 January 2020, www.theguardian.com/australia-news/datablog/ng-interactive/2019/dec/07/how-big-are-the-fires-burning-on-the-east-coast-of-australia-interactive-map (last accessed 14 April 2020); Sigal Samuel, 'A staggering 1 Billion Animals are Now Estimated Dead in Australia's Fires' (*Vox*, 7 January 2020), www.vox.com/future-perfect/2020/1/6/21051897/australia-fires-billion-animals-dead-estimate (last accessed 14 April 2020).

[50] Ben Butler, 'Economic Impact of Australia's Bushfires Set to Exceed $4.4bn Cost of Black Saturday' *The Guardian*, Sydney, 8 January 2020, www.theguardian.com/australia-news/2020/jan/08/economic-impact-of-australias-bushfires-set-to-exceed-44bn-cost-of-black-saturday (last accessed 14 April 2020).

[51] Will Steffen, Annika Dean and Martin Rice, 'Weather Gone Wild: Climate Change-Fuelled Extreme Weather in 2018' (Climate Council, 2019) 4.

[52] Fergus Hunter and Zoe Samios, 'Increasing Fire Threat to Vulnerable Telecommunications Networks' *The Sydney Morning Herald*, Sydney, 11 January 2020, www.smh.com.au/politics/federal/increasing-fire-threat-to-vulnerable-telecommunications-networks-20200110-p53qcy.html (last accessed 14 April 2020).

NEM going down, meaning that energy consumers have been asked to urgently reduce their energy consumption in an attempt to prevent blackouts or rolling brown-outs.[53]

Dr Kerry Schott, the Chair of the Australian Energy Security Board, said that the failure to integrate energy and climate policy and the lack of a national policy had made it increasingly difficult to maintain a secure, reliable and resilient energy sector. This was even more so during Australia's bushfire crisis and as a result Schott said 'national leadership' was needed on emissions policy.[54] Meanwhile, Audrey Zibelmann, the head of the Australian Energy Market Operator responsible for running the NEM, and previously the head of the New York Public Service Commission, likened the impact of the bushfires on the electricity sector to that experienced by the North-east of the United States following Hurricane Sandy in 2012.[55] More recently, there have been heightened calls for a comprehensive national emissions policy and the urgent need to integrate energy and climate law. There was widespread condemnation of the failure of the Commonwealth Government's response to the bushfires. This was especially in light of the disclosure in the media that a number of the country's emergency services leaders had requested urgent meetings with the Government about their growing concerns regarding the impact of climate change on the frequency and serious nature of bushfires. In response to this, Prime Minister Scott Morrison has defended his decision to decline meeting with the emergency services leaders as well as his handling of the bushfire crisis, acknowledging 'the link ... between the broader issues of global climate change and what that means for the world's weather and the dryness of conditions in many places' but that 'no response by any one government anywhere in the world can be linked to any one fire event'.[56] He maintains that he does not plan to change Australia's emissions reduction policy. In contrast, the opposition Labor Party has called for the NEG to be re-introduced to help reduce greenhouse gas emissions to mitigate the impacts of climate change in the

---

[53] Rex Martinich, 'Urgent Call to Reduce Power Use as Snowy Region Bushfires Cut Interstate Lines' *The Canberra Times*, 4 January 2020, www.canberratimes.com.au/story/6566220/urgent-call-to-reduce-power-use-as-bushfires-cut-interstate-lines/?cs=14231 (last accessed 14 April 2020).

[54] Fergus Hunter, Dominic Powell and Simon Johanson, 'Government Energy Adviser Calls for "National Leadership" on Emissions' *The Sydney Morning Herald*, Sydney, 13 January 2020, www.smh.com.au/politics/federal/government-energy-adviser-calls-for-national-leadership-on-emissions-20200113-p53r2a.html (last accessed 14 April 2020).

[55] Nick Toscano, '"Like New York after Sandy": Bushfires a "Wake-Up Call" for Power Grid' *The Sydney Morning Herald*, Sydney, 10 January 2020, www.smh.com.au/business/the-economy/like-new-york-after-sandy-bushfires-expose-major-power-grid-risks-20200109-p53q5o.html (last accessed 14 April 2020).

[56] Stephanie Convery, 'Morrison's Government on the Bushfires: From Attacking Climate "lunatics" to Calling in the Troops' *The Guardian*, Sydney, 4 January 2020, www.theguardian.com/australia-news/2020/jan/04/morrisons-government-on-the-bushfires-from-attacking-climate-lunatics-to-calling-in-the-troops (last accessed 14 April 2020).

energy sector. Given the noticeable changes in public sentiment regarding the urgent need for climate action and the need to integrate energy and climate laws, perhaps this will be the much-needed driver for change?

VII. Conclusion

Australia's transition from a traditional reliance on coal-fired generation to an integrated energy mix that incorporates more renewable energy and energy storage has not been a smooth one. Despite a clear desire among the Australian populace for renewable energy investment, Australian energy law has always been subject to the whims of the fossil fuel industry which is severely opposed to a coordinated transition towards renewable generation as well as efforts to reduce greenhouse gas emissions. A failure of the Australian Government to integrate climate policy when considering energy law has also been particularly damaging to this transition. Australia's fraught history with climate action has seen Australia ranked the worst of 57 countries on climate change policy, labelling the Morrison Government as a 'regressive force' in international climate negotiations.[57] In light of the unprecedented drought and bushfire disasters which have ravaged the nation, it is now more important than ever that a consideration of the climate crisis takes place when proceeding with energy and climate laws.

---

[57] Jan Burck and others, 'Climate Change Performance Index: Results 2020' (Germanwatch, Climate Action Network and New Climate Institute, 2019) 23.

15
Canada's Emerging LNG Export Industry and the Project Approval Challenge

RUDIGER TSCHERNING[1]

I. Introduction

Canada, despite abundant hydrocarbon resources such as crude oil and natural gas, has historically had only one international energy market, the United States of America (US). In the wake of the shale revolution in the mid-2000s, increasing US domestic production has reduced the need for Canadian energy imports. At the same time, Asian economies experienced increasing demand for energy and looked to diversify their energy suppliers. Given the limited opportunities in North America, the Canadian energy industry considered a number of new projects for Asian markets. With these emerging opportunities, tidewater access to the coastal province of British Columbia became a key priority for the energy industry, especially in the resource-rich, but land-locked province of Alberta.

In the mid-2000s, Canada seemed to have awoken from slumber to become a global energy exporter. The Canadian energy industry planned greenfield pipeline projects to provide new tidewater access to resources in Western Canada, and also contemplated brownfield pipeline projects to expand the capacity of existing energy infrastructure. Both domestic and foreign oil and gas companies were keen to invest on the assumption that pipelines would be built, opening access to Asian markets. Along the Pacific coast in British Columbia, an emerging liquefied natural gas (LNG) export industry had proposed various LNG projects. The high prices of natural gas and crude oil globally, and the relatively high price of LNG in Asia, further incentivised the development of energy infrastructure projects.

Since the heydays of the mid-2000s, more than a decade has passed. Today, Canada is domestically divided over energy infrastructure projects and a number

---

[1] The author would like to thank Kenryo Mizutani, JD Candidate 2020, for his helpful research assistance. All errors remain those of the author.

of crude oil and natural gas pipeline projects, and many LNG export projects, are either delayed or cancelled. Canada, to date, has only one major LNG project for export to Asia that has reached the final investment decision (FID),[2] and has only one crude oil pipeline that connects resource-rich Alberta to the Pacific cost of British Columbia. One could say that Canada has become a difficult place to complete energy infrastructure projects.

Why then, does Canada, a potential energy superpower, face such protracted challenges to securing project approval for critical energy infrastructure, including to access tidewater? To make sense of these issues facing Canada's emerging LNG export industry, this chapter examines the broader question of development of energy infrastructure in Canada. As this chapter argues, the delay in project approval and other regulatory and political challenges to facilitate Canada's LNG export industry are a symptom of deeper issues that share commonalities with the Canadian energy industry as a whole.

The underlying reasons for what this chapter terms the 'project approval challenge' may be found in a legitimacy crisis in the project approval process and in challenges arising from so-called 'proxy clashes' waged by stakeholders over broader environmental concerns and historically strained Indigenous relations. The objective of this chapter is therefore to provide a critical examination of this project approval challenge, aimed at an international readership that may not be familiar with the regulatory landscape in Canada. To deliver on this objective, this chapter examines issues facing the emerging LNG export industry and also draws upon the project approval process in the broader Canadian energy industry. While there has been much written on individual aspects of Canada's project approval challenges, the current literature lacks a macro-perspective analysis that contextualises Canada's regulatory struggles within the global energy market, in particular in the context of an emerging LNG export industry directed at the Asian markets. This chapter seeks to address this gap.

This chapter is structured as follows. After this Introduction, section II sets out Canada's position in the global energy market. Section III examines a number of domestic infrastructure projects that have faced significant challenges to project approval, preventing access to the Asian markets. Section IV analyses the underlying reasons for challenges in the project approval process, including environmental concerns and Indigenous relations. The chapter concludes that the challenges faced by Canada's LNG export industry reflect the wider struggles of Canada's energy industry. The reality is that the project approval process suffers from a legitimacy crisis, which has exposed it to interferences from 'proxy clashes' over environmental and Indigenous issues.

---

[2] LNG Canada is the only large-scale LNG project that received FID in 2018 and is the largest private investment project in the history of Canada. See further, LNG Canada, 'About LNG Canada', www.lngcanada.ca.

II. Canada in the Global Energy Market

A. Canada's Resource Potential

To understand the motivation behind Canada's emerging LNG export industry, Canada's resource potential must briefly be examined. In terms of natural gas, Canada is the fourth largest producer and fifth largest exporter of natural gas, with average marketable production of 16.7 Bcf/d (2.4 Bcm/d).[3] Due to Canada's endowment of shale plays, 71 per cent of Canada's natural gas production is derived from unconventional sources, such as tight gas, coalbed methane, and shale gas.[4] Close to 69 per cent of production is from the province of Alberta, 29 per cent from the province of British Columbia, and the remaining two per cent from the province of Saskatchewan, all provinces in Western Canada.[5] In 2018, Canada exported 46 per cent of produced natural gas that amounted to 7.8 Bcf/d (0.22 Bcm/d), exclusively to US markets.[6]

As the issues facing the LNG export industry share commonalities with energy infrastructure projects for crude oil, it is worthwhile highlighting Canada's export potential in terms of crude oil. Canada has the third largest proven reserves for crude oil after Venezuela and Saudi Arabia. Currently, Canada is the fourth largest producer and fourth largest exporter of oil in the world, 96 per cent of which is from the oil sands, mostly located in the province of Alberta.[7] Producing 4.6 MMb/d of crude oil, Canada is a net exporter, exporting 3.7 MMb/d abroad, 96 per cent of which is transported to the US markets.[8]

Despite an abundant resource potential, the common theme in the Canadian energy industry (whether natural gas or crude oil) is the lack of access to energy infrastructure. In light of this, Canada currently lacks access to any true export market other than to the US.[9]

With traditional dependence on US markets for its natural gas and crude oil exports,[10] Canada has missed out on the regional differences in the prices of crude oil and natural gas by not being able to export globally. Canada historically exported its natural gas to the US through an extensive pipeline network,

---

[3] Government of Canada, Natural Resources Canada, 'Natural Gas Facts' (9 August 2019), www.nrcan.gc.ca/natural-gas-facts/20067.
[4] Ibid.
[5] Ibid.
[6] Ibid.
[7] Government of Canada, Natural Resources Canada, 'Crude Oil Facts' (9 August 2019), www.nrcan.gc.ca/crude-oil-facts/20064.
[8] Ibid.
[9] Alastair R Lucas and Chidinma B Thompson, 'Infrastructure, Governance and Global Energy Futures: Regulating the Oil Sands Pipelines' (2016) 28:3 *Journal of Environmental Law and Practice* 355 at 367.
[10] Alastair R Lucas, 'Canada's Role in the United States' Oil and Gas Supply Security: Oil Sands, Arctic Gas, NAFTA, and Canadian Kyoto Protocol Impacts' (2004) 25 *Energy Law Journal* 403.

yet in recent years, the increasing supply of unconventional gas from domestic US sources has decreased the price of natural gas in North America.[11] As a result, Canada's traditional market is shrinking fast: the US imported 5.9 Bcf/d of natural gas from Canada in 2018, but imports will decline to zero by 2040.[12] Moreover, the recent development of the Permian Basin in West Texas has increased domestic oil production, which will reduce the need for Canadian crude oil, as the US becomes the largest producer of both crude oil and natural gas.[13]

In the meantime, the price of natural gas exhibited a different trend elsewhere in the world.[14] Regional price differentials exist for natural gas because natural gas markets are geographically segmented, given that natural gas is difficult to transport.[15] While the development of natural gas liquefaction technology has improved global market integration,[16] regional price differentials persist. In Asia, natural gas is predominantly imported as LNG and is priced relative to crude oil.[17] For instance, the Japan Crude Cocktail (JCC) index sets the LNG price for LNG imported into Japan.[18] Given Japan's historical position as the world's single largest LNG importer,[19] the JCC is an influential pricing mechanism in Asia, used by other Asian economies with some modifications.[20]

The fact that the Asian LNG price is linked to crude oil while the North American natural gas price is not, creates an opportunity for arbitrage. Between 2010 and 2019, the Henry Hub index oscillated between 1.73 US Dollars per MMBtu at the low end and 6.00 US Dollars per million Btu at the high end,[21] whilst during the same period, the natural gas price under the JCC index increased

---

[11] Satish Kumar et al, 'Current Status and Future Projections of LNG Demand and Supplies: A Global Prospective' (2011) 39 *Energy Policy* 4097 at 4103.

[12] Canadian Energy Research Institute, *Study No 172: Competitive Analysis of Canadian LNG* (Canadian Energy Research Institute, 2018) at 1.

[13] A Simienski, 'Implications of the US Shale Gas Regulation' (Presented at the US-Canada Energy Summit on 17 October, 2014 in Chicago), www.eia.gov/pressroom/presentations/sieminski_10172014.pdf.

[14] Boriss Siliverstovsa et al, 'International Market Integration for Natural Gas? A Cointegration Analysis of Prices in Europe, North America and Japan' (2005) 27 *Energy Economics* 603 at 614.

[15] Ruchdi Maalouf, 'The Essential Evolution of LNG Trading – Moving to GTCs' (2018) 11 *Journal of Energy & Natural Resources Law* 410 at 411.

[16] Paul Griffin, 'Changing Markets and Contracts of the LNG Business' (2003) 21 *Journal of Energy & Natural Resources Law* 85 at 86. See also Michael Coates, 'LNG Receiving Terminals – Some Key Legal Issues' (2010) 28 *Journal of Energy & Natural Resources Law* 207 at 209.

[17] United States Energy Information Administration, 'Natural Gas Prices in Asia Mainly Linked to Crude Oil, but Use of Spot Indexes Increases' (*Today in Energy*, 29 September 2015), www.eia.gov/todayinenergy/detail.php?id=23132.

[18] United States Energy Information Administration, *Perspectives on the Development of LNG Market Hubs in Asia Pacific Region* (United States Energy Information Administration, 2017) 32.

[19] United States Department of Commerce, International Trade Administration, 'Japan Country Commercial Guide' (6 September 2018), www.export.gov/article?id=Japan-Liquefied-Natural-Gas-LNG.

[20] United States Energy Information Administration (n 17) 32. See also Mike Fulwood, *Asian LNG Trading Hubs: Myth or Reality* (Columbia University School of International Public Policy Centre on Global Energy Policy, 2018) 27.

[21] United States Energy Information Administration, 'Natural Gas' (7 August 2019), www.eia.gov/dnav/ng/hist/rngwhhdm.htm.

to a high of 16.75 US Dollars per MMBtu.²² This regional price differential provides Canada with a strong incentive to capitalise on market differentials.

A regional price differential also affects Canadian crude oil. For instance, the key price index for Canadian crude oil is Western Canadian Select (WCS), which is for a blend consisting of diluted bitumen from Western Canadian oil sands.²³ Generally, North American crude oil prices are determined by pipeline capacity and transportation costs.²⁴ For Canadian crude oil, there is an additional discount as diluted bitumen tends to be heavier and have higher processing costs compared to West Texas Intermediate (WTI), a blend of lighter crude oil from the US.²⁵

In addition, the US Midwest and the US Gulf Coast have been the primary markets for Canadian crude oil exports,²⁶ as these areas have specialised refineries capable of handling heavier Canadian oil.²⁷ However, with the recent boom in the US production of crude oil, these markets increasingly became saturated.²⁸ As a result, the lack of alternative markets has resulted in a significant price discount for Canadian crude oil, by as much as 28 US dollars per barrel in the third quarter of 2018.²⁹

Given these changes in the North American markets and the increasing market opportunities in Asia, the Canadian energy industry has considered alternative markets for its natural gas and crude oil production.

B. Asia as a Potential Market for Canada

With its traditional US market shrinking, Canada has sought access to Asian markets where prices are more lucrative compared to the North American market.³⁰ Historically, there have been a number of pipeline project proposals to gain tidewater access to the Pacific coast with a view to exporting Canadian energy to Asia.

---

[22] Maha Kamal, 'Dynamics of Natural Gas pricing: The Critical Need for a Natural Gas Hub in South Asia' (2016) 69:1 *Journal of International Affairs* 70 at 74.

[23] MC Moore et al, 'Catching the Brass Ring: Oil Market Diversification Potential for Canada' (2011) 4:16 *The University of Calgary The School of Public Policy SPP Research Papers* 1 at 1.

[24] Emil D Attanasi, 'Bitumen Prices and Structural Changes in North American Crude Oil Markets' (2016) 25:4 *Natural Resources Research* 487 at 488.

[25] Moore (n 23) 41.

[26] Moore (n 23) 2.

[27] Perry Sadorsky, 'Risk Factors in Stock Returns of Canadian Oil and Gas Companies' (2001) 23 *Energy Economics* 17 at 27.

[28] Elimira Aliakbari and Ashley Stedman, 'The Cost of Pipeline Constraints in Canada' (*Fraser Research Bulletin*, 8 May 2018), www.fraserinstitute.org/sites/default/files/cost-of-pipeline-constraints-in-canada.pdf.

[29] Oil Sands Magazine, 'Oil Price Differentials Explained: Why Alberta Crude Sells at a Depp Discount' (*Oil Sands Magazine*, 2018), www.oilsandsmagazine.com/market-insights/crude-oil-pricing-differentials-why-alberta-crude-sells-at-deep-discount-to-wti.

[30] Nigel Bankes, 'Pipelines and the Constitution: a Special Issue of the Review of Constitutional Studies' (2018) 23 *Review of Constitutional Studies* 1 at 17.

In particular, Japan, China, and South Korea have been key players in the global energy markets. In terms of natural gas, Japan is the largest LNG importer, historically importing about 70 per cent of the globally available LNG.[31] Japan's relative share has since declined with the growth of other Asian economies, in particular China. Estimates for when China will overtake Japan as the world's largest LNG importer vary, with the most recent figures ranging from 2022 to 2040.[32]

For Asian economies, diversification of supply sources is a key strategic consideration,[33] which may include taking equity interests in projects at source, as in the case in the LNG Canada mega-project. These diversification policies present a strategic window of opportunity for the Canadian energy industry as it casts its eyes towards Asia. This is especially noticeable in Canada's LNG export industry, where Asian interests dominate the LNG Canada project.[34]

But what makes the Western Canadian energy industry so attractive for exports to the lucrative Asian markets? A brief discussion of the key advantages enjoyed by Canada over its global competitors must follow.

i. Geographic and Geopolitical Advantages

Shipments from Canada can access Asian markets faster than global competitors, including from the US. For instance, to reach Asia from the Middle East, a tanker must use the traditional shipping lanes of the Strait of Hormuz and the Strait of Malacca, which may take up to three weeks.[35] Alternatively, to reach Asia from the US Gulf of Mexico, a tanker must travel through the Panama Canal, a global chokepoint that has limited handling capacity, especially for larger LNG tankers, and may take approximately three weeks.[36] For a tanker to travel from Australia to Asia, it would typically take about 15 days. In comparison, it only takes 10 days for a tanker to travel from an LNG export terminal in British Columbia to the port of Yokohama, a key Japanese LNG import terminal.[37]

---

[31] Vlado Vivoda, 'LNG Import Diversification in Asia' (2014) 2 *Energy Strategy Reviews* 289 at 289. International Energy Agency, *Global Energy Outlook 2018* (International Energy Agency, 2018) 183.

[32] Wood Mackenzie, 'Japan to Lose Top LNG Importer Position to China by 2022', <www.woodmac.com/press-releases/japan-to-lose-top-lng-importer-position-to-china-by-2022/; see also International Energy Agency, *ibid* 183.

[33] Vivoda (n 31) 290.

[34] LNG Canada, 'About LNG Canada: Joint Venture Participants', www.lngcanada.ca/about-lng-canada/joint-venture-participants/. LNG Canada is a joint venture of Shell (Canada), Petronas (Malaysia), PetroChina (China), and Mitsubishi Corporation (Japan) and Kogas (South Korea).

[35] Kapil Narula, *The Maritime Dimension of Sustainable Energy Security* (Springer Singapore, 2019) 105.

[36] Yohei Muramatsu and Yuta Sugiura, 'Asian Energy Groups Join Shell in $14bn Canada LNG Project: Mitsubishi, PetroChina and Petronas to Supply Energy-Hungry Asia' (*Nikkei Asian Review*, 3 October 2018), https://asia.nikkei.com/Business/Markets/Commodities/Asian-energy-groups-join-Shell-in-14bn-Canada-LNG-project.

[37] Ken Koyama, *Japan: A High-Value Market for Canadian LNG* (Asia Pacific Foundation of Canada, 2014) 14.

Reduced travel times and distances also have advantages in terms of lower fuel costs and shorter shipping routes directly translate into reduced greenhouse gas emissions from maritime transportation. Thus, Canadian LNG exports not only gain strategic 'climate change advantages' in terms of marketability, but can also translate these advantages into real cost advantages in the export chain. These advantages will become even more relevant as global efforts to reduce greenhouse gas emissions from maritime fuels and shipments, spearheaded by the International Maritime Organisation, continue to intensify.

Canada's northern location is also ideal for the liquefaction of natural gas and offers strategic production cost advantages. A colder climate is an inherent advantage in LNG production, as natural gas needs to be cooled to −162 degrees Celsius to produce LNG.[38] Lower ambient temperatures increase the energy efficiency of the production process. Proposed LNG plants in British Columbia enjoy natural energy efficiency advantages compared to international competitors, with estimates ranging from 35 per cent compared to LNG projects in Australia, 32 per cent for projects in Qatar, and 26 per cent for projects in the US Gulf of Mexico.[39]

Another strategic advantage of Canadian LNG exports to Asia is Canada's geopolitical position. For example, the shipping lane that extends from the Strait of Hormuz to the Strait of Malacca is the dominant shipping route used to transport approximately 61 per cent of the world's petroleum trade in 2015.[40] The same shipping lane is used by LNG tankers to transport LNG from Qatar to Asia. In the event of any disruption in the Strait of Hormuz, upward of 75 per cent of the current Middle Eastern hydrocarbon production – including about 18 per cent of global LNG production – would be disrupted.[41] The heavy reliance of this shipping lane by Asian importers would make their economies particularly vulnerable to any disruption,[42] as was seen by the recent attacks on tankers in the summer of 2019 in the Strait of Hormuz and the nearby Gulf of Oman.[43] Closer to Asia, tankers then must pass through the Strait of Malacca, which has traditionally been the hotbed of maritime piracy.[44] North of the Strait of Malacca, energy shipments travel through the South China Sea, where regional geopolitical tensions pose an additional risk-factor along the shipping route.[45]

---

[38] Government of Canada, National Energy Board, 'Market Snapshot: LNG Projects have an Energy Efficiency Advantage Compared to the other LNG Producers in Warmer Locations' (3 August 2018), www.neb-one.gc.ca/nrg/ntgrtd/mrkt/snpsht/2017/10-01lngprjcts-eng.html?=undefined&wbdisable=true.

[39] *Ibid*.

[40] United States Energy Information Administration, 'World Oil Transit Chokepoints' (25 July 2017), www.eia.gov/beta/international/regions-topics.php?RegionTopicID=WOTC.

[41] J Peter Pham, 'Iran's Threat to the Strait of Hormuz: A Realist Assessment' (2010) 32 *American Foreign Policy Interests* 64 at 65.

[42] Vivoda (n 31) 295–96.

[43] Riad A Ajami, 'Global Oil Supplies and Asia Pacific Economies: Dependencies and Challenges' (2019) *Journal of Asia-Pacific Business* 1 at 1.

[44] Robert C Beckman et al, 'Acts of Piracy in the Malacca and Singapore Straits' (1994) 1:4 *International Boundaries Research Unit – Maritime Briefing* at 1.

[45] Robert D Blackwill and Meghan L O'Sullivan, 'American's Energy Edge: The Geopolitical Consequences of the Shale Revolution' (2014) 93:2 *Foreign Affairs* 102 at 109.

ii. Competitive Advantages

Canada may be able to benefit from regional price differentials between North America and Asia, while offering Asian markets an alternative LNG pricing mechanism that is not tied to the price of crude oil. This would be highly attractive to Asian consumers and make Canadian LNG exports increasingly competitive. As noted earlier, the LNG in Asia is priced in relation to crude oil price, mostly a modification of Japan's JCC.[46] The JCC index links LNG and crude oil prices, causing the two to fluctuate together. While Japan has been the most vocal proponent for pricing reforms, since the JCC index in its modified forms is used in other Asian economies, similar concerns have been expressed.[47]

Canada may therefore become an alternative supplier to Asian LNG markets if it can offer Asian economies a pricing formula that is decoupled from crude oil indexing. In fact, the US, which is ahead of Canada in preparing to enter Asian markets, has already developed and offered a pricing formula that is attractive to Asian importers: 80 per cent of the LNG projects in the US do not use crude oil indexing, but rather a pricing formula that is either based solely on the Henry Hub index or a hybrid based on the Henry Hub index.[48]

Despite Canada's resource potential and attractive economic rationales for entering Asian LNG markets, the Canadian energy industry faces increasing challenges to the approval of critical energy infrastructure. The following section examines the current challenges of securing approval for energy infrastructure projects in the context of Canada's developing LNG export industry.

III. Regulatory and Political Challenges in Canada

A. Contentious Energy Infrastructure Projects

As discussed in section II, shrinking US markets, emerging Asian markets for LNG export, and attractive regional price differentials are three core motivations for Canadian energy exporters to focus on Asian markets. But the lack of domestic infrastructure to provide critical access to tidewater on the Western Canadian coastline is a clear obstacle to these ambitions. The focus of this section is to examine the challenges that currently exist in Canada to securing project approval and how these may impact the approval of strategic LNG energy infrastructure projects.

Contentions over energy infrastructure projects have been a historic issue in Canada. In fact, the current Canadian federal regulator, the Canadian Energy

---

[46] James Henderson, *The Potential Impact of North American LNG Exports* (Oxford Institute for Energy Studies, 2012) 6.
[47] Fulwood (n 20) 27. See also United States Energy Information Administration (n 18) 32.
[48] United States Energy Information Administration (n 17).

Regulator (which used to be called National Energy Board, but was renamed in fall 2019), was founded because the TransCanada Pipeline Project to connect Western and Eastern Canada created such social and political tensions that it was considered necessary to establish an arms-length, independent regulator.[49] Most recently, the Mackenzie Gas Pipeline Project, which sought to connect Arctic Canada with US markets, attracted significant negative attention and public scrutiny[50] during its 17-year approval process. Due to changing market conditions, most notably the reduced need for Canadian natural gas in the US, the project proponents cancelled the project in 2017.[51]

Yet, the challenges facing contemporary energy infrastructure projects in Canada are on a different scale. Today, the issue of the elusive 'social license' is central to the approval process, even though there is no accepted understanding of what the concept actually entails.[52] The most salient issues on 'social license' relate to environmental concerns and Indigenous relations, but these issues are, in fact, 'classic proxy issues – matters over which, primarily for constitutional reasons [the regulators] have little or no legal authority'.[53]

For large-scale energy infrastructure projects, projects which have impacts beyond provincial or national boundaries, points of contention often concern broader global issues such as climate change and an energy transition away from fossil fuels. As currently stands, these important questions are beyond the jurisdiction and mandate of regulators in Canada.[54]

Moreover, the increasing public awareness is not limited to new build energy infrastructure projects. Expansion of existing brownfield projects face 'significant (and taken in its totality, unprecedented) opposition from members of civil society as well as from Indigenous communities, cities, towns and provincial governments'.[55] The tensions have escalated and, as discussed further below in section IV, the majority of brownfield projects now also attract 'significantly increased litigation'.[56]

B. The Regulatory Framework for Energy Infrastructure Projects in Canada

Before describing the challenges to obtaining project approval for recent Canadian energy infrastructure development, it may be helpful to provide a high-level

---

[49] Lucas and Thompson (n 9) 368.
[50] Lucas and Thompson (n 9) 361.
[51] Imperial Oil, News Release, 'Mackenzie Gas Project Participants end Joint Venture' (22 December 2017), https://news.imperialoil.ca/press-release/mackenzie-gas-project-participants-end-joint-venture.
[52] Peter Forrester et al, 'Energy Superpower in Waiting: New Pipeline Developments in Canada, Social License, and Recent Federal Energy Reforms' (2015) 53:2 *Alberta Law Review* 419 at 429.
[53] Lucas and Thompson (n 9) 369.
[54] Lucas and Thompson (n 9) 370.
[55] Bankes (n 30) 1–2.
[56] Bankes (n 30) 1–2.

introduction to the Canadian regulatory framework. In Canada, the Constitution Act 1867 allocates areas of responsibility for the federal and the provincial governments.[57] Section 92 (10) of the Act provides provincial governments the power to regulate works and undertaking that are of a local nature and within each province, but there is a carve-out of provincial jurisdiction for works and undertaking that connect provinces or extend beyond a provincial boundary, where federal jurisdiction arises.[58] Nigel Bankes has summarised the process as follows:

> In sum, federal jurisdiction is principally confined to the interconnected physical interjurisdictional transmission facilities. It will only extend beyond those transmission facilities – either upstream to processing and gathering facilities, or downstream to distribution or storage facilities – in cases where those facilities are integral to the transmission function.[59]

However, in practice, energy infrastructure projects often face jurisdictional questions since pipelines are 'linear projects that frequently stretch considerable distances',[60] including provincial and national boundaries. This raises jurisdictional issues, as a pipeline system within a province may be interconnected with another regional pipeline system, thereby crossing provincial boundaries and making it a federally regulated project.

The Supreme Court of Canada articulated the constitutional framework to divide regulatory powers in *Westcoast Energy Inc v Canada (National Energy Board)*.[61] The Supreme Court of Canada ruled that the test to determine jurisdiction is twofold: first, a pipeline or its related facilities, would fall under the federal jurisdiction if, together with all its gathering pipelines and processing plants, such facilities 'constitute a single federal work or undertaking'.[62] Second, even if the first category is not satisfied, a pipeline or its related facilities can still fall under the federal jurisdiction if such facilities are 'integral to the mainline transmission pipeline'.[63]

Once federal jurisdiction is established, the National Energy Board (to be renamed the Canadian Energy Regulator) acts as the federal regulator. In addition, the provinces maintain their provincial regulators. This may create a 'duplication of regulation across various jurisdictions and levels of government',[64] adding an administrative burden and regulatory costs to the project approval process.[65] It is also possible for the regulators to coordinate their regulatory review processes, as was the case on the Mackenzie Gas Pipeline Project.

---

[57] Constitution Act 1867, 30 & 31 Victoria, c 3 (UK), s 91 and s 92.
[58] *Ibid* s 92(10) and s 91(29).
[59] Bankes (n 30) 13.
[60] Bankes (n 30) 2.
[61] *Westcoast Energy Inc v Canada (National Energy Board)* [1991] 1 SCR 322, [1998] SCJ No 27.
[62] *Ibid* para 45.
[63] *Ibid*.
[64] Canadian Energy Pipeline Association and Ernst Young, *Regulatory Competitiveness in Canada's Pipeline Industry* (Ernst & Young LLP, 2019) 3.
[65] *Ibid* 6.

Moreover, the project approval process for energy infrastructure projects necessarily triggers related areas of regulation, in particular environmental impact assessment. After extensive consultation and lengthy review (what can be termed the 'Bill C-69 reform process'), the Impact Assessment Act came into force on 28 August 2019.[66] These reforms recast the National Energy Board into the Canadian Energy Regulator, and also established a new single assessment body, the Impact Assessment Agency of Canada.

C. Recent Examples of Contentious Energy Infrastructure

A decade ago, Canada seemed to be on the verge of becoming a global energy exporter. Since 2011, 24 proposed LNG projects obtained long-term export licence from Canada's federal regulator, varying between 20 to 40 years.[67] Moreover, pipeline companies planned to expand Canada's pipeline networks to the Pacific shores, including the Enbridge Northern Gateway Pipeline Project to carry diluted bitumen from Alberta's Athabasca Basin to the marine terminal of Kitimat in British Columbia,[68] and the Kinder Morgan Trans Mountain Pipeline Expansion Project to increase the existing capacity of crude oil pipelines connecting Edmonton, Alberta to Burnaby, British Columbia.[69] Many of these projects faced significant delays or have subsequently been cancelled. To better understand the common challenges faced by proponents of energy infrastructure development in Canada as examined in section IV below, a brief description of the most high-profile and contentious energy infrastructure projects is necessary.

i. Energy East Pipeline Project

The Energy East Pipeline Project is not a pipeline to the Pacific coast, but its experience illustrates the common challenges in Canadian project approval. In 2014, TransCanada (now known as TC Energy) proposed to construct a 4,600 kilometre pipeline to carry 1.1 million barrels of crude oil per day from Alberta and Saskatchewan to Ontario, Quebec, and New Brunswick.[70] The project was intended to open Western Canadian access to markets in Eastern Canada and the Northeast US.

---

[66] Impact Assessment Act (SC 2019, c 28). See also Bill C-69, *An Act to Enact the Impact Assessment Act and the Canadian Energy Regulator Act, to amend the Navigation Protection Act and to make consequential amendments to other Acts*, 1st Sess, 42nd Parl, 2018 (assented to 21 June 2019).

[67] Government of Canada, Natural Resources Canada, 'Canadian LNG Projects' (31 December 2018), www.nrcan.gc.ca/energy/natural-gas/5683.

[68] Forrester et al (n 52) 420.

[69] Forrester et al (n 52) 421.

[70] Government of Canada, Canadian Environmental Assessment Agency, 'Energy East Project' (10 October 2017), www.ceaa-acee.gc.ca/050/evaluations/proj/80073.

Environmental groups raised concerns over the habitat of beluga whales in the St Lawrence River, and in 2015, TransCanada decided to abandon a planned oil export terminal as political opposition from the Provincial Government of Quebec mounted.[71] Because of the increasing public interest, the Federal Government extended the review timeline for added consultation with stakeholders.[72] In the end, TransCanada cancelled the project in October 2017, after the National Energy Board changed the environmental assessment procedure to include both upstream and downstream emissions associated with new oil production realised by the project.[73]

ii. Northern Gateway Pipeline Project

The project history of the Northern Gateway Pipeline Project by Enbridge is a vivid example of the challenges of building a pipeline across British Columbia. The project is intended to transport 400,000 barrels per day of diluted bitumen from Alberta to British Columbia for Asian markets.[74] Enbridge filed the formal project for review in 2010 with the National Energy Board, and after some delay in the process, the Federal Government approved the project in 2014 as a project in the public interest.[75]

Similar to previous energy infrastructure projects, the Northern Gateway Pipeline Project attracted much criticism from stakeholders, including the Provincial Government of British Columbia, Indigenous groups, and environmental groups because of the fear of oil spills in the sensitive ecological areas near the tidewater port of Kitimat. Due to these mounting public concerns, Prime Minister Trudeau issued a mandate letter to the Federal Transport Minister in 2015, calling for a moratorium on crude oil tanker traffic in northern British Columbia, including Kitimat.[76] By banning tanker traffic around Kitimat, the moratorium effectively killed the project; even if the pipeline was to be built and diluted bitumen could be transported, the tanker ban would deprive the project of the

---

[71] Government of Canada, National Energy Board, *Energy East Pipeline Ltd. TransCanada Pipelines Ltd. – Consolidated Application, Volume 1: Application and Project Overview* (National Energy Board, 2016).

[72] Daily Commercial News, 'NEB Releases Preliminary Timeline for Energy East Pipeline Hearing' (2 May 2016), https://canada.constructconnect.com/dcn/news/resource/2016/05/neb-releases-preliminary-timeline-for-energy-east-pipeline-hearings-1015497.

[73] Government of Canada, National Energy Board, *Filing A86594 Energy East Pipeline Ltd. and TransCanada Pipeline Ltd. – TransCanada withdraws Energy East and Eastern Mainline Project Applications* (National Energy Board, 5 October 2017).

[74] Robert Hage, *Risk, Prevention, and Opportunity: Northern Gateway and the Marine Environment* (Macdonald-Laurier Institute, 2015) 14.

[75] Government of Canada, Natural Resources Canada, News Release, 'Recommendation to Impose 209 Conditions on Northern Gateway Proposal' (17 June 2014), https://web.archive.org/web/20140701151400/http://news.gc.ca/web/article-en.do?nid=858469.

[76] Government of Canada, Office of the Prime Minister, 'ARCHIVED--Minister of Transport Mandate Letter' (12 November 2015), https://pm.gc.ca/en/mandate-letters/2015/11/12/archived-minister-transport-mandate-letter.

necessary access to Asia. Furthermore, the final blow to the project was a Federal Court of Appeal decision in 2016, which quashed the original project approval by the Federal Government (granted by the previous Harper administration in 2014) and referred the matter for reconsideration to the current Federal Government, which subsequently found that the project was no longer in the public interest.[77]

iii. Trans Mountain Pipeline Expansion Project

The Trans Mountain Pipeline Expansion Project by Kinder Morgan illustrates that securing project approval is challenging, even for a brownfield project.[78] Kinder Morgan operates the Trans Mountain Pipeline between Edmonton, Alberta and Burnaby, British Columbia. Kinder Morgan sought to increase the carrying capacity of the existing pipeline from 300,000 barrels per day to 890,000 barrels per day.[79] The company filed the application for expansion with the National Energy Board in May 2013.[80] In May 2016, the National Energy Board considered the project to be in the public interest[81] and following the recommendations of the National Energy Board,[82] the Federal Government officially approved the expansion in November 2016.[83]

However, opponents challenged both the administrative process of the National Energy Board and the subsequent governmental approval by way of judicial review, which resulted in the quashing of the regulatory permits and licences by the Federal Court of Appeal in 2018. The Federal Court of Appeal ruled that the evaluation of marine traffic as the result of the expansion was inadequate, and that the Crown (which embodies the constitutional monarchy of Canada and represented by the Federal Government) failed to discharge its duty to consult with the affected Tsleil-Waututh First Nation.[84] The duty to consult will be examined in further detail in section IV below.

Eventually, the National Energy Board recommended the approval of the project after re-assessment of the impact of marine shipping, but imposed 156 conditions.[85] To ensure the viability and completion of the project, the Federal Government purchased the pipeline for 4.5 billion Canadian Dollars with the

---

[77] Government of Canada, Natural Resources Canada, 'Northern Gateway Pipelines Project' (24 July 2017) www.nrcan.gc.ca/energy/resources/19184.

[78] Bankes (n 30) 1–2.

[79] Government of Canada, Canada Energy Regulator, Trans Mountain Expansion Project – Project Background, www.cer-rec.gc.ca/pplctnflng/mjrpp/trnsmntnxpnsn/hrngprcss-eng.html.

[80] Forrester et al (n 52) 421.

[81] National Energy Board Act, RSC 1985 c N-7, s 52.

[82] Government of Canada, National Energy Board, *National Energy Board Report: Trans Mountain Expansion Project OH-001-2014* (National Energy Board, 2014).

[83] Government of Canada, Major Projects Management Office, 'Trans Mountain Expansion Project' (6 February 2019), https://mpmo.gc.ca/measures/256.

[84] *Tsleil-Waututh Nation v Canada (Attorney General)* 2018 FCA 153 at paras 4–7.

[85] Government of Canada, National Energy Board, News Release, 'The Government of Canada has Approved the Trans Mountain Expansion Project' (18 June 2019), www.neb-one.gc.ca/pplctnflng/mjrpp/trnsmntnxpnsn/mdsttmnt2019-06-18-eng.html.

intent of eventually selling the approved project to private companies.[86] Currently, despite major delays, the project is still being pursued under the ownership of the Government of Canada.

iv. Coastal GasLink Pipeline Project

The Coastal GasLink Pipeline Project aims to supply natural gas from interior British Columbia to the port of Kitimat on the Pacific coast, where LNG Canada will use the transported natural gas to make LNG.[87] The project proponent is Coastal GasLink, a subsidiary of TransCanada, and the project is regulated provincially by British Columbia. Subsequently, an environmental activist challenged the project at the National Energy Board by arguing that, because the project is connected to the federally regulated NGTL Pipeline in Alberta, it must be a part of the same federal undertaking and ought to be regulated as a federal project.[88] The National Energy Board ruled in the summer of 2019 that there is no basis to conclude that the project 'forms part of a single indivisible undertaking with the NGTL System or any other federal undertaking'[89] and thus declined to assume federal jurisdiction.[90]

D. The Cost of Regulatory Challenges to the Canadian Economy

The above examples of contentious energy infrastructure projects illustrate that proponents struggle with increasing public scrutiny and vocal stakeholder opposition. In addition, uncertainty over project approval is not without cost and Canada's global competitiveness is at stake. Foreign investors have aggressively withdrawn from their land-locked Canadian investments that cannot easily export capacity to market.[91] Canadian companies are also seeking opportunities elsewhere and divesting domestic assets.[92] As a result, Canada currently has only one operating

---

[86] Government of Canada, Prime Minister's Office, 'Prime Minister's Statement on the Trans Mountain Pipeline Project' (15 April 2018), https://pm.gc.ca/en/news/speeches/2018/04/15/prime-ministers-statement-trans-mountain-pipeline-project.

[87] TC Energy, Coastal GasLink, 'Overview', www.tcenergy.com/operations/natural-gas/coastal-gaslink/.

[88] Government of Canada, National Energy Board, *C00715 National Energy Board – Letter Decision – Jurisdiction over the Coastal GasLink Pipeline Project MH-053-2018* (29 July 2019) 22.

[89] *Ibid* 46.

[90] *Ibid* 47.

[91] Chris Varcoe, 'International Stampede out of Oilsands Grows, as Devon Energy Set to Exit Canada' (*Calgary Herald*, 21 February 2019), https://calgaryherald.com/business/energy/varcoe-a-sign-of-the-times-oilsands-exodus-expands-petrochemical-incentives-spread.

[92] Ted Morton, 'Another Canadian Oil Company Flees Trudeau and Notley for the US: Encana is the Latest Example of the Exodus of Capital Since 2015' (*Financial Post*, 6 November 2018), https://business.financialpost.com/opinion/ted-morton-another-canadian-oil-company-flees-trudeau-and-notley-for-the-u-s.

major crude oil pipeline (the Trans Mountain Pipeline), which requires urgent expansion of capacity. Furthermore, only two LNG projects on Canada's Pacific Coast have reached the milestone of a final investment decision, and only one of these projects can be considered a large-scale investment.[93]

Regulatory uncertainty has costs to Canada in terms of international trade, foreign investment, as well as direct economic costs. The following section undertakes an analysis of the underlying tensions that give rise to this regulatory uncertainty, which this chapter has termed the project approval challenge.

IV. Underlying Challenges in the Canadian Project Approval Process

A. Causes of Uncertainty

Why is Canada such a difficult energy market to obtain regulatory approval for any energy infrastructure project, be it a pipeline project or an LNG project? Currently, the three most common challenges to securing approval for an energy infrastructure project in Canada can be identified as challenges relating to the project approval process, broader environmental and social concerns, and challenges arising from relations with Indigenous peoples.

i. A Legitimacy Crisis in the Project Approval Process

Today, the established method of obtaining project approval, whereby 'regulators, authorized by legislation, having the final say on whether or not a new pipeline project is in the public interest'[94] is no longer fully functional. Stakeholders can significantly delay or even cancel a project if they have an upper hand in the balance of power surrounding the regulatory and political processes by identifying and exploiting critical veto points.[95] In addition to following the black-letter law and regulations of the project approval process, proponents and the regulatory process have to accommodate various stakeholders and address broader issues relating to the so-called 'social license to operate'.[96]

---

[93] Aside from the small-scale 0.3 bcf/d Woodfibre LNG, which has already taken the final investment decision (FID) in 2016, LNG Canada reached the FID in 2018.
[94] Forrester et al (n 52) 426.
[95] George Hoberg, 'The Battle Over Oil Sands Access to Tidewater: A Political Risk Analysis of Pipeline Alternatives' (2013) 39:3 *Canadian Public Policy* 371 at 374.
[96] John Colton et al, 'Energy Projects, Social License, Public Acceptance and Regulatory Systems in Canada: A White Paper' (2016) 9:20 *University of Calgary School of Public Policy SPP Research Papers* at 5.

While public attention and scrutiny of energy infrastructure projects in Canada has 'waxed and waned over time',[97] recent judicial challenges of formally approved projects reflect a growing legitimacy crisis in the approval process.[98] This is a new reality, of which the regulators themselves are painfully aware.[99]

ii. 'Proxy Clashes' Relating to Broader Social Issues

It could be argued that the regulatory process itself has turned into a battleground for so-called 'proxy clashes' between stakeholders of divergent interests.[100] Often in Canada, a debate over the construction of a pipeline turns into a 'much broader debate about climate and energy policy'.[101] As a result, in regulatory hearings, there is a risk that energy infrastructure becomes 'the vessel into which ... the entire carbon economy's sins [are] stuffed'.[102]

Concerns raised by stakeholders in the regulatory process are no longer about the approval of the particular energy infrastructure project under review, but instead may fall outside the true jurisdictional mandate, competence and scope of the regulatory process.[103] Thus, the National Energy Board has become increasingly aware of the gap between what the public expects it to address, and what the federal regulator can actually address pursuant to its jurisdiction.[104]

Relations with Indigenous peoples are one area that often appears as a flashpoint in the regulatory approval process in Canada. To realise exports to Asia, projects need to pass through British Columbia, where there are unresolved land claims.[105] Often, the construction of energy infrastructure will become contentious with local Indigenous groups that may claim land title and rights to project areas, in addition to tensions relating to Indigenous sovereignty and the process of reconciliation.[106] Ensuring effective citizen engagement and addressing

---

[97] Angela V Carter et al, 'Environmental Policy Convergence in Canada's Fossil Fuel Provinces? Regulatory Streamlining, Impediments, and Drift' (2017) 43:1 *Canadian Public Policy* 61 at 67.

[98] Forrester et al (n 52) 420.

[99] Peter Watson, 'National Energy Board Technical Briefing for the NEB Modernization Expert Panel' (Opening remark of the Chair and CEO of the NEB, delivered at the meeting of the NEB Modernization Expert Panel, 29 November 2016), www.canada.ca/en/national-energy-board/news/2017/02/national-energy-board-technical-briefing-modernization-expert-panel.html.

[100] Chris Turner, *The Patch: The People, Pipelines and Politics of the Oil Sands* (Simon & Shuster, 2017) 119.

[101] *Ibid*.

[102] *Ibid* 255.

[103] Guy Holburn and Margaret Loudermilk, *Risks and Costs of Regulatory Permit Applications in Canada's Pipeline Sector: Submission to the National Energy Board Modernization Expert Panel* (Ivey Business School, 2017) 5.

[104] *Ibid*.

[105] Government of Canada, Indigenous and Northern Affairs Canada, Indigenous Services Canada, 'INAC Map of First Nations in British Columbia' (27 May 2013), www.aadnc-aandc.gc.ca/eng/1100100 021015/1100100021021.

[106] Kim Stanton, 'Looking Back: The Canadian Truth and Reconciliation Commission and the Mackenzie Valley Pipeline Inquiry' (2012) 27:1 *Canadian Journal of Law and Society* 81 at 84.

stakeholder concerns has been a challenge for the National Energy Board,[107] yet many issues before regulators are actually beyond the regulator's mandate, as discussed below in the context of environmental concerns and Indigenous relations. Indigenous relations are examined in further detail below.

B. Environmental Concerns and Challenges

i. Climate Change and the Regulation of Energy Infrastructure

One of the key themes in recent contentions over energy infrastructure projects in Canada are environmental concerns in the wider context. Recently, the focus has not been on the impacts of the energy infrastructure projects *per se*, but rather on subsequent and indirect effects. One of the biggest challenges in regulating Canadian energy infrastructure is how to address the issue of greenhouse gas emissions and climate change, in particular arising from downstream emissions.

As set out in section III above, federal Bill C-69[108] became the Impact Assessment Act in August 2019, which replaced the National Energy Board with the new Canadian Energy Regulator. When Bill C-69 was being drafted, a key area of contention was how to accommodate concerns over greenhouse gas emissions and climate change in the project approval process reforms. The Senate proposed to explicitly exclude 'greenhouse gas emissions generated from another physical activity or designated project located downstream from the designated project' from the definition of 'direct or incidental effects' in the new impact assessment regime.[109] However, the Federal Government rejected this proposal, and the final version of Bill C-69 does not explicitly allow for greenhouse gas emissions facilitated by the energy infrastructure project in question to be excluded from consideration.[110] Global warming and climate change will therefore be factored into the project approval process of energy infrastructure projects in Canada.

ii. The Provinces and Municipalities as Stakeholders

Energy infrastructure projects have impacts beyond provincial or even national boundaries, and because of these ramifications, non-traditional stakeholders in Canada, such as the provinces or municipalities, are increasingly involved in broader discussions relating to climate change and environmental concerns.[111]

---

[107] Lucas and Thompson (n 9) 369.
[108] Bill C-69 (n 66).
[109] Senate of Canada, Standing Senate Committee on Energy, the Environment and Natural Resources, *Nineteenth Report: Bill C-69, An Act to Enact the Impact Assessment Act and the Canadian Energy Regulator Act, to amend the Navigation Protection Act and to make consequential amendments to other Acts*, 1st Sess, 42nd Parl, 2018 (28 May 2019) at 1(b)(ii).
[110] Bill C-69 (n 66) s 2.
[111] Lucas and Thompson (n 9) 369.

A province that has repeatedly clashed with the Federal Government on the approval of energy infrastructure projects is the strategically located province of British Columbia. British Columbia has repeatedly asserted its jurisdiction over energy infrastructure projects proposed in the province, but it has sent mixed signals, in particular on developing Canada's LNG export industry. On the one hand, British Columbia supports the LNG export industry and natural gas pipelines.[112] On the other hand, British Columbia has vehemently opposed crude oil pipelines (including expansion of existing infrastructure) to carry diluted bitumen from Alberta to British Columbia for export to Asia. To recall, British Columbia opposes the Trans Mountain Pipeline Expansion Project on the grounds of 'risks of a seven-fold increase in tanker traffic, or the catastrophic effect a diluted bitumen spill would cause to British Columbia's economy and environment'.[113] British Columbia also challenged the Trans Mountain Pipeline Expansion Project by filing a reference to the British Columbia Court of Appeal in 2018, asking whether it can enact a provincial environmental law that would require the transport of diluted bitumen via pipeline to require a provincial hazardous substances permit.[114] The province lost the appeal as British Columbia's attempt to change its law was found to be directed at blocking a federal undertaking and therefore encroaching upon federal jurisdiction.[115]

At a more local level, Canadian municipalities derive their power from respective provincial governments.[116] A number of municipalities have been fierce advocates against pipeline projects, for example the City of Vancouver and the City of Burnaby have been active opponents to the Trans Mountain Pipeline Expansion Project, taking legal actions against it.[117] The City of Burnaby attempted to use its municipal bye-laws to stop the construction of the pipeline,[118] and unsuccessfully challenged the National Energy Board's federal jurisdiction,[119] all the way to the Supreme Court of Canada.[120]

---

[112] Government of British Columbia, Office of the Premier, News Release, 'B.C.'s New LNG Framework to Deliver Record Investment, World's Cleanest LNG Facility' (2 October 2018), https://news.gov.bc.ca/releases/2018PREM0073-001910. See also Richard Zussman, '"A Spectacular Day for British Columbians": Premier Horgan Vows to Hit Climate Targets even with LNG Emissions' (*Global News*, 2 October 2018), https://globalnews.ca/news/4509526/a-spectacular-day-for-british-columbians-premier-horgan-vows-to-hit-climate-targets-even-with-lng-emissions/.

[113] Government of British Columbia, Office of the Premier, News Release, 'Premier's Statement on Proposed Purchase of the Trans Mountain Pipeline' (29 May 2018), https://news.gov.bc.ca/releases/2018PREM0080-001060.

[114] *Reference re Environmental Management Act (British Columbia)*, 2019 BCCA 181 at para 41.

[115] *Ibid* para 105.

[116] Constitution Act 1867 (n 57) s 92(8).

[117] See *Tsleil-Waututh Nation* (n 84).

[118] Olivia C Dixon et al, 'Recent Judicial Decisions of Interest to Energy Lawyers' (2018) 56:2 *Alberta Law Review* 479 at 548. See also *Burnaby (City) v Trans Mountain Pipeline ULC*, 2015 BCSC 2140, affirmed *Burnaby (City) v Trans Mountain Pipeline ULC*, 2017 BCCA 132, leave of appeal dismissed, *City of Burnaby v Trans Mountain Pipeline ULC et al*, docket SCC 38104.

[119] *Burnaby (City) v Trans Mountain Pipeline ULC*, 2017, *ibid* at para 1.

[120] See *City of Burnaby v Trans Mountain Pipeline ULC et al* (n 118).

C. Indigenous Relations and Challenges

i. Indigenous Peoples and Energy Infrastructure Projects

Proponents of energy infrastructure projects in Canada should pay careful attention to Indigenous relations.[121] Historically strained relations with Indigenous peoples may pose significant surface risks, adding complexities to an already lengthy project approval process. Failure to accommodate Indigenous relations will expose the proposed project to the potential risk of delays or outright cancellations.[122]

ii. Indigenous Peoples as 'Rights and Title Holders'

The rights of Indigenous peoples in Canada were historically overlooked and denied.[123] This began to change in 1982 with the constitutional protection of indigenous rights under section 35 of the Constitution Act 1982.[124] The Canadian Constitution 'guarantees consultation and participation by affected First Nations in natural resource projects on aboriginal lands, which gives First Nations legal rights and political clout unimagined in the 1970'.[125]

Constitutionally protected rights include 'aboriginal rights', which are 'practices, traditions and customs integral to the distinctive cultures of aboriginal peoples',[126] and 'treaty rights', which are a codified version of the aboriginal rights whereby 'a treaty represents an exchange of solemn promises between the Crown and various Indian nations'.[127] When aboriginal rights concern land, these may become 'aboriginal title', a concept that 'encompasses the right to exclusive use occupation of the land held pursuant to that title for a variety of purposes'.[128]

These various rights are considered to be unique and deviate from the standard legal concepts of Anglo-Canadian common law, existing 'by reason of the fact that aboriginal peoples were once independent, self-governing entities in possession of most of the lands now making up Canada'.[129] In Canada, Indigenous peoples are not mere stakeholders, but rather constitutionally protected 'rights and title holders'.

---

[121] Rachel Davis and Daniel Franks, *Costs of Company-Community Conflict in the Extractive Sector* (Cambridge, CSR Initiative at the Harvard Kennedy School, 2014) 8.
[122] William M Maurin and Joann P Jamieson, 'Aligning Energy Development with the Interests of Aboriginal Peoples in Canada' (2015) 53:2 *Alberta Law Review* 453 at 466.
[123] See, eg, Truth and Reconciliation Commission of Canada, *Honouring the Truth, Reconciling for the Future: Summary of the Final Report of the Truth and Reconciliation Commission of Canada* at 1.
[124] Constitution Act 1982, being Schedule B to the Canada Act 1982 (UK), 1982, c 11, s 35.
[125] Lucas (n 10) 418.
[126] *R v Van der Peet* [1996] 2 SCR 507, 137 DLR (4th) 289 at para 68.
[127] *R v Badger* [1996] 1 SCR 771, [1996] 4 WWR 457 at para 41.
[128] *Delgamuukw v British Columbia* [1997] 3 SCR 1010, [1997] SCJ No 108 at para 117.
[129] B Slattery, 'The Constitutional Guarantee of Aboriginal and Treaty Rights' (1983) 8 *Queen's Law Journal* 232 at 242.

There are, however, instances when rights of Indigenous peoples may be infringed. For example, the Crown can infringe rights when there is a valid objective for the contemplated Crown conduct[130] including general economic development, mining, protection of the environment or endangered species, hydroelectric power, and the development of infrastructure.[131] In determining whether an infringement can be justified, Canadian courts consider whether the infringement in question achieves the necessary objective in the least impairing manner possible, whether there is necessary compensation, and whether there was adequate consultation.[132] The courts have applied the concept of proportionality to see if the infringement can be justified.[133]

iii. The Duty to Consult and Accommodate

The single most important interaction with Indigenous peoples in the development of energy infrastructure projects in Canada is the 'duty to consult and accommodate' the affected peoples. As alluded to briefly in section III above, the duty to consult governs the relations between the Crown and the affected indigenous group. The duty is a unique concept in the Canadian law, where the Crown owes fiduciary obligations to Indigenous peoples.[134] In this instance, the Crown means the Canadian state and its Government. The duty arises from the honour of the Crown[135] and the need to reconcile the Crown's sovereignty with the pre-existing sovereignty of the Indigenous peoples of Canada.[136]

Failure of adequate consultation and accommodation is often raised in legal challenges of proposed energy infrastructure projects.[137] When there is an alleged infringement of rights held by Indigenous peoples, the courts will examine whether there was adequate consultation as one of the first factors of assessment.[138]

This raises the key initial question of when the duty to consult and accommodate is triggered. It is triggered 'when the Crown has knowledge, real or constructive, of the potential existence of the Aboriginal right or title and contemplates conduct that might adversely affect it'.[139] Canadian courts have refined their understanding of the duty, which is understood to contain several elements: the Crown must have either real or constructive knowledge of a potential claim or right by Indigenous

---

[130] *R v Sparrow* [1990] 1 SCR 1075, [1990] 4 WWR 410 at para 64.
[131] *Delgamuukw* (n 128) para 165.
[132] *Sparrow* (n 130) para 62.
[133] *Tsilhqot'in Nation v British Columbia* 2014 SCC 44 at para 87.
[134] *R v Guerin* [1984] 2 SCR 335, 13 DLR (4th) 321 at 383. See also Michael Coyle, 'Loyalty and Distinctiveness: A New Approach to the Crown's Fiduciary Duty toward Aboriginal Peoples' (2003) 40:4 *Alberta Law Review* 841 at 857.
[135] *Haida Nation v British Columbia (Minister of Forests)* 2004 SCC 73 at para 32.
[136] *Ibid* para 16.
[137] See *Tsleil-Waututh Nation* (n 84). See also *Dene Tha' First Nation v Canada (Minister of Environment)*, 2006 FC 1354, appeal dismissed 2008 FCA 20.
[138] *Sparrow* (n 130) para 62.
[139] *Haida Nation* (n 135) para 3.

peoples; there must be a Crown conduct in contemplation; and the conduct may adversely affect this right or claim in question.[140] The Crown bears the ultimate burden of discharging the duty, but it may use its independent regulators (eg the Canadian Energy Regulator) as 'a vehicle through which the Crown acts'.[141]

While the duty to consult and accommodate can easily be triggered, the extent of such consultation and accommodation measures depends on the strength of the claim of the right(s) and the potential adverse impact on the Indigenous group in question.[142] The Supreme Court of Canada has stated in the past that the duty is 'spectral'.[143] Critically, the duty does not provide a right to a veto, particularly where the claimed rights are not yet proven.[144] There is also no duty to agree, but rather the duty requires a commitment to a meaningful process of consultation of the parties.[145]

Whether the Crown has adequately discharged the duty to consult is circumstantial and determined on a case-by-case basis.[146] For instance, in 2017, the Supreme Court of Canada considered the adequacy of consultation conducted by the National Energy Board in preparation of a petroleum seismic survey in Nunavut as completely inadequate,[147] whilst consultation in preparation of a pipeline project in Ontario to have been adequate.[148] These cases illustrate that compliance with the duty cannot, typically, be resolved until litigated, which results in further uncertainty and delay-risks for project proponents.[149]

It is no surprise then that there has been a significant increase in legal uncertainty since 1982, in particular for natural resources and extractive sector activities in Canada.[150] In addition, The Supreme Court of Canada has been cautious to define what exactly the duty to consult and accommodate entails.[151]

In response to the potential uncertainties and risks arising from Indigenous relations, project proponents have resorted to so-called 'impact and benefit agreements' (IBAs) with Indigenous peoples. With an IBA, a project proponent contractually reaches an agreement with the affected communities in the hope of

---

[140] *Rio Tinto Alcan Inc v Carrier Sekani Tribal Council* 2010 SCC 43 at para 31.
[141] *Clyde River (Hamlet) v Petroleum Geo-Services Inc* 2017 SCC 40 at para 29.
[142] *Haida Nation* (n 135) para 39.
[143] *Haida Nation* (n 135) paras 43–44.
[144] *Tsleil-Waututh Nation* (n 84) para 494. See also Peter W Hogg, 'The Constitutional Basis of Aboriginal Rights' (2019) 15:1 *Lex Electronica – Édition spéciale Mélanges en l'honneur d'Andrée Lajoie* 177 at 192.
[145] *Haida Nation* (n 135) paras 42, 48 and 62. See also *Taku River Tlingit First Nation v British Columbia (Project Assessment Director)* 3 SCR 550 at para 22.
[146] *Sparrow* (n 130) para 66. See also *Delgamuukw* (n 128) para 87.
[147] *Clyde River (Hamlet)* (n 141) para 52.
[148] *Chippewas of the Thames First Nation v Enbridge Pipelines Inc* 2017 SCC 41 at para 64.
[149] Dwight Newman, *The Rule and Role of Law: The Duty to Consult, Aboriginal Communities, and the Canadian Natural Resource Sector* (Macdonald-Laurier Institute, 2014) 7.
[150] Dimitrios Panagos and J Andrew Grant, 'Constitutional Change, Aboriginal Rights, and Mining Policy in Canada' (2013) 51:4 *Commonwealth & Comparative Politics* 405 at 414.
[151] Derek Inman et al, 'We Will Remain Idle No More: The Shortcomings of Canada's Duty to Consult Indigenous Peoples' (2013) 4 *Göttingen Journal of International Law* 251 at 248.

avoiding legal uncertainty and project delays caused by protracted litigation.[152] IBAs are discussed in further detail below.

D. The Future of Indigenous Relations in the Project Approval Process

Today, there is a view held by Indigenous peoples and commentators that the duty to consult and accommodate in Canadian law is inadequate, given that it does not require consent, but rather, only an attempt to reach consent. This adds to the already complex understanding of the duty. In light of the uncertainties and risks arising from Indigenous relations, project proponents have developed IBAs[153] to address these uncertainties and risks. IBAs set out to establish a degree of contractual certainty where regulatory certainty is lacking.[154]

There is a strong incentive for a project proponent to enter into an IBA with the affected indigenous group, as the project may be subjected to delays or cancellation,[155] due to inadequate consultation. An IBA can also provide the added certainty in the event that the non-contractual route of the duty to consult and accommodate will not provide the necessary certainty to the project proponent.[156]

An IBA is a private contract entered into between the project proponent and the affected indigenous group and the contents of IBAs vary but are typically subject to stringent confidentiality obligations. These agreements may include a non-objection clause to the proposed energy infrastructure project, contractual provisions on on-going consultation obligations, provisions on financial and economic benefits that typically include training, employment opportunities, business and procurement opportunities, as well as provisions that govern the mechanism to address environmental concerns arising from the proposed activity of the project in question.[157]

In recent years, many successful Canadian energy infrastructure projects have concluded IBAs with respective Indigenous groups.[158] Most importantly,

---

[152] Newman (n 149) 12.
[153] Ken S Coates and Blaine Favel, *Understanding FPIC: From Assertion and Assumption on 'Free, Prior and Informed Consent' to a New Model for Indigenous Engagement on Resource Development* (Macdonald-Laurier Institute, 2016) 19.
[154] Panagos and Grant (n 150) 415.
[155] Newman (n 149) 12.
[156] Brad Gilmour and Bruce Mellett, 'The Rule of Impact and Benefits Agreements in the Resolution of Project Issues with First Nations' (2013) 51:2 *Alberta Law Review* 385 at 399
[157] *Ibid* 390–98.
[158] Government of British Columbia, 'Natural Gas Benefits Agreements', www2.gov.bc.ca/gov/content/environment/natural-resource-stewardship/consulting-with-first-nations/first-nations-negotiations/natural-gas-pipeline-benefits-agreements. See also Government of British Columbia, Ministry Indigenous Relations and Reconciliation, News Release, 'Kitsumkalum to Share in LNG Benefits after Agreements Reached with B.C.' (29 March 2019), https://news.gov.bc.ca/releases/2019IRR0030-000529.

LNG Canada and its natural gas supplier Coastal GasLink signed a number of IBAs with neighbouring Indigenous groups in British Columbia.[159]

Yet, IBAs are not without problems. IBAs can reduce uncertainty so long as the contractual parties are willing to adhere to the agreement. But to ensure the legitimacy and the durability of IBAs, proponents must be certain that they negotiate, and enter into an IBA, with the correct parties.[160] This may be easier said than done. Internal differences may arise within the Indigenous peoples signing the IBA,[161] as was the case experienced by Coastal GasLink pipeline in the spring of 2019. Coastal GasLink had signed an IBA with the elected chief and council of Wet'suwet'en First Nation.[162] However, the hereditary chiefs started protests and blockades adjacent to the project site, claiming that the authority of the elected leaders was limited to the reserve and that the hereditary leaders in fact had ultimate jurisdiction over the traditional territories in question.[163] This experience highlights the limitations of entering into IBAs and the challenges of ensuring that at any time, the project proponent is engaging with the authorised representatives of the identified contractual party.

V. Conclusion

Canada, despite its abundant natural resources including natural gas, and a pre-eminent strategic geographical location to the attractive Asian export markets, has struggled to obtain tidewater access to the Pacific coast due to what this chapter has termed the 'project approval challenge'. As this chapter has illustrated, crude oil pipeline infrastructure projects have experienced considerable regulatory and political challenges and are often the subject of public scrutiny, if not costly and time-consuming litigation. Proposed LNG export projects share commonalities with Canada's crude oil pipeline projects and as such, important conclusions can be drawn for Canada's emerging LNG export industry with respect to the project approval challenge.

---

[159] Hayley Woodin, 'B.C. First Nations to Reap Benefit from LNG Canada' (*JWN*, 10 October 2018), www.jwnenergy.com/article/2018/10/bc-first-nations-reap-multibillion-dollar-benefit-lng-canada/. See also Government of British Columbia, "Natural Gas Benefits Agreements" (n 158).

[160] Sandra Gogal et al, 'Aboriginal Impact and Benefit Agreements: Practical Considerations' (2005) 43 *Alberta Law Review* 129 at 143.

[161] Dwight Newman, *Political Rhetoric Meets Legal Reality How to Move Forward on Free, Prior and Informed Consent in Canada* (Macdonald-Laurier Institute, 2017) 15.

[162] Maham Abedi, 'Band Councils, Hereditary Chiefs – Here's What to Know about Indigenous Governance' (*Global News*, 10 January 2019), https://globalnews.ca/news/4833830/band-councils-hereditary-chiefs-indigenous-governance/.

[163] Chantelle Bellrichard 'Wet'suwet'en Hereditary Leaders, Supporters Call for Stop Work Order on Coastal GasLink pipeline' (*CBC News*, 3 February 2019), www.cbc.ca/news/indigenous/wet-suwet-en-stop-work-coastal-gaslink-pipeline-1.5003495.

The underlying reason for Canada's challenges to obtain project approval can be identified as a legitimacy crisis in the approval process combined with so-called 'proxy clashes' on broader environmental and social concerns, including climate change. Related to these concerns, historically strained relations with Indigenous peoples may pose challenges as contentious energy infrastructure projects, including LNG projects, are proposed and developed and may have an impact on Indigenous peoples and traditional lands. The rise of public awareness over the environment and broader social issues has also resulted in an increase of provinces and municipalities increasingly challenging federally approved energy infrastructure projects. The constitutional enshrinement of the rights of Indigenous peoples in 1982, and an increasing awareness and assertion of these rights, have added a further dimension to the project approval challenge in Canada.

In an attempt to address these issues, Canada has undertaken reforms of the regulatory process, both federally and provincially. Frustration with ongoing delays in the project approval process and the risk of judicial intervention on the all-important duty to consult with Indigenous peoples, has resulted in project proponents resorting to impact and benefit agreements. These are a contractual mechanism to resolve relations between the affected Indigenous group and the project proponents.

It remains to be seen whether Canada's efforts to reform the project approval mechanism will be adequate in addressing many of the components making up the project approval challenge examined in this chapter. Overcoming the critical question of project approvals would not only re-establish Canada as an investor-friendly environment but, critically, facilitate and support the emerging LNG export industry to ship Canadian LNG from Western Canadian tidewater to the attractive long-term markets in Asia.

16

Challenges and Opportunities for Energy Transitions and Decarbonisation in Southern African Countries

VICTORIA R NALULE AND SMITH I AZUBUIKE

I. Introduction

Transitioning to a low carbon economy has been a marked feature of the twenty-first century following the adoption of the 2015 Paris Agreement with the aim of reducing greenhouse gas emissions and strengthening the global response to the threat of climate change.[1] In the energy sector, this implies a shift from fossil fuels to renewable energy and investment in technologies or innovative ways of capturing, removing or curbing emissions from energy systems. Transitioning to a low carbon economy, although necessary, is complex and challenging, especially for developing countries that are still faced with energy poverty and access to reliable energy services. Indeed, it becomes imperative to understand what energy access means for us to clearly understand the challenges and opportunities in transitioning to a low carbon economy in Southern Africa.

Basically, energy is central to the economic development of a country, it is used in everyday life for lighting, heating, cooking and transport, etc.[2] Given the central role of energy in our economies, it becomes clear that energy transition is highly capable of affecting the social, economic and political atmosphere of a country. Additionally, the influence of the energy sector on other major sectors such as mining cannot be ignored considering the central role of minerals in most of the

---

[1] Victoria R Nalule, 'Transitioning to a Low Carbon Economy: Is Africa Ready to Bid Farewell to Fossil Fuels?' in Geoffrey Wood and Keith Baker (eds), *The Palgrave Handbook of Managing Fossil Fuels and Energy Transitions* (Palgrave Macmillan, 2020) 261–86.
[2] Victoria R Nalule, *Energy Poverty and Access Challenges in Sub-Saharan Africa: The Role of Regionalism* (Springer Nature, 2018).

countries in Southern Africa. We note that most of the challenges faced in the mining sector are in some way attributed to the lack of adequate modern energy, moreover there are now various initiatives to ensure utilisation of renewables in mining.[3] Other sectors including the transport sector, industry, education, health and many others are all reliant on energy. Moreover, Goal 7 of the UN Sustainable Development Goals (SDGs) also emphasises access to affordable, reliable, sustainable and modern energy for all.[4]

Goal 7 of the UN SDGs in brief highlights what energy access really means. We note that there is no globally agreed definition of energy access, although international organisations have been influential in developing this definition. The International Energy Agency (IEA) defined energy access as

> a household having reliable and affordable access to both clean cooking facilities and to electricity, which is enough to supply a basic bundle of energy services initially, and then an increasing level of electricity over time to reach the regional average.[5]

In simple terms, energy access means access to modern energy which is reliable, sustainable and affordable.

One may ask what does modern sources of energy entail? Modern energy can be distinguished from traditional sources of energy by considering the quality of sources used. For instance, with regard to traditional energy, candles, kerosene and lamps are used for lighting; and fire-wood for cooking.[6] On the other hand, with regard to modern energy, electricity and by-products of natural gas such as liquefied petroleum gas (LPG) are used for lighting and cooking, respectively.[7] We however note that a transition to a low carbon economy emphasises the deployment of renewable energy sources and also efforts to decarbonise the energy sector. Countries, however, are at different stages of implementing these initiatives.

In the European Union (EU) for instance, although there are common and regional efforts, we cannot ignore the fact that Member States have specific measures and face different challenges when it comes to the deployment of renewable energy; energy efficiency; promotion of electric vehicles; deployment of smart grids and smart meters and other features of transitional energy markets.[8] Thus, both developed and developing countries do face different energy challenges and as such a transitioning to a low carbon economy presents different challenges and

---

[3] Victoria R Nalule, *Mining and the Law in Africa: Exploring the Social and Environmental Impacts'* (Springer Nature, 2020).

[4] See, Sustainable Development Goal 7. Can be accessed at https://sustainabledevelopment.un.org/sdg7.

[5] See International Energy Agency, 'World Energy Outlook, Special Report, 2017', p 21.

[6] Nalule (n 1).

[7] Nalule (n 2).

[8] For a full discussion on EU decarbonisation efforts, see Rafael Leal-Arcas, Mariya Peykova, Victoria Nalule and Pinar Kara, 'Decarbonizing the Energy Sector' (2019) *Michigan State Journal of Animal and Natural Resource Law* 15.

opportunities in these countries. In this chapter, the focus will be on the Southern African Development Community (SADC). The chapter addresses the challenges and opportunities in transitioning to a low carbon economy in SADC with a specific focus on the regional initiatives to enable this transition.

A. A Panoramic Overview of the Energy Sector in the SADC

Established under Article 2 of the 1992 Treaty, SADC is a regional intergovernmental organisation of 15 countries.[9] The main objective of SADC is to achieve development, economic growth and alleviate poverty through regional integration. Access to modern energy is indeed essential in achieving most of the objectives of the SADC Member States. Historically, the SADC is the successor to the Southern African Coordinating Conference (SADCC) – which was formed in Lusaka, Zambia in 1980 with the adoption of the Lusaka Declaration.[10] Six institutions are established under the SADC Treaty, these include the Summit of Heads of States or Governments, the Council of Ministers, Commissions, the Standing Committee of Officials, the Secretariat, and the Tribunal. The Summit is the supreme policy-making institution of SADC; it consists of the Heads of States or governments of each Member State, and it is responsible for the overall policy direction and control of the functions of SADC. Although there are several developments in the region, the focus of this chapter is on the regional and national efforts of the countries in Southern Africa in the energy transition. Given the increasing role of regionalism in the development of the energy sector globally, while seeking to promote energy access in the region, SADC has set up several initiatives aimed at supporting the transition to a low carbon economy and these will be highlighted in the following sections.[11]

In energy terms, the region has massive energy resources including coal, oil, gas and renewable energy resources such as solar, hydropower, wind energy, etc. Similar to other sub-regions, the focus for Southern African countries is mostly to ensure access to modern energy especially reliable electricity.

---

[9] SADC countries include Angola, Botswana, the Democratic Republic of the Congo (DRC), Eswatini, Lesotho, Madagascar, Malawi, Mauritius, Mozambique, Namibia, Seychelles, South Africa, Tanzania, Zambia and Zimbabwe.

[10] SADCC was formalised by a Memorandum of Understanding (MOU) on the Institutions of the Southern African Development Coordination Conference, dated July 1981. In an effort to formalise SADCC and give it an appropriate legal status, the MOU was replaced by a Treaty. In this regard, the SADC Declaration and Treaty was signed on 17 August 1992 and this effectively transformed SADCC into SADC.

[11] For a full discussion on regionalism in the African energy sector, see Victoria R Nalule, 'Regionalism in Addressing Energy Access Challenges' in *Energy Poverty and Access Challenges in Sub-Saharan Africa* (Palgrave Macmillan, 2019) 41–89.

At this juncture it is worth noting that the dominant source of electricity in SADC is coal contributing to over 60 per cent, followed by hydro, which contributes 21.02 per cent of the electricity generation capacity. With respect to the Southern African Power Pool (SAPP), we note that South Africa is a country that is highly dependent on coal which dominates the power generation as it accounts for 76 per cent of the overall generation capacity. As of 2019, coal made up 65.7 per cent of the primary energy in South Africa followed by crude oil at 21.6 per cent and renewables covering the remainder. The situation is similar in other Southern African countries including Botswana and Zimbabwe where coal is the dominant source of energy. However, we note that the region has enormous hydropower potential which can be an option for coal as evidenced in Congo and Mozambique. Additionally, other SADC countries including the Democratic Republic of the Congo (DRC), Lesotho, Malawi, and Zambia solely rely on hydropower for electricity generation. Besides the option of hydroelectricity to replace coal, other cleaner electricity generation options such as imported natural gas feeding into combined-cycle gas turbines (CCGTs) and the pebble bed modular reactor (PBMR) have also been suggested for South Africa especially due to their low greenhouse gas (GHG) emissions.

Taking stock of the above therefore, we note that most countries in Southern Africa are heavily reliant on fossil fuels and large-scale hydropower to meet their energy needs. In this chapter therefore, the main question to be addressed is what are the challenges and opportunities in transitioning to a low carbon energy mix and economy in Southern Africa? The other issue to be addressed is, what are the existing initiatives to decarbonise the energy sector in Southern Africa? In addressing these issues, a four-step framework is employed in the form of sections. Section I is the Introduction; section II examines the literature on transitioning to a low carbon economy; section III examines the concept of a just transition and energy justice in Southern Africa; section IV analyses the decarbonisation efforts in Southern Africa; section V highlights the challenges and opportunities in transitioning to a low carbon economy in Southern Africa; and section VI gives the concluding remarks.

II. Understanding the Transition to a Low-Carbon Energy Mix

This section reviews the existing literature on a transition to a low-carbon economy with the main aim of establishing how this transition differs in different countries. The section also highlights new concepts that are relevant to the transition, including energy justice, a just transition and geographies of energy transitions. Prior to discussing a transition to a low carbon economy, it is pertinent to ask what energy transition means for the countries in Southern Africa? The next sub-section therefore addresses this question.

A. What does Energy Transition Mean for Southern African Countries?

Although recent literature defines energy transition as a shift from fossil fuels to renewables, it is important to know what the concept of 'transition' entails. In simple terms, a transition means the process or a period of changing from one state or condition to another. In energy terms, this could be a structural change in which a previously state-controlled and vertically-integrated energy supply industry, in which a government-owned or public utility corporation has a monopoly across the value chain, evolves into a more liberalised value chain in which some form of private sector participation and competition is introduced in electricity generation and retail, as seen in some countries such as Nigeria since the 2000s.[12] Energy transition could also be considered in the context of centralised energy markets becoming more decentralised in terms of planning and organisation of energy supply. For example, countries in which electricity is supplied to consumers mainly from energy generated from sources such as coal and large-hydro dams by large vertically-integrated utilities are now benefitting from more off-grid sources of energy from facilities like roof-top solar, biogas plants and other renewables, where consumers are increasingly becoming energy suppliers and market participants.[13]

In the Southern African context, we need to be aware of what we are really transitioning from and this necessitates understanding the energy situation of the countries concerned.[14] As noted in the previous section, different countries face different energy challenges. For instance, most countries in Southern Africa such as South Africa, Zimbabwe and Botswana are dependent on coal for electricity generation and yet other countries such as the DRC do utilise their abundant hydropower resources. Malawi, on the other hand, has many people who are still reliant on traditional biomass, especially in rural areas. So, even in regions such as SADC, it is not practical to have a general definition of energy transition. These countries face common energy challenges including unreliable electricity, heavy reliance on traditional biomass, inadequate energy infrastructure, inadequate finances and lack of adequate expertise and technology needed for the required large-scale deployment of modern sources of energy to fill the access gap.

---

[12] See Tade Oyewunmi, *Regulating Gas Supply to Power Markets: Transnational Approaches to Competitiveness and Security of Supply* (Wolters Kluwer, 2018) 360 at 111–71: Tade Oyewunmi, 'International Best Practices and Participation in a Private Sector Driven Electricity Industry in Nigeria: Recent Regulatory Developments' (2013) 8 *International Energy Law Review* 306–14.

[13] Heather Dziedzic and Tade Oyewunmi, 'Decarbonization and the Integration of Renewables in Transitional Energy Markets: Examining the Power to Gas Option in the United States' (2019) *Oil, Gas and Energy Law Journal*, www.ogel.org/journal-advance-publication-article.asp?key=622; Raphael J Heffron, Penelope Crossely and Tade Oyewunmi, 'OGEL Special Issue on "Energy Law and Regulation in Low-Carbon and Transitional Energy Markets" – Editorial' (2018) *Oil, Gas and Energy Law Journal*, www.ogel.org/article.asp?key=3801.

[14] For a full discussion on what energy transition means in an African perspective, see Nalule (n 1).

The situation is no different in other African regions such as East Africa, Central Africa and West Africa. This is understandable since they are all African countries and most of them tend to face common challenges. However, in the energy sector the progressive nature of energy transitions is also evident in the developed world, including in the European Union as a regional body.[15] The EU is often celebrated for its efforts in transitioning to a low carbon economy, which is reflected in the various efforts made by the Member States to decarbonise the energy sector.[16] Despite the various initiatives at the EU level to shift from fossil fuels to clean energy, some member countries are still heavily reliant on coal for electricity generation. Despite being a host of the 24th Conference of the Parties to the United Nations Framework Convention on Climate Change (COP24), which was held from the 2nd to the 14th December 2018, Poland is one such country which is still heavily dependent on coal.[17]

It is noted further that Poland's energy supply is mainly dominated by coal at 50.8 per cent followed by oil at 24.5 per cent. Other low carbon sources including gas, wind and hydro are represented in the energy mix though at a low rate.[18] Similarly, when you look at Southern African countries, we note that coal is the dominant source of energy as it contributes to over 50 per cent of the SAPP electricity generation. So, is it fair to say that energy transition for these countries entails a shift from coal to oil and gas? This question can be answered in the affirmative if we are to consider the progressive nature of energy transitions. Nonetheless, this is not to say that such countries are climate change deniers but rather we must be aware of the economic and social situation of such countries, all of which have an influence on energy transition.

In this respect therefore, energy transition for the countries in Southern Africa should focus on a shift from coal and traditional biomass to oil, gas and renewables. With respect to traditional biomass, it is imperative to note that most people in rural areas in countries such as Malawi, Tanzania and Zambia rely heavily on traditional energy such as firewood and candles for cooking and lighting respectively. In fact, estimates show that in the SADC region more than 153,000 people die each year from household pollution resulting from indoor burning of solid fuels, such as traditional biomass for cooking and heating.[19]

Taking stock of the above, it can be argued that energy transition in Southern Africa should focus on a shift from coal and traditional biomass to oil, gas and other renewable sources. The focus should also be on the employment of clean

---

[15] For a detailed discussion on the progressive nature of energy transition, see Nalule (n 1).

[16] Rafael Leal-Arcas, Mariya Peykova, Victoria Nalule and Pinar Kara, 'Decarbonizing the Energy Sector' (2019) *Michigan State Journal of Animal and Natural Resource Law* 15.

[17] COP24 involved the most important climate talks and negotiations since the COP21 Paris Agreement reached in 2015. Leal-Arcas et al, *ibid*.

[18] Leal-Arcas et al, *ibid*.

[19] See SADC, 'SADC Energy Monitor 2016: Baseline Study of the SADC Energy Sector' (SADC) and Southern African Research and Documentation Centre (SARDC), 2016) p 58, www.sardc.net/books/SADC_Energy_Monitor_final.pdf.

technology to utilise coal resources. In the next section, general literature on what a transition to a low-carbon economy means from a global perspective is analysed.

B. What Constitutes a Global Transition to a Low-Carbon Economy?

In the discussion about how society should move towards the use of energy sources with a low-carbon footprint, there arises the question of what energy transition is about and the challenges it might present for the global South whose economy and livelihood depends on proceeds from fossil fuel and other carbon-intensive sources. Two aspects are critical in the transition process. The first aspect is that the transition should be fair and the second is that it should consider issues relating to the distributional impacts of low-carbon energy transitions on poorer households or communities that depend on carbon-intensive energy sources or environmentally impacting sources. Energy transition entails three core elements: a shift away from fossil fuel to electrically powered devices; electricity generation from renewable sources and the implementation of energy efficiency measures.[20]

C. Definition and Components of the Energy Transition

Energy transition, as considered in this chapter, is a pathway towards transforming the global energy sector from carbon-intensive hydrocarbon to low-carbon or net-zero-carbon economies during the twenty-first century.[21] It consists of a shift from a system controlled by finite energy onto a system mostly dependent on renewable energy sources and taking advantage of the opportunities available from energy efficiency and improved management of energy demand. Before the twenty-first century, fossil fuel, coal, firewood and other non-renewable energy and heating sources were used to provide heating and lighting for homes, power industrial machines and the transport sectors of many economies.[22] But as the discussion about climate change gains momentum, societies are beginning to move towards an economy free of carbon dioxide (CO_2) emission, thus towards less carbon-intensive sources.[23] A decarbonised economy is one that uses low-carbon energy and heating sources which has negligible output of GHG or CO_2

---

[20] Christopher Kennedy, Iain D Stewart and Michael I Westphal, 'Shifting Currents: Opportunities for Low-Carbon Electric Cities in the Global South' (*World Resources Institute*, January 2019), https://wrirosscities.org/sites/default/files/19_WP_Shifting_Currents_final.pdf.
[21] International Renewable Energy Agency (IRENA), 'Energy Transition', www.irena.org/energytransition.
[22] Phebe A Owusu and Samuel Asumadu-Sarkodie, 'A Review of Renewable Energy Sources, Sustainability Issues and Climate Change Mitigation' (2016) 3(1) *Cogent Engineering* 1167990.
[23] Raphael J Heffron and Darren McCauley, 'What is the Just Transition?' (2018) 88 *Geoforum* 74–77.

emissions on the environment to limit climate change.[24] This means the use of more environmentally friendly energy sources against carbon-based sources in energy generation. It has been noted that GHG emissions due to anthropogenic activity is the dominant cause of observed global warming since the mid-twentieth century.[25]

A move away from using fossil fuels has been considered a crucial facilitator for the low-carbon transition necessary to attain climate goals, but delivering this transformation has extensive consequences across local communities. It is essential that the decarbonisation process be fair,[26] and should consider social, environmental and economic approaches to achieve the goal of decarbonisation.[27] In this regard, the International Labour Organisation (ILO) noted that a just transition should be

> a bridge from where we are today to a future where all jobs are green and decent, poverty is eradicated, and communities are thriving and resilient. More precisely, it is a systemic and whole economic approach to sustainability. It includes both measures to reduce the impact of job losses and industry phase-out on workers and communities and measures to produce new, green and decent jobs, sectors and healthy communities. It aims to address environmental, social and economic issues together.[28]

The ILO insight outlays three policy pillars that a just transition should incorporate – macroeconomic and sectoral, employment, and social aspect. There is broad agreement as to what transition means, albeit, it presents implications, especially for local communities. Thus, the meaning and effect of transiting, the balance it should achieve and the opportunities it presents, take centre stage in the discussion as to what constitutes transition to a low-carbon economy, especially as it relates to geography and local economy.

The shift in energy type is part of a future event in a dynamic political economy, covering social and spatial geographies along a global value chain. It consists of processes (how) and performances (what) and a growing focus on unequal economic and financial systems.[29]

---

[24] IRENA (n 21).

[25] Intergovernmental Panel on Climate Change, 'Climate Change 2014: Synthesis Report Summary for Policymakers', www.ipcc.ch/site/assets/uploads/2018/02/AR5_SYR_FINAL_SPM.pdf.

[26] Fairness in these circumstances refers to a consideration of the economic, social and current energy conditions of local communities in Southern African countries whose major access to electricity comes from fossil fuel sources subsidised by government.

[27] Leah Worrall, Leo Roberts and Shelagh Whitley, 'Enabling a Just Transition to a Low-Carbon Economy in the Energy Sector: Progress and Lessons in Emerging Markets' (HSBC Centre of Sustainable Finance, December 2018), www.sustainablefinance.hsbc.com/reports/enabling-a-just-transition-to-a-low-carbon-economy-in-the-energy-sector.

[28] International Labour Organisation, 'A Just Transition to Climate-Resilient Economies and Societies: Issues and Perspectives for the World of Work' (Technical Paper, The Green Initiative, International Labour Organisation, December 2016), www.ilo.org/wcmsp5/groups/public/---ed_emp/---gjp/documents/publication/wcms_536552.pdf.

[29] Ibid.

In the pursuit of a decarbonised society, the concept of justice is considered a crucial aspect of the transition process. Although environmental,[30] energy[31] and climate change[32] scholars view the justice scholarship differently, there exists an element of justice in their discussion about the drive for low carbon economy. Energy scholars agree that the justice conception is a vital component to achieve the decarbonisation objective.[33] Thus, the concept of 'just transition' has been advanced as a critical concept that encapsulates environmental, energy and climate change perspectives of justice.[34] As a result, issues about sustainability, justice and fairness, especially for those who stand to lose in the transition process, are raised. These issues call into question the extent to which a fast low-carbon transition could adversely impact specific economic sectors, communities and regions.[35] This creates the need to consider an energy justice[36] dimension in the transition to a low-carbon economy, and particularly about recognitional justice, in the energy justice trilemma.[37]

Energy transition requires an active social dialogue to explore and invest in new jobs, new industries, new skills, new investment and the opportunity to create a resilient and equal economy. It requires a transition that achieves a balance between continuing the exploration and exploitation of hydrocarbon resources and the development of renewable energies and energy efficiency.[38] A recognition of the present energy situation of fossil fuel-based developing economies and what challenges they may face in the transition to a low-carbon economy, especially in the global South, is vital in the transitioning process. A case in point is Southern African countries. Accordingly, an understanding of the challenges and building

---

[30] Stella M Capek, 'The Environmental Justice Frame: A Conceptual Discussion and an Application (1993) 40(1) *Social Problems* 5–24. Environmental justice advances equal treatment for everyone and to involve them in the process of developing, implementing and enforcing environmental policies, regulations and laws.

[31] Darren McCauley, Raphael J Heffron, Hannes Stephan and Kirsten Jenkins, 'Advancing Energy Justice: The Triumvirate of Tenets' (2013) 2(3) *International Energy Law Review* 107–110. Energy justice seeks to apply human rights throughout the energy life-cycle.

[32] Simon Caney, 'Two Kinds of Climate Change: Avoiding Harm and Sharing Burden' (2014) 22(2) *Journal of Political Philosophy* 125–49. Climate change justice seeks to share the benefit and burden of climate change from a human rights standpoint.

[33] Raphael J Heffron, 'The Just Transition to a Low-Carbon Economy' (2018) 4 *Renewable Energy Law and Policy Review* 39–41; Stephen Williams and Andréanne Doyon, 'Justice in Energy Transitions' (2019) 31 *Environmental Innovation and Societal Transitions* 144–153.

[34] Heffron and McCauley (n 23) 74.

[35] Ajay Gambhir, Fergus Green, Peter JG Pearson, 'Towards a Just and Equitable Low-Carbon Energy Transition' Grantham Institute Briefing Paper No 26 (Imperial College, London, August 2018), www.imperial.ac.uk/media/imperial-college/grantham-institute/public/publications/briefing-papers/26.-Towards-a-just-and-equitable-low-carbon-energy-transition.pdf.

[36] Williams and Doyon (n 33) 145.

[37] Raphael J Heffron, Darren McCauley, Gerardo Zarazua de Rubens, 'Balancing the Energy Trilemma through the Energy Justice Metric' (2018) 229 *Applied Energy* 1191–1201.

[38] Nick Robins, Vonda Brunsting and David Wood, 'Investing in a Just Transition: Why Investors Need to Integrate a Social Dimension into their Climate Strategies and How They Could Take Action' (Graham Institute Policy Insight, 1 June 2018), www.lse.ac.uk/GranthamInstitute/wp-content/uploads/2018/06/Robins-et-al_Investing-in-a-Just-Transition.pdf.

upon the opportunities that the transition will present is necessary. An effective transition process will entail close coordination between policy, technology and capital, and mostly partnership between the public and private sector as well as opportunities to collaborate with countries around the world.[39] To attain the transition, the key focus would be to achieve access to electricity especially for rural dwellers living 'under the grid' and lacking access.[40] It would also mean speeding up the deployment of mini-grids and single systems, which is the least expensive way to ensure that half the population has access to power by 2030. This practice will enable the delivery of electricity in an integrated way and would support economic growth and all-inclusive development, especially through new sources of productive employment in rural areas, in particular for women.[41]

D. Assessing the Literature on Transitioning to a Low-Carbon Economy

The core discussions on energy transition have been about decarbonisation as against the implication of the change to low-carbon energy systems in carbon-emitting climes. The leading papers in energy transition reflect this perspective. In the low-carbon transition discussion, some scholars identified energy justice as a cardinal principle of energy law which developed in the late twentieth and early twenty-first centuries and is now a growing moral, philosophical and ethical movement.[42] They identified the essential themes of energy justice – distributional justice, procedural justice and recognition justice – and note that it looks beyond traditional concerns about energy security, technology and economic development to consider issues on morality in decision-making.[43]

André Silveira and Paul Pritchard note that although decarbonisation is an urgent challenge facing society today with more compelling evidence and rapidly emerging technology to support it, there is a need to consider the fairness of the economic, social and environmental effects associated with the transition.[44] Both scholars stressed the importance of incorporating a justice dimension that would help us to recognise the challenges that other communities may face in the transition process. However, their focus was on the UK energy sector and its transition trajectory. Their approach supports a focus on a just transition that encourages participation and legitimacy in decision-making by stakeholders.

---

[39] Gambhir, Green and Pearson (n 35).
[40] International Energy Agency (IEA), 'Africa Energy Outlook 2019' (Country report – November 2019), www.iea.org/reports/africa-energy-outlook-2019#energy-transitions.
[41] Ibid.
[42] Raphael J Heffron, Anita Ronne, Joseph P Tomain, Adrian Bradbrook and Kim Talus, 'A Treatise for Energy Law' (2018) 11 *Journal of World Energy Law and Business* 34–48.
[43] Ibid.
[44] Andre Silveira and Paul Pritchard, 'Justice in the Transition to a Low-Carbon Economy' (University of Cambridge Institute for Sustainability Leadership (CISL), Working Paper 04/2016, June 2016), www.cisl.cam.ac.uk/resources/working-papers-folder/justice-in-transition-low-carbon-economy.

Raphael Heffron and Darren McCauley ask the question 'What is the Just Transition', apparently to advance a conceptualisation that encapsulates just transition from a climate change, energy and environmental law perspective.[45] They view 'just transition' from the standpoint of participation in decision-making in the decarbonisation process as governments and businesses seek to move away from carbon-intensive energy sources, technology and practices. Within the just transition scholarship, some scholars note that energy transition presents a positive momentum from a climate change perspective, but they question how beneficial this energy shift could be for stakeholders.[46] This consideration informs their assessment of a 'just transition' and other aspects concerning the distributional impacts of decarbonisation on low-income households that benefit from fossil fuel subsidies.

From a market perspective, some scholars highlight the need for decarbonisation efforts to take firm root now as fossil fuel prices are low and likely to stay that way for some time.[47] These scholars see challenges and prospects in the pursuit of a decarbonised economy as they note that the transition process involves disruptions that must be addressed through energy policies, overhauling the existing infrastructure, and training and retooling the labour force for sustainable growth. In their market-based perspective, Rabah Arezki and others acknowledge the social and economic disruptions of transitioning in general and highlights the benefit it may bring to society. However, they did not provide any theoretical underpinning for their market approach except that they note that countries could take advantage of the low oil prices now to transit to renewable energy sources. These authors recognise that for energy transition to occur, a justice dimension should be considered in the transition process to accommodate communities that could be affected.

A look at the literature on energy transition from the Southern African region provides further insight into the decarbonisation scholarship. In their discussion about energy mobility, Monyei and others noted that the push by the global North for the global South to transit to a decarbonised economy amounts to 'energy bullying', and that the former has failed to identify the constant contribution of 'dirty energy' sources in sustaining the economy of the North as well as the assumed benefits of research and development for alternative energy sources.[48] It must be noted that the clamour for a decarbonised economy has not been met with a corresponding level of study focusing on the environmental impacts and proper regulation of mining for the resources used in producing some of the technologies

---

[45] Heffron and McCauley (n 23).
[46] Gambhir, Green, Pearson (n 35).
[47] Rabah Arezki, Christian Bogmans, Rachel Yuting Fan and Akito Matsumoto, 'The Energy Transition in an Era of Low Fossil Fuel Prices' in Arezki Rabah and Akito Matsumoto (eds), *Shifting Commodity Markets in a Globalized World* (International Monetary Fund, 2018).
[48] Chukwuka G Monyei, Kirstein EH Jenkins, Viriri Serestina and Aderemi Adewumi 'Examining Energy Sufficiency and Energy Mobility in the Global South through the Energy Justice Framework' (2018) 119 *Energy Policy* 68–76.

used in global decarbonisation efforts such as solar PVs, electric vehicles and batteries.[49] Most of the metals and minerals critical for clean energy technologies such as cobalt, platinum and manganese are found in Africa.[50] Responsible development of these resources is crucial to support Africase economic prosperity and global energy transitions, especially as these minerals have not been extracted in a health-friendly and properly regulated regime.[51] Responding to Todd and other scholars, Monyei and others stressed the need for more concrete contributions that will facilitate environmental protection and electrification, alongside justice and progress for the global South. Arguably, this entails alignment with a transition that ensures a fair process and outcome for the global South, mainly the SADC region with a vulnerable group that is still struggling with energy access.[52]

Relatedly, Monyei and others identified policy vagueness as a challenge to renewable energy efforts and called for a policy framework that set out a clear roadmap for the global South.[53] Samarakoon points out that in the transition scholarship, the triumvirate of tenets in energy justice arise in the course of provisioning energy services for populations in the global South. Samarakoon also highlights that a failure to recognise and address these injustices has negative consequences for the wellbeing of a number of people, including forthcoming generations.[54] Kate Altieri and others discuss development and mitigation objectives through decarbonisation[55] as against the challenges and implications of decarbonisation and how developing economies, such as the Southern African region, could transit to a decarbonised economy with less challenges. From a climate change perspective, the Congress of South African Trade Unions (COSATU) explores the unjust and unsustainable way energy, goods and services are being produced and calls for a low-carbon economy to create and preserve the planet for future generations.[56]

---

[49] IEA Africa Energy Outlook 2019 (n 40).
[50] IEA Africa Energy Outlook 2019 (n 40).
[51] Siddharth Kara, 'I Saw the Unbearable Grief Inflicted on Families by Cobalt Mining. I Pray for Change' *The Guardian*, Monday 16 December 2019, www.theguardian.com/global-development/commentisfree/2019/dec/16/i-saw-the-unbearable-grief-inflicted-on-families-by-cobalt-mining-i-pray-for-change.
[52] Chukwuka G Monyei, Kirsten EH Jenkins, Chukwuemeka G Monyei, Okechukwu C Aholu, Kingsley O Akpeji, Olamide Oladeji and Serestina Viriri, 'Response to Todd, De Groot, Mose, McCauley and Heffron's Critique of "Examining Energy Sufficiency and Energy Mobility in the Global South through the Energy Justice Framework"' (2019) 133 *Energy Policy* 110917.
[53] Chukwuka Monyei, Lukumon Oyedele, Olugbenga Akinade, Anuoluwapo Ajayi and Xiaojun Luo, 'Benchmark for Energy Access: Policy Vagueness and Incoherence as Barriers to Sustainable Electrification of the Global South' (2019) 54 *Energy Research & Social Science* 113–16.
[54] Shanil Samarakoon, 'A Justice and Wellbeing Centered Framework for Analysing Energy Poverty in the Global South' (2019) 165 *Ecological Economics* 106385.
[55] Kate E Altieri, Hilton Trollip, Tara Caetano, Alison Hughes, Bruno Merven and Harald Winkler, 'Achieving Development and Mitigation Objectives through a Decarbonization Development Pathway in South Africa' (2016) 16 *Climate Policy* 578–91.
[56] Congress of South African Trade Unions (COSATU), 'A Just Transition to a Low-Carbon and Climate Resilient Economy' COSATU Policy on Climate Change – A Call to Action (2017), www.sagreenfund.org.za/wordpress/wp-content/uploads/2017/05/Naledi_A-just-transition-to-a-climate-resilient-economy.pdf.

However, COSATU does not include how the transition may affect present economic activities and livelihood in South Africa.

Lucas Satterlee presents an analysis of the fast growth of renewable energy in South Africa which challenges the notion that a healthy economic future is dependent on growth through fossil fuels.[57] Lucas, discussing the National Development Plan (NDP) and the Integrated Resources Plan, writes that the success of South Africa's renewable energy policy could be a model for implementing sustainable energy market for Africa and other emerging markets. This article promotes the success of renewable energy and notes the challenges that the transition may bring. Other scholars note that decarbonisation will present social and economic costs for the poor who use power in a variety of ways in South Africa.[58] However, these authors did not show how the poor will be affected in the transition, but contend that the economic condition of urban communities will be a challenge. Relatedly, some scholars highlight the need to make provision for carbon-intensive sectors to enable a just transition,[59] while others highlight Botswana's plan to retain CO_2 emitting sources in their energy mix given the high cost of renewable energy technology compared to the costs of relying on such other sources.[60] Matthew Huxham and others examine transition from an energy finance and investment risk perspective and note that energy transition should be fair, leaving no one behind.[61]

Several vital texts on energy transition discuss the shift away from carbon-emitting sources to renewable energy sources to align with climate change goals. Only a few articles highlight the social and economic implication of decarbonisation on economies in developing countries. But these texts have not considered the challenges it might present for the global South whose economy and livelihood depends on fossil fuel and other environmentally impacting sources or suggest a theoretical framework or advance a guiding principle to base their discussion. This is a fundamental aspect of energy transition which this chapter approaches from an energy justice perspective. The Southern Africa region is made up of countries namely Namibia, Botswana, South Africa, Swaziland, Lesotho and others. This chapter focuses on these countries and examines the challenges, impacts and opportunities they will face in their effort to transit to a decarbonised economy. These questions recognise their current situation and relate to justice consideration in the transition process.

---

[57] Lucas Satterlee, 'Cautious Optimism: Renewable Energy in South Africa as a Sustainable Model for the Region' (2017) 32 *Journal of Environmental Law and Litigation* 213–46.

[58] Thuli N Mdluli and Coleen H Vogel, 'Challenges to Achieving a Successful Transition to a Low-Carbon Economy in South Africa: Examples from Poor Urban Communities' (2010) 15 *Mitigation and Adaptation Strategies for Global Change* 205–22.

[59] Herald Winkler and Andrew Marquand, 'Changing Development Paths: From an Energy-Intensive to Low-Carbon Economy in South Africa' (2009) 1(1) *Climate and Development* 47–65.

[60] Yong Jun Baek, Tae Yong Jung and Sung Jin Kang, 'Low Carbon Scenarios and Policies for the Power Sector in Botswana' (2019) 19(2) *Climate Policy* 219–30.

[61] Matthew Huxham, Muhammed Anwar and David Nelson, 'Understanding the Impact of a Low Carbon Transition on South Africa' (A Climate Policy Initiative Energy Finance Report, March 2019) https://climatepolicyinitiative.org/wp-content/uploads/2019/03/CPI-South-Africa-ES-final.pdf.

III. Energy Justice in the Transition Context

A. Recognition Justice in the Energy Justice Framework

The concept of energy justice is fast becoming a research and policy tool by which the justice scholarship could be applied to energy policy, energy production and systems, energy consumption, energy activism, energy security and climate change.[62] As society evolves and responds to the dynamic posture of the energy sector and climate change, it is crucial to ensure that justice becomes part of the decision-making process in the industry.[63] Justice is a combination of ensuring and recognising the fundamental equal value of all human beings in addition to a commitment to the 'distribution of good and bad things',[64] and energy justice pursues principles of fairness and social equity into energy systems and energy system transitions.[65]

Enhancing justice in the transition process could reduce inequality in society and facilitate the decarbonisation process. In this regard, the triumvirate of tenets – *procedural justice, distributional justice and recognition justice*.[66] In the triumvirate of doctrines, procedural justice highlights the need for due process, representative justice, and public participation in decision-making, and concerns itself with questions about fairness and transparency of decision, the adequacy of legal protections, and the legitimacy and inclusivity of institutions involved in decision-making[67] around energy system infrastructures and technologies.

Relatedly, distributional justice focuses on assessing where the key impacts are located[68] and raises questions about the siting of energy infrastructure and economic issues of benefits and burdens ('who gets what').[69] It also includes other intersecting dimensions such as need, vulnerability and responsibility and seeks to address questions about access to resources and opportunities that are considered critical to compensate social injustices.[70] An example of this intersecting dimension has been observed in South Africa where the Government's renewable policy objective is focused on low carbon energy access, price stability, and independent

---

[62] Kirsten Jenkins, Darren McCauley Raphael Heffron, Hannes Stephan and Robert Rehner, 'Energy Justice: A Conceptual Review' (2016) 11 *Energy Research & Social Science* 174–82.

[63] Heffron, McCauley and Zarazua de Rubens (n 37).

[64] Tom Campbell, *Justice*, 3rd edn (Palgrave Macmillan, 2010).

[65] Ramazan Sari, Ebru Voyvoda, Max Lacey-Barnacle, Eminegul Karababa, Cagatay Topal and Demet Islambay, 'Energy Justice – a Social Sciences and Humanities Cross-Cutting Theme Report' (Cambridge SHAPE ENERGY, June 2017) https://shapeenergy.eu/wp-content/uploads/2017/09/SHAPE-ENERGY_ThemeReports_ENERGY-JUSTICE.pdf.

[66] McCauley, Heffron, Stephan and Jenkins (n 31) 107–16.

[67] McCauley, Heffron, Stephan and Jenkins (n 31) 107–16.

[68] Darren McCauley, Vasna Ramasar, Raphael J Heffron, Benjamin K Sovacool, Desta Mebratu and Luis Mundaca, 'Energy Justice in the Transition to Low Carbon Energy Systems: Exploring Key Themes in Interdisciplinary Research' (2019) *Applied Energy* 233–34 and 916–21.

[69] Sari, Voyvoda, Lacey-Barnacle, Karababa, Topal and Islambay (n 65).

[70] Williams and Doyon (n 33) 147.

power production to reduce the social and economic costs for the poor who use energy in a variety of ways.[71] The essence is to develop a cost-effective renewable energy-based alternative to traditional fuels and technologies,[72] to address issues of distributional justice in the transition process. In Botswana, the Government plans to allow coal-based power while gradually adding renewables to the energy mix to forestall any distributional, cost and affordability impact that may arise from a swift low carbon transition.[73]

To address the challenges and implications and examine the opportunities that Southern African countries may experience, a recognition of their present energy situation is crucial, especially considering that geographies of energy systems are not the same and that energy transition is fast becoming a global agenda. As a result, we examine recognition justice in the energy justice scholarship for a broader understanding. Justice as recognition is concerned with the identification, misrecognition or non-recognition of several groups, and is linked with bias and various forms of discrimination.[74] At the foundation of these injustices lie cultural and institutional processes and legacies that have clearly or indirectly given individuals, communities or social groups unequal recognition.[75] Recognition is thought to better interact with pluralist needs, issues and solutions, providing a complete scholarship of justice useful for energy transition.

Justice as recognition extends to identifying where inequalities emerge and make us reflect upon who precisely we should focus on when we think of energy victims in the transition process. This recognition-based justice analysis of distributional inequalities includes a profound reflection upon where injustice emerges with regards to the impact on parts of society. It emphasises the need to recognise and consider different technological needs across social groups and communities, acknowledge and address a variety of the needs of women, children, elders and various ethnic groups in the relational process and improve the reflective nature of organisations, bearing in mind the assumptions and rules entrenched in decision-making models.[76] The essence is to avoid worsening the discrimination or disadvantage that may support other forms of energy injustice or impede energy access and affordability, especially for the poor.

Recognition, therefore, considers the present condition of energy usage by communities with a strategy to align with the future transition plan especially for poor homes in Southern African communities that may not be able to immediately access the subsidies that are available under a fossil fuel energy regime. Most households depend on CO_2 emitting sources for heating and lighting. Several jobs in these areas are linked to these environmentally impacting sources. A transition

---

[71] Satterlee (n 57) 213.
[72] Gaylor Montmasson-Clair and Georgina Ryan, 'Lessons from South Africa's Renewable Energy Regulatory and Procurement Experience' (2014) 7 *Journal of Economic and Financial Sciences* 507–26.
[73] Yong Jun Baek, Tae Yong Jung and Sung Jin Kang (n 60) 222.
[74] Williams and Doyon (n 33) 147.
[75] Gordon Walker, *Environmental Justice: Concept, Evidence and Politics*, 1st edn (Routledge, 2012).
[76] Silveira and Pritchard (n 44).

B. Geographies of Energy Systems

In the decarbonization discourse, an understanding of where transitions take place, and the spatial configurations and dynamics of the networks within which it will evolve, is crucial in energy transition scholarship.[78] The geography of energy draws from many philosophical and thematic traditions, but it is mainly placed at the interface of environmental and economic concerns. It unpacks social, cultural and political dimensions of energy production and consumption, and the ways by which space, place, landscape and territory account for such energy processes.[79] Energy geography responds to the modern debate on climate change, low-carbon transition, resource constraints and security and the rise of renewable energy sources. It puts forward 'a way of doing sources. ecurity and the rise of consumption, and the ways by which space, place, landscapenetworks within which it will evoly combining discursive, governance, and technological domains'.[80]

It has been noted that energy transition should be viewed as a geographical process, involving the resetting of current forms and scales of economic and social activity,[81] and not a process understood from the perspective of developed economies. This argument finds support in the fact that the global location of natural resources such as oil, gas and coal set the parameters for energy needs, especially in Southern African countries. In the global South, both urban and rural dwellers mostly use a non-renewable source of energy to meet their energy needs. Their economies depend on revenue from these sources, and income from these environmentally impacting sources drive social engagements. Again, renewable energy aligns with spatial variation because of geomorphic (hydroelectric) and climate (solar and wind) factors.

Among communities of the global South, there exists inequality and disparity in the use of energy resources between urban and rural dwellers, and the rich and poor in society. A country's dependence on fossil fuel and coal, its size and climate, its economic development, and the average quality of life of its inhabitants

---

[77] The process – recognition justice – in energy transition is about how the transition was achieved and a consideration of any likely impact on local communities. The outcome is about achieving energy transition. The two elements – process and outcome – must work together in the transition process.

[78] Lars Coenen, Paul Benneworth and Bernhard Truffer, 'Toward a Spatial Perspective on Sustainability Transitions' (2012) 41(6) *Research Policy* 968–79.

[79] Andres Luque-Ayala, 'Geographies of Energy' (*Oxford Bibliographies*, June 2016), <www.oxfordbibliographies.com/view/document/obo-9780199874002/obo-9780199874002-0132.xml#obo-9780199874002-0132-div1-0005.

[80] *Ibid*.

[81] Gavin Bridge, Stefan Bouzarovski, Michael Bradshaw and Nick Eyre, 'Geographies of Energy Transition: Space, Place and the Low-Carbon Economy' (2013) 53 *Energy Policy* 331–40.

are vital variables that determine the patterns of fuel and energy consumption. A transition that recognises this geographical difference, human behaviour and consumption choices when it comes to energy use, is necessary for the global quest for decarbonisation.

IV. Decarbonisation Efforts in Southern Africa

In the decarbonisation process, countries of the Southern African region have been making efforts to reduce energy-related carbon footprints through policies, practices and establishing energy organisations that can promote energy transition. One such union is the Southern African Development Community (SADC) Centre for Renewable Energy and Energy Efficiency (SACREEE), a regional co-operation created to contribute towards increased access to new energy sources and improved energy security across the SADC Region through the promotion of market-based uptake of renewable energy and energy-efficient technologies and energy services.[82] While some progress has been made, there exist technical, social, economic and financial barriers in the expansion of renewables in the SADC region. A typical challenge is how to provide the high proportion of the rural and peri-urban population that currently does not have access to electricity with access to electricity, by establishing off-grid solutions that are feasible to establish and maintain. To address this problem as well as the challenge of dealing with growing financial constraints, rural electrification efforts in the SADC region are moving strongly towards incentivising the use of mini-grids and/or household solar systems. Again, the introduction of more-efficient cooking technologies has had only limited success, and as a result deforestation caused by excessive harvesting of fuelwood is still a problem in SADC Member States.[83]

A. Deployment of Renewable Energy in SADC Countries

Despite identified challenges, solar photovoltaic (PV) projects are being introduced at a fast rate through utility-scale projects such as in South Africa and the use of Feed-in Tariffs (FITs) and auctions. Cases in point include the 40 megawatt (MW) Mocuba project in Mozambique, a 37 MW project and 14 5 MW renewable energy feed-in tariff (REFIT) projects in Namibia, two 50 MW projects in Zambia based on competitive auctions, and more than 800 MW of solar PV projects approved in South Africa's most recent bid window.[84] There are also some ongoing

---

[82] SACREEE, 'SADC 2018 Renewable Energy and Energy Efficiency Status Report' (SADC Centre for Renewable Energy and Energy Efficiency, 24 October 2018), www.sacreee.org/document/sadc-2018-renewable-energy-and-energy-efficiency-status-report.
[83] Ibid 12.
[84] Ibid.

wind energy projects in the SADC region such as in South Africa where 3,366 MW was approved in the newest bid window, and even in Namibia and Tanzania where smaller projects are either functional or pending financial closure.[85]

Apart from Botswana, hydroelectric projects at all levels constitute the primary source of both existing and planned renewable energy development in the SADC region. In states such as Angola, the DRC and Zambia, hydropower is almost the only renewable energy source currently in use, despite the presumable abundance of other renewable sources such as solar, bioenergy and wind. As at mid-2018, the SADC region had 21,760 MW of installed renewable energy, of which 15,996 MW was hydropower. Another 17,361 MW of renewables capacity had reached financial closure and was pending commissioning, of which 8,305 MW was largescale hydropower.[86]

SADC states are progressively considering the option of distributed generation and mini-grids as part of their rural electrification schemes. Swaziland, Malawi, Mozambique, Namibia, Tanzania, Zambia and Zimbabwe have met this challenge by developing specialised agencies to implement these policies.[87] Zambia is making an effort to move from the traditional to the contemporary use of biomass to protect its environment and improve energy security.[88] Within the SADC region, biomass is a vital source of energy, with traditional biomass such as wood and charcoal accounting for over 45 per cent of final energy usage in the region.[89]

B. Deployment of Electric Vehicles in SADC Region

The transport sector constitutes one of the most significant sources of GHG emissions. Renewable energy use in the transport sector has been slow in the region, lagging behind the electricity sector. Meanwhile, both Mozambique and Tanzania have launched new public transport schemes, with Mozambique trying compressed natural gas for buses and considering a Bus Rapid Transit (BRT) system for use in Maputo, the capital city. In Zambia, there is a plan to mainstream different renewable energy and electric vehicles under varying degrees of redistribution, although the choice of electric vehicle charging policy has substantial cost implications of seeing this strategy through.[90]

---

[85] *Ibid.*
[86] *Ibid.*
[87] *Ibid.*
[88] Mwansa Kaoma, Mabvuto Mwanza and Shadreck Mpanga, 'Biomass Resource Potential and Enabling Environment for Bioenergy Production in Zambia' in Levy Siaminwe and Grain M Munakaamp (eds), *Industrialisation: Sustainability and Efficiency* (Engineering Institution of Zambia, 2017)
[89] SADC Energy Monitor 2016 (n 19).
[90] Madeleine McPherson, Malik Ismail, Daniel Hoornweg and Murray Metcalfe, 'Planning for Variable Renewable Energy and Electric Vehicle Integration under Varying Degrees of Decentralization: A Case Study in Lusaka, Zambia' (2018) 15 *Energy Policy* 332–46.

Some SADC Member States are developing initiatives to enhance transport effectiveness. In South Africa, these initiatives have assumed the form of electric bus programmes, light rail systems, and the installation of solar power at some bus and maintenance depots. In Madagascar, there is a project that seeks to remove vehicles with over 25 years of service from traffic, and a new customs code now proscribes selling cars which are more than ten years old in the local market.[91]

C. Energy Efficiency in SADC

The energy objective of the SADC Member States is to guarantee the availability of adequate, least cost, environmentally sustainable energy services in the region;[92] realising the importance of energy efficiency as a cost-effective approach to ensure energy security and reduce GHG emissions. This objective is evidenced in the launch of the Renewable Energy and Energy Efficiency Strategy and Action Plan (REEESAP) which sees energy efficiency as the region's 'first fuel'.[93]

New methods and business models for energy efficiency also are being applied across the SADC region, intended to attract and involve private sector participants. This is intended to support the SADC Industrialization Strategy and Roadmap 2015–2063. The Revised Regional Indicative and Strategic Plan (RISDP) (2015–2020) recognises energy efficiency as a 'key enabler' for industrial development that can bring about increased competition in the industrial sector.[94]

Energy efficiency is part of the overall mandate of SADC, but support for projects in this area has been minimal. There is an initiative to replace Compact Fluorescent Lamps (CFL) to improve energy efficiency in the region. This initiative has led to the design of specific programmes for CFL replacement involving 11 national utilities and initiated an expanded Energy Efficiency Framework covering four technologies: CFLs, commercial lighting retrofits, solar water heating and distribution, and transformer retrofits. This initiative resulted in an expected demand reduction of 4500 MW by the end of 2015.[95]

A significant objective of the region is to phase out incandescent bulbs, and the least option is to apply the demand market participation (DMP). Namibia and South Africa have used the DMP initiative, while Mauritius, South Africa has established full national energy efficiency programmes with supportive policy initiatives.[96] In Zimbabwe, the electricity supply authority (ZESA) has executed a CFL roll-out, with project performance monitoring and verification.[97] The utility

---

[91] SACREEE (n 82) 13.
[92] SADC Energy Monitor 2016 (n 19) 17.
[93] SACREEE (n 82) 14.
[94] SACREEE (n 82) 14.
[95] SADC Energy Monitor 2016 (n 19) 17.
[96] SADC Energy Monitor 2016 (n 19) 17.
[97] SADC Energy Monitor 2016 (n 19) 17.

company also has a strategy to reward individuals, students, companies or other institutions that engage in systematic energy use. In the DRC, the national utility company, SNEL, is in the process of setting up a committee which will be responsible for energy efficiency. Mauritius has introduced a National Energy Efficiency Programme, as well as an incremental duty on sub-standard appliances, voluntary labelling scheme, pre-paid meters and distribution loss reduction.[98]

D. Smart Grids and Smart Meters in SADC

In the SADC region, there is a commitment to provide electricity access to both the rural and semi-urban population that does not presently have access, by launching off-grid solutions that are practicable to set up and maintain. To address the energy challenge and deal with the growing financial limitations, rural electrification efforts in the SADC region are encouraging the use of mini-grids and/or household solar systems and other minis – and pico-scale technologies.[99] Some countries offer subsidies to households to enable them to install off-grid systems, to increase the rate of acceptance in the region knowing that rural households may not have the financial capacity to pay for the technologies. These schemes help in facilitating the transition to low carbon energy by making the technology available and accessible to rural dwellers, thus recognising that these people need to be incorporated in the transition process.

For instance, the energy regulatory board in Zambia has joined forces with the Bureau of Standards and the Revenue Authority to regulate the quality of renewable energy products at the point of entry. This strategy is intended to lower the costs of these products and encourages consumers to purchase items only from licensed service providers.[100] It must be noted that renewable energy policies in the region are evolving due to the economics of wind and solar energy, and the need to allow the Member States to access the global experience regarding which strategies are most effective and suitable to local conditions.

In discussing the decarbonisation efforts in the region, energy justice plays an important role. From a broad perspective, energy justice seeks to entrench principles of justice, fairness and social equity into energy systems and energy system transitions. These systems and transitions operate at different levels, just as energy justice can be local, regional, national and global in both approach and application. In this regard, energy justice is therefore underpinned by a decision-making framework, and the triumvirate of energy justice. The decision-making framework involves key principles such as availability, affordability, due process, transparency

---

[98] SADC Energy Monitor 2016 (n 19) 17.
[99] SACREEE (n 82) 14.
[100] SACREEE (n 82) 14.

and accountability and sustainability, while energy justice involves tenets such as distributional, procedural and recognition justice. These key values should guide investment and decision-makers when formulating energy policy, to provide more equitable and just energy policy outputs in the pursuit of decarbonisation in Southern African region.

An equitable output in the energy scholarship highlights the need to recognise and integrate issues of gender inequality, economic condition of rural dwellers and energy access into the transition process. Evidence of the decarbonisation effort in the region recognises the social and economic conditions of local communities in the region and the need to help them move to low carbon energy. The introduction of FITs in South Africa, mini grids and subsidies aligns with the recognition just in the energy justice scholarship. However, more needs to be done to enable a just transition to a low-carbon economy. This includes the introduction of subsidies, single mini-grids and cost-effective solar PVs. Given the level of social inequality within many Southern African states, the region's energy policy needs to pay attention to the social and economic implications of energy transition. As a result, one needs to pay more attention to energy justice in order to effectively meet Southern Africa's future energy challenges.

V. Challenges and Prospects for Southern African Countries in Transitioning to a Low-Carbon Economy

Transitioning to a low-carbon economy presents both a significant opportunity and a considerable challenge. As an opportunity, it could engender widespread global policy action and facilitate an important emerging market. It could also support the transformation of the worldwide energy sector through the commercialisation of low-carbon solutions, including clean energy technologies. Concurrently, this transition could result in a considerable challenge given the substantial capital required to transform economies that have relied mainly on energy systems that are fossil fuel-based.[101] The transition challenge is even more when you consider the investment requirements today against benefits that will accrue in the future.[102] Low-carbon transition provides dimensions for investors to consider the negative and positive social and employment implication given that energy transition is a global activity that will affect developed and developing economies, and cover sectors far beyond the energy sector.[103] In this section, these opportunities and challenges are highlighted, drawing examples from Southern African countries.

---

[101] Goldman Sachs, 'Transition to a Low-Carbon Economy' (Goldman Sachs, 2010), www.goldmansachs.com/insights/archive/archive-pdfs/trans-low-carbon-econ.pdf.
[102] *Ibid.*
[103] Robins, Brunsting and Wood (n 38).

A. Opportunities for Transitioning to a Low-Carbon Economy

The obvious opportunities for transitioning to a low-carbon economy in Southern Africa include the creation of jobs; technological transfer; improved regional co-operation; tackling both climate change and energy access challenges.

With respect to job creation and technological transfer, we note that there are many renewable energy companies that have made their way in Southern African countries. The activities of these companies not only create jobs but also have made it possible for the local people to acquire specialised skills. In South Africa for instance, there are various renewable energy companies involved in solar and wind energy. These companies include among others: Juwi Renewable Energies; Treetops; Phelan Energy Group; GreenCape to mention just a few.

Besides creating jobs and technological transfer, renewable energy companies are also tackling the challenge of energy access. As noted in the previous sections, SADC countries just like other African countries, do face energy poverty and access challenges as there are many people who are still relying on traditional biomass. Renewable energy companies are therefore contributing to tackle this challenge. For instance, GreenCape, a non-profit organisation operating in Cape Town, accounts for more than 6,300 MW of installed renewable energy capacity in the area, and almost 3,000 MW of generation capacity tied to the national grid. In Zimbabwe, in a bid to ensure a transition to a low-carbon economy, the Zimbabwe Energy Regulatory Authority (ZERA) in early 2019 processed 39 solar power projects with an estimated investment requirement of over $2.3bn that have the capacity to generate 1,151.87 MW.[104] Other countries in Southern Africa indeed have renewable energy projects and initiatives taking place. In Tanzania for instance, the Tanzania Renewable Energy Association (TAREA) has been established to promote sustainable development of renewable energy technologies in Tanzania by ensuring co-operation amongst the relevant stakeholders.[105]

Another advantage of transitioning to a low-carbon economy in SADC is the improved regional co-operation in the region. For instance, the SADC Centre for Renewable Energy and Energy Efficiency (SACREE) was approved by the SADC energy ministers on 24 July 2015. SACREE supports the SADC Member States in the achievement of sustainable development by promoting the use of renewable energy (RE) and energy efficiency (EE) technologies. SACREE is also involved in resource mobilisation, capacity building and promotion of investments in RE and EE projects for the SADC region. All these initiatives are not only ensuring a transition to a low-carbon economy, but also promoting regional co-operation in Southern Africa. There are indeed several opportunities and advantages of transitioning to a low-carbon economy. In this section, focus is given to the issue of tackling climate change as discussed below.

---

[104] See Power Engineering International, https://www.powerengineeringint.com/2019/09/27/zimbabwe-commits-to-39-solar-projects-worth-2-3b/. Last accessed 20 November 2019.
[105] See, TAREA, www.tarea-tz.org/.

i. Tackling Climate Change

One of the main drivers of initiatives to transition to a low-carbon economy is the need to tackle climate change. The Intergovernmental Panel on Climate Change (IPCC) defines climate change as the state of climate that can be identified by changes in the mean and/or the variability by its properties and that persists for an extended period, typically decades or longer.[106] These changes affect the general environment and this in turn not only affects humans but also other species and the biosphere. Southern Africa is one of the regions that has been hit hard by climate change impacts, as evidenced in the current disruptions in water and food systems, public health and agricultural livelihoods, not to mention causing enhanced droughts, sea level rise, and changes in the incidence and prevalence of vector-borne disease. Rapid urbanisation in this region is high as many people in rural areas see urban areas as an 'escape' from the deteriorating agricultural productivity presumably caused by factors that could be attributed to climate change.

The impacts of climatic events including droughts have also been witnessed in the energy sector of SADC countries. For instance, Zambia was left facing a 560 MW power deficit due to reduced water levels at the Kariba lake reservoir. There have also been increasing worries that the dry climate is likely to affect the Zambezi River Basin points as it is likely to reduce hydropower generation for both new and existing plants. We cannot also ignore the El Niño climate event in Southern Africa which left approximately 21.3 million people in the region requiring emergency assistance due to the drought it has caused since 2015. The countries which were mostly affected by this were Lesotho, Madagascar, Malawi, Mozambique, Swaziland, Zambia and Zimbabwe.

There are indeed various issues to discuss with respect to climate change impacts in Southern Africa. However, the focus in this section is to highlight how a transition to a low-carbon economy is essential in tackling climate change and ensuring energy access in the region. In summary therefore, the main prospects/opportunities include the creation of jobs; technological transfer; tackling energy access and climate change.

B. Challenges for Transitioning to a Low-Carbon Economy

The main challenges encountered in transitioning to a low-carbon economy in Southern Africa include lack of finances; lack of necessary energy infrastructure; lack of advanced technology; differences in energy priorities at a regional level. There are also issues in some countries with respect to the favourable legal and regulatory framework for renewable energy investments. In Tanzania for instance, the regulatory framework doesn't include the development of geothermal and there are no FITs or clear incentives for renewable energy larger than 10 MW.

---

[106] Intergovernmental Panel on Climate Change (IPCC), 2007.

There is also an issue of limited expertise in countries such as Malawi (with a substantial rural population) with respect to undertaking feasibility studies and designs for renewable energy projects.

Another challenge relates to the disadvantages associated with renewable energy. For instance, geothermal energy projects are costly to establish and maintain; marine energy has various negative impacts to wildlife; hydropower projects pose social and ecological risks, especially large dams; solar and wind energy are variable and intermittent.[107]

All these are valid challenges, however the focus in this section is on the continued role of fossil fuels in the region, which is making it hard to effectively transition to a low-carbon economy. We note that most countries in Southern Africa are still developing and as such urbanisation and population growth are expected to increase, thus necessitating more demand for reliable access to affordable energy, which presupposes a reliance on available and abundant fossil fuels. In the 2018 BP Energy Outlook, it is estimated that the demand for fossil fuels and renewables in different sectors will grow by around a third by 2040 globally.[108] This increase is also supported by population growth, estimated to increase by around 1.7 billion to reach nearly 9.2 billion people in 2040.[109] These developments will also be experienced in Southern Africa implying that these countries will still need to heavily rely on fossil fuels including coal. This therefore weighs down on the goal of effectively transitioning to a low-carbon economy in these countries.

VI. Conclusion

Transitioning to a low-carbon economy presents many opportunities and challenges. As discussed in the sections above, different countries face different energy challenges. Developed and developing countries are at different stages of this transition. For countries such as those in Southern Africa, the need to tackle energy access and climate change should be at the centre of this transition. Whereas most of the countries in the region are still dependent on fossil fuels, these countries have also successfully managed to invest in technologies aimed at decarbonising the energy sector, including renewable energy, electric vehicles, energy efficiency, smart grids and smart meters, to mention just a few. Whereas it is essential to tackle climate change and protect the environment, it is also necessary to ensure that these countries achieve their economic development goals. In this respect therefore, in addition to clean energy, the focus should also be on clean technology to utilise the coal and oil resources in these countries.

---

[107] Nalule (n 2).
[108] See, BP Energy Outlook, 2018.
[109] *Ibid.*

Conclusion: An Exposition of a Contextual Approach to Energy and Decarbonisation

PENELOPE CROSSLEY, TADE OYEWUNMI, KIM TALUS
AND FRÉDÉRIC SOURGENS

I. Introduction

The decarbonisation of the energy sector will be one of the most fundamental shifts to industry and the economy since the Industrial Revolution. It will require new ways of working, new ways of thinking and significant technological innovation. However, managing a transition on the scale required to mitigate and adapt to climate change, is unlikely to be smooth or straightforward. In the Introduction to this book, we noted that a more holistic approach to the energy transition was needed. One that recognised that for the foreseeable future, many countries will continue to use both conventional fossil fuel generation and energy sources, while also increasingly expanding their use of low-carbon and decarbonised energy sources. This approach also recognises that while in some countries the transition will be faster as they have ageing coal-fired generators which are due to be retired and can be replaced by renewable and/or gas-fired generators, this process is capital intensive and that different countries have different abilities to make this change quickly. Even though chapter 14 briefly discussed the scrapping of a national carbon tax in Australia; and chapter 12 highlighted the introduction of a 'carbon emissions trading scheme' in China; the handbook does not delve into the complexities of climate-centred debates such as international climate finance and carbon taxation or international carbon trading and the different carbon funds in specific detail.

Considering the adopted theme and approach highlighted in the Introduction to this handbook, the authors focused primarily on the institutional and regulatory dynamics of evolving energy transitions as the decarbonisation agenda gains traction. In this regard, the three dimensions of energy law and policy, ie securing reliable, affordable and sustainable access to modern energy systems and energy services interact not as mutually-exclusive goals, rather they are counterbalancing dimensions of a trilemma that has stirred the development of law and policy over the years. Throughout the analysis in this book, the authors have presented their take on the lessons that must be learnt if the decarbonisation of the energy sector is to be successful.

II. A Brief Exposition of Lessons Learnt

We need to accept that tradeoffs will need to be made throughout the decarbonisation process: In chapter one, David Spence discussed the need for tradeoffs between affordability, security and environmental performance to be made in public policies seeking to decarbonise the energy sector in the United States. For example, one of the key challenges posed by the energy transition is that the low wholesale prices associated with large volumes of intermittent renewable energy generation entering the grid may make it difficult to secure sufficient dispatchable capacity for back-up generation for those periods when renewable energy sources may not be available. This is because absent government intervention in the form of some kind of regulatory and financial support, the market may not send the appropriate signals to procure sufficient investment in the mix of generation sources needed to provide a well-balanced, stable, secure and reliable electricity transmission and distribution network. However, such a decision will involve tradeoffs, because if additional dispatchable capacity is procured to enhance the security of supply, additional costs will potentially be imposed on end-users and this may also have environmental impacts. Thus, Spence identified that each tradeoff will have winners and losers, which will need to be carefully managed through sensible debate to ensure that the costs and benefits are distributed fairly. If done well, this process could serve as an important tool to educate the public and reduce the likelihood of political conflict. However, if this process is done poorly or not at all, the creation of winners and losers may only serve to further polarise both public and political opinion around the energy transition and may make the transition more fraught.

Regulatory institutions will play an important role in addressing climate change within the energy sector but they must provide regulatory and policy coherence and work with all stakeholders to reduce emissions: In chapter two, Tade Oyewunmi examined how carbon dioxide and methane emissions are being controlled along the supply chain within the United States and in Nigeria. Oyewunmi argued that a range of international and domestic regulatory institutions such as the United Nations Framework Convention on Climate Change (UNFCCC), the US Environmental Protection Agency (EPA) and the Bureau of Land Management have sought to play a role in addressing climate change within the energy sector. He argued that the ideal scenario would recognise that regulatory institutions and industry should work to share information and thus reduce information asymmetries, would avoid institutions being captured by particular interest/sectoral groups with vested interests and would provide the energy sector with much needed policy coherence. However, even if all of these conditions are met,

Oyewunmi argued that operators, stakeholders and institutions will still need to work together to reduce the emissions attributable to the gas production and supply chain to as low as is reasonably practicable.

There is a need for regulatory solutions that realise the full range of benefits that emerging technologies can provide so as not to stifle innovation: Tade Oyewumi considered the potential role of renewable natural gas (RNG) and power to gas (P2G) in the decarbonisation of the gas used in power generation in chapter three. He argued that the current scope of Renewable Portfolio Standards (RPS) in the US states is too narrow and that they should be amended to reflect the benefits that RNG and P2G offer in terms of their carbon profile, ability to provide liquid fuel sources and role in integrating intermittent renewable generation. This chapter also discussed carbon capture and storage technologies and negative emissions technologies and the need for innovative regulatory solutions to ensure their potential is fully realised.

In the context of natural gas flaring, a longer-term view is needed with respect to economic gains, and greater attention must be paid to the climate considerations: In chapter four, Kim Talus and Cheri R Hasz discussed how the position of the Texas Railroad Commission in permitting increased volumes of natural gas flaring in Texas has led to the economic wastage of a valuable commodity. They further established that the relaxation of the applicable environmental standards will lead to increased greenhouse gas emissions and thereby contribute to climate change. In this chapter, Talus and Hasz argued that a longer-term view is needed with respect to economic gains, and that in balancing economic gains and the potential risk of climate change, greater attention must be paid to the climate considerations, which have historically been subject to lax regulatory oversight in Texas.

The governance of decarbonisation will rely on interacting governance networks made up of multiple actors: In chapter five, Frédéric Gilles Sourgens outlined the process that makes up the global governance of climate change and energy investment. He argued that decarbonisation is a continuous process made up of multiple actors with differing stakes in the regulatory enterprise. Sourgens noted that this process is not linear but reflects the competing interests of different stakeholders and international institutions operating within the space. In particular, he noted the importance not just of state actors in formal climate negotiations but also non-state responses which are reliant on self-regulation and private sources of regulation to affect their aims. As a result, networked decision-making around converging interests will play a critical role in supporting decarbonisation.

International investment law and decarbonization of energy systems: In chapter six, Diane Desierto and Frederic G Sourgens expound on a new outlook to international investment law frameworks as a means of guaranteeing and supporting the much need international investments in renewable and low-carbon sources and energy systems such as large-scale solar and wind developments and nuclear. Such developments are springing up in several countries such as in the UK, EU, Africa and Asia. Some are regions considered to have a stable and investor-friendly regulatory climate; while some countries are perceived to have a high regulatory and political risk profile. Regardless, recent history gathered from renewable energy related investment dispute cases in Spain and Portugal shows that international investment protection has a relevant and important role to play in channeling and securing 'green' finance and investments.

Arguably, investment law and energy regime should strive to act as a catalyst for human development rather than simply as an aggregator of economic growth. The chapter appraises the role of investment law in global policy processes aimed at decarbonisation. It expounds on the concept of positive invocation of investment law for green energy development and the role of investment law in the reliance of investment protection to bind states to their promises to incentivise 'green' energy generation capacity such as solar power. Desierto and Sourgens conclude among other things that investment law as a whole could be both helpful and harmful to the quest for decarbonisation, even though the extent of investment law's problematic effects are not due to investment law processes themselves; rather due to the underlying policy decisions preceding an investment claim.

Civic shares could provide a valuable mechanism to unlock the potential of shale gas within the African region and thereby support sustainable energy for all and increase access to energy: Emeka Durugibo analysed the role of private mineral rights in the context of the development of Africa's shale gas resources in chapter seven. He argued that while the use of private mineral rights has worked in the United States, an alternative approach may be needed within African nations that do not permit the private ownership of mineral rights. He proposed the use of civic shares in shale gas projects as an effective strategy to overcome opposition to projects, which in turn could then benefit local communities through enhancing energy access and reducing energy poverty.

International oil and gas operators will increasingly be required to consider decarbonisation strategies to reduce the climate impacts of their operations: In chapter eight, Peter Kayode Oniemola examined the impact of climate change and decarbonisation on the oil and gas sector, with a particular focus on exploration and production activities. He noted that many of the oil rich countries within the global North are least developed and often have lax enforcement of environmental laws. Oniemola also noted that these same countries which are trying to discover petroleum resources, are at the same time seeking to exploit their indigenous renewable energy sources and reduce their greenhouse gas emissions in accordance with their commitments under the Paris Agreement.

The Carbon Tax Conundrum: In chapter nine, Frederic G Sourgens and Lori A McMillan examine carbon taxation as a tool of regulation and means of realising energy-related decarbonisation policy objectives. The chapter highlights the ingenuity of a tax approach to internalising the cost of emissions and spurring an efficient switch towards decarbonised technologies and energy systems. However, the authors contend that carbon taxation has significant difficulties in accounting for the deep disruptions that pricing carbon through taxation brings with it. For instance, carbon taxation assumes economic efficiencies that do not currently exist, including the assumption that the market is able to bring about the desired result of decarbonisation in an efficient manner once people are forced to make choices internalising the cost of carbon emission. Carbon taxation further assumes technological efficiencies that do not currently exist at all or at the right scale to make the scheme fully effective. Pointing out that there is currently no viable removal technology that could be paid through carbon taxation, it seemingly 'banks' money and imposes hardships that cannot deploy a corresponding benefit either as economic or as a technological matter. The chapter concludes that carbon taxation on its own is not currently an effective policy tool to support the decarbonisation effort. It is important to note that in setting a carbon price through taxation, a price that is significantly less than the 'true costs' would most likely not achieve the necessary goals of decarbonisation it sets out to meet. Rather, it would create externalities of its own without absorbing the externalities of carbon emissions. Conversely, setting a price that is higher than the already exorbitant costs or required measures has considerable equity and fairness implications.

In a political environment where Federal Government support for decarbonisation in the United States is waning, there are still significant gains being achieved at state and local levels: Troy A Rule analysed the impact of the US energy and decarbonisation policies in chapter ten. He stated that despite waning Federal Government support, and perceptions of a growing conflict with some conventional fossil fuel producers, there are continuing efforts to decarbonise the American economy. These efforts to reduce greenhouse gas emissions and increase the deployment of renewable energy are particularly notable at state and local levels, as well as through the corporate procurement of renewable energy.

The European Union has adopted significant legislative reforms to support the integration of renewable energy and decentralised energy resources, as well as increase the system flexibility of the grid: In chapter 11, Sirja-Leena Penttinen and Leonie Reins shifted attention to the European Union, considering how the EU has sought to increase power sector flexibility and better integrate large volumes of renewable energy into the transmission and distribution grid. This chapter provided a comprehensive overview of the eight legislative instruments contained in the Clean Energy for all Europeans package, which were designed to help EU Member States meet the revised EU renewable energy target of 32 per cent by 2030. These changes to the existing legislative framework were necessary with the advent of increasingly decentralised energy resources operated by more active energy market participants. The changes enabled by the new legislation have been designed to encourage empowerment of energy consumers and the development of energy communities, the greater deployment of energy storage, sector-coupling, as well as new roles for distribution transmission system operators in facilitating the integration of renewable energy and managing increased flexibility on the grid.

China has become the undisputed world leader in clean energy industries through a combination of the strategic use of industrial and energy policies: Philip Andrews-Speed analysed how the political, legal and economic dimensions of energy governance in China have facilitated the remarkable growth of the renewable energy sector in chapter 12, particularly in the areas of wind and solar generation and changes to improve energy efficiency. He stated that many of these achievements were made possible by the pragmatic approach adopted by the organs of the Chinese Government through their energy laws and policies towards achieving security of supply, energy self-sufficiency and abating pollution. In particular, Andrews-Speed noted the ability of the Chinese Government to rapidly learn from their policy successes and failures.

The energy transition will prove particularly challenging in resource-rich developing nations and thus any approach to decarbonise the economy will need to be fair, just, affordable and pragmatic: In chapter 13, Ivie Ehanmo and Tade Oyewunmi studied how the regulatory framework governing the electricity supply industry in Nigeria will have to adapt in order to integrate an increasing volume of renewable generation and incorporate off-grid developments, while still ensuring reliable access to electricity. Ehanmo and Oyewunmi argued that this posed a particular challenge in Nigeria given its developing nation status, wealth of hydrocarbons and reliance upon natural gas for its domestic electricity generation. Regulatory developments to facilitate better access to modern energy services within rural communities include the development of a policy and regulatory framework governing off-grid power supply. However, the uptake of off-grid supply still appears to be hampered by a range of market barriers including a lack of access to finance, unfavourable government policies, a lack of technical expertise and public distrust for these new solutions. These barriers will need to be addressed in order for all Nigerians to be able to access modern energy services, especially through the use of off-grid renewable energy solutions within rural communities.

Countries must integrate their energy and climate laws and policies to enable the decarbonisation of their economies and support the energy transition: Penelope Crossley began chapter 14 by noting the inherent conflict between Australia's traditional role as the world's largest exporter of coal and liquefied natural gas (LNG), and a significant exporter of uranium and the strong growth of its domestic renewable energy sector. In particular, Crossley argued that many of the problems associated with the Australian energy sector stem from the importance of the fossil fuel sector to the economy; Australia's low population, geography and relative isolation; and the Constitutional settlement with respect to energy. These factors have made the establishment of a truly national National Electricity Market impossible and have long hampered efforts to the adoption of a national approach to decarbonisation. Crossley argued that conflict had been exacerbated by the ongoing failure of the Commonwealth Government to integrate Australia's energy and climate laws. However, she also suggested that in light of the worst bushfires and drought in Australia's history in 2019/2020, this may force government action at all levels to support decarbonisation and the energy transition.

Crises of legitimacy can undermine public confidence in key approval processes within the energy sector, which in turn may hamper global efforts to transition to low-carbon fuels: In chapter 15, Rudiger Tscherning focused attention on the Canadian LNG industry and the challenges faced in achieving project approval, including environmental concerns and Indigenous relations. He argued that the increasingly contentious nature of project approvals and delays have hampered Canada in fully realising its ambitions as a LNG exporter to Asia. In particular, Tscherning noted that both foreign and domestic project companies are struggling to transport their product to ports for export due to the difficulties experienced by pipeline projects in gaining approvals. This is the result of both a legitimacy crisis and the impact of proxy wars with respect to broader environmental issues such as climate change and social issues such as the rights of Indigenous people.

While the energy transition and decarbonisation presents serious challenges for developing countries, it also presents new opportunities, particularly with respect to access to energy for all, tackling climate change and improved regional cooperation: In chapter 16, Victoria R Nalule and Smith I Azubuike examined the challenges and opportunities presented to the 15 countries that make up the South African Development Community (SADC) through their transition to a low carbon economy. They noted that the SADC countries have availed themselves of a combination of regional and national initiatives in their shift from coal and traditional biomass to oil, gas and renewable energy sources. Nalule and Azubuike considered these decarbonisation efforts in the context of the 'just transition' literature and argued that the energy transition could be used to further energy justice and thereby reduce inequality. They conclude by noting that developed and developing nations are at different stages of the energy transition and that it is important that developing countries can still achieve their economic development goals while decarbonising their economies.

III. Final Thoughts

Throughout this book, it is evident that many senior scholars in the energy sector believe that more needs to be done in addressing the global challenge of how to decarbonise the energy sector. The lessons presented by the contributing authors throughout this book are varied, yet they also present a coherent approach to managing the global energy transition and decarbonisation of the energy sector. It is clear that low-carbon fuels such as natural gas will continue to play a role in supporting the transition away from more carbon intensive fossil fuel sources, and that with the advent of new removal, storage and negative carbon technologies, may in fact be an integral part of the solution in the future. There will also need to be an integrated approach to energy and climate laws, and significant improvements to facilitate the increased volume of intermittent renewable energy generation on transmission and distribution networks. A further important take-away message is that for the transition to be just, it must recognise that different countries have the ability to decarbonise at differing rates of change and at least initially, to differing degrees. However, each author has also highlighted some of the opportunities presented by this challenge, including improved access to modern energy services for all, financial benefits from new markets, and the ability to reduce the energy sector's greenhouse gas emissions and address climate change. It is the view of the authors that these benefits outweigh the challenges posed.

INDEX

A
acid rain 51n
Adams, Henry 31
Africa *see* **Africa's shale gas; South Africa; Southern Africa Development Community**
Africa's shale gas
  Algeria 178, 182–183, 196
  civic shares, proposals for 11, 178, 192–195, 198, 404
  development 182–183
  energy access and 178–182, 198–199
  energy security 177
  environmental challenges 195–196
  environmental gains offered by 177, 196
  incentivising development 178, 187, 192–195
  international operators 214
  investment in 186
  obstacles to development 177–178, 184–187, 199
  ownership of mineral rights 177–178, 186–188, 199, 404
  pipeline infrastructure and capacity 185
  rational for development 178–182
  recoverable reserves 182–185
  renewable energy transition and 197–198
  resistance from surface owners 177
  South Africa 178, 182, 183–184, 187, 195–196
  sustainable energy 178–181
  water supply, access to 185, 195–196
aggregators 273, 274
Agreement on Subsidies and Countervailing Measures 217
agricultural sector
  greenhouse gas emissions 4, 45, 79
  waste gases 87
Algeria
  shale gas reserves 178, 182–183, 196
Altieri, KE et al 388
ammonia production
  CCUS technology 98, 100
  power-to-gas (P2G) technology 82–83

anaerobic digestion 86
Angola *see* **Southern Africa Development Community**
Arctic oil and gas reserves 145
Arezki, R et al 387
Argentina
  shale gas reserves 182
Australia
  battery storage 337, 338, 341
  bushfire crisis 9, 337, 338, 339, 349–352
  carbon pricing 348, 401
  carbon tax scrapped 7, 348, 401
  Clean Energy Act, repeal 348
  climate change 9, 337, 338, 339, 340, 349–352
  climate and energy policies 9, 337, 338–339, 347–350, 406
  COAG Energy Council 344
  coal exports 338, 406
  coal-fired power plants 337–338, 347–349, 352339–352340
  conflicting objectives 338
  constitutional settlement 341–342, 345
  consumer protection 344
  Direct Action scheme 348
  distributed energy sources 345–346
  embedded networks 341
  Emissions Reduction Fund 348
  Emissions Reduction Obligation 348–349
  energy mix 339–341
  energy pricing 338, 340–341, 343, 347
  energy sector transition 227–228, 339, 340–341, 345–346, 352
  Finkel Review 349
  gas exports 338, 406
  gas-fired power plants 340, 347–349
  geothermal power 338
  greenhouse gas emissions 338, 345, 346, 347–349, 351, 352
  hydroelectric power 340
  inter-state transmission 342, 343, 345, 350–351
  islanded grid 338–339, 341
  Kyoto Protocol 349
  legal framework 341–347

market competition   343
National Electricity Law   343–344, 351–352
National Electricity Market   338, 339, 341–346
National Electricity Objective   343–344
National Energy Guarantee   348–349
Ombudsman Schemes   344
Paris Agreement   349
peer-to-peer trading   341
politicised energy and climate debate   337
population densities   339
privatisation   344
renewable energy   337–338, 340–341, 345–346, 347–348, 352
Renewable Energy Targets   346, 347–348
Retailer Reliability Obligation   349
Rudd Government Review   347
self-generation   340–341
shale gas reserves   182, 185n
solar power   338, 340–341, 346
state government-owned monopolies   342, 344, 345
subsidies and incentives   344
sustainability   346
uranium exports   338
Warburton Review   347–348
wind power   338, 340
Averch-Johnson effect   17–18

B
Bankes, N   362
battery storage technology   2, 6, 71–72, 84, 99, 276–278
Australia   337, 338, 341
Benvenisti, E   138, 153
best available control technology (BACT)   39, 50, 53, 56, 67
best system of emissions reduction (BSER)   39, 57–58, 67
biochar   103
bioenergy with carbon capture and storage (BECCS)   104–105
biogas/biofuels
generally   6, 39, 72, 381
integration in conventional systems   92
power plants   92, 104–105
renewable natural gas (RNG)   5, 72, 75–76, 86–88, 97, 105, 403
sector growth   70–71
biomass fuels   181, 199, 307–308, 309–310, 381, 394, 398, 407
Nigeria   307, 308, 309
SADC   381, 382–383, 393, 394

Birol, F   337
Botswana *see* **Southern Africa Development Community**
Brazil
shale gas deposits   182
Brown, Jerry   20
Bush (GW) Administration   51, 63, 134

C
Canada
Asian market   353–354, 355–360
Canada–Renewable Energy/Feed-In Tariff   217
carbon tax   147, 235–237
climate change concerns   361, 369
coalbed methane   355
Coastal GasLink Pipeline Project   366, 375
contentious infrastructure projects   360–367, 370–376
Energy East Pipeline Project   363–364
environmental concerns   9, 354, 361, 364, 366, 367, 369–370, 406–407
environmental impact assessments   363, 364
foreign investment   366–367
gas export potential   353–354, 355–360, 370, 375–376
gas reserves   353, 355, 375
global energy market position   354, 355–360
greenhouse gas emissions   9, 369
Impact Assessment Agency   363, 369
impact and benefit agreements   373–375
indigenous population   354, 361, 364, 365, 367, 368, 371–375, 376, 406–407
Kyoto Protocol   133
legitimacy crisis   367–368, 378, 406–407
liquefied natural gas (LNG)   9, 353–376
Mackenzie Gas Pipeline Project   361, 362
mineral rights, ownership   186
Northern Gateway Pipeline Project   363, 364–365
oil exports   355, 357
oil and gas pipelines   353–354
oil reserves   353, 355, 375
opposition to infrastructure projects   9, 354, 360–376, 406–407
Paris Agreement   137
project approval challenges   9, 354, 360–376, 406–407
provinces and municipalities as stakeholders   9, 369–370
'proxy clashes'   354, 361, 368–369, 376
regulatory framework   360–361, 367, 369

regulatory uncertainty, effect on
    economy   366–367
shale gas deposits   182, 196
social concerns   367, 368–369
social license to operate   361, 367
tidewater access   353–354, 357, 360, 364, 375
Trans Mountain Pipeline   367
Trans Mountain Pipeline Expansion
    Project   363, 365–366, 370
TransCanada Pipeline Project   361
*Westcoast Energy Inc v Canada
    (National Energy Board)*   362
cap-and-trade schemes
carbon taxes compared   221–222, 226, 228, 229
carbon capture, utilisation and storage (CCUS)
afforestation/reforestation   103
ammonia production   98, 100
bioenergy with (BECCS)   104–105
direct air capture technologies   105
enhanced natural processes   103–104
enhanced oil recovery   6, 98, 100
enhanced weathering   103–104
generally   5, 6, 7, 39, 45, 47, 67, 70, 72, 92, 97–98, 123, 403
Inventys Project   99–100
legal and policy issues   100–102
London Protocol   102
methanisation   98
negative carbon emissions   103–105, 403
ocean fertilisation   103–104
offshore storage   101, 102
Oil and Gas Climate Initiative   99–100
permanent storage   98–102, 104–105, 123
power-to-gas technology   5, 8, 88–89, 91
risk allocation   101–102
Solidia Project   100
United Kingdom   100, 105
United States   8, 98–100, 101–102, 105, 137
uses   98, 104–105
carbon credits
self-regulation   149
carbon dioxide
air pollutant, as   52–53
atmospheric lifespan   124
capture *see* carbon capture, utilisation and storage
carbon dioxide removal (CDR)   47, 70, 231, 234, 240
climate change mitigation   383–384
coal combustion   38
curbing emissions   49

enhanced oil recovery   6, 98, 100
gas combustion   38–39
gas flaring   6, 8–9, 107, 117, 403
greenhouse gas, as   4, 44–45, 44n, 52, 55, 87, 123–124
hydrocarbons, combustion   38
IPCC Special Report   141–142
negative emissions   8, 103–105, 403
renewable natural gas (RNG)   5, 72, 75–76, 86–88, 97, 105, 403
sequestration   44n, 98–99
storage   97–102, 104–105, 123
US emissions   51, 54–55, 76–78, 251, 253, 402
carbon emissions trading schemes   7, 9, 219, 348, 349, 401
carbon footprint   383
ISO principles and guidelines   149
carbon monoxide   86
natural gas flaring   6, 8–9, 107, 403
US Clean Air Act   50, 211
carbon pricing
Australia   348, 401
carbon taxes and   12, 112, 228–232, 233, 234–235, 238, 239–240, 405
France   233
infrastructure, costs of switching   232, 235
output-based pricing system (OBPS)   235–237
carbon taxes
assumptions underlying   229–230, 234–235
Australia   7, 348, 401
Canada   147, 235–237
cap-and-trade schemes compared   221–222, 226, 228, 229
carbon pricing   7, 12, 112, 228–232, 233, 234–235, 238, 239–240, 405
conceptual case for   226–227, 228–230
difficulties   3, 238–241
disparate impact   238–239
economic cost of decarbonisation   23–29, 222–226, 234–235, 238
economic inequality and   3, 238–239
efficiency   229
feasibility of decarbonisation   223, 225–235
financing decarbonisation   142–144, 221–241
France   3, 147, 233, 237
generally   11–12, 24, 221–222, 404–405
goal   221, 222, 225
limitations   235
market mechanism, as   24, 221–222, 225, 227
negative externalities   12, 222, 227
opposition to   147

Output-Based Pricing
    System (OBPS)   235–237
  regressive nature   238, 240
  regulatory tool, as   7–8, 12, 221
  UK Climate Change Levy   211
cement production   44, 56
  BECCS technology   104–105
  Solidia Project   100
China
  abuse of market power   289
  banking sector   288, 289, 296
  carbon dioxide emissions   283
  carbon emissions trading scheme   7, 9, 401
  carbon trading markets   302
  Central Leading Committee   285
  Central Leading (Leading Small)
    Groups   284–285, 290–291
  city gas companies   302
  Clean Development Mechanism   301
  clean energy, transition to   283, 284, 293, 294, 297, 299, 405–406
  climate change mitigation   285, 295, 298
  coal   9, 283, 284, 291, 292–293, 294, 295, 297, 300, 302–304, 305
  Coal Law   295
  coalbed methane   303
  Communist Party of China   284, 285, 287, 292
  Confucian school   286
  corruption   289
  decarbonisation   283, 284
  economic governance   288–290, 294
  economic liberalisation   288, 293, 294
  Electric Power Law   295
  electricity sector   292, 293
  energy conservation policy and
    technologies   294–295, 297–299, 305, 405–406
  energy efficiency   284, 294, 297–299
  energy policy   292–297
  energy pricing   292, 293, 295, 298, 303, 304
  energy sector governance   288–289, 290–297
  energy security   292, 293
  Environmental Protection Law   295
  Environmental Protection Tax Law   295
  environmental regulation   289, 291
  gas, substitution of coal by   9, 284, 291, 292, 297, 302–304, 305
  gas resources   303
  greenhouse gas emissions   283, 293
  grid access   301
  hydroelectricity   283
  imported of natural gas   303
  industrialisation   134, 135, 143
  infrastructure inflexibility   301–302
  institutional inflexibility   301–302
  intellectual property   286
  internationalisation of
    Chinese companies   289
  Kyoto Protocol   301
  land rights   291
  legal system   284, 286–288, 304–305
  Legalist school   286
  LNG imports   358
  Made in China 2025 strategy   289, 294
  marketisation   9, 291, 293, 295, 296, 298, 302, 304
  Mineral Resources Law   295
  mining sector   289
  National Development and Reform
    Commission   288, 290, 291, 292, 294, 301, 302, 303
  National Energy Administration   290, 291
  National Energy Commission   290, 291
  national energy intensity   283, 292, 297–299
  national oil companies   302, 303
  National People's Congress   284, 285–286, 295
  National Petroleum Corporation   214
  National Supervision Commission   285, 288, 291
  nuclear power plants   283, 295
  oil industry   291, 292, 293
  Paris Agreement   137, 138–139
  pipeline infrastructure and
    capacity   302–304
  planning and coordination
    failures   297, 301, 304
  political system   284–286, 304
  pollution   143, 283, 293, 296, 297, 300, 304
  property rights   287, 291
  renewable energy   9, 253, 295, 297, 300–302, 405–406
  renewable energy equipment exports   283, 284, 300, 301, 405–406
  Renewable Energy Law   295, 300–301, 305
  safety regulation   289
  shale gas   182, 185, 303
  solar power   4–5–6, 283, 284, 300–302
  state-owned enterprises   9, 289, 292, 296, 298, 305
  subsidies and protectionist measures   301
  technological innovation   289, 294, 296
  Ten Thousand Enterprise Programme   299
  underuse of renewable energy capacity   302

water rights   291
wind power   283, 294, 300–302, 405–406
Christian, Wayne   119
Clean Development Mechanism (CDM)   219, 301
Clean Technology Fund   143–144
climate change
   adaptation costs   241
   associated risks for energy industry   218
   Australia   9, 337, 338, 339, 340, 347, 349–352, 406
   economic cost   227
   predicted timeline   233–234, 241
   United States   261
climate change mitigation
   see also environmental protection; greenhouse gas emissions
   African countries   210
   all-electric pathway   6, 7
   Canada   369
   cap-and-trade schemes   221–222, 226, 228
   carbon sinks   4, 98–102, 104–105, 123
   carbon taxes *see* carbon taxes
   CCUS *see* carbon capture, utilisation and storage
   China   285, 295, 298
   Copenhagen Accord   134–136, 143, 152
   cost   223–226
   decarbonisation *see* decarbonisation
   developing countries   210–214, 215, 377
   differentiation principle   131–132, 133, 135, 136
   energy transition driven by   338, 361, 377, 383–384
   European public opinion   15
   European Union   264, 266, 405
   exploration activities and   6, 202, 203, 204
   financing   142–144
   gas flaring and venting *see* gas flaring and venting
   generally   2, 7, 38, 44–45, 72–74, 91–92, 123, 204, 383–384
   GHG atmospheric lifespans   124
   global consensus on need for   128
   human rights and   146–147
   indigenous rights and   147–148
   integrating climate and energy policies   337, 338–339, 347–350, 406
   international cooperation   213
   international governance *see* international governance networks
   international oil and gas operators   202, 203–205, 220

IPCC   45, 70, 74, 103, 128, 140–142, 143
   Kyoto Protocol   50, 125, 132–134, 150, 212, 219
   nationally determined contributions   137, 138–139, 140, 205, 212–213
   negative externalities   222, 227
   north-south dynamic   130, 131, 133, 383, 385, 387–389, 392, 404
   obstacles to   3
   ozone layer depletion   125–126
   Paris Agreement *see* Paris Agreement
   policy push towards   205–209, 216
   politicised debate in Australia   337, 406
   polluter pays principle   3, 122, 129–130
   precautionary principle   129
   public interest litigation   204–205
   Rio Declaration   129
   Rio Earth Summit   125, 127–130
   SADC   399
   scientific initiatives   125–126, 140–141
   shale gas fracking   196, 197–198
   subsidising renewable energy   240
   Sustainable Development Scenario   75
   UK Climate Change Levy   211
   UNFCCC   45, 49–50, 125, 127–128, 130–132, 134, 139–140, 202, 205, 402
   US public opinion   15, 35
   US regulatory framework   49–67, 210
Climate Investment Fund   143–144
climate refugees   144
Clinton, Bill   50
coal
   see also coal-fired power plants
   Australian exports   338, 406
   Chinese reserves   283–284, 292–293, 294
   generally   4
   greenhouse gas emissions   4, 5, 38, 69
   Nigerian reserves   307
   pollution, generally   4, 51n
   primary energy source, as   1
   SADC   379, 380
   US reserves   247, 249
coal-fired power plants
   associated costs   23–24
   Australia   337–338, 339–340, 347, 352, 406
   centralised systems   271, 381
   China   9, 283, 291, 292–293, 294, 297, 300, 302–304, 305
   cost, generally   23–24, 25
   emission reduction   83
   environmental externalities   38
   generally   1, 4, 5
   Germany   142

greenhouse gas emissions 4, 5, 38, 69
investor protection 172
obsolescence 172–173
percentage of electricity generated by 246
Poland 382
replacement 154
SADC 10, 380, 381, 382, 391
shale gas, replacement by 196, 197–198
South Africa 184
United Kingdom 46
United States 43–44, 46, 51n, 55, 76–78, 172, 230, 246–247, 249, 252, 257–258
combined-cycle gas turbines 2, 41, 380
Comer v Murphy Oil USA Inc 204
community initiatives
EU energy market 273
compensation
communities affected by decarbonisation 175
oil spills 210–211
competition
Australia 343
energy supply, generally 2, 381
international oil and gas operators 203, 213–214
Nigeria 313
open access networks 2, 18–19, 42, 86
price-competitiveness of renewable energy 39, 245–246, 257
United States energy market 18–20, 42, 85–86
compressed air storage 26
confidentiality agreements
international oil and gas operators 203
Congress of South African Trade Unions (COSATU) 388–389
conservation regulation
United States 96–97, 101, 115–116
Convention on Biological Diversity 145
Copenhagen Accord 134–136, 143, 152
corruption
China 289
international investment law 166, 168
Cuomo, Mario 33

D

decarbonisation
see also greenhouse gas emissions
adaptation costs 232
afforestation/reforestation 103
bilateral treaties 216
binding states to their commitments 159, 176, 210–214, 215, 216
bordering countries and 237
cap-and-trade schemes 221–222, 226, 228
carbon dioxide removal 47, 70, 231, 234, 240
carbon mitigation costs 230–231
carbon removal costs 231
carbon taxes *see* carbon taxes
CCUS *see* carbon capture, utilisation and storage
climate change mitigation 44–45, 72–74, 123
communities affected by 175, 223, 224–226, 232–233
conflicting values 128–130
cost distribution 224–226
cross-sectoral coordination 75
decarbonised economies 383–384
differentiation principle 131–132, 133, 135, 136
economic cost 8, 23–29, 222–226, 230–233, 234–235, 238
employment aspect 384
energy security and 202, 204
energy transition *see* energy transition
energy operators' role 73
enhanced natural processes 103–104
enhanced weathering 103–104
European Union 206, 210, 378, 405
feasibility 223, 225–235
financial incentives *see* financial incentives
financing 142–144, 221–241
fossil fuels in the energy mix 226
gas networks 5, 75
global collaboration 386, 387–388, 391, 397
gradual process, as 239–240, 401
green energy development 11, 159, 169–171, 218–220, 221
hydrogen as energy source 70
incentivising international operators 218
industry opposition to 245–246
infrastructure replacement costs 223–224, 230–231, 232, 234, 235, 238
international governance *see* international governance networks
international investment law *see* international investment law
international oil and gas operators 11, 201–220
investment law, necessity for 15, 4049
investment law as catalyst for 11, 169–171, 404
investment law as potential brake 171–173
IPCC 45, 70, 74, 103, 128, 140–142, 143
justice and 5, 6, 385, 386–389, 390–393, 396–397

Kyoto Protocol 50, 125, 132–134, 136, 150, 212, 219
Lofoten Declaration 209
low-carbon energy 27, 46, 293, 377–378, 379–400
macroeconomic aspect 384
market mechanisms enabling 24, 221–222, 225, 227
nationally determined contributions 137, 138–139, 140, 205, 212–213
negative carbon emissions 103–105, 403
north-south dynamic 130, 131, 133, 383, 385, 387–389, 392, 404
obstacles to green grid 28–29
ocean fertilisation 103–104
Oil and Gas Climate Initiative 47, 99–100
out-of-pocket costs 23–24, 27
Paris Agreement *see* Paris Agreement
personal costs 224
policy push towards 205–209, 216
political volatility of energy policy 159, 170–172, 176, 217
polluter pays principle 3, 122, 129–130
power-to-gas (P2G) *see* power-to-gas technology
precautionary principle 129
private investment, need for 169–171, 241
recycling technologies 5, 7, 47
renewable energy *see* renewable energy
renewable natural gas 5, 72, 75–76, 86–88, 92, 97, 105, 403
Rio Earth Summit 125, 127–130
risks associated with move towards 208
SADC 393–397
self-regulation 149
social aspect 384, 385
social costs 23
stakeholder engagement 73
subsidising 240, 391, 396, 397
United States 15–16, 20–35, 39, 43–44, 45–46, 76–84, 87–88, 91–97, 210, 246, 249, 250–262, 405
zero carbon gas 92
demand-side management programmes 2
Deng Xiaoping 288
development
Africa's shale gas *see* Africa's shale gas
economic growth and 164–165, 180–181
energy access and 10, 178–182, 198–199
energy poverty and 178–181, 198–199, 377, 398
energy transition in developing countries 10, 400, 406, 407
freedom of political choice 173
green, investment as catalyst for 11, 169–171, 404
human right to 11, 159, 165–166
international investment law and 158–159, 164–169
investment, impact of 167–169
lack of regulatory expertise in transitional economies 174
private investment, need for 169–171
resource-rich developing countries 211
UN Declaration on Right to 159, 166
UN Development Programme 165–166
UN Draft Convention on Right to 166
urbanisation 4, 399, 400
dispute resolution
changing patterns of 215–217
International Centre for Settlement of Investment Disputes 217
international investment law 161, 162–164, 215
WTO mechanism 161, 217
distributed energy 2, 4, 6, 28, 88–89, 95, 214–215, 256, 381
Australia 345–346
European Union 270–273, 270n, 279–282
Nigeria 320
DRC *see* **Southern Africa Development Community**

E
economic growth
development and 164–165, 178–179, 180–181
economic shock therapy 234, 235
Edison, Thomas 247
electricity sector
Africa 180, 378
aggregators 273, 274
battery storage 2, 6, 71–72, 84, 99, 276–278, 337, 338, 341
centralised 2, 270–272
climate change mitigation 6
coal-fired *see* coal-fired power plants
combined-cycle gas turbines 2, 41, 380
competition and market pricing 18–19, 46
compressed air storage 26
curtailment 80–81, 91
decarbonisation 91–97
deregulated markets 248–249
development 1–2
dispatch order 18

distributed and decentralised   2, 4, 6, 28,
    88–89, 95, 214–215, 256, 270–273,
    270n, 279–282, 381
dynamic pricing contracts   273–274, 286
efficiency   2, 264, 378, 383, 385, 395–396
electric vehicles   2, 70, 82, 91, 205–206,
    223–224, 278–279, 387–388,
    394–395, 400
excess   72
falling costs   15
fluctuating demand, meeting   18, 71,
    80, 274
fuel cell electric vehicles (FCEVs)   82
gas-fired *see* gas-fired power plants
generally   1
geothermal power   26, 253, 309–310, 338
greenhouse gas emissions   4–5
grid congestion   81, 91
hydrocarbons, combustion   23–24
hydroelectric power *see* hydroelectric power
increasing use   2, 70
integration of renewable energy   74–84,
    91–97, 263–264
interconnectedness with other sectors   2
islanded grids   338–339, 341
low-carbon   27
marginal costs   18
microgrids   28, 88, 89, 271
monopoly providers   17–18, 271
municipally-owned utilities   250
net metering   28, 256
Nigeria   307–308
nuclear power *see* nuclear power
obstacles to green grid   28–29
off-grid systems   2, 10, 74, 88–89, 307, 308,
    310–311, 313, 320, 324–329, 393
open access networks   2, 18–19, 86, 301
pollution   2, 4, 23–24
power system flexibility   263, 264,
    273–281, 405
power-to-gas (P2G) *see* power-to-gas
    technology
primary sources   37, 69
prosumers   88, 273, 381
pumped storage hydroelectricity   26, 79, 276
reducing reliance on   28
regulation *see* regulation of energy supply
reliability of renewables   23–29, 71–72,
    79–80, 88, 91, 269, 402
renewable sources *see* renewable energy
rural areas   17
secondary energy source, as   1, 37, 43
sector-coupling   278–279

security constrained economic
    dispatch rule   18, 19
security of supply *see* energy security
smart grids   88, 378, 396–397, 400
smart meters   6, 88, 273–274, 378,
    396–397, 400
solar power *see* solar power
storage   2, 25, 26, 43, 71–72, 79–80, 84, 88,
    99, 259, 260, 262, 276–278
stranded cost problems   25
transmission constraints   81
transport sector, electrification   2, 70, 91
wind power *see* wind power
zero-carbon renewables   4–5
electrolysis   88
emission trading schemes   7, 9, 219, 348,
    349, 401
energy
    definition   1
    primary sources   1
energy access
    definition   378
    generally   404, 406–407
    inequality and disparity   382–383
    reliable and affordable   6, 8, 10,
        20, 23–29, 78, 324, 349, 378,
        391, 400, 401, 402
    rural areas   17, 324
    SADC   10, 386, 388, 390–391, 393, 395, 396,
        397, 398–399
Energy Charter Treaty   216–217
energy efficiency
    China   284, 294, 297–299
    energy transition   4, 5, 383, 395–396, 400
    EU Energy Efficiency Directive   264
    increasing   2, 70, 264, 378
    SADC   383, 395–396, 400
energy justice
    energy transition and   5, 6, 385, 386–389,
        390–393, 396–397
energy operators
    see also international oil and gas operators
    decarbonisation and   73
    net metering   28, 256
    stranded cost problems   256
    United States   19, 25–26, 84–86, 256
energy sectors
    development and interconnectedness   1–2
energy security
    Africa   177, 199
    China   292, 293
    decarbonisation and   202, 204
    generally   2, 3, 37–38, 69, 74, 269, 271, 402

oil price rises 202
shale oil and gas 199
energy supply
  access to *see* energy access
  active consumers 6, 88, 273–275, 381
  advanced storage battery 2, 71–72, 84, 99
  Africa 177–182
  changes in mix 214–215, 226
  changes in structure 214–215
  competitiveness 2, 18–19
  distributed and decentralised *see* distributed energy
  electricity *see* electricity sector
  energy poverty 178–181, 198–199, 377, 398
  excess 88–89
  fluctuating demand, meeting 18, 71, 80, 274
  goal of international community 198–199
  integration of renewable energy 74–84, 91–97
  islanded grids 338–339, 341
  microgrids 28, 271
  off-grid 2, 74, 88–89, 307, 308, 310–311, 313, 320, 324–329, 393
  Power Africa initiative 180
  power-to-gas (P2G) *see* power-to-gas technology
  primary sources 37, 69
  regulation *see* regulation
  reliability, generally 3, 37, 69, 74, 88, 91, 401
  reliability of renewables 23–29, 71–72, 79–80, 88, 301–302, 402
  renewable energy *see* renewable energy
  secondary sources 1, 37, 43
  sector-coupling 278–279
  security *see* energy security
  shale oil and gas 178–179, 181–182, 198–199
  supply and demand mismatch 4, 23, 71–72, 75, 79–80, 91
energy transition
  see also decarbonisation
  Africa's shale gas 197–198
  Australia 9, 227–228, 338, 339, 340–341, 345–346, 352
  Canada 9, 361
  China 9, 283, 284, 293, 294, 297, 299
  components 383
  decarbonised economies 383–384
  decentralisation 381
  definition 381, 383
  developing countries 10, 400, 406, 407
  employment aspect 384
  energy efficiency 4, 5, 383, 385, 395–396

  European Union 263–264, 270–282, 382, 405
  fairness and equity 6, 384, 389, 390, 396–397, 406
  generally 2–7
  geographical process, as 392–393
  global collaboration 386, 387–388, 391, 397
  gradual process, as 239–240, 401
  greenhouse gas emissions 383–384
  holistic approach 401
  justice and 5, 6, 385, 386–389, 390–393, 396–397, 406
  lack of regulatory expertise 174
  literature on 386–389
  macroeconomic aspect 384
  Nigeria 10, 308, 335, 381, 406
  policy vagueness 388
  private sector participation 381
  renewable energy 199, 377, 378, 381–390
  SADC 10, 377–378, 379, 380–400, 407
  social aspect 384, 385
  tradeoffs *see* tradeoffs
  United States 15–16, 21–22, 34–35, 43–44, 46, 46n, 76–84
Enhanced Oil Recovery (EOR) 6, 98, 100
enhanced weathering 103–104
environmental externalities
  protection from 38, 44, 69, 74
environmental protection
  see also climate change mitigation; international governance networks
  bilateral treaties 215–216
  bio-diversity 145
  economic policy and 129
  indigenous rights and 147–148
  international law of the sea 145
  ownership of mineral rights and 196
  polluter pays principle 3, 122, 129–130
  precautionary principle 129
  regulation, generally 3, 37, 38–39, 69
  Rio Declaration 129
  shale gas fracking 195–196, 197–198
  transboundary harm 129
Ethiopia
  shale gas reserves 180
European Convention on Human Rights (ECHR) 204
European Union
  20-20-20 targets 264, 267
  Agency for Cooperation of Energy Regulators 264, 266
  aggregators 273, 274
  cap-and-trade system 237
  carbon neutrality framework 206, 210

citizens energy communities   274–275
Clean Energy for All Europeans   264–265, 266, 268, 270–282, 405
climate change policy   264, 266
consumer role in energy market   272, 273–275, 281
coordination between market parties   279–281
decarbonisation   206, 210, 378
decentralised (distributed energy system)   270–273, 270n, 279–282
Distribution System Operators (DSOs)   266, 275, 277–278, 279–281, 405
double tariffs   276, 277
dynamic pricing   273–274, 281
Electricity Market Directive   264, 268, 273–275, 277–278, 280–281
Electricity Market Regulation   276, 277, 280–281
Energy Efficiency Directive   264
Energy Performance of Buildings Directive   264, 278
energy storage technologies   276–278
energy transition   263–264, 270–282, 382
Energy Union Strategy   272
Green New Deal   21, 24, 27, 231, 259
Green Deal   231
grid balancing   269
Paris Agreement   264
policy push towards electric vehicles   278–279
power system flexibility   9, 263, 264, 272, 273–281, 405
regulatory framework   9, 264–282, 267n, 405
renewable energy   9, 142, 214–215, 263–282, 378, 405
renewable energy communities   275
Renewable Energy Directive   264, 266–267, 269–270, 279, 281
Risk-Preparedness in electricity sector   265, 268
sector-coupling   278–279
shared competences   267
smart grids   378
smart meters   273–274, 378
solar power   264, 269, 272, 273
TFEU energy policy   267–268
Third Energy Package   264
wind power   264, 269, 272
exports
Australia   338, 406
Canada's export potential   353–354, 355–360, 370, 375–376

China, renewable energy equipment   283, 284, 300, 301, 405–406
cross-border pipelines   41, 42
Nigeria   48, 307
United States   41, 42

F
farm-in/farm-out agreements   203
financial incentives
China   300
civic shares   11, 178, 192–195, 198, 404
European Union   264
generally   7, 190–191
SunShot Initiative   254
United States   251, 253–257
floating LNG (FLNG) facilities   41
floating storage and regasification units (FSRUs)   41
fluorinated gases   44n
France
carbon taxes   3, 147, 233, 237
yellow vest protests   3, 233, 237
Friedkin, NE and Bullo, F   32
fuel cell electric vehicles (FCEVs)   82

G
gas
see also gas-fired power plants
Canadian reserves   353–376
China   291
cross-border pipelines   41
decarbonised   5, 75, 91–97
decreased cost   70
developing countries   210–214
environmental externalities   38–39
exploration activities   6, 201n, 202, 203, 216
exploration and production licences/leases   218
exports   41, 42, 48, 307, 338, 353–354, 355–360, 370, 375–376, 406
flaring *see* gas flaring and venting
floating LNG (FLNG) facilities   41
floating storage and regasification units (FSRUs)   41
fugitive emissions and leaks   38, 46–47, 49, 54, 57, 58, 60, 62, 65, 66, 117–118
generally   4
green completions   47, 58
greenhouse gas emissions   4, 44–49
horizontal drilling   40
hydraulic fracturing   40, 58, 181–182, 199, 245, 247

international operators *see* international oil and gas operators
liquefied natural gas (LNG)   9, 41, 47, 48, 353–376
liquefied petroleum gas (LPG)   41, 378
maintenance operations emissions   49, 49n
methane *see* methane
natural gas price differentials   356–357, 360
Nigeria   307, 308
Oil and Gas Climate Initiative   47, 99–100
open access pipelines   2, 40, 86
pipeline capacity   108, 110–111, 118, 121
pipeline condition   38, 65
power-to-gas (P2G) *see* power-to-gas technology
pressure surge relief systems   49n
primary energy source, as   1, 37, 69
production, generally   201n, 202, 203, 216
production costs   23–24, 25, 41, 42, 201n
renewable natural gas (RNG)   5, 72, 75–76, 86–88, 92, 97, 105, 403
renewables competing with   39
shale gas *see* shale oil and gas
Southern Africa   379
storage and transportation   41–44, 65, 84, 91, 117
supply chain and market   40–42
thermal efficiency   41
transitional fuel, role as   7
US decarbonisation   76–78
US gas supply boom   37, 40–44, 46, 49, 56–61, 181–182, 353
US pipeline infrastructure   83–84
US regulation   249
US reserves   247, 259
venting *see* gas flaring and venting
waste prevention   62, 96–97
zero carbon   92
gas flaring and venting
carbon dioxide   107, 117
cost-benefit analysis   118–119, 120–121
developing countries   211
generally   4, 6, 8–9, 38, 42, 46n, 47–48, 49, 54, 57, 58, 62, 65, 96, 107–108, 403
greenhouse gas emissions   6, 107
methane   107, 117
Penalise or Commercialise   47
pipeline capacity   108, 110–111, 118, 121
private parties, rights of   119–120
Texas shale oil industry   8–9, 107–121
United States   107–121, 137
unitisation agreement   114–116
US Clean Air Act   117, 211

US Environmental Protection Agency   117
US litigation   113–116, 118–119
volatile organic compounds (VOCs)   117
gas-fired power plants
Australia   340
back-up supply, as   26
centralised systems   271
China   9, 292, 297, 302–304, 305
combined-cycle gas turbines   2, 41, 380
cost, generally   23–24, 25, 41
decarbonised natural gas   5
generally   1, 4–5
Nigeria   10, 309–312, 313, 315
power-to-gas (P2G) technology   5, 7, 82–83, 91–97
shale gas   196, 197–198
United Kingdom   46
United States   43–44, 75–76, 83–84, 91–92, 230, 249
General Agreement on Tariffs and Trade (GATT)   217
geothermal power   26, 253, 309–310, 338
Germany
coal-fired power plants   142
renewable energy   268
Ghana
greenhouse gas reduction   212–213
international operators   214
oil reserves   180, 203
pollution, regulation   211
rural energy access   324, 334–335
Global Environment Facility   143–144
global warming *see* climate change mitigation; greenhouse gas emissions
global warming potential (GWP)   44
globalisation, economic   134
Green Climate Fund   144
green completions   47, 58
Green Cornerstone Bond Fund   206
greenhouse gas (GHG) emissions   50, 125, 132–134
see also climate change mitigation; environmental protection; pollution
atmospheric lifespans   124
Australia   338, 345, 346, 347–348, 351, 352
best available control technology (BACT)   39, 50, 53, 56, 67
best system of emissions reduction (BSER)   39, 57–58, 67
Canada   9, 369
cap-and-trade schemes   221–222, 226, 228
carbon dioxide   4, 44–45, 44n, 52, 55, 87, 107, 123–124, 197, 204, 383–384

carbon dioxide equivalent   123
carbon monoxide   50, 107, 204
carbon removal technology   47, 70, 231, 234, 240
carbon taxes *see* carbon taxes
causes, generally   73
CCUS *see* carbon capture, utilisation and storage
China   283, 293
climate change and   3, 72–73, 123
coal combustion   4, 38, 69
communities affected by   227
decarbonisation *see* decarbonisation
developing countries   210–214, 215
economic cost   222–226, 227
electric power sector   4–5
estimating and reporting   133
EU targets   266
European public opinion   15
exploration activities and   6, 202, 203, 204
fugitive emissions and leaks   46–47, 49, 54, 57, 58, 60, 62, 65, 66, 117–118
gas flaring and venting   6, 8–9, 107–121, 137, 403
gas supply systems and   4, 38–39, 44–49
generally   2, 3, 69, 204, 383–384
global warming potential (GWP)   44
international oil and gas operators   202
IPCC Special Report   141–142, 143
ISO standards for accounting   149
Kyoto Protocol   125, 132–134, 136, 219
maritime fuels and shipments   359
measurement   123
methane   4, 44, 48–49, 87, 107, 137, 197
monitoring   49, 57
negative emissions   8, 103–105, 403
negative externalities   222, 227
nitrous oxides   107
offsetting   4
oil combustion   4, 69
Oil and Gas Climate Initiative   99–100
Output-Based Pricing System   235–237
Paris Agreement   205, 212
penalty regimes   47–48
power-to-gas (P2G) technology   5, 91, 403
production activities and   202, 203, 204, 216
public interest litigation   204–205
regulation   39, 69
renewable natural gas   5, 72, 75–76, 87–88, 403
reporting requirements   54–55
shale gas industry   196, 197–198
sulphur dioxide   50, 107

sulphur   204
UNFCCC   125, 127–128, 130–132, 134, 139–140, 202, 205, 402
United Kingdom   46, 211
United States   45–46, 49–56, 76–78, 79, 137, 211, 251, 253, 402, 405
US Clean Air Act   50–53, 54, 55–56, 78, 117, 211
US public opinion   15
Gulf of Mexico oil spill   210

H
Heffron, R and McCauley, D   387
Hefner, Robert A III   189, 190
Hempling, S   38
Howlett, M and Ramesh, M   296, 305
human rights
climate change and   11, 146–147, 154
public interest litigation   204–205
right to development   159, 165–166
Huxham, M et al   389
hydraulic fracturing
development   245, 247
US gas boom   40, 108, 181–182, 199
US regulation   58
hydrocarbons
coal *see* coal; coal-fired power plants
environmental externalities   38–39
gas *see* gas; gas flaring and venting; gas-fired power plants
greenhouse gases   6, 44, 73
modern economy built on   4
oil *see* oil
pollution by   4, 23–24
hydroelectric power
associated risks   400
Australia   340
centralised systems   381
China   283
generally   1, 271
Iceland   26
Nigeria   305, 307, 308, 309
plant construction times   142
pumped storage hydroelectricity   26, 79, 276
SADC   10, 379, 380, 381, 394
sector growth   701
United States   248
hydrofluorocarbons   52–53
hydrogen as energy source   5, 70
energy storage   95
fuel cell electric vehicles   82
integration in conventional systems   92
low-carbon hydrogen   6

power-to-gas (P2G) technology   5, 7, 72, 76, 81–83, 87, 88–89, 97, 276, 403
renewable natural gas   5, 86–88, 97, 403

I
Iceland
  geothermal power   26
  hydroelectric power   26
India
  industrialisation   135
indigenous rights
  Canada   354, 361, 364, 365, 367, 368, 371–375, 376
  climate change issues and   147–148, 154
innovation and risk-taking
  conditions conducive to   189
integrated energy providers   39, 47
Intergovernmental Panel on Climate Change (IPCC)   128, 140–142, 399
  independence   141
  predicted climate change timeline   234
  Special Report   45, 70, 74, 103, 141–142, 143
International Energy Agency (IEA)   70, 98–99, 203, 378
International Finance Corporation (IFC)   207
international governance networks
  see also international investment law
  bio-diversity, protection   145
  climate change mitigation   11, 124, 129–130, 403
  climate finance   142–144, 146
  competitive pressures   153
  Conference of the Parties (COP) Process   128, 130–132, 134
  constitutive processes, generally   126–127
  Convention on Biological Diversity   145
  Copenhagen Accord   134–136, 143, 152
  data exchange   137
  differentiation principle   131–132, 133, 135, 136
  diplomatic conferences   125–126, 130–131
  human rights   146–147, 154
  indigenous rights   147–148, 154
  Intergovernmental Panel on Climate Change   45, 70, 74, 103, 128, 140–142
  international law of the sea   145
  international trade law   146
  investment treaties *see* international investment law
  ISO standards   149

Kyoto Protocol   50, 125, 132–134, 136, 150, 212, 219
  legal fragmentation   152
  Montreal Protocol   126
  Nagoya Protocol   145
  nationally determined contributions   137, 138–139, 140, 212–213
  networked decision-making   149–154, 403
  non-state   148–154
  north-south dynamic   130, 131
  Paris Agreement   45, 50, 73, 78, 125, 136–140, 150
  policy coherence   402
  polluter pays principle   3, 122, 129–130
  resistance to change   153
  Rio Declaration   129, 131, 207
  Rio Earth Summit   125, 127–130
  soft law provisions   206–209
  state sovereignty and   129
  transboundary harm   129
  transnational legal processes   151
  UN, generally   206–207
  UNFCCC   125, 127–128, 130–132, 134, 139–140, 202, 205, 402
  value conflicts   128–130, 131
  Vienna Convention (1985)   126
  voluntary commitments   150
  World Trade Organisation   146
international investment law
  catalyst for green development   11, 159, 169–171, 404
  compatibility with decarbonisation   164, 175–176
  conduct of investor   163
  corporate investors   157–158
  counterclaims or set off   164
  criticism of   157–158, 161–164
  damages awarded under   163–164, 175, 176
  dispute resolution mechanism   161, 162–164, 215, 217
  fair and equitable treatment   162–163
  foreign investments   157–158
  good faith as *Grundnorm*   163, 164, 167–168, 174
  indigenous rights and   148
  influence on decarbonisation governance   146
  international treaties   146, 148, 160–161, 160n, 162, 169, 173–174, 210, 215–217
  investment protection binding states to commitments   159, 176, 215, 216
  investor liability   164

investor protection   3, 157–159, 164–169
legal fragmentation   152
necessity for   159, 403–404
need for large scale energy investment   146
networked decision-making   149, 150–151, 154, 403
neutrality   172–173
Paushok v Mongolia   162
policy decisions underlying investment claims   176
political policy goals and   164–165, 167
potential brake on decarbonisation   171–173
reasonable reliance interests   164
reform, need for   173–175, 176
state liability   163–164
transnational legal processes   151
transparent global scrutiny under   167, 173
treaty interpretation   162–163
use of term   160–161
violation of treaty commitments   170–171, 215, 216
International Labour Organisation (ILO)   384
international law
soft law provisions, generally   206–209
international oil and gas operators
capital-intensive nature   203
clean energy technologies, development   218–220
climate change issues   11, 202, 203–205, 220
competition   203, 213–214
corporate disclosure   218
decarbonisation and   11, 201–220
developing countries   210–214
diversification into renewables   206, 209
dominance   201, 201n
exploration and production licences/leases   218
host governments and   203
host state commitments, regulation   203, 210–214, 216
host state contracts   203
incentivising to decarbonise   218
influence   203
international soft law   206–209
legal preparedness for decarbonisation   217–219, 220
nationalisation of assets of   216
Paris Agreement   11, 202, 209, 217–219, 220
pollution by   210–214
public interest litigation against   204–205
sanctions imposed on   210–213

International Organization for Standardization (ISO)   149
Inventys Project   99–100
investment
clean energy technologies, development   218–220, 240–241
coal-fired power plants, in   172
economic growth and   164–165
financial reporting   207–208
Green Cornerstone Bond Fund   206
impact on development   158–159, 164–169
innovation and risk-taking   189
international law *see* international investment law
international operators   201, 201n, 203
investor claims against state policy changes   170–171, 217
investor protection, generally   3, 157–159, 164–169
lack of regulatory expertise in transitional economies   174
Multilateral Investment Guarantee Agency   207
Norwegian Sovereign Wealth Fund   207–208
policy push towards decarbonisation   205–209, 216
political dimension   164–165
private   169–171, 203, 261
public-private partnerships   241
renewable energy, in   263
returns, generally   74
risks associated with decarbonisation   208
shale gas fracking   191
subsidising   240
violation of state law   167
violation of treaty commitments   170–171, 215, 216
World Bank Climate Change Action Plan   206
World Bank Equator Principles   207
investor-owned utilities (IOUs)
United States   16–17, 18, 19, 25, 35

J
Japan
LNG imports   356, 358
joint bidding agreements   203

K
Kazakhstan   131–132
Kenya
Euro Partial Risk Guarantee programme   215
renewable energy sources   215

rural energy access 324
shale gas reserves 180
Kivalina v ExxonMobil Corporation & Ors 204
Koh, Harold 151, 152
Kyoto Protocol 50, 125, 132–134, 136,
    150, 212, 219
  Australia 349
  China 301
  Joint Implementation 219
  United States 50, 133, 251

L
lead pollution
  US Clean Air Act 50, 211
Lee, K et al 324
Lesotho *see* **Southern Africa**
    Development Community
letters of intent 203
Li Keqiang 285, 291
Liberia
  shale gas reserves 180
lifting agreements 203
liquefied natural gas (LNG) 9, 41, 47, 48,
    353–376
liquefied petroleum gas (LPG) 41
Lofoten Declaration 209
London Protocol 102

M
Madison, James 31
Malawi *see* **Southern Africa Development**
    Community
Mao Zedong 290
marketing Agreements
  international oil and gas operators 203
Markey, Ed 259
Mauritius *see* **Southern Africa Development**
    Community
methane
  air pollutant, as 52–53
  atmospheric lifespan 124
  CCUS technology 6, 98
  coalbed 303, 355
  curbing emissions 38, 47, 48–49, 56
  gas venting 6, 107, 117
  global warming potential (GWP) 44, 44n
  greenhouse gas, as 4, 44, 48–49, 87, 107
  leaks 38, 49, 54, 56, 58, 60, 65, 66, 117–118
  Oil and Gas Climate Initiative 99–100
  power-to-gas (P2G) technology 5, 7, 72, 76,
    81–83, 87, 88–89, 92, 97, 98, 403
  recycling 5
  reformation 5, 39

renewable natural gas 5, 72, 75–76, 86–88,
    92, 97, 105, 403
  shale gas fracking 197
  synthetic 72, 81–83, 86–89, 92, 98
  thermal oxidisers 56
  US Bureau of Land Management (BLM) 2016
    Rule 61–65, 62n
  US Bureau of Land Management (BLM) 2018
    Rule 64–65
  US emissions 48–49, 51, 52, 54–58, 61–66,
    67, 117, 137, 302
Mexico
  rural energy access 324
  shale gas deposits 182
microgrids
  decentralised electricity systems 28, 88,
    89, 271
mineral rights
  Africa 10, 177–178, 186–188, 199, 404
  Canada 186
  United States 186–191, 249
mining sector
  China 289
  regulation 387–388
  Southern Africa 377–378
  utilisation of renewables 378
Mitchell, George 247
modern monetary theory
  Green New Deal 24n, 28
monopoly providers
  European Union 271
  United States 17–18
Montreal Protocol 126
Monyei, CG et al 387, 388
Morrison, Scott 351, 352
Mozambique *see* **Southern Africa**
    Development Community
Multilateral Investment Guarantee Agency
    (MIGA) 207

N
Nagoya Protocol 145
Namibia *see* **Southern Africa Development**
    Community
Natural Resource Charter 209
negative externalities
  carbon taxation 12, 222, 227
negative pricing
  renewables 25
net metering 28, 256
Netherlands
  renewable energy 267–269
  Urgenda case 146–147

Index

Netherlands-UAE bilateral treaty   216
networked decision-making *see* **international governance networks**
Nigeria
   ancillary services rates   316
   Associated Gas Reinjection Act   211
   biomass fuels   307, 308, 309
   Bulk Electricity Trading Co   312, 313, 316, 321, 323, 332
   captive power generation   320, 327
   coal   307
   competition in electricity sector   313
   consumer protection   320
   distributed generation   320
   efficiency of energy system   324
   Electric Power Sector Reform Act   10, 309
   Electricity Corporation   307, 308, 322
   electricity distribution   318–320, 322, 324
   electricity distribution franchising   330–331
   electricity generation   313–317, 318, 320, 323
   Electricity Regulatory Commission   309, 320–321, 326
   electricity supply industry   307, 308–322, 331, 332, 334–335
   Electricity System Operator   321
   electricity transmission   317–318, 322, 324
   electricity value chain   311–320
   Electrification Project   333
   Electrification Roadmap   317, 318, 320
   eligible customer regime   320, 327, 330
   energy mix   308, 309–311
   energy pricing   10, 319, 322–323, 324
   Energy Support Programme   330, 334
   Extractive Industry Transparency Initiative   211
   Flare Gas Commercialisation Programme   47–48, 107
   gas-fired power plants   10, 309–312, 313, 315
   gas reserves   307
   geothermal power   309–310
   German government partnership   317, 322, 329–330
   grid-based energy supply   10, 307, 308, 310–311, 312–313, 322–324
   hydroelectric power   307, 308, 309, 315
   imported equipment   325, 328, 329
   independent power producers   312, 313, 320, 327
   infrastructure   313–316, 318, 319
   institutional framework   308–309
   international development financing   329–330, 333
   international operators   208, 214, 312
   investment   310, 315, 318–319, 322–323, 324, 326, 327–328, 329, 330–331, 332, 334
   licensing system   320
   LNG Project   48
   mini-grids   320, 327–328, 329, 334
   Minister of Power   320
   National Electric Power Policy   10, 309
   National Power Training Institute   321
   nuclear power   325
   off- and under-grid electricity systems   10, 307, 308, 310–311, 313, 320, 324–329, 333, 334, 335, 406
   oil and gas exports   48, 307
   oil reserves   307
   Operator of the Nigerian Electricity Market   321
   pollution, regulation   211
   Presidential Task Force on Power   322
   privatisation of energy sector   10, 309, 309n, 310, 313, 314–315, 319, 321, 323, 334, 381
   regulatory framework   308–309, 320–322, 326–328
   renewable energy   307–308, 325, 328–329, 332, 334–335, 406
   Renewable Energy Master Plan   325
   Rural Electrification Agency   321, 326, 332–334
   Rural Electrification Fund   326–327
   rural energy access   324, 334–335
   shale gas reserves   180
   solar power   307, 309, 325, 329, 334
   supply and demand mismatch   310–311, 314–316, 318, 322
   total primary energy consumption   307–308
   Transmission Company of Nigeria   312–313, 318–320
   USAID Nigeria Power Sector Program   334
   wind power   307, 309, 325
nitrous oxides
   air pollution by   52–53
   greenhouse gas, as   44, 44n, 107
   natural gas flaring   107
   US Clean Air Act   50, 51n, 54, 211
North American Free Trade Agreement   216–217
North Sea
   international operators   214
Norway
   greenhouse gas reduction   212

nuclear power
  China 283, 295
  climate change mitigation 6
  cost 25
  international investment law 403–404
  Nigeria 325
  plant construction times 142
  United States 43–44, 46, 46n, 91, 142, 230, 247, 248

O
Obama Administration 20, 45, 50, 53, 59–60, 62, 65, 78, 117, 134, 135, 180, 251
Ocasio-Cortez, Alexandria 259
ocean fertilisation 103–104
oil
  Canadian reserves 355, 356, 357
  China 291, 292, 293
  crude oil price differentials 357
  developing countries 210–214
  energy security and 202
  environmental externalities 38
  exploration activities 6, 201n, 202, 203, 216
  exploration and production licences/leases 218
  fugitive emissions and leaks 46–47, 57, 60, 62, 65
  gas flaring and venting 107–121
  generally 4
  greenhouse gas emissions 4, 69, 107
  Gulf of Mexico oil spill 210
  hydraulic fracturing 40, 58, 108, 181–182, 199, 245, 247
  international operators *see* international oil and gas operators
  Nigeria 307, 308
  Oil and Gas Climate Initiative 47, 99–100
  price rises 202
  primary energy source, as 1, 37, 69
  production 201n, 202, 203, 216
  SADC 10, 379, 380
  shale oil *see* shale oil and gas
  storage and transportation 41–42, 117
  US oil industry 46, 49, 55, 56–61, 78, 107–121, 192, 247
  US regulation 46, 49, 55, 56–61, 249
  US reserves 247
Omorogbe, Y 325
open access networks
  China 301
  competition and 2, 18–19, 42, 86
  gas pipelines 40
  United States 18–19, 40, 42, 86

optical gas imaging (OGI) 57
Organisation of Petroleum Exporting Countries (OPEC) 202, 203
Output-Based Pricing System (OBPS) 235–237
ozone 44
  ground level 51, 51n
  ozone layer depletion 125–126
  ozone-forming VOCs 117
  US Clean Air Act 50, 51, 211

P
Paris Agreement
  Australia 349
  Canadian withdrawal 137
  domestic regimes complementing 218
  European Union 264
  greenhouse gas reduction 205, 212
  international oil and gas operators 11, 202, 209, 217–219, 220
  monitoring 137, 212
  nationally determined contributions 137, 138–139, 140, 205, 212–213, 349
  operation, generally 150
  ratification 217–218, 377
  Secretariat 139–140
  target limit 136, 141
  US withdrawal 45, 50, 78, 137, 138–139, 148, 154, 252
  World Bank Climate Change Action Plan 206
pebble bed modular reactor (PBMR) 380
Perezcano, Hugo 167
Pielke, R 180
pipelines
  cross-border 41
  leak detection 65, 66
  open access 2, 40, 42, 86
  regulation 54, 65, 249
pneumatic pumps and compressors
  proposed standards 57–58
Poland
  coal-fired power plants 382
  shale gas deposits 182
political choice, freedom of
  investor protection and 173
political influence
  fossil fuel stakeholders in US 251–252, 257
political instability
  impediment to resource development 185
political opinion
  US hyper-polarisation 8, 16, 20, 29–35
political volatility of energy policy
  generally 171–173

investor claims against state policy
  changes   170–171, 217
 regulation of state
  commitments   210–214, 216
 state commitments, investment law
  binding   159, 176, 215, 216
 United States   250–252
polluter pays principle   3, 122, 129–130
 carbon taxes *see* carbon taxes
pollution
 best available control technology
  (BACT)   39, 50, 53, 56, 67
 best system of emissions reduction
  (BSER)   39, 57–58, 67
 bordering countries and   237
 cap-and-trade schemes   221–222, 226, 228
 CCUS *see* carbon capture, utilisation
  and storage
 China   283, 293, 296, 297, 300, 304
 communities affected by   227
 developing countries   210–214, 215
 economic cost   222–226, 227
 electricity sector   2, 4, 23–24
 flaring *see* gas flaring and venting
 greenhouse gases *see* greenhouse
  gas emissions
 hydrocarbon-powered   4, 23–24, 38, 73
 international operators, by   210–214
 London Protocol   102
 negative externalities   222, 227
 oil spills   210–211
 Output-Based Pricing System
  (OBPS)   235–237
 particulate matter (PM)   50, 51n
 penalty regimes   47–48
 sanctions   210–214
 shale gas fracking   195–196, 197–198
 US Clean Air Act   50–53, 54, 55–61, 78,
  117, 211
 US NAAQS   50
 venting *see* gas flaring and venting
Poole, KT and Rosenthal, H   29–30
Power Africa initiative   180
power-to-gas (P2G) technology
 ammonia production   82–83
 carbon capture   88–89, 91
 distributed energy source, as   95
 energy input   88
 energy storage   91, 94–95, 97
 generally   5, 7, 72, 76, 81–83, 87, 90, 97,
  105–106, 276, 403
 hydrogen   72, 76, 81, 87, 88–89
 integration in conventional systems   91–97

methane   72, 76, 81–83, 87, 88–89
 potential uses   82–83
 regulatory oversight   89–90
 sector-coupling   278–279
 synthetic methane   72, 76, 81
 United States   8, 72, 77, 81–90, 97
power-to-heat technology   278–279
power-to-mobility technology   278–279
Pöyry   92
pressure surge relief systems   49n
production sharing contracts   203
public interest litigation
 international operators, against   204–205
public opinion
 digital information
  dissemination   16, 29, 32–34
 Europe   15
 social media, influence   16, 29, 32–34, 35
 United States   15, 16, 29
pumped storage hydroelectricity   26, 79, 276
pyrogasification   86

R
recycling technologies
 carbon removal   5, 7, 47
reduced emissions completions
  (RECs)   47, 58
regulation
 accountability of regulators   38
 assessment and evaluation   38
 Australia   341–347
 carbon taxes *see* carbon taxes
 China   284–290
 developing countries   210–214
 dispute resolution   161, 162–164, 215–217
 domestic   212–213
 environmental protection and   37, 38
 European Union   9, 264–282, 267n, 405
 generally   3, 7–12, 37–39, 402–403
 greenhouse gas emissions   39
 independent regulators   38
 information asymmetries   38
 international governance *see* international
  governance networks
 international oil and gas operators   203,
  210–214
 international treaties   146, 148, 160–161,
  160n, 162, 169, 173–174, 210,
  215–217
 investment law *see* international
  investment law
 lack of expertise in transitional
  economies   174

Nigeria   308–309, 320–322, 326–328
over-regulation   39
penalty regimes   47–48
permitting requirements   50, 53, 54, 55–56
policy coherence   402
power-to-gas (P2G) technology   89–90, 403
pricing   17–20, 37, 38
regulatory capture   61
reliability of supply   3, 37–38, 69, 74, 401
reporting requirements   54–55
sanctions, imposition   210–213
security of supply   3, 37–38, 69
soft law provisions   206–209
stakeholder engagement   38, 73
sustainability, ensuring   3, 37–38, 215–216
taxation as regulatory tool   7–8, 12, 221
Texas shale oil industry   109–110, 192
transparency   38, 137, 212
treaty commitments   159, 176, 210–214, 215, 216
United Kingdom   211
United States   39, 43, 49–67, 211, 245, 247, 248–250, 260–262

renewable energy
  see also hydroelectric power; solar power; wind power
  Australia   337–338, 340–341, 345–346, 347–348, 406
  backup supply   26
  biomass fuels   72, 75, 92, 103, 104–105, 181, 199, 307–308, 309–310, 381, 382–383, 394, 398, 407
  China   9, 253, 295, 297, 300–302, 405–406
  corporate energy procurement   261
  curtailment   80–81, 91, 96
  decarbonisation, generally   6, 71
  developing countries   215, 377
  European Union   142, 214–215, 263–282, 378, 405
  excess   72
  falling costs   2, 5, 15, 22, 23–29, 70, 83, 245–246
  financial incentives *see* financial incentives
  Green New Deal   21–22, 24, 24n, 27–28, 33–34, 231, 259
  grid balancing   269
  increasing use   70–71
  industry opposition to   245–246
  integrated energy providers   39, 47
  integration in conventional systems   23–29, 74–84, 91–97, 263–264
  intermittent generation   6, 23, 71–72, 75, 79–80, 91, 142, 269, 301–302, 402

international energy companies   206
investment law, necessity for   159, 169–171, 403–404
low carbon economy   378
market participation   381
mostly renewables systems   23–29
negative pricing   25
new transmission capacity   22
Nigeria   307–308, 325, 328–329, 332, 334–335, 406
off-grid   2, 10, 74, 325, 393
out-of-pocket costs   23–24, 27
policy vagueness   388
power system flexibility   263, 264, 273–281
power-to-gas (P2G) *see* power-to-gas technology
price-competitiveness   39, 245–246, 257
private investment in   169–171, 261
reliability   23–29, 71–72, 79–80, 88, 301–302, 402
renewable natural gas   5, 72, 75–76, 86–88, 92, 97, 105, 403
resistance from energy industry stakeholders   245–246, 257, 258, 262
SADC   379, 380, 381–390, 391, 393–394, 396, 398, 400
sector growth   2, 70–71, 74
shale gas industry and   197–198
South Africa   389, 393
state support, disputes arising from   217
stimulating investment in   263
storage   25, 26, 79–80, 91, 94–95, 97, 259, 260
subsidising   217, 240, 391, 396, 397
supply and demand mismatch   4, 23, 71–72, 75, 79–80, 91
transition to, generally   3–4, 199, 377, 378, 381–390
transmission constraints   81
transport sector   394–395
United Kingdom   46
United States   15–16, 21–22, 34–35, 43–44, 46, 46n, 76–84, 245–246, 250–262, 405
variable   75, 77, 79–80, 92
waste-to-energy technology   39, 72, 75–76, 86–88, 96–97
zero carbon   4–5, 92
renewable portfolio standards (RPS)   77–78, 79, 97, 255–256, 403
Rio Declaration   129, 131, 207
Rio Earth Summit   125, 127–130

Russia
  shale gas deposits 182

S
Samarakoon, S 388
Sanders, Bernie 24n, 27
Satterlee, L 389
Saudi Arabia
  greenhouse gas reduction 213
Schott, Kerry 351
secondary energy sources 1, 37, 43
sector-coupling 278–279
security *see* **energy security**
security constrained economic dispatch (SCED) rule 18, 19
sewage treatment plants 56
shale oil and gas
  Africa *see* Africa's shale gas
  benefits 199
  Canada 355
  China 182, 185, 303
  civic shares, proposals for 11, 178, 192–195, 198, 404
  earthquakes 195, 196
  energy access 178–182, 198–199
  energy security 199
  environmental challenges 195–196, 197
  environmental gains offered by 177, 196
  flaring and venting 8–9, 107–121
  horizontal drilling 40, 108, 181, 199
  hostility towards 185, 195–196, 197
  hydraulic fracturing 40, 58, 108, 181–182, 185, 199, 245, 247
  incentivising development 178, 187, 192–195
  investment in 186
  low price 181–182
  methane release 197
  mineral rights 10–11, 177–178, 184, 186–191, 199, 249, 404
  obstacles to development 177–178, 184–187, 199
  pipeline infrastructure and capacity 185
  pollution caused by 195
  recoverable reserves 182–185
  technology transfer 186
  Unconventional Gas Technical Engagement Program 186
  United Kingdom 196
  United States 39, 40–44, 108, 181–191, 196, 199, 247, 259, 353, 356, 357
  unitisation agreements 114–116
  water contamination 185, 195
  water supply, access to 185, 195–196

Shurtz, N 226
Slaughter, Anne Marie 151, 152
Soifer J 119
solar power
  Australia 338, 340–341, 346
  China 283, 284, 300–302, 405–406
  costs 2, 23–29, 34, 70, 83
  curtailment 80–81, 96
  European Union 264, 269, 272, 273
  intermittent nature 6, 23–29, 71–72, 75, 79–80, 91, 142, 269, 301–302, 402
  investor claims against state policy changes 170–171, 217
  negative pricing 25
  net metering 28, 256
  Nigeria 307, 309, 325, 329, 334
  out-of-pocket grid costs 28
  prosumers 88, 273, 381
  SADC 393, 394, 395, 396, 398
  sector growth 2, 4, 70–71
  solar plus storage projects 25
  Southern Africa 379
  storage 25, 26, 79–80, 88
  SunShot Initiative 254
  United States 23–29, 34, 35, 71, 77, 79–80, 91, 154, 249, 250–251, 254, 256–258, 260, 261
Solidia Project 100
South Africa
  see also Southern Africa Development Community
  coal-fired power plants 10, 380
  energy access 10, 390–391
  feed-in tariffs 393, 397
  generally 389
  Integrated Resources Plan 389
  National Development Plan 389
  oil 10, 380
  renewable energy 389, 393, 395
  shale gas reserves 178, 182, 183–184, 187, 195–196
  transport sector 395
South Korea
  LNG imports 358
Southern Africa Development Community (SADC)
  Angola 394
  biomass energy 393, 394
  Botswana 380, 381, 389, 391, 394
  climate change mitigation 399
  coal-fired power plants 10, 380, 381, 382, 391
  coal reserves 184, 379

combined-cycle gas turbines 380
decarbonisation 393–397, 407
deforestation 393
demand market participation 395–396
DRC 380, 381, 394, 396
electric vehicles 394–395, 400
electricity 379–380
energy access 10, 388, 390–391, 393, 395, 396, 398
energy efficiency 383, 395–396, 400
energy justice 385, 386–389, 390–393, 396–397
energy objective 10, 395
energy poverty 377, 398
energy resources 379
energy sector overview 379–380
energy transition 10, 377–378, 379, 380–400, 407
establishment 379
gas reserves 379
hydroelectric power 10, 379, 380, 381, 394, 400
industrialisation strategy 395
Lesotho 380, 389, 399
Madagascar 399
Malawi 380, 381, 382, 399, 400
Mauritius 395, 396
membership 379
mini-grids 393, 397
mining sector 377–378
Mozambique 203, 380, 393, 399
Namibia 389, 393, 394
off-grid systems 10, 393, 396
oil reserves 10, 379
pebble bed modular reactors 380
policy-making institutions 379
population growth 400
REEESAP 395
Regional Indicative and Strategic Plan 395
renewable energy 379, 381–390, 391, 393–394, 396, 398, 400
SACREEE 393, 398
smart grids and smart meters 396–397, 400
solar power 379, 393, 394, 395, 396, 398
Southern African Power Pool 10, 380, 382
Swaziland 389, 394, 399
Tanzania 382, 394, 398, 399–400
transition to low carbon economy 377–378, 379, 380–400
urbanisation 399, 400
wind power 379, 394, 396, 398
Zambia 380, 382, 393, 394, 396, 399
Zimbabwe 380, 381, 394, 395–396, 398, 399

Southern African Coordinating Conference (SADCC) 379
Stevens J 52
Stockholm Declaration 207
storage
  battery 2, 6, 71–72, 84, 99, 276–278, 337, 338, 341
  carbon *see* carbon capture, utilisation and storage
  electricity 2, 25, 26, 43, 71–72, 84, 88, 99, 259, 260, 262
  gas 41–43, 65, 84, 91
  oil 41
  power-to-gas (P2G) technology 91, 94–95
Strategic Climate Fund 143–144
subsidising renewable energy 240, 391, 396, 397
  Agreement on Subsidies and Countervailing Measures 217
sulphur dioxide (SO$_2$)
  acid rain 51n
  natural gas flaring 8–9, 107
  US Clean Air Act 50, 211
sustainability
  all-electric pathway 6, 7
  Australia 346
  bilateral treaties 215–217
  energy access 378, 401
  energy supply regulation and 3, 37–38, 74, 91
  financing oil and gas sectors 206–209
  international oil and gas operators 209
  Natural Resource Charter 209
  policy push towards 3, 205–209, 216
  Rio Declaration 129
  shale gas 178–181
  Sustainable Development Goals 179, 378
  Sustainable Development Scenario 75
  UN Sustainable Energy for All 177, 179–180, 207, 208
  UNFCCC measures 202, 205
Swaziland *see* **Southern Africa Development Community**
Sweden
  renewable energy 268

T
Tanzania
  see also Southern Africa Development Community
  rural energy access 324
  shale gas reserves 180
taxation *see* **carbon taxes**

430   Index

Technical Barriers to Trade
    Agreement   217
technology transfer
    shale gas development   186
Tillerson, Rex   154, 155
tradeoffs
    affordability   23–29, 402
    energy security   3, 402
    energy transition, generally   2–3
    political-economic dynamic   16, 29–34
    reliability   3, 23–29, 71
    United States   16, 23–34, 402
transmission constraints   81
transparency
    energy sector regulators   38
    Paris Agreement   137, 212
    procedural justice   390, 396–397
transport sector
    decarbonisation   79, 91
    electric vehicles   2, 70, 82, 91, 205–206,
        223–224, 278–279, 341, 387–388,
        394–395, 400
    fuel cell electric vehicles   82
    greenhouse gas emissions   4
    power-to-gas (P2G) technology   82, 91
    renewable energy   394–395
Trudeau, J   364
Trump Administration   20, 32, 45, 59–60,
    63–64, 78, 117, 135, 148, 252, 254,
    258

U
Uganda
    oil reserves   180, 203
    rural energy access   324
United Kingdom
    CCUS technology   100, 105
    Climate Change Levy   211
    decarbonisation   46
    electricity consumption   46
    greenhouse gas emissions   46
    renewable energy sources   46
    shale gas fracking banned   196
    subsidies   240
    wind power   240
United Nations
    Conference of the Parties (COP)   128,
        130–132, 134
    Declaration on the Right to
        Development   159, 166
    Development Programme   165–166
    Draft Convention on the Right to
        Development   166

Framework Convention on Climate Change
    (UNFCCC)   45, 49–50, 73, 125,
    127–128, 130–132, 134, 139–140,
    202, 205, 402
    IPCC   128, 140–142
    north-south dynamic   130, 131
    Rio Declaration   125, 127, 128–130, 131, 207
    Stockholm Declaration   207
    Sustainable Development Goals   378
    Sustainable Energy for All   177, 179–180,
        207, 208
United States
    Administrative Procedure Act   60, 63–64
    Affordable Clean Energy Rule   20, 78
    air pollutants   51–53, 54, 56–61
    *American Electric Power Co v
        Connecticut*   53
    automobile tailpipe emissions   248
    best available control technology   39, 50,
        53, 56, 67
    best system of emissions reduction   39,
        57–58, 67
    BLM 2016 Rule   61–65, 62n
    BLM 2018 Rule   64–65
    Bureau of Land Management   40, 54,
        61–65, 96
    Bureau of Ocean Energy Management   40
    carbon dioxide emissions   51, 54–55, 76–78,
        251, 253, 402
    carbon-heavy economy   245–246
    CCUS technology   8, 98–100, 101–102,
        105, 137
    *Citizens United v Federal Election
        Commission*   258
    Clean Air Act   50–53, 54, 55–56, 78,
        117, 211
    Clean Power Plan   20, 78, 137, 172
    climate change   261
    climate policy, generally   15, 16, 35, 210
    coal-fired power plants   43–44, 46, 51n, 55,
        76–78, 172, 230, 246–247, 249, 252,
        257–258
    coal reserves   247, 249
    *Coalition for Responsible Regulation v
        EPA*   211
    competition and market pricing   18–20, 42,
        85–86
    Congressional Review Act   63
    conservation regulation   96–97, 101,
        115–116
    Consolidated Appropriations Act   54–55
    cooperative federalism   50–51
    cost-minimisation rule   17–18

decarbonisation   15–16, 20–35, 39, 43–44, 45, 76–84, 87–88, 91–97, 210, 246, 249, 250–262, 405
decentralised regulation   248
Department of the Interior   248
deregulated markets   248–249
electric grid   17, 18, 80, 83–86, 249–250
electricity co-ops   17
electricity markets   19–20
electricity sector   8, 16–20, 28, 43–44, 46, 83–86, 91–97, 230–231, 248–250
Energy Information Administration   71, 112
Energy Mapping System   43
energy policy   246, 248, 250–252
Energy Policy Act   85, 253
energy resources   247
energy sector tradeoffs   16, 23–34, 402
energy supply infrastructure   247, 248, 249
energy supply systems and operators   19, 25–26, 84–86, 245–246
Environmental Defense Fund   108, 112
Environmental Protection Agency   20, 39, 50–62, 78, 117, 211, 248, 252, 402
Federal Energy Regulatory Commission   17, 18–19, 41, 43, 85–86, 94–96, 248
Federal Land Policy and Management Act   61
fuel economy standards   248
gas exports   41, 42
gas extraction, regulation   249
gas-fired power, generally   43–44, 75–76, 83–84, 230, 249
gas flaring and venting   8–9, 107–121, 137
gas infrastructure network   42, 43–44, 54, 83–84
gas reserves   247, 259
gas storage facilities   42, 43, 65, 84
gas supply boom   8, 37, 40–44, 46, 49, 56–61, 181–182, 189–191, 356
GHG Reporting Programme   54–55
global influence in energy industry   245–247, 250–251
Green New Deal   21–22, 24, 24n, 27–28, 33–34, 231, 259
greenhouse gas emissions   45–46, 49–56, 76–78, 79, 137, 211, 251, 253, 402, 405
grid operators   80
hydroelectricity   248
Independent System Operators   19, 25–26, 80, 85, 86
industry opposition to renewables and decarbonisation   245–246
Information Collection Requests   117

integrated policy framework, developing   91–97
Inventory of US Greenhouse Gas Emissions and Sinks   55
Investment Tax Credit   253, 254
investor-owned utilities   16–17, 18, 19, 21, 25, 35
IRC report on emerging technologies   93–94
Kyoto Protocol   50, 133, 251
local government decarbonisation programmes   260–261, 262
low-carbon energy   27, 45–46
lowest achievable emissions rate   50
Massachusetts v EPA   51–53, 54, 211
methane emissions   48–49, 51, 52–53, 54–58, 61–66, 67, 117, 402
Mineral Leasing Act   54, 61–62, 64
mineral rights   186–191, 249
monopoly providers   17–18
municipally-owned electric utilities   250
national ambient air quality standards   50
Natural Gas Pipeline Safety Act   54
net metering programmes   256
New Source Performance Standards   56–61, 117
New Source Review programme   55–56
NTL-4A   62, 65
nuclear power   43–44, 46, 46n, 91, 142, 230, 247, 248
obstacles to green grid   28–29
oil extraction, regulation   249
oil and gas well siting   250
oil industry   46, 49, 55, 56–61, 78, 107–121, 192, 247
oil reserves   247
open access networks   18–19, 40, 42, 86
Paris Agreement   45, 50, 78, 137, 138–139, 148, 154, 252
permitting requirements   50, 53, 54, 55–56
pipeline capacity   108, 110–111, 118, 121
Pipeline and Hazardous Materials Safety Administration   54, 65
pipelines, regulation   249
political hyper-polarisation   8, 16, 20, 29–35
political influence of fossil fuel stakeholders   251–252, 257, 258, 262
power-to-gas (P2G) technology   8, 72, 77, 81–90, 91, 97
Prevention of Significant Deterioration permits   50, 53, 56

price regulation   17–20
Production Tax Credit   253–254
public opinion on decarbonisation   15, 16, 20, 29–34, 251–252
Public Utilities Regulation Act   85
public utility commissions   248, 249
Railroad Commission v Flour Bluff Oil Corp   115
Railroad Commission v Sterling Oil & Refining Co   115
Regional Transmission Organisations   19, 25–26, 80, 85, 86
regulatory framework   39, 43, 49–67, 211, 245, 247, 248–250, 260–262
renewable energy credits   261
renewable energy generating capacity   253
renewable energy incentives   251, 253–257
renewable energy industry   245–246, 252, 257, 258, 405
renewable energy policy   251–252, 255–262
renewable natural gas   86–88, 92, 97
renewable portfolio standards   77–78, 79, 97, 255–256, 403
reporting requirements   54–55
Rural Electrification Act   17
security constrained economic dispatch rule   18, 19
shale oil and gas   39, 40–44, 108, 181–182, 186–191, 196, 199, 247, 259, 353, 356, 357
solar power   23–29, 34, 35, 71, 77, 79–80, 91, 154, 249, 250–251, 254, 256–258, 261, 262
state decarbonisation programmes   20–21, 252, 255–257, 260–261, 262
SunShot Initiative   254
technological innovation   245–247, 250
Texas Railroad Commission v Rowan Oil Co   116
Texas shale oil industry   8–9, 107–121, 192
Title V permits   55, 56
Utility Air Regulatory Group v EPA   53, 55
vacillating commitment to decarbonisation   250–252, 259
vertically integrated utilities   248
volatile organic compounds   57, 58, 61, 62n, 117
waste prevention   62, 96–97
wind power   21, 23–29, 34, 35, 46, 46n, 77, 79–80, 91, 249, 251, 253–254, 257, 258, 261
Wyoming v US Dep't of Interior   64

unitisation agreements
international oil and gas operators   203
Texas shale oil industry   114–116
Urgenda Foundation v The Netherlands   204–205

V
variable renewable energy (VRE)   75, 77, 79–80, 92
see also solar power; wind power
vertically integrated utilities   2, 248, 271, 293, 381
volatile organic compounds (VOCs)   57, 58, 61, 62n, 117

W
Wang, Z and Krupnick, A   191
Warburton, Dick   347–348
waste management
conservation regulation   96–97
greenhouse gases   44, 45
landfill gases   87
natural gas flaring   8–9, 107–121
United States   62, 96–97
waste-to-energy technology
generally   39, 72, 96–97
renewable natural gas   5, 72, 75–76, 86–88, 97, 105, 403
water supply
China   291
shale oil and gas industry   185, 195–196
water vapour   44
Wen Jiabao   290
West African Gas Pipeline   48
wind power
Australia   338, 340
China   283, 294, 300–302, 405–406
costs   2, 23–29, 34, 70, 83
curtailment   80–81, 96
European Union   264, 269, 272
generally   1, 4
intermittent nature   6, 23–29, 71–72, 75, 79–80, 91, 142, 269, 301–302, 402
Lake Turkana Wind Power Project   215
negative pricing   25
Nigeria   307, 325
offshore installations   145
SADC   394, 396, 398
sector growth   4, 70–71
Southern Africa   379

storage 25, 26, 79–80
United Kingdom 240
United States 21, 35, 46, 46n, 77, 79–80, 91, 249, 251, 253–254, 257, 258, 261
World Bank
  Climate Change Action Plan 206
  Equator Principles 207
  International Finance Corporation 207
  Multilateral Investment Guarantee Agency 207

World Trade Organisation (WTO) 146
  dispute resolution mechanism 161, 217

X
Xi Jinping 284–285, 287, 289–290, 293

Z
Zahar, A 142–143
Zambia *see* **Southern Africa Development Community**
Zibelmann, Audrey 351

Milton Keynes UK
Ingram Content Group UK Ltd.
UKHW050049260324
439952UK00005B/132